GROUP PROCESSES

Eugene Burnstein

Fred E. Fiedler

Dean G. Pruitt

Robert B. Zajonc

Philip G. Zimbardo

SEX ROLES, SEX DIFFERENCES

Sandra L. Bem

Kay Deaux

Alice H. Eagly

Janet T. Spence

SOCIAL COGNITION

Susan T. Fiske

E. Tory Higgins

Shelley E. Taylor

Robert S. Wyer, Jr.

Thomas K. Srull

(Continued to inside back cover)

SOCIAL PSYCHOLOGY:
Understanding Human Interaction

5th Edition

ROBERT A. BARON

Purdue University

DONN BYRNE

State University of New York
at Albany

Allyn and Bacon, Inc.

Boston   London   Sydney   Toronto

Managing Editor: Bill Barke
Senior Editorial Assistant: Alicia Reilly
Text Design and Production: Nancy Murphy/
East of the Sun
Composition Buyer: Linda Cox
Photo Research: Laurel Anderson/Photosynthesis
Cover Coordinator: Linda K. Dickinson
Cover Designer: Design Ad Cetera
Manufacturing Buyer: William J. Alberti

Library of Congress Cataloging in Publication Data

Baron, Robert A.
  Social psychology.

  Bibliography: p.
  Includes index.
  1. Social psychology. I. Byrne, Donn Erwin.
  II. Title.
HM251.B435   1987   302   86-26609
ISBN 0-205-10313-8

           Printed in the United States of America
10 9 8 7 6 5   91 90 89

Photo Credits

Chapter 1: p. 2 Stock, Boston/Gale Zucker; p. 8 Stock, Boston/Ira Kirschenbaum; p. 9 (left) Stock, Boston/Owen Franken, (right) Fredrik D. Bodin; p. 18 (top) The Picture Cube/Jeff Dunn, (left) Stock, Boston/Gale Zucker, (right) The Picture Cube/J. D. Sloan.
Chapter 2: p. 41 (left) Woodfin Camp & Associates/Koen Wessing, (right) Stock, Boston/Ira Kirschenbaum; p. 44 (left) The Image Works/Alan Carey, (right) UPI/Bettmann Newsphoto; p. 66 Paul Johnson.
Chapter 3: p. 74 Woodfin Camp & Associates/Lynne J. Weinstein; p. 81 Stock, Boston/Barbara Alper; p. 82 (top) The Picture Cube/Gary Goodman, (bottom) Stock, Boston/Donald Dietz; p. 87 (top) Woodfin Camp & Associates/Lynn J. Weinstein, (bottom) Stock, Boston/Cary Wolinsky.

Chapter 4: p. 114 Stock, Boston/Patricia Hollander Gross; p. 117 Stock, Boston/Jean-Claude Lejeune; p. 125 (top) Stock, Boston/Bohdan Hrynewyck, (bottom) Stock, Boston/Patricia Hollander Gross; p. 139 Omni-Photo Communications/Frances M. Cox.
Chapter 5: p. 148 Omni-Photo Communications/David Chalk; p. 151 Nawrocki Stock Photo/Jason Laure; p. 157 (top) The Bettmann Archive, (bottom) Woodfin Camp & Associates/Alon Reininger; p. 167 Omni-Photo Communications/David Chalk; p. 171 Stock, Boston/Peter Southwick.

(Photo credits continue on the page following the index, which constitutes an extension of the copyright page.)

To Jessica, who's always close, even when she's far away

To Lindsey, Robin, and Keven — three exceptional offspring

CONTENTS

PREFACE: SIXTEEN YEARS OF FOLLOWING THE "TWO PERCENT RULE"; Or, Why Edison Was Right

THE FIFTH edition — zounds, how time flies! More than sixteen years have elapsed since we sat down to plan, and then prepare, the original version of this text. To say that these years have been turbulent is a definite understatement. Oil crises and oil gluts, wild swings in the political pendulum, economic recessions and recoveries — the world around us has been anything but placid during this period. Social psychology, too, has changed dramatically, as new topics, theories, and approaches have risen to the fore. Despite all this change, though, here we are again, back for yet another try at summarizing the knowledge base of social psychology, and transmitting its appeal and excitement to our students. While neither of us enjoys counting the intervening years (!), we do take great pride in the longevity and popularity of our text. According to reports from our publisher, it has been chosen by more of our colleagues and has been read by more students (perhaps twice as many), as any other text in the history of social psychology. We feel that the fifth edition — a true milestone for any book — is an appropriate point at which to express our appreciation for this support and to offer our views about why, precisely, *Social Psychology: Understanding Human Interaction* has enjoyed such continued acceptance. Briefly, we feel that two factors are most important in this respect.

The first of these derives from a somewhat surprising source: Thomas Edison, inventor of the electric light, phonograph, and many other useful items. When asked to account for his impressive record of accomplishments, Edison remarked that success consists of "ninety-eight percent perspiration and two percent inspiration." Call us Type As, but we firmly endorse this formula: there is no substitute for hard work. Consistent with this view, we have tried with each edition to "do our homework"—to read the latest journals, to examine the latest books, and to ask our colleagues for their newest ideas and publication pre-prints. The result, we feel, has been well worth the effort: a text that reflects modern social psychology broadly, accurately, and in an up-to-date manner. Of course, we have also tried, in each edition, for that extra two percent—new features, new ideas, and shifts in organization that we hope will enhance our ability to communicate with readers. While making such efforts, though, our attention has never wandered from Edison's basic principle.

The second factor in the continuing success of our text is closely related to the first. It concerns our approach to each new edition. In revising this book, we have never assumed that what's already present is somehow sacred and should remain unchanged. On the contrary, we proceed from the viewpoint that almost everything can (and perhaps should!) be improved. Thus, instead of retaining existing content and merely adding something new to reflect recent developments, we've followed a radically different process—one in which large sections and even entire chapters are thoroughly rewritten. This has certainly added to our "perspiration quotient," but, again, in our view it has been effort well spent.

These, then, seem to be the factors responsible for the widespread and (for us) gratifying acceptance of our text. Have we followed them once more in this new edition? Our answer is "You bet!" This time, too, we've made many major changes, and—as in the past—virtually all these changes reflect one or both of the principles outlined above. The most important of these modifications are summarized below.

Changes in content: The specifics

Once again, we've tried to reflect what's new in social psychology. Thus, we've thoroughly up-dated virtually every section of the text. The result: over 38 percent of the references are from 1984, 1985, and 1986. In addition, we've added dozens of new topics not considered in the previous edition in order to cover new lines of investigation and important new findings. A small sampling of these new topics includes:

practical applications of attribution theory
fallacies and biases in social judgment
choking under pressure
action identification
cognitive response analysis of persuasion
elaboration likelihood model

negative effects of tokenism
racial slurs as activators of negative racial schemata
mindlessness and prejudice
status and sex role stereotypes
the social influence (SIM) model
maintaining relationships
dealing with terrorists
effects of pollution on behavior

self-monitoring behavior
aggression in close relationships
alcohol and aggression
effects of repeated exposure to pornography
effects of framing on bargaining
comparable worth
biased sampling of information
minority influence

biased sampling of information in
group discussions
differences in the pay expectations of
males and females
reactions to Three-Mile Island
psychoneuroimmunology
societal barriers to female need for
achievement

Changes in content: Two shifts in emphasis

In addition to the specific changes mentioned above, two more general shifts in content have been undertaken to represent corresponding changes in the focus of social psychology. These involve (1) greater emphasis on the cognitive bases of social behavior, and (2) more attention to the practical application of social psychological knowledge.

More emphasis on the "cognitive side" of social psychology. In recent years, interest in social cognition and related topics has continued and perhaps even increased. To reflect this fact, we've devoted more attention to the cognitive foundations of social psychology throughout this edition. This can be seen most clearly in chapters 3 (Social Cognition) and 4 (Attitudes), which have been extensively revised, but it is also reflected in many other chapters. We feel that this shift in emphasis (which, is, of course, *evolutionary* rather than revolutionary in nature) helps us capture the orientation and flavor of modern social psychology in a timely and accurate manner.

More attention to the application of social psychological knowledge. In recent years, social psychologists have become increasingly concerned with the task of applying their knowledge to practical issues and topics. This trend, too, is reflected in our new edition. Throughout the text, we call attention to practical implications of the findings and principles of our field, and to concrete examples of the use of this knowledge in a wide variety of applied settings. Again, we feel that this shift in emphasis is appropriate and that it mirrors developments in social psychology itself.

Changes in special features

We feel that in the late 1980s social psychology can be proud of its record of accomplishments: it has gathered an impressive body of basic knowledge about social behavior and social processes, and it is continuing to do so at an accelerating rate. To reflect this conviction, we have included two new types of special insert labeled, respectively, **Focus on Research: Classic Contributions** and **Focus on Research: The Cutting Edge.**

Focus on Research: Classic Contributions.   As the title suggests, inserts of this type describe investigations that are generally viewed as "classics" in social psychology. These are included to help put the development of our field in historical context, and to counter the impression among some students that social psychology was invented only last year, and began serious research just last week!

Focus on Research: The Cutting Edge.   To balance the picture, we also present another set of inserts that report studies and findings that seem to fall along the boundary of current progress in social psychology — at its "cutting edge," so to speak. We feel these types of special features will provide readers with a balanced overview of research in our field — one which has been adding significantly to human knowledge for several decades, and which continues to do so in impressive ways at present.

On the Applied Side.   A third type of insert, designed to highlight the practical implications and applications of social psychological knowledge, has been retained. While the title is the same as in previous editions, all inserts of this type are new.

We should add that, as in the previous edition, all inserts are carefully cited in the text so that readers will know just when each is to be read, and how each relates to other text materials.

Changes in ancillary materials

Ancillary materials, too, have been improved. The Instructor's Manual has been expanded, and now includes many new exercises and suggestions for enhancing class discussion. The Study Guide includes a wider range of questions (e.g., matching, definitions, completion), and the answers for all self-tests are cross-referenced to their location in the text. Finally, a computerized testbank containing 1,500 multiple-choice items is available. All items in this testbank are categorized by type and difficulty level. Together, this package of materials should help make the tasks of teaching social psychology — and mastering it — even more pleasurable than in the past.

Inclusion of "major contributors to social psychology"

Progress in social psychology, like progress in any other any branch of science, rests primarily on the insight and inspiration of individual researchers. To reflect this fact, the book endsheets (the pages inside the front and back covers) present a new feature: photos of many key contributors to our field. These individuals, who were chosen through feedback provided by several hundred colleagues, are grouped according to the area of their contributions. (Many have contributed to several areas of the study, so this placement is somewhat arbitrary.) We regret that space limitations prevent us from including more individuals whose work we also admire. Together, though, the persons shown do represent a broad sample of the scientists whose work has helped make social psychology what it is today.

ACKNOWLEDGEMENTS:
Some Words of Thanks

IN PREPARING this "silver" edition of our text, we have been assisted by many hard-working, talented people. While we can't possibly hope to thank all of them here, we'd like to express our sincere appreciation to a few whose help has been most valuable.

First, our heartfelt thanks to Roy F. Baumeister, Kathryn Kelley, and Jerry M. Suls, who assisted us by preparing drafts of several chapters (chapters 3, 4, 12, and 13). Their expertise, skill, and enthusiasm were major "pluses" for the project, and we gratefully acknowledge these esteemed colleagues here.

Second, we wish to thank the persons listed below, who read and commented upon various portions of the manuscript. Their suggestions were thoughtful, constructive, and informative, and we have tried to follow them as closely as possible:

Robert S. Baron
University of Iowa

Russell D. Clark, III
Florida State University

Herbert C. Fink
State University of New York at Brockport

Jeffrey D. Fisher
University of Connecticut

Robert Gifford
University of Victoria

Daniel Gilbert
University of Texas at Austin

Steven Prentice-Dunn
University of Alabama

Daniel M. Wegner
Trinity University

Third, our special thanks to Nancy L. Murphy for yet another outstanding design, help with photo selection, and so many other contributions it would be impossible to mention all of them here. Thanks, Nancy —as always, it's been a pleasure working with you. We should also specially mention Laurel Anderson's fine job of photo research.

Fourth, we want to thank Paula Carroll at Allyn and Bacon for her outstanding efforts as production manager, to Linda Dickinson for devising a very attractive cover, and to Linda Cox for her help in securing excellent typesetting.

Fifth (and appropriately so, given that this is the *fifth* edition!), some warm words of thanks to our good friend, editor, and one-man support group, Bill Barke. It wouldn't be half as much fun without you!

Sixth, we wish to express our appreciation to Alicia Reilly for her invaluable aid in pulling the entire "package" for the fifth edition together.

And last, but certainly not least, our thanks, once again, to Gene F. Smith and Bem P. Allen for preparing an excellent set of ancillaries to accompany our text (a comprehensive instructor's manual, an extensive test bank, and a very helpful study guide).

To all of these outstanding people, and to many others as well, our warmest personal *"Thank You!"*

A CONCLUDING COMMENT and Yet Another Request for Help

It is our hope that you, our colleagues and readers, will find the fifth edition changes to be helpful ones. Looking back, we can honestly say that, once again, we have followed Edison's rule and have spared no effort in preparing this new edition. Yet we are equally certain that now, as in the past, there is still room for improvement. We would appreciate it greatly, therefore, if you would share your reactions with us. We *do* pay close attention to such feedback and always find it helpful. So please don't hesitate — send us your comments and suggestions whenever you can, and as often as you wish. In this respect, the more the better!

Robert A. Baron
Department of Psychological
  Sciences
Purdue University
West Lafayette, IN 47907

Donn Byrne
Department of Psychology
The University at Albany
State University of New York
Albany, NY 12222

ABOUT THE AUTHORS

ROBERT A. BARON is currently Professor of Psychological Sciences at Purdue University. A 1968 Ph.D. (University of Iowa), he has also held academic positions at the University of Washington, Oxford University, Princeton University, the University of Texas, the University of Minnesota, and the University of South Carolina. Winner of numerous awards for teaching excellence, he is the author of more than fifteen books and seventy-five articles in professional journals. From 1979 to 1981, Professor Baron was the Program Director for Social and Developmental Psychology at the National Science Foundation. A Fellow of the American Psychological Association since 1978, he has served as an Editor or member of the Editorial Board for several journals (e.g., *Journal of Personality and Social Psychology, Journal of Applied Social Psychology, Aggressive Behavior*). His current research interests are focused on applying the principles and findings of social psychology to key aspects of organizational behavior (e.g., organizational conflict, self-presentation during interviews). A long-time runner, his hobbies include woodworking, coin-collecting, and music.

DONN BYRNE is currently Professor of Psychology and Chairman of the Department of Psychology at the State University of New York at Albany. He received the Ph.D. degree in 1958 from Stanford University and has held academic positions at the California State University at San Francisco, the University of Texas, Stanford University, the University of Hawaii, and Purdue University. A past president of the Midwestern Psychological Association and a Fellow of two divisions of the American Psychological Association, he has written more than twenty books, twenty-five invited chapters, and one hundred twenty-five articles. He was invited to deliver a G. Stanley Hall lecture at the 1981 meeting of the American Psychological Association in Los Angeles and a State of the Science address at the 1981 meeting of the Society for the Scientific Study of Sex. He has served on the Editorial Boards of thirteen journals, including *Psychological Monographs, Journal of Experimental Social Psychology, Journal of Research in Personality, Journal of Applied Social Psychology, Journal of Personality*, and *Motivation and Emotion*. His current research interests include interpersonal attraction and the prediction of sexually coercive behavior. Leisure-time activities include literature, the theater, and landscaping.

SOCIAL PSYCHOLOGY:
Understanding Human Interaction

5th Edition

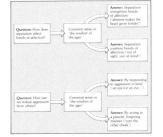

UNDERSTANDING SOCIAL BEHAVIOR: An Introduction

It's a beautiful, bright summer day, and four friends — Julie Frank, Tom Bell, Sue Pilkowski, and Lou Santini — are on their way to the beach. Tom's at the wheel, but everyone is so busy laughing, talking, and having a good time that no one pays much attention to his driving. During a momentary pause in the conversation, though, Julie notices a strange fact: they are being passed by more than half of the other vehicles on the road.

"Hey, Tom, have you gone to sleep?" she asks with a smile. "Even the campers are passing us!"

"I'm doing 58," Tom answers at once. "That ought to be fast enough."

"Fast enough!" Lou replies, shaking his head. "Heck *nobody* drives that slowly any more. The state troopers don't even look at you until you break 65."

"Maybe so," Tom answers. "But I promised my Dad I'd stay pretty close to 55, and I don't like to go back on my word."

"Just listen to him, people," Lou continues, "Mr. Goodbar himself!"

"Yeah, Tom," Julie chimes in, "speed up, why don't you. We don't want to miss all the fun. I always go 65 at least. Last week I drove down to the beach with Bill Thompson. We made it in under two hours, so he must have averaged over 70. Speed up!"

"Right, look alive, man!" Sue comments with a giggle. "You're not *that* old yet! No one pays any attention to that 55 speed limit anymore. Get with it."

"OK, OK," Tom answers, a note of reluctance still in his voice, "just don't make a big deal out of it." And with this remark, he presses down on the accelerator and watches as the speedometer needle moves smoothly up to 65. He's not happy to be going back on his agreement with his father, but he doesn't want to be teased by his friends, either. And after all, if everyone is doing it, why shouldn't he . . . ?

Clearing his throat, Charlie Hastings begins: "OK, now we come to the moment of truth. Do we promote Fred or Claire?"

"That's easy," Helen Simon answers. "Everyone knows that Fred's done a much better job for us. He ought to get the nod."

"You really think so?" Charlie asks with surprise.

"You bet," Helen answers with conviction. "I've had a chance to watch both of them, and in my opinion Fred's a much better worker. Always at his desk, always busy. I wish we had more like him in the department."

"Then how do you account for this?" Charlie asks, tossing the personnel folders for the two people onto the table in front of her. "The numbers show that Fred's actually turned out less than half of what Claire's produced during the last two periods."

"There must be some mistake," Helen replies. But, in fact, there is no error: the numbers speak for themselves. Claire *has* turned out nearly twice as much as Fred. Moreover, her work has also been of higher quality; fewer errors and complaints are noted in her folder. Now it's Helen's turn to be surprised.

"I don't understand it," she mutters. "I've always had the impression that Fred was doing more."

"Sure you have," Charlie replies, a note of sarcasm in his voice. "And I can tell you why. You've got this thing about people over forty-five. As far as you're concerned, Claire's got two strikes against her just because she's pushing fifty. You're convinced she can't cut it, so you don't notice when she does good work. But, boy! do you ever pounce on her every little mistake. No, Helen, you haven't been fair."

Helen denies Charlie's claim, and defends herself as best she can. After she leaves, though, she begins to wonder whether he might be right. Could her beliefs about older people — most of which really *are* pretty negative — have influenced her judgment? The possibility is far from flattering, but there are the figures, in black and white. Maybe there's something to it after all. . . .

HAVE YOU ever experienced situations such as these? Whether you have or not, the following fact is probably true: at some time or other you *have* thought about questions similar to those faced by the characters in these stories. Like the driver in the first incident, you have been exposed

FIGURE 1.1.   Because other persons play a central role in our lives and provide many of our most important rewards, we are keenly interested in our social relations with them. As shown here, authors are certainly no exception to this general rule! (Source: Drawing by Koren; ©1975 The New Yorker Magazine, Inc.)

Other persons: Often, they're the center of our world

"A brilliant achievement . . . Unflinching . . . Writing at its most illuminating . . . Gripping . . . Explosive . . . Long overdue . . . True vision . . . Plain speech . . . Proclaims the failure of our civilization as a whole."

to pressure from others to act in ways you don't prefer. At such times, you have wondered whether you should give in and go along with the crowd, or *dig in* and refuse. Similarly, like the woman in the second anecdote, you have had to make judgments or decisions about others, and you may have wondered whether you are always entirely fair in performing this task. Interest in such matters is only natural, for other persons play a key role in our lives. Indeed, they usually provide our most important forms of pleasure and our most upsetting types of pain (refer to Figure 1.1). For these reasons, most of us think about other persons and our relations with them on a fairly regular basis. In this respect, we are in excellent company. Over the centuries poets, philosophers, playwrights, and novelists have filled countless volumes with their thoughts about human social affairs. Since many of these thinkers were brilliant and talented, their work is often insightful. Thus, there seem to be basic truths in such age-old principles as "misery loves company," "soft words turneth away wrath," and "it is better to give than to receive."

In many cases, though, such informal knowledge seems both confusing and inconsistent. For example, consider the following illustration. The "wisdom of the ages" informs us that prolonged separation may strengthen bonds of affection between two persons: "absence makes the heart grow fonder." At the same time, though, it tells us that such separation can also produce the opposite effect: "out of sight, out of mind." Which view is correct? Can both be true? Common sense offers no clear-cut answers. As a second example, consider the recommendations of such informal knowledge with respect to handling provocations from others. On the one hand, we are urged to "turn the other cheek." On the other, we are informed that vengeance and counterattacks are effective: "an eye for an eye, a tooth for a tooth." Again, can both of these proposals be useful? Common sense offers no clue. We could go on to list several other examples of a similar, inconsistent nature (e.g., "birds of a feather flock together"; "opposites attract"), but by now the main point is probably clear. Often, our common sense or even the so-called "wisdom of the ages" provides us with a confusing picture of human social relations (refer to Figure 1.2).

At this point, we should hasten to insert a word of caution: we certainly do not mean to imply that such information is totally useless. On the contrary, it can serve as a rich source of suggestions for further study, and often provides reasonable explanations for social phenomena after the fact—after they have occurred. By itself, though, informal knowledge cannot stand alone; it fails to provide an adequate basis for fully understanding the complex nature of our social relations with others.

FIGURE 1.2. Common sense or the "wisdom of the ages" frequently offers contradictory answers to questions about human social relations.

Common sense: An imperfect guide to human social behavior

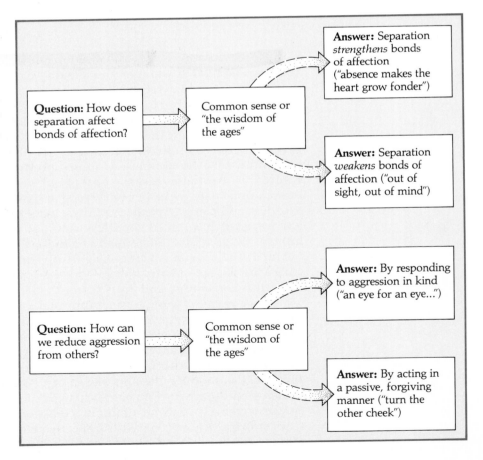

Of course, it is one thing to reject these traditional sources of knowledge about social behavior, and quite another to offer alternative means for acquiring such information. How, aside from speculation, insight, and intuition, can this crucial task be accomplished? One answer — and a successful one, we believe — is provided by the field of **social psychology.** In simplest terms, this answer rests on the following assertion: accurate and useful information about human social relations can be readily acquired through use of scientific methods. In short, social psychologists contend that we can indeed come to understand even complex aspects of social behavior, provided we are willing to study them in an essentially scientific manner.

Given the rapid progress that has often resulted from the application of scientific methods in other areas, this suggestion seems reasonable. Thus, you may be surprised to learn that it was not adopted until quite recent times. Indeed, a science-oriented approach to the study of social relations took root only during this century, and has flourished primarily during the past three or four decades. Despite its recent arrival on the scene, though, social psychology has already made considerable progress. Perhaps the breadth of the valuable information it has uncovered is best suggested by the following list, which offers a small sample of the topics currently under investigation by social psychologists:

(1) How are stereotypes formed? How can they be changed?
(2) How does alcohol affect human social behavior?
(3) Does our present mood affect our evaluations of others or the information about them that we later remember?
(4) What are the causes of shyness? Do individuals sometimes use this behavior as a means of protecting their self-image?
(5) Does exposure to pornography — especially violent pornography — contribute to the occurrence of sexual assaults and related crimes?
(6) How do people react when they feel they have been treated unfairly?
(7) Do males and females differ in their performance of various tasks? In their creativity? In their leadership potential?
(8) How do intimate relationships form, develop, and sometimes dissolve?
(9) Why do some individuals behave consistently across a wide range of social situations, while others seem to change their behavior (and even their personalities) as they move from one setting to another?
(10) Why do individuals tend to take credit for favorable outcomes but tend to blame others for unfavorable ones?
(11) When jury members are told to disregard information they have previously received, can they really do so?
(12) Why are the members of large crowds often willing to engage in actions they would never perform as individuals?

As even this short list suggests, social psychologists have turned their attention to a wide range of issues. Indeed, if modern social psy-

ON THE APPLIED SIDE

Understanding Social Behavior: Why, Ultimately, It's Essential

Social behavior is fascinating. Further, enhanced knowledge about it is certainly valuable from a purely scientific point of view. But what about practical benefits—will these, too, follow from increased understanding of social relations? We believe the answer is "yes." The major reason for this reply, simply, is that in our opinion none of the most serious problems facing humanity today—overpopulation, a rising tide of violence, growing industrial pollution—can be solved through purely technological approaches. Rather, solutions to these dangerous problems will require important shifts in human behavior and attitudes, in addition to impressive advances in engineering and technology (refer to Figure 1.3). To see why this is so, let's take them one at a time.

First, consider overpopulation. Even if to-

FIGURE 1.3. Can problems such as overpopulation, rising levels of violence, and pollution be solved entirely through technological means? We sincerely doubt it.

Solving social problems: Technology alone is not enough

chology has a "middle name," *diversity* is it! Before we turn to these intriguing topics, however, we feel it will be useful to pause briefly, in order to provide you with certain background information. In the remainder of this chapter, then, we will focus on completing three preliminary tasks. First, we will present a formal *definition* of social psychology —our view of what it is and what it seeks to accomplish. Second, we will

tally safe and completely effective contraceptives are developed, there is no guarantee they will be used. And they will certainly have little impact on population growth unless millions of people decide to adopt them. Second, consider pollution. While new techniques for dealing with toxic wastes and rendering them harmless are certainly essential, they will not be put to large-scale use unless millions of persons (including government and industry leaders) decide that the huge costs of doing so are justified. Finally, turning to human violence, it is clear that neither super weapons nor super defenses will eliminate warfare or senseless acts of violence; only shifts in human attitudes and values concerning such behavior can accomplish this goal.

In sum, there appear to be powerful grounds for seeking increased scientific knowledge about human social behavior. Indeed, in our view, advances in such knowledge may ultimately prove just as essential to continued human survival as gains in technology and engineering.

offer a capsule summary of social psychology's *history* — how it began, how it developed, and where it is today. Finally, we will examine some of the basic methods used by social psychologists in their *research*. Our goal here is simple: helping you to understand just how the facts and principles presented throughout this text were obtained. (Why, precisely, should we seek to understand social behavior? Does such knowledge have any practical importance or value? For some comments on these issues, please see the special insert on pages 8–9.)

SOCIAL PSYCHOLOGY: A Working Definition

Suggesting a formal definition of almost any field is a complex task. In the case of social psychology, these difficulties are intensified by two factors: (1) the field's diversity and (2) its rapid rate of change. Despite the broad sweep of topics they choose to study, though, most social psychologists seem to focus the bulk of their attention on the following central task: understanding the behavior of individuals in social contexts. In short, they are primarily concerned with comprehending how and why individuals behave, think, and feel as they do in situations involving the presence (actual or symbolic) of others. Taking this central focus into account, our working definition of social psychology is as follows: *Social psychology is the scientific field that seeks to understand the nature and causes of individual behavior in social situations.* (Please note that by the term "behavior" we mean feelings and thoughts as well as overt actions.) Since this definition, like all others, is a bit abstract, please bear with us for a few moments while we clarify several of its major features.

Social psychology is scientific in orientation

In the minds of many persons, the term "science" refers primarily (or even exclusively) to specific fields of study such as chemistry, physics, and biology. Such individuals, of course, will find somewhat puzzling our suggestion that social psychology, too, is scientific. How, they may wonder, can a field that seeks to investigate the nature of love, the causes of interpersonal violence, and everything in between be scientific in the same sense as nuclear physics or neuroscience? The answer is surprisingly simple. In reality, the term "science" does *not* refer to a select group of highly advanced fields. Rather, "science" refers to a general set of methods—techniques that can be used to study a wide range of topics. In deciding whether a given field is scientific, therefore, the crucial question is this: does it make use of such procedures? To the extent it does, it may be viewed as scientific in orientation; to the extent it does not, it can be perceived as falling outside the realm of science. When this basic criterion is applied to social psychology, there can be little doubt that it fits into the first of these two categories. In their efforts to understand social behavior, social psychologists rely heavily on the same basic methods as other scientists. Thus, while the topics they study are certainly different from those in older and more established fields, their overall approach—and so social psychology itself—is clearly a scientific one.

Social psychology focuses on the behavior of individuals

Societies may differ in terms of their overall level of bigotry, but it is individual persons who hold stereotypes about specific groups, experience negative feelings toward them, and seek to exclude them from their neighborhoods, jobs, and schools. Similarly, it is specific persons who give aid to others, who commit acts of violence, and who fall in or out of love. In short, social behavior, ultimately, is performed by specific persons. With this basic fact firmly in mind, social psychologists have chosen to focus the bulk of their attention upon the actions and thoughts of individuals in social situations (ones involving the real or symbolic presence of others). They realize, of course, that such behavior always occurs against a backdrop of sociocultural factors (e.g., group membership, culturally shared standards and values). But their major interest is that of understanding the factors that shape and direct the actions of individual human beings in a wide range of social settings.

Social psychology seeks to comprehend the causes of social behavior

In a key sense, this is the most central aspect of our definition: it specifies the very essence of our field. What it means is this: social psychologists are primarily concerned with understanding the wide range of conditions that shape the social behavior of individuals — their actions, feelings, and thoughts with respect to other persons. Interest in this issue, in turn, stems from a basic belief: knowledge about these conditions will permit us both to predict social behavior and, perhaps, to change it in desirable ways. Thus, it may have important practical as well as scientific outcomes.

As you can readily guess, the task of identifying all the factors that affect our behavior with respect to others is one of huge proportions. Social behavior is shaped by a seemingly endless list of variables, so in this sense social psychologists truly have their work cut out for them! While the number of specific factors influencing social reactions is large, however, it appears that most fall into five major categories. These involve (1) the behavior and characteristics of other persons, (2) social cognition (our thoughts, attitudes, and memories about the persons around us), (3) ecological variables (direct and indirect influences of the physical environment), (4) the sociocultural context in which social behavior occurs, and (5) aspects of our biological nature relevant to social behavior (Georgoudi and Rosnow, 1985). Perhaps a few words on each of these categories will clarify their basic nature. (Also, please refer to Figure 1.4, page 12.)

That social behavior is strongly affected by the actions and characteristics of other persons is obvious. For example, consider how your feelings, behavior, and thoughts would be affected by each of the following events: (1) a teller in a bank places a "closed" sign in front of her

FIGURE 1.4. Social behavior stems from many different causes. Among the most important of these are (1) the behavior and characteristics of others, (2) social cognition, (3) ecological (environmental) variables, (4) sociocultural factors, and (5) biological factors.

Social behavior: A summary of its major causes

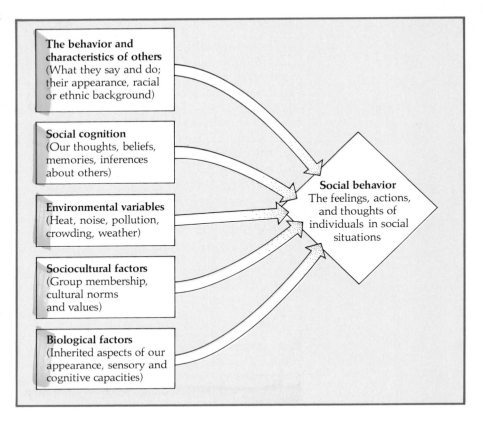

window just as you step up to the counter; (2) another driver recklessly cuts you off in traffic and then makes an obscene gesture when you honk your horn in warning; (3) your date whispers into your ear, "My place or yours?" Clearly, each of these actions by another person would exert strong effects upon you.

In a similar manner, the observable characteristics of others, too, strongly affect our feelings, thoughts, and subsequent behavior (e.g., Warner and Sugarman, 1986). We often react differently to highly attractive persons than to unattractive ones; we treat well dressed and well groomed people differently from those who are not so well turned-out; and we even respond to others' style of speech, apparent age, and ethnic backgrounds.

While the behavior and characteristics of others play an important part in shaping behavior, however, they are only part of the total picture. In addition, we are also influenced by **social cognition**—our own thoughts, beliefs, attitudes, and memories about other persons. For example, imagine that during a phone conversation with a business associate the line suddenly goes dead. How do you react? Clearly, this depends on your interpretation of the causes behind this event. If you conclude that you were simply cut off by faulty equipment, you will respond in one manner. If, instead, you decide that the other person purposely hung up on you, your reaction will be quite different! In these and countless other settings, our behavior toward others is determined by our thoughts, memories, inferences, and beliefs about them. Thus, such factors are of major interest to social psychologists.

The impact of the physical environment upon social behavior, too, is readily illustrated. For some personal insight into such effects, simply recall how you have felt and behaved on hot, humid days and on cool, dry ones. If you are like most persons, you probably remember being more irritable, and perhaps harder to get along with, when uncomfortably hot than when comfortably cool. In a similar manner, many other environmental variables, such as noise, pollution, excessive crowding, and even many aspects of weather all seem to affect our moods, cognitive processes, and overt actions toward others (e.g., Rotton and Frey, 1985).

Finally, we should note that social behavior definitely does *not* unfold in either a cultural or a biological vacuum. With respect to the former, such factors as cultural norms (rules about how people should behave in specific situations), our membership in various groups, and shifting societal standards or values can influence many aspects of our behavior — everything from our political attitudes on the one hand through our choice of marriage partner on the other. Similarly, some biological factors (e.g., inherited aspects of our physical appearance, built-in limits to our capacity to process social information) affect key aspects of our behavior in many social settings. It is probably fair to conclude that in the past, both sociocultural and biological factors have received less attention from social psychologists than the other types of potential causes. However, they, too, often play a role in shaping social behavior and so fall within the scope of both our field and this text.

Social psychology: Summing up

To conclude: social psychology focuses mainly on the task of understanding the causes of social behavior — identifying factors that shape our feelings, behavior, and thought in social situations. Further, it seeks to accomplish this goal through the use of essentially scientific methods. The remainder of this text is devoted to the task of summarizing the findings uncovered by social psychologists in their studies of social interaction. This information is intriguing, so we're sure you'll find it to be of interest. But please be warned: it is also full of surprises, and what you learn will challenge many of your current views about people and relations between them. Thus, it's probably safe to predict that after exposure to it, you'll never think about social relations in quite the same way as before. If you value such change, and look forward to new insights, read on; if not, now is the time to turn back!

SOCIAL PSYCHOLOGY: A Capsule Memoir

When precisely, did social psychology begin? This is a difficult question to answer, for speculation about social behavior has continued since the days of antiquity (Allport, 1985). Thus, any attempt to present a complete survey of its historical roots would quickly bog us down in endless lists of names and dates. Since we definitely wish to avoid that pitfall, this discussion will be limited in scope. Specifically, we will focus on the emergence of social psychology as an independent field, its growth during the middle decades of this century, and its current status and trends.

The early years: Social psychology emerges

Few fields of science mark their beginnings with formal, ribbon-cutting ceremonies. Instead, most develop in a gradual manner, as growing numbers of scholars become interested in certain topics, or develop new methods for studying old ones. This was certainly the pattern for social psychology. No bottles of champagne were uncorked to mark its entry upon the scientific scene. Thus, it is difficult to choose a specific date for its "official" arrival. As a rough guess, though, the years between 1908 and 1924 seem to qualify as the period when it first emerged as an independent entity. Each of these dates represents a year in which an important text containing the words "social psychology" in its title was published. Comparison of the two volumes is informative. The first, published in 1908 by William McDougall, was based largely on the view that social behavior stems from a small number of innate tendencies or *instincts*. This view is currently rejected by almost all social psychologists, so it is clear that the field had not assumed its modern form at that time.

The second volume, published in 1924 by Floyd Allport, provides a sharp contrast. In fact, it is much closer in orientation to that of social psychology as it exists today. Basically, this text argued that social behavior stems from — and is influenced by — many factors, including the presence of other persons and their specific actions. Further, it contained discussions of actual research which had already been performed on topics such as the ability to recognize the emotions of others from their facial expressions, social conformity, and the impact of audiences on task performance. The fact that we will return to each of these topics in later chapters points to the following conclusion: by the middle of the "Roaring Twenties," social psychology had appeared on the scene and begun to focus on many of the issues and topics it still seeks to study today.

The years following publication of Allport's text were marked by rapid growth. New issues were studied, and systematic methods for investigating them were rapidly developed. Especially important was the work of two major figures in the history of social psychology: Muzafer Sherif and Kurt Lewin. Sherif (1935) began the study of *social norms* — rules informing individuals how they should or ought to behave. We will consider these in more detail in Chapter 7. Lewin and his colleagues (Lewin, Lippitt, and White, 1939) began the systematic study of *leadership* and related *group processes* (see Chapter 11). Further, they urged the adoption of an approach in which careful scientific methods are applied to the study of key social problems — a tradition that has persisted within social psychology to the present time (refer to Chapter 13). By the end of the 1930s, then, social psychology was clearly an active, growing field.

Decades of growth: The 1940s, 1950s, and 1960s

After a pause produced by World War II, social psychology continued its progress during the late 1940s and 1950s. During this period, it expanded its scope in several directions. First, it focused much attention upon the influence of groups and of group membership on individual behavior (Forsyth, 1983). Second, it examined the link between various personality traits and social behavior. Perhaps the major event of the period, however, was the development of the theory of **cognitive dissonance** (Festinger, 1957). This framework proposed that human beings dislike inconsistency and will strive to reduce it. Specifically, it argues that we find inconsistency between our attitudes — or inconsistency between our attitudes and our behavior — disturbing, and seek to eliminate it. While these ideas may not strike you as very surprising, they actually lead to many unexpected predictions. For example, they suggest that offering individuals small rewards for stating views they don't really hold may often be much more effective in getting them to change their opinions than offering them larger rewards for engaging in such behavior — a principle sometimes known as the "less leads to more" effect. Festinger's theory captured the interest of many social psychologists, and it remained a major topic of research for several decades. (We will return to this theory in Chapter 4.)

In an important sense, the 1960s can be viewed as the time when social psychology "came into its own." During this turbulent decade the number of social psychologists rose dramatically (see Figure 1.5 on page 16), and the field expanded its scope to include virtually every imaginable aspect of social interaction. So many lines of research either began or developed during these years that we could not possibly list all of them here. Among the topics and questions receiving major attention, though, were these: *social perception* (how do we form first impressions of others? how do we determine the causes behind others' behavior?); *aggression* (what are the roots of this dangerous type of behavior? how can it be controlled?); *attraction* and *love* (why do individuals like or dislike others? what is the nature of romantic love?); *group decision making* (how do groups go about making decisions? do such decisions differ from ones made by individuals?); *equity* and *inequity* (how do people react when they feel that they are being treated unfairly by others?); and *proso-*

FIGURE 1.5. As shown here, the number of social psychologists in the U.S. rose more rapidly during the 1960s than at any other time. (Note: Figures shown are the number of social psychologists belonging to Division 8 of the American Psychological Association. Social psychologists who were not members of this organization are not included in the totals.)

Social psychology's own "population explosion"

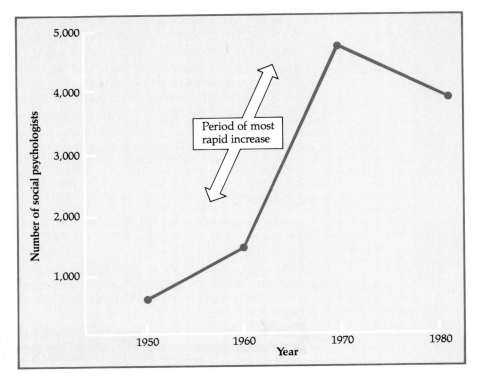

cial behavior (why do people sometimes fail to come to the aid of others during emergencies?). As you can see from even this brief list, social psychology moved into many new areas during the 1960s.

The 1970s, 1980s and beyond: Where we are and where we're going

The rapid pace of change we have just described did not slacken during the 1970s. If anything, it accelerated! Many lines of study begun during the 1960s were continued and expanded. Second, several new topics rose to prominence, or were investigated from a new and more sophisticated perspective. Among the most important of these were: *attribution* (how do we infer the causes behind others'—and our own—behavior?); *sex roles* and *sex discrimination* (how are sex roles and sex role stereotypes acquired? what forces work against full equality for females in many societies?); *environmental psychology* (what is the impact of the physical environment—heat, noise, crowding, pollution—upon social behavior?).

In addition, two larger-scale trends took shape in the 1970s and have expanded in the 1980s. Since these are of great importance, we will consider them separately here.

Growing influence of the cognitive perspective.   As we noted earlier, social psychologists have long been aware of the fact that cognitive factors — attitudes, beliefs, values, inferences — play a key role in social behavior. Starting in the late 1970s, however, interest in such topics has taken an exciting new form. At present, many of our colleagues believe that our understanding of a wide range of social phenomena can be greatly enhanced through adoption of a strategy in which we first seek to comprehend the basic cognitive processes that underlie them (Markus and Zajonc, 1985). Consistent with this view, they have investigated a wide range of social processes, including stereotypes (Hamilton, Dugan, and Trolier, 1985), group decision making (Lurigio and Carroll, 1985), and persuasion (Rule, Bisanz, and Kohn, 1985) from a cognitive perspective. What this involves, in essence, is efforts to apply basic knowledge about such issues as (1) how memory operates, (2) how reasoning occurs, and (3) how information is integrated by the human mind, to complex social processes. Thus, to mention just one example, the formation and persistence of stereotypes is understood in the context of certain aspects of memory, which lead us to recall only certain types of information about others, and several aspects of social inference (reasoning), that lead us to jump to false conclusions about others.

The results of research conducted within this general perspective have been impressive, to say the least. Major insights into key aspects of social behavior have been gained, and new phenomena previously overlooked have been brought sharply into focus (Fiske and Taylor, 1984). Thus, it is far from surprising that the volume of work concerned with cognitive factors and cognitive processes has risen sharply in recent years.

On the other side of the coin, some critics have noted that the current emphasis on cognition in social psychology has diverted attention away from other basic tasks, for example, efforts to study social behavior in naturally occurring situations, and concern with important current social issues (Carlson, 1984). While we do see some basis for such complaints, it is our view and that of many of our colleagues (e.g., Kenrick, 1986) that the situation will prove largely self-correcting. As information about the cognitive processes underlying social interaction grows, it will gradually spread until it is applied to virtually all topics that have traditionally been of interest to social psychologists. Thus, it may ultimately play an *integrative* role, pulling diverse lines of research and contrasting bodies of knowledge together into a unified whole. To the extent it yields such results, the cognitive perspective will certainly prove to be a major "plus" for our field.

Growing emphasis on application: The "exportation" of social knowledge.   The 1970s and especially the 1980s have also been marked by a second major trend where social psychology is concerned: growing interest in the application of social knowledge (Oskamp, 1984). An increasing number of social psychologists have turned their attention to questions concerning *personal health* (e.g., what factors help individuals resist the harmful effects of stress?), the *legal process* (e.g., how valid is eyewitness testimony?), and the functioning of large *organizations* (e.g., how can performance in various jobs best be evaluated or appraised?). (Refer to Figure 1.6.) In addition, many other social psychologists have actually moved from positions within departments of psychology to jobs in schools of business, law, and medicine, or to posts in government agencies or private corporations. In such locations, they apply their unique skills and knowledge to a wide range of practical issues, and also serve a major educational function as well. We view this "exportation" of social knowledge to other fields, and to society as a whole, as a healthy development; further, we look forward to many practical benefits from it in the years ahead.

FIGURE 1.6. In recent years social psychologists have shown increasing interest in applying their special skills and knowledge to a wide range of practical problems. Thus, they have made growing contributions to such fields as law, health care, and business.

Social psychology: Increasing interest in application

So where do we go from here? A brief glance at the future.   Earlier in this chapter, we noted that *diversity* is social psychology's "middle name." For this reason, guesses about its future development are risky — perhaps as risky as trying to predict the up-and-down motions of the stock market! Even with this warning firmly in mind, though, we are still willing to make several predictions about where social psychology may, perhaps, go from here.

First, we believe that the cognitive perspective described above will continue to grow and prosper. Indeed, we expect it to spread to all areas of the field, and to provide it with a degree of conceptual unity it has not enjoyed before. Second, we believe that the shift toward application, too, will continue. This will be the case both because of economic necessity (sources of financial support for "pure" social research have decreased sharply in recent years), and also because increasing maturity in any field of science tends to foster growing interest in application of the knowledge gained. Third, and probably riskiest of all, we predict that social psychologists will gradually direct increasing attention to the study of social behavior in natural settings, and to the impact of sociocultural factors (e.g., cultural norms, socioeconomic status). The major basis for this belief is the recent emergence of what has been termed the *contextualist view* — a perspective suggesting that no form of social behavior can be understood apart from the context in which it occurs (Georgoudi and Rosnow, 1985). Since sociocultural factors form a backdrop for much of social behavior, it seems only reasonable to expect that greater attention will be focused on such variables in the years ahead.

These, then, are our predictions. Only time will tell whether and to what extent they will be confirmed. Regardless of their fate, however, there is one additional prediction we are willing to make with considerably greater conviction: no matter how social psychology changes in the years ahead, it will remain an active, vital field — one with considerable potential for contributing in essential ways to overall human welfare.

ADDING TO WHAT WE KNOW: *Research Methods in Social Psychology*

By now, we hope you are convinced of two facts: (1) social behavior is truly fascinating; (2) learning more about it is worthwhile. If you agree with these points, you will also be interested in the next question we will address: how, precisely, do social psychologists "do their thing"? How, in short, do they attempt to add to existing knowledge about social interaction? Answering this question will require three steps. First we will describe the major *methods* in social psychological research — the experimental and correlational approaches. Next we will examine the role of *theory* in such research. Finally, we will consider some of the complex *ethical issues* that often arise in the context of systematic research on human social behavior.

The experimental method: Knowledge through intervention

Because it is the research method preferred by most social psychologists, we will begin with **experimentation.** Unfortunately, our past experience suggests that many persons view this approach as both mysterious and complex. Actually, this is far from the case. In its basic logic, experimentation is surprisingly simple. To help you understand its use in social research, we will first describe its basic nature — how it actually proceeds. Then we will comment briefly on two conditions essential for its success.

Experimentation: Its basic nature.   A researcher who decides to employ the experimental method generally begins with a clear-cut goal: determining whether a given factor (variable) influences some aspect of social behavior. In order to answer this question, such a researcher follows two basic steps: she or he (1) varies the presence or strength of this factor in a systematic manner and (2) tries to determine whether these variations have any impact upon the aspect of social behavior under investigation. The central idea behind these procedures can be put as follows: if the factor varied does exert such effects, individuals exposed to different levels or amounts of the factor should show different patterns of behavior. That is, exposure to a small amount of the factor should result in one level of behavior, exposure to a larger amount should result in another level, and so on.

Generally, the factor systematically varied by the researcher is termed the *independent variable,* while the behavior (or aspect of behavior) studied is termed the *dependent variable.* In a simple experiment, then, subjects in different groups are exposed to contrasting levels of the independent variable (e.g., low, moderate, high). The behavior of these persons is then carefully examined and compared to determine whether it does in fact vary with different levels or amounts of the independent variable. If it does — and if two other conditions we shall mention below are met — it can be tentatively concluded that the independent variable does indeed affect the form of behavior being studied.

Since our discussion so far has been somewhat abstract, perhaps a concrete example will now prove useful. Let's consider an experiment designed to examine the *hypothesis* (an as yet unverified suggestion) that being touched by a stranger in a nonthreatening way induces positive reactions on the part of the persons being touched. The independent variable in such research would be the presence (and perhaps amount) of touching. Thus, we might arrange to expose three different groups of subjects to contrasting levels of this factor (e.g., no touching, being touched briefly, being touched for a longer period of time). This could be accomplished in many different ways, but for the sake of argument, let's assume that we decide to perform our study in a natural setting — restaurants. Here, we may enlist the aid of several waiters and waitresses, and arrange for them to avoid touching customers in one condition, to touch them briefly (0.5 seconds) in another, and to touch them for a longer period (1.0 seconds) in a third. Since the waiters and waitresses would assist in the research, they would serve as *accomplices* or *confederates*. (This is a common arrangement in many social psychological experiments; social psychologists often need the aid of other persons in carrying out their projects.) The dependent variable would then be some measure of subjects' (i.e., customers') reactions to the waiters and waitresses. For example, it might be the size of the tip they left, or their responses to a brief questionnaire where they rate the service they received. If touching does indeed affect reactions on the part of the persons receiving such treatment, we would expect differences among the three groups to appear. For example, we might find that those in the no-touch condition leave the smallest tips, or report the lowest ratings. Those in the brief-touch group might leave the largest tips and provide the highest ratings. And those in the prolonged-touch condition might fall somewhere in between on both of these dependent measures (refer to Figure 1.7). If such results were obtained (or if the three groups differed in any other way), we could conclude, at least tentatively, that touching does affect reaction to a stranger, at least in the way measured here. (Actually, several studies concerned with this topic have already been conducted,

FIGURE 1.7. In the study illustrated here, the *independent variable* was the extent to which waiters or waitresses touched customers in restaurants. The *dependent variable* was the size of the tips left by these persons. Results indicated that tips were largest in the brief-touch condition, smallest in the no-touch condition, and intermediate in the prolonged-touch condition.

Experimentation: A simple example

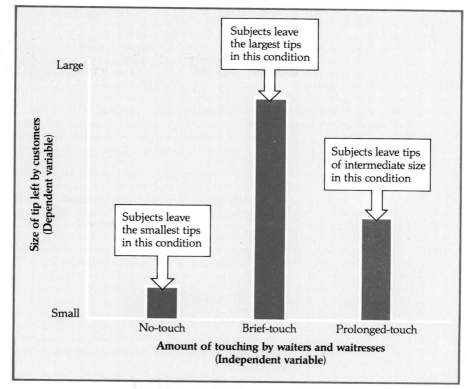

e.g., Crusco and Wetzel, 1984. They are discussed in Chapter 2.)

At this point we should note that the example just presented describes an extremely simple case — the simplest type of experiment one could conduct. In many instances, researchers wish to examine the impact of several independent variables at once. For example, in the study just described, the sex of the customers and the attractiveness of the persons doing the touching might also be considered, along with touch itself. When several variables are included in an experiment, a larger amount of information can usually be obtained. Even more important, potential *interactions* between two or more of the variables under study can be examined. We can determine whether the impact of one independent variable is affected in some manner by one or more other variables. For example, in the experiment described above, we might find that touch has different effects when it comes from a member of one's own sex as opposed to a member of the opposite sex, or that it operates differently when delivered by an attractive than by an unattractive person. Because social behavior is usually affected by many factors and conditions operating at once, knowledge of such interaction is important. Thus, we will discuss many of them in later parts of this book.

Successful experimentation: Two basic requirements. Earlier, we noted that before we can conclude that an independent variable has affected some form of behavior, two important conditions must be met. Because a basic understanding of these is essential for evaluating the usefulness of any experiment, we will now describe them for you.

The first involves what is generally termed **random assignment of subjects to groups.** According to this principle, each person taking part in a study must have an equal chance of being exposed to each level of the independent variable. The reason for this rule is simple: if subjects are *not* randomly assigned to each group, it may prove impossible to determine whether differences in their later behavior stem from differences they brought with them to the study, or from the impact of the independent variable. For example, returning to the study just described, imagine that for some reason all of the customers assigned to the brief-touch condition were businessmen and businesswomen dining on expense accounts, while customers in the other two groups (no-touch, prolonged-touch) were paying for their meals themselves. Further, suppose that once again, we found that those in the brief-touch condition left the largest tips. Does this mean that touching others briefly produces more favorable reactions in them than touching them for longer periods of time or not at all? Not necessarily. It may simply be that people dining on expense accounts tend to leave bigger tips than those who must pay for their meals out of their own pockets. In order to avoid problems such as these, it would be necessary to assure that those on expense accounts and those not enjoying such benefits have an equal chance of receiving any of the three experimental treatments — that is, that they be *randomly assigned* to each of these groups.

The second condition we referred to above may be stated as follows: insofar as possible, all other factors that might also affect subjects' behav-

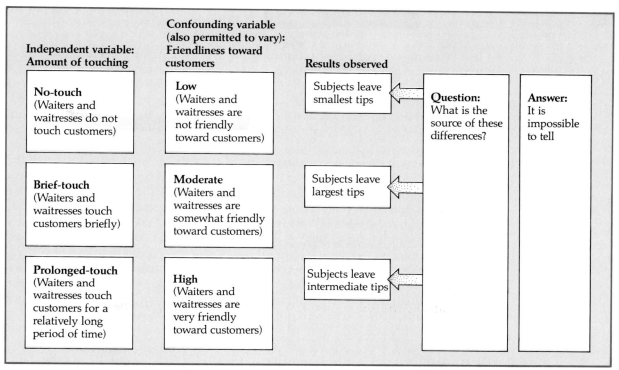

Independent variable: Amount of touching	Confounding variable (also permitted to vary): Friendliness toward customers	Results observed		
No-touch (Waiters and waitresses do not touch customers)	**Low** (Waiters and waitresses are not friendly toward customers)	Subjects leave smallest tips	**Question:** What is the source of these differences?	**Answer:** It is impossible to tell
Brief-touch (Waiters and waitresses touch customers briefly)	**Moderate** (Waiters and waitresses are somewhat friendly toward customers)	Subjects leave largest tips		
Prolonged-touch (Waiters and waitresses touch customers for a relatively long period of time)	**High** (Waiters and waitresses are very friendly toward customers)	Subjects leave intermediate tips		

FIGURE 1.8. When factors other than the independent variable are also permitted to vary in an experiment, it may be impossible to interpret obtained results. In the example shown here, the independent variable was the amount of touching of customers by waiters and waitresses. However, waiters and waitresses also varied their level of friendliness toward customers, without any instructions to do so from the experimenter. Because of such *confounding* it is impossible to tell whether the observed results stemmed from the impact of the independent variable (touching), this other factor (friendliness), or some combination of the two.

Confounding of variables in an experiment

ior, aside from the independent variable, must be held constant. To see why this is so, consider the following situation. In the study on the impact of touching, the waiters and waitresses decide to "help the study along." Thus, when they don't touch the customers, they also treat them in a cold and distant manner. When they touch them briefly, they are a little friendlier. And when they touch them even more, they also do their best to be as friendly as possible. Results are now as follows: subjects in the no-touch group leave the smallest tips, those in the brief-touch group leave larger ones, and those in the prolonged-touch condition leave the biggest tips of all. What do these findings mean? Actually, we can't really tell. There is no way of knowing whether these results stem from the impact of being touched, the increasing friendliness shown by the waiters and waitresses in the two touch conditions, or some combination of these factors. In short, the independent variable of interest — touching — is **confounded** with another variable the experimenter never meant to introduce: degree of friendliness. The potential effects of each cannot be separated or disentangled (refer to Figure 1.8).

In the case we have just described, confounding between variables is relatively easy to spot. Often, though, it can enter in more subtle and hidden ways. For this reason, researchers wishing to conduct successful experiments must always be on guard against it. Only when such confounding is prevented can the results of an experiment be interpreted with confidence.

The correlational method: Knowledge through systematic observation

Earlier, we noted that experimentation is usually the preferred method of research in social psychology. (We will comment on why this is so shortly.) Sometimes, though, it simply cannot be used. This can be true for either of two general reasons. First, systematic variation of some factor of interest may simply lie beyond a researcher's control. For example, imagine that a would-be experimenter has reason to believe that height plays a major role in political elections; taller candidates have an important edge and usually win. Clearly, he or she could not vary the stature of persons running for public office or arrange to have candidates of different height compete against each other in the same elections. Second, ethical constraints may prevent a researcher from conducting what might otherwise be a feasible experiment. It may be possible to vary some factor of interest, but doing so would violate basic ethical standards accepted by all social psychologists. For example, imagine that a researcher suspects that certain events play a key role in triggering dangerous riots. Certainly, it would be unethical to stage such events in some locations but not in others in order to determine if collective violence actually erupts more frequently under the first set of conditions than under the second. Similarly, consider the dilemma faced by a social psychologist who believes that certain kinds of jealousy are especially damaging to romantic relationships. It would clearly be unethical to test this suggestion by conducting an experiment in which happy couples are exposed to varying amounts of such jealousy, and then counting the number who break up or get divorced!

When faced with such restrictions, social psychologists do not simply give up and shift their attention elsewhere. Instead, they often adopt an alternative technique of research known as the **correlational method**. In this approach, efforts are made to determine whether two or more variables are related by engaging in careful observation of both. If changes in one are found to be consistently associated with changes in the other, evidence for a link between them is obtained. Please note: in contrast to the experimental method, *no attempt is made to vary one of the factors in a systematic manner in order to observe its effect on the other.* Rather, *naturally occurring* variations in both are observed to determine whether they tend to occur together in some fashion (hence, the term *co*-relation.).

Perhaps the best way of illustrating the correlational method, and indicating how it differs from experimentation, is by returning to the topic discussed earlier — the impact of touch — and demonstrating how it might be studied through systematic observation.

Procedures here would be relatively simple. First, we would obtain the permission of a large number of restaurant managers to observe interactions between waiters or waitresses and customers during some period of time (e.g., several days or weeks). Then, we would carefully observe a large number of such interactions. Specifically, we would make systematic records of (1) whether and to what extent waiters and waitresses touch their customers, and (2) reactions of customers to these persons. (This could be assessed in terms of the size of tips left by patrons, the number of complaints they make about the service they received, and similar measures.) If being touched does indeed produce positive reactions among persons who receive it, we might observe an increase in tips and a reduction in complaints, in cases where touching occurs relative to instances where it does not.

Note again that in such an investigation we would *not* attempt to control the amount or frequency of touching by waiters or waitresses. Rather, we would simply observe naturally occurring variations in such behavior, and determine whether these are related in any manner to reactions on the part of customers.

The correlational method offers several key advantages. It can be employed to study behavior in many real-life settings. It is often highly efficient and can yield large amounts of interesting data in a short period of time. And, as we noted earlier, it can be used to study topics that, because of practical or ethical constraints, simply can't be studied through experimentation. Unfortunately, though, this approach suffers from one major drawback that greatly lessens its appeal: in contrast to experimentation, the findings it yields are often somewhat uncertain with respect to cause-and-effect relationships. That is, the fact that changes in one variable are accompanied by changes in another does not in any sense guarantee that there is a causal link between them — that changes in the first *caused* alterations in the second. (See Figure 1.9 for an

FIGURE 1.9. The fact that changes in one variable are accompanied by changes in another in no way guarantees a causal link between them (i.e., that changes in one cause changes in the other). Thus, the character in this cartoon has no real basis for his conclusion that the weather is responsible for problems with his car. (Source: Copyright, 1985 Universal Press Syndicate. Reprinted with permission. All rights reserved.)

Correlation: A shaky basis for assuming causation

amusing illustration of this fact.) Rather, in many cases, a tendency of two variables to rise or fall together simply reflects the fact that both are caused by a third, perhaps less visible, factor.

Sometimes this fact is obvious and easy to spot. For example, it has long been observed that the greater the number of storks nesting on rooftops in Holland during the winter, the greater the number of human births nine months later. Does this mean that ancient myths are correct: the presence of storks somehow increases human fertility? Obviously not. Rather, both factors (an increased number of storks and the human birth rate) are related to a third: severity of winter weather. The colder the winter, the more storks seek the warmth of roofs. And the colder the weather, the more human beings stay indoors and cuddle—hence, a rise in births.

In other cases, though, it may be more tempting to assume causality where none actually exists. For example, it has sometimes been observed that in major cities, crime rates increase with degree of crowding. Does this mean that crowding causes crime? Not necessarily. Again, both factors may be related to a third: personal income. The poorer people are, the more crowded their living conditions. And the poorer they are, the more likely they may be to become desperate and turn to crime. Similarly, it is frequently noted that as people grow older, they adopt more conservative political beliefs. Does this imply that age causes conservatism? Again, we can't be sure. It may be that as people age, they also get richer. And this factor—not simply mounting "miles"—may be the major cause of their shifting political views.

By now, the main point of this discussion should be clear. The existence of even a strong correlation between two factors should not be interpreted as a definite indication that they are causally linked. Such conclusions are justified only in the presence of additional confirming evidence.

Theory: Essential guide to research

"How do social psychologists come up with the ideas for their studies?" This is a question we often hear from students in our classes. Our reply touches on several points. First, we note that ideas for research projects are often suggested by observation of the social world around us. Researchers notice some aspect of social behavior that is puzzling or surprising, and plan investigations to shed new light upon it. Second, we call attention to the fact that successful experiments tend to raise more questions than they answer. Thus, the problem facing social psychologists is usually not that of coming up with interesting ideas for further study; rather, it is choosing among the many enticing possibilities. Third, and most central of all, we point to the essential role of **theory**. In our view, this is the most important single source of research in social psychology. For this reason alone, it is worthy of our careful attention here.

Put very simply, theory represents efforts, by scientists in any field, to answer the question "why?" In short, it involves attempts to understand precisely *why* certain events or processes occur as they do. In this sense, theory goes beyond mere observation or description of various aspects of social behavior; it seeks to *explain* them. The development of comprehensive, accurate theories is a major goal of all science (Howard, 1985), and social psychology is no exception to this basic rule. Thus, a great deal of research in our field is concerned with efforts to construct, refine, and test such frameworks. But what precisely are theories? And what is their value in social psychology? Perhaps the best means of answering such questions is, again, through a concrete example.

Imagine that we observe the following: when people work together in a group, each member exerts less effort on the joint task than when they work alone. (This is known as *social loafing,* and is discussed in Chapter 11.) The observation just described is certainly useful by itself. After all, it allows us to predict what will happen when individuals work together, and it also suggests the possibility of intervening in some manner to prevent such outcomes. These two accomplishments — *prediction* and *intervention* (sometimes known as *control*) — are major goals of science. Yet, the fact that social loafing occurs does not explain *why* it takes place. It is at this point that theory enters the picture.

In older and more advanced fields such as physics or chemistry, theories are often phrased as mathematical equations. In social psychology, however, they are usually verbal statements or assertions. For example, a theory designed to account for social loafing might read as follows. When persons work together, they realize that their outputs will not be individually identifiable, and that all participants will share in the responsibility for the final outcome. As a result, they conclude that they can get away with "taking it easy," and so exert less effort on the task. Note that this theory, like all others, consists of two parts: several basic concepts (e.g., individual effort, shared responsibility) and statements concerning the relationships between these concepts (e.g., as belief in shared responsibility increases, individual effort decreases).

Once a theory has been formulated, a crucial process begins. First, predictions are derived from the theory. These are formulated in accordance with the basic principles of logic, and are known as *hypotheses.* For example, one such prediction that might be derived from the theory of social loafing outlined above would be as follows: to the extent members of a group believe their work will be individually identifiable, social loafing will decrease.

Next, such predictions are tested in actual research. If they are confirmed, confidence in the accuracy of the theory is increased: it is viewed as providing an adequate explanation for the phenomena with which it deals. If, instead, such predictions are disconfirmed, confidence in the theory is weakened. Then, the theory itself may be altered so as to generate new predictions, and these, in turn, can be subjected to test. In short, the process is a continuous one, involving the free flow of information

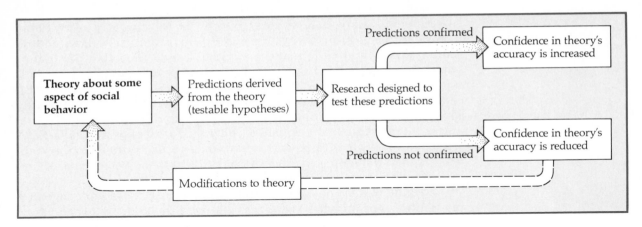

FIGURE 1.10.   Once theories are formulated in social psychology (or any other branch of science), they are put to empirical test. This involves a process in which predictions derived from the theory are examined in actual research. If these predictions are confirmed, confidence in the theory's accuracy is increased. If they are disconfirmed, confidence in the theory's accuracy is reduced. In the latter case, the theory may be modified so as to generate new predictions, and these, in turn, may be tested.

Putting theories to the test: An ongoing process

between a theory, predictions derived from it, and the findings of ongoing research. (Please see Figure 1.10 for a summary of this process.)

Please note, by the way, that theories are useful, from a scientific point of view, only to the extent that they lead to testable predictions. Indeed, if they do not generate hypotheses that can be examined in actual research, they should not be viewed as scientific in nature. For example, consider the following "theory": the reason you recently had a run of bad luck (lost your job, had a minor traffic accident, caught the flu) is that one of your ex-lovers has put a hex upon you. Obviously, hexes, evil spells, and similar events lie outside the realm of science. Thus, such a "theory" is not a theory at all; it does not generate predictions testable by scientific means (i.e., by the experimental or correlational methods described earlier).

In sum, theories serve as important guides to research in social psychology, just as they do in other branches of science. Thus, we will have reason to consider many theories in the pages that follow. As each theory is presented, try to keep the following points in mind: (1) theories are designed to explain key aspects of social behavior, and (2) they should be accepted as valid or useful only to the extent that the predictions they generate are confirmed by research findings. (What role, if any, should scientists' values play in the research process? For some thoughts on this important issue, please see the **Focus** insert on pages 30–31.)

The quest for knowledge and the rights of individuals: In search of an appropriate balance

In their use of experimentation and systematic observation, and in their reliance on comprehensive theories, social psychologists do not differ from researchers in many other fields. There is one technique, however, that seems to be unique to research in our field: **deception.** Basically, this involves efforts by researchers to conceal the true purpose of their studies from the persons participating in them. The reason behind this procedure can be simply stated: many social psychologists are convinced that if subjects know the true purposes behind an investigation, their behavior will be changed by such knowledge. Then, the research itself will be doomed to fail; it will have little chance of adding to our knowledge of human social behavior.

On the face of it, this is an eminently reasonable suggestion. For example, imagine that, in a study designed to examine the impact of flattery upon their liking for a stranger, subjects are informed of this purpose. Clearly, they may then react differently to the compliments they receive than would otherwise be the case. Similarly, imagine that subjects taking part in a study of racial prejudice are told that this is the topic under investigation. With this information in their possession, they may lean over backwards to avoid showing any trace of prejudice whatsoever. Because of such considerations, many social psychologists feel that deception — at least on a temporary basis — is essential for their research. Thus, they employ it on a regular basis (Gross and Fleming, 1982). The adoption of this technique, though, is not without its costs. Deceiving or misleading research participants, no matter how justified this may seem, raises important ethical issues that should not be overlooked.

First, it is possible that at least some persons exposed to such treatment will resent having been led astray. As a result, they may adopt a negative attitude toward social research generally. Second, deception, even when temporary, may result in some type of harmful outcome for the persons exposed to it (Kelman, 1967). For example, they may experience discomfort, stress, negative shifts in their self-esteem, or related effects. Finally, there is the very real question of whether scientists, committed to the search for knowledge, should place themselves in the position of deceiving persons kind enough to assist them in this undertaking.

In short, the use of deception does pose something of a dilemma to social psychologists. On the one hand, it seems essential to their research. On the other, its use raises serious problems. How can this issue be resolved? At present, opinion remains somewhat divided. Some of our colleagues feel that deception, no matter how useful, is inappropriate and must be abandoned (Baumrind, 1979). In contrast many others (perhaps a large majority), believe that temporary deception *is* acceptable, provided certain safeguards are followed (Baron, 1981). The most important of these are **informed consent** and thorough **debriefing.**

Informed consent involves providing research participants with as full a description of the procedures to be followed as feasible, prior to their decision to take part in a given study. In short, the guiding principle is "Research participants should know what they are getting into before they make a commitment to assist." In contrast, thorough debriefing *follows* rather than precedes each experimental session. It consists of providing participants with a full explanation of all major aspects of the

FOCUS ON RESEARCH:
The Cutting Edge

Values: What Role Should They Play in Social Research?

Suppose we asked you the following question: "What, precisely, do scientists do?" How would you reply? While we can't be certain, we're willing to bet your answer would go something like this: "Why, they search for *truth*." In other words, you might well indicate that in your eyes, scientists are dispassionate seekers of knowledge — they strive to increase our understanding of the natural world around us.

If you hold this view — and most people do — we can also predict your reply to a second question: "What role should values play in scientific research?" Here, your answer might be, "None. They shouldn't enter into the picture." This position seems reasonable; after all, values refer to personal conceptions of what is good or useful. Presumably, scientists should *not* be affected by such matters. Rather, they should search for "the truth," pure and simple.

In the past, this suggestion was widely accepted both by scientists and by philosophers of science (McMullin, 1983). Recently, though, the situation has begun to change — and to change radically. At the present time, many experts believe that since it is a human enterprise carried out by specific persons, science can *never* be totally value-free. In fact, values can and do enter the process in several different ways. The key question, then, is not, "Do values influence scientific research?" but rather, "How do they affect this process, and which of these potential influences are acceptable?" While total agreement has not as yet emerged, there does seem to be growing consensus about the following basic points (Howard, 1985).

First, it seems appropriate for scientists to hold certain values relating directly to their work (e.g., "knowledge is valuable"; "nature is lawful"). Indeed, such views are part-and-parcel of the scientific process, and adherence to them is essential before any field can be viewed as scientific in orientation.

Second, it is also appropriate for scientists to apply certain values to the task of choosing among competing theories or explanations. Such values as *predictive accuracy* (the best theory is the one which predicts most accurately), *internal coherence* (the best theory is the one which hangs together most consistently), and *unifying power* (the best theory is the one which can pull together previously unrelated bodies of knowledge) fit under this general heading. They, too, are an essential aspect of the scientific process, and facilitate its progress.

Third, and perhaps most controversial, it has recently been argued by several experts (e.g., Howard, 1985), that psychologists should also allow another value to play a guiding role in their research: the value of enhancing human welfare. Obviously, this value is shared with scientists working in several other fields (e.g., the health sciences). However, it has been suggested that in psychology it may have unique implications. The argument goes something like this.

People, unlike chemicals or atoms, think; thus, they usually realize that they are being studied when they take part in psychological research. Further, they care about the findings of such projects. For example, if they learn, from reports of social research, that most persons are adversely affected by televised violence, or that many individuals show unquestioning obedience to authority, they may attempt to change their own actions in the light of such knowledge. Because of this tendency, it is suggested, psychologists should build the value of enhancing human welfare directly into their research. Specifically, they should refer to this value when deciding what topics to study, how to go about conducting their projects, and how to publicize their results. We should hasten to note that not all social psychologists agree with this value-guided approach to their field; in fact, some take strong exception to it, and urge retention of the older, "neutral seeker-after-truth" perspective. The ideas outlined above do at least seem worth considering, however, and represent yet another way in which values can play a role in the ongoing work of social psychology.

Finally, there are important ways in which values should *not* enter into social research. First, and most obviously, such views should never be permitted to affect the results of specific studies. Rather, researchers should do everything in their power to assure that their own values do not intrude on data they collect. They should avoid revealing their views to subjects, who may be strongly affected by them. And they should take great pains to assure that their studies are not designed in ways guaranteed to yield results consistent with the researchers' personal values. For example, an investigator who feels strongly that traditional sex-role stereotypes are harmful should take care to avoid designing studies certain to show in an unfavorable light persons who hold tra-

ditional views of masculinity and femininity. Second, values should not be permitted to distort the interpretation of research findings. Even if the results of a project are directly contrary to a researcher's own political, social, or moral values, they should be reported accurately — not "bent" to be more consistent with these views. As you can probably guess, the vast majority of social psychologists concur with these ideas, and conduct their research accordingly. However, some critics outside our field have suggested that social psychology has not always been successful in this respect. They believe that social psychologists have sometimes permitted their own political or social values to affect the nature and interpretation of their research (Hatch, 1982). We feel that this charge is mainly unfounded; but, given its serious nature, it is certainly one deserving of careful thought.

To conclude: whether we like it or not, values do appear to play a key role in the scientific process. As we have tried to note, however, their impact in this regard is not necessarily harmful. On the contrary, in certain ways it can be constructive and beneficial. The key task for social psychologists, as for other scientists, then, is not that of eliminating all values from their work. Rather, it is that of assuring that they enter only in scientifically appropriate ways.

study, including its true goals, the hypotheses under investigation, and an explanation of the need for temporary deception. The basic principle here is that all research participants should leave the session in *at least* as favorable or positive a state as when they arrived.

That informed consent and thorough debriefing go a long way toward eliminating the potential dangers of deception is suggested by the findings of several studies concerned with this issue. First, an overwhelming majority of subjects view temporary deception as acceptable, and do not resent its use (Rogers, 1980). Second, there is some indication that individuals who have participated in studies involving deception actually report more positive feelings about the value of psychological research than subjects who have not taken part in such research (Smith and Richardson, 1983). Third, it appears that effective debriefing does eliminate many negative effects experienced by subjects as a result of temporary deception (Smith and Richardson, 1985). Of course, even in light of such results, it is unwise to take the safety or appropriateness of deception for granted. As noted recently by Rubin (1985), this would be a serious error indeed. Rather, it appears that the key phrase for all researchers wishing to use deception in their studies must remain: "Danger: Complex ethical issues ahead. Proceed with extreme caution."

USING THIS BOOK: A Displaced Preface

Before concluding, we'd like to comment briefly on several features of this text. Often, such information is included in the preface, but since many readers seem to skip such messages from authors, presenting it here seems to make good sense.

First, we should mention several steps we've taken to make our text easier and more convenient for you to use. Each chapter begins with an outline of the major topics covered, and each ends with a summary. Key terms are printed in **boldface type** and are defined in a glossary that follows each chapter. All figures and graphs contain special labels designed to call your attention to the key findings they present. Finally, a list of sources for further information is offered at the end of each chapter.

Second, we wish to call your attention to the fact that we've included two distinct types of special inserts throughout the text. The first of these, labeled FOCUS ON RESEARCH, examines specific studies performed by social psychologists. Such inserts appear in two basic forms. The first is subtitled Classic Contributions, and describes investigations now widely considered to be "classics" in our field — ones that initiated new lines of research or changed the thinking about important social phenomena. The second type is subtitled The Cutting Edge, and focuses on recent projects carried out at the frontiers of our field (see pages 30 and 31). The presence of these two types of FOCUS inserts reflects our desire to maintain a balance between contemporary trends in social psychology and its past history and progress.

The second type of insert is titled ON THE APPLIED SIDE (see the one on pages 8 – 9 for an example). These focus primarily on the practical implications of social psychology — ways in which the knowledge it yields can contribute to the solution of a broad range of practical problems.

It is our hope that these and other features of our text will help us communicate knowledge about social behavior in a manner you will find interesting and enlightening. We also hope that they will permit some of our own excitement about the field to come through in an undistorted way. To the extent we succeed in these basic tasks — and only to that extent — will we be satisfied that as authors, teachers, and representatives of social psychology, we have done our part.

SUMMARY

Social psychology may be defined as the scientific field that seeks to understand the nature and causes of individual behavior in social situations. Informal speculation about social interaction has gone on since ancient times, but a science-oriented field of social psychology emerged only in the early decades of this century. Once established, it grew rapidly and today seeks to examine every conceivable aspect of social behavior. Two recent trends in the field have involved the growing influence of a *cognitive perspective* — efforts to understand complex social behavior in terms of the basic cognitive processes that underlie them, and an increasing emphasis on *application* — applying the knowledge and principles of social psychology to many practical problems.

In conducting their research, social psychologists generally employ either the **experimental** or the **correlational method.** The first involves procedures in which one or more factors are systematically varied in order to examine the impact of such changes upon one or more aspects of social behavior. The second involves careful observation of existing relationships between two or more variables. In selecting the topics of their research and planning specific studies, social psychologists are often guided by **theories.** These are logical frameworks designed to explain why certain events or processes occur as they do. Predictions derived from theories are tested in ongoing research. If they are confirmed, confidence in the accuracy of the theory is increased. If they are disconfirmed, such confidence is reduced. At one time it was believed that *values* should play absolutely no role in scientific research. Now, however, it is realized that they always exert some impact upon it. The key task for social psychologists, then, is not eliminating all impact of values upon their research, but rather assuring that this influence is beneficial and appropriate.

Social psychologists often attempt to conceal the true purpose of their studies from the persons participating in them. That is, they make use of temporary **deception.** Use of this technique stems from the belief that if subjects know the true purpose of a research project, their behavior may be altered, thus rendering results invalid. Use of deception raises important ethical issues, but most social psychologists believe that it is permissible, provided proper safeguards (e.g., informed consent, thorough debriefing) are adopted.

GLOSSARY

cognitive dissonance
An unpleasant state that occurs when individuals notice inconsistency between their attitudes or between their attitudes and their overt behavior.

cognitive perspective
The view that many complex social phenomena can best be understood in terms of the cognitive processes (e.g., memory, social inference) that underlie them.

confounding (of variables)
Occurs in situations where factors other than the independent variable under investigation in an experiment are permitted to vary. Confounding makes it impossible to determine whether results stem from the independent variable or from other factors.

contextualist view
A new perspective on social behavior suggesting that no action can be adequately interpreted or understood apart from the context in which it occurs.

correlational method
A method of research based on careful observation of two or more variables. If changes in one are consistently associated with changes in another, evidence for a link between them is obtained.

debriefing
Procedures at the end of an experimental session in which research participants are informed about the true purpose of the study and the major hypotheses under investigation.

deception
Efforts by researchers to conceal the true purpose of their studies from persons participating in them. Use of this technique stems from the belief that if subjects know the purpose of a study, their behavior may be changed by this knowledge.

experimentation (experimental method)
A method of research in which one factor (the independent variable) is systematically changed or adjusted in order to determine whether such variations affect a second factor (the dependent variable).

informed consent
Procedures in which subjects are told, in advance, about the activities they will perform during an experiment. They then participate in the study only if they are willing to engage in such activities.

interaction (between variables)
Occurs when the impact of one variable is affected by one or more other variables. For example, being touched by a stranger might produce positive reactions when this person is highly attractive, but negative reactions when he or she is unattractive.

random assignment of subjects to groups
A basic requirement for the conduction of valid experiments. According to this principle, research participants should have an equal chance of being exposed to each level of the independent variable. In short, they should be randomly assigned to various conditions within the study.

social psychology

The scientific field that seeks to comprehend the nature and causes of individual behavior in social situations.

theory

Systematic efforts by scientists to explain natural phenomena. Theories generally consist of two major parts: basic concepts and assertions regarding the relationships between these concepts.

FOR MORE INFORMATION

Allport, G. W. (1985). The historical background of social psychology. In G. Lindzey and E. Aronson (eds.), *Handbook of social psychology.* New York: Random House.

> If you'd like to know more about how social psychology came into being, this is an excellent source to consult. It is written by a well-known scholar who was witness to social psychology's earliest days.

Baron, R. A. (1986). *Behavior in organizations: Understanding and managing the human side of work,* 2nd ed. Boston: Allyn and Bacon.

> This text provides a broad survey of the field of organizational behavior. By skimming through it, you can get an idea of how the findings of social psychology have been applied to the solution of many practical problems in businesses and other organizations (e.g., enhancing employee morale, providing effective leadership).

Drew, C. J., and Hardman, M. L. (1985). *Designing and conducting behavioral research.* Elmsford, N. Y.: Pergamon Press.

> A clear and relatively brief description of how psychologists and other behavioral scientists actually conduct their research. If you'd like to learn more about this topic, this is a good source to consult.

Oskamp, S., ed. (1980–1985). *Applied social psychology annuals.* Beverly Hills, Cal.: Sage.

> The books in this continuing series illustrate the many ways in which social psychological knowledge can be applied to solving practical problems. Each volume differs in content, but together they provide a thorough picture of how social psychologists seek to apply the principles and findings of their field.

CHAPTER 2

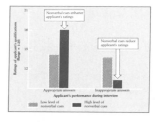

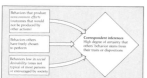

SOCIAL PERCEPTION: Knowing Others — and Ourselves

"Oh well, I may as well get this over with," Joan Manuso thinks to herself. And with this thought in mind, she opens the door to her office and invites Sue Landeen, who's waiting outside, to enter. It's time for the annual performance reviews at Joan's company, so all this week she's been conducting feedback sessions with the people who work under her supervision. She never likes this task — telling others what they've been doing wrong is far from her favorite activity. But for some reason (she's not sure just why) Joan has been especially dreading her encounter with Sue.

"Have a seat," Joan remarks, "and we'll get started right away. I've got a pretty hectic morning ahead."

"I understand," Sue replies, a sweet smile on her face. "We all know how busy you've been lately." And with this comment, she sits down and folds her hands in front of her respectfully. In fact, everything about her posture seems to proclaim "You're the boss. . . . I know I'm just the underling."

Clearing her throat, Joan begins. "Well, Sue, I have to give you a mixed report this time around. You certainly did a good job on the Thompson project — first rate all the way . . . "

Sue interrupts. "Oh *thank* you, Ms. Manuso. I really appreciate that," she states, smiling broadly.

"But," Joan continues, "there are some problems too. First, there's this repeated lateness. I hate to say it, but you've really got about the worst record in the department on that score. You know how we feel about being on time."

"Oh, I know, I know," Sue answers, looking upset. "But believe me, it's not my fault. They've been working on Highway 70, and there's a huge traffic jam every morning, just when I start for work. It's awful. Anyway, I'm moving in a couple of weeks, and the trip from my new place should be much easier. So I really think I can improve on that score."

"Good," Joan answers. "I really hope so. But there's another problem I have to mention, too. I've gotten some complaints from other people in the department who've worked with you. I'm not going to name any names, but they all seem to say the same thing: you don't hold up your end on joint projects. I'd like to hear your side of it."

Sue looks hurt, puzzled, and upset all at once. "How can they say that?" she exclaims, pouting her lips. "Why, *I* usually do most of the work! And it seems as if other people in the department are always giving me the hardest parts, too. No, it's just not fair. Ooh — it makes me so mad!" And at this point, she tries to choke down a sob.

Hastily, Joan retreats. "O.K., let's not get too excited about it. I'll keep an open mind. But do give it some thought; that's all I ask."

Now Joan shifts to another tactic. "Look, Sue," she begins, "I want to ask you a more general question. Just how committed are you to staying here? I mean, sometimes I get the impression that you really don't plan to be around very long. Is that true?"

There's a slight pause before Sue replies — slight, but definite. Then, in a noticeably higher-pitched voice, she states: "Absolutely not! Why, I love it here. I like my job, and I really enjoy working for you, Ms. Manuso. You're so fair and easy to get along with . . . "

These remarks, plus the look of open admiration on Sue's face, really get to Joan, so she quickly brings the interview to a close. After Sue has left, however, she finds that as usual, she feels puzzled. What kind of person is Sue, really? The sweet, respectful, conscientious victim of circumstances (traffic jams, unfair co-workers) she claims to be? Or a lazy, irresponsible manipulator? She certainly *seems* sincere, but is she? "There's something about her smile and something about her voice that makes me wonder," Joan reflects. "I guess that's why I dread these sessions with her. I can never figure her out. Thank goodness all of them aren't like her!"

ADMIT IT: Other people are often something of a mystery. They say and do things we don't expect, have motives we don't readily understand, and seem to perceive the world in ways very different from ourselves. Yet, because they play such a key role in our lives, this is one mystery we cannot afford to leave unsolved. Thus, we often engage in efforts to understand other persons — to comprehend their major motives and traits (see Figure 2.1). Like Joan, the character in the story above, we try to figure out what they are *really* like, and why they behave in the ways that they do. Social psychologists generally term the process through

FIGURE 2.1. While we can't really know what other organisms think about, we *do* know what human beings ponder much of the time: other people! (Source: Drawing by Lorenz; © 1980 The New Yorker Magazine, Inc.)

Social perception: An important part of daily life

which we seek such knowledge about others **social perception,** and it will serve as the major focus of the present chapter.

While our efforts to understand the people around us (and ourselves, too) focus on many different issues, two of these are most important. First, we often seek to grasp the current, temporary causes behind others' behavior — their present moods, feelings, and emotions. Information on this issue is often provided by *nonverbal cues* relating to others' facial expressions, eye contact, and body posture or movements. Second, we attempt to comprehend the more lasting causes behind others' actions — their stable traits, motives, and intentions. Information pertaining to this second task is usually gained through a complex process known as **attribution,** in which we observe others' behavior, and then try to *infer* the causes behind it in a relatively systematic way (Harvey and Weary, 1984). Because nonverbal communication and attribution provide us with somewhat different kinds of information about others, we will consider them separately here. But please note: they usually proceed simultaneously in actual social settings.

NONVERBAL COMMUNICATION: *The silent — But Often Eloquent — Language of Expressions, Gazes, and Gestures*

In many situations, behavior is strongly affected by temporary factors or causes. Shifting moods, fleeting emotions, fatigue, and various drugs can all exert strong effects on individual behavior. To mention just a few examples, most persons are more willing to do favors for others when in a good mood than when in a bad one (Isen, 1984), and many are more likely to lose their tempers and lash out at others when feeling irritable than when feeling mellow (Geen and Donnerstein, 1983). Further, many forms of behavior, and even the basic ways in which we think or reason, are strongly affected by alcohol and other widely used drugs (e.g., Steele and Southwick, 1985). Because these temporary factors produce important effects upon social behavior, it is useful to know something about them. But how can we obtain such knowledge? How can we know whether others are in a good or bad mood, whether they are experiencing anger, joy, or sorrow, and whether they are calm or tense? One answer is deceptively simple: we can ask them directly. Unfortunately, this strategy doesn't always work. Sometimes others are willing to reveal their inner feelings or moods, and sometimes they are not. Indeed, they may often actively seek to deceive or mislead us in this regard (e.g., DePaulo, Stone, and Lassiter, 1985a). (If you've ever tried to conceal your own anger, or your own attraction to another individual, you are already well aware of this basic fact.) In such cases, it is not necessary for us to give up in despair, for there is another revealing source of information about these temporary causes of behavior: *nonverbal cues*. In short, we can learn much about others' current moods and feelings from a silent language that often accompanies, but exists independent from, their spoken words. Such **nonverbal communication** is quite complex, and has been studied from many perspectives. For purposes of this discussion, however, we will focus on two major issues: (1) what are the basic channels through which such communication takes place? and (2) what is its role in ongoing social interaction?

Nonverbal communication: The basic channels

How do individuals communicate nonverbally? Several decades of research suggest they do so in many different ways. The most important of these seem to involve: facial expressions, eye contact, body movements and posture (body language), and touching.

Unmasking the face: Facial expressions as guides to the moods and emotions of others.   More than 2,000 years ago the Roman orator Cicero noted, "The face is the image of the soul." By this comment he meant that human feelings and emotions are often reflected on the face, and can be "read" there from various specific expressions. Modern research suggests that, in this respect, Cicero and many other observers of human behavior were correct: often it *is* possible to learn much about the current moods and feelings of others from their facial expressions. In fact, it appears that six different — and basic — emotions are represented clearly on the human face: happiness, sadness, surprise, fear, anger, and disgust (Buck, 1984; Izard, 1977). Please note: this does not imply that we are capable of demonstrating only six different facial expressions — far from it. Emotions occur in many combinations (e.g., anger along with fear, surprise together with happiness). Further, each of these reactions can vary greatly in intensity. Thus, although there appear to be only six basic "themes" in facial expressions, the number of variations upon them is truly huge.

The fact that facial expressions do indeed often reflect our inner feelings raises another intriguing question: are such expressions themselves universal in nature? For example, if you traveled to a remote part of the globe and visited a group of people who had never before met an outsider, would their facial expressions in various situations resemble your own? Would they smile when they encountered events that made them happy, frown when exposed to conditions that made them sad, and so on? Further, would you be able to recognize their facial expressions in such situations as readily as you can recognize those of persons belonging to your own culture? The answer to both questions appears to be "yes." People living in widely separated geographic areas do seem to demonstrate similar facial expressions in similar, emotion-provoking situations; and they show an impressive ability to recognize each other's expressions accurately (Ekman and Friesen, 1975). Moreover — and importantly — this is true even when they have had no direct contact with one another. Thus, it appears that when experiencing basic emotions, human beings all over the world tend to show similar facial expressions, and the meaning of such expressions, too, is universal (refer to Figure 2.2). For this reason, the language of the face, in contrast to that of spoken words, rarely requires an interpreter.

Gazes and stares: The language of the eyes.   Have you ever had a conversation with someone wearing dark glasses? If so, you may remember that this was an uncomfortable situation. The reason for your discomfort is

FIGURE 2.2. Can you recognize the emotions being experienced by each of these persons? Despite the fact that they come from very different cultures, you can. This is because facial expressions, in contrast to spoken language, are quite universal in nature.

Facial expressions: No interpreter needed

simple: you could not see this person's eyes, and so you were denied access to an important source of information concerning her or his feelings. Ancient poets often described the eyes as "windows to the soul," and in an important sense, they were correct. We *do* often learn a great deal about others' internal states—and so the causes behind their behavior—from their eye contact with us. For example, we often interpret a high level of gazing from another as a sign of liking or friendliness (Kleinke, Meeker, and LaFong, 1974). In contrast, if others avoid eye contact with us, we usually conclude that they are unfriendly, don't like us, or, perhaps, are simply shy (Zimbardo, 1977).

While a high level of eye contact from others is usually interpreted as a sign of liking or positive feelings, there is one important exception to this general rule. If another person gazes at us in a continuous manner, and maintains such contact regardless of any actions we perform, he or she may be said to be **staring**. As you probably know from your own experience, this is a decidedly unpleasant experience—one that makes us feel nervous or tense (Strom and Buck, 1979). Thus, it is not surprising that when confronted with such treatment by a stranger, many individuals seek to withdraw from the situation in which the staring occurs (Greenbaum and Rosenfield, 1978). Even worse, some evidence suggests that stares are often interpreted as a sign of hostility or anger, both by people and animals (Ellsworth and Carlsmith, 1973).

Together, these findings seem to imply that staring always produces negative effects. After all, people become upset when they are stared at, view such treatment as a sign of hostility, and often react to it with anger or attempts to flee the scene. Additional evidence suggests, however, that occasionally staring can yield more positive outcomes. For example, it can sometimes increase offers of aid from passersby (Ellsworth and Langer, 1976). You have probably experienced one form of this yourself. Recall how much harder it is to walk past persons collecting for various charities without making a donation once they have stared at you and caught your eye. It is for this reason that we often try to look down when approaching such individuals. These and other instances suggest that stares, while often unpleasant, are not always negative in their effects. The fact remains, though, that usually, staring is a potent and potentially dangerous nonverbal cue—one that should be used with a great deal of caution.

Body language: Gestures, movements, and postures.   Before reading further, try this simple demonstration. First, try to remember some incident that made you angry (the angrier the better!). After thinking about this event for about a minute, try to remember another incident—one that made you sad (again, the more intense the emotion, the better). Now consider your behavior: did you change your posture or move your hands, arms, or legs as your thoughts shifted from the first event to the second? The chances are good that you did, for our current moods or emotions are often reflected in the posture, position, and movement of our bodies. Nonverbal cues from such sources are usually termed **body**

language, and can provide us with several useful types of information about others.

First, as we just noted, body language often reveals much about other persons' emotional states. Large numbers of movements — especially ones in which a particular part of the body does something to another (e.g., scratching, stroking) — suggest emotional arousal. The greater the frequency of such behavior, the higher others' level of arousal or nervousness seems to be (Knapp, 1978).

Second, more specific information about others' feelings is often provided by *gestures*. These fall into several different categories, but perhaps the most important are *emblems* — body movements carrying a highly specific meaning in a given culture. For example, in the United States (and elsewhere), rubbing one's stomach with an open hand signifies a favorable response to food or other items (yum-yum!). In contrast, seizing one's nose with the thumb and index finger indicates disgust. Emblems vary greatly from culture to culture (Morris et al., 1979). However, all human societies appear to have at least some signals of this type for greetings, departures, insults, and the description of various physical states (hunger, thirst, fatigue).

Finally, body language can also reveal others' reactions to *us*. Certain body movements or postures signify liking, while others signal disliking or rejection (Mehrabian, 1968). For example, research on this topic reveals that when others sit facing us directly, lean in our direction, or nod frequently while we speak, we conclude that they like us. When, in contrast, they sit so as to avoid facing us directly, lean away, or look at the ceiling while we speak, we may reach the opposite conclusion (Clore, Wiggins, and Itkin, 1975). Clearly, then, there is often much to be learned from careful attention to others' body language.

Touching: Physical contact as a nonverbal cue.   Suppose that during a conversation with another person, she or he touched you briefly. How would you react? And what information would you view this behavior as conveying? The answer to both questions is, "It depends." And what it depends upon is several factors relating to who does the touching (a friend or stranger; a member of your own or the opposite sex), the nature of this physical contact (is it brief or prolonged, gentle or rough, what part of your body is involved), and the context in which it takes place (a business or social setting; a public or private location). Thus, depending on such factors, touch can suggest affection, sexual interest, dominance, or even aggression (Knapp, 1978; refer to Figure 2.3, p. 43). Further, it has been found that touching does not occur in a random manner. On the contrary, it follows clear-cut patterns. Thus, males touch females more than twice as often as females touch males, and high-status persons touch low-status ones much more often than vice versa (Henley, 1973).

Despite these and other complexities, however, a growing body of evidence points to the following conclusion: when one person touches another in a noncontroversial manner (i.e., gently, briefly, and on a nonsensitive part of the body), positive reactions generally result (Alagna,

FIGURE 2.3. The meaning of physical touching can vary, depending on how and where it takes place. At different times and under different conditions, touching can signify affection, sexual interest, dominance, or even aggression.

Touching: Different contexts, different meanings

Whitcher, and Fisher, 1979; Smith, Gier, and Willis, 1982). This fact is clearly illustrated by an ingenious study carried out by Crusco and Wetzel (1984), to which we alluded in Chapter 1.

These investigators enlisted the aid of waitresses working in two restaurants, who agreed to treat customers in one of three distinct ways when giving them their change: they either refrained from touching these persons in any manner, touched them briefly on the hand, or touched them for a longer period of time on the shoulder. The effects of these treatments were assessed by examining the size of the tips left by the patrons. Results were clear. First, males left larger tips than females (15.3 percent of the bill versus 12.6 percent). Second, and of greater interest, both a brief (approximately one-half second) touch on the hand and a longer (about one second to one and a half seconds) touch on the shoulder significantly increased tipping over that in the no-touch condition (refer to Table 2.1). Thus, consistent with previous findings, being

TABLE 2.1. Both brief and more prolonged touching by waitresses increased the size of the tips left by customers. Thus, in this nonthreatening context, touching seemed to induce positive reactions among its recipients. Numbers shown indicate percent of bill left by subjects. (Source: Based on data from Crusco and Wetzel, 1984.)

No Touching	Brief Touching	More Prolonged Touching
12.2%	16.7%	14.4%

touched in an innocuous, nonthreatening way seemed to generate positive rather than negative reactions among recipients.

We should emphasize, once again, that touching does not always produce such effects. Indeed, when it is perceived as a status or power play, or when it is too prolonged or intimate, it may evoke anxiety, anger, or other negative reactions. Thus, in most cases, it is a form of nonverbal cue that should be used sparingly, and with great restraint.

Nonverbal cues and social interaction: Their role in self-presentation

Almost everyone wishes to make a good impression on others when meeting them for the first time. As a result, many persons engage in fairly elaborate tactics of *self-presentation* or **impression management** in such contexts (Schlenker, 1980). For example, they flatter others, pretend to agree with them about various issues, or feign great interest in what they are saying—all in an attempt to create a favorable first impression (Jones, 1964; Wortman and Linsenmeier, 1977). Not surprisingly, persons who are skilled in self-presentation often make better first impressions on others than persons who are less adept in this regard. For example, in one recent study (Riggio, 1986), the higher subjects scored on a measure of this particular social skill (labeled by Riggio *social control*), the more they were liked by two accomplices who engaged them in a brief conversation.

While skillful self-presentation often involves tactics such as the ones listed above (flattery, pretended interest), it may also rest, to an important degree, on the effective use of nonverbal cues. As we noted above, certain facial expressions, patterns of eye contact, and specific body postures or movements convey liking or positive reactions to others. Persons who are successful at self-presentation seem to be well aware of this fact. Thus, they often seek to manage such impressions by controlling their own nonverbal behavior. While interacting with target persons (ones they wish to impress), they smile frequently, lean forward, maintain a high level of eye contact, and nod in agreement on many occasions. The result: they often succeed in producing positive first impressions. Of course, a high level of nonverbal expressiveness is not always the result of calculated efforts to curry favor with others. Individuals vary greatly on this dimension, so that some are simply more expressive than others, quite apart from any overt efforts at self-presentation (Riggio and Friedman, 1986). In general, such expressiveness seems to be a "plus": persons high on this dimension generally receive more favorable ratings than persons low on this dimension when meeting others for the first time (Riggio, 1986). Despite such large individual differences, though, the emission of many positive nonverbal cues *is* often a conscious tactic, employed by specific persons to enhance their impression on others. Reliance on such tactics is visible in many different contexts, ranging from blind dates on the one hand through customer-salesperson interactions on the other. But perhaps their impact is most apparent—and also most disturbing—in formal interviews.

Many studies have been conducted to examine the impact of nonverbal cues in such settings, and in general results have been consistent: applicants for various jobs or positions who demonstrate high levels of positive nonverbal cues receive better ratings from interviewers than ones who show lower levels of such cues (e.g., Imada and Hakel, 1977; McGovern, Jones, and Morris, 1979). Indeed, in one correlation study, Forbes and Jackson (1980) found that individuals actually selected for engineering apprenticeships showed more smiling, eye contact, and head-nodding during actual interviews than persons who were rejected. Additional evidence indicates, however, that where the use of nonverbal cues during interviews is concerned, there can often be "too much of a good thing." First, when applicants "lay it on too thick" and demonstrate too many positive nonverbal cues, they may arouse negative reactions on the part of interviewers, who come to realize that they are being misled or manipulated (Baron, 1986a). Second, it appears that a high level of nonverbal cues will exert positive effects upon the ratings received by applicants only when they also possess relatively good qualifications for the job in question. This conclusion is supported by an investigation conducted by Rasmussen (1984).

In this study, male and female subjects watched taped interviews of what seemed to be an actual job interview. In fact, the interview was staged so that several factors relating to the applicant could be systematically varied. First, in different versions of the interview (watched by different groups of subjects), the applicant emitted either a high level or a low level of positive nonverbal cues. In one version he smiled and nodded his head frequently, and maintained a high level of eye contact with the interviewer. In the other, he rarely performed such actions. Second, in answering the interviewer's questions, the applicant either responded in an appropriate manner (by presenting relevant information), or in an inappropriate manner (by presenting irrelevant information). Finally, before watching one of the tapes, subjects read a résumé which indicated that the applicant was either well or poorly qualified for the job in question.

After observing one version of the taped interview, subjects rated the applicant in terms of his qualifications for the job. As expected, the applicant received higher ratings when he had a strong résumé than when he had a weak one. In addition, though, this person's performance during the interview and the level of nonverbal cues he emitted interacted in affecting such ratings. As shown in Figure 2.4, a high level of nonverbal cues enhanced ratings of the applicant when he answered the interviewer's questions appropriately. However, such cues actually *reduced* his ratings when he answered the interviewer's questions inappropriately. One possible explanation for these findings is as follows: when the applicant responded poorly during the interview, subjects may have perceived his use of nonverbal causes as a manipulative tactic—an attempt to make up for his lack of credentials. Thus, they reacted negatively. In

FIGURE 2.4.   When an applicant answered an interviewer's questions appropriately, a high level of nonverbal cues enhanced the ratings he received. However, when he answered inappropriately, a high level of nonverbal cues actually reduced the applicant's ratings. These findings suggest that nonverbal cues are not always a "plus" in social situations. (Source: Based on data from Rasmussen, 1984.)

Nonverbal cues: Their role in interviews

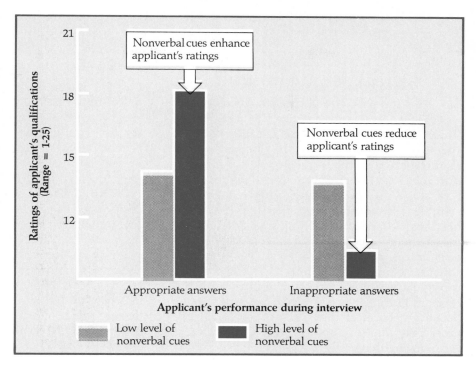

contrast, when he responded well during the interview, subjects may have viewed his use of nonverbal cues as natural — another reflection of his general competence. Regardless of the precise basis for these results, when combined with the other findings mentioned above (e.g., Baron, 1986a), they contain a practical message for anyone facing an interview: be careful not to overdo it. Too many efforts at impression management via positive nonverbal cues can often be as bad as too few. (For a discussion of another important way in which nonverbal cues affect social interaction, please see the **Focus** insert on pages 48–50.)

ATTRIBUTION: Understanding the Causes of Behavior

Accurate knowledge about others' current moods or feelings can be useful — it helps us interact with them effectively. Yet, where social perception is concerned, it is usually only part of the total picture. In addition, we usually want to know something about others' lasting traits — the stable characteristics they bring with them from situation to situation. And, more generally, we wish to understand the *causes* behind their behavior — to know precisely *why* they have acted in certain ways under certain conditions. The process through which we attempt to gain

Nonverbal Cues: An Effective Tool for Exposing Deception?

Sadly, deception is an all too common part of social life. Individuals try to mislead others about their true feelings or beliefs for many different reasons, and with great frequency. A key task we all face, therefore, is recognizing such deception when we meet it. What is the best way of accomplishing this goal? Since most persons are capable of exerting fairly precise control over what they say, it seems reasonable to suggest that nonverbal cues might provide a better source of information in this respect. Perhaps we can recognize attempts at deception from changes in others' facial expressions, body language, or eye contact. Growing evidence suggests that this is actually the case.

First, many studies suggest that when provided with sufficient nonverbal cues, most persons *can* discriminate truth from lies with better than chance success (e.g., DePaulo, Stone, and Lassiter, 1985b). Second, additional evidence points to the specific nonverbal cues that may be most useful in performing this task. These seem to include *microexpressions* — fleeting facial expressions lasting only a few tenths of a second (Ekman and Friesen, 1975), changes in *voice pitch* (Frick, 1985), and shifts in overall patterns of eye contact (Knapp, 1978). Microexpressions appear on the face very quickly after an emotion-provoking event — before the person involved can get his or her "mask" in place. If they are noticed, therefore, they can be quite revealing about true underlying feelings, and can call attention to subsequent efforts at concealment. With respect to voice pitch, several studies indicate that when individuals tell lies, such pitch rises slightly (e.g., Streeter et al., 1977). This is not always the case, but it occurs often enough to

provide another useful clue to deception. Finally, as we noted earlier, when individuals seem to purposely avoid eye contact with us, this is often a sign that they are engaging in deception. Given that our eyes are often a revealing source of information about our feelings and reactions, this is hardly surprising.

The findings outlined above are quite comforting. Together, they suggest that careful attention to appropriate nonverbal cues can help us recognize deception when we encounter it. Perhaps even more encouraging, though, is the following fact: the harder others try to deceive us, the more apparent is such deception in their nonverbal behavior. Evidence for this conclusion has recently been provided by DePaulo, Stone, and Lassiter (1985b). These researchers arranged for male and female subjects to describe their own views on several controversial issues (e.g., should wives pay alimony to their ex-husbands?) to another unseen person, whose views on these issues were made known to them. In reality, this "partner" did not exist, but subjects were led to believe either that this individual was a member of their own sex or the opposite sex, and that he or she was attractive or unattractive. On half of the issues, subjects were asked to express their true views, while on the others, they were instructed to lie — to falsely represent their attitudes. Further, one of these lies was ingratiating (subjects pretended to agree with the fictitious partner when in fact they disagreed), while the other was noningratiating (subjects pretended to disagree when in fact they agreed).

DePaulo and her colleagues predicted that the higher subjects' motivation to lie successfully, the more readily would such deception be apparent in their nonverbal cues. Thus, they expected that subjects' efforts at deception would be more obvious under conditions

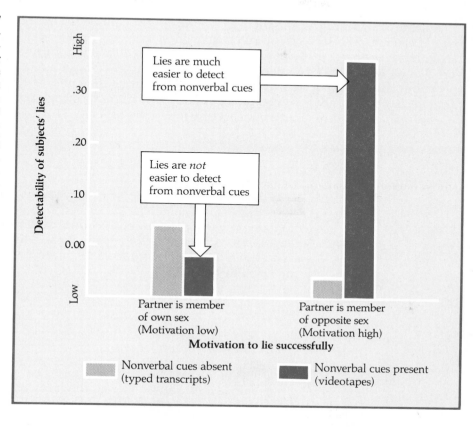

FIGURE 2.5. Subjects' lies were more detectable from their nonverbal cues when their motivation to lie successfully was high than when it was low. Thus, their lies were more detectable when they thought they were addressing a member of the opposite sex rather than a member of their own sex, and when they feigned agreement with this person (ingratiating lies) rather than disagreement. (Source: Based on data from DePaulo, Stone, and Lassiter, 1985b.)

Motivation to deceive: Sometimes, it backfires

where they told ingratiating lies and believed that their partner was an attractive member of the opposite sex than when they told noningratiating lies and believed that their partner was an unattractive member of their own sex. To test these predictions, records of subjects' behavior that either contained or did not contain nonverbal cues (e.g., complete videotapes versus typed transcripts of their words) were given to another group of persons (judges). These persons were asked to rate subjects' sincerity. As shown in Figure 2.5, results offered support for the major hypothesis. When subjects' motivation to lie successfully was high,

their efforts at such deception were actually *easier* to detect than when their motivation to accomplish this task was low.

One possible explanation for these results is as follows. As individuals become more and more concerned with lying effectively, they tend to focus increasing attention on what they say. The result: crucial nonverbal channels are left relatively unguarded and become "leakier"—more revealing of deceit. Whatever the precise mechanism involved, however, one fact seems clear: where interpersonal deceit is concerned, the harder people try, the worse they often do.

Before concluding, we should insert a final note of caution. While we do seem capable of recognizing attempts at deception from non-verbal cues, we are far from perfect in this respect. Our ability to spot such deception is better than chance, but not much better (about 60 percent in many studies). Further, expecting to encounter deception does not seem to improve our ability to spot it. In fact, it may actually reduce it to a slight degree (Toris and DePaulo, 1985). So, in sum, while nonverbal cues can help, they are far from the final word in our efforts to recognize, and deal with, deception by others.

such information is known as **attribution**, and it has been of major interest to social psychologists for several decades. Because attribution is complex, several theories designed to explain its operation have been proposed (e.g., Heider, 1958). Here, we will focus on two that have been especially influential — frameworks proposed by Jones and Davis (1965) and by Kelley (1972).

From acts to dispositions: Using others' behavior as a guide to their lasting traits

The first of these theories is concerned with a basic — and very reasonable — issue: how do we go about inferring the lasting characteristics of other persons from their behavior? Such inference is necessary because individuals do not carry signs proclaiming their central traits. Indeed, they are often quite unaware of these, and in other cases they are unwilling to share such knowledge with us even if they possess it. (After all, how many persons would admit, openly, that they are stingy, manipulative, prejudiced, or cruel?) Thus, if we wish to understand the persons around us, we must usually observe their behavior and use the information observation provides as a basis for reaching conclusions about them.

At first glance, it might appear that our task in this regard is quite simple — others' behavior *does* provide us with a rich source of input. Actually, though, it is complicated by the following fact: often, other people act in certain ways not because of their own traits or dispositions, but because of the influence of factors outside their control. For example, imagine that you observe a state trooper giving one speeding ticket after another to passing motorists. Does this mean that she is a "tough cookie" who enjoys punishing hapless strangers? Not necessarily. She may have been given a high quota for tickets that week, and feels she has no choice. In cases such as this, using others' behavior as a guide to their lasting traits or motives can lead us seriously astray.

How do we cope with such complications? How do we decide either that others' actions reflect their "true" characteristics or, alternatively, that these actions stem from other factors? Jones and Davis provide an answer in their theory of **correspondent inference** (Jones and Davis, 1965; Jones and McGillis, 1976). According to this theory, we accomplish this difficult task by focusing our attention on certain types of actions — those most likely to be informative in this regard.

First, we consider only behaviors that seem to have been freely chosen; those that were somehow forced on the persons in question tend to be ignored. Second, we pay careful attention to behaviors that produce unique or *noncommon effects* — outcomes that would not be produced by any other action. The advantage offered by such behaviors is readily illustrated. For example, imagine that one of your friends has just gotten married. Further, suppose that her spouse is (1) highly attractive, (2) pleasant and friendly, and (3) incredibly rich. Would the fact that your friend married this man tell you much about her personality? Probably not. There are so many potential reasons for having married him (his good looks, charm, wealth) that it is impossible to determine which was most important to her. But now, in contrast, imagine that your friend has just married someone who is (1) highly unattractive, (2) grumpy and irritable, and (3) incredibly rich. In this case, there is only one apparent reason for your friend's decision to marry: her mate's great wealth. Under these conditions, your friend's decision *does* tell you something about her major traits or motives. Thus, you may conclude that she values money more than other things such as getting along with her spouse or a good sex life. By comparing these situations, you should be able to see why we can usually learn more about others from actions on their part that produce noncommon effects than from actions without any distinctive consequences.

Finally, Jones and Davis suggest that we also pay greater attention, in our efforts to understand others, to actions they perform that are low in *social desirability* than to actions that are high on this dimension. In short, we learn more from actions by others that depart from the ordinary and are not encouraged by society than from actions that are typical of most persons or that *are* widely encouraged. For example, consider the state trooper mentioned previously. If you see her helping a stranded motorist, you may be reluctant to form any conclusions about her stable traits; after all, this is part of her job, and other officers would probably act in the same manner. If you see her refuse to help a motorist in distress, or observe her drinking beer while tooling down the highway in her patrol car, you may be more willing to reach such conclusions. These actions are both unusual and against rules she's supposed to follow.

In sum, the theory proposed by Jones and Davis suggests that we are most likely to conclude that others' behavior reflects their stable traits (i.e., we are likely to reach *correspondent inferences* about them) when these actions (1) occur by choice; (2) yield distinctive, noncommon effects; and (3) are low in social desirability. (Please refer to Figure 2.6, page 52, for a summary of these principles.)

FIGURE 2.6. According to a theory proposed by Jones and Davis, when others' behavior produces noncommon effects, appears to be freely chosen, and is low in social desirability, we attribute it to their traits or personal dispositions. (Source: Based on suggestions by Jones and Davis, 1965.)

Correspondent inference: Attributing others' behavior to their traits and dispositions

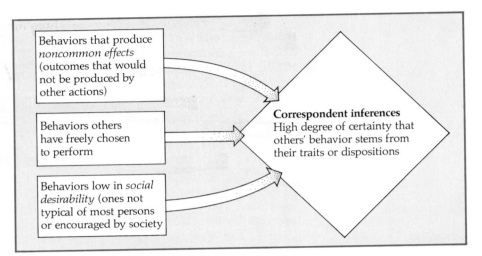

Behaviors that produce *noncommon effects* (outcomes that would not be produced by other actions)

Behaviors others have freely chosen to perform

Behaviors low in *social desirability* (ones not typical of most persons or encouraged by society

Correspondent inferences
High degree of certainty that others' behavior stems from their traits or dispositions

Kelley's theory of causal attribution: How we answer the question "Why?"

Consider the following events: you apply for membership in a social organization but are rejected; your boss announces, unexpectedly, that he is giving you a big raise; you ask someone special for a date but are refused. What question would arise in your mind in each of these situations? If you are like most people, your answer can be stated in a single word: "Why?" You would wonder *why* the organization has rejected you, *why* your boss is giving you that raise, and *why* your advances have been spurned. In countless life situations, this is the central attributional task we face. We want to know why other persons have behaved the way they have. Such knowledge is of crucial importance, for only if we understand the causes behind their actions can we adjust our own behavior accordingly, and make sense out of the social world around us. Obviously, the number of specific causes behind others' behavior is very large— perhaps almost infinite. To make this task more manageable, therefore, we often begin with a preliminary question: has others' behavior stemmed mainly from *internal causes* (their own characteristics, motives, intentions), mainly from *external causes* (some aspect of the social or physical world), or from a combination of the two? For example, with respect to your raise, you might first wonder whether your boss has decided to reward you in this manner because of internal causes (he is a kind, benevolent person sensitive to your dire need!), external causes (he was told to do so by *his* supervisor), or some combination of causal factors. Revealing insights into just how we carry out this initial— but central—attributional task are provided by a major theory proposed by Kelley (Kelley, 1972; Kelley and Michela, 1980).

According to Kelley, in our attempts to answer the question "why" about others' behavior, we focus on three major dimensions. First, we consider **consensus** — the extent to which others react in the same manner to some stimulus or event as the person we are considering. Second, we consider **consistency** — the extent to which this person reacts to this stimulus or event in the same way on other occasions. And third, we examine **distinctiveness** — the extent to which he or she reacts in the

FIGURE 2.7. According to a theory proposed by Kelley (1972), we focus on information about three central factors when attempting to determine whether others' behavior stemmed from internal or external causes. These factors are *consensus, consistency,* and *distinctiveness.*

Kelley's theory of causal attribution: Its major predictions

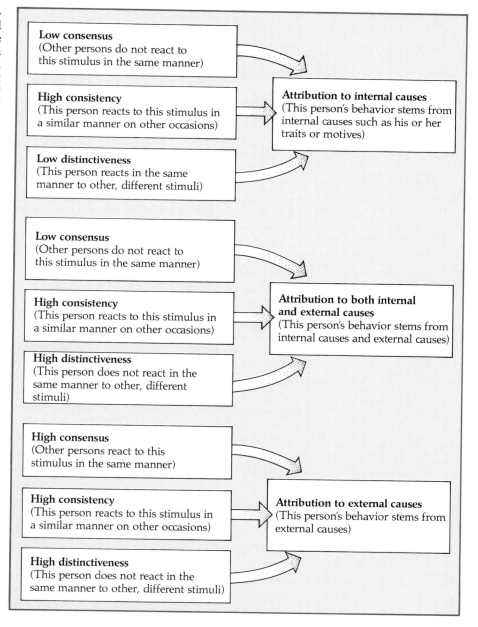

Low consensus
(Other persons do not react to this stimulus in the same manner)

High consistency
(This person reacts to this stimulus in a similar manner on other occasions)

Low distinctiveness
(This person reacts in the same manner to other, different stimuli)

Attribution to internal causes
(This person's behavior stems from internal causes such as his or her traits or motives)

Low consensus
(Other persons do not react to this stimulus in the same manner)

High consistency
(This person reacts to this stimulus in a similar manner on other occasions)

High distinctiveness
(This person does not react in the same manner to other, different stimuli)

Attribution to both internal and external causes
(This person's behavior stems from internal causes and external causes)

High consensus
(Other persons react to this stimulus in the same manner)

High consistency
(This person reacts to this stimulus in a similar manner on other occasions)

High distinctiveness
(This person does not react in the same manner to other, different stimuli)

Attribution to external causes
(This person's behavior stems from external causes)

same manner to other, different stimuli or events. (Note: please don't confuse consistency and distinctiveness. Consistency refers to the extent to which an individual reacts similarly to the *same* stimulus or event at different times. Distinctiveness refers to the extent to which he or she reacts in a similar manner to *different* stimuli or events. If an individual reacts in the same way to a wide range of stimuli, distinctiveness is *low*.)

Kelley's theory suggests that we are most likely to attribute another's behavior to *internal* causes under conditions of low consensus, high consistency, and low distinctiveness. In contrast, we are most likely to attribute another's behavior to *external* causes under conditions of high consensus, high consistency, and high distinctiveness. And we generally attribute it to a combination of these factors under conditions of low consensus, high consistency, and high distinctiveness. (Please refer to Figure 2.7, page 53.) Perhaps the reasonable nature of these proposals can best be illustrated by means of a simple example.

Imagine you are dining in a restaurant with some friends and one of them acts in the following manner: she takes one bite of her food and then shouts loudly for the waiter. When he appears, she claims that the dish is inedible, and demands that it be replaced. Why has your friend acted in this manner — because of internal or external causes? In other words, is your friend a fussy eater, almost impossible to please, or is the dish really so terrible that it deserves to be returned? According to Kelley's theory, your decision would depend on the three factors mentioned above. First, assume that the following conditions prevail: (1) no one else at your table complains (consensus is low); (2) you have seen your friend return this dish on other occasions (consistency is high); and (3) you have seen your friend complain loudly in other restaurants (distinctiveness is low). In this case, Kelley's theory indicates that you would probably attribute her behavior to internal causes. For example, you might conclude that your friend is a perfectionist, or just likes to complain.

In contrast, assume that the following conditions exist: (1) several other diners at your table also complain about their food (consensus is high); (2) you have seen your friend return the same dish on other occasions (consistency is high); and (3) you have *not* seen her complain in this manner in other restaurants (distinctiveness is high). Under these conditions, you would attribute her behavior to external causes (i.e., the food really *is* terrible).

As we noted earlier, Kelley's theory is a reasonable one, and this fact becomes clear when it is applied to concrete social situations such as the one described above. Further, it has been confirmed by the findings of a large number of studies (e.g., Harvey and Weary, 1984; McArthur, 1972). We should note, though, that research on this framework also suggests the need for certain modifications. Several of these are described below.

Unexpected versus expected events: When we engage in causal attribution and when we don't.   There's an old saying to the effect that people generally take the "path of least resistance." In other words, they do as little work as they can. Unfortunately, the type of causal analysis described by Kelley takes a lot of effort; after all, obtaining relevant information about consensus, consistency, and distinctiveness may be both time-consuming and difficult. Thus, it is not surprising to learn that people tend to avoid such cognitive work whenever they can. In many situations, they are all too ready to jump to quick and easy conclusions about the causes of others' actions. They can do so because they know, from past experience, that certain kinds of behavior generally stem from internal factors while other kinds usually derive from external causes (Hansen, 1980). For example, they may have come to believe that success, in many spheres of life, is often due largely to talent and effort — two internal causes. Thus, when they encounter someone enjoying success, they quickly (and blithely) assume that these outcomes have derived from such internal causes, without any careful attention to the factors mentioned by Kelley. Only when behavior is unexpected and does not fit with what they know about a specific person, or about people generally, does extensive causal analysis occur (Hastie, 1984). In other words, Kelley's theory appears to be an accurate description of causal attribution *when it takes place.* It may not be applicable to many situations, though, because people simply don't wish to bother: they prefer to save their "cognitive energy" for situations that seem unusual or novel.

Actions and occurrences: Using different kinds of information to explain different types of behavior.   Consider the following two events: Bill practices his parachute jumping; Andrea is overwhelmed by a powerful wave of passion. Both describe behaviors by specific persons, but they differ in a key respect. The first is largely voluntary, while the second is not (our feelings, after all, are not always under our direct control). Do you think that in attempting to understand the causes behind these two types of behavior you might concentrate on different types of information? Research findings indicate that you would. It appears that in attempting to interpret voluntary behaviors (often known as *actions*), we tend to emphasize information about distinctiveness, while in seeking to interpret less voluntary actions (often known as *occurrences*), we pay more attention to information about consensus (Zuckerman and Feldman, 1984). The reason for this difference is as follows. Since actions are largely voluntary in nature, they can often be understood in terms of intentions. And information about intentions can more readily be inferred from distinctiveness (how an individual has acted in different situations) than from consensus (how different people act in a given situation). Conversely, since occurrences are only partly voluntary, they can be better understood in terms of the external conditions that evoke them. And such information can be more readily inferred from consensus than from distinctiveness. In sum, our differential use of information about consensus and about distinctiveness in interpreting actions and occurrences makes a great deal of sense. Indeed, it can be viewed as yet one more example of our general tendency to employ whatever information is most useful in a given situation.

Discounting and augmenting: Dealing with multiple potential causes. Imagine that one of your friends is taking a course with one of the toughest instructors at your school. She complains bitterly and frequently about how poorly she's doing. How would you explain her poor performance? The chances are good that you would do so in terms of the instructor. That is, you might assume his unfair grading policies and excessive demands account for your friend's problems. But now imagine that you also know that your friend has never cracked a book and goes to class only once a month. Would you still be so certain about the impact of the instructor on her performance? In all likelihood, you would not. The reason for this is simple: you now realize that there are at least *two* potential causes (the instructor, her own laziness) rather than only one. This example illustrates the **discounting principle,** an attributional principle suggesting that we tend to downplay the importance of any potential cause of another person's behavior to the extent that other possible causes, too, exist (refer to Figure 2.8).

Now, assume that the situation is somewhat different. Your friend is taking the same course with the same tough instructor, but is doing well. In fact, she's about to receive the first *A* given by this professor in the past five years. What is the cause behind her success? Obviously, something about your friend herself — her intelligence, hard work, and so on. Further, under these circumstances, you would probably have a great deal of

FIGURE 2.8. The *discounting principle* (upper diagram) suggests that we attach less importance to a given cause of some behavior when other potential causes of the behavior are also present. The *augmenting principle* (lower diagram) indicates that when a given behavior occurs in the presence of both facilitory and inhibitory factors, we assign added weight to the facilitory factor.

Discounting and augmenting: Reacting to multiple causes

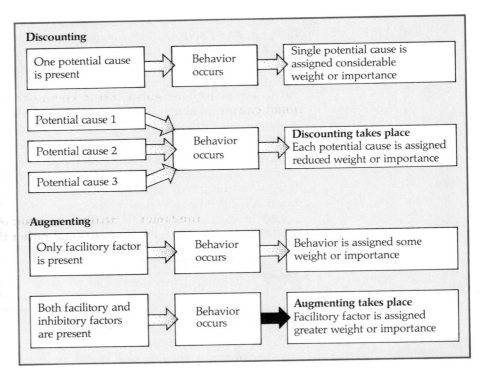

confidence in this conclusion. After all, she's doing well despite the instructor's harshness. This incident illustrates a second attributional principle — **augmenting**. It suggests that when a factor that might *facilitate* a given behavior and a factor that might *inhibit* it are both present, yet the behavior still occurs, we assign added weight to the facilitative factor. As you can readily see, this makes good sense. After all, the facilitative cause has succeeded in producing the behavior in the face of important barriers (the inhibitory factors; refer to Figure 2.8).

Both augmenting and discounting play an important role in attribution, especially in situations where we can't observe others' actions over an extended period of time or in several situations (i.e., when information on consistency and distinctiveness is lacking). Thus, they should be taken into careful account in many situations where, with respect to others' behavior, we attempt to answer the question "why?"

Attribution: Some major sources of bias

So far in this discussion, we have seemed to imply that attribution is a highly rational process. Whether we adopt the framework proposed by Jones and Davis or the view offered by Kelley, the overall picture is much the same: individuals seeking to unravel the causes behind others' behavior focus on certain key factors and then follow an orderly process en route to their conclusions. In general, this view is correct; attribution *is* logical in several respects. We should also note, though, that it is subject to important types of bias — tendencies that can lead us into serious errors about the causes of others' behavior (or even our own). Several of these are summarized below.

The fundamental attribution error: Overestimating the role of dispositional causes.

Suppose that during a visit to a park, you witness the following scene: a young woman picks up a plate of potato salad and dumps it on the head of another woman sitting at the same picnic table. How would you explain this unusual behavior? Research evidence points to an intriguing answer: the chances are good that you would conclude (however tentatively) that the first woman has a violent temper — she is someone to be avoided at all costs. This example illustrates what is often described as the **fundamental attribution error:** our tendency to explain others' actions in terms of dispositional rather than situational causes. Often, we seem to perceive others as acting as they do largely because they are "that kind of person"; the many situational factors which may also have affected their behavior tend to be ignored, or at least downplayed. Thus, in the example mentioned above, we tend to attribute the woman's actions to her temper, impulsiveness, or other traits; potential situational causes, such as strong provocation from the victim of her potato-salad assault, are overlooked.

This tendency to overemphasize dispositional causes while underestimating the impact of situational ones appears to be quite strong. Indeed, it even seems to come into play in situations where we know that others' actions were *not* under their own control. For example, if we read an essay written by a stranger, we tend to assume that it reflects this person's views, even if we are told that the author was instructed to write it in a particular way (Yandrell and Insko, 1977). One explanation for the fundamental attribution error involves the following fact: when we observe another person's behavior, we tend to focus on his or her actions; the context in which these occur often fades into the background. As a result, the potential influence of situational causes is not recognized. A second interpretation is that individuals do, in fact, notice situational factors, but fail to assign them sufficient weight. In other words, they do not perceive them as being as important as they actually are (cf. Gilbert and Jones, 1986; Johnson, Jemmott, and Pettigrew, 1984).

Whatever the precise basis for the fundamental attribution error, it has important implications. For example, it suggests that even if individuals are made aware of the situational forces that adversely affect minorities and other disadvantaged groups (e.g., poor diet, broken family life), they may still perceive these persons as largely responsible for their own plight. Clearly, then, this basic attributional bias can have important social consequences.

The actor-observer effect: You trip; I was pushed.   A second and closely related type of attributional bias can be readily illustrated. Imagine that while walking along the street, you see another person stumble and fall. How would you explain this behavior? Probably, in terms of characteristics of this individual. For example, you may assume he is clumsy. But now suppose that the same thing happens to *you*. Would you explain your own behavior in the same terms? Probably not. Instead, you may well assume that you tripped because of situational causes—uneven pavement, slippery heels on your shoes, and the like.

This tendency to attribute our own behavior to external or situational causes but that of others to internal ones is generally termed the **actor-observer effect** (Jones and Nisbett, 1971), and has been demonstrated in many different studies (e.g., Eisen, 1979). It seems to stem, in part, from the fact that we are quite aware of the situational factors affecting our own behavior, but less aware of these factors when we turn our attention to the actions of others. Thus, we tend to perceive our own behavior as stemming largely from situational causes but that of others as deriving more heavily from their dispositions (Fiske and Taylor, 1984).

While the actor-observer effect is both frequent and general, it can be eliminated under certain conditions. For example, if we *empathize* with another person—try to see the world as he or she does—our attributions about his or her behavior become more situational in nature (Gould and Sigall, 1977). Similarly, if the situational causes behind others' behavior are made very clear, we may assign these more weight (Monson and Hesley, 1982). Finally, the actor-observer effect can also be overcome by yet another type of attributional bias, discussed below. (Before reading the next section, though, please turn to the **Focus** insert on pages 60–61).

The self-serving bias: On the tendency to assume that we (unlike others) can do no wrong.   Suppose, at some future time, you write a report for your boss. After reading it, she provides you with glowing feedback — she's very pleased. To what will you attribute this success? The actor-observer effect seems to suggest that you will explain it in terms of situational factors (e.g., the task was easy, your boss is lenient, you had plenty of time to complete the report). But would this be the case? We doubt it. If you are like most persons, the chances are good that you will explain your success in terms of *internal* causes — your high level of intelligence, good judgment, and so on. Now, in contrast, imagine that your boss is unhappy with your report and criticizes it harshly. How will you explain *this* type of outcome? Here, the probability is high that you will focus mainly on situational factors — the difficulty of the task, your boss's unfairly high standards, and so on. In short, the actor-observer bias may well be overturned, in this context, by yet another form of attributional bias: our tendency to take credit for positive behaviors or outcomes, but to blame external causes for negative ones (refer to Figure 2.9). This tendency is generally known as the **self-serving bias** (Miller and Ross, 1975), and its existence has been confirmed by the results of many different experiments (e.g., Arkin, Gleason, and Johnston, 1976; O'Malley and Becker, 1984; Van Der Pligt and Eiser, 1983). An especially revealing illustration of this attributional bias in action is provided by the results of a study conducted by Baumgardner, Heppner, and Arkin (1986).

These researchers asked individuals who viewed themselves either as effective or ineffective at solving personal problems to offer solutions to six hypothetical problems of this type (e.g., wanting to be more popular, feeling nervous, being lazy). After proposing their solutions, subjects were provided with false feedback suggesting that they had done either very well or very poorly on this task. At this point, they were asked to indicate the extent to which their performance stemmed from various causes (their ability, their effort, the difficulty of the task, or luck). Results indicated that both groups of participants demonstrated a self-serving bias: they tended to attribute success to internal factors such as

FIGURE 2.9. As suggested by this cartoon, most persons have a strong tendency to attribute favorable outcomes to internal causes (e.g., their own talent or effort), but unfavorable outcomes to external ones (e.g., unreasonable actions by others, forces beyond their control). (Source: Reprinted by permission: Tribune Media Services, Inc.)

The self-serving bias strikes again!

FOCUS ON RESEARCH:
Classic Contributions

Actors and Observers: Different Perspectives, Different Attributions

The actor-observer effect has been demonstrated in many different studies. One of the first and clearest illustrations of its impact, however, was provided about fifteen years ago by a series of studies conducted by Nisbett and his colleagues (Nisbett et al., 1973). In the first of their investigations on this topic, Nisbett and his colleagues asked some subjects (those who served as actors) to volunteer their time to assist a charitable organization (one concerned with helping underprivileged people). Other subjects in the study (observers) were simply instructed to watch these proceedings; they were *not* asked to volunteer themselves. After the actor had either agreed to volunteer or refused, both subjects (the actor and observer) were asked to rate the likelihood that the actor would later agree to help a different charitable organization (the United Fund). In accordance with the actor-observer effect, it was predicted that observers would interpret the actors' behavior toward the first organization in more dispositional terms than would the actors themselves. Thus, observers would expect greater consistency in the actors' future behavior than actors would. Specifically, observers

would rate actors as *more* likely to help the second organization if they had agreed to help the first, but *less* likely to help the second if they had initially refused, than would actors. As you can see from Figure 2.10, results offered support for these predictions.

Although the findings of this first study were encouraging, the investigators realized that they were obtained under conditions where actors and observers did not know one another. Would similar results also occur when these persons were well acquainted? To find out, they conducted a second study in which male subjects wrote short paragraphs describing the reasons why *they* had chosen their current girlfriends and college majors, and paragraphs describing why their best friend had chosen *his* girlfriend and college major. These paragraphs were then carefully analyzed to determine whether, as the actor-observer effect predicts, subjects would explain their own choices largely in terms of situational causes (e.g., something about their girlfriend or the field they had chosen to enter), but would explain their friend's choices largely in terms of dispositional causes (i.e., his own traits, interests, dispositions). Results indicated that this was in fact the case. Subjects focused on situational factors in explaining

their own ability, but failure to external factors such as luck or task difficulty. However, subjects who viewed themselves as generally effective at solving personal problems showed stronger tendencies in this regard than those who viewed themselves as relatively ineffective at coping with such problems. It is interesting to speculate that perhaps it is this greater tendency to engage in the self-serving bias that permits persons in the former group to obtain more success in actually dealing with such problems. As we will soon see, additional findings offer support for this possibility (refer to page 64.)

FIGURE 2.10. Observers perceived actors' behavior as stemming from dispositional factors to a greater extent than did the actors themselves. Thus, they predicted that actors would behave in the future as they had in the past, while actors made less extreme judgments in this respect. (Source: Based on data from Nisbett et al., 1973.)

The actor-observer effect: A classic demonstration

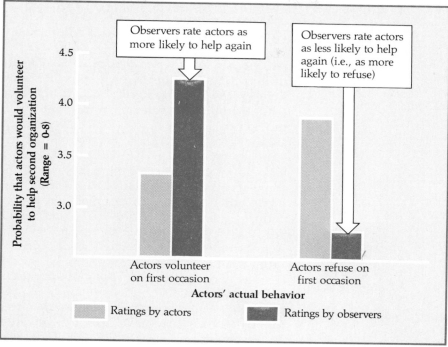

their own behavior, but dispositional causes when accounting for the behavior of their friends.

Together, the results reported by Nisbett and his co-workers offered convincing evidence for the existence of the actor-observer effect. Their intriguing research was then followed by many studies designed to uncover the mechanisms responsible for this attributional bias, and to establish the conditions under which it does or does not occur.

Additional evidence suggests that the self-serving bias stems from two different but related sources. First, this "tilt" in our attributions allows us to protect or enhance our self-esteem. After all, if we are responsible for positive outcomes but are not to blame for negative ones, our feelings about our own worth may be bolstered (Greenberg, Pyszcynski, and Solomon, 1982). Second, the self-serving bias permits us to improve our public image—to "look good" in the eyes of others. Regardless of its precise origins, however, this common attributional error can be the cause of much interpersonal friction. For example, consider what happens when two or more persons work together on a task. Because of the self-serving bias, each may perceive any success resulting from their joint efforts as stemming mainly from his or her own contributions. In contrast, each may perceive failures as primarily the fault of the others. Clearly, to the extent such reactions develop, the chance for future cooperation flies quickly out the window. (Please refer to Chapter 10 for further discussion of this and related topics.)

Attitudes and values as determinants of attributions.   The final source of bias in attributions we will consider is not really a "bias" at all. It involves the fact that attributions do not exist in isolation from individuals' attitudes and values. On the contrary, they are shaped and determined by these key aspects of social thought. A dramatic illustration of such effects has recently been provided by Feather (1985). This researcher asked Australian college students to rate the importance of various potential causes for unemployment. Some of these involved personal factors (e.g., a lack of motivation among unemployed people), while others referred to external causes (e.g., economic recession). In addition, subjects also completed a questionnaire designed to assess their political views (the extent to which they were conservative or liberal). Results indicated that such attitudes were indeed related to subjects' ratings of the various potential causes. Specifically, the more conservative the participants were, the more importance they assigned to internal, personal causes of unemployment (e.g., lack of motivation, self-indulgence). And the less conservative they were, the greater importance they assigned to external causes (e.g., government policies, general economic conditions). In a follow-up study Feather (1985) found similar relationships between the values held by teenagers (e.g., the importance of being honest or responsible), and their views concerning the causes of unemployment. These findings, and those of other studies (e.g., Feather and Tiggermann, 1984) suggest that our explanations of others' behavior, as well as important social events, can be strongly affected by our beliefs, attitudes, and values. Thus, this is yet another way in which our attempts to make sense out of the social world around us differ from the completely rational, information-based process described by Kelley's theory.

Applying what we know: Practical applications of attribution theory

Kurt Lewin, one of the founders of modern social psychology, often remarked, "There's nothing as practical as a good theory." What he meant by this comment was that once we have a solid, scientific understanding of some aspect of social behavior, we can put this knowledge to practical use. Where attribution is concerned, this has definitely been the case. In recent years, growing understanding of this aspect of social perception has been followed, quite closely, by its application. The range of topics to which attribution principles have been applied is vast, so we could not possibly hope to describe all of these here. What we can do, however, is to mention several that seem most important, and which have already yielded encouraging and informative results.

First, basic knowledge about attribution has been applied to the task of understanding reactions to the victims of rape and other serious crimes (e.g., Kanekar, Pinto, and Mazumdar, 1985). Unfortunately, such persons are often perceived as somehow responsible for the harm they have suffered — having failed to take proper precautions, or having done something that actually encouraged the attack. Because they are aware of such reactions, rape victims are often reluctant to report this crime to police or other authorities. Recent findings suggest that such reluctance is greatest under conditions where the faulty attributions mentioned above are most likely (e.g., when the victim has no physical injuries, or was acquainted with the rapist; Feldman-Summers and Norris, 1985). By helping to identify such conditions, and by suggesting steps that can be taken to counter their impact, attribution theory has shed considerable light on a disturbing phenomenon with important societal implications.

Second, attribution principles have recently been applied to the reduction of interpersonal conflict (Baron, 1985). In this context, it has been found that when persons taking part in negotiations indicate *why* they have adopted the positions they hold (e.g., because they sincerely believe that these positions are fair), conflict is reduced, and the likelihood of an agreement is enhanced. Thus, attribution theory suggests techniques that may be of considerable value in resolving costly conflicts.

Third, knowledge of attribution has added to our understanding of the origins of serious marital difficulties (Holtzworth-Munroe and Jacobson, 1985). Couples experiencing such maladjustment are more likely than their better-adjusted counterparts to attribute negative actions by their partner to lasting traits and characteristics. Thus, they see little hope of change. In contrast, couples not experiencing marital distress tend to attribute such actions to external causes or temporary factors. These findings suggest that important benefits may result if couples can be induced to shift their perceptions of the causes behind each other's behavior.

Finally, attribution has been used to assist individuals cope with personal problems; in short, it has found application as a form of individual therapy. One use of such procedures has focused on students experiencing difficulties in their college studies (Wilson and Linville, 1982). Apparently, one problem faced by such persons is that they attribute these difficulties to lasting, internal causes (e.g., their own lack of ability). When such persons are induced to shift their attributions so that they now perceive their low grades as stemming mainly from external or temporary causes (e.g., adjustment to college), important benefits follow. Their grades improve, and they are less likely to drop out of school than comparable students not exposed to such "treatment." Perhaps an even more dramatic use of attribution as a form of therapy involves efforts to combat the negative effects stemming from low self-esteem. An investigation performed by Brockner and Guare (1983) illustrates the surprising results that can sometimes be attained in this manner.

These researchers began with an intriguing idea: perhaps many of the difficulties faced by low self-esteem persons stem from faulty attributions. Specifically, they proposed that persons suffering from low self-esteem may show a pattern of personal attributions directly opposite to that suggested by the self-serving bias. In contrast to most individuals, they tend to attribute their failures to internal causes (e.g., their own real or imagined weaknesses), but attribute their successes to external causes (e.g., good luck, an easy task). To the extent this is actually the case, an interesting possibility follows: perhaps the often devastating effects of low self-esteem can be reduced by somehow inducing such persons to reverse these attributions—to attribute their failures to external factors (causes beyond their control), and their successes to internal ones (their own abilities or effort).

In order to examine this possibility, Brockner and Guare had college students who had previously been found to be either low or high in self-esteem work on insoluble concept formation problems. (Subjects were told that some stimuli they examined shared a common characteristic, and they were asked to identify it. In fact, the stimuli did *not* share a single characteristic, so there was no right answer.) Following this failure experience, subjects worked on an anagrams task that *was* solvable. At this time, some individuals were provided with information suggesting that their previous poor performance stemmed from *external* causes (they were led to believe the task was very hard). In contrast, others were provided with information suggesting that their previous failure stemmed largely from *internal* causes (they were led to believe the task was quite easy and that they were responsible for their own poor performance). Finally, subjects in another condition received no information designed to affect their attributions; they were left to their own devices in this regard. It was predicted that among low self-esteem subjects, those induced to attribute their past failure to external causes would now do better on the anagrams task than those induced to attribute it to internal causes. Since high self-esteem subjects would tend to attribute failure to external causes regardless of what information they received (recall the self-serving bias), no such effects were predicted among this group. As shown by Figure 2.11, results offered support for both of these predictions.

These findings, and those of related studies, suggest that getting individuals who suffer from the effects of low self-esteem to change their attributions about the causes of their own performance may be a very useful strategy. Indeed, under appropriate conditions, it can help them to escape from the vicious, self-fulfilling circle generated by their negative self-concepts. To the extent basic knowledge about attribution can contribute to such outcomes, of course, it will prove to be of major practical benefit.

FIGURE 2.11. When low self-esteem individuals were induced to attribute their failure on one task to external causes, they did much better on a second task. In contrast, information about the causes behind their failure had little impact upon the performance of high self-esteem persons, who normally attribute negative outcomes to external factors. (Source: Based on data from Brockner and Guare, 1983.)

Countering the harmful effects of low self-esteem: An attributional approach

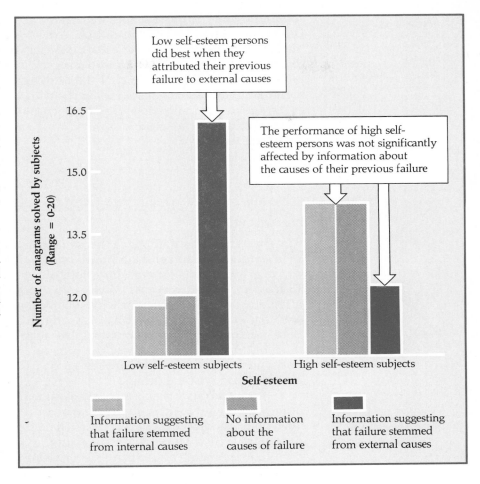

Low self-esteem persons did best when they attributed their previous failure to external causes

The performance of high self-esteem persons was not significantly affected by information about the causes of their previous failure

Number of anagrams solved by subjects (Range = 0-20)

16.5

15.0

13.5

12.0

Low self-esteem subjects   High self-esteem subjects

Self-esteem

Information suggesting that failure stemmed from internal causes

No information about the causes of failure

Information suggesting that failure stemmed from external causes

SELF-ATTRIBUTION: Understanding Ourselves

So far, in our discussion of attribution we have focused mainly on the manner in which we come to know and understand others. At this point, then, it makes sense to turn to a related question of equal importance: how do we come to know and understand *ourselves*? At first glance, you might assume that this is a simple task. After all, our own feelings, motives, and intentions are open to our direct observation; thus, it should be easy to obtain information about them by turning our attention inward (Carver, Antoni, and Scheier, 1985; Carver and Scheier, 1981). To a degree, this is true. But think again: there are at least two important complications in this process. First, we are often unaware of at least some of the factors that affect our own behavior (Nisbett and Ross, 1980). We may know that we acted in a given manner but are uncertain — or even wrong — about *why* we did so. Second, it is often difficult, if not impossible, to evaluate our own traits, abilities, or attitudes without reference to the persons around us. Are we intelligent or dull, sexy or lacking in sex appeal, successful or unsuccessful? Usually, we can't tell merely by looking inward, or into a mirror. Instead, we must rely upon social information — comments and feedback provided by others or, occasionally, by additional sources in the world around us (refer to Figure 2.12). Social psychologists have long been aware of this fact, but perhaps it has been stated most forcefully by Daryl Bem in an influential theory of **self-perception.**

Bem's theory of self-perception: Behavior as a source of self-knowledge

The central idea behind Bem's theory is this: often, we do *not* know our own attitudes, feelings, or emotions directly. Rather, we find it necessary to infer them from observations of our own behavior (Bem, 1972). If we have acted in some manner, we seem to reason, then we must hold an attitude or feeling consistent with such behavior. What we *do*, in short, serves as a useful guide to what is happening inside! Further, according to Bem, we draw inferences about ourselves in much the same manner as we do about other persons. Thus, the process through which we come to know ourselves is very similar to the process through which we come to know and understand others.

We should quickly add that Bem assumes that we use observations of our own behavior to infer our feelings or attitudes primarily in situations where our internal cues concerning such matters are weak or ambiguous. For example, if we violently dislike another person, we generally don't have to infer such feelings from the fact that we usually avoid her company. Similarly, Bem suggests that we will use our behavior as a guide to our attitudes or emotions only in cases where these actions were freely

FIGURE 2.12.   Unfortunately, devices such as this one don't actually work. To obtain information about our own traits and characteristics we must usually rely on social information — comments and feedback provided by other persons.

An amusing — but ineffective — means for gaining self-insight

chosen. If, instead, they were somehow forced upon us, we refrain from drawing such conclusions.

Although Bem's theory may strike you as being counter-intuitive, it is supported both by informal observation and by research findings. To illustrate the former, try to recall incidents in your own life when you were surprised to find that your behavior was not consistent with what you thought were your own feelings. For example, have you ever found, once you started eating, that you were hungrier than you thought? Or have you ever been in a situation where, once you lost your temper, you found that you were angrier than you realized? In such cases we discover that we really don't know our own internal states as well as we think we do. And in such cases our overt actions often help us gain a more accurate picture of these hidden processes.

Turning to research findings, Bem's theory has been supported by the results of several different lines of work. For example, it has been found that when individuals perform some action consistent with an attitude they hold, they may then come to hold it even more strongly than they did before (Kiesler, Collins, and Miller, 1969). Perhaps the most intriguing investigations deriving from Bem's theory, though, have been concerned with the topic of **intrinsic motivation.**

Self-perception and intrinsic motivation: The overjustification effect. Individuals perform many activities simply because they find them enjoyable. Behaviors ranging from hobbies and amateur sports through gourmet dining, playing video games, and lovemaking all fit under this general heading. Such activities may be described as stemming largely from *intrinsic motivation.* That is, the persons who perform them do so largely because of the pleasure they yield — *not* because of any hope of external rewards. But what would happen if individuals performing such behaviors were suddenly provided with extra payoffs for doing so? For example, what would happen if we were actually to pay someone for sipping vintage wines, for playing their favorite video game, or for pursuing a favorite hobby? Bem's theory offers an intriguing answer. It predicts that under at least some conditions, the persons involved would actually experience a *drop* in their intrinsic motivation. In short, they would be less motivated to engage in such activities than was the case before. The reasoning behind this prediction is as follows. Upon observing their own behavior, such "overrewarded" persons may conclude that they chose to engage in these activities partly to obtain the external rewards provided. To the extent they do, they may then perceive their own intrinsic interest as lower than was previously the case. In short, such persons may shift from explaining their behavior in terms of intrinsic motivation ("I engage in this activity simply because I enjoy it") to accounting for their actions in terms of external rewards ("I engage in this activity partly to obtain some external reward"). In other words, such persons may have too many good reasons (justifications) for performing such behavior to continue to view it as intrinsically motivated

FIGURE 2.13. When individuals perform some activity they enjoy in the absence of external rewards, their intrinsic motivation to engage in this behavior is maintained (upper panel). When they receive extrinsic rewards for performing this activity, however, their perceptions about why they do so may change. As a result, their intrinsic motivation may be reduced (lower panel).

Self-perception: Its role in intrinsic motivation

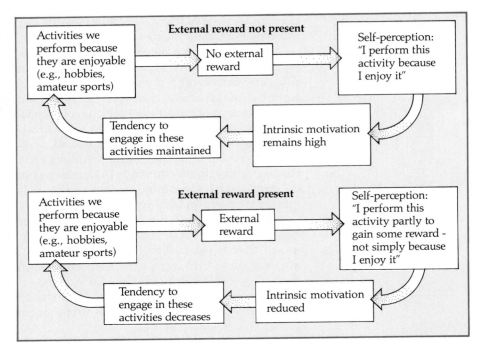

(refer to Figure 2.13). Along these lines, consider the following statement by Reggie Jackson, a baseball player whose salary at the time was $975,000 per year: "A lot of it is the money, but I'd be playing if I was making $150,000." (*Newsweek*, 1986). Given the impact of external rewards on intrinsic motivation, our summary comment is: "We wonder!"

Note, by the way, that the discounting principle, which we discussed earlier, also seems relevant here. Since subjects now have two potential causes to explain their behavior (their intrinsic motivation and the external rewards), they may discount (downplay) the role of the former. The result: they experience a drop in intrinsic motivation.

Support for the reasoning outlined above has been obtained in many experiments (e.g., Deci, 1975; Lepper and Greene, 1978; Pretty and Seligman, 1984). In these and other studies, subjects provided with extrinsic rewards for engaging in some task they initially enjoyed later demonstrated lower quality performance and reduced tendencies to perform these activities voluntarily than did other subjects not given such rewards. Thus, it appeared that the intrinsic interest of rewarded subjects in such tasks had in fact been reduced. Further, additional evidence suggests that such effects are most likely to occur under the conditions predicted by Bem's theory—when internal cues relating to the tasks at hand (e.g., attitudes toward them) are unclear or low in salience (Fazio, 1981).

Recently, though, another possible explanation for such findings has been suggested. According to this view, offering individuals external rewards for activities they enjoy may cause them to experience *negative affect* — unpleasant feelings or moods. These may stem from subjects' beliefs that they are being bribed or coerced in some way (Pretty and Seligman, 1984), or simply from the fact that they now feel that their performance is being evaluated (Harackiewicz, Manderlink, and Sansone, 1984). In any case, such negative affect may then interfere with subjects' enjoyment and so tend to reduce intrinsic motivation. If this is indeed the case, then it should be possible to eliminate the overjustification effect by somehow countering these negative feelings. Evidence that this is so has recently been provided by Pretty and Seligman (1984).

These investigators asked subjects to work on puzzles they found highly enjoyable. Some participants were told that they would receive a reward (a lottery ticket) for each puzzle they completed (the expected reward condition). Others were informed about the reward only after completing their work (unexpected reward condition), while still others never received any reward whatsoever (no reward). After completing the puzzles, subjects were asked to perform a different task. This consisted of reading statements designed to place them in a positive, neutral, or negative mood. In accordance with the reasoning described above, Pretty and Seligman predicted that the overjustification effect would fail to occur among subjects who read the positive statements; the pleasant feelings generated by this experience would prevent a reduction in their intrinsic motivation. In order to test this hypothesis, subjects were left alone in the experimental room for eight minutes, while the researcher ostensibly used the computer next door. The room contained the puzzles plus various magazines, and subjects were free to do whatever they wished during this period. A measure of their intrinsic motivation to work on the puzzles was then obtained by observing how much time they spent performing this activity. As you can see from Figure 2.14 (page 70), results offered support for the prediction that positive feelings would prevent occurrence of the overjustification effect. In this condition, subjects who received rewards for working on the puzzles in the first part of the study did *not* choose to work on them less during the free-choice period than those who received no such rewards. In contrast, the overjustification effect did occur when subjects read only neutral statements; here, those in the expected reward group worked on the puzzles for less time than those in the unexpected reward or no reward groups.

While countering negative affect appears to be an effective technique for preventing the overjustification effect from occurring, additional findings suggest that it is not the only procedure useful in this regard. For example, it appears that when external rewards are offered as a sign of competence or effectiveness, rather than as a bribe, they may fail to reduce intrinsic motivation. In fact, they can actually increase it (Rosenfield, Folger, and Adelman, 1980). Similarly, when the external rewards provided to individuals for engaging in enjoyable activities are both large and satisfying, they can maintain, rather than reduce, intrinsic motivation (Fiske and Taylor, 1984). Finally, if individuals are reminded of the enjoyable nature of various tasks, offering them external rewards

FIGURE 2.14. When individuals who received external rewards for performing a task they enjoyed were also induced to experience positive affect, the overjustification effect failed to occur. That is, these persons did *not* experience a reduction in intrinsic motivation. In contrast, subjects who did not experience positive affect demonstrated the usual overjustification effect. (Source: Based on data from Pretty and Seligman, 1984.)

Countering the overjustification effect: The role of positive affect

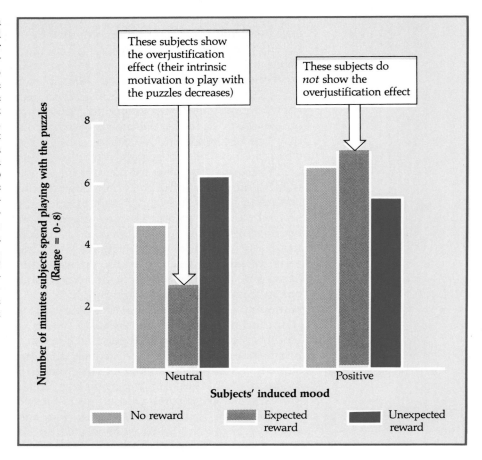

for engaging in them may fail to reduce their intrinsic motivation (Fazio, 1981).

In sum, several factors play a role in determining whether, and to what extent, external rewards will reduce intrinsic motivation. Given the widespread use of such rewards in many different settings, careful attention to these factors seems justified. If they are ignored, costly rewards may reduce intrinsic motivation, and so may actually reduce the frequency of behaviors they are designed to encourage. Clearly, this is an outcome few individuals, organizations, or societies can afford.

SUMMARY

The process through which we attempt to understand the persons around us is known as **social perception.** In order to gather information on the temporary causes of others' behavior, we often focus on *nonverbal cues* provided by their facial expressions, eye contact, body posture or movements, and touching. Such cues can reveal others' moods or feelings even when they wish to conceal them. Individuals often attempt to control their nonverbal cues in order to create favorable impressions on others. Such *impression management* plays an important role in interviews and other forms of social interaction.

Knowledge about the more lasting causes of others' behavior is gained through the process of **attribution**. In this key aspect of social perception, we attempt to infer others' traits, motives, and intentions from observation of their overt actions. In order to determine whether others' behavior stems mainly from internal or external causes, we focus on information relating to three factors: *consensus, consistency,* and *distinctiveness.* Detailed causal analysis of others' behavior involves considerable cognitive work. Thus, individuals perform it only under certain conditions (e.g., when confronted with unexpected actions by others). Recent evidence indicates that we tend to emphasize different types of information in our efforts to understand the causes of fully voluntary behaviors (*actions*) and ones that are only partly voluntary (*occurrences*). Our attributions are also affected by *discounting* and *augmenting.* Attribution is far from a totally rational process. In fact, it is subject to a number of biases, such as the *fundamental attribution error,* the *actor-observer effect,* and the *self-serving bias.* Attributions are also affected by attitudes and values.

The task of understanding the causes of our own behavior is more difficult than might be suspected. According to Bem's theory of *self-perception,* we often infer our attitudes or emotions from our overt actions. This theory helps explain why providing individuals with external rewards for engaging in activities they enjoy often reduces their motivation to participate in these activities. However, negative affect, too, seems to play a role in this surprising phenomenon, often known as the *overjustification effect.*

GLOSSARY

actor-observer effect

Refers to our tendency to attribute our own behavior largely to situational causes, but the behavior of others to internal (dispositional) causes.

attribution

The process through which we seek to determine the causes of others' behavior and gain knowledge of their stable traits and dispositions.

augmenting principle

Our tendency to attach greater importance to a facilitory causal factor if it succeeds in producing some behavior in the presence of one or more inhibitory causal factors.

body language
Cues provided by the position, posture, and movement of others' bodies or body parts.

consensus
The extent to which actions shown by one person are also shown by others.

consistency
The extent to which an individual responds to a given stimulus or situation in the same way on different occasions (i.e., across time).

correspondent inferences
Inferences concerning the stable traits of others about which we have a high degree of confidence.

discounting principle
Our tendency to reduce the importance we assign to one potential cause of some behavior when other potential causes are also present.

distinctiveness
The extent to which an individual responds in a similar manner to different stimuli or different situations.

fundamental attribution error
Our tendency to overestimate the impact of dispositional causes on others' behavior.

impression management
Efforts by individuals to present themselves in the most favorable light to others.

intrinsic motivation
Motivation to perform various activities simply because they are enjoyable in themselves.

nonverbal communication
Communication between individuals that does not involve the content of spoken language. It relies, instead, on a "silent language" of facial expressions, eye contact, body language, and touching.

overjustification effect
Reductions in intrinsic motivation that are produced by external rewards.

self-perception
The process through which we seek to understand our own feelings, traits, and motives. We must often infer these from observation of our overt behavior.

self-serving bias
Our tendency to view positive outcomes as stemming from internal causes (e.g., our own effort or ability) but negative outcomes as stemming largely from external factors.

social perception
The process through which we seek to know and understand the persons around us.

staring
Eye contact in which one person continues to gaze at another for an extended period of time regardless of what the recipient of such treatment does.

FOR MORE INFORMATION

Buck, R. (1984). *The communication of emotion.* New York: Guilford.
While this excellent book considers emotion and the communication of emotion generally, it contains a wealth of valuable information about nonverbal aspects of this process. In particular, the chapter on the role of nonverbal communication in social interaction is both thought-provoking and intriguing. This is a good source to consult if you want to know more about many aspects of nonverbal communication.

Harvey, J. H., and Weary, G. (1981). *Perspectives on attributional processes.* Dubuque, Iowa: Wm. C. Brown.
In our opinion, this is still the best brief introduction to the topic of attribution. The book is clearly written and covers a great deal of ground. Major theories are reviewed, and important applications of attribution (e.g., to the treatment of personal problems) are described.

Ross, M., and Fletcher, G. J. O. (1985). *Attribution and social perception.* In G. Lindzey and E. Aronson (eds.), *Handbook of social psychology.* New York: Random House.
A comprehensive, thorough discussion of many aspects of social perception by two experts in this general area. While the book is primarily intended for a professional audience, it is clearly written and contains much fascinating information.

CHAPTER 3

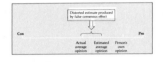

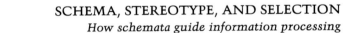

MENTAL SHORT-CUTS: Heuristics, Biases, and Fallacies
Some major cognitive strategies: Short-cuts to understanding the social world • Exceptions to fallacies and biases • Affect and cognition: How feelings shape thought and thought shapes feelings

SCHEMA, STEREOTYPE, AND SELECTION
How schemata guide information processing

SELF-AWARENESS: The Effects of Looking Inward
Alcohol, paranoia, and pressure: Three applications of self-awareness

SPECIAL INSERTS

FOCUS ON RESEARCH: The Cutting Edge — Action identification: Knowing what you're doing

ON THE APPLIED SIDE — Sadder but wiser? Depression and information processing

FOCUS ON RESEARCH: The Cutting Edge — What happens when reality doesn't fit your schema? A recent controversy

SOCIAL COGNITION: Understanding the Social World

"Well, what do we do?" Stan Lomm asks, opening his hands in a gesture of despair. "Is he in or out?"

His question is addressed to his old friends Phil Watson and Jerry Rigley, and concerns Frank Baxter, a fellow they've met just this semester. Frank wants to join Stan and his friends in renting a two-bedroom condo next year, and right now they're trying to decide if he's the kind of person they want as a roommate.

"I'm for him," Jerry answers. "I mean, he's a pretty easy-going guy, right? And that's the kind of person we want around."

"Yeah, he's easy-going OK," Phil agrees. "But man, is he ever sloppy. He was in my chem lab, and he made a mess every week. His partner was really sore."

"Oh come on," Stan responds with annoyance. "How can you tell a guy is sloppy just because he makes a mess of his lab experiments? Anyone can do that. He might be a lot different at home."

"Maybe, but I have my doubts," Phil comments. "Besides, you're just for him because he introduced you to Becky. I guess you expect him to provide you with one wild red-head after another."

At this remark, everyone laughs — everyone except Phil, that is. He waves his arm and says, "No way! I can meet my own women. I just think he's a regular guy and would fit right in, that's all. And I think *you're* against him just because of his East Coast accent. Come on, man, shape up!"

"OK, OK," Jerry interjects before the argument can continue.

"Let's not get upset—that won't help any. We've got to make a decision. If we don't take Frank, we'll have to get someone else, and that would be a real pain at this late date. Anyway, we need someone who'll pay the rent on time, and do their share of the chores. From what I can tell, he's a pretty organized guy."

"Organized? Where did you get *that* idea?" Stan asks. "Why, he can't even find his way around campus half the time! And he's always forgetting things, like meetings and assignments. *Dis*organized is more like it."

At this, there's a pause in the conversation, as everyone tries to put this mixed bag of "facts" about Frank together. Then, after a moment, Stan continues. "Gee, it looks as though we don't really know the guy at all. I don't see how we're going to make a decision if we can't even agree on what he's like. . . ."

HOW DO people make judgments about others? As suggested by the example above, this task is more complex than it might at first seem. Even when we don't know someone well, we have a lot of information about them at our disposal. We know how they look, what they've said at various times, and how they've acted in different situations. Somehow, we must then boil this information down into a few essential impressions, and base our judgments on these. As Stan, Phil, and Jerry discovered, though, different persons often interpret "facts" about others in contrasting ways, or combine them in unique ways, with the result that they reach sharply different conclusions. In recent years, social psychologists have directed increasing attention to this issue — to the ways people sort and store information about others and then make judgments about them on the basis of such input. The study of these processes is part of the new field of **social cognition.** Social cognition evolved out of research on *attributions* which, as we saw in Chapter 2, provided important insights into the ways in which people interpret social life. Social cognition borrowed some methods and ideas from cognitive psychology and applied them to the problems of social psychology. In general, social cognition is the study of how people interpret, analyze, remember, and use information about the social world.

The basic fact of social cognition is **information overload.** Stop for a moment and think about the last time you went out with friends, or took an exam, or ate lunch in a public place. How many thousands of stimuli confronted you — all the sights and sensations, all the words spoken by everyone present, all the possible implications of everything that happened? Multiply that by a lifetime's worth of such experiences, and it becomes obvious that the normal human mind could not possibly notice — let alone analyze and use — every bit of social information we encounter. And, in fact, adult minds are marvelously efficient at screening, sorting, and storing social information. But this efficiency sometimes means being less than fully logical, thorough, or accurate. To put it simply, the human mind uses numerous short-cuts to handle the immense amount of information that confronts it every day. A large part of social cognition is the study of those short-cuts.

The use of short cuts is so pervasive and so necessary that many social psychologists think the human mind is always looking for the easiest way to understand the events of social life. This view portrays the individual as a "cognitive miser" (Fiske and Taylor, 1984), which means that as a general rule people actually think as little as necessary, and that once they have a certain belief or idea they are reluctant to give it up.

Another basic fact of social cognition is that people are often unaware of their own mental processes. In a famous article, two social psychologists (Nisbett and Wilson, 1977) argued that people are generally unable to report the true reasons for their behavior, and that when

FIGURE 3.1. People's explanations for their own behavior cannot always be trusted. (Source: Doonesbury, copyright, 1982, G. B. Trudeau. Reprinted with permission of Universal Press Syndicate. All rights reserved.)

Explanations for our own behavior: Often unreliable

people do explain their behavior, their explanations are often wrong. In one study designed to show people's inability to report the causes of their behavior, Nisbett and Wilson pretended they were conducting a consumer survey. Shoppers were asked to pick the best one out of four stockings. In reality, they tended to pick the last stocking they saw, regardless of the order in which they were arranged. Thus, shoppers' selections were determined largely by which stockings they saw last. But were they aware of this? No! When asked why they made their choice, subjects gave reasons based on texture, color, and so forth, but no one ever mentioned the order in which the stockings were arranged. And when the experimenter asked shoppers whether they had picked that particular stocking because it was the last one they saw—which was the real cause of their selection—everyone denied it. In fact, they usually looked at the experimenter as if he must be demented to ask such a question.

People spend a lot of time explaining how they made a decision and explaining why they acted as they did. Social psychologists, however, are suspicious of such explanations for a variety of reasons (see Figure 3.1, page 77). If Nisbett and Wilson are right, such explanations are often worthless. At the very least, researchers know they cannot rely fully on people's self-reports about their mental processes. Social cognition researchers therefore have to conduct complex, detailed experimental studies to learn about how the mind makes sense of the social world.

(Nisbett and Wilson's argument does not mean, of course, that people *never* understand their own actions at all. To learn more about how people think about their behavior, please read the **Focus** insert on pages 80–81.)

MENTAL SHORT-CUTS: Heuristics, Biases, and Fallacies

Now let's begin looking at some of the short-cuts the mind uses to reduce information overload and make sense of human social life. These short-cuts, also called **cognitive strategies,** need to have two features in order for people to use them. First, they must provide a quick and simple way of dealing with social information. Second, they must be reasonably accurate most of the time. If a cognitive strategy always leads you to make wrong decisions, you will probably switch to a different strategy sooner or later. Often these cognitive strategies represent a tradeoff between these two features—accuracy (or reliability) and speed (or simplicity).

First, a word about terminology. Social cognition researchers often label the phenomena they study as heuristics, biases, and fallacies. **Heuristics** are decision-making principles used to make inferences or draw conclusions quickly and easily. **Fallacies and biases** refer to the errors and distortions that crop up in the way people use social information and think. The terms are related, for using heuristics often involves fallacies and biases.

Some major cognitive strategies: Short-cuts to understanding the social world

In our efforts to make sense out of the social world around us, we make use of many different short-cuts and strategies. Several of the most important of these are described below.

Representativeness heuristic: Judging by resemblance.   The **representativeness heuristic** means making a judgment or inference based on resemblance to typical cases (Tversky and Kahneman, 1982). Imagine that you have just met your next-door neighbor for the first time. On the basis of a brief conversation with her, you ascertain that she is exceptionally neat, has a good vocabulary, reads many books, is shy, and dresses conservatively. During the conversation, though, she never got around to mentioning her occupation. Is she a business executive, a librarian, a waitress, an attorney, or a dancer? One quick way of making a guess would be to compare her traits with the typical traits that go with each of those occupations. In other words, you might simply ask yourself how well she resembles the typical or average executive, librarian, waitress, attorney, or dancer. If you proceeded in this fashion (and concluded that she was probably a librarian), you would be using the *representativeness heuristic*. This heuristic allows one to make a "best guess" based on resemblance to typical patterns or general types, but of course it is far from infallible. It might turn out that your neighbor was a dancer after all.

When people have to make judgments or inferences about the probable nature of some person or event, they tend to rely on the representativeness heuristic more than on some other kinds of information. One possible alternative way to make such judgments would be to rely on how *common* each option is in the general population. In America today there are many more lawyers than librarians, so another way to guess your neighbor's occupation would be to pick the most common occupation. In this case you would be relying on *base-rate information* — that is, information about how common some pattern is in the general population. In practice, though, it turns out that people rarely use base-rate information in making decisions. This common failure to make use of information about the patterns and probabilities in the general population is called the **base-rate fallacy.**

A famous experiment by Tversky and Kahneman (1973) pitted representative information against base-rate information. Subjects learned that an imaginary person named Jack had been selected from a group of 100 men, and subjects had to guess the probability that Jack was an engineer. Some subjects were told that 30 of the 100 men were engineers (thus, the base rate of engineers was 30 percent), while others were told

FOCUS ON RESEARCH:
The Cutting Edge

Action Identification: Knowing What You're Doing

Do people know what they are doing? You may be inclined to answer "Of course!" because people couldn't act without some knowledge of their own behavior. Then again, you may be inclined to say "Of course not!" after watching someone act in a bewildered or self-destructive pattern, or after reading a social psychology textbook about some of the subtle factors that affect human behavior. Maybe both answers are partly correct — in different senses, people do and don't know what they are doing. This is the position taken by Vallacher and Wegner (1985, 1986) in their new theory of **action identification**. Action identification is the process of labeling and interpreting one's own behaviors.

Vallacher and Wegner start with the observation that any given behavior can potentially be described on many different levels. For example, consider what you are doing right now. Is it "reading a box in a psychology book"? How about "learning about some new theory"? Or try these: "looking at lines of print," "studying," "learning social psychology," "moving my eyes," "getting an education." All of those may be valid at the same time. Thus, the question is not *whether* people know what they are doing, but rather *how* and *in what way* people know what they are doing.

Vallacher and Wegner point out that the various ways of talking about each behavior can be arranged in a hierarchy, with higher and lower levels. The low levels are the mundane, mechanistic, and immediate ones, as in "looking at lines of print" or "moving my eyes." The high levels refer to abstract, general descriptions, often involving long-range goals, such as "getting an education." (For another example, see Figure 3.2.) Many of the interesting features of Vallacher and Wegner's theory center around hierarchy levels, and the causes and

consequences of considering actions in high- or low-level terms.

People may generally prefer to consider their actions in high-level terms, but they are often forced to go down to lower levels. In learning a skill, for example, you have to start with the details and mechanics. Imagine playing tennis for the first time while focusing on a *high*-level goal such as "impressing the crowd." Probably you wouldn't do very well! Instead, beginners at tennis usually focus on low levels of action identification, such as "gripping and swinging the racquet" or "trying to hit the ball."

Another central part of action identification theory is that when people change the way they think about behavior from one high level to another, they tend to drop down to lower levels first. Vallacher and Wegner provided a vivid illustration of this process in some studies done on couples about to get married. The researchers contacted people a month before their wedding, and then called them again a day or two before their wedding, and then again a few months later. Each time, they asked the couples how they thought about getting married. A month before the marriage, the responses were phrased in terms of high levels: "expressing my love," "building a life together," "starting a family." Just before the wedding, however, people described getting married in low-level terms such as "saying vows," "wearing a special outfit," "meeting new relatives," and so forth. When questioned some time after the wedding, the couples described the act of getting married in high-level terms again, but these were different high-level terms from the earlier ones. Unfortunately, the most common response at this time was some variation on the theme of "getting myself into a mess of problems!" This study showed that the same behavior (getting married) was described by the same people in different ways at different times. From a distance,

FIGURE 3.2. If you asked the people shown here, "What are you doing?" they might provide very different answers. Some would say, "Standing in line." Others would reply, "Waiting my turn." And still others might comment, "Taking care of my family's needs." These answers would reflect contrasting levels of *action identification.*

Action identification: Interpreting our own behavior

it was described in high-level terms, but just before the wedding people described it at low levels. And, as the theory specified, moving to a low level was an intervening step in the process of changing from one high-level interpretation to another.

Considering your actions in low-level terms, then, goes with high-level change. This implies that people may be more susceptible to external influence when they are operating at a low rather than at a high level, as shown in another study by Vallacher and Wegner. Subjects were offered a free computer analysis of their personalities. Half the subjects were asked to describe their typical behavior in low-level terms (e.g., particular comments and movements), while the others were told to use high-level terms (e.g., expressing certain basic values). This manipulation focused their attention on either the high- or the low-level aspects of their acts. Subjects then received the "computer analysis," which was actually generated at random. Half the subjects (selected at random) were told that they were cooperative, while the others were told they were competitive. Participants were then given a chance to respond to the feedback. Who do you think accepted the analysis as valid? The subjects who were focused at the low level were most swayed by the random analysis, as shown by

how they described themselves afterward. They believed it. High-level subjects, in contrast, tended to be skeptical of the computer analysis, and their views of themselves were unaffected by it. Thus, thinking about your actions in low-level, immediate terms makes you more open to influence and more ready to change how you see yourself.

A final application concerns criminal behavior. Have you ever wondered how people can deliberately do things they know are illegal or immoral? Wegner and Vallacher (1986) show that when committing a crime, people tend to focus on low levels of action identification. It would indeed be hard to rob someone if all the while you thought about it in high-level terms such as "committing the crime of burglary," "violating the property of another human being," or "being dishonest." Instead, criminals use low levels to think about their activities: "climbing the fence," "opening the window," "finding the money." By focusing on these mechanical, low-level details the criminals are able to avoid thinking about the unpleasant implications of their actions. So, do criminals know what they are doing? The answer is yes and no — *yes*, they are aware of the details and techniques, but *no*, they remain comfortably unaware of the broader and higher meanings of their acts.

that 70 of them were engineers. Half the subjects were given no further information other than these base rates, but other subjects received a personal description of Jack. The researchers found that subjects did use the base rates (30 percent or 70 percent) when they had no other information. But if they had any other information to work with, they ignored the base rates. They gave estimates based only on whether Jack resembled their stereotype of an engineer. People apparently prefer to use representativeness information instead of base-rate information.

FIGURE 3.3. Which of these events poses a more serious threat to your own safety or well-being? Although most people express greater concern about the situation at the top, the one on the bottom is actually much more likely. This is an illustration of the *base-rate fallacy*.

The base-rate fallacy: Ignoring information about probabilities

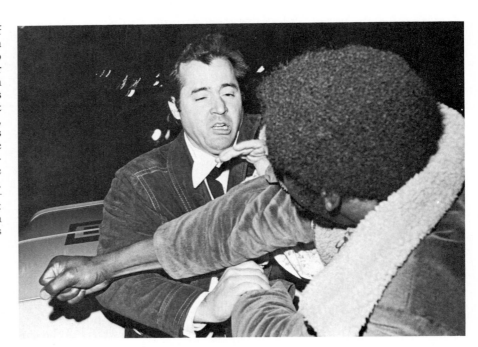

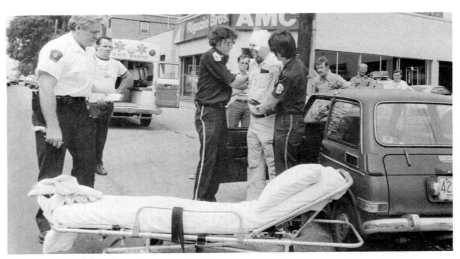

An important application of the base-rate fallacy concerns the impact of the mass media on individuals' personal fear of being victims of crime or accidents. It is well known that fears of victimization are often grossly out of line with the actual base rates of various crimes and accidents. For example, people tend to express great concern and fear about murder and AIDS; but, in reality, car crashes and emphysema are far more common causes of death (refer to Figure 3.3). Tyler and Cook (1984) gave groups of experimental subjects articles from the mass media to read, such as "Drunk Driving: A License to Kill" and "A Shooting Gallery Called America." These articles were chosen because they dramatized the dangers of death or injury caused by drunk drivers and firearms, respectively. Sure enough, reading these articles made subjects more likely to see drunk drivers and guns as serious national problems. Yet personal worries about these risks were unaffected by reading the articles. Thus, once again people appear to separate judgments about particular events (in this case, their own lives) from base-rate information about national trends and patterns.

Availability heuristic: What comes to mind first? Which is more common—words that start with the letter *k* (e.g., *king*) or words that have *k* as the third letter (e.g., *awkward*)? Tversky and Kahneman (1982) put this question to over 100 people in a demonstration of the **availability heuristic,** which means making judgments based on how easily instances come to mind. In English there are more than twice as many words having *k* for the third letter as words starting with *k*, but most people wrongly judge that *k* is more commonly the first letter. The reason, presumably, is that it is easy to think of words starting with *k* but harder to think of words having *k* in the third position.

Judging the frequency of words may not be a crucial part of social life, but the availability heuristic probably guides many important judgments, too. When a professor assigns grades for class participation, she may rely on how easily she can remember each student's making a comment in class. When a boss evaluates an employee's reliability, he may be guided by how easy it is to remember the employee's missing a deadline. In 1985 a series of highly publicized airplane crashes made many citizens afraid to fly. Note the base-rate fallacy involved in the airplane example: millions of people fly innumerable miles all over the world, and the base rate of accidents per miles travelled shows flying to be one of the safest modes of travel. But many people ignore this and become reluctant to fly because the reports of plane crashes are so readily available in memory.

False consensus effect: Thinking that others think as we do. Several other patterns in social cognition are related to the availability heuristic. One is the **false consensus effect,** which denotes an individual's tendency to overestimate how many other people would make the same judgments and choices and would hold the same attitudes, as the individual (Ross, Greene, and House, 1977). For example, high school boys who smoke estimated that 51 percent of their fellow male students smoke, but non-smoking boys estimated that only 38 percent smoke (Sherman et al., 1983). College students who sometimes think about dying estimate that 66.2 percent of other students think about death, too, whereas students who themselves rarely think about death estimate that only 32.7 percent of other students think about death (Sanders and Mullen, 1983). Similarly, students tend to overestimate the proportion of other students who would agree with their attitudes about drugs, abortion, university policies, the President's record, hamburgers, Brooke Shields, and Ritz crackers (Nisbett and Kunda, 1985). The false consensus effect is thus very common and broad, although it is not large. A student's estimate of the average opinion of other students will often be surprisingly accurate, although slightly distorted toward his or her own opinion (see Figure 3.4).

Why does the false consensus effect occur? There are two reasons. The *motivational* explanation is that people want to believe others agree with them because that makes them feel their own actions and judgments are normal, correct, and appropriate (e.g., Sherman et al., 1983; Sherman, Presson, and Shassin, 1984). A second view, the *perceptual distortion* explanation is based on the availability heuristic. It may be easier to notice and recall examples of people agreeing with you than people disagreeing with you. Indeed, to the extent that groups of friends have the same attitudes and preferences, each person is mostly exposed to people who agree with him or her. That alone could make agreement with your own attitudes and choices more available than disagreement, producing a false consensus effect.

Recent evidence has underscored the importance of the availability heuristic in producing the false consensus effect. If subjects are asked to consider the view opposite their own, they subsequently are less likely to show the false consensus effect (Goethals, 1986; Mullen et al., 1985). This argument assumes, in other words, that the false consensus effect occurs because instances of agreement with oneself are easiest to recall (that is, are most *available* in memory). If the opposite view is made more available, the false consensus effect is reduced or eliminated.

FIGURE 3.4. When estimating the average opinion of others, most people give an estimate that is fairly accurate but slightly distorted, being closer to their own views than is actually the case. This is the *false consensus effect.*

The false consensus effect: Its basic nature

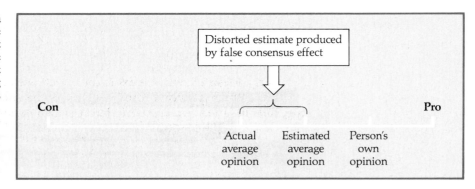

The false consensus effect is not universal, although it is quite common. Sometimes people want to think that others agree with their opinions, but sometimes they want to be unique. Campbell (1986) showed opposite effects for opinions and abilities. With opinions, people overestimate consensus, but with abilities, they underestimate it. In other words, people like to think their abilities stand out and make them special. In general, individuals seem to distort their views of others so as to flatter themselves: "My opinions are correct because everyone thinks like I do; my abilities are special because no one is as good as I am." People with high self-esteem seem especially prone to show this type of self-serving pattern in estimating consensus (Campbell, 1986).

Vividness effect. Consider two fund-raising appeals for donations to feed hungry children overseas (Fiske and Taylor, 1984). The first appeal presents statistics on food supply, child mortality rates, numbers of orphans, and so on. The other gives no statistics but describes little Felicia, an orphan with twelve brothers and sisters, living off the sale of firewood they gather by hand and carry on their little backs into the city to sell. Which ad would bring in more donations? Although the first ad offers more (and more reliable) information, common sense suggests that the second ad would be more effective. Presumably, this would be the case because it is higher in *vividness* — it is more noticeable and so presumably more persuasive than dry facts and numbers. Certain principles of social cognition, too, seem to point to the same conclusion. After all, vivid information, which is characterized by emotional appeal, concrete imagery, and the capacity to touch us personally in some way, should stand out from other information and be more readily noticed. As a result, it should be entered into memory more strongly, and be higher in availability at later times (Nisbett and Ross, 1980; Fiske and Taylor, 1984).

Surprisingly, though, it has proven extremely difficult to demonstrate such a **vividness effect** in systematic research. The impact of vividness, if it exists, seems to be weak, subtle, and unreliable (Taylor and Thompson, 1982). The only exception to this pattern is that case histories are often more persuasive than general statistics. Since case histories differ from general statistical reports in several ways, though, it is hard to evaluate the meaning of such results. Further, as we noted earlier in our discussion of the base-rate fallacy, statistical information often has little impact upon individuals. On the basis of existing evidence, then, it seems safest to conclude that vividness, in and of itself, has relatively little effect on how people make decisions and process social information.

Why doesn't vividness exert the effects we might expect? One possibility is as follows: vivid information may be entertaining and stimulating, but this in no way assures that it is also persuasive. Put very simply, we may be touched without being swayed by such materials. (We will see just how complex the process of persuasion can be in Chapter 4.) In a situation where we are bombarded with lots of information from various sources, our attention may be drawn to the most vivid messages. But that may exhaust the value of vividness. Once we focus on a given message, its vividness or lack of vividness may be irrelevant to its success at persuasion. Indeed, sometimes vividness can even interfere with persuasion, perhaps by being distracting. Fiske and Taylor (1984) describe several television commercials that were highly noticeable and memorable due to sexy or funny images — yet viewers could not remember the brand of the product being advertised! (Refer to Figure 3.5). The vivid images were remembered, but the sponsor's message itself was quickly forgotten.

Illusory correlation: Seeing patterns that aren't there.   Clinical psychologists often have to decide whether a given patient is sane or insane, is dangerous or not, should be locked up or released from the hospital, and so forth. Often they don't have much reliable information on which to base these decisions. Even the question of whether a patient is paranoid, manic-depressive, hysterical, or schizophrenic can be quite difficult, for there are no techniques comparable to a medical X-ray to see if a bone is broken. One of the few tests that is available is called the *draw-a-person test (DAP)*. The patient draws a human figure and the therapist interprets the meaning of various features. A drawing with large eyes, for example, is taken as a sign of paranoia.

Chapman and Chapman (1982) challenged the validity of the DAP test. In their view, clinicians using the DAP are succumbing to **illusory correlation.** In an illusory correlation, you expect a certain pattern to exist, and that expectation causes you to believe you are seeing proof of that pattern when in fact the pattern is not objectively confirmed. In other words, illusory correlation means seeing relationships that aren't really there, because your expectations distort the way you process information. Chapman and Chapman reviewed all the evidence pertaining to the DAP and concluded that most of the supposed signs of mental illness did not hold up as valid. In one study, for example, the eyes of figures drawn by paranoid schizophrenic mental patients were no different from the eyes of figures drawn by a normal group of student nurses.

A series of studies showed how illusory correlations can crop up in clinical judgments, regardless of whether subjects were expert clinical psychologists or students in introductory psychology. Chapman and Chapman prepared a stack of test results, randomly pairing drawings showing various features (e.g., large eyes, elaborate genitals) with various symptoms of mental illness. They made sure that the pairings were completely random — for example, the symptom "suspiciousness of others" was no more likely than any other symptom to be paired with drawing large eyes. Nonetheless, most subjects who looked through the stack of test results concluded that suspiciousness had mainly been paired with large eyes. In short, their expectations led them to "see" a pattern that wasn't actually there. The Chapmans even tried preparing the stack of drawings with the opposite pattern — suspiciousness was thus less likely than other symptoms to be paired with large eyes — but

FIGURE 3.5. Ads such as these are certainly *vivid*—they stand out from their backgrounds and catch our attention. Surprisingly, though, vivid ads do not seem to be more effective than other ads in changing our buying habits.

Vividness: Not necessarily linked to persuasion

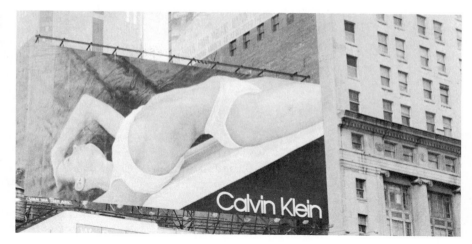

people still thought they saw large eyes and suspiciousness together most often. The illusory correlation was very difficult to break.

Why do people succumb to illusory correlations? One reason has to do with what is sometimes called the **confirmation bias:** People tend to seek out, notice, and recall things that support their beliefs more than things that disconfirm their beliefs. The great biologist Charles Darwin was well aware of the confirmation bias and the danger it presented to scientific progress. His rule was always to be sure to write down immediately any observation that failed to fit his theory, because such observations are easily forgotten by a scientist looking for observations to support their views.

Priming: Increasing availability. During the first year of medical school, many students experience the "medical student syndrome." They begin to suspect themselves (and their families and friends) of having various serious illnesses. An ordinary headache, for example, may cause the medical student to worry about a possible brain tumor. The medical student syndrome occurs presumably because the readings and lectures about various diseases plant the idea of those diseases in students' minds, so when a minor symptom occurs, the student's first thoughts are guided by the high availability of the disease categories. This is an example of **priming,** which is perhaps the most direct application of the availability heuristic (Gabrielcik and Fazio, 1983). Priming means exposing the person to certain ideas or categories in order to increase their availability in memory. In simpler terms, priming means planting certain ideas or categories in people's minds, causing them to use such ideas or categories to interpret subsequent events. (For example, after watching a movie or television show in which key characters act in an extremely competitive manner, we may be more likely to notice signs of competitiveness on the part of persons with whom we subsequently interact. Similarly, after reading a romantic novel, we may perceive others as being more flirtatious than would be the case if we had not just read the book.)

Priming was first applied in social psychology by Higgins, Rholes, and Jones (1977). They planted various traits in subjects' minds by having them do a cognitive task that required them to memorize various trait names (e.g., adventurous, reckless, independent). Later, in what they thought was a completely separate experiment, subjects were asked to form an impression of an imaginary person named Donald based on descriptions that portrayed him climbing mountains and crossing the Atlantic in a sailboat. Subjects' impressions of Donald were shaped by the trait names they had memorized during the cognitive task. That task had made those traits highly available in the subjects' minds, so, when reading about Donald, they naturally interpreted his behavior in those terms. Moreover, their general impression of Donald was favorable if they had been primed with good traits, such as "adventurous," but it was unfavorable if they had been primed with bad traits, such as "reckless." The same information about Donald, in other words, led to quite different impressions depending on what the subject had been thinking about earlier.

The direct effects of priming gradually wear off. Priming is more likely to influence judgments made on the same day that the priming occurred than on the next day (Srull and Wyer, 1979). The indirect effects of priming may persist indefinitely. If priming the trait "reckless" causes you to infer that Donald is reckless, you may continue to see Donald as reckless later on, even though the priming ceases to affect your first impressions of other people you meet. Still, the fact that priming wears off probably explains why the medical student syndrome mainly affects first-year students, which is good news for their families and friends!

Theory perseverance: When conclusions outlast their evidence.   We have seen that ideas planted in people's minds can affect their subsequent thinking. What happens if a false idea is planted in someone's mind and the person later learns it was false? The answer is that, sadly, the effects of that false idea may hang on. People seem to cling to their conclusions even after the supporting evidence is discredited, as depicted in Figure 3.6. This durability of false beliefs has been studied under the label of **theory perseverance** (Anderson and Sechler, 1986; Ross, Lepper, and Hubbard, 1975).

Theory perseverance was demonstrated in a well-known experiment by Anderson, Lepper, and Ross (1980). They gave half their subjects stories to read which led them to think that people who like to take risks make the best firefighters. Their other subjects read stories suggesting the opposite — that the best firefighters are by nature cautious people. Subjects then thought up reasons why effective firefighting ability should be associated with the trait of riskiness or cautiousness. Anderson then informed subjects that the stories they had seen were completely untrue. Did they abandon their theories linking riskiness or caution to being a good firefighter? Hardly! People continued to believe their theories about what made a good firefighter even when the basis for their theories had been destroyed. This is the cognitive miser in action — once the mind has a definite idea, it is reluctant to give it up.

Availability is one of the main reasons for theory perseverance. Thinking up reasons for a certain pattern, such as the pattern of risky firefighters being most successful, makes those reasons very available in memory. Even if you learn that the pattern is not true (firefighters aren't

FIGURE 3.6. Once a conclusion is drawn, it may persist despite the fact that the evidence on which it was based is shown to be false. This is known as *theory perseverance.*

Theory perseverance: One reason why false ideas persist

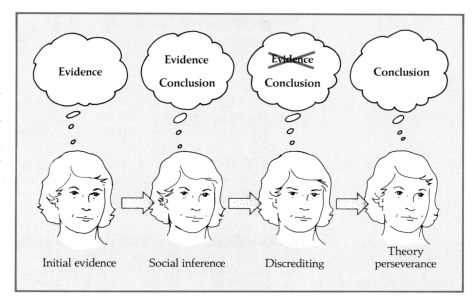

Initial evidence   Social inference   Discrediting   Theory perseverance

necessarily risky), your explanation is still there in your memory and may crop up in the future.

Availability isn't the only cause of theory perseverance, although it is an important one (Anderson, New, and Speer, 1985; Anderson and Sechler, 1986). Another reason is that once people have a theory, they may look for more information to support their theory. Thus, they process other information in a biased way, causing them to think their theory is generally true (Lord, Ross, and Lepper, 1979). The confirmation bias (described above under "illusory correlation") could produce that effect. The end result is a kind of vicious circle. A little bit of initial evidence makes someone form a general belief, which causes the person to see other evidence in a distorted fashion, which strengthens the belief. Even if the initial evidence is discredited, the person still thinks there is plenty of other support for that belief. Thus, once the mind draws a conclusion, it tends to disregard the basis for it. The conclusion can outlast the evidence on which it was based.

Regression fallacy.   Suppose you took an exam and scored much better than your usual grade. How would you expect to do on the next test? The odds are that you wouldn't repeat that high score. The reason is that part of any test grade involves luck. To score much better than usual, you had to know the material well, but probably you also had to be lucky on most of the questions that required guesses. Luck is not permanent, though, and the next time you couldn't count on such extremely good fortune. By the same token, if one score is much below your usual grade, you would probably do better the next time. These examples illustrate the basic statistical principle of *regression toward the mean,* which holds that extreme scores (high or low) will tend to be followed by less extreme (more average) scores the next time around.

People tend to be unaware of regression toward the mean. As a result, they tend to think up other explanations for the regression pattern when it occurs. This is called the **regression fallacy.** For example, consider two typical parents and their little boy. Like most parents, they will praise their child whenever he is even slightly good and punish him whenever his behavior is very bad. Regression toward the mean predicts that after being exceptionally good, the boy won't be quite so good the next time. Likewise, right after being very bad he probably won't be quite so bad. The parents, though, will tend to think that their reactions changed the boy's behavior. The result? They will think that punishment works better than praise, for the boy's behavior improved after punishment but got worse after praise. Over time, therefore, parents may come to rely more and more on punishment (Schaffner, 1985).

Sympathetic magic: Primitive thinking in modern life.   Thus far we have focused on how modern individuals adopt mental strategies to cope with information overload. Not all mental short-cuts are modern, of course. In fact, recent work suggests that some of the fallacies of primitive thinking still operate in the minds of people today.

Rozin, Millman, and Nemeroff (1986) reviewed the evidence about how people in primitive societies think, and came up with two principles of "sympathetic magic." One is the *law of contagion,* which holds that things that have once been in contact with each other have a permanent connection via some mysterious transfer of essences. For example, a primitive might think that someone's hair clippings or garments contain part of the person's essence, so burning or shredding these things will harm the person. The other principle is based on *similarity,* and it holds that things that resemble each other are somehow connected. For example, by burning a picture or small statue of someone, you can harm that person, according to some primitive beliefs.

Do modern people still have vestiges of these beliefs? Rozin and his colleagues conducted a series of experiments to demonstrate that they do. To show contagion, the experimenter gave subjects a glass of apple juice and then dropped a sterilized, dead cockroach into it. The roach was then removed with a sterile plastic spoon, leaving the drink in exactly the same physical condition as before. But subjects no longer wanted to drink the apple juice. In fact, most subjects even rejected a new drink of apple juice, served in a clean glass! The disgusting roach had contagiously and irrationally managed to "contaminate" all apple juice, in subjects' minds.

Several other studies were conducted by the same authors to demonstrate the operation of "magical" similarity. In one, participants were given a piece of chocolate fudge and then offered a second piece of fudge which had been shaped like either a round muffin or a piece of dog feces. Not surprisingly, subjects rejected the fudge in the latter case, when it resembled something unpleasant. In yet another study, subjects learned to throw darts at a target, and then pictures of various people were placed on the target. When the picture was of someone the subjects liked or admired, they were unable to throw the darts accurately. Apparently they felt that harming the photo might harm the person it depicted. Together, the data collected by Rozin and his colleagues suggest that primitive patterns of thought and information processing are still very much with us today, even in the modern "computer age."

Exceptions to fallacies and biases

In our discussion of mental short-cuts, we have seen that people typically overuse some kinds of information and underuse other kinds. Can these fallacies be overcome? Some evidence suggests that they can. For example, the regression fallacy can be avoided if people know about it and remember to apply it. Kruglanski, Friedland, and Farkesh (1984) tried telling subjects that a basketball team's scores fluctuated widely from one game to the next, and asked the subjects to predict the next score after a very high score. In this case, subjects predicted (correctly) that an unusually high score would probably be followed by a slightly lower score.

People can also learn to avoid the base-rate fallacy. Zukier and Pepitone (1984) put a base-rate problem both to first-year medical students and to medical residents who were about to become fully licensed physicians. The students succumbed to the base-rate fallacy, but the residents didn't. The implication is that part of learning to become a doctor teaches one to use base-rate information. In making a diagnosis, physicians have to rely heavily on the frequency that a given disease occurs. A patient's headache could mean a brain tumor or a virus, but the base rates suggest that a virus is far more likely to be the cause. Learning to use such information in diagnosis helps physicians appreciate the value of base-rate information.

Still, one should not be too optimistic about people overcoming these fallacies. Tversky and Kahneman (1971) found that even professional statisticians and mathematical psychologists were prone to some of these errors. It seems a safe bet that in normal life, many decisions and judgments are affected by the heuristics, biases, and fallacies identified by research on social cognition.

Affect and cognition: How feelings shape thought and thought shapes feelings

Thus far, we have mainly looked at social *thinking*, but *feelings* play a role in social cognition, too. Emotional states affect our judgment and our memory processes. For example, Baron (1987) had people conduct a job interview after putting them into either a good or a bad mood. Not surprisingly, the interviewers' mood affected their evaluations of the candidate, with good moods producing more favorable evaluations than bad moods. This difference was partly due to the effects of mood on memory for what was said in the interview. Although the same information was presented in all interviews, people in a good mood were more likely to forget the candidate's weaknesses and drawbacks. Similarly, people in a bad mood were more likely to forget the candidate's good points.

An influential theory of emotion was originally proposed by Schachter and Singer in 1962. According to this theory, emotion has two components: *bodily arousal* and *cognitive label*. The arousal part is largely the same for all emotions. A pounding heart, a warm and flushed face, and a few tears could apply equally well to someone experiencing anger, distress, or joy. The cognitive label comes from interpreting the situation. If you are watching a horror movie, you may interpret your arousal as fear, but if you just won the lottery, you will probably interpret the same physical signs as joy. A good way to remember the two components of Schachter's theory of emotion is to think of emotion as being like a television program. The bodily arousal is the on-off (and volume) control, which decides *whether* there will be any emotion or not (and if so, how strong it will be). The cognitive part is like the channel selector, deciding *which* of the various possible emotions is taking place.

One important implication of Schachter's theory is that it is possible to switch emotions by changing the label. For example, most people experience some arousal prior to an important exam. It might help to label your arousal as "feeling excited and eager" rather than as "feeling terrified!" Research on switching emotional labels has produced mixed results. At present, the safest conclusion is that switching works best with similar emotions and with people who may be uncertain of what they are feeling. It may not work at all with very dissimilar or unambiguous emotions. If someone insults you, for example, it is unlikely that you could be persuaded to re-label your anger as joy.

A current debate in social psychology concerns whether cognition is a necessary part of emotion. Schachter's theory, for example, clearly included cognition as part of emotion. Zajonc (1984), however, argues that people form emotional preferences they can't explain and may scarcely be aware of. He concludes that *some* emotions occur without cognitive processes. Lazarus (1984) disagrees with Zajonc, claiming that a certain amount of interpretation is always involved in emotion. Probably this disagreement arises from different meanings of the word "emotion." Zajonc thinks of emotion very broadly, as something akin to mood states. He claims that everyone is always in some emotional state. Lazarus takes a more limited view of emotion and says that having a preference is not necessarily the same as having an emotion. Both sides agree, however, that emotion can have effects on cognitions.

Several general conclusions about the effects of feelings on social cognition emerged in a recent review by Isen (1984). Good feelings seem to have effects that are more consistent and reliable than those of bad feelings. People who feel good find it especially easy to remember good things about themselves and others. They tend to judge things in a more positive or favorable light than people with neutral or bad feelings. They tend to be more optimistic about the future. They tend to produce more unusual word associations, which suggests that good moods may help people think and work creatively (Isen et al., 1985). And they tend to use quick, efficient, simple, and intuitive approaches to solving problems.

Bad feelings (or "negative affect") have complex effects (Isen, 1984). One reason is that bad feelings set off conflicting tendencies. Feeling bad can cause people to see the bad side of everything, but sometimes people actively try to overcome their negative feelings by deliberately looking at the good side of things. Moreover, different bad feelings have different effects. Anger and sadness, for example, are both bad feelings, but they have contrasting effects on what sorts of material gets remembered (e.g., Nasby and Yando, 1982). We still have much to learn about how bad feelings influence cognitive processes.

The intimate and personal quality of emotion is a powerful feature. If someone wants to get to know you, would that person do better to observe your behavior or to try to understand your private feelings? Most people answer strongly in favor of feelings (Andersen and Ross, 1984). And, in fact, there is evidence that feelings are more important than behavior in getting to know someone. In one study, subjects listened to

FIGURE 3.7. Do we learn more about others from their behavior or from information about their feelings and thoughts? Findings reported by Anderson (1984) suggest that the latter are more revealing. Subjects formed more accurate impressions of strangers who described their past thoughts and feelings than of strangers who described their past behavior. (Source: Based on data from Anderson, 1984.)

Forming impressions of others: Emotions are more revealing than behaviors

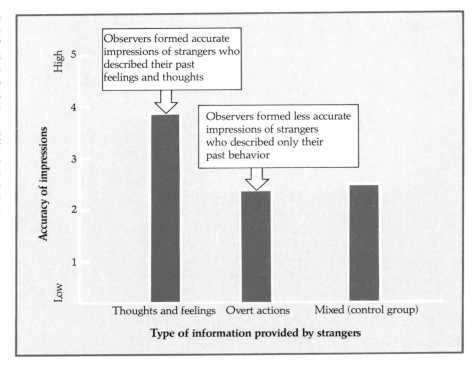

tape-recorded interviews in which speakers described either their past actions, their past thoughts and feelings, or a mixture of both. Subjects formed the most accurate impressions of the speakers who had discussed just their thoughts and feelings (Andersen, 1984; please see Figure 3.7). Emotion reflects the inner self, so understanding emotion can be helpful in understanding what someone is really like.

This special relation between emotion and the inner self can be disrupted. Some people have to show certain emotions as part of their jobs. For example, airline flight attendants are supposed to be cheerful and friendly, and bill collectors have to show anger and indignation. Hochschild (1983) coined the term *emotional labor* to refer to feeling certain ways as part of one's job. Her research suggests that emotional labor can be harmful, for it can alienate people from their own feelings or can make them emotionally numb.

SCHEMA, STEREOTYPE, AND SELECTION

One of the main concepts in social cognition is **schema.** A schema is an organized collection of one's beliefs and feelings about something. Stereotypes, preconceptions, and generalizations are schemata (psychologists prefer the Greek plural *schemata* instead of *schemas*). The basic idea is that your mind isn't just a hodge-podge of isolated facts about everything in the world. The mind organizes its contents very carefully and elaborately. Schemata are what the mind uses to organize the wealth of its information about the world. There are many types of schemata, including *self-schemata, person schemata, role schemata,* and *event schemata.* Let's consider each of these briefly.

Self-schemata. What is the self? Psychologists have been working on that question from many angles, and there is no single answer. Social cognition has provided its own perspective on what the self is. The self is in part a schema that helps us process information. The self, in other words, is something that helps us interpret certain events and understand their implications.

For example, imagine failing a course, or getting the highest grade in the class. Your self-schema leaps into action to interpret that experience. What does the grade signify about your knowledge of the topic? About your intelligence in general? How will it affect your chances for getting the kind of job you want after graduation? How will it affect what your friends or family think of you? Does it change how you feel about yourself? And so forth.

Early evidence of the importance of self-schemata for processing information was provided by Rogers, Kuiper, and Kirker (1977). In their study, the subject sat in front of a computer screen. A word would flash on the screen, and then a question about the word would appear. There were actually four types of questions: (1) was the word written in capital letters? (2) did the word rhyme with some particular other word? (3) did the word mean the same as a certain other word, and (4) did the word describe the subject? Different words were paired with different questions. At the end, the experimenter popped a surprise quiz to the subject, who was asked to write down as many of the words as he or she could remember. Which words do you think were remembered best? The principle is that the more deeply the subject thinks about a word, the more likely it is to be remembered. These researchers found that subjects remembered best the words that were paired with the question, "Does this word describe you?" In order to answer that question, unlike the other questions, the subject had to use his or her self-schema. Bringing the self-schema into play resulted in superior memory for the word (refer to Figure 3.8, page 96).

The implication of these results is that the self-schema is a powerful factor in the way people understand their social world. Events that bear on the self attract more attention, produce more thought, and are remembered better than other events. Other researchers have begun to study how self-schemata determine the way we form impressions of other people (Markus and Smith, 1982) and how the self-schemata of depressed people differ from those of normal people. (For some surprising—and unsettling—information on the role of self-schemata in depression, see the **On the Applied Side** insert on pages 98–99.)

FIGURE 3.8.   When subjects' self-schemata were activated, their memory was enhanced. They remembered more words paired with the question "Does this word describe you?" than words paired with other types of questions. (Source: Based on data from Rogers, Kuiper, and Kirker, 1977.)

Self-schemata and memory

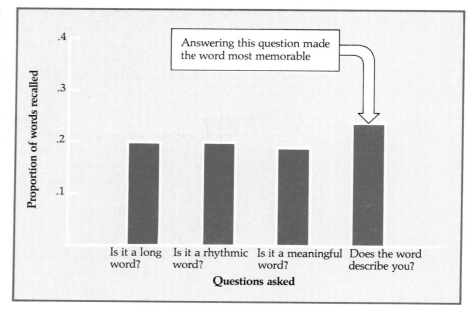

Person schemata and role schemata.   Obviously, the self is not the only person about whom an organized impression is formed. For each person whom we know well, we have a *person schema* that organizes what we know and feel about this individual. Sometimes a person will behave in a way that surprises you, even though that same behavior would not be so surprising if done by someone else. For example, it strikes you as perfectly normal to see George mopping the floor and making his bed if your schema portrays him as a neat housekeeper, but those same actions would surprise you if you had come to think of him as a slob. The surprise, then, occurs because that behavior violates the way you have come to expect that person to act — in other words, it doesn't fit your schema for that person.

We also have *role schemata*, or organized sets of expectations about how people in certain roles are supposed to act (for example, see Figure 3.9). Imagine the first time you go to hear a new rock band and the first time you go to a new dentist. You will have some definite expectations about how these people will act, even though you never met them before. If the dentist starts singing at the top of his lungs, or if the band's guitarist tries to peer into your mouth, your role schemata will tell you that something is wrong.

Event schemata.   Last, we have organized beliefs about the normal or typical course of events in various familiar situations, called *event schemata* or *scripts* (e.g., Schank and Abelson, 1977). These schemata enable us to know in advance what will happen when we go to take an exam, get a haircut, or go on a picnic. We don't need to be told specifically to bring a pen rather than a harmonica to an exam, because our exam-taking script tells us that we will have to write and that the professor usually brings paper but rarely supplies the pens. As this example suggests, event schemata can often be quite specific and elaborate.

How schemata guide information processing

What do schemata do? What are they good for? To answer these questions, we will look at schema effects on three main cognitive processes: attention, encoding, and retrieval. **Attention** refers to what you notice. **Encoding** refers to what gets stored in memory. **Retrieval** (that is, retrieval from memory storage) refers to what actually gets remembered later on. A basic principle is that some information gets lost during each of these processes. You notice only a small part of the world that confronts you; you encode only a small part of what you notice; and you retrieve only part of what was previously stored in your memory. (This

FIGURE 3.9. As you can readily see, the character in this cartoon has definitely violated a *role schema!* (Source: "The Far Side" cartoon by Gary Larson is reprinted by permission of Chronicle Features, San Francisco.)

Role schemata: Expectations about how persons occupying certain roles should behave

"Now let me get this straight . . . We hired you to babysit the kids, and instead you cooked and ate them BOTH?"

ON THE APPLIED SIDE

Sadder but Wiser? Depression and Information Processing

One aspect of depression is having a "negative attitude" about oneself and about life in general. Compared with normal people, depressed people blame themselves when things go wrong, attribute faults to themselves, and are pessimistic about the future. One way of summing this up is that the *self-schema* of a depressed person includes more negative and undesirable traits than a normal person's self-schema (Kuiper, MacDonald, and Derry, 1983). For most of the twentieth century, clinical psychology has acted on the assumption that these negative attitudes of depressed people are the result of cognitive distortions that make life seem worse than it is. Therapies have tried to correct these distortions, and clinical research has investigated how depressed people developed these distorting patterns in the first place.

But stop for a minute and think about what you have read in this chapter and in Chapter 2. Normal people do quite a lot of distorting too, don't they? Normal people take all the credit for success but deny responsibility for failures; they overestimate the accuracy and consensus for their opinions, and so forth. In view of all this, Alloy and her colleagues (e.g., Alloy, 1986) have recently put forward a surprising new theory that is changing the way psychologists understand depression. The central idea in Alloy's theory is that it is normal (i.e., nondepressed) people who often have a distorted view of life. Depressed people are often seeing life as it really is, without the biases that affect normal people.

One approach to testing Alloy's theory was to use *judgments of contingency* — that is, people's assessment of the degree to which their successes and failures were due to their own efforts. In life, contingency is usually partial. Whether a salesman makes a sale, for example, is partly due to his own skill but partly due to the customer's actual need for the product or service. Likewise, whether a difficult operation saves a patient's life is only partly contingent on the surgeon's skill and effort, for the degree of injury and the patient's recuperative strength also play a role. Alloy and Abramson (1979) programmed a computer to present subjects with a situation in which they had partial control. In one condition, whether a subject got a reward depended 75 percent on the subject's responses, but the other 25 percent was decided at random by the computer. Alloy and Abramson then asked subjects to estimate the contingency — that is, how much the outcome was due to their own efforts. Sure enough, depressed people were more likely than normals to say that failure had been a result of their own actions, consistent with the usual pattern. But it was the depressives who were closest to the true judgment (75 percent, in that condition). Normal people underestimated their responsibility when the outcome was failure and overestimated their role in success. Depressives were pretty accurate and even-handed, regardless of success or failure. Interestingly, depressives seem to show distortions when asked to make judgments about someone else. Their greater accuracy shows up mainly in interpreting their own lives and experiences (Martin, Abramson, and Alloy, 1984).

Other evidence shows that depressives are less susceptible to the false consensus effect than normal people (Tabachnik, Crocker, and Alloy, 1983). Thus, again, a common distortion in the way normal people process social information is reduced or absent in depressed people. Alloy is not saying, of course, that it is better to be depressed. There may be important advantages to using distorted ways of thinking, for the biases of normal people may contribute to feelings of happiness, confidence, and well-being. Christopher Columbus might never have set sail if he had accurately appreciated the dangers and difficulties that lay ahead, so one might say that overconfidence led to the discovery of America! Still,

Alloy's work underscores the difference between normal human thinking and correct (i.e., totally logical) thinking. It is ironic that depression, a form of mental illness, should increase the correctness of mental processes.

FIGURE 3.10. At each stage of cognitive processing, some information is lost.

Information loss during cognitive processing

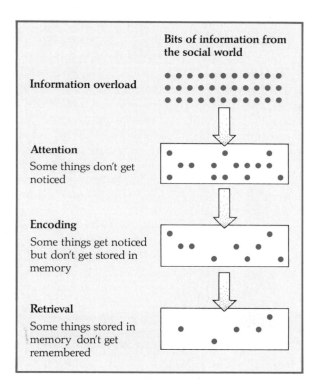

loss of information is depicted in Figure 3.10.) Another way to think of this loss of information is that each of the three processes requires *selection* among all the possible things that could be noticed, encoded, and retrieved. This selection is not random. Rather, the mind has ways of choosing what to notice and remember. This is where *schemata* enter the picture. Schemata guide the selective processing of social information. Schemata are among the mind's main weapons for coping with information overload. But schemata do not operate simply as "cognitive filters." In addition, they play a more active role, changing or distorting incoming information (or at least, our understanding of it), filling in gaps in such input, and, in general, shaping our comprehension of the social world. Some of the major effects of schemata upon information processing are summarized below.

Attention.   Attention comes before encoding and retrieval; obviously, you can't remember something you never noticed in the first place. Attention is also the hardest of the three processes to study, because it is difficult for a researcher to know whether something was never noticed or was noticed but forgotten. For this reason, we know less about attention than about encoding and retrieval. Still, there is some evidence about how schemata guide attention.

A schema tells you what to expect, and things that violate these expectations may stand out. There may be a hundred people at a wedding reception — far too many to pay attention to all of them. If one is stark naked, however, you are much more likely to notice that person, because your event schema for wedding receptions says that everyone will be fully and formally clothed. In the early 1970s a fad called *streaking* spread through American universities, which capitalized on this schematic expectation that people wear clothes in public. The streaker would run naked through a library, a class, a party, a sports event, or whatever. Although the streaker was only there for a brief moment, he or she usually captured everyone's attention!

On the other hand, another possible effect of schemata on attention is that the person will ignore whatever doesn't fit the schema. Recent work has focused on what makes people notice things or ignore things that don't fit their schemata. The more dependent you are on someone, for example, the more you attend to subtleties of that person's behavior, and the more you notice deviations from your schema for that person (Erber and Fiske, 1984). Thus, if a casual acquaintance were to act in a slightly unusual fashion, you might not notice it as much as you would notice the same amount of unusual behavior in your boss.

Encoding.   Not everything that is noticed gets stored in memory. Attention does not lead to encoding in all cases. Instead, much information "goes in one ear and out the other." Schemata are a powerful influence over what gets encoded.

The role of schemata in selective encoding was demonstrated in a well-designed study by Darley and Gross (1983). The schemata they used were *stereotypes*, which are schemata about social groups (see Chapters 4 and 5). Specifically, Darley and Gross used the common stereotype that children from poverty-stricken backgrounds do poorly in school compared to children from well-to-do families.

Subjects in Darley and Gross's experiment saw a videotape of a fourth-grade girl named Hannah. At the end of the tape subjects were asked to estimate how well she was doing in school. The first part of the tape showed Hannah's home and school. Half the subjects saw a tape showing that Hannah was from a poor neighborhood and school, and that her parents were uneducated. The other subjects saw a tape showing that

Hannah was from an upper-middle-class neighborhood with a well-furnished school, and that her parents were both college graduates.

Some of the subjects (in the stereotype-only condition) saw only this first part of the tape. The other subjects (in the stereotype-plus-test condition) saw a second part too. In this second part, Hannah was shown taking an oral exam on various topics. It was a long exam. Hannah got many questions right and many others wrong — both hard and easy questions. Which subjects do you think rated Hannah the highest?

One prediction might be that people apply stereotypes when that's all the information they have but not when they have direct evidence about ability. This prediction suggests that stereotypes would make a difference in the stereotype-only condition but not in the stereotype-plus-test condition. But the results of the experiment were exactly the opposite of this prediction. The stereotypes alone did not produce different estimates of Hannah's ability in school, but the different stereotypes did affect these estimates when combined with evidence — even though the evidence was the same for everyone (refer to Figure 3.11).

Consider what went on in the subject's mind. Knowing Hannah's social class background activated subjects' stereotypes about social class and school abilities, and these schemata led to the formation of hunches

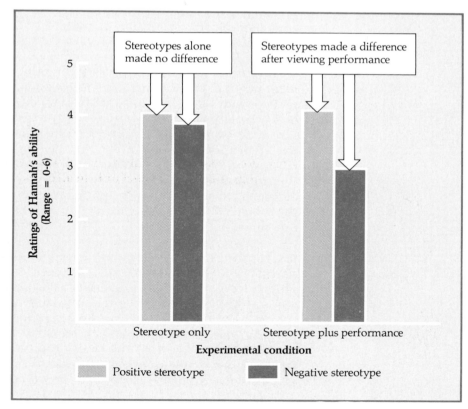

FIGURE 3.11. Subjects' ratings of a fourth-grader did not differ when all they knew about her was that she came either from a poor or an upper-middle-class background. However, when they also received information about her performance, stereotypes relating to these different backgrounds did affect such ratings. These findings illustrate the impact of schemata on the encoding of social information. (Source: Based on data from Darley and Gross, 1983.)

Evidence for the impact of schemata upon encoding

about Hannah, such as that her school abilities may be below average if she is from a lower class background. People weren't willing to leap to the conclusion that Hannah was academically slow just because of her social class, but they suspected it. If they received no more information about Hannah, they did not rate her on the basis of these hunches. When they received more information, these schema-based hunches apparently led subjects to encode her exam performance in a biased fashion. People who knew Hannah was from a poor background encoded more of her wrong answers than those who thought she was from a well-off family. Thus, ironically, the same evidence — that is, the same tape of Hannah giving the same answers to the same questions — led to different conclusions, because of selective encoding. This is another example of the confirmation bias.

In general, then, schemata work as guides as to what should be stored in memory. In many cases you encode whatever information fits your schema best. Sometimes, though, information that clearly or obviously contradicts your schema gets encoded. (Please see the **Focus** insert on pages 104 – 105 for more information about how we process information inconsistent with existing schemata.)

Retrieval.   Finally, schemata affect what is retrieved from memory on a particular occasion. Out of all the information you have encoded in memory, your mind will select some and distort some in order to fit whatever schema is active at the moment. This selective, distorted retrieval was demonstrated in a clever article entitled ''Getting What You Want by Revising What You Had,'' by Conway and Ross (1984).

These researchers started out by looking at a study-skills improvement program at their university. Most universities have such programs to help students learn how to study more effectively. The objective evidence usually fails to show that these programs succeed, at least when measured by possible improvements in grades as compared with students who don't take the program. The fact that these programs don't really work is not widely known, of course, and participants often claim to have benefited from them. There is thus a discrepancy between the objective evidence — that such programs do not improve grades — and the subjective evidence — that people feel they have benefited from the programs.

Conway and Ross proposed that people have an *event schema* for participating in a study skills improvement program, and that part of this schema says that one's skills do improve. The schema may therefore produce selective and distorted recall. The program participants in Conway and Ross's experiment rated their study skills both before and after the program. Control subjects, drawn from a waiting list for the same programs, also rated themselves. Before the program, participants and control subjects averaged the same level of study skills, as would be expected. After the program, participants and control subjects (those who had not had any study skills training) still rated their study skills about the same, which is consistent with the general pattern that study skills programs don't really work. But when asked to recall their earlier ratings, a significant difference emerged between the two groups. Control subjects recalled their earlier skill levels accurately, whereas program participants "recalled" having much poorer skills before the program (see Figure 3.12). In other words, the study skills program did not raise the participants' rating of their current skills, but it did lower their rating of their skills before the program. Their schema said that the program would improve their skills, and it didn't — but they persuaded themselves that their skills had improved. They did this by exaggerating their memory of how bad they had been beforehand.

Another of Conway and Ross's findings also demonstrates how schemata bias retrieval. Right after the program, participants expected better grades than control subjects, because the event schema for such a program includes improvement in grades. These expectations were unwarranted, for in fact participants' grades turned out to be no better than the control group's. Nevertheless, when contacted half a year later and asked to recall their grades, participants (falsely) recalled higher grades than control subjects. Their schema said their grades would improve after the study skills program, and that's what they said had happened. The only problem is, in reality it had *not* happened.

FIGURE 3.12. Subjects do not raise their ratings of their own study skills after participating in a study-skills program. However, they *do* lower their ratings of their skills prior to the program. Such findings point to the important impact of schemata upon retrieval of information previously stored in memory. (Source: Based on data from Conway and Ross, 1984.)

Getting what you want by revising what you had

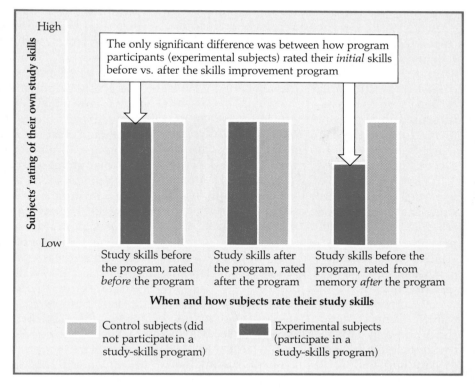

FOCUS ON RESEARCH:
The Cutting Edge

What Happens When Reality Doesn't Fit Your Schema? A Recent Controversy

Schemata guide how people process social information. Information that is consistent with a schema may be noticed quickly and remembered well. But what about information that directly contradicts a schema — is it especially noticeable and memorable, or is it likely to be ignored and forgotten? Over the last several years, researchers have debated this issue.

One argument is that schemata simply exert a massive *confirmation bias*, filtering out whatever is irrelevant or contradictory (e.g., Taylor and Crocker, 1982). This view is supported by studies demonstrating that individuals remember information consistent with their schemata better than information inconsistent with these cognitive frameworks (Cohen, 1981). On the other hand, additional research has found that what *contradicts* our schemata is recalled best (e.g., Hastie and Kumar, 1979). Together these seemingly contradictory results suggest that schemata filter primarily on the basis of *relevance*. Irrelevant information is screened out, but relevant information is noticed and encoded regardless of whether it supports a given schema or contradicts it.

As you can see, this conclusion is somewhat puzzling. It seems only reasonable to assume that it matters, at least in some respects, whether specific events "fit" or "break" the pattern suggested by schemata. Many recent studies have focused on this issue, and now, after several years of active research, a clearer picture is beginning to emerge.

Whether an event fits a schema or contradicts it seems to determine how much people think about it. This fact is demonstrated by an interesting study carried out by Stern, Marrs, Millar, and Cole (1984). These researchers gave subjects a schema for a person who was supposed to be aggressive, careless, and honest. Subjects then read a series of brief stories about this individual. In some, his behaviors conformed to the schemata of aggressiveness, carelessness, and honesty. In others, he acted in a manner opposite to these schemata. And in yet others, his acts were neutral or irrelevant to these schemata. The researchers timed how long subjects spent reading about each event. Results indicated that subjects spent the most time reading stories in which the target person acted in a way contrary to the schemata (that is, stories in which he behaved nonaggressively, carefully, or dishonestly). Later, when asked to recall the person's behaviors, subjects were best able to remember actions that contradicted their schemata. The implication of these findings is that when something goes directly against a schema, we stop and think about it more carefully than usual (see Figure 3.13).

What is it that we think about when something runs counter to our (schema-based) expectancies? Partly, we try to explain away the contradiction, but also, we seem to spend time reviewing past evidence that *supported* the schema (O'Sullivan and Durso, 1984). This may be one reason that schemata such as stereotypes are so resistant to change: evidence that contradicts them ironically makes them stronger, because people mentally review the stereotype and the past evidence for it. For example, consider a racial bigot who thinks that all blacks are lazy, who then meets a black person who works harder than anyone else around. Does the bigot revise her prejudiced stereotype now that it has been contradicted by this case? Hardly. More likely, the bigot will rack her brains to recall evidence of laziness in other black people she has known. These results underscore once again the "cognitive

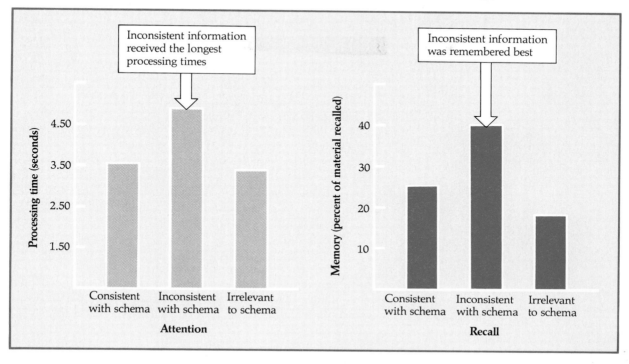

FIGURE 3.13. Information that was inconsistent with subjects' schemata received more processing time than information that was either consistent with or irrelevant to these schemata (left bars). Similarly, schema-inconsistent information was also recalled more effectively (right bars). (Source: Based on data from Stern et al., 1984.)

Processing information consistent or inconsistent with existing schemata

miser" model. Apparently, the mind will go to great lengths to preserve its schemata, even if this means ignoring evidence suggesting that they are wrong!

In sum, the studies by Stern and by O'Sullivan and Durso provide added insight into the ways we handle information that contradicts an existing schema. Such contradictory information gets extra attention—we think about it more than we think about information that reinforces our beliefs or information that is irrelevant to our views. And part of the mental effort we expend on schema-contradicting information goes to bolster our schema: we convince ourselves that there is still ample evidence for it, despite contradictory input. In this context, the old phrase "having a closed mind" takes on new, and perhaps even more disturbing, meaning.

SELF-AWARENESS: The Effects of Looking Inward

Up to now, we have focused mainly on the processing of information from the social world around us. The external world is not the only focus of our interest, however — sometimes our attention is directed inward, toward the self. Many psychologists have studied the causes and consequences of *self-focused attention*, also called self-attention or **self-awareness.**

One of the first systematic views of the process of self-awareness was offered by Duval and Wicklund (1972). These researchers suggested that attention can be directed either inward or outward, and that it sometimes oscillates back and forth between the self and the external world. According to Duval and Wicklund, then, self-awareness involves comparing oneself to one's ideals and goals. They further reasoned that, since we don't usually measure up to our ideals completely, self-awareness must usually be unpleasant. Later research on self-awareness, though, has abandoned the idea that self-awareness is typically unpleasant. When we succeed, when we stand up for our beliefs, or when we do anything else that makes us feel good about ourselves, we tend to seek out self-awareness (Greenberg and Musham, 1981). And, obviously, many people enjoy having their pictures taken, being on television, or looking at themselves in a mirror — all events that increase self-awareness.

A more complex theory of self-awareness was proposed by Carver and Scheier (1981, 1982). They treat self-awareness as a *feedback loop,* similar to regulatory mechanisms in guided missiles and thermostats. Carver and Scheier suggest that self-awareness involves checking our current self against our goals and then altering our behavior (if necessary) to fit more closely with these goals. This is analogous to the way a thermostat "checks" the temperature in a room and turns on the heat or air conditioning.

Scheier and Carver (1981) also distinguish between two distinct types of self-awareness (or self-consciousness): *public self-consciousness* and *private self-consciousness.* The first of these refers to our awareness of ourselves as social objects — how we appear to others. The second (private self-consciousness) involves awareness of our own feelings, attitudes, and values. (We will have more to say about these two types of self-awareness, and their effects, in Chapter 12, when we consider *deindividuation.*)

Evidence for the feedback loop model has been provided by several different studies. For example, Gibbons (1978) first gave female subjects a questionnaire designed to measure sex guilt (guilt or anxiety over sexual matters). Two weeks later, he had them read and evaluate pornographic descriptions of sexual acts. Some of the women read the sexual passages while sitting in front of a mirror, a procedure that raises self-awareness. Their reactions to the pornographic materials were consistent with their personal standards: women with high sex guilt disliked the passages, whereas women with low sex guilt liked them. In contrast, among the women who read the sexual passages in the absence of a mirror, there was no relationship between personal standards and ratings of the pornography. Without self-awareness, subjects' reactions were not strongly determined by their inner attitudes or beliefs.

So far, we have discussed self-awareness as *attention* to the self, but attention is not the only cognitive process involved in self-awareness. Hull and Levy (1979) point out that self-awareness often pertains to *encoding*, not attention. They treat self-awareness as a matter of processing information about the self, rather than just noticing the self. Self-awareness can also be approached as a *personality trait* (Fenigstein, Scheier, and Buss, 1975). Some people are frequently self-conscious, think about themselves, enjoy looking in mirrors, and often consider how others perceive them. Other people are not like that at all.

Alcohol, paranoia, and pressure: Three applications of self-awareness

While self-awareness is interesting in its own right, it also has several practical applications. Among the most interesting of these are its implications for alcohol use, paranoid thinking, and performance under pressure.

Alcohol use.   Why do people drink alcohol? There are many different reasons, but Hull and his colleagues have identified a factor common to a lot of them. Alcohol apparently reduces one's self-awareness, even with just a drink or two, and people turn to the bottle partly for that effect. Remember that self-awareness entails thinking about how events bear on the self and comparing oneself with goals and standards. When something bad happens — losing your job, failing an exam, breaking up with your lover — you may want to stop brooding about being a failure, and alcohol helps accomplish this. People say that alcohol helps you "forget your troubles," but in fact its effect is to reduce self-awareness so you cease to think about how these troubles reflect on the self. Conversely, when you want to cease matching your behavior to standards of proper conduct — for example, to enjoy a wild party, unconstrained by normal inhibitions — alcohol helps accomplish this too, again by reducing self-awareness (Hull, 1981).

Various laboratory studies have supported Hull's theory. In one study, Hull and Young (1983) reasoned that people who tend to have high self-awareness would want to drink more alcohol after failure, because it is painful to focus on oneself after failing. Male subjects were given an IQ test. The questions were difficult, so subjects could not be sure how well they were doing. Afterwards, half of them were told they had scored very high, while the rest were told they had done very poorly. Then the subject went to another room, ostensibly to participate in a second experiment on taste perception of alcoholic beverages. The subject had to rate a series of wines. Hull and Young were not interested in how the subject rated the wines but rather in how much wine he drank while doing the rating task.

FIGURE 3.14. Following a failure experience, subjects high in self-consciousness drank more wine. In contrast, subjects low in self-consciousness did not demonstrate similar effects. These findings suggest that at least some persons consume alcohol to reduce their self-awareness. (Source: Based on data from Hull and Young, 1983.)

Alcohol as an escape from self-awareness

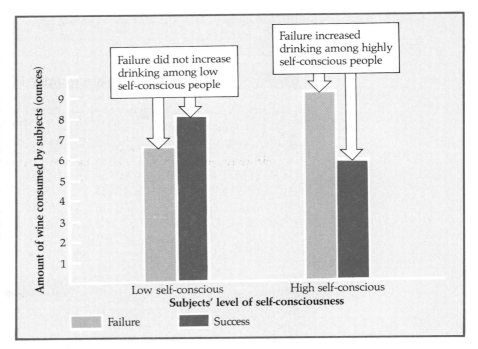

The results (see Figure 3.14) depended on the personality trait of *self-consciousness*, which had been assessed earlier. People high in self-consciousness drank far more wine after supposedly failing than after succeeding at the IQ test. The reason, presumably, is that they wanted to escape from the self-focused thinking about the implications of their failure. People whose personality included a low level of self-consciousness, however, drank about the same amount of wine regardless of prior success or failure.

A field study made a similar point (Hull, Young, and Jouriles, 1986). The researchers surveyed alcoholics who had just been "cured" by an alcohol detoxification program. Based on this survey, each subject was classified as having high or low trait self-consciousness, and as having current life situations that were either positive and successful, or stressful and negative. After three months, the researchers checked with each subject to ascertain whether he had resumed drinking. Which subjects do you think had the highest relapse rate? The clear answer was people with stressful and negative life situations combined with a personal tendency to be highly self-aware. People who are low in self-awareness presumably drink for reasons unrelated to a need to reduce self-awareness. Sure enough, the researchers found these people's relapse rate was unaffected by their good or bad life situation.

Self-as-target of paranoid thinking. The professor is about to return the exam papers, but first he says that one exam in particular was among the worst papers he has ever seen. How likely is it that he is talking about your exam paper? (Suppose he had said it was one of the *best* he had ever seen?) One day you notice two of your friends standing at some distance from you, talking. They notice you, and shortly afterwards they both laugh. Are they laughing at you? Another time, your date asks to go home early, saying he or she is not feeling well. Could the real reason be that your date does not want to spend any more time with you?

Most people tend to exaggerate the likelihood that "yes" is indeed the answer to the above questions. Fenigstein (1984) calls this tendency the **self-as-target phenomenon,** meaning a tendency to exaggerate the belief that external events are directed at the self. For example, when Fenigstein tried out the first scenario (the one miserable exam paper) in his own psychology class, his students individually gave 22 percent as the average estimated likelihood that the professor was referring to their own paper, when the true average probability should have been 4 percent (because there were about twenty-five people in the class). The self-as-target phenomenon, although normal, resembles the thought processes of *paranoids*, who think, to an extreme degree, that many external events are directed specifically at them. The mass murderer Charles Manson, a seriously disturbed paranoid, believed that the lyrics on Beatles' records — records that sold millions of copies all over the world — were really intended as messages specifically for him.

Self-awareness contributes to the self-as-target phenomenon. Fenigstein found that people who were highly self-conscious (as a personality trait) were the most likely to answer "yes" to the type of questions listed above. Thus, if you tend to focus attention on yourself, you'll tend to think external events are directed at you. What role self-awareness may play in genuine paranoia is unknown, but it is an exciting area for future research.

Performance under pressure.   When the pressure is on, people try very hard to perform well. But what is the result — do they usually come through with their best work, or do they "choke" and perform badly? Research by Baumeister (1984, 1985) shows that self-awareness helps determine the outcome of performance under pressure. *Pressure* means the importance of performing well, and **choking under pressure** means performing badly precisely when it is most important to do well.

Baumeister's theory is that pressure increases self-awareness, which then interferes with skills. Skills normally work automatically, without conscious attention, and attending to them can destroy that automatic quality. For example, if you are highly skilled at the piano or typewriter, you don't usually pay attention to your individual finger movements while playing or typing. If you were to start paying such close attention, you would probably find yourself making more mistakes than usual, or slowing down a lot. That is how choking under pressure occurs.

In one experiment, male students competed at a skilled task against a female confederate. In one condition, she performed better than the male subject, creating competitive pressure on him to keep up. Ironically, the subjects under pressure performed worse than other subjects who were not under pressure to do well. Choking was most common among people whose personalities were low in self-consciousness. If pressure increases self-awareness, that should be less of a problem for people who often feel self-aware, because they are familiar with the feeling and know how to cope with it. People who are unaccustomed to feeling self-aware may be most prone to choke.

Simply having an audience can cause choking. People playing video games at an arcade performed about 25 percent worse when someone stood and watched them than when no one was watching (Baumeister, 1984). And knowing that other people expect you to do well creates pressure that can cause choking, if you feel some need to live up to their expectations (Baumeister, Hamilton, and Tice, 1985).

Perhaps the most surprising finding is that choking under pressure can eliminate the familiar "home court advantage" in sports. Baumeister and Steinhilber (1984) reasoned that pressure, and therefore self-awareness, would be highest when playing for the championship in front of a supportive home audience. They tallied the results of World Series base-

FIGURE 3.15. Home teams are more likely than visiting teams to win the first two games in the World Series. However, they are *less* likely to win the last game — the most crucial one of all. In short, they tend to choke under pressure. (Source: Based on data from Baumeister and Steinhilber, 1984.)

Choking in the World Series: Fifty years of results

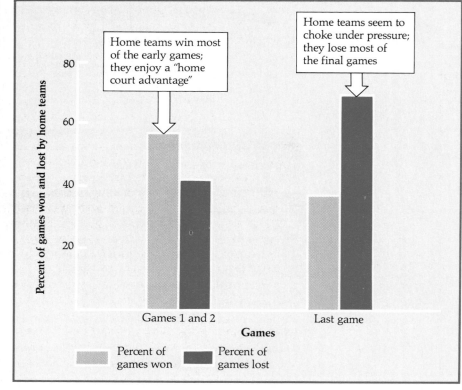

ball games for over half a century. In the early games of the World Series, home teams are more likely to win than visitors, but in the final game of the Series, when the championship is decided, the reverse occurs (see Figure 3.15). Home teams tend to choke during the final game of the World Series, when the championship is at stake and the home crowd demands a victory.

SUMMARY

Social cognition is the study of how people interpret, analyze, remember, and use information about the social world. Because of information overload, it is necessary for the human mind to develop ways of sorting information and making judgments quickly and easily. These cognitive strategies include the use of *heuristics* and *schemata.* Heuristics apply decision rules that are quick, easy to use, and often correct, although they do sometimes lead to errors. Schemata guide information processing by providing a model of what to expect. The person then notices, encodes, and remembers material in relation to his or her schema.

Use of **cognitive strategies** leads to some systematic fallacies, biases, and errors. For example, people tend to ignore base-rate information, to overestimate others' agreement with them, to draw false conclusions about expected patterns of events, and to cling to a schema or belief despite contradictory evidence.

Moods and emotions also influence mental processes. Good moods produce positive, optimistic judgments, and they increase memory for good things. The effects of bad moods are less clear-cut, partly because some people try to overcome their bad moods by positive thinking and by good deeds. People suffering from depression seem to lack many of the cognitive biases of normal people, with the ironic result that depression often increases the accuracy of people's judgments and inferences.

Self-awareness is a state in which attention is focused inward on the self. This state is associated with the use and abuse of alcohol, with "choking" under pressure, and with believing that external events are directed at the self.

GLOSSARY

action identification
The process of labeling and interpreting one's own behaviors.

attention
The first step in social cognition. It refers to the act of noticing something.

availability heuristic
A strategy of making judgments based on how easily information comes to

mind. Information we can remember quickly or easily is used as if it were
especially important or frequent.

base-rate fallacy
In making social judgments, people tend to ignore or underuse *base-rate
information*, which is information about how prevalent or frequent something
is in general.

choking under pressure
Performing below the level of one's ability in a situation in which it is
important to perform well.

cognitive strategies
Techniques the mind uses to sort, analyze, and use information; "mental
short-cuts."

confirmation bias
The tendency to pay most attention to information that supports our
preconceptions and beliefs. Information that contradicts our beliefs may be
overlooked.

encoding
The second step in social cognition: putting something into memory.

fallacies and biases
Typical errors in human social judgment that are caused by systematic use of
cognitive strategies.

false consensus effect
The individual's tendency to overestimate how many other people would
make the same judgments and choices and hold the same attitudes as the
individual.

heuristics
Basic principles or rules that allow us to make social judgments easily and
rapidly (see *cognitive strategies*).

illusory correlation
Because one expects a certain pattern or relationship, one tends to believe it is
confirmed, even though the pattern or relationship is not objectively valid.

information overload
The social world is too complex and has too many stimuli for the mind to
handle. Hence the need for cognitive strategies.

priming
Planting ideas or categories in someone's mind, causing the person to use
them to interpret subsequent events, due to increased availability.

regression fallacy
The common tendency to forget that extreme events are most likely followed
by less extreme events.

representativeness heuristic
Making judgments on the basis of resemblance to typical patterns or general
types.

retrieval

The third step in social cognition (after *attention* and *encoding*): remembering something that has been stored in memory.

schema

An organized collection of one's beliefs and feelings about something. Types of schemata include self-schemata, person schemata, role schemata, and event schemata (scripts).

self-awareness

A state in which one's attention is focused on oneself.

self-as-target phenomenon

A tendency to exaggerate the belief that external events are directed at the self.

social cognition

The study of how people interpret, analyze, remember, and use information about the social world.

theory perseverance

The tendency to keep beliefs or conclusions even after the evidence for them has been shown to be false.

vividness effect

Refers to the greater persuasive power and greater noticeability of information that has emotional appeal, concrete imagery, and the capacity to touch us personally. Research generally has failed to confirm the vividness effect.

FOR MORE INFORMATION

Fiske, S. T., and Taylor, S. E. (1984). *Social cognition.* Reading, Mass.: Addison-Wesley.

> A well-written, thorough review of recent research on social cognition, starting with attribution theory and covering the major cognitive processes.

Nisbett, R. E., and Ross, L. (1980). *Human inference: Strategies and shortcomings of social judgments.* Englewood Cliffs, N.J.: Prentice-Hall.

> A classic book that generated many of the ideas guiding subsequent research.

Kahneman, D., Slovic, P., and Tversky, A., eds. (1982). *Judgment under uncertainty: Heuristics and biases.* Cambridge: Cambridge University Press.

> A collection of articles and chapters that focus on heuristics, biases, and fallacies. This is the best source on mental short-cuts.

Wyer, R. S., and Srull, T. K. (1984). *Handbook of social cognition.* Hillsdale, N.J.: Erlbaum.

> This is a good reference source, with self-contained chapters for each of the major topics in social cognition. Use this text as a source of information on specific topics.

CHAPTER 4

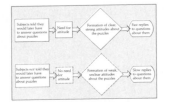

ATTITUDES:
Evaluating the Social World

The day starts when your clock radio clicks on, wrenching you out of your deep sleep. As you struggle out of bed, you are reminded once again how much you hate waking up when it is dark outside and you must get out of a warm bed into a cold room. You pull on your clothes: a favorite sweater, your worn and friendly blue jeans, the shoes you like so much because they are so comfortable. As you head for the door, one of your favorite songs comes on the radio, so you sit and listen to it before leaving.

Heading for breakfast, you think ahead to your schedule for the morning. Economics class with that boring old professor — maybe it would be a good day to cut! Later, you have social psychology which (of course) you always enjoy. Meanwhile, you have arrived at the cafeteria. Everything looks so unappetizing — why can't breakfast foods be as appealing as pizza, ice cream, french fries? You make your selections and find a table, preferring an isolated spot that may be a little bit quieter than the others. You begin to contemplate the upcoming weekend and this makes you feel better. You have tickets for a concert featuring one of your favorite bands, and then there's one of those parties you usually enjoy, and of course you can sleep in on Sunday morning. . . .

EVEN IF your morning doesn't begin quite like this, you probably use at least half a dozen **attitudes** before lunch. Attitudes are a basic and pervasive part of human life. Without attitudes, we wouldn't know how to react to events, we wouldn't be able to make decisions, and we wouldn't even have much to talk about. It is no wonder that attitudes have been a major concern of social psychologists since the early days of the field. Over half a century ago, Gordon Allport (1935) wrote that the attitude was social psychology's most important concept. Many social psychologists today would agree that this is still true.

Attitudes can be defined as *lasting, general evaluations of people* (including oneself), *objects, or issues* (e.g., Petty and Cacioppo, 1985). Saying that an attitude is *lasting* means that it tends to persist across time. A momentary feeling does not count as an attitude. Saying that an attitude is *general* means that it involves at least some degree of abstraction. If you drop a book on your toe and find that particular experience to be unpleasant, that is not an attitude, because it applies only to one event. But if the experience makes you dislike books or clumsiness *in general*, that dislike is an attitude.

Of course, attitudes do not have to be extremely general. They can be as specific as liking brown mustard with Swiss cheese, or being a fan of a particular movie or football star. At the other extreme, attitudes can be as general as being a political conservative, or believing that women are generally superior to men. As we shall see, the level of specificity turns out to be an important factor in determining how attitudes guide behavior. Another important dimension is *active versus passive processes* for forming and changing attitudes. For example, retired U.S. senators and Russian elementary school pupils may have attitudes about the American government, but there is a big difference. The Russian children's attitudes are acquired passively, according to what their teachers and parents tell them about American government, whereas the senators' attitudes are shaped by years of firsthand, direct, active experience.

Most social psychologists accept the **ABC model of attitudes**, which suggests that an attitude has three components: affect, behavior, and cognition (e.g., Breckler, 1984). The *affect* component refers to positive or negative emotions — our gut-level feelings about something. The *behavior* component involves our intentions to act in certain ways, to engage in behaviors that are somehow relevant to our attitudes. Finally, the *cognition* component refers to the thinking and interpreting that goes into forming or using an attitude. Each attitude, then, is made up of a cluster of feelings, likes and dislikes, behavioral intentions, thoughts, and ideas (see Figure 4.1). Although the ABC model is a handy way in which to remember that an attitude involves all three components, please don't forget that the three are closely interrelated.

Social psychologists have quite a lot to say about attitudes. To present this information, we'll use the following organizational scheme. First, we examine how attitudes are *created*. We'll look at how children learn their attitudes, and later look at how individuals form attitudes out of their personal experiences. Next, we consider how attitudes are *changed*. We'll start with the passive forms of persuasion and proceed to the most active type of attitude change, in which people revise their

FIGURE 4.1. Can you spot evidence of affect, behavior, and cognition in this photo? These people's attitudes about the issue in question include feelings, actions, and thoughts or ideas.

The ABC model of attitudes

opinions to justify their own behavior. Finally, we consider evidence about how attitudes affect *behavior,* a complex issue with some rather surprising evidence.

FORMING ATTITUDES: *Learning and Experience*

Heroes and heroines may be born, but liberals, bigots, conservatives, and baseball fans are clearly made. Hardly any psychologist would suggest that babies enter the world with political preferences, racial hatreds, or religious views already fully formed. Rather, such attitudes are acquired over a long period of time. But how, precisely, are they gained? What processes account for their formation and development? Research has suggested several. We will look first at some learning processes, in which the individual acquires attitudes in a rather passive fashion. Then we'll consider direct experience, in which the individual participates actively in the formation of his or her attitudes. Please note: the terms *active* and *passive* are relative; people are almost never completely passive.

Social learning: Acquiring attitudes from others

Learning attitudes is a large part of **socialization,** the process by which a wild, helpless creature (a newborn baby) is transformed into a responsible and capable member of human society. As we saw at the beginning of this chapter, adult human social life is practically unthinkable without

FIGURE 4.2. Parental teachings and influences are a potent source of attitudes formed during childhood. (Source: Reprinted with special permission of King Features Syndicate, Inc.)

Socialization: A key source of attitudes

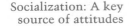

attitudes. It is no mystery *where* children get their attitudes. They get them everywhere—from parents (see Figure 4.2) and later from teachers, from the media, from friends and acquaintances. *How* children learn attitudes is a little harder to answer, but psychologists have identified at least three main processes that play a role in this regard: **classical conditioning, instrumental conditioning,** and **modeling**.

Classical conditioning means learning by association. Imagine a child's first encounter with "wabble"—the child doesn't know what wabble is, so she asks her mother about it. Mother frowns or acts upset while answering. The odds are that the mother's negative emotions will be noticed by the child, who will then develop negative associations to wabble. As the child grows up, that negative attitude toward wabble may continue. This is especially likely if the association is strengthened by similar parental reactions on other occasions. Now cross out "wabble" and substitute work, sex, a certain TV program, or Democrats, and you can appreciate the potential power of parental attitudes in shaping children's attitudes by classical conditioning.

Instrumental conditioning refers to learning in which responses that yield positive outcomes or eliminate negative ones are acquired or strengthened. A father who is a Democrat may praise his son for claiming to be one, too, and he may punish his son for expressing contrary views. Probably, most children identify themselves as Republicans or Democrats long before they understand the real historical and philosophical differences between these two parties. Essentially, children want to hold the "right" views, and parents are able to have the final say about what the right views are, at least before their youngsters reach adolescence. By rewarding and punishing their children, parents can shape their attitudes on many issues.

Modeling refers to learning by observation. Even when parents aren't trying to influence their child's attitudes directly, they may be setting examples the child will imitate. For example, little girls' career ambitions sometimes depend on their mothers' examples. If the mother is employed outside the home, the daughter is more likely to want her own career than if the mother is a full-time homemaker (cf. Hoffman, 1979).

Parents aren't the only ones to guide the passive formation of attitudes, of course. Much learning of attitudes goes on in schools, churches, and elsewhere. In recent decades social scientists have become increasingly aware of the power of the mass media to shape attitudes. This power has led to some public concern over whether the media are fair or biased in how they present events and shape public opinion. The issues of media bias are complex, and social psychologists are just now uncovering some of the basic facts about how it operates. (Please see the **Focus** insert on page 120 for more information on this topic.)

Forming attitudes by direct experience

So far we have considered how parents and others teach attitudes to children. People also form attitudes as a result of their own experience. They actively draw conclusions or make generalizations based on what has happened to them. Don't be surprised if this section uses the material on social cognition covered in Chapter 3. Social cognition tells us how people come to such conclusions, so it contributes heavily to our understanding of how attitudes are formed.

Attitudes as heuristics.   Why do we have attitudes in the first place? What are they good for? One major answer is that attitudes help us make decisions by reducing *information overload.* Attitudes help simplify human social life, which can be complicated and full of information. Even simple acts like stopping at the supermarket to pick up something for dinner would be enormously difficult if you tried to perform them without attitudes. You'd end up looking at everything in the store, considering various criteria such as price and nutritional value, and it would be very late by the time you got home. Attitudes such as preferences for certain foods make the job much simpler.

Saying that attitudes help reduce information overload is another way of saying that attitudes are *heuristics,* that is, cognitive strategies for processing information quickly and easily. Bodenhauser and Wyer (1985) showed that stereotypes — attitudes suggesting that all members of a given social group share the same characteristics — can operate as heuristics. (We consider stereotypes in detail in Chapter 5.) In their study, Bodenhausen and Wyer had subjects read a hypothetical description of a crime, either a forgery and embezzlement or a brutal physical assault. Common stereotypes associate forgery with upper-middle-class white criminals and associate physical violence with lower-class Hispanic criminals (among others). In the cases people read, the criminal either fit these stereotypes or didn't. When the stereotypes fit, people relied heavily on stereotype-relevant information to make their judgments about the case. Identical information was ignored when the stereotypes didn't fit. In other words, whenever they could, people used their stereotypes as a basis for sorting and evaluating all the complex information regarding the case and for inferring why the crime occurred.

FOCUS ON RESEARCH:
The Cutting Edge

Bias in the News?

Is there bias or distortion in the way the news is presented on TV, in newspapers, and on the radio? And if there is bias, does it change people's opinions? There are several ways to interpret these questions, and the answers depend on how you approach them.

One approach is to consider whether the reporting of facts is slanted one way or the other. Robinson (e.g., 1985) tried this by analyzing the content of the news on the major TV networks, looking for liberal or conservative biases. He found the three networks are pretty fair and pretty equal. In Presidential elections there is a tendency to emphasize stories that reflect badly on the incumbent President, but that could just be because an incumbent President is easier to attack than an unknown challenger. And news reporters rarely make biased editorial statements about these issues.

So far, so good. But presenting the facts is not the only way to shape attitudes. As we saw, attitudes can be shaped by associating good or bad feelings with various sides of an issue, as in classical conditioning. Suppose that what the newscaster says is impartial and fair, but he smiles when talking about one candidate and frowns when talking about the other. Viewers' attitudes may be affected even if what the newscaster *says* is impartial. Do such facial expressions show bias? Mullen and his colleagues (1987) found evidence of such bias and its consequences.

The first step in their research was to see whether any emotional bias existed in the facial expressions of newscasters. The researchers videotaped the evening news on the major networks during the 1984 Presidential election campaign between Ronald Reagan and Walter Mondale. At random, they selected brief excerpts from these newscasts, deleted the sound, and played the tapes (which showed only facial expressions) for audiences who were asked to rate the degree of good or bad feeling in the newscaster's expression. The audience never knew whether the newscaster was talking about Reagan, Mondale, or some unrelated event, nor did the audience know what he was saying. When Mullen tallied the ratings, he found that Tom Brokaw (NBC) and Dan Rather (CBS) showed no pattern of bias, but Peter Jennings (ABC) showed a pro-Reagan bias in his facial expressions. In other words, Jennings was more likely to have been smiling or looking happy when talking about Reagan than about Mondale.

After the election, Mullen's group then conducted surveys in several American cities. People were randomly selected from the phone book and asked two questions: which national evening news show do you watch on TV? and which presidential candidate did you vote for? Sure enough, people who had watched the most pro-Reagan news program (ABC) were also most likely to end up voting for Reagan (see Figure 4.3). It looks, therefore, as if subtle emotional biases in the media can shape attitudes. Remember, there was no evidence that the content of the news was biased, so it seems unlikely that the viewers were deliberately choosing their news program to hear what they wanted to hear. It is disturbing, though, to think that the newscaster's smile can help elect a president even if what he or she says is unbiased.

Evidence that the content of the news is unbiased seems to contradict the common opinion that the news often *is* biased. Many people think newscasters fail to do justice to the side they favor while being too lenient on the opposing side. Vallone, Ross, and Lepper (1985) suspected that viewers may think the news is biased even when it's not, because the

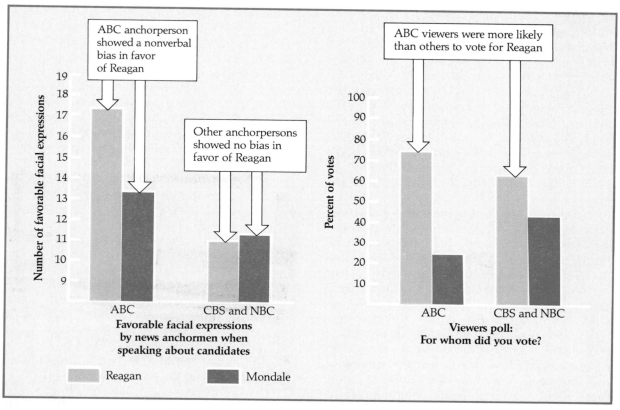

FIGURE 4.3. Peter Jennings (the ABC anchorperson) showed more favorable facial expressions when talking about Reagan than when talking about Mondale. The anchorpersons for NBC (Tom Brokaw) and CBS (Dan Rather) did not show a similar pattern of reactions. Interestingly, people who reported watching ABC News were more likely to vote for Reagan than viewers who reported watching the NBC or CBS news programs. These findings suggest that subtle forms of bias in the media can shape political attitudes. (Source: Based on data from Mullen et al., 1987.)

Facial expressions: A subtle form of media bias

viewers are themselves biased. Vallone et al. (1985) coined the term the **hostile media phenomenon** to refer to the common tendency to believe, incorrectly, that the media are biased against one's side.

To demonstrate the hostile media phenomenon, these researchers used televised coverage of a tragic and controversial news event. In 1982 the conflict between Arabs and Israelis in the Middle East escalated to high levels, and at one point led to a military massacre of civilians in several refugee camps in Lebanon. The researchers selected several news excerpts dealing with the massacre and showed them to American college students who had indicated strong opinions about the conflict. Pro-Israeli students rated the news as being pro-Arab, whereas pro-Arab students rated the same newscasts as pro-Israel. Also, each side predicted these newscasts would sway neutral viewers against their side. Finally, both sides believed that the media's hostile coverage derived from a clear and deliberate bias on the part of the editorial staffs who created the news programs.

Clearly, with the hostile media phenomenon we are no longer dealing with a case of viewers' attitudes being passively shaped by biased news media. Viewer bias is active and potent in determining how the news programs are received. Further evidence for the extent and power of viewer bias was recently provided by Sweeney and Gruber (1985). These researchers noted that people do not simply sit and absorb whatever the media decide to present. Instead, viewers change channels or tune out when confronted with news coverage that seems biased against their opinions. Thus, when the news supports a viewer's attitude, the viewer pays considerable attention. When the news threatens the viewer's attitude,

though, the viewer ignores it, such as by shutting off the TV set or by turning the page.

The findings of Sweeney and Gruber (1984) can be understood in terms of social cognition (see Chapter 3). Attitudes guide the selective processing of information. Some people show **selective avoidance,** directing their attention away from information that challenges their attitudes. Others show **selective exposure,** deliberately seeking out information that supports their views.

Although we don't yet have all the facts about media bias, the final picture is beginning to emerge. At present, it seems that TV networks do a reasonably fair job of avoiding bias in their objective coverage of the news, as far as content is concerned, although in small ways they tend to attack whoever is in power. Subtle biases do exist, such as in facial expressions and in other hidden ways—and these may exert some influence over public opinion. On the other hand, viewers are often clearly and strongly biased. Their own biases lead viewers to seek out and avoid various news items so as to strengthen and preserve their own attitudes. And viewer bias helps produce the final irony: even if the networks present unbiased news coverage, many viewers will think it is biased anyway.

The idea that attitudes are handy ways of dealing with information overload implies that people will form attitudes when they expect to need them. Imagine that you have to drive to another town for an interview for law school. A friend comes along for the ride, to help with the driving. Even if you tour the campus together, *you* are more likely to form opinions about the place than your friend is, because you may need to make a decision about whether to spend several years there, while your friend may never set foot there again. In other words, you form opinions because they may help you in case you have to make a decision. This principle was shown in a series of studies by Fazio, Lenn, and Effrein (1984) on why people spontaneously form attitudes. In their experi-

FIGURE 4.4. Subjects told that they would later have to answer questions about some puzzles they worked on formed stronger and clearer attitudes about these puzzles than subjects who had no similar need for such attitudes. These findings offer support for the view that attitudes often operate as *heuristics*, mechanisms that help us to process information about the social world in a rapid and efficient manner. (Source: Based on data from Fazio, Lenn, and Effrein, 1984.)

Attitudes as heuristics

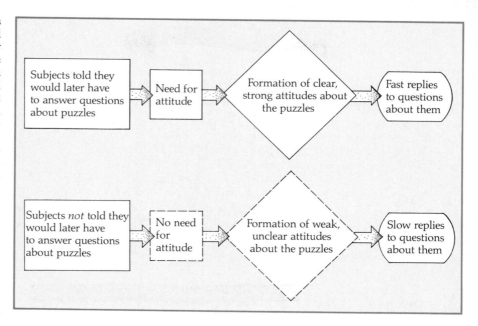

ments, subjects first played with various puzzles. The "need" to form an attitude was created by telling some subjects that they would have to answer questions about the puzzles later. (In a second experiment, subjects were told they would have to decide later which types of puzzles they wanted to spend more time doing.) These subjects formed clearer and stronger attitudes than other subjects, who spent the same amount of time with the puzzles but didn't expect any further questions or decisions about them. The way the experimenters verified the formation of attitudes was to wait until after subjects had finished with the puzzles. Then, they asked everyone how interesting or boring they were. Those subjects who expected to receive such questions answered faster than those who were not told to expect questions (refer to Figure 4.4). The conclusion from this study is that attitudes are sometimes created on purpose for their value as heuristics — that is, as cognitive short-cuts. If we expect to have to make a decision some time in the future, we start forming our attitudes now, so that they'll be in place, ready to help, when it's time to decide.

Forming stereotypes. Granted, stereotypes can influence judgment once they exist, but how do they get started? Social cognition researchers have some of the answers. *Illusory correlation* is an important part of the process (e.g., Hamilton and Gifford, 1976). As you may recall from Chapter 3, an illusory correlation occurs when expectations cause someone to infer a pattern or relationship that is not really there. Consider a majority and a minority group — for example, white people and black people in modern America. Suppose that both commit crimes at the same rate. Illusory correlation processes may cause people to develop the stereotype that the minority group commits more crimes. The key is salience, or noticeability. There are more whites than blacks in society, so being black is more unusual—hence more salient. And crimes are relatively rare, so it is salient when someone commits a crime. After all, you never see a newspaper headline saying "Harry Smith Didn't Commit a Crime Today"! The two factors combine, so it is most salient when a black person commits a crime. Crimes by blacks are therefore more available in memory than (1) crimes by whites or (2) non-crimes by blacks. As we saw in research on the availability heuristic (Chapter 3), people tend to overestimate the frequency of things that are easy to remember. As a result, people will tend to overestimate the frequency of crimes by minorities, and a stereotype (in this example, the idea that blacks tend to be dangerous criminals) gets created despite the lack of any valid or factual grounds for it (Hamilton, Dugan, and Trolier, 1985).

PERSUASION: Changing Attitudes

In the 1980s the business of changing attitudes is definitely a big one. If you have any doubts on this score, simply switch on your TV or radio or flip through the pages of any magazine. Almost at once, you will be flooded by attempts to alter your opinions. Commercials urge you to buy various products; political candidates plead for your vote; and public service organizations caution you against smoking, drinking, speeding, or overeating. In short, you will encounter attempts to change your attitudes at every turn (see Figure 4.5). Sometimes these attempts succeed; on other occasions they fail. For a long time now, social psychologists have studied the causes of successful versus unsuccessful persuasion. Let's take a look at what they've found.

Passive persuasion

One major approach to studying persuasion was developed more than three decades ago by a group of social psychologists at Yale University. These researchers would measure someone's attitude, try to change it by various means, and then measure it again. By comparing different ways of attacking the attitude, they could see what worked best. Here are some of the findings of this approach, which is still used to some extent in today's research.

First, experts are more persuasive than nonexperts (Hovland and Weiss, 1952). The same arguments carry more weight when delivered by someone who presumably knows all the facts. Second, we are more easily persuaded if we think the message is not deliberately intended to persuade or manipulate us (Walster and Festinger, 1962). Probably that's why you don't succumb to every TV commercial you see: when you know others are trying to persuade you, you tend to be on your guard. Third, people with low self-esteem are persuaded more easily than people with high self-esteem (Janis, 1954). Fourth, popular and attractive communicators are more effective than unpopular and unattractive ones (Kiesler and Kiesler, 1969). People are more easily swayed by someone they like than, say, by someone they don't know or someone they dislike, even if the same arguments are used. Fifth, people are sometimes more susceptible to persuasion when they are distracted than when paying full attention, at least when the persuasive message is simple (Allyn and Festinger, 1961). The distraction effect though, brings up some tricky issues to which we'll return later. Sixth, when persuasion is tough — that is, when the audience has attitudes contrary to what the speaker is trying to get them to believe — it is more effective to present both sides of the issue than just one side (Hovland, Lumsdaine, and Sheffield, 1949). Seventh, people who speak rapidly are more persuasive than people who

FIGURE 4.5. How many attempts at persuasion do you encounter each day? If your experience is like that of most persons, you would probably find it hard to keep count!

Attempts to change our attitudes: A common part of social life in the 1980s

FIGURE 4.6.   As this cartoon suggests, individuals can sometimes be frightened into changing their attitudes. (Source: Drawing by Dedini; ©1977 The New Yorker Magazine, Inc.)

Persuasion through fear

"Tell him I couldn't agree with him more."

speak slowly (Miller et al., 1976). This is contrary to the common view that people are distrustful of "fast-talking" salespeople and seducers. One reason, apparently, is that rapid speech conveys the impression that the person knows what she or he is talking about. Eighth, persuasion can be enhanced by messages that arouse fear in the audience (Leventhal, Singer, and Jones, 1965). To persuade people to stop smoking, for example, it may be best to create high fear of dying from lung cancer, such as by showing them what a smoker's lung looks like when it is operated on for cancer. (Or see Figure 4.6 for another example.)

That is quite a list! Table 4.1 summarizes it for you. Obviously, there are plenty of ways to try to persuade someone. Different advertisers use different principles in their ads. Hence, one commercial may use a medical doctor to plug its product, relying on the value of expertise. Another may use a famous athlete or movie star, hoping to capitalize on popularity and attractiveness. Still others may try to distract the audience with humor or sexual suggestion, while yet others may try to arouse fear by warning that if you don't use their product you'll end up unloved, rejected, sick, or fired!

Not all the findings based on the early Yale research on persuasion have stood the test of time. Baumeister and Covington (1985), for example, challenged the conclusion that people with low self-esteem are more easily persuaded. They found that people with high self-esteem are just as persuaded as those with low self-esteem, but they don't want to admit it. Acknowledging that you have changed your attitude can often seem like an admission of gullibility, indecisiveness, or lack of personal conviction, so sometimes people may resist persuasion. And when persuasion does occur, people may deny it. Indeed, one classic study showed that when people do succumb to persuasion they conveniently "forget" what their original opinion was (Bem and McConnell, 1970). Instead of saying, "Yes, you are right, I was wrong, and now I have changed my mind," they say, in effect, "Yes, you are right — but I already believed that before I heard your argument"! Let's consider some of the evidence about resisting persuasion.

TABLE 4.1. A summary of some of the major findings uncovered in research on passive persuasion.

Persuasion: Some key results

Factor	More Attitude Change (successful persuasion)	Less Attitude Change	Comment
Characteristics of the person who is trying to persuade someone	Expert	Nonexpert	
	Popular	Unpopular	
	Attractive	Unattractive	
	Speaks fast	Speaks slowly	Rapid speech suggests expertise
	Persuasive intent is not obvious	Obviously trying to persuade	
Characteristics of the persuasive message	Considers both sides of the issue	Presents only one side	When audience is initially opposed
	Fear arousing	No fear	
Characteristics of the person who is being persuaded	Distraction	Not distracted	Distraction may determine whether persuasion occurs via central or peripheral routes
	Low self-esteem	High self-esteem	High self-esteem persons may be persuaded, but don't want to admit it

When attitude change fails: Resistance to persuasion

On any given day, we are exposed to a large number of persuasive messages. Commercials, political speeches, editorials—all are designed to alter our views in some manner. Given the frequency of such attempts, and the fact that they are often contradictory in nature, one point is clear: if we yielded to all of these appeals—or even to a small fraction of them—we would soon be in a pitiable state. Our attitudes would change from day to day, or even from hour to hour; and our behavior would probably show a strange pattern of shifts, reversals, and re-reversals! Obviously, this does not happen. Usually, our attitudes are quite stable and do not change from moment to moment. In fact, we generally show a great deal of stability in this respect. Thus, it is probably safe to conclude that far more attempts at persuasion fail than succeed. Why? What factors arm us with impressive resistance to even powerful efforts to change our views? As you can probably guess, many play a role. Among the most important, however, seem to be **reactance, forewarning, and inoculation.**

Reactance: Protecting your personal freedom.   Have you ever been in a situation where, because you felt that someone was trying to exert undue influence on you, you leaned over backwards to do the opposite of what he or she wanted? If so, you are already familiar with the operation of *reactance.* In social psychology this term refers to the unpleasant, negative reactions we experience whenever we feel that someone is trying to limit our personal freedom. Research findings suggest that when we perceive this is the case, we often tend to shift in a direction directly opposite to that being recommended—an effect known as *negative attitude change* (e.g., Brehm, 1966; Rhodewalt and Davison, 1983). Indeed, so strong is the desire to resist undue influence that, in some cases, individuals shift away from a view being advocated even if it is one they might normally accept.

Regardless of the basis for reactance and negative attitude change, the existence of these processes suggests that "hard-sell" attempts at persuasion will often fail. When individuals perceive such appeals as direct threats to their personal freedom (or their public image), they may be strongly motivated to resist. And such resistance, in turn, may result in total failure for many would-be persuaders.

Forewarning: Prior knowledge of persuasive intent.   On many occasions when we receive a persuasive message, we know full well that it is designed to change our views. Indeed, situations in which a communicator manages to catch us totally unprepared are probably quite rare. But does such advance knowledge of persuasive intent help? In short, does it aid us in resisting later persuasion? A growing body of research evidence suggests that it may (e.g., Cialdini and Petty, 1979; Petty and Cacioppo, 1981). When we know that a speech, taped message, or written appeal is designed to alter our views, we are often less likely to be affected by it than if we do not possess such knowledge. Moreover, this seems to be especially true with respect to attitudes and issues that we consider important (Petty and Cacioppo, 1979). The basis for these beneficial effects seems to lie in the impact of forewarning upon key cognitive processes. When we receive a persuasive message, especially one that is contrary to our current views, we often formulate counterarguments against it. Knowing about the content of such a message in advance, then, provides us with extra time in which to prepare such defenses. Similarly, forewarning may also give us more time in which to recall relevant facts and information from memory — facts that may prove useful in refuting a persuasive message (Wood, 1982). For these and related reasons, to be forewarned is indeed to be forearmed, at least in cases where we care enough about the topics in question to make active use of knowledge.

Inoculation: Protection against persuasive ideas.   A third factor that sometimes helps us resist attempts at persuasion was suggested by McGuire (1969) some years ago. Briefly, he proposed that exposing individuals to arguments against their views — but which are then strongly refuted — may serve to "inoculate" them against later persuasive appeals. That is, having heard various arguments against their attitudes demolished, individuals may be better equipped to withstand later attempts at persuasion.

In order to test these suggestions, McGuire and Papageorgis (1961) conducted a well-known study in which subjects in two groups were exposed to contrasting procedures. The first (a *supportive defense*) involved the presentation of several arguments supporting their views on various issues (e.g., the benefits of penicillin). The second (a *refutational defense*) involved the presentation of several weak arguments against the subjects' initial views, all of which were then strongly refuted. (Participants in a third condition did not receive either type of "immunization.") Several days later, subjects were exposed to strong attacks against their attitudes. Following these, their views were assessed once again. As McGuire and Papageorgis (1961) predicted, the refutational defense was quite effective in protecting participants against later attitude change. Indeed, it proved to be much more successful in this respect than the supportive defense. These and related findings point to an intriguing conclusion: previous exposure to "bad" ideas (views contrary to our own) in a weak or readily refuted form may indeed serve to immunize us against later attempts at persuasion.

To conclude: because of the operation of reactance, forewarning, and several other factors, our resistance to persuasion is great. Of course, attitude change does occur in some cases; to deny this fact would be to suggest that advertising, propaganda, and persuasive messages always fail. But the opposite conclusion — that we are helpless pawns in the hands of powerful communicators — is equally false. Resisting persuasion is an ancient human art, and there is every reason to believe that it is just as effective today as it was in the past. Because of this fact, attitude change is often much easier to plan or imagine than it is to achieve.

Two routes to persuasion

More recent research has replaced the Yale group's question, "What kinds of messages produce the most attitude change?" with the question, "What mental processes determine whether someone is persuaded?" This approach was first promoted by several researchers who described it as **cognitive response analysis** (e.g., Petty, Ostrom, and Brock, 1981). Recently, this cognitive approach to studying persuasion has been influenced by ideas from social cognition.

Cognitive response analysis emphasizes that what makes you change your mind is how and what you think about a persuasive message. People don't just passively absorb persuasive messages (such as speeches, arguments, and advertisements). Instead, they often actively think about them, and their thoughts lead either to attitude change or to resistance. While thinking, people often *elaborate* on the content of the persuasive message — in other words, they consider arguments and ideas that may not have been part of the original message.

The latest version of cognitive response analysis is a theory called the **elaboration likelihood model** (Petty and Cacioppo, 1985). **Elaboration** means scrutinizing the arguments in a persuasive message and thinking about them, (which includes considering relevant arguments the message may have left out). According to this theory, there are two different kinds of persuasion processes, or rather there are two different "routes" to persuasion. The **central route** involves careful and thoughtful consideration of the issue and of arguments that are being used to persuade. The attitudes in question are at the center of the person's attention at the moment, so to speak (hence the name "central route"). In contrast, the **peripheral route** leads to attitude change without careful or deliberate thinking, such as persuading someone who is distracted. High elaboration puts you on the central route to attitude change; low elaboration refers to the peripheral route.

One prediction of the elaboration likelihood model is that when the persuader has good, strong, convincing arguments, he or she should use the central route, but if the persuader can't make a strong case then the peripheral route should work best. One experiment showed this, using distraction to manipulate which route persuasion would follow (Petty, Wells, and Brock, 1976). The researchers tried to persuade students that their tuition should be raised by 20 percent. (As you can imagine, most students were initially opposed to the idea!) One persuasive message had strong and convincing arguments, such as that higher tuition would enable the school to hire better professors and improve the libraries. The other persuasive message had weak arguments, such as that higher tuition would enable the university to get new shrubs for campus buildings. Half the subjects heard one of these messages without distraction, but the others heard the message while simultaneously watching a computer screen to see whether certain letters would flash — a distracting task that had nothing to do with the tuition issue.

When the researchers checked their data to see how much attitude change had been produced, they found two opposite patterns. The strong

Persuasion: Changing Attitudes   131

arguments produced more attitude change when there was no distraction, because subjects were able to think about (i.e., elaborate on) the arguments and see their merit. Distracting subjects prevented them from being able to think about the arguments, so the strong message was less effective. In contrast, the weak message was slightly more effective with distracted subjects than with subjects who could devote their full attention to it. When weak arguments try the central route, such as in the no-distraction condition, the person is able to think about them and see their flaws, so attitude change does not occur. Weak arguments can produce some persuasion in someone who is not able to think about them carefully — in other words, via the peripheral route. Another way to think about these results is that the quality of someone's arguments is an important determinant of whether persuasion occurs on the central route, but argument quality seems to make no difference on the peripheral route (see Figure 4.7).

What *does* make a difference on the peripheral route? When you're not really paying any attention to a message or thinking about it, persuasion depends on subtle *persuasion cues.* Eagly and Chaikin (1984) put these effects in terms of social cognition in their **heuristic model of persuasion.** As you may recall from our earlier comments, a heuristic is a mental short-cut. So if the mind can't think carefully about a message, it relies on short-cuts to evaluate the message. In the peripheral route, then, the mind relies on cues such as how long the message is, how much

FIGURE 4.7. Strong arguments produced more attitude change among subjects in the absence of distraction. However, weak arguments were more effective in this respect when distraction was present. These findings support the view that persuasion can occur through either of two different routes. (Source: Based on data from Petty, Wells, and Brock, 1976.)

Persuasion: Two different routes

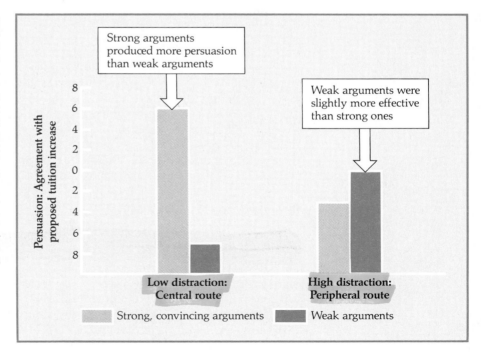

expertise the persuader appears to have, and whether the message is bolstered by statistics or multiple reasons. The person does not really think about what the arguments actually say — rather, he or she just operates on the basis of how many arguments there are or how likely it seems that the arguments are good. The heuristics in this case are general assumptions such as "the more arguments there are, the more likely the conclusion is correct" or "experts usually know what they are talking about, so they must be right," or "statistics don't lie" (Eagly and Chaikin, 1984).

In short, the elaboration likelihood model says that persuasion depends on how the mind reacts to the message. In the central route, the mind evaluates the quality of the arguments used and often considers other possible arguments. Persuasion is most likely if the arguments are intrinsically strong and if the person is able to think about and appreciate them fully. On the peripheral route, however, the mind evaluates the message based on simple and superficial cues, without really thinking about the arguments. In this case, persuasion is most likely if the message seems to resemble a type that is usually correct — regardless of how strong its specific arguments really are.

COGNITIVE DISSONANCE: Changing Your Own Attitudes

Remember the last time you had a difficult decision to make, such as choosing between two different but appealing colleges? Perhaps one college offered a great climate, friendly students, and a relaxed and easygoing atmosphere, but the other had a better academic program in the field you wanted to study. You wavered between the two, and even after you made your choice you still felt some regrets about forsaking the advantages of the other place. If you are like most people, you probably wonder now and then whether you made the right choice after all.

Remember the last time your actions deviated from your inner convictions? This, too, is a common experience. Perhaps you had resolved to diet, but you succumbed to temptation and ate a chocolate sundae, or cheesecake with whipped cream. Or perhaps your boss asked you whether you liked the new policy, and you said yes even though you really didn't. Or perhaps someone gave you an unattractive gift and you had to pretend you were glad and grateful for it.

What all these examples have in common is **cognitive dissonance, feelings of discomfort generated by conflicts among a person's beliefs or by inconsistences between a person's actions and attitudes.** You wanted a college with a relaxed atmosphere, but you chose the more academically rigorous one — so you have dissonance because your choice didn't mesh with your attitude about having a relaxed environment. Your choice did mesh with some of your other attitudes, such as the desirability of a good program: but it's often hard to satisfy all of one's attitudes. That's why dissonance is such a common experience. Each person has many attitudes, which often don't agree as to the best course of action. Similarly, you felt dissonance because eating cheesecake was inconsistent with your intention to diet, or because pretending you liked the gift was inconsistent with your belief in being honest. Dissonance is the struggle with personal inconsistencies, and social psychologists have given this struggle considerable attention (e.g., Festinger, 1957; Cooper and Fazio, 1984).

Dissonance: Its basic nature

Most researchers agree that cognitive dissonance can be viewed as a motivational state. That is, individuals experiencing dissonance are motivated to reduce it. There are three main ways in which this can be accomplished (refer to Figure 4.8). The first is to *change your attitudes and/or behavior*, so as to make them more consistent. Imagine a forty-five-year-old man who has dissonance because every day he goes to work at a job he hates. To reduce dissonance, he can try to convince himself that he doesn't really hate his job (changing his attitude), or he could quit and become a beach bum (changing his behavior).

The second way to reduce dissonance is to *get new information*—specifically, information that supports your attitude or your behavior. The information reassures you that there really is no problem or inconsistency to worry about, so you don't have to change your attitude or behavior. People who smoke cigarettes or take drugs may feel dissonance because these habits can harm their health. Risking one's health is inconsistent with most people's attitude that they want to have a long, healthy

FIGURE 4.8. Dissonance can be reduced in many different ways, but among the most important are: (1) changing one's attitudes or behavior, (2) acquiring new information that supports one's attitudes or behavior, and (3) minimizing the importance of the dissonance.

Techniques for reducing dissonance

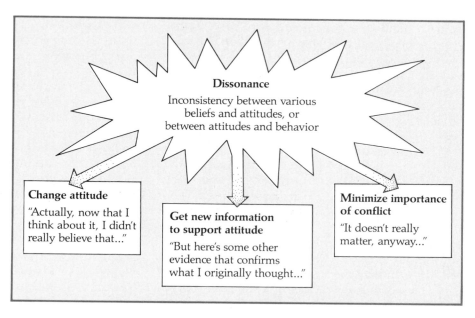

Dissonance
Inconsistency between various beliefs and attitudes, or between attitudes and behavior

Change attitude
"Actually, now that I think about it, I didn't really believe that..."

Get new information to support attitude
"But here's some other evidence that confirms what I originally thought..."

Minimize importance of conflict
"It doesn't really matter, anyway..."

FOCUS ON RESEARCH:
Classic Contributions

Lying, Suffering, and Dissonance

The theory of cognitive dissonance was proposed by Leon Festinger in 1957, and several researchers raced to provide initial tests of its accuracy. Two of the most famous early experiments concerned with this theory are described below.

CASH, BOREDOM, AND ATTITUDES

The first dissonance study to be published was one by Festinger and Carlsmith (1959). Their strategy was to create dissonance by putting subjects through an incredibly boring procedure and then getting them to tell others that it was a fascinating experience.

Subjects signed up for a study called "Measures of Performance." When they arrived, the experimenter explained that he was studying how people perform routine tasks. The subject was then shown a tray with twelve spools on it. He was instructed to take them off the tray one at a time. When they were all off the tray, he was to put them back on it, again one at a time. And then he took them off again, over and over, for half an hour. Next, the subject was shown a large board with forty-eight square pegs. His task was to turn each peg one quarter-turn clockwise, and then do them all another quarter-turn, and another, and so on for half an hour. By now the subject was probably very sorry he had signed up for this experiment, for a more boring and repetitive task could scarcely be imagined!

At this point the experimenter explained that there was really more to the experiment. Actually, said the experimenter, the purpose of the research was to motivate people to perform routine tasks. He said that some subjects had been told in advance by an assistant that the experiment would be exciting, interesting, and enjoyable, to see whether that motivated them to perform better.

Then came the crucial part of the experiment. The lab supervisor came in and informed the experimenter that the assistant had failed to show up, and he was supposed to be there now to tell the next subject that the experiment was interesting. The experimenter asked the subject to fill in, offering a cash payment for doing so. All subjects consented, and each then went out to the waiting room, where the subject told the person there (actually an accomplice pretending to be the next subject) that the study was exciting, intriguing, and a lot of fun. Later, in another setting, subjects were asked how much they had in fact enjoyed the experiment. Some had been given twenty dollars for lying—for telling the accomplice the experiment was a lot of fun—while others had been paid only one dollar for such counterattitudinal behavior. Who do you think changed their attitudes most? Common sense seems to suggest that the bigger reward should produce the larger change. Surprisingly, though, the opposite actually occurred (refer to Figure 4.9). Subjects paid one dollar ended up liking the task more than subjects paid twenty dollars. Why? According to cognitive dissonance theory, people feel dissonance when they can't justify their actions by making them fit their attitudes. Nobody approves of lying, but subjects paid $20—a lot of money in those days—felt that their behavior was justified by the large reward. Consider the people who lied for one dollar, however. They couldn't tell themselves, "I said it was interesting because they paid me a lot of money to do so." To reduce their dissonance, they had to change their attitudes: "I said it was interesting because I really found it kind of interesting" (see Figure 4.10, page 136).

This study set a pattern that many dissonance experiments have followed. The subject is paid to perform counterattitudinal behavior, and the subject's attitude is measured. Typically, the smaller payment produces the greater attitude change.

FIGURE 4.9. Subjects who told another person that they had enjoyed a boring task later reported liking it more when they engaged in this counterattitudinal behavior for a small reward (one dollar) than for a large one (twenty dollars). These findings offer support for dissonance theory. (Source: Based on data from Festinger and Carlsmith, 1959.)

Dissonance and counterattitudinal behavior

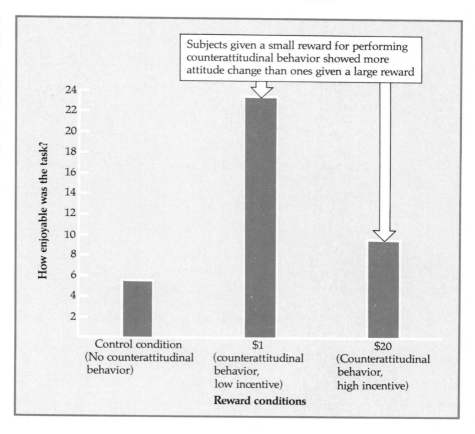

Subjects given a small reward for performing counterattitudinal behavior showed more attitude change than ones given a large reward

How enjoyable was the task?

Control condition
(No counterattitudinal behavior)

$1
(counterattitudinal behavior, low incentive)

$20
(Counterattitudinal behavior, high incentive)

Reward conditions

THE SEXUAL EMBARRASSMENT TEST: ON SEVERE INITIATIONS

Like today, college students of the 1950s often joined fraternities and sororities. Unlike today, however, these institutions often had drastic and strenuous initiation rituals. A new member might have to submit to being blindfolded, stripped naked, spanked with a paddle, sprayed with paint, driven several miles from campus, and tossed out into the night to find the way home (alone, painted, and naked). Controversies about these initiation practices led some psychologists to wonder what value they might have. Applying cognitive dissonance theory, Aronson and Mills (1959) reasoned that initiations may strengthen group bonds. They proposed that people would certainly feel dissonance over voluntarily submitting to unpleasant and humiliating treatment. To reduce dissonance, people might convince themselves that they were submitting for a good cause — to become a member of the desired sorority or fraternity. Ironically, then, the more the person suffered for the group, the more the person would end up liking it, in order to justify having suffered.

Aronson and Mills performed their experiment on college women who wanted to join a study group on "the psychology of sex." When the subject arrived, the experimenter greeted

	Attitude	Justification incentive	Counterattitudinal behavior	Effect of such behavior	Final attitude
Large reward	I don't like it!	They'll pay me $20 to say I like it	I like it!	No dissonance ("I had a good reason for lying")	I don't like it!
Small reward	I don't like it!	They'll pay me only $1 to say I like it	I like it!	Dissonance ("I had a pretty weak reason for lying")	I like it!

FIGURE 4.10. When subjects receive small rewards (incentives) for engaging in counterattitudinal behavior, dissonance occurs, and attitude change follows. When they receive large rewards, however, dissonance is not aroused, and attitude change fails to take place.

The impact of counterattitudinal behavior: A closer look

her, talked a little about the group, and then said he wanted to be sure the subject would be able to talk about sex without embarrassment. Could she? The subject always asserted that she could indeed discuss sex without embarrassment. In the control condition, the experimenter accepted the answer and allowed her to join the group. In the severe initiation condition, however, the subject was first put through an unpleasant "embarrassment test" before being allowed to join the group. First, the experimenter held up a series of index cards with obscene words on them, and the subject had to read them aloud. Next, the subject had to read aloud some vivid, explicit passages from pornographic novels, while the experimenter watched her closely for any signs of embarrassment. The subject was always told that she passed the test. Most subjects disliked the test, but they ended up liking the group better than control subjects who hadn't suffered through it. In another condition, a mild test did not increase liking for the group. It was the unpleasantness of the initial experience that made people like the group, presumably because of dissonance over having submitted to the embarrassing initiation. Thus, dissonance can help explain why people often come to like the things for which they suffer.

These two early examples show dissonance reduction in action. People change their own attitudes in order to justify their behavior. When they say something for low pay, they convince themselves that they meant what they said. And when they suffer for something, they justify this by convincing themselves that they like it.

life. These people may reduce their dissonance by looking for evidence that cigarettes or drugs are not dangerous — such as research studies that fail to prove health damage, or old grandpa who lived to be eighty-seven despite smoking a pack every day.

The third way to reduce dissonance is to *minimize the importance of the conflict*, so that it can safely be ignored. A young smoker may tell herself, for example, that it really doesn't matter if she takes a chance on getting lung cancer, because there is likely to be a nuclear war before she ever gets that old. Or she may decide that the risk is unimportant because a cure will probably be found by the time she's old enough to get the disease.

How much dissonance someone feels depends on the magnitude of the inconsistency and on the importance of the issue. The three approaches to reducing dissonance, therefore, try to reduce either the inconsistency or the importance. Although all three modes of reducing dissonance are viable, social psychologists have been mainly concerned with dissonance as a way of changing attitudes. Much research has focused on getting a person to behave in a way that contradicts his or her beliefs, and then determining whether this **counterattitudinal behavior** led to attitude change as a means of reducing dissonance. (To learn about the early research on cognitive dissonance, please read the **Focus** insert on page 134.)

Dissonance: Some factors that affect it

What factors contribute to dissonance? Researchers have identified several. One is choice. If you hate oatmeal but someone holds a gun to your head and forces you to say you love oatmeal, will your attitude toward it become more favorable? It's unlikely. Being forced to do something is a lot like being paid a huge amount to do it — you have ample external justification, so you don't feel dissonance and you don't have to revise your opinion. Normally, dissonance only occurs when people feel that their inconsistent behavior was done by their own free choice.

The importance of choice was first demonstrated in a study by Linder, Cooper and Jones (1967). They asked students to write a counterattitudinal essay arguing that controversial speakers should not be permitted on campus. Half their subjects were simply told that that was the task assigned them in the experiment. The other half were told that the decision to write the essay was entirely up to them, although the experimenter said he would appreciate their help. Everyone consented to write the essay. Initially, nearly all students were opposed to prohibiting controversial speakers. When attitudes were surveyed after writing the essays, the students who had simply been *told* to write the essay were still opposed. The students who had been told the decision was up to them, however, had changed their attitudes and become more favorable toward prohibiting such speakers on campus. Apparently, dissonance had only been aroused when the person had been reminded of having free choice and personal responsibility.

There are additional causes of dissonance. First, the inconsistent behavior has to have some foreseeable, possibly bad consequences (e.g., Goethals, Cooper, and Naficy, 1979). You don't feel dissonance if your behavior doesn't cause any harm, or if its consequences were an accident and could not have been anticipated. Second, the inconsistent actions have to involve the self in some important way. This can come about either because the behavior was performed by free choice, which creates inner feelings of personal responsibility for the behavior, or because the behavior is witnessed by others so that one's reputation is involved (e.g., Baumeister and Tice, 1984). In other words, the inconsistent behavior must be linked either to the private self-concept, through inner feelings of personal responsibility, or to the public self, through other people's knowledge of what you did — or else dissonance will not be created. Third, dissonance seems to depend on physiological, bodily arousal (e.g., Croyle and Cooper, 1983). Getting at least mildly upset seems to be part of dissonance. In one study, dissonance and attitude change were prevented by giving people tranquilizers before they performed the counterattitudinal behavior! (Cooper, Zanna, and Taves, 1978).

Thus, many factors contribute to dissonance: personal choice, foreseeable consequences, the public or private self, and arousal. No doubt others will be found in the future. Dissonance has been one of the most intensively studied topics in social psychology. One reason for its popularity is that its active approach to changing attitudes (by getting people to change their own attitudes) has such a reliable, powerful effect. You might think that if dissonance works so well, other people would have used it to change real attitudes — and they have. To learn about one way in which techniques resembling those suggested by cognitive dissonance theory have been put to use, please see the **On the Applied Side** insert on page 139.

Cults, Brainwashing, and Behavior

Cults are deviant religious groups who think quite differently from mainstream society. To recruit new members, therefore, cults often have to bring about major changes in the attitudes and beliefs of the potential members. The process by which these changes are effected, which cult members regard as learning but which outsiders often label as *brainwashing*, is a fascinating area for psychological study. Based on recent analyses of brainwashing (e.g., Baumeister, 1986), it appears that the most effective techniques rely heavily on cognitive dissonance. Brainwashing is not passive persuasion; it requires active participation, just like cognitive dissonance.

Have you ever been approached in a public place by a cult member? (Refer to Figure 4.11.) Probably you just brushed him or her off, wondering why these people waste their time courting rejection. But think for a minute about the effects on the *cult member* of accosting strangers to speak about the cult. The cult member is publicly advocating his or her beliefs, with low external incentives or justification. That is precisely the situation that makes people's attitudes fall into line with their behavior, according to dissonance theory. Members are made to feel their actions derive from their own free choice instead of from coercion, another important feature of dissonance theory. Arousal is kept high by various means — at first, by the excitement of meeting

many new people (the other cult members) and learning new ideas, later by the nervousness that goes with approaching total strangers to tell them about the cult. Feelings of inconsistency are generated by ascertaining that the potential member has high ideals and values but has often fallen short of them in actual behavior. Although most people fall short of their ideals, brainwashers emphasize these inconsistencies to build up strong feelings of guilt and dissonance which can be resolved by committing oneself to the cult — a major change in behavior.

Cults are well aware that suffering and sacrifice build commitment, as dissonance theory also holds (remember the experiment on severe initiations). Cult members have to give up some or all of their possessions, often including giving large sums of money to the cult. They often have to sacrifice contacts with friends and family. Long days of physically grueling labor are common. Sometimes even embarrassment and humiliation are used. For example, Charles Manson and Jim Jones — two cult leaders whose activities resulted in the shocking deaths of many innocent people — are said to have required their cult members to participate in deviant sexual acts, often with others watching. Once a person has submitted to all that, it is hard for him or her to begin questioning the cult. Such individuals feel that if they were going to decide the cult was not for them, they should have done so *before* they endured so much for it.

FIGURE 4.11. How do cults create desired attitudes in new members? Evidence suggests that they use various techniques to create *cognitive dissonance* among these persons, and so place them in a situation where they experience internal pressure to adopt the attitudes favored by the cult.

Dissonance: Its role in cults

ATTITUDES AND BEHAVIOR: The Essential Link

Do attitudes shape behavior? Your first answer is likely to be, "Of course!" After all, you can recall many incidents in which your own actions were strongly determined by your opinions. Besides, social psychologists wouldn't have spent so much time and energy studying attitudes if they didn't predict behavior. Behavior is the bottom line in social psychology. Without behavior, attitudes become irrelevant whims.

But is there proof that attitudes shape behavior? Many studies have examined attitude-behavior relationships. Some years ago Wicker (1969) reviewed all these studies and arrived at a shocking conclusion: Attitudes and behavior are at best very weakly related, and often there is no relationship between them. The scientific community was stunned, but they couldn't argue with the mass of evidence Wicker had assembled. In study after study the correlation between attitude and behavior was found to be weak or negligible. Wicker even suggested that the concept of attitude should be abandoned as useless!

At this point, you're probably wondering why you bothered to read this chapter, or perhaps why we even included a chapter on attitudes in the first place. Fortunately, there has been new evidence that attitudes *can* predict behavior effectively under some conditions. Wicker had challenged social psychology to show that attitudes predict behavior, and our field responded to the challenge. Often attitudes don't predict behavior well, but sometimes they do. Let's look at what factors determine the strength of the essential link between attitudes and behaviors.

Attitude specificity

Consider two of your attitudes. Suppose, for example, that you like pickles on your hamburger (a specific attitude) and that you oppose racial discrimination and prejudice (a general attitude). Which one will show a stronger, more consistent relationship with your actual behavior? Probably you don't always take every opportunity to work for racial equality — you don't always take part in every demonstration, you don't sign every petition that comes along, you don't always seek out the companionship of people of other races. Sometimes you do those things, but sometimes you don't — which translates into a *weak* (inconsistent) relationship between your attitude and your behavior. In contrast, if you like pickles, you may order them almost every time you have a hamburger. Thus, your behavior is highly consistent with your attitude. No doubt you would say that racial equality is more important than pickles, but the link between attitude and behavior is nonetheless stronger (more consistent) for pickles — that is, for the specific attitude than for the general attitude.

Most attitude researchers have studied general attitudes, such as ones about religion, political issues, or groups of people, because these seem the most important and interesting ones. Ajzen and Fishbein (1977) suspected that the emphasis on general, global attitudes may have led to the weakness of the attitude-behavior link that Wicker described. They argued that it may be unreasonable to expect *general* attitudes to predict *specific* behaviors with high statistical reliability. For example, they suggested, a researcher might look at attitudes toward Christianity to see how these are linked to attending church on a particular Sunday. A weak relationship might be found, indicating that not all devout Christians attended church that day, and that some of the relatively indifferent Christians happened to show up. Ajzen and Fishbein noted that instead of looking at general attitudes about Christianity, the researchers should have focused on the narrow and specific attitude about attending that church on that day. The specific attitude would show a much higher correlation with actual church attendance than would the general or global attitude.

Ajzen and Fishbein reviewed considerable research on the attitude-behavior problem (sometimes called the **"A-B problem"**). Their conclusion strongly supported the advantages of attitude specificity for predicting behavior. Research studies that measured very specific attitudes showed high correlations with behavior. Research studies that measured global and general attitudes, however, found the weak or negligible correlations that Wicker had criticized. So the conclusion is this: to predict overt behavior from attitudes, it is usually more effective to look at specific, narrow, and precise attitudes instead of general or global ones.

Attitude strength and accessibility

Obviously, strong attitudes predict behavior better than weak ones. That is no surprise. There are several less obvious factors related to attitude strength, however. One is direct experience. At the beginning of this chapter we compared attitudes formed by direct personal experience with attitudes acquired passively by observation. That difference is related to the A-B problem. Attitudes formed by direct personal experience tend to be stronger and tend to predict behavior better than other attitudes. For example, in one study half the subjects formed their attitudes about some puzzles by playing with them while the other subjects formed their attitudes by watching someone else play with the puzzles. The first (direct experience) group ended up with attitudes that affected their behavior more than the second (observer) group, even though both groups had the same amount of information about the puzzles (Fazio et al., 1982).

A second factor is whether the person has a **vested interest** in the issue. A vested interest means that the events or issues in question will have a strong effect on the person's own life. Having a vested interest increases the relation between attitudes and behavior, as shown in an experiment by Sivacek and Crano (1982). They contacted students and pretended to solicit their help in campaigning against a proposed state law that would raise the drinking age from eighteen to twenty. Nearly all students were opposed to the law, regardless of their own age. But some of them had a vested interest—those young enough so that the law would interfere with their social lives if it passed. Students who were a little older had no vested interest, for even if the law passed they would already be over age twenty by the time it took effect. Who do you think agreed to campaign against the law? The younger students, of course. The older students were equally opposed to the law in principle but lacked any vested interest. Their attitudes did not lead to the corresponding behavior.

Remember the importance of *availability* in social cognition, from Chapter 3? Attitude researchers have a similar concept, called **accessibility,** that ties together the evidence about attitudes and behavior (e.g., Fazio, 1986; Fazio et al., 1986). Attitude accessibility means bringing the attitude to mind. Strong attitudes come to mind more readily, so they exert more influence over behavior than do weak attitudes. Direct experience and vested interests also make the attitude accessible, and that is why those two factors increase the attitude's effects on behavior. The more often you have thought about a particular attitude, the more likely it is to come up again and to influence your behavior. In one study, attitude accessibility was increased simply by asking subjects six different times what their attitude was, as opposed to asking them only once (Powell and Fazio, 1984).

If accessibility is high, then, even general attitudes can exert a strong influence on behavior. This has to occur through a three-step process. First, something calls the general attitude to mind. Second, the general attitude influences how the person perceives the situation, "coloring" judgments and interpretations. The general attitude operates like a *schema* in creating expectations and guiding attention, encoding, and retrieval. Third, behavior is determined by these judgments and interpretations of the immediate situation (Fazio, Powell, and Herr, 1983). If the general attitude is never accessed, it won't affect behavior (see Figure 4.12).

Perhaps the earliest evidence for the three-step process model was provided in an experiment by Snyder and Swann (1976), which was actually published before the three-step model was formulated. Subjects read a simulated court case regarding sex discrimination. In one condition, subjects' attitudes about affirmative action favoring women were accessed: the experimenter asked them to consider these attitudes before they read the case. These subjects' judgments in the case followed from their attitudes. People favoring affirmative action were harsher on the university accused of sex discrimination than were people opposed to affirmative action. In contrast, other subjects were not specifically asked to consider how they felt about affirmative action, and their judgments were not affected by these attitudes. Thus, general attitudes *can* influence specific behaviors, but only if something brings the attitude to mind and enables it to influence how the person interprets the situation.

Making people consider their attitudes, as in the Snyder and Swann experiment, sounds a lot like increasing self-awareness: in both cases, attention is directed inward to some feature or part of the self. To con-

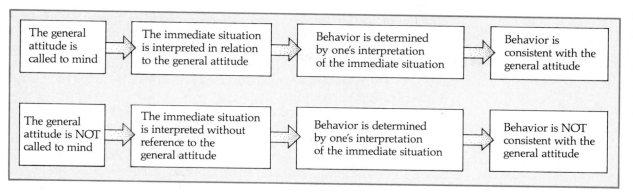

FIGURE 4.12. When general attitudes are *accessed* (called to mind), they can affect behavior in specific situations. When they are not accessed, however, their impact upon overt behavior will be minimal. (Source: Based on a theoretical model proposed by Fazio, Powell, and Herr, 1983.)

General attitudes and specific behavior: A three-step model

clude this chapter, let's look briefly at how the attitude-behavior link is affected when attention *is* focused inward.

Self-attention and the A-B problem

In Chapter 3 we discussed one study showing that self-awareness can strengthen the A-B link. Self-awareness made women's reactions to pornography more consistent with their general attitudes about sex (Gibbons, 1978). Other studies have likewise shown that heightened self-awareness increases consistency between attitudes and behavior (e.g., Pryor et al., 1977). There are two reasons why self-awareness increases such consistency. First, self-awareness increases people's access to their own attitudes, so they report their attitudes more accurately when self-aware than when not self-focused. Second, in a behavioral setting, self-awareness can "remind" the person of his or her attitude, enabling the attitude to guide behavior. Increasing someone's self-awareness is like saying to the person, "Before you act, stop for a moment and consider who you are and what you believe in. What course of action suits you best?" That makes subsequent behavior more likely to follow from the person's own inner attitudes and less likely to be determined mainly by external, situational factors.

But there is a catch to all this. In Chapter 3 we also saw that people are often unaware of their own mental processes (Nisbett and Wilson, 1977). If people don't know their own minds, how can we ever expect them to tell us their attitudes accurately enough to predict their behavior? The answer is that there is a difference between knowing attitudes (and other mental states) and knowing the *processes* that go on inside the mind. People may not know the process by which they arrived at a judgment, but they know the outcome of it. Likewise, they may not be aware of all the complex processes of attitude formation that we discussed earlier in this chapter, but they do know their attitudes that are the final result of those processes. So focusing on your attitudes may increase consistency between attitudes and behavior, because the mind is quite capable of knowing its attitudes. Focusing on its processes, however, may be too hard a task to accomplish. Trying to analyze all the reasons behind your attitudes may just confuse the issue and *reduce* attitude-behavior consistency. This was demonstrated in a clever series of studies by Wilson and his colleagues (1984).

In the first couple of experiments, the researchers had subjects form attitudes about some games. Half the subjects were asked to analyze their reactions to each game and give reasons why they liked it or disliked it, while other subjects simply stated their opinion without explaining it. Later, when their behavior was checked for consistency with these attitudes, it turned out that consistency was *lower* for the subjects who had analyzed their reasons than for those who had simply expressed opinions. In the final experiment, the researchers then turned their attention to dating relationships. Young couples were brought into the lab. All were unmarried college students having a serious, exclusive relationship that had been going on for an average of six to seven months. The two lovers were put in separate rooms. Half the couples were instructed to analyze their relationship and list all the reasons they could think of for why it was good or bad. Other couples did not analyze their relationship.

All couples were then asked for their bottom-line evaluation of the relationship — how happy they were with it, how well the couple had adjusted to each other, and how they felt about the relationship's future. Of course, some couples felt their relationship was good, and others felt theirs was not so good. The control and the reasons-analysis groups were about equal in their average evaluations of the relationships.

Eight months later, the researchers contacted each of the couples to see whether they had broken up or were still going together. About one-third of the couples in each group had broken up. The key question, though, is whether the attitudes toward the relationship predicted who would break up. In the control condition, the attitudes were very predictive: those who had said they were happy in the relationship were still together eight months later, and those who were unhappy tended to have split up. But the couples who analyzed the relationship in detail before expressing their attitudes showed no consistent pattern. Once again, analyzing reasons lowered the consistency between attitude and behavior. Why? Because the mind doesn't really know its true reasons. So when it tries to analyze them, it misleads and confuses itself. The attitudes people reported after analyzing reasons were simply unreliable.

To sum up: the effects of focusing attention inward on the self depend on what aspects of the attitude are involved. The mind is capable of knowing its attitudes, but if often cannot know the reasons and processes that underlie these attitudes. When attention is focused on the attitude itself, the link between attitude and behavior is strengthened. Focusing attention on the attitude makes the attitude more accessible, so it exerts more influence on behavior. But when the person tries to focus attention on the underlying reasons and processes, the attitude gets distorted, and the link between attitude and behavior is weakened (refer to Figure 4.13).

FIGURE 4.13. When attention is focused on specific attitudes, the link between these attitudes and overt behavior may be strengthened. When, instead, attention is focused on the reasons or processes underlying such attitudes, their impact on behavior may actually be lessened.

Focus of attention and the attitude-behavior link

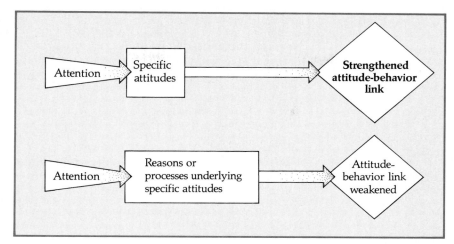

SUMMARY

We have numerous **attitudes,** and we use them constantly. Attitudes enable us to evaluate our experiences by guiding positive and negative reactions to things (and to people). Each attitude is made up of certain thoughts or labels (cognition), the good or bad feelings (affect) associated with these thoughts, and behavioral patterns or at least intentions to behave in certain ways.

There are several ways in which attitudes can be created. Children learn many attitudes in the course of *socialization.* Such learning can occur when they are taught to associate good or bad feelings with certain actions or things, or it can occur simply when they are rewarded or punished for expressing certain views. It can also occur when they copy the example set by parents or other people. Adults form attitudes spontaneously based on their personal experiences.

Persuasion is the process of influencing someone to change his or her attitude. According to the *elaboration likelihood model,* there are two routes to persuasion. The *central* route to persuasion involves careful thought about the issue and about the arguments, so persuasion is most likely if there are strong, convincing arguments. The *peripheral* route, however, involves convincing someone without having his or her full attention, so the strength of the arguments is less important than superficial cues or distractions. Sometimes, of course, people resist persuasion, such as when they know in advance that someone will attack their beliefs, or when they feel someone is trying to take away their freedom to make up their own minds.

Cognitive dissonance is an unpleasant feeling that results from conflict or inconsistency between one's thoughts and/or actions. People want to avoid cognitive dissonance, so they will often change their attitudes in order to justify their behavior. For example, people may come to like the things they have suffered for, because the liking justifies the suffering — it is worth suffering for something if you like it.

Surprising as it may seem, the connection between attitudes and behavior is sometimes very weak. Specific attitudes, strong attitudes, easily accessible attitudes, and attitudes involving a vested interest seem to have the most direct influence on behavior. Self-awareness can increase consistency between actions and attitudes, but analyzing the reasons behind one's attitude reduces such consistency.

GLOSSARY

A-B problem
The research issue concerned with whether or how strongly attitudes are related to behavior.

ABC model
Each attitude is composed of affect, behavior, and cognition.

accessibility
The ease with which an attitude is brought to mind.

attitudes
Lasting, general evaluations of people, objects, or issues.

central route
When persuasion occurs by means of careful and thoughtful consideration of the issue and arguments (opposite of peripheral route).

classical conditioning
Learning by association.

cognitive dissonance
The feeling of discomfort caused by conflicts or inconsistencies between a person's attitudes and/or behaviors.

cognitive response analysis
Studying how people's thought processes mediate persuasion.

counterattitudinal behavior
Actions that seem contrary to one's attitudes. Counterattitudinal behavior often causes cognitive dissonance.

elaboration
Thinking about and analyzing the arguments relevant to the persuasive message.

elaboration likelihood model
The theory that there are two routes to persuasion, the *central* route and the *peripheral* route, which are distinguished by the amount of cognitive *elaboration* they involve.

forewarning
Advance knowledge that one is to be the target of the persuasion attempt. Forewarning often produces resistance to persuasion.

heuristic model of persuasion
The theory that attitude change sometimes occurs when the person evaluates the persuasive message on the basis of superficial cues.

hostile media phenomenon
The common tendency to believe that news coverage is biased against one's own side or attitude.

inoculation

Exposing people to arguments against their attitudes, then refuting those arguments. Inoculation strengthens resistance to persuasion.

instrumental conditioning

A form of learning in which responses that yield positive outcomes or eliminate negative ones are acquired or strengthened. (Also known as *operant conditioning.*)

modeling

Learning by observation of someone else's behavior.

peripheral route

When persuasion occurs without careful or deliberate thinking about the issue or the arguments (opposite of central route).

reactance

Unpleasant, negative reactions to threats to one's freedom. Reactance often entails resisting external influence.

selective avoidance

Directing one's attention away from information that challenges one's attitudes.

selective exposure

Deliberately seeking out or attending to information that supports one's attitudes.

socialization

The process of teaching a child the basic beliefs, values, and practices of society. This process makes the child into a responsible and capable member of society.

vested interest

Refers to instances in which events or issues will have a strong effect on the person's own life.

FOR MORE INFORMATION

Festinger, R., Riecken, H. W., and Schachter, S. (1956). *When prophecy fails.* Minneapolis: University of Minnesota Press.

> One of the earliest works to deal with issues of cognitive consistency and dissonance, this classic book provides an absorbing case study. A small group predicted the end of the world on a precise date, but, of course, it never happened. Three social psychologists infiltrated the group to learn how it would deal with disconformation of its basic beliefs.

Petty, R. E., and Cacioppo, J. T. (1986). *Attitude change: Central and peripheral routes to persuasion.* New York: Springer-Verlag.

> This book provides the most up-to-date account of this fascinating approach to persuasion research.

Zanna, M. P., Olson, J. M., and Herman, C. P. (1986). *Social influence: The Ontario symposium,* vol. 5. Hillsdale, N.J.: Erlbaum.

> The chapters in this volume deal with a variety of current topics related to attitudes. You may find some of them to be difficult, because they are written primarily for an audience of experts, but it is a good way to become acquainted with the latest ideas of several leading researchers.

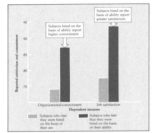

PREJUDICE AND DISCRIMINATION: When "Different" Is Definitely Not "Equal"

"Well, honey, how do you like working in the big city?" These words are uttered by Lola Williams's Uncle Bill, in the midst of one of his famous bear hugs.

"It's OK, I guess," Lola replies, a forced smile on her face. "It has its ups and downs, just like anything else."

Lola's smile can't fool her uncle — he's known her all her life. So, holding her at arm's length and looking her straight in the eye, he continues. "Hey, hold on a minute. From what I hear, you've had a lot more ups than downs. Didn't your mama tell me that you just got another promotion? You seem to be doing *real* good."

"I am, I am," Lola replies. "Really, I've got no complaints."

"Then why do you look like a grey day in December? Come on, you can tell your old Uncle Bill. Are those white folks giving you a hard time? Lord knows they can be *mean* when they want to! But don't you stand for nothing from them. You're the *best*, and they better believe it. Hmmph! The first black woman from this whole part of the state to get a degree at that fancy Harvard College. Why, they're darn lucky to have you!"

"No, no, Uncle Bill," Lola quickly replies. "It's nothing like that. They're real nice to me all the time."

"So what's the problem? I know you're a big executive and all, but I still might know a thing or two you didn't study about in college."

"Well, it may sound kind of strange, but the fact is, they're a little *too* nice. Whenever I do something right, they just praise it up and down. And when I make a mistake, everyone bends over backwards to ignore it, or to reassure me. You know, saying it happens to everyone, not to worry about it, stuff like that."

"Hmm . . ." Bill murmurs, stroking his chin. "That don't sound so bad. Anyway, it's sure better than what your cousin Mel had to face when *he* went looking for his fortune about ten years back. No one wanted to hire him. And when they did, 'cause they had no choice, they did everything they could to trip him up so they could get rid of him. Yup, black people had a tough time in those days.''

"I know, Uncle Bill. Things *are* different now. But you see, I *know* I'm good and that I can do my job as well as anyone else. So it really hurts when I feel that they're treating me different just because I'm black. I want to make it on my own, not because they have to fill some quota or need a good public image.''

At these words, Bill sticks his hands in his pockets and rocks back and forth on his heels — a sure sign, Lola knows, that he's deep in thought. When he finally continues, it's with a serious expression on his face. "Well, Lola, I sure see what you mean. That *is* a bad situation. You want to get ahead because you're *you*, not because those fools where you work have a guilty conscience or who knows what. Lord give us strength; won't those people *ever* run out of ways to give us a hard time? Seems like they're all pretty much the same, and that they'll *never* change.''

Then, brightening a bit, and with a twinkle in his eye, he adds: "If only they'd all just go back where they came from, life would sure be a lot simpler.''

CONSIDER THE following list: blacks, Hispanics, Yankees, conservatives, Russians, Jews.

Do you have an "image" of persons belonging to each of these groups? For example, if you learned that someone you were about to meet was a member of one of these groups, would you have any expectations about the kind of person he or she would be? If you are completely honest, your answer is probably "Yes." Despite the age-old warning against jumping to conclusions, most of us do just that where other persons are concerned. We form judgments about them, assume that they possess certain traits, and predict that they will act in certain ways simply because they belong to specific groups. Our tendency to jump to "social conclusions" about others in this manner plays a central role in the topics we will consider in this chapter: **prejudice** and **discrimination**.

As we're sure you already realize, these processes pose a serious and continuing threat to human welfare all over the globe. Indeed, it is virtually impossible to pick up a newspaper or tune in the evening news without learning of new atrocities stemming from their impact (refer to Figure 5.1). For this reason alone, prejudice and discrimination have long been of major interest to our field. In their efforts to understand these unsettling processes, social psychologists have focused on many issues. Among the most important of these, though, have been the following: (1) what is the basic nature of prejudice and discrimination? (2) what factors account for their occurrence? and (3) what steps can be taken to reduce their impact? We will consider each of these questions below. In addition, we will also focus on one type of prejudice that seems especially

FIGURE 5.1. Today, as in the past, prejudice and discrimination are major causes of human suffering.

Prejudice and discrimination: The costs are high

pervasive, which has recently been the subject of a great deal of research interest: prejudice based on sex (**sexism**).

CHAPTER 5

PREJUDICE AND DISCRIMINATION: *What They Are, How They Differ*

In everyday speech, many persons seem to use the terms *prejudice* and *discrimination* interchangeably, as synonyms. Are they really the same? Most social psychologists feel that they are not. Prejudice refers to a special type of attitude — generally, a negative one toward the members of some distinct social group. In contrast, discrimination refers to negative actions directed toward these individuals. Since this is an important distinction, we will now expand upon it in more detail.

Prejudice: Group membership and social rejection

Let's begin with a more precise definition: *prejudice is an attitude (usually negative) toward the members of some group based solely on their membership in that group.* In other words, when we state that a given person is prejudiced against the members of some social group, we generally mean that she or he tends to evaluate its members in some characteristic manner (again, usually negatively) merely because they belong to that group. Their individual traits or behavior play little role; they are liked or disliked simply because they belong to a specific social group.

When prejudice is defined as a special type of attitude, two important implications follow. First, as we noted in Chapter 4, attitudes often operate as *schemata* — cognitive frameworks for organizing, interpreting, and recalling information (Fiske and Taylor, 1984). Thus, when individuals are prejudiced against the members of some group, they tend to notice, to accurately encode (i.e., store in memory), and later to remember certain kinds of information — for example, information consistent with their prejudice (e.g., Bodenhausen and Wyer, 1985).

Second, as an attitude, prejudice involves the three major components described in Chapter 4. That is, it encompasses affective, cognitive, and behavioral aspects. The affective component refers to the negative feelings or emotions prejudiced persons experience when in the presence of members of specific groups, or merely when they think about them for some reason. The cognitive component involves beliefs and expectations about members of these groups, plus the ways in which information about them is processed. Finally, the behavioral component involves tendencies to act in negative ways toward the groups who are the object of prejudice, or intentions to do so. When these tendencies or intentions are translated into overt actions, they constitute *discrimination* — the next major topic we will consider.

Discrimination: Prejudice in action

As we noted in Chapter 4, attitudes are not always reflected in overt actions. Indeed, there is often a substantial gap between the views individuals hold and their actual behavior. Prejudice is no exception to this general rule. In many cases, persons holding negative attitudes toward the members of various groups find that they cannot express these views directly. Laws, social pressure, and the fear of retaliation all serve to prevent them from engaging in openly negative actions against the targets of their dislike. In other instances, however, such restraining forces are absent. Then, the negative beliefs, feelings, and behavior tendencies described above may find expression in overt actions. Such *discriminatory behaviors* can take many different forms. At relatively mild levels, they involve simple avoidance. At stronger levels, they can produce exclusion from jobs, education, or residential neighborhoods. And in extreme cases, discrimination may take the form of overt aggression against the targets of prejudice. Regardless of their precise form, however, the ultimate outcome is always the same: members of the target group are harmed in some fashion.

Subtle forms of discrimination: Hitting below the belt.   Bigots, like other persons, prefer to "have their cake and eat it, too." If possible, they prefer to harm the targets of their prejudice without any cost to themselves. How do they seek to accomplish this goal? One answer is through the use of several *subtle forms of discrimination* — ones that permit their users to conceal their underlying negative views. A number of these exist, but here we will focus on three that seem to be most common: (1) withholding aid from persons who need it, (2) various forms of *tokenism*, and (3) *reverse discrimination.*

RELUCTANCE TO HELP: "LET SOMEONE ELSE DO IT": The first of these tactics — withholding aid from the members of disliked groups — is often used with considerable finesse. Contrary to what you may expect, prejudiced persons do not engage in blanket refusals to assist the objects of their bigotry. Rather, they act in this manner only when they feel they can get away with such actions — when there are other plausible explanations for their failure to help, aside from prejudice. Thus, such persons are more likely to refrain from aiding members of groups they dislike in situations where other potential helpers are present than in situations where they are absent (Gaertner and Dovidio, 1977). The reason for this is simple: when other helpers are present, bigoted persons can attribute their own failure to act to the belief that *these* individuals will take any necessary action. In this manner, they get neatly off the hook. Fortunately, some evidence suggests that the use of this particular subtle form of discrimination may be on the wane (Shaffer and Graziano, 1980). However, it probably persists in at least some settings, and it continues to exact a high cost from persons who could be aided by help but do not receive it simply because they belong to a particular social group.

TOKENISM: SMALL BENEFITS, HIGH COSTS? A second form of subtle discrimination involves **tokenism.** The basic mechanism here is simple. Prejudiced individuals engage in trivial, positive actions toward the members of groups they dislike (e.g., they hire or promote a single "show" black, Jew, or Hispanic). Then, they use these actions as a rationale for refusing other, more important actions (e.g., the adoption of truly fair hiring or promotion practices) or as a justification for later discrimination. "Don't bother me," they seem to say. "Haven't I done enough for those people already?" Evidence for the use of such tactics has been reported in several studies (e.g., Dutton and Lake, 1973; Rosenfield et al., 1982). In these experiments, white subjects who had performed a small favor for a black stranger were less willing to engage in more effortful forms of helping at a later time than those who had not performed such a favor. Moreover, this was especially likely to be the case when the small (token) favor activated negative stereotypes about blacks (e.g., when the favor involved giving money to a black panhandler).

Unfortunately, various forms of tokenism do more than deny groups who are the object of prejudice important forms of aid. Being the recipient of such grudging help — for example, being hired as a "token" black, woman, or Hispanic — can also play havoc with the self-esteem and careers of the persons involved. Evidence for such conclusions has been reported by Chacko (1982). He asked young women holding managerial jobs to rate the extent to which several different factors (their ability, experience, education, or sex) had played a role in their hiring. In addition, they completed questionnaires designed to measure their organizational commitment (favorable attitudes toward their companies) and their satisfaction with various aspects of their jobs (e.g., satisfaction with their supervisors, with the work itself). When subjects who rated their ability as the most important factor in being hired were compared with those who rated their sex as most important, unsettling differences emerged. Those who felt they were mere "tokens" (that they had been hired mainly because they were female) reported significantly lower commitment and satisfaction (refer to Figure 5.2). These and related findings suggest that the impact of tokenism is largely negative, even for those few individuals who seem to profit from its existence.

REVERSE DISCRIMINATION: GIVING WITH ONE HAND, TAKING AWAY WITH THE OTHER.   At the start of this chapter, we described an incident in which a bright young woman felt that she was receiving special, favored

FIGURE 5.2.   Women who felt that they had been hired primarily because of their sex (i.e., those who felt that they were the victims of *tokenism*) expressed less satisfaction with their jobs and lower commitment to their organizations than women who felt they had been hired because of their ability. (Source: Based on data from Chacko, 1982.)

Tokenism: Some unsettling effects

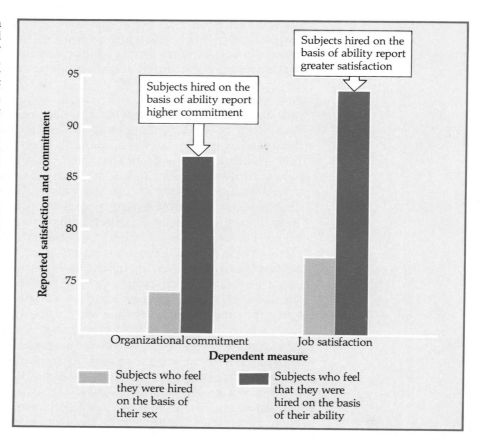

treatment on the basis of her race. Not surprisingly, she found this situation disturbing; after all, she wanted to succeed because she was talented and hard-working, *not* because she happened to fit into a particular racial category.

This incident illustrates yet another subtle form of discrimination: **reverse discrimination.** It occurs in situations where persons holding at least residual prejudice toward the members of some social group actually lean over backwards to treat these persons favorably — more favorably than would be the case if they did not belong to this group. Such effects have been observed in several investigations. For example, Chidester (1986) had subjects engage in a brief "get-acquainted" conversation with a stranger who was described as being either black or white. (The conversation took place through sound equipment — a microphone and headphones.) When subjects later evaluated this person, they reported more favorable reactions toward strangers who were ostensibly black than ones who were supposedly white. (All participants were white; only subjects' beliefs about the race of their partner were varied.) Unless one assumes that these white subjects actually held more favorable views of blacks than of members of their own race, these findings point to the occurrence of a "lean-over-backwards" or "demonstrate my lack of prejudice" approach among participants.

At first glance, such behavior may not seem to fit our definition of discrimination; after all, it yields positive rather than negative outcomes for its "victims." On one level, this is certainly true; individuals exposed to reverse discrimination do receive raises, promotions, and other benefits. At the same time, though, such favorable treatment may actually prove harmful, especially over the long haul. For example, while individuals who acquired prejudicial attitudes early in life may successfully hold them in check in many situations, such reactions may rise to the fore and encourage negative actions toward their target groups when emotions and arousal run high (e.g., Rogers and Prentice-Dunn, 1981). Similarly, consider what happens to minority students whose work is evaluated more leniently than that of other students by their teachers. Such youngsters may be passed on from grade to grade until graduation — when they discover that they are severely lacking in basic skills. In this and many other cases, what seems to be kind or benevolent treatment may actually prove harmful.

Both the operation and potential negative impact of reverse discrimination are forcefully illustrated by a recent study conducted by Fajardo (1985). In this investigation, teachers were asked to grade essays designed, in advance, to be either poor, moderate, or excellent in quality. Information attached to the essays indicated that they were prepared either by white or by black students. If reverse discrimination exists, it would be expected that the teachers (all of whom were white) would rate the essays more favorably when they were supposedly prepared by black than by white students. (The essays themselves were identical in both cases; only the supposed race of the authors was varied.) Results indicated that this is precisely what happened. Moreover, as shown in Figure

5.3, the tendency of white teachers to favor black students was strongest under conditions where the essays were of moderate rather than excellent or poor quality. In short, it was when the students in question appeared to be of average ability that reverse discrimination was most likely to occur.

Comments by the teachers indicated that they used a number of different tactics to generate favorable ratings for black authors (e.g., they reported reading such essays more carefully, and grading them more leniently). As you can readily see, while such practices may help minority students in the short run, they can set the stage for later problems. For example, they may lead some students, at least, to develop inflated opinions of their own abilities, and unrealistic expectations about the likelihood of future success. The anguish that results when such hopes collide with reality can be devastating. Similarly, reverse discrimination may prevent minority students from seeking the help they sometimes need early in their academic careers. As a result, they may later face an especially difficult task in compensating for their disadvantaged back-

FIGURE 5.3.   White teachers rated essays supposedly written by black students higher than identical essays supposedly written by white students. Thus, they showed *reverse discrimination.* This tendency was strongest when the essays were average in quality. (Source: Based on data from Fajardo, 1985).

Reverse discrimination: An example

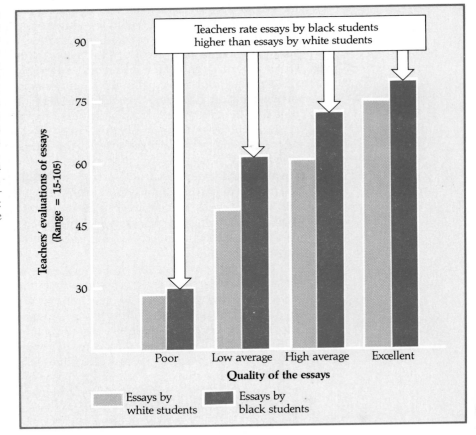

FIGURE 5.4. Prejudice seems to have been part of human society throughout recorded history.

Prejudice: An ever-present danger

grounds. Needless to say, when reverse discrimination produces such effects, it can be as harmful as other, more obvious forms of discrimination.

WHY PREJUDICE OCCURS: *Some Contrasting Views*

That prejudice exists is an all too obvious fact. Indeed, it seems to have been present in all societies throughout recorded history (refer to Figure 5.4). This fact raises an important question: how do such attitudes origi-

FOCUS ON RESEARCH:
Classic Contributions

Intergroup Conflict in a Summer Camp: The Robbers Cave Experiment

It was the relatively peaceful days of the mid-1950s. Yet, Sherif and his colleagues (Sherif et al., 1961) were deeply concerned with the questions of intergroup conflict and prejudice. In order to understand these important processes more clearly, they decided to conduct an ingenious field investigation. The study involved sending eleven-year-old boys to a special summer camp in a remote area where, free from many external influences, the nature of conflict and other group processes could be carefully observed.

When the boys arrived at the camp, they were divided into two separate groups and were assigned to different cabins located quite far apart (refer to Figure 5.5). For one week, the campers in each of these groups lived and played together, engaging in such enjoyable activities as hiking, swimming, and various sports. During this initial phase, the boys quickly developed strong attachments to their own group. Indeed, they soon named them-

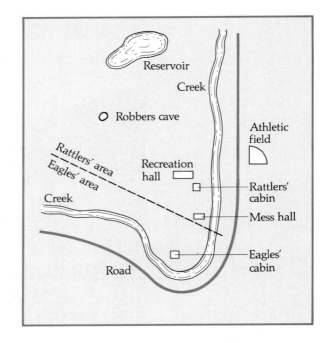

FIGURE 5.5. The summer camp that served as the site of the famous Robbers Cave experiment. Note the distance between the cabins in which the two groups (the Rattlers and Eagles) lived. (Source: Based on information in Sherif et al., 1961.)

Scene of the Robbers Cave experiment

nate? Why, in short, do so many persons hold negative views about people belonging to specific social groups — especially ones different from their own? The answer seems to involve a number of different factors, but among these the following seem most important: (1) direct *intergroup conflict*, (2) *social categorization*, (3) *early learning experiences*, and (4) several aspects of *social cognition*.

selves the Rattlers and the Eagles, stenciled these names onto their shirts, and made up separate flags.

At this point, the second phase of the study was begun. The boys in both groups were told that they would now compete in a tournament consisting of a series of competitions. The winning team would receive a trophy, and its members would earn prizes (pocket knives and medals). Since these were outcomes the boys strongly desired, the stage was set for intense competition. Would such conflict generate prejudice? The answer was quick in coming. As the boys competed, the tension between the groups rose. At first, it was limited to verbal insults, teasing, and name-calling. Soon, though, it escalated into more direct acts. For example, the Eagles burned the Rattlers' flag. The next day, the Rattlers retaliated by attacking their rivals' cabin, overturning beds, tearing out mosquito netting, and taking personal property. Such actions continued until the researchers intervened to avoid any serious consequences. At the same time, the two groups voiced increasingly negative views of one another. They labeled their opponents "sissies," "bums," and "cowards," while perceiving their own group as superior in every way. In short, after only two weeks of conflict, the groups developed all the key components of strong prejudice toward each other.

In a final phase of the study, Sherif and his colleagues attempted to reduce these negative reactions. Merely increasing the amount of contact between the groups failed to accomplish this goal. However, when conditions were arranged so that the groups worked together to reach *superordinate goals* — ones they both desired, dramatic shifts occurred. After working together to restore their water supply (which was "sabotaged" by the researchers), pooling their funds to rent a movie, and jointly repairing a broken-down truck, tensions between the groups largely vanished. Indeed, after six days of such treatment, the boundaries between the groups melted away, and many cross-group friendships were established.

Needless to state, there are major limitations to even this intriguing research. The study took place during a relatively short period of time, the camp setting was a special one, and, perhaps most important of all, the boys were quite homogeneous in background — they did not belong to different social groups. However, taken as a whole, the findings reported by Sherif and his colleagues do provide a chilling picture of how competition over scarce, desired resources can quickly escalate into full-scale conflict and strong feelings of prejudice. In this respect, their research is enlightening indeed.

Direct intergroup conflict: Competition as a source of bias

Unfortunately, the things that most people value — good jobs, money, status — are in short supply: there's never quite enough to go around or keep everyone happy. This basic fact serves as the foundation for one influential explanation of prejudice — **realistic conflict theory.** According to this view, prejudice stems from competition between various social groups over valued commodities. In short, prejudice develops out of the struggle over jobs, adequate housing, good schools, and many other desirable outcomes. The theory further suggests that as such competition continues, the members of the groups involved come to view each other in increasingly negative ways (White, 1977). They label one another as "enemies," view their own group as totally in the right, and draw the boundaries between themselves and their opponents ever more firmly. The result, of course, is that what begins as simple competition soon develops into full-scale prejudice, with all that this implies.

Evidence for the occurrence of this process has been obtained in many different studies. For example, Blake and Mouton (1979) observed its development among corporate executives who, as part of a management-training program, worked in competing small groups. The groups soon entered into intense conflicts, and came to view each other in highly negative ways. Perhaps the most dramatic illustration of the negative impact of intergroup conflict, however, has been provided by Sherif and his colleagues in a famous field study. Please refer to the **Focus** insert on pages 158–159 for a description of this research.

"Us" versus "them": Social categorization as a basis for prejudice

A second perspective on the origins of prejudice begins with a basic fact: often, individuals divide the social world around them into two distinct categories—"us" and "them" (refer to Figure 5.6). In short, they view other persons either as belonging to their own group (usually termed the **ingroup**) or to some other category (an **outgroup**). Moreover, individuals are usually quite expert at making this distinction. Thus, in Northern Ireland, where the population is physically homogeneous, Catholics and Protestants are highly successful in determining whether a stranger belongs to their own group or to the other on the basis of such subtle cues as his or her name, place of residence, and school (Stringer and Cook, 1985).

If this process of **social categorization** stopped there, it would have little bearing upon prejudice. Unfortunately, though, it does not. Sharply contrasting feelings and beliefs are usually attached to members of the ingroup and members of various outgroups. While persons in the former ("us") category are viewed in favorable terms, those in the latter ("them") category are often seen in a negative light. They are assumed to possess undesirable traits, and are strongly disliked (e.g., Hemstone and Jaspars, 1982).

That strong tendencies to divide the social world into these contrasting groups exist has been demonstrated by several revealing studies (e.g., Locksley, Ortiz, and Hepburn, 1980; Tajfel and Turner, 1979). In these investigations, subjects generally expressed more negative attitudes toward members of outgroups and treated them in less favorable ways than members of their own ingroup. Further, this was true even under conditions where these categories were purely arbitrary in nature (they had no existence outside the experiment), and "group" members never met in a face-to-face context. Such findings suggest that in some settings, at least, prejudice may well stem from our tendency to perceive others as belonging either to our own or some other group.

But what forces lie behind this powerful propensity, and behind the corresponding tendency to view people in the two categories in very different ways? One intriguing answer is provided by Tajfel and his colleagues (e.g., Tajfel, 1982a). They suggest that individuals seek to enhance their self-esteem by becoming identified with specific social groups. This tactic will succeed, however, only to the extent that they can perceive these groups as somehow superior to other, competing groups. Since all individuals are subject to the same forces, however, the final result is inevitable: each group seeks to view itself as somehow better than its rivals, and prejudice arises out of this clash of social perceptions. Tajfel terms this process *social competition* to distinguish it from the type of realistic intergroup conflict discussed in the preceding section.

Support for the accuracy of these suggestions has been obtained in several experiments (e.g., Skevington, 1981). For example, in one recent study Meindl and Lerner (1985) reasoned that a failure experience would intensify individuals' needs for enhancing their self-esteem, and so would lead to stronger social categorization. Specifically, they predicted that persons who have just experienced failure will evaluate members of an outgroup in a more extreme manner. To test this possibility, English-speaking Canadians were exposed or not exposed to conditions designed to threaten their self-esteem. They were then asked to express their opinions toward French-speaking Canadians. (In the reduced self-esteem condition, subjects were asked to get a chair and while taking it, "acci-

FIGURE 5.6. Contrary to what this cartoon might suggest, our tendency to divide the social world into two basic categories —"us" and "them" is no laughing matter. In fact, it may play an important role in the occurrence of intergroup prejudice. (Source: Drawing by Ziegler; ©1983 The New Yorker Magazine, Inc.)

Social categorization: One potential cause of prejudice

"I'm surprised, Marty. I thought you were one of us."

dentally" caused a large pile of computer cards to fall onto the floor. Needless to say, the chair was placed so that the slightest movement of it produced this event.) Results offered support for the major hypothesis: subjects who had endured the self-esteem-lowering experience did in fact rate members of an outgroup more extremely than those who had not undergone this event. These and other results offer support for the view that our basic tendency to divide the social world into two camps — us" and "them"— often plays a role in the development of racial, ethnic, and religious prejudice.

Early experience: The role of social learning

You will probably find a third explanation for the occurrence of prejudice far from surprising. It suggests that such reactions are *learned*, and that they develop in much the same manner, and through the same processes, as our other attitudes (refer to our discussion in Chapter 4). Thus, this **social learning view** holds that children acquire negative attitudes toward specific social groups because they are exposed to such views on the part of others (e.g., their parents, friends), or because they are specifically rewarded for adopting them (e.g., with praise for expressing the "right" views).

While parents, teachers, and friends seem to play a key role in this process, the mass media, too, are important. For example, until quite recently members of racial and ethnic minorities appeared infrequently in movies or on television. And when they did appear, they were usually shown in low-status or comic roles. Given repeated exposure to such materials, it is far from surprising that many children soon came to believe that members of such groups must be inferior. After all, why else would they always be shown in such contexts?

Fortunately, the situation has changed greatly in recent years in the United States and elsewhere. Members of various racial and ethnic minorities now appear more frequently than was true in the past, and are often represented in a more favorable manner. Whether these shifts will contribute to reduced racial and ethnic prejudice, however, remains uncertain. Given the tremendous impact of television and other mass media upon both attitudes and behavior (Bandura, 1986; Liebert, Sprafkin, and Davidson, 1982), such benefits seem plausible. However, only time — and systematic research — will reveal whether they do in fact materialize.

Cognitive sources of prejudice: Stereotypes, illusory correlation, and acceptance of outgroup homogeneity

A final source of prejudice is, in some ways, the most unsettling we will consider. It involves the basic ways in which we think about other persons—in short, the key process of *social cognition.* Unfortunately, growing evidence points to the conclusion that several basic aspects of this process may contribute to the development and maintenance of prejudice. Among the most important of these are **stereotypes, illusory correlation,** and the **illusion of outgroup homogeneity.**

Stereotypes: Negative schemata for social groups.   We have already examined the nature of stereotypes in Chapter 3, where we noted that they can be viewed as a special type of *schema*—a kind of cognitive framework for interpreting and processing social information. Specifically, stereotypes consist of knowledge and beliefs about specific social groups, much of it negative in nature. Like other schemata, stereotypes strongly affect the ways in which we deal with (i.e., process) incoming information. For example, information relevant to a particular stereotype is processed more quickly than information not related to that stereotype (Dovidio, Evans, and Tyler, 1986). Similarly, stereotypes lead the persons holding them to pay attention to specific types of information—usually input that is consistent with the stereotypes. Or, if inconsistent information does become the subject of attention, strongly entrenched stereotypes may induce the individuals involved to engage in efforts to refute it, perhaps by recalling facts that *are* consistent with their schemata (O'Sullivan and Durso, 1984). Third, stereotypes also determine what we remember; usually, again, we remember information that is consistent with them.

Now, consider how these effects apply to prejudice. Once an individual has acquired a stereotype (a negative schema) for some social group, he or she tends to notice information that fits readily into this cognitive framework, and to remember "facts" that are consistent with it. Thus, the stereotype is, to a large degree, self-confirming: even exceptions to it make it stronger, for they simply induce the person in question to bring supporting information to mind! (Refer to our discussion in Chapter 4.)

Evidence for the operation of such negative schemata has been reported in several recent studies. For example, Dovidio, Evans, and Tyler (1986) presented subjects with the words "white" and "black," and then asked them to decide whether various traits (also presented one at a time) could ever be true of each of these racial groups. The subjects—all of whom were white—were faster in deciding whether positive traits described whites, but faster in deciding whether negative traits described blacks. Thus, their cognitive representations of these two groups appeared to differ sharply. An even more disturbing illustration of the operation of racial stereotypes has recently been reported by Greenberg and Pyszcynski (1985). These researchers arranged for white students to watch a debate between a black and a white. For half the subjects the black seemed to lose the debate, while for the other half he appeared to win. At the conclusion of the debate, subjects were asked to evaluate the performance of both participants. Before having a chance to do so, one-third heard another person (an accomplice) make a racist remark ("There's no way that n——r won the debate.") A second third heard a

FIGURE 5.7.   When white subjects heard an accomplice make a racial remark about a black debator, they lowered their evaluation of this person. However, this was the case only when he appeared to lose the debate. (Source: Based on data from Greenberg and Pyszcynski, 1985.)

Racial slurs and the activation of negative racial schemata

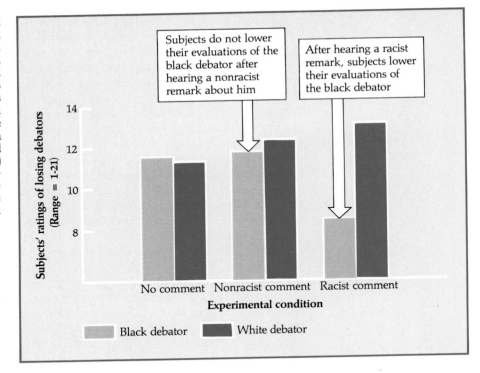

nonracist remark ("There's no way that debator won the debate.") Finally, subjects in a control group heard no remark by the accomplice. Greenberg and Pyszcynski reasoned that the racial slur would activate negative racial schemata (stereotypes) among subjects, and so lower their evaluations of the black debator. However, this would be the case only when he lost. When, in contrast, he appeared to win, subjects would compensate for the impact of their schemata, and would not lower their ratings of this person. As you can see from Figure 5.7, results confirmed these predictions. Overhearing a racist comment did in fact lower subjects' evaluations of the black debator, but only when he lost.

Illusory correlation: Perceiving relationships that aren't there.   Unfortunately, negative schemata are not the only cognitive source of prejudice and discrimination. Another involves *illusory correlation* — a topic we have already considered in Chapters 3 and 4 (Hamilton, Dugan, and Trolier, 1985; Hamilton and Gifford, 1976). As you may recall, illusory correlation refers to our tendency to perceive associations (correlations) between variables that do not, in fact, exist. It seems to stem primarily from the co-occurrence of distinctive stimuli or events. For example, consider the following facts. Violent crimes are fairly rare events, even in the United States, which has a higher rate of such events than other developed nations. For this reason, violent crimes are quite distinctive. Similarly, being a member of a minority group is also a distinctive event;

there are, after all, many more members of the majority. Because these two events are relatively unusual, their co-occurrence is highly distinctive. Thus, a report of a violent crime committed by a person of Cuban descent will draw the attention of majority readers. Such heightened attention, in turn, assures that the event is entered strongly into memory. As a result, it will be readily recalled on later occasions — more readily than other, less distinctive events (e.g., the report of a violent crime by a white person). Because of this process, an illusory correlation may develop: individuals may come to perceive that ethnic identity is closely linked to violent crime. Moreover, and here is the important point, they may reach this conclusion even if the rate of violent crime is equal in both the minority and majority groups. In short, illusory correlations, which seem to develop because of our basic tendency to pay most attention to unusual or distinctive events, can sometimes play a role in the development of stereotypes and prejudice (Spears, van der Pligt, and Eiser, 1985).

The illusion of outgroup homogeneity.   A third cognitive factor worthy of our attention involves what has sometimes been termed the *illusion of outgroup homogeneity*. Briefly, this refers to our tendency to perceive the members of outgroups as much more similar or homogeneous than members of our own ingroup (Linville, 1982). At first glance, it is tempting to assume that this tendency stems from a simple fact: we have more contact with members of our own group, and so develop richer and more differentiated cognitive representations of them. However, research findings suggest that this is not the only factor involved. The illusion of greater homogeneity among persons belonging to groups other than our own seems to exist even in cases where we have a great deal of contact with them. For example, males perceive women as more homogeneous in their attitudes and behavior than men, while females perceive men as being more homogeneous than women, despite the fact that the two groups are in continuous, intimate contact with one another (Park and Rothbart, 1982). Apparently, then, our tendency to perceive the members of groups other than our own as all "very much alike" reflects a very basic type of bias in the way we think about others.

Together, stereotypes, illusory correlations, and perception of outgroup homogeneity go a long way toward explaining the occurrence — and persistence — of prejudice. Such attitudes, it appears, rest upon basic aspects of social cognition as well as intergroup conflict, early social learning, and the desire to enhance one's self-esteem. The practical message contained in such findings seems clear: in order to be successful, techniques designed to combat prejudice and reduce its negative impact must take careful account of its cognitive as well as its social foundations.

COMBATING PREJUDICE: *Some Plans of Action*

Prejudice, wherever and whenever it occurs, poses serious problems. In its least harmful forms, it can be viewed as a thorn in the side of society

—one producing unnecessary annoyance, friction, and irritation. At worst, it is like an open wound—one through which a given culture or nation can be drained of its vitality, precious human resources, and social conscience. Reducing prejudice and combating its negative effects, therefore, are important tasks. But how can they be accomplished? Fortunately, several strategies for reaching these goals exist. While none, by itself, can totally eliminate prejudice or discrimination, together they seem capable of making substantial "dents" in these persistent problems. Four of these tactics will now be described.

Breaking the chain of bigotry: On learning not to hate

At several points in this book, we have noted that parents play a key role in shaping their children's attitudes. Included among the many views that they transmit in this respect are various forms of prejudice. In short, children are certainly *not* born with hatreds for persons belonging to various social groups. On the contrary, they acquire these from their mothers and fathers through the basic learning processes described in Chapter 4 (e.g., modeling, operant conditioning; refer to Figure 5.8). Given this central fact, one useful technique for combating prejudice and discrimination is obvious: somehow, discourage parents from providing their offspring with training in ethnic or racial bigotry. As we're sure you realize, this is a difficult task. Psychologists cannot intervene directly in parent-child relations. Doing so would be unethical, if not simply illegal. What they *can* do, however, is call parents' attention to their own crucial role in maintaining the chain of bigotry. While some die-hard fanatics may actually wish to turn their children into hate-filled copies of themselves, most parents genuinely wish to provide them with a more positive view of the social world. Thus, campaigns designed to enhance parents' awareness of this process, and to discourage them from demonstrating prejudice in their own behavior, may yield positive results.

There is no reason why attempts to "nip prejudice in the bud" must end there, however. Teachers, too, can play a positive role. One dramatic illustration of this fact was provided some years ago by Jane Elliot, an Iowa schoolteacher. In an attempt to help her all-white class of third-graders grasp the negative impact of prejudice, Ms. Elliot divided her students into two groups on the basis of eye color. On the first day of the demonstration, the brown-eyed group was assigned an inferior status. They were ridiculed by the teacher, who stated that they were duller, lazier, and sloppier than blue-eyed children. They were denied classroom privileges, and as a sign of their low status, were made to wear a special collar. This treatment continued for several days, and then was reversed, so that blue-eyed students now became the victims of totally irrational prejudice.

As you can probably guess, youngsters in both groups found the experience of being the victims of unfair discrimination quite upsetting. Indeed, it even lowered their performance on standard classroom tasks.

FIGURE 5.8. As suggested by this picture, children often acquire various forms of prejudice from their parents. Both modeling and operant conditioning seem to play an important role in this process.

Prejudice: How, often, it's acquired

The purpose of the demonstration, of course, was that of providing the children with an opportunity to experience the evils of discrimination in a direct manner. It was hoped that in this way, their own tendency to engage in such behavior in the future would be sharply reduced. (A vivid pictorial record of the entire demonstration is presented in the documentary film, *The Eye of the Storm*.)

Direct intergroup contact: The potential benefits of acquaintance

Answer honestly: how frequently do you have contact with people from outside your own racial, ethnic or religious group? For example, if you are white, how often do you interact with blacks? If you are Christian, how often do you interact with individuals who are Jews? Unless you are different from most persons, or live in an environment that actively encourages such cross-group contacts, your reply is probably "Not very often." Even in the late 1980s most people have most of their social contacts with persons belonging to their ingroup. Of course, the situation is partially reversed for members of various minority groups; many of their contacts are, by necessity, with persons belonging to the majority (Ickes, 1984). Even here, however, a high proportion of social interaction takes place with other members of their own group.

This basic fact raises an intriguing question: can prejudice be reduced by somehow increasing the degree of contact between different groups? The idea that it can is known as the **contact hypothesis,** and there are several good reasons for predicting that such a strategy might prove effective (Stephan, 1985). First, as individuals belonging to different social groups become better acquainted, they may come to realize that they are more similar than they initially believed. As we will see in Chapter 6, growing recognition of such similarity, in turn, may generate increased mutual attraction. Second, while stereotypes *are* resistant to change, they can be altered when sufficient information inconsistent with them is encountered. Thus, as persons from different groups get to know one another better, these negative schemata may begin to crumble, or at least to change. Third, increased contact may help counter the illusion of outgroup homogeneity described above. For these and other reasons, it seems possible that direct intergroup contact may be effective in combating prejudice. Is it? The answer, unfortunately, is somewhat mixed. Such contact does seem capable of producing beneficial effects, but only when it occurs under highly specific conditions (Cook, 1985).

First, the groups interacting must be roughly equal in social, economic or task-related status. If, instead, they differ sharply in such respects, communication between them may be difficult, and prejudice can actually increase. Second, the contact situation must involve cooperation and interdependence, so that the groups work toward shared goals. Third, contact between the groups must be informal, so they can get to know each other on a one-to-one basis. Fourth, contact must occur in a setting where existing norms favor group equality and increased association between persons belonging to each category. Fifth, the groups must interact in ways that permit disconfirmation of negative, stereotyped beliefs about each other. And finally, the persons involved must view one another as typical of their respective groups; only if they do will they generalize their pleasant contacts to other persons or situations, and demonstrate more positive reactions toward the outgroup (Wilder, 1984).

When contact between initially hostile groups occurs under the conditions just described, prejudice between them does seem to decrease (Cook, 1985; Riordin, 1978). For example, in a series of related studies, Aronson and his colleagues have employed increased contact under cooperative conditions as a means of reducing racial prejudice among children (e.g., Aronson, Bridgeman, and Geffner, 1978). The basic procedure they used—the jigsaw method—was simple. Groups of six students worked together on a specific lesson. Each member of the group was required to master a single portion and present it to the others. Successful group performance could be attained only if each person performed adequately. Thus, all members had to cooperate in order to attain a shared group goal. The results achieved with this simple procedure were impressive. Following exposure to the jigsaw method (and the cooperative intergroup contact it involved), students showed reduced racial stereotyping and increased liking for members of the other race.

Additional encouraging results along these lines have been reported by Cook and his co-workers (e.g., Cook, 1984a). In this research, subjects participate along with two accomplices — one black and one white — in a management game involving the movement of imaginary railroad cars over several different routes. The game is complex and requires a number of difficult decisions. While results, too, have been complex, they generally point to the following conclusion: friendly, cooperative contact between persons belonging to different social groups *can* promote respect and liking between them. Thus, if used with care and considered judgment, direct group contact may be an effective tool for combating cross-group hostility and prejudice. (In the United States, the contact hypothesis has been put to actual use in the context of *school desegregation*. For some comments on how it has fared — and why — please see the **Applied Side** insert on pages 170–171.)

Mindfulness or mindlessness? Reducing prejudice by learning to make distinctions

In Chapter 3 we noted that people are "cognitive misers": they do as little thinking or other cognitive work as they can get away with. Langer and her colleagues (Langer, 1983) summarize this fact by the term **mindlessness.** This means that most of the time we process information in a passive, automatic manner. For example, when meeting someone for the first time, we rely on categories or distinctions we already have at our disposal, rather than actively formulating new ones. Unfortunately, this tendency has direct bearing on prejudice. Once we notice that another person belongs to a specific social group, our reactions may be dominated by this single characteristic. Indeed, we may fail to notice other important facts about this individual. As we have already seen, such biased, stereotyped thinking often lies at the heart of various types of prejudice. Can anything be done to counter this tendency and to induce people to behave more *mindfully* toward others? A study conducted by Langer, Bashner, and Chanowitz (1985) offers a positive reply.

In this experiment, one group of sixth-grade children was exposed to procedures designed to increase their tendency to think about handicapped persons in a mindful way. This training consisted of showing subjects slides of handicapped people, and then asking them to answer complex questions about them. For example, one such question required subjects to list four reasons why a specific handicapped person might make a good newscaster, and four reasons why she might make a poor one. Another task required explaining how a handicapped person might be able to drive a car. In contrast, subjects in a second group answered simpler questions, designed to leave them in their usual "mindless" state.

After these procedures were completed, subjects' reactions to handicapped persons were assessed. Langer and her colleagues predicted that those who had been trained to adopt a mindful set would demonstrate less prejudice toward such persons, and results supported this hypoth-

ON THE APPLIED SIDE

The Contact Hypothesis in Action: School Desegregation in the United States

During the 1960s and 1970s, the United States embarked on what can be viewed in some respects as one of the largest social experiments in history. This "experiment" involved efforts to desegregate the nation's schools which, prior to that time, had been sharply divided along racial lines. (Blacks attended some schools, while whites attended others.) These efforts were the direct result of a U.S. Supreme Court decision declaring that segregated schools were illegal, and to say that they were greeted with mixed reactions is a huge understatement. At one extreme was a large group of persons who felt that forced busing and other practices often used to achieve desegregation infringed on their basic rights. Further, such individuals often felt — perhaps because of racial prejudice — that increased contact between black and white children would yield undesirable rather than beneficial results. For example, they predicted that the educational achievements of both groups would suffer, and that forced contact would intensify rather than reduce racial prejudice. At the other end of the continuum was another group who believed that desegregation was a moral necessity in a nation committed to equal opportunity for all. In addition, such persons also expressed hope that desegregation would improve the opportunities of minority children, and might also reduce prejudice on the part of both blacks and whites.

What have been the results of this vast undertaking? Have the hopes of its supporters been realized? Or have the fears of its opponents proved valid? The answer, once again, is something of a mixed bag. Studies undertaken to assess the results of desegregation (some of them long-term and large-scale in nature) have yielded a confusing picture (e.g., Gerard, 1983; Miller and Brewer, 1984). On the one hand, it is clear that educational achievement among both blacks and whites has *not* improved in the decades since efforts at school desegregation were begun. If anything, it has declined. Is this due to the disruptions associated with efforts to attain fully integrated schools, or are other factors to blame? At present, it is impossible to say.

In contrast, evidence with respect to shifts in racial attitudes is a bit more promising. Here, some indication that desegregation has resulted in better cross-race relations, and in at least some reductions in stereotyping and prejudice, exists (e.g., Cook, 1984a, 1984b; Miller and Brewer, 1984). Results have certainly not been uniformly positive, but some findings, at least, point to beneficial outcomes.

So, in sum, we are left facing a mixed picture. But this in itself is puzzling: after all, the contact hypothesis described earlier seems to suggest that increased contact between social groups will often reduce prejudice between them. Why has this prediction not been strongly confirmed? The answer, it seems, lies in the following fact: in arranging for desegregation, government and school authorities have often overlooked several of the conditions that are essential if direct intergroup contact is to yield beneficial effects (Cook, 1985). For example, little attention has been directed to assuring that the students in contact are of roughly equal status. On the contrary, the typical pattern has been one in which minority children from disadvantaged backgrounds are suddenly placed in schools where the white youngsters enjoy higher socioeconomic status. Similarly, far from supporting intergroup contact, the norms surrounding such schools have often been dead set against it; indeed, integration has frequently taken place within a context of angry demonstra-

FIGURE 5.9. School desegregation has failed to yield some of the benefits predicted by its advocates. One reason for these disappointing results is that it has often taken place under the conditions shown here.

Schools desegregation: One reason for its disappointing results

tions and protests (refer to Figure 5.9). Given such conditions, it is hardly surprising that school desegregation has often failed to yield the benefits predicted by its advocates. Indeed, it is hard to see how results could be otherwise.

To conclude: while school desegregation has not, as yet, yielded many of the benefits its supporters once predicted, there is still considerable room for hope. If key factors determining the ultimate impact of intergroup contact are taken carefully into account, the effects of this "grand social experiment" may yet be positive. If they are not, it may continue to prove disappointing in the years ahead.

esis. Thus, subjects exposed to the mindfulness training reported being much more willing to go on a picnic with a handicapped person than subjects not given such training. Similarly, they showed a greater tendency to choose handicapped persons as their partners in tasks where the handicap might actually be an advantage (e.g., a blind child as partner in a game of pin the tail on the donkey). This suggested that they were thinking about these persons in terms of their abilities and disabilities, *not* simply as members of a particular social category.

These results, and those obtained in related studies (e.g., Langer and Imber, 1980) suggest that teaching individuals to think actively about others, rather than to go along with previously established categories or distinctions, can be a useful strategy for overcoming prejudice. Paradoxically, the more discriminating we are in our thinking about others, the less likely we may be to treat them as members of some abstract social category rather than as unique individuals.

SEXISM IN THE 1980s: A Closer Look at One Form of Prejudice

Females constitute a clear majority of the world's population. Yet, they have often been treated much like a minority in many cultures. They have often been excluded from economic and political power. They have been the subject of pronounced negative stereotyping, and they have had to confront overt discrimination in many spheres of life (e.g., exclusion from certain jobs, kinds of training, social organizations). Fortunately, the situation appears to be changing in many nations. Overt discriminatory practices are decreasing, and there has been at least some shift toward more egalitarian sex-role attitudes on the part of both men and women (Helmreich, Spence, and Gibson, 1982). Despite such changes, though, prejudice based on sex persists in many settings (e.g., Crosby, 1982; Steinberg and Shapiro, 1982). Because this type of prejudice affects more individuals than any other kind, and because it produces negative outcomes for both men and women (refer to Figure 5.10), it is a serious problem, fully deserving of our special attention.

Prejudice toward females: Its nature and origins

As we noted earlier, females have often been the object of widespread stereotyping. To an extent, this is also true of males; they, too, are perceived as being "all alike"—all possessing certain traits. Usually, though, stereotypes concerning females are more negative in content than those for males. For example, in several cultures males are assumed to possess such traits as assertiveness, ambition, self-confidence, decisiveness, and dominance. In contrast, the corresponding stereotype for females includes such characteristics as submissiveness, concern with

FIGURE 5.10. Overt discrimination on the basis of sex has decreased in recent years. However, many persons continue to hold sexist attitudes, at least to some degree. (Source: *Crock* by Rechin & Wilder ©Field Enterprises, Inc. 1981. Permission of News America Syndicate.)

Sexist attitudes: Still with us in the 1980s

others, dependence, emotionality, and passivity (Williams and Best, 1982).

That such stereotypes exist is no longer open to question: their presence is supported by a large body of research evidence (e.g., Deaux and Lewis, 1986). Two important questions relating to them, however, are these: (1) to what extent are they accurate? and (2) why do they persist?

Stereotypes about women and men: Myth or reality?   To what extent do men and women actually differ, either in their behavior or in their traits? This is a complex question that can be addressed on several different levels. Thus, no simple or clear-cut answer yet exists. Existing evidence, however, seems to point to the following general conclusion: where differences between the sexes are concerned, "common sense" probably overstates the case. Males and females do indeed seem to differ in several respects (e.g., Parsons, Adler, and Meece, 1984), but the number and size of such differences is less than prevailing stereotypes suggest.

For example, in a series of related studies, Rice and his colleagues (e.g., Rice, Instone, and Adams, 1984) have compared the behavior of male and female cadets at West Point (the United States Military Academy). Results indicated that few, if any, differences could be observed. Similarly, in other investigations (e.g., Steinberg and Shapiro, 1982) male and female managers have been compared in terms of a large number of personality dimensions. In general, results offer little support for the view that they differ in important ways.

Together, such findings suggest that stereotypes concerning differences between the sexes are only partly true at best (Eagly and Carli, 1981). While the behavior of males and females does differ in some respects, these differences are smaller, both in degree and number, than has often been assumed. In sum, there appears to be more myth than reality in such cultural stereotypes.

Gender stereotypes: Why do they persist?   If, as we have just seen, stereotypes about the supposed traits of males and females are largely inaccurate, why do they exist? If men and women really don't differ very much, in either behavior or traits, why do so many people continue to believe that they do? Again, this is a complex question, with no simple answers. However, research conducted recently by Eagly and her associates (e.g., Eagly and Steffen, 1983) points to an intriguing possibility:

perhaps these stereotypes have their foundations in the fact that males and females often occupy somewhat different roles in society. Even today, after several decades of rapid social change, a larger proportion of males are employed in full-time jobs outside the home. It may be that individuals who fill such positions, *regardless of their sex*, are perceived as possessing the traits often ascribed to males (e.g., assertiveness, self-assurance, decisiveness). Correspondingly, a larger proportion of females than males are homemakers, with no employment outside this context. Persons filling this role may be perceived as possessing the traits often attributed to females (e.g., selflessness, concern with others). In short, gender stereotypes may persist because men and women are not equally distributed across these contrasting social roles.

In order to investigate this possibility, Eagly and Steffen (1984) asked male and female students to rate imaginary persons described as being employed either full time outside the home or as a homemaker, and as being either a man or a woman. The traits on which subjects rated these persons were ones included in traditional stereotypes for both sexes. (In a third condition, no information about occupation was given, but each individual was still identified as being either a man or a woman.) Results offered strong support for the view that stereotypes persist because

FIGURE 5.11. Individuals who were described as holding full-time jobs were rated as more masculine in their traits than individuals who were described as being homemakers. Further, this was true regardless of whether they were men or women. (Source: Based on data from Eagly and Steffen, 1984.)

Social roles: A basis for gender stereotypes

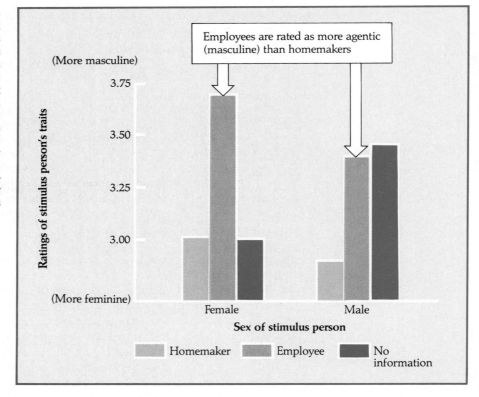

males and females occupy different roles in society. As shown in Figure 5.11, homemakers were rated as being more feminine (in their traits) than persons employed full-time outside the home, *regardless of whether they were men or women.* Similarly, employed persons were rated as being more masculine (in their traits) than homemakers, again regardless of whether they happened to be men or women. Thus, it was the role individuals played, not their actual sex, that determined how they were perceived.

As we're sure you can readily appreciate, these findings are quite optimistic in their implications. They suggest that as women enter new fields and take on new roles, traditional stereotypes about them may fade. They will come to be perceived (and evaluated) mainly in terms of the roles they fill, rather than on the basis of their sex. To the extent this is the case, substantial changes in prevailing gender stereotypes may well lie ahead.

Discrimination against females: Subtle, but sometimes deadly

Although the Equal Rights Amendment failed to gain passage in the United States, other legislation and court rulings have gone a long way toward eliminating overt discrimination on the basis of sex. It is no longer feasible for businesses, schools, or other organizations to reject applicants for jobs or admission simply because they are female (or male). Yet, despite this fact, women continue to occupy a relatively disadvantaged position in society, at least in some respects. For example, they still tend to be concentrated in relatively low-paying and low-status jobs. As Steinberg and Shapiro (1982, p. 306) have noted: "Women populate corporations but they rarely run them." Why is this the case? The answer seems to involve a number of subtle, but often damaging, forces that operate against success and achievement by females in many settings. Several of these are considered below.

Subjective task value and career choice. In recent years, only 6 percent of the bachelor's degrees in engineering and 18 percent of those in computer science were awarded to women, despite the fact that females make up approximately 50 percent of college enrollment. Clearly, such differences are not due to overt discrimination: few colleges or universities currently tolerate barriers designed to prevent persons of either sex from choosing specific majors. What, then, accounts for this state of affairs? Findings reported by Parsons and her colleagues (Parsons, Adler, and Meece, 1984) indicate that it may stem from differences in the *subjective value* attached by males and females to different fields of study.

When these researchers questioned a large group of junior high school students, they found that females rated English as more important than math, while males rated the two subjects as equally important. Similarly, females expressed stronger interest in taking further English courses than did males. Since jobs in many high-paying fields (e.g., engineering, information science) require considerable background in mathematics, and since top executives are often drawn from such areas, these findings point to one potential reason why women often hold second-class status in the world of work: they select career routes that lead to less rewarding jobs. The question of *why* they choose such paths is very complex, and probably involves contrasting socialization practices for males and females (e.g., little boys are encouraged to work with tools and numbers, while little girls are not), as well as persisting stereotypes about the relative abilities of the two sexes (e.g., many persons assume that males possess superior quantitative skills and that females possess superior verbal ones). Regardless of the precise mechanisms involved, though, the tendency of females and males to value certain kinds of tasks differentially probably plays an important role in their selection of contrasting careers, and in the levels of work-related status and success they ultimately attain (Parsons and Goff, 1980).

Denying credit where credit is due: Attributions about male and female achievement. Suppose that you were asked to evaluate the performance of two subordinates. Both were performing at the same satisfactory level, but the causes behind these outcomes were somewhat different. The first person was doing well because she was working as hard as possible — she was investing a great deal of effort in her job. The second was doing well because, just by accident, she had been given relatively easy tasks to perform. To whom would you give the higher evaluation? The chances are good that you would choose the first individual; after all, effort seems more worthy of praise than simple good luck. In short, you would view good performance that seemed to stem from ability or effort as more deserving of recognition than similar performance deriving from luck or an easy task (e.g., Mitchell and Kalb, 1982).

All of this probably strikes you as quite reasonable, and it is. But now consider the following fact: research findings suggest that many persons demonstrate a tendency to attribute successful performance by males to *internal* factors, such as effort or ability, but similar performance by females to *external* causes, such as luck or an easy task (e.g., Deaux, 1982; Nieva and Gutek, 1981). In short, if a man succeeds in performing some task, it is assumed that he worked hard or that he possessed a high level of ability. If a female attains the same level of performance, however, it is assumed that she merely "lucked out" or that the task wasn't very difficult (refer to Figure 5.12).

Since important rewards such as raises and promotions usually depend on such evaluations, it is clear that these tendencies operate against success by females in many business settings. Fortunately, they do not seem to exist in all contexts. In particular, when the attention of persons making such evaluations is directed firmly to the actual performance of those being judged, such bias may vanish (Izraeli, Izraeli, and Eden, 1985). In other contexts, though, it may persist, and continue to exert damaging effects upon the careers of deserving female employees. (For

FIGURE 5.12. When males succeed at some task, their performance is often attributed to internal causes, such as high ability or effort. In contrast, when females succeed, *their* performance is often attributed to external causes, such as luck or an easy task. Recent findings indicate that these tendencies may be fading, but their impact still persists in at least some settings.

Contrasting attributions for successful performance by males and females

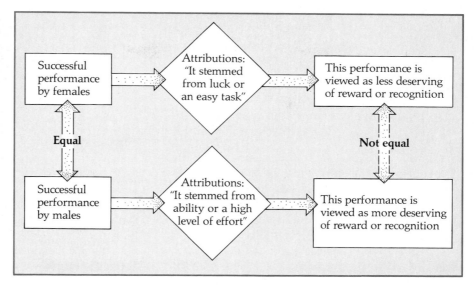

discussion of a third factor that may operate against females in many employment settings—lower expectations—please refer to the **Focus** insert on pages 178–179.)

An optimistic conclusion: Sexism in the world of work —going, going . . . ?"

OK, now that we're near the end of this chapter, it's about time for a personal admission. On a scale ranging from pessimism on the one hand through optimism on the other, we fall pretty far along toward the latter. We feel that few persons are really hardened bigots, so filled with hatred toward specific social groups that they will do everything in their power to harm the targets of their prejudice. On the contrary, we strongly believe that most people are basically reasonable and decent. They do *not* wish to harm others who have done nothing to injure them and, at the very least, adopt a live-and-let-live attitude toward the members of groups outside their own. When they demonstrate prejudice, they often do so because, as we noted earlier, their cognitive systems are on "automatic": they simply haven't thought through the implications of their beliefs or behaviors. Once the unreasonable or harmful nature of these tendencies becomes clear, many *are* willing to change, at least to a degree.

We believe that this has been the case with respect to sexism in recent years. As many persons of both sexes have come to understand the basic unfairness of many existing practices, considerable change has taken place. Perhaps nowhere is this shift more visible than in the world of work. For example, while less than 5 percent of first-line managers were females two decades ago, about 30 percent are females at present. That

Getting What You Expect
and Expecting What You Get:
Differences in the Pay Expectations of
Males and Females

Expectations, it seems, often have a self-fulfilling impact. When people expect others to like them, they often behave in ways that cause these beliefs to be confirmed. Similarly, when they expect others to reject them, they act in ways that confirm *these* predictions (Snyder, 1985). Extending this principle to the realm of discrimination based on gender, it seems possible that this is another factor operating against females in many settings. Put simply, they may have lower expectations concerning rewards or outcomes than males (e.g., Major and Deaux, 1982). Unsettling evidence that this is the case has been reported by Major and Konar (1984).

These researchers asked male and female business students to estimate their future starting and peak salaries. In addition, these subjects were also asked to estimate the starting and peak salaries of other persons in their fields. Still other questions asked them to rate the importance of several career outcomes(e.g., high pay, interesting work, promotional opportunities). Results pointed to the existence of important differences between the sexes on all of these measures. For example, as you can see from Figure 5.13, females expected starting and peak salaries considerably lower than did males. Similarly, they offered lower estimates for the starting and peak salaries of others in their field. That such differences really count is suggested by the re-

sults of follow-up research (Major, Vanderslice, and McFarlin, 1985). Here, it was found that the higher the starting salaries individuals requested, the more money they were actually paid.

Insight into the factors responsible for these differences was provided by subjects' responses to other questions. Females rated high salary and promotional opportunities as *less* important to them than did males, but rated interesting work as *more* crucial. Together, these findings suggest that one reason females frequently attain lower outcomes and less financial success than males in employment settings involves their expectations: women receive smaller benefits because this is what they expect. The question of *why* females hold lower expectations than males, of course, remains puzzling. One possibility, suggested by Major and Konar (1984), is that this difference simply reflects social reality: women realize, from what they see around them, that females usually *do* receive less pay than men. Thus, they adjust their expectations accordingly. To the extent this is true, current efforts to eliminate sex discrimination in the world of work may well yield double benefits. On the one hand they may lessen the pay gap that now exists between men and women, while on the other, they may help overcome one of the internal barriers that prevents full equality in this respect.

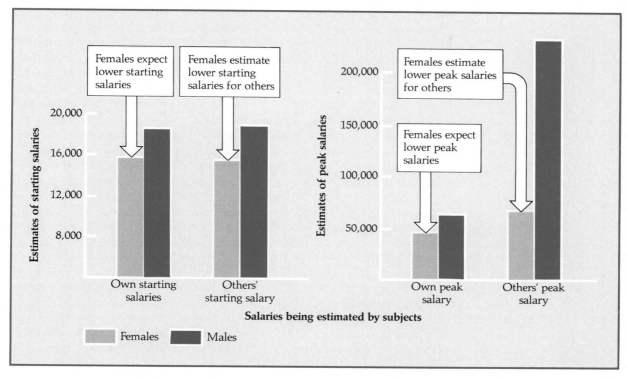

FIGURE 5.13. Female business students expected to receive lower starting and peak salaries than male business students. In addition, they also offered lower estimates for starting and peak salaries for other persons in their field. (Source: Based on data from Major and Konar, 1984.)

Sex differences in pay expectations: One factor operating against females

such shifts have been accompanied by corresponding reductions in prejudice toward women is suggested by a growing number of studies reporting little, if any, evidence for sexism in several areas, including ones where such bias was formerly noted. For example, contrary to earlier findings (e.g., Bartol and Butterfield, 1976), a recent investigation by Izraeli and Izraeli (1985) found no tendency for their male or female managers to evaluate female leaders less favorably than males. Similarly, in a large-scale study involving evaluations of the performance of more than six hundred male and female store managers by their male and female supervisors, Peters and his colleagues (Peters et al., 1984) found no indication of discrimination against females. Indeed, both male and female supervisors actually assigned *higher* performance ratings to female managers than to male managers. Finally, Schwab and Grams (1985) recently noted that experts in employment compensation did *not* rate jobs filled predominantly by females as less compensable (i.e., less deserving of various rewards) than ones filled mainly by males.

When these and other findings are combined, a picture of major change — and a shift toward reduced sex discrimination — emerges. Females, it appears, *are* receiving more equitable treatment in many employment settings than was true in the past. Of course, this is not to suggest that the battle for full equality is over, and that victory is already at hand — far from it. Women still face serious barriers and problems in work settings (e.g., they continue to be the victims of sexual harassment to a much greater extent than males; Gutek, 1985). We do feel, though, that the campaign is going well, and that further progress is likely to occur in the years ahead. Of course, only time will reveal whether such optimism on our part is justified. Unless (or until) we are confronted with convincing evidence to the contrary, though, we intend to remain quite hopeful.

SUMMARY

Prejudice involves the tendency to evaluate others negatively simply because they belong to a specific social group. **Discrimination** refers to specific harmful actions directed toward the persons or groups that are the targets of prejudice. Discrimination is sometimes overt, but frequently it takes subtle forms. Among the most damaging of these are reluctance to offer aid to members of disliked groups, *tokenism*, and *reverse discrimination.*

Several explanations for the existence of prejudice have been offered. *Realistic conflict theory* suggests that it derives primarily from competition between various groups for possession of valued resources (e.g., jobs, status). *Social categorization* — our tendency to divide the social world into two distinct groups ("us" and "them") also plays a role. Prejudice may also stem from early *social learning experiences*, in which children are exposed to prejudiced attitudes on the part of others, or are actively rewarded for holding them. Finally, prejudice seems to derive, in at least in part, from basic aspects of *social cognition.* These include the operation of *stereotypes, illusory correlation,* and the *illusion of outgroup homogeneity.*

Several tactics appear to be effective in reducing prejudice. Changes in child-rearing practices and in the way members of various groups are depicted in the mass media may be useful. *Increased contact* between persons belonging to different groups can succeed, but only when such contacts occur under favorable conditions (e.g., equal status, in the context of norms supporting cross-group ties). Teaching individuals to adopt a *mindful* rather than a *mindless* approach in evaluating others may also yield beneficial effects.

Sexism, prejudice based on sex, has received a great deal of attention from social psychologists in recent years. Stereotypes concerning the supposed traits of the two sexes appear to be misleading; males and females do not differ to the extent that they suggest. Such views persist, however, because males and females occupy different roles in society (e.g., a greater proportion of males is employed outside the home). While overt discrimination against females has decreased, some factors continue to operate against their success. These include a tendency on the part of many persons to attribute successful performance by females to external factors (e.g., luck) but similar performance by males to internal causes (e.g., effort or ability), and lower reward expectations on the part of females.

GLOSSARY

contact hypothesis
The suggestion that increased contact between members of various social groups will be effective in reducing prejudice between them. Such effects seem to occur only when contact takes place under specific, positive conditions.

discrimination
Negative behaviors directed toward members of social groups who are the object of prejudice.

illusion of outgroup homogeneity
The tendency to assume that members of various outgroups are more similar to one another than are the members of one's own ingroup.

illusory correlation
The perception of an association (correlation) between two variables when in fact no such relationship exists. This form of cognitive bias appears to be based primarily on the co-occurrence of highly distinctive events.

ingroup
The social group to which an individual perceives herself or himself as belonging.

mindlessness
Our tendency to process information about other persons in a passive,

automatic manner (e.g., on the basis of previously established categories and distinctions).

outgroup
A group other than the one to which individuals feel they belong.

prejudice
Negative attitudes toward the members of specific social groups.

realistic conflict theory
The view that prejudice often stems from direct competition between various social groups over valued outcomes (e.g., jobs, status).

reverse discrimination
The tendency to evaluate or treat members of outgroups (especially racial or ethnic minorities) more favorably than members of one's own ingroup.

sexism
Prejudice based on gender.

social categorization
Our basic tendency to divide the social world into two separate categories: "us" and "them."

social learning view (of prejudice)
The view that prejudice is acquired through basic mechanisms of learning (modeling, operant conditioning).

stereotypes
Beliefs and expectations (generally negative) about the members of specific social groups. Stereotypes can be viewed as negative schemata relating to such groups.

tokenism
Instances in which individuals perform trivial positive actions for members of groups toward whom they are prejudiced, and then use such behavior as an excuse for avoiding more meaningful beneficial actions toward them.

FOR MORE INFORMATION

Gutek, B. A. (1985). *Sex and the workplace.* San Francisco: Jossey-Bass.
> A thoughtful analysis of sexual harrassment and related issues in work settings. Individual chapters examine the causes of sexual harrassment, the attitudes of men and women toward such behavior, and techniques for coping with this important problem.

Miller, N., and Brewer, M. B. (1984). *Groups in conflict; The psychology of desegregation.* New York: Academic Press.
> This book focuses primarily on the *contact hypothesis* — the view that increased contact between groups can reduce the level of prejudice between them. Separate chapters describe attempts to investigate this hypothesis in a wide range of situations. Suggestions for enhancing the outcomes of desegregation are also considered.

Stephan, W. G. (1985). Intergroup relations. In G. Lindzey and E. Aronson (eds.), *Handbook of social psychology*, 3rd ed. New York: Random House.
   A thorough review of current knowledge about intergroup relations by a well-known researcher in this area. Many processes that play a role in the development of prejudice, as well as several techniques for combating such reactions, are examined. This is an excellent place to begin if you'd like to know more about prejudice and related topics.

CHAPTER 6

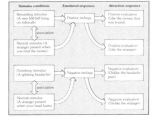

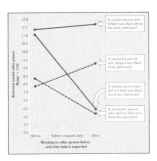

INTERPERSONAL ATTRACTION:
Friendship, Love, and Relationships

Scene I.   The setting is the front seat of a car at a drive-in movie on a clear summer evening. Two college students are munching on French fries and sipping soft drinks.

MARK: You really looked beautiful when I picked you up tonight.

JUDY: Not the way I usually look?

MARK: You know what I mean. You always look great, but tonight you positively glowed.

JUDY: Being in love must be good for the complexion.

MARK: Then I must look great, too, because I love you more than anything in the world.

JUDY: I feel the same way, and you know it. You're cute when you're so serious.

MARK: I'm also hot for your body.

JUDY: I want you, too, Mark. But . . . I wouldn't feel right unless we do this the old-fashioned way. I hate to shock our friends, but I want to save all that until we're married. It's just a few more weeks until our wedding at the end of August.

MARK: (*sighing*) I know. You're very special, and I'll do anything you say.

JUDY: Wipe the grease off of your mouth and kiss me.

MARK: It's my pleasure, Madame.

Scene II.   Three years have passed, and the same two individuals are sitting in a small, shabbily furnished apartment. A baby is in the next room, crying.

MARK: (*loudly folding up his newspaper*) Can't you do something to shut that kid up?

JUDY: (*angrily*) Can't you? Why do you think taking care of our son is all up to me? Why should it be my job?

MARK: Just what do you think your job is? I work like a dog at that damn service station six days a week while you sit here and watch the boob tube.

JUDY: (*going out to get the baby*) If you think that's all I do, you're as dumb as your father.

MARK: What does my father have to do with it?

JUDY: Total male insensitivity seems to run in your family, but I wouldn't expect you to notice.

MARK: I wish something ran in your family besides overeating like your mother.

JUDY: (*beginning to cry*) You don't even like to look at me any more.

MARK: What I don't like is to come home every night to a mess and so much noise I can't even relax (*standing up*). I'm going over to see Ed. He's getting up a poker game.

JUDY: (*wiping her tears as anger takes over*) I'm really terribly glad that we can afford for you to go out gambling. Take the garbage with you and don't bother to wake me up when you get back.

MARK: Don't worry about that! (*slamming the door as he leaves*).

MUCH OF our time is spent interacting with others—strangers, acquaintances, friends, and those with whom we are most intimate. In choosing our friends, in falling in love, and in establishing and trying to maintain close relationships, we each respond to specific determinants that have been of interest to social psychology since its earliest beginnings. The general question has been, "What are the determinants of interpersonal evaluations?" That is, why does a given individual like one person, dislike another, and feel indifferent about a third? We tend to react to others on the basis of such attitudes. **Attraction** is based on the direction and the strength of interpersonal evaluations, as summarized in Figure 6.1.

In addition to identifying the determinants of attraction, social psychologists have become increasingly interested in how relationships develop and change (Duck, 1985; Duck and Gilmour, 1981; Hatfield and Walster, 1985). For example, it is important to know how friendships grow out of acquaintanceships and how people fall in love. It is also crucial to know why some close relationships are maintained over long periods of time, while others are unsuccessful. We will touch on each of these major issues in the following pages.

In this chapter we first examine the process by which strangers become acquaintances on the basis of such variables as proximity, emotions, and the need to affiliate. Then, we look at what determines the way in which some acquaintances become friends in response to such factors

FIGURE 6.1. *Interpersonal attraction* refers to the attitude we hold about another person. Such attitudes fall along a negative-positive dimension that ranges from *hate* to *love*. These attitudes reflect how we respond to others emotionally, and how they strongly influence our interpersonal behavior.

Interpersonal attraction: Attitudes toward others

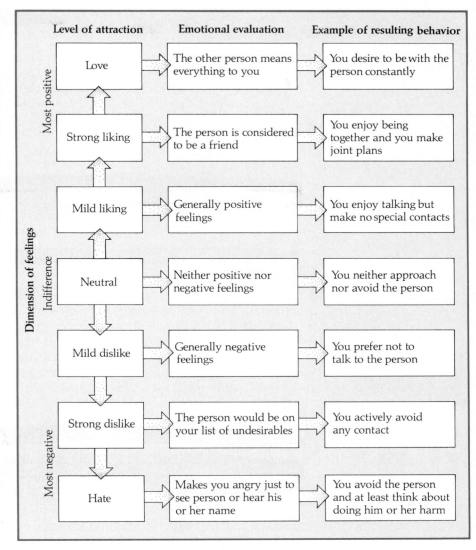

Level of attraction	Emotional evaluation	Example of resulting behavior
Love	The other person means everything to you	You desire to be with the person constantly
Strong liking	The person is considered to be a friend	You enjoy being together and you make joint plans
Mild liking	Generally positive feelings	You enjoy talking but make no special contacts
Neutral	Neither positive nor negative feelings	You neither approach nor avoid the person
Mild dislike	Generally negative feelings	You prefer not to talk to the person
Strong dislike	The person would be on your list of undesirables	You actively avoid any contact
Hate	Makes you angry just to see person or hear his or her name	You avoid the person and at least think about doing him or her harm

Dimension of feelings — Most positive / Indifference / Most negative

as physical attractiveness, similarity, and reciprocal judgments of one another. In the final section of the chapter, we take a close look at what it means to fall in love and the complexities involved in maintaining an ongoing relationship. Three special topics will also be covered: the way seating arrangements can influence attraction toward a fellow worker, Theodore Newcomb's classic study of friendship development among undergraduates, and a discussion of how close relationships may best be maintained.

EVALUATING STRANGERS: Physical Proximity, Emotional States, and the Need to Affiliate

There are over four billion people on our planet, and each of us is likely to come into extended contact with only a very small proportion of these people during a lifetime, perhaps several thousand. Of these thousands of potential friends, enemies, and lovers, we tend to limit those we know at any given time to a handful of individuals. On what basis do we select whom to know and to ignore, whom to like and to dislike? To some extent we react to specific aspects of others, but we are also influenced by factors having nothing to do with the other person. The stage is set for acquaintanceships to form if two people are brought in contact through physical proximity or **propinquity,** if each is experiencing positive rather than negative **emotions,** and if each has strong **affiliative needs.**

The role of propinquity: Physical contact, familiarity, acceptance

Acquaintanceship most often begins as the result of a series of accidental contacts. Strangers are assigned adjoining seats in a classroom, rent apartments across the hall from one another, or walk down the same sidewalk on the way to catch a bus or to buy groceries. Propinquity in such instances leads to a gradual increase in familiarity. We feel more comfortable with a familiar face and are more likely to exchange greetings. Even infants respond more positively to a stranger after several exposures to that individual (Levitt, 1980).

Propinquity: The role of the physical environment.   In research stretching back to the 1930s, it has been established that any aspect of the environment that increases the *propinquity* (physical proximity) of two individuals on a regular basis increases the probability that they will gradually get to know and to like one another (Festinger, Schachter, and Back, 1950). In universities, for example, students often become acquainted on the basis of classroom seating assignments or dormitory room location, regardless of whether they have similar academic majors, religious backgrounds, or hobbies (Caplow and Forman, 1950). In married student housing areas, propinquity is an overwhelming factor in determining attraction patterns; couples assigned apartments whose entrances are 22 feet or less from one another are very likely to become friends. Those with apartments 88 feet or more apart almost never become friends (Festinger, Schachter, and Back, 1950).

Students sitting side-by-side in a classroom are also very likely to become acquainted as the school term progresses. When seats are assigned alphabetically by the instructor, friendships are most likely to form between those whose last names begin with the same letter or nearby letter of the alphabet (Segal, 1974). During your college years, such physical factors may well help to determine some of your friendships, some of your romantic relationships, and maybe even your future spouse.

These environmental effects are by no means confined to a college campus. In a housing project for the elderly in a large city, the residents were most likely to become friends if they were given rooms on the same floor (Nahemow and Lawton, 1975), precisely the same pattern that holds true in college dormitories (Evans and Wilson, 1949). A similar trend is found in non-university apartment complexes; also, the closer two people live, the more likely they are to become "best friends" rather than simply "good friends" (Ebbesen, Kjos, and Konecni, 1976).

Why? Repeated exposure is the key.   Classroom or apartment locations lead to liking because certain physical arrangements lead strangers to experience **repeated exposure.** That is, because of spatial arrangements, some individuals are more likely to see one another time after time as part of their regular daily routines. As was discussed in Chapter 4, Zajonc and his colleagues have consistently shown that repeated exposure to a given stimulus usually leads to increasingly favorable attitudes toward that stimulus (Zajonc, 1968).

In one experiment, subjects were shown the photograph of a male college student once a week for four weeks to test the effect of repeated exposure on attraction (Moreland and Zajonc, 1982). Half of the subjects saw the same photograph each week and half saw a different photograph each week. At the end of each experimental session, subjects indicated how much they liked the person in the photograph. As shown in Figure 6.2, liking for a given stranger increased as the number of exposures to that person's photograph increased.

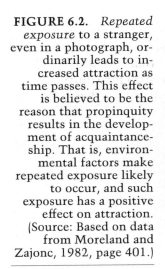

FIGURE 6.2. *Repeated exposure* to a stranger, even in a photograph, ordinarily leads to increased attraction as time passes. This effect is believed to be the reason that propinquity results in the development of acquaintanceship. That is, environmental factors make repeated exposure likely to occur, and such exposure has a positive effect on attraction. (Source: Based on data from Moreland and Zajonc, 1982, page 401.)

Repeated exposure increases attraction

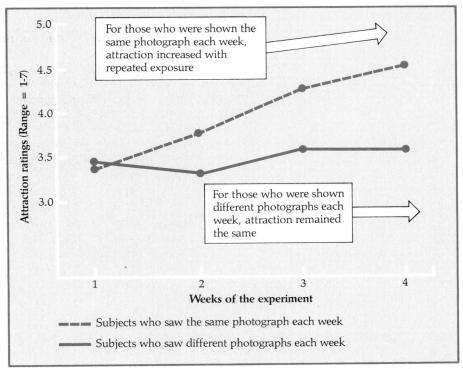

For those who were shown the same photograph each week, attraction increased with repeated exposure

For those who were shown different photographs each week, attraction remained the same

Attraction ratings (Range = 1-7)

Weeks of the experiment

- - - - Subjects who saw the same photograph each week

———— Subjects who saw different photographs each week

FOCUS ON RESEARCH:
The Cutting Edge

Visual and Verbal Contact with Fellow Workers as Influences on Attraction

Much of one's adult life is spent outside the home in a work setting, and it matters a great deal whether we like or dislike our fellow workers. Eight hours a day, five days a week spent with individuals you dislike can be a demoralizing experience.

Among the specific determinants of emotions (and hence interpersonal relations) in the workplace is the way in which fellow workers are able to interact. Consider the office depicted in Figure 6.3. In the photo, the desks are arranged in a face-to-face position; in other office situations, the employees are seated back-to-back. Does it matter? One could argue that it may be disconcerting to have another person facing you *or* that having someone behind you could be even worse because you never know for sure what they are doing.

Think of another aspect of such an environment. In some organizations, the rule is silence except during coffee breaks or the lunch hour. Other employers allow as much conversation as the employees desire, so long as the work gets done. Which would you prefer — the chance to talk or the chance to do your work without interruption?

To explore these variables (seating arrangement and amount of verbal contact), Dixit (1985) set up an experimental situation in which an undergraduate subject was paired with a confederate and assigned the task of assembling a series of objects out of paper. The experimental room was arranged like a small office with desks placing the two "workers" face-to-face, side-by-side, or back-to-back as they carried out the assignment. In addition, a rule was imposed indicating that they were or were not permitted to talk while working.

It was found that the subjects' feelings were strongly influenced both by seating arrangements and by the chance to converse or not in this temporary work environment. Male and female undergraduates felt most positively when they were seated face-to-face or side-by-side and when they were allowed to

FIGURE 6.3. In any work environment, such as an office, several alternative physical arrangements are possible. For example, desks can be placed face-to-face, as shown here, or they may be back-to-back. Research suggests that such variations have an effect on the emotional state of the employees and on their attraction toward one another.

Desk arrangement as a determinant of emotions and attraction

FIGURE 6.4. How much a fellow worker is liked has been found to be influenced by seating arrangements on the job and by rules about talking. Attraction is most positive when workers are seated face-to-face and when they are allowed to talk to one another. (Source: Based on data from Dixit, 1985.)

Attraction on the job: The effect of seating and verbal contact

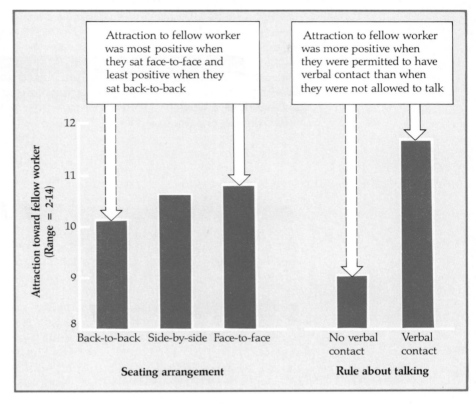

talk. The most negative emotional responses occurred in the back-to-back condition and when verbal contact was forbidden.

Even though the "fellow worker" obviously had nothing to do with the seating arrangement or with the rules about talking, he or she was liked best when feelings were positive and least when feelings were negative. The attraction results are shown in Figure 6.4.

As is often found in such research, productivity and emotional satisfaction are not necessarily related. That is, in this experimental situation, more work was accomplished in the back-to-back seating arrangement than in the other two, and more was accomplished when there was no talking than when verbal contact was possible. What should be done in an actual office or factory depends on the relative value one places on interpersonal relationships and work output. In terms of attraction research, however, the main point is that it was shown once again that when emotions are affected by external factors, interpersonal attraction is also affected.

Despite the importance of propinquity and repeated exposure, these factors do not *always* have a positive effect. For example, repeated exposure to a stranger who acts unpleasantly each time you are together is not a likely basis for friendship. To test this proposition, Swap (1977) conducted an experiment in which female undergraduates interacted with one another either once or on two, four, or eight occasions. When the interaction took place, the stranger either rewarded or punished the subject. Repeated exposure to a rewarding stranger led to increased attraction, while repeated exposure to a punishing stranger led to *decreased* attraction. We would expect that close propinquity and repeated exposure to an unpleasant individual would lead to more and more intense feelings of dislike.

Feelings: Conditioned emotional responses

Most of us are aware that positive and negative events in our daily lives can have an immediate and intense effect on our general mood (Stone and Neale, 1984). A growing body of research indicates that mood, in turn, affects many aspects of behavior, including interpersonal attraction.

Music, emotions, and attraction.   Music is pervasive in our society, and the selections played may or may not be under one's control. Anthropologist James Schaefer visited more than one hundred taverns and observed that sad songs on the jukebox (e.g., "I'm So Lonesome I Could Cry") led to an increase in alcohol consumption, while fast and loud music (e.g., "Disco Duck") resulted in very little drinking (Littlel, 1981). Given such findings, does it follow that an emotion-arousing stimulus, such as music, also has an effect on interpersonal behavior?

In a study of emotions and attraction, May and Hamilton (1980) first determined that the best-liked music among female college students was rock, while avant-garde classical material was liked least. For the attraction experiment itself, other female students were asked to rate male strangers after examining their photographs. While the ratings were being made, there was either silence or one of the two types of music was playing in the background. Compared to the silent condition, there was less attraction when avant-garde music was playing and more attraction during rock music. In addition, the same males were rated as more physically attractive with rock music in the background and less physically attractive with the disliked classical selections playing. So, music affected mood, and mood affected interpersonal judgments.

Other sources of emotion.   Many experiments have consistently indicated that events eliciting positive feelings increase interpersonal attraction, while negative events decrease attraction. Examples range from hot, uncomfortably humid rooms (Griffitt, 1970) to happy versus sad movies (Gouaux, 1971). In a similar fashion, depressed individuals make us feel uncomfortable, and we like them less (Winer et al., 1981).

Even good versus bad news on radio and television can affect interpersonal behavior. To test this prediction, Veitch and Griffitt (1976) arranged for subjects to hear a news broadcast just before the study supposedly started. The "radio" was actually a cassette recording containing a series of either good or bad news stories. The good news caused a positive emotional reaction, and subjects exposed to it expressed greater liking toward a stranger. Bad news had the opposite effect — negative feelings and decreased attraction.

In many instances, we may not be aware of the source of our positive and negative feelings, but they affect our behavior nevertheless. The **Focus** insert on pages 190–191 provides an example of this.

Why? Our emotional responses to other people can be conditioned. According to one of the theories developed to explain interpersonal attraction, all our likes and dislikes are based on emotional responses (Clore and Byrne, 1974). At its simplest level, this means that when anyone makes us feel good, we respond with liking; we dislike whoever makes us feel bad. Any variable (such as repeated exposure) that leads to greater attraction does so because positive feelings are aroused.

This general formulation, known as the **reinforcement-affect model** of attraction, has an additional element, as shown in Figure 6.5 (page 194). We not only respond to the person who *arouses* such feelings in us, but also to anyone who is simply *associated with* such feelings. This conditioning of emotional responses to those around us explains why attraction is influenced by music, heat, movies, radio news, seating arrangements, and so forth. These factors arouse positive or negative feelings; these feelings become associated with any individual who happens to be present; and we tend to like or dislike that person accordingly.

Need for affiliation: People differ in their desire to have friends

We spend much of our time interacting with other people. Such activities as making new friends, being with friends, and being able to share personal feelings are rated as *very important* by most Americans who are surveyed (Research and Forecasts, Inc., 1981). It has been proposed that having friends is intrinsically positive (Wright, 1984). It is also true that individuals differ in their **need for affiliation**. That is, some people prefer to be alone much of the time while others behave in a very sociable fashion, as in Figure 6.6 (page 196). Presumably, such personality differences help to determine whether propinquity and positive emotions actually lead two strangers to interact.

FIGURE 6.5.   According to the *reinforcement-affect model* of attraction, our likes and dislikes are based on the feelings aroused by rewarding and punishing events. Rewards elicit positive feelings and are liked; punishments elicit negative feelings and are disliked. In addition, conditioning can occur. When a stranger (or any other neutral stimulus) is present when feelings are aroused, that person is associated with the reward or punishment. As a result, feelings are *conditioned* to the stranger. Thus, a person to whom we might have responded in a neutral way is now evaluated either positively or negatively.

Feelings and conditioned feelings: The reinforcement-affect model of attraction

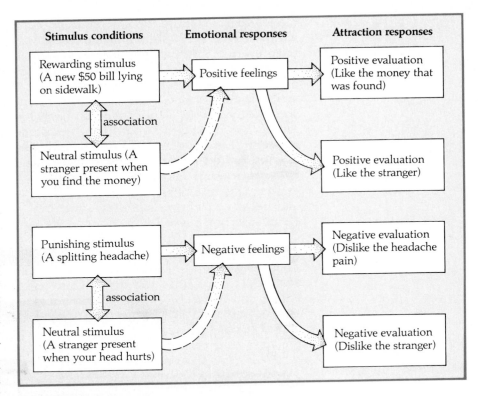

Need for affiliation as a trait.   Beginning with the pioneer work of Murray (1938), several measures of the *need for affiliation* have been constructed. Research with these tests has revealed, for example, that males high in affiliation need are relatively self-confident, and they tend to talk more to attractive females than do males whose affiliation need is low (Crouse and Mehrabian, 1977). In a college classroom, students whose need for affiliation scores are high tend to make more friends in the course of a semester than do students whose scores are low (Greendlinger and Byrne, 1985).

The general need to affiliate has been refined somewhat as **friendship motivation** in work by McAdams and Losoff (1984). The assumption is that some people are more strongly motivated than others toward the goal of warm and friendly interpersonal relationships. In a study of elementary school children, compared to subjects with low scores, those highest in friendship motivation knew more about their friends, had more stable friendships, and were rated by teachers as more friendly, affectionate, co-operative, happy, and popular.

Individuals differ not only in their motives involving affiliation and friendship but in their *social skills*. It has been found that birth order plays a role. Compared to first-borns, the **youngest members of the fam-**

FIGURE 6.6. An important determinant of whether acquaintanceships and friendships develop is the *affiliative needs* of those involved. There are individual differences in the motivation to form close relationships, and there are also situational variables that can increase the need to affiliate.

Need for affiliation: Differences among individuals and across situations

ily are more skillful socially (Ickes and Turner, 1983). Those who have an older, opposite-sex sibling are found to have the most rewarding interactions with members of the opposite sex.

After a relationship actually forms, students high in need for affiliation are increasingly satisfied as the relationship progresses over the first several months (Eidelson, 1980). Those with low affiliative needs tend to feel less satisfied over time, especially if they have a high need for independence. You can see that two individuals with different need patterns might be puzzled by one another as their friendship grows. One might be pleased by the tightening bonds of a close relationship while the other becomes unhappy, feeling tied down.

Need for affiliation as a response to arousing situations.   You are sitting in your social psychology class when suddenly you hear a scream through the window, followed by a great deal of shouting. What do you do? Does such a potentially frightening situation have any effect on interpersonal behavior?

In a series of now-classic experiments, Schachter (1959) was able to show that anxiety and fear increase one's desire to affiliate with others.

When experimental subjects were led to believe they would receive painful electric shocks, they preferred waiting with other subjects rather than alone. When no painful shock was involved, subjects preferred waiting alone or had no preference.

The explanation for the effect of fear on affiliation seems to be that frightened individuals desire to communicate with others about the situation. People seek out others — even total strangers — to talk about what is happening, to compare perceptions, and to decide what, if anything, to do. The ability to engage in this kind of *social comparison* process leads to a reduction in anxiety. Once you share your fears with others, you are actually less afraid. This process was clearly shown in an experiment in which college students were waiting for what they had been told was an electric shock experiment. Compared to controls who were not expecting to be shocked, the experimental subjects actually did interact more and spent more time discussing the upcoming experiment (Morris et al., 1976).

WHY ACQUAINTANCES BECOME FRIENDS: *Attractiveness, Similarity, and Reciprocity*

Once two individuals are brought together by such variables as propinquity, and if their feelings are generally positive, and if each has sufficiently strong affiliative needs, they may be expected to begin interacting. At this point in the process, however, some additional variables become important. Whether friendship (or even an ongoing acquaintanceship) develops now depends on the *physical attractiveness* of each member of the potential pair, their *similarity* on a variety of characteristics, and the extent to which they demonstrate *reciprocity* with respect to positive evaluations of one another. We will take a look at the research that has dealt with each of these factors.

Physical attractiveness: Judging others on the basis of appearance

First impressions rest in large part on appearances. When we encounter others for the first time, we notice such things as race, height, weight, clothing, facial features, hair color, and so forth. We tend to have various beliefs and prejudices about such factors on the basis of our past experiences and on the basis of stereotypes we have developed. Whatever the basis of these reactions and whatever their validity, we nevertheless are strongly affected by them.

One of the most powerful, and most studied, of such factors is **physical attractiveness.** This aspect of others turns out to be a primary determinant of whether others seek to form a relationship.

The effects of attractiveness.   When males and females interact, the attractiveness of the other person affects the behavior of both sexes (Folkes, 1982; Hatfield and Sprecher, 1986). In a commercial video-dating service, attractive males and females are most likely to be chosen as dates, though females also respond positively to high-status males (Green, Buchanan, and Heuer, 1984). There are some individual differences in the importance of attractiveness. For example, traditionally sex-typed males and females respond more positively to physically attractive strangers than do androgynous individuals (Andersen and Bem, 1981).

There is a general assumption that attractive people also possess a number of other positive qualities, just as you yourself may react to the two people depicted in Figure 6.7. Both males and females indicate that attractive individuals are also poised, interesting, sociable, independent, exciting, and sexually warm (Brigham, 1980). Less attractive individuals are believed to be deviant in a variety of ways including psychopathology, political radicalism, and homosexuality (Jones, Hannson, and Phillips, 1978; Unger, Hilderbrand, and Madar, 1982). Physically attractive males are judged to be more masculine, and attractive females to be more feminine, than those who are less attractive (Gillen, 1981). Those low in attractiveness respond to these various negative reactions by evaluating themselves in a negative way; for example, less attractive college students are more likely to believe they will become mentally ill in the future (O'Grady, 1982).

Being with attractive people seems to "rub off"; the friends of an attractive same-sex peer are rated more positively than the friends of someone who is unattractive (Kernis and Wheeler, 1981). This effect even holds when subjects rate sets of photos of unassociated individuals (Geiselman, Haight, and Kimata, 1984).

FIGURE 6.7.   Physical attractiveness has a strong effect on the assumptions we make about other people and on the degree of attraction we feel toward them. However unreasonable this may be, we attribute more positive and desirable qualities to those who are attractive than to those who are not.

Physical attractiveness: A major determinant of attraction

Beliefs about attractive and unattractive individuals are generally thought to be based on cultural biases and therefore to be unrelated to the actual qualities people possess. Nevertheless, there are some behavioral and personality differences related to appearance (Erwin and Calev, 1984), perhaps in part because of the way others react to attractive versus unattractive individuals (Adams, 1977). As you might expect, for example, attractive males and females interact well with the opposite sex and have more dates (Reis et al., 1980). Attractive males have more social interactions with females and fewer interactions with other males; they are more assertive and have less fear of rejection. Attractive females, however, don't interact with others any more than unattractive ones, and they are less assertive and less trusting of males (Reis et al., 1982). Attractive people expect to succeed in social situations (Abbott and Sebastian, 1981), and they apparently *do* succeed. In a large sample of several thousand adults, Umberson and Hughes (1984) found that attractiveness is positively related to educational attainment, income, occupational prestige, and psychological well-being. Those who are attractive also spend more time gazing at themselves when they pass a mirror (Lipson Przybyla, and Byrne, 1983; McDonald and Eilenfield, 1980).

It might seem logical to expect that attractive individuals would be higher in self-esteem than unattractive ones, but the relationship between these two characteristics is actually very weak and not entirely consistent across studies (Maruyama and Miller, 1981). One explanation is that attractive people receive so much praise they tend to question or discount it; "People only pay attention to the way I look, not to what I do or say." Unattractive individuals, on the other hand, would assume that any praise they receive is genuine and deserved. Major, Carrington, and Carnevale (1984) tested these general propositions by arranging for attractive and unattractive undergraduates to write a brief essay that was to be evaluated by another student. The evaluator was supposedly able to observe them as they wrote or was unable to observe them. Actually, all subjects received a positive evaluation from an opposite-sex observer. As shown in Figure 6.8, attractive subjects were more likely to attribute the praise to the quality of their work if they were not seen by the evaluator, while unattractive subjects felt the praise was related to work quality if they *had* been observed. The authors point out that in real life most social interactions take place with others who *are* aware of how we look. If less attractive people receive less praise, they give a lot of weight to it; in contrast, more attractive individuals receive more praise but discount it. For that reason, attractiveness and self-esteem are not strongly related.

What do we mean by "physically attractive"?   Though we have no problem deciding who is attractive and unattractive, it is difficult to pin down the variables responsible for such judgments. Probably a number of physical and behavioral factors are involved. For example, in a study of lonely hearts ads, more responses were received by those describing themselves as having red hair than by blondes or brunettes (Lynn and Shurgot, 1984). This would mean that having red hair leads to loneliness, but it is more likely that those who advertise believe that red hair is a positive attribute.

FIGURE 6.8.   Those who are physically attractive tend to discount praise from those who can see them, because they may assume that it probably is based on their looks. In contrast, those who are unattractive are more impressed by positive evaluations from those who can see them than from those who cannot, because they assume it is actually based on how well they did — in spite of their looks. These opposite tendencies may explain the lack of relationship between attractiveness and self-esteem. Attractive individuals receive more praise than unattractive ones, but unattractive individuals place more weight on such praise than attractive ones. The end result is equivalent levels of self-esteem. (Source: Based on data from Major, Carrington, and Carnevale, 1984.)

Interpreting praise: Attractive and unattractive persons react differently

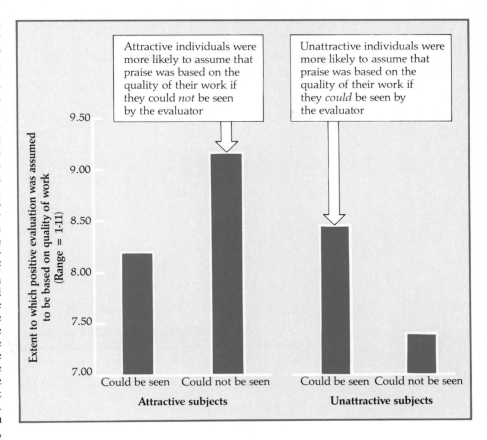

Females are found to respond positively to males with Robert Redford physiques — thin legs, a thin waist, broad shoulders, and small buttocks (Beck, Ward-Hull, and McLear, 1976; Horvath, 1979; Lavrakas, 1975). Though a tall male may seem to be an ideal romantic partner (Gillis and Avis, 1980), female college students actually prefer males of medium height (Graziano, Brothen, and Berscheid, 1978).

Males (despite what they see in magazine centerfolds) are attracted to females with medium-sized breasts (Kleinke and Staneski, 1980) and medium-sized legs and buttocks (Wiggins, Wiggins, and Conger, 1968). For both sexes, obesity is perceived as unattractive (Harris, Harris, and Bochner, 1982).

Some aspects of external behavior play a role in addition to physical appearance. Smiling is generally attractive to both males and females, while sad expressions evoke judgments of unattractiveness (S. Lau, 1982; Mueser et al., 1984). Females in a video-dating situation prefer expressive, outgoing males, while men react negatively to expressive, extroverted women (Riggio and Woll, 1984). Beyond physical appearance and style, even one's name can affect the perception of attractiveness. In one study, equally attractive female photographs were judged to be more beautiful when their names were Kathy, Jennifer, or Christine than when named Ethel, Harriet, or Gertrude (Garwood et al., 1980).

There may also be some situational determinants of perceived attractiveness. Males who had just been watching the glamorous "Charlie's Angels" on television rated a female stranger as less attractive than males who had not been watching that show (Kenrick and Gutierres, 1980). In a barroom situation, potential partners were found in one study "to get prettier at closing time," presumably because scarcity led to a reevaluation of looks (Pennebaker et al., 1979). This finding has not been consistently replicated and may depend on the type of bar, the size of the bar, and the actual characteristics of early evening versus late evening patrons (Nida and Koon, 1983; Sprecher et al., 1984).

Similarity of attractiveness: The matching hypothesis. People may *prefer* the best-looking of all possible friends and marriage partners, but not everyone can obtain such a partner. Males tend to be afraid of being rejected by extremely attractive females; they need some extraneous excuse even to approach them (Bernstein et al., 1983). Because people differ in physical attractiveness, who is actually chosen as a friend, lover, or spouse? There is a tendency to select partners similar to oneself in physical attractiveness—the **matching hypothesis** (Berscheid et al., 1971). This matching tendency influences casual dates, engagements, and marriages (Murstein, 1972). Married couples, regardless of age or length of marriage, are similar in attractiveness (Price and Vandenberg, 1979). The importance of matching is shown by the fact that mismatched couples are more likely to break up than couples similar in attractiveness (White, 1980b).

More surprising, perhaps, than male-female matching is the fact that same-sex friends also tend to resemble one another in attractiveness (Cash and Derlega, 1978), though this is apparently more characteristic for male pairs than for female pairs (McKillip and Riedel, 1983).

Similarity: Liking those who are like ourselves

When two people first meet, they are more inclined to ask one another questions than is true in established relationships (Kent et al., 1981). One reason is that we want to know one another's likes and dislikes. As has been suggested since the days of Aristotle, we tend to accept those who agree with us and reject those who differ. Most people are quite aware of this social norm (Jellison and Oliver, 1983), as are the cartoon characters shown in Figure 6.9. Thus, it has long been assumed that **attitude similarity** leads to attraction. In a more general sense, we respond positively to those who most closely resemble ourselves. Before reading about the most recent research on attitude similarity, you may find it valuable to read the **Focus** insert on page 202 to learn about an important study that dealt with this topic over a quarter of a century ago.

FIGURE 6.9. It has been observed for several thousand years that people tend to be attracted to those who are similar to themselves. There may be changes over the years in the specific details as to *which* attitudes, behaviors, and other characteristics are important, but the general principal remains constant. (Source: *Cathy*, copyright, 1985, Universal Press Syndicate. Reprinted with permission. All rights reserved.)

As similarity increases, attraction increases

Attitude similarity and attraction. Beyond formal and informal observations of the effect of similarity on attraction, a great many experiments have established the way in which this relationship operates. In typical laboratory investigations, attitude similarity toward a stranger is manipulated to determine the effect on attraction (for example, Schachter, 1951; Smith, 1957). Despite occasional controversy (Byrne, Clore, and Smeaton, 1986; Rosenbaum, 1986), the effect is a powerful and very consistent one, so it is possible to predict with reasonable accuracy how much one person will like another on the basis of the *proportion* of attitudinal topics on which they agree (Byrne and Nelson, 1965).

FOCUS ON RESEARCH:
Classic Contributions

Attitude Similarity and Attraction: Newcomb's Field Study of Friendship Formation

The *observation* that similarity leads to attraction is thousands of years old. Research *data* indicating that pairs of friends, engaged couples, and spouses are more similar than random pairs of individuals began with the work of Sir Francis Galton in 1870 and was well established in the first half of the twentieth century (for example, Schuster and Elderton, 1906; Winslow, 1937).

Both the observations and the research involved a correlational approach. For that reason, it was not possible to determine whether similarity leads pairs of individuals to like one another, or whether two people who like one another tend to become more similar. The *direction* of the similarity-attraction association could only be established by means of laboratory experimentation in which similarity was manipulated or a field study that examined the process of friendship development over a period of time. Both approaches were undertaken for the first time in the 1950s. The pioneering *field work* dealing with this issue was conducted by the late Theodore Newcomb (1961) at the University of Michigan.

In the fall semester of 1954 Newcomb set up a special dormitory for seventeen male transfer students who were total strangers to one another. They were provided free rent for a semester in exchange for serving as research subjects for several hours each week. One year later, the entire process was repeated with a new group of seventeen transfer students.

Because two individuals who meet for the first time have little information about one another, you would expect any relationship to be fairly unstable at the beginning. As time passes, however, each person gains more (and

more accurate) information about others. As a result, some early relationships fade away, new ones are established, and friendship pairs should begin to stabilize. This is precisely what occurred. Though there were many changes in who liked whom at the beginning of the semester, more permanent friendship patterns became evident after about eight weeks of sharing the same residence. What was found with respect to attitude similarity?

The subjects' attitudes about a wide variety of topics (from church attendance to President Eisenhower) were assessed by mail before the subjects arrived at Ann Arbor and again at the end of the semester-long project. Attitudes were found to be quite consistent over this time span. In examining attitudes and attraction, the investigators were able to show that attitude similarity existing *before* two individuals had even met formed the basis for predicting attraction *after* they became acquainted. That is, it was established that attraction develops as a consequence of the fact that two strangers agree about various issues.

Another type of attitude similarity was also examined. One of the more common topics any of us discuss is the way we feel about mutual acquaintances. And, it makes someone very uncomfortable if you dislike his or her friends and are fond of his or her enemies. In Newcomb's research, agreement about the likeability of the remaining fifteen house members in each group of subjects was determined for all pairs of subjects. As was predicted, agreement about fellow residents was greater among those persons who were highest in attraction than among those who were lowest in attraction, as shown in Figure 6.10. Later research has confirmed that it is important for friends to agree in assessing other people (Neimeyer and Neimeyer, 1981).

Newcomb concluded that stable interper-

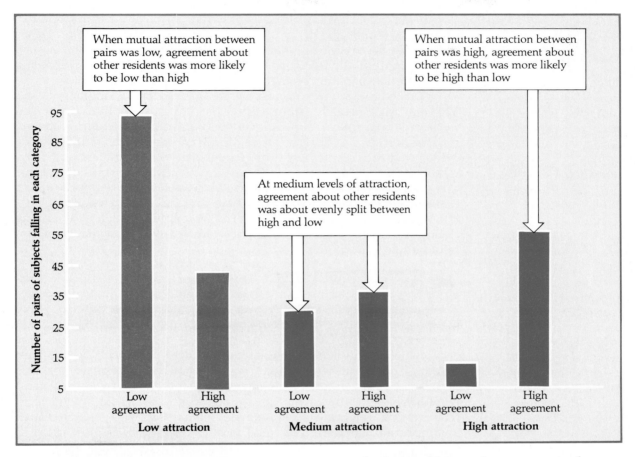

When mutual attraction between pairs was low, agreement about other residents was more likely to be low than high

When mutual attraction between pairs was high, agreement about other residents was more likely to be high than low

At medium levels of attraction, agreement about other residents was about evenly split between high and low

Number of pairs of subjects falling in each category

95
85
75
65
55
45
35
25
15
5

Low agreement | High agreement
Low attraction

Low agreement | High agreement
Medium attraction

Low agreement | High agreement
High attraction

FIGURE 6.10. A major topic about which people agree or disagree is the way they evaluate mutual acquaintances. In a dormitory setting, there is more agreement than disagreement about other residents when attraction is high, and more disagreement than agreement when attraction is low. (Source: Based on data from Newcomb, 1961.)

Attraction and agreement about the evaluation of others

sonal relationships tend to grow out of agreement about many aspects of our world. People with high levels of agreement tend to become friends and to associate with one another. Those who disagree tend to stay away from one another.

Along with other interesting findings, Newcomb's research provided evidence for the validity of the many subsequent laboratory experiments that also found a similarity-attraction effect. Such similarity clearly is an important determinant of how actual relationships are established in everyday life.

These laboratory findings were verified in field studies involving such situations as computer dating (Byrne, Ervin, and Lamberth, 1970) and sharing a fall-out shelter with same-sex strangers (Griffitt and Veitch, 1974). For socially anxious subjects, these effects are eliminated, possibly because they are too upset to pay attention to the characteristics of others (Heimberg, Acerra, and Holstein, 1985). The attraction generated by the discovery of similar attitudes leads to behavioral effects, such as being more likely to return to a laboratory to work with an agreeing than with a disagreeing stranger (Gormly and Gormly, 1981).

We tend to assume that most people agree with us (Campbell, 1986). This effect is especially strong with respect to those we like. If a person feels attraction toward someone on the basis of non-attitudinal characteristics, such as physical attractiveness (Marks and Miller, 1982; Marks, Miller, and Maruyama, 1981) or general charisma (Granberg and King, 1980), that other individual is perceived as attitudinally similar. It seems that positive responses to the superficial characteristics of others lead us to the often mistaken belief that we have the same attitudes and values. It is not difficult to find unhappy examples of this tendency when one chooses the wrong mate or votes for a political candidate whose stands on issues do not match one's own.

Why do we like similar others?   Most theorists agree that attitude similarity is positive because it confirms one's judgments about the world. There is a *social comparison* process in which we find out whether some other person "validates" what we have already concluded about politics or religion or whatever by agreeing with us (Sanders, 1982). If someone believes what you believe, he or she provides "evidence" that you are correct. This affirmation of your good judgment is a positive affective experience, and you like the one who made you feel that way. Disagreement has just the opposite effect; it suggests you are wrong, elicits negative emotions, and causes you to dislike the person who generated such uncomfortable feelings. For these reasons, we tend to seek sources of information (including other people) who validate what we already believe. For example, Nixon supporters were much less interested in the Watergate hearings, and paid less attention to them, than those who were anti-Nixon (Sweeney and Gruber, 1984).

Another approach to explaining the similarity effect is provided by **balance theory.** Newcomb (1981) and others have suggested that human beings have a natural inclination to organize their likes and dislikes in a symmetrical fashion that results in **balance** (Cacioppo and Petty, 1981; Insko, Sedlak, and Lipsitz, 1982; Rodrigues and Newcomb, 1980). There is balance when two people like one another and agree about whatever they are discussing. When two people like one another and disagree, there is **imbalance,** and this unpleasant state motivates each individual to do something (such as changing attitudes about the topic) in order to restore balance. When two people do not like one another, there is **nonbalance,** and either agreement or disagreement results in indifference.

Keep in mind that we do not *always* reject those with dissimilar views. Though we wish to validate our beliefs, we have other needs as well. Interactions with a dissimilar stranger can provide new information (Gormly, 1979), reduce one's confusion (Russ, Gold, and Stone, 1980), and make a person feel special and unique instead of being just like everyone else (Snyder and Fromkin, 1980). Dissimilarity is threatening, and people assume that those who disagree with them will dislike them (Gonzales et al., 1983). This threat can be eliminated if we know in advance that the dissimilar other is not going to reject us and that he or she is open to discussing alternative points of view (Broome, 1983; Sunnafrank and Miller, 1981).

Similarity of other characteristics.   Even though most social psychologists are in agreement that attitude similarity leads to attraction, the effects of personality or behavioral similarity are the subject of some controversy. Put in its simplest form, do birds of a feather flock together, or do opposites attract? Convincing arguments can be — and have been — made for both suggestions.

In the first place, there are some personality characteristics that are liked by almost everyone, *regardless* of degree of similarity. For example, relatively dominant individuals are preferred to relatively submissive ones by both dominant and submissive others (Palmer and Byrne, 1970). In a similar way, competitive individuals are liked by both men and women (Riskind and Wilson, 1982), and strangers who are willing to disclose information about themselves are preferred to those who are unwilling to reveal much (McAllister and Bregman, 1983).

For many characteristics, though, we tend to choose friends who are similar to ourselves. For example, heterosexual males are fairly negative toward homosexual ones, regardless of how much their attitudes on other topics are in agreement (Aguero, Bloch, and Byrne, 1984; Krulewitz and Nash, 1980), presumably because sexual preference is judged to be a matter of overriding importance. College women prefer roommates who are similar to themselves socially and with respect to values (Hill and Stull, 1981). Friends are similar to one another in their ability to understand facial cues to emotion (Brauer and DePaulo, 1980). After age seven or eight, there is an increasing tendency for children to seek companions close to their own age (Ellis, Rogoff, and Cramer, 1981; Rubin, 1980). Among high school best friends, there is greater than chance similarity in age, sex, religion, and race (Kandel, 1978). On various personality characteristics (such as androgyny versus traditional sex roles, degree of masculinity and femininity, sensation-seeking, and cognitive style), similarity is preferable to dissimilarity (Antill, 1983; Lesnik-Oberstein and Cohen, 1984; Pursell and Banikiotes, 1978). The personality similarity effect is generally weaker than the attitude similarity effect, and it also seems to be true that personality similarity increases when people interact (Blankenship et al., 1984). On those personality dimensions on which friends are actually no more similar than random strangers, they *believe* themselves to be similar (Feinberg, Miller, and Ross, 1981).

We also like those who behave as we do. With college students paired in a series of games, partners with similar game behavior liked one another (Knight, 1980). Those who are similar in disclosing—or not disclosing—intimate information about themselves tend to be attracted (Daher and Banikiotes, 1976). Elementary school children prefer peers who perform about as well as they do in academics, sports, music, and the like (Tesser, Campbell, and Smith, 1984). We even like those who imitate our behavior and make the same choices and decisions we do (Roberts et al., 1981; Thelen et al., 1981). Among high school students, friends tend to be similar with respect to engaging in deviant behavior such as drug use (Kandel, Single, and Kessler, 1976), and, for females at least, smoking, drinking, and premarital sex (Rodgers, Billy, and Udry, 1984). When two people live together (for example, college roommates or spouses), similarity of circadian activity rhythms is important. Roommates who differed in being morning-active versus evening-active evaluated one another more negatively than when they were similar in this respect (Watts, 1982).

The greatest amount of controversy about the effect of personality variables involves *needs*. It has been proposed that **need compatibility** (having similar needs) is a positive factor in a relationship. It has also been proposed that **need complementarity** (having opposite needs) leads to liking because both individuals find it rewarding. For example, someone who is motivated to talk a lot should like a good listener, and vice versa. As reasonable as the complementarity idea seems, research generally supports the importance of similarity. In one study, Meyer and Pepper (1977) found that husbands and wives who were similar in their needs tended to have better adjusted marriages than spouses with dissimilar needs. Need compatibility seems to be important in an ongoing relationship.

Reciprocal evaluations: I like you if you like me

One of the most influential factors affecting your attraction toward a given person is that individual's evaluation of you (Byrne, 1971). For example, when a female interacts positively with a male by maintaining eye contact, leaning toward him, and engaging in conversation, he is attracted to her even if he and she are dissimilar in their attitudes (Gold, Ryckman, and Mosley, 1984). Friendships are strengthened by verbal and nonverbal signs of mutual respect, consideration, interest, wanting to be together, wanting to communicate, affection, and liking (Hays, 1984). Almost everyone likes a positive response from others and dislikes any indication of negative feelings. Even if a positive evaluation is inaccurate and consists of flattery from someone who has something to gain, we are pleased to receive it (Drachman, de Carufel, and Insko, 1978). With negative evaluations, we tend not to like the person who voices them, even when other people are the targets (Amabile, 1983).

Once relationships are established, we expect our friends to like us, to evaluate us positively, and to behave kindly toward us. For those we dislike, we have the opposite expectancies. What happens when such expected reciprocity is *not* fulfilled? To pursue this question, Riordan, Quigley-Fernandez, and Tedeschi (1982) manipulated initial liking by presenting female subjects with information that another female student held either similar or dissimilar attitudes. Next, each subject had a time-consuming task that involved placing decks of index cards in alphabetical order; the other subject (a confederate) had a much easier task. The experimenter suggested that the subject request help from the confederate when she was finished. For half the subjects, the confederate agreed to help, while for the other half, the response was "no." Changes in attraction measured before and after this interaction indicated what happened when expectancies were or were not met. As you can see in Figure 6.11, the greatest change was in liking for a similar person who refused the request — attraction dropped sharply in this instance. In contrast, when

FIGURE 6.11. One indication of how positively another person feels about you is his or her willingness to provide help when you request it. When we know others have similar attitudes, we like them, expect them to like us, and assume that they will be helpful if asked. When attitudes are dissimilar, one's attraction, expectations, and assumptions are negative. When we request help and the other person's response does not match what we expect, there is a dramatic decrease in liking for a similar person who does not help, and an increase in liking for a dissimilar person who does help. When helping behavior matches expectations, a similar person who helps is still liked while a dissimilar person who does not is liked even less afterward. (Source: Based on data from Riordan, Quigley-Fernandez, and Tedeschi, 1982.)

Attraction and expectations for friendliness: When helpfulness is not consistent with similarity

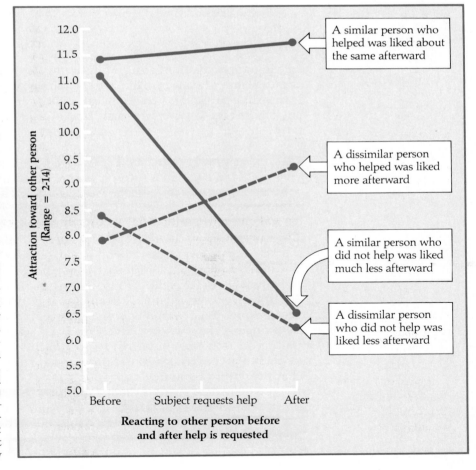

A similar person who helped was liked about the same afterward

A dissimilar person who helped was liked more afterward

A similar person who did not help was liked much less afterward

A dissimilar person who did not help was liked less afterward

Attraction toward other person (Range = 2-14)

12.0
11.5
11.0
10.5
10.0
9.5
9.0
8.5
8.0
7.5
7.0
6.5
6.0
5.5
5.0

Before   Subject requests help   After

Reacting to other person before and after help is requested

the subject expected a negative response (from a dissimilar confederate), her willingness to help *increased* attraction. It seems that we expect the words and deeds of others to match our feelings about them, and attraction can change markedly when these expectations are not met. When two people provide rewards for one another over time, liking and satisfaction with the relationship increase (Berg, 1984).

IT'S SO EASY TO FALL IN LOVE and So Difficult to Maintain a Relationship

Whenever two people perceive one another as potential sexual partners, a relationship can move beyond acquaintanceship and friendship. There is the possibility of **love**. Only in the last fifteen years or so have social psychologists made attempts to study this emotional state. We will describe what is now known about what it means for one person to "fall in love" with another.

Passionate love versus companionate love

In the course of interacting with members of the opposite sex, there comes a time when we are likely to ask ourselves whether or not we are in love with a particular person. Because there are at least two quite different kinds of love, the answer may depend on exactly what we mean by the term.

Passionate love: I've got a feeling I'm falling.   The majority of the recent theoretical and research interest has centered on **passionate love.** This refers to an intense, sometimes overwhelming emotional state in which a person thinks about a lover constantly, wants to spend as much time as possible with that individual, and is often quite unrealistic in his or her judgments about that person (Murstein, 1980). Contacts with other friends become less frequent, and attention is focused on one, all-important individual (Milardo, Johnson, and Huston, 1983). One measure of passionate love (Hatfield, 1983a) includes items that indicate the intensity of the feelings involved. Examples are: "Since I've been with ____, my emotions have been on a roller coaster." "Sometimes I can't control my thoughts; they are obsessively on ____." Our language (for example, "falling in love" or "head over heels in love") suggests some sort of accidental process much like slipping on a banana peel (Solomon, 1981). That may be an accurate description.

   A widely held current theory of passionate love indicates that three major conditions are necessary (Hatfield and Walster, 1981). First of all, one must be raised in a culture that believes in the concept and teaches it to young people in fiction and in real life depictions (see Figure 6.12). The idea of love arose in Europe in the Middle Ages, and it was thought to be a

FIGURE 6.12. In order to experience romantic love, it is necessary to learn that such a thing exists. This emotion seems to occur only in cultures that expose their citizens to the appropriate models in fictional presentations and in real life. In Europe and the Western Hemisphere, for example, from earliest childhood we are provided with examples in which couples fall in love, marry, and live happily ever after.

Learning about love

pure and holy emotion unrelated to sexual desire. It was not until the end of the seventeenth century in England that it became generally accepted that an ideal marriage was based on love (Stone, 1977). In present day India, romantic love is just now replacing arranged marriages among the middle class. Popular Indian movies have begun to depict couples who fall in love and defy their parents to get married (Kaufman, 1980). In western nations, most adolescents raised on stories and songs about love are well prepared to undergo such an experience in their own lives (Dion and Dion, 1975). It has even been found that the more a person thinks about love, the more likely he or she is to fall in love (Tesser and Paulhus, 1976).

The second condition for passionate love to occur is the presence of an appropriate love object. For most people, that means a physically attractive member of the opposite sex, about the same age, with the male taller than the female, and neither deeply involved in another relationship. If one believes strongly that it is possible to experience "love at first sight," that can happen, too. Approximately 50 percent of the adults in one study reported having this happen to them at least once (Averill and Boothroyd, 1977).

The third condition is probably crucial to intense infatuation. Any emotional arousal can be *interpreted* as love. It has been found that the way we label emotional excitement can depend on external cues. In Chapter 9 we will describe how one kind of emotional arousal can transfer to another. Various types of arousal have been found to influence romantic feelings, attraction, and sexual interest in experiments focusing on fear (Dutton and Aron, 1974), on erotic excitement (Istvan, Griffitt, and Weidner, 1983), and on embarrassment (Przybyla, Murnen, and Byrne, 1985). Even anger at parents' attempts to break up an affair leads to increased feelings of love (Driscoll, Davis, and Lipetz, 1972).

Though the mislabeling hypothesis has been the most widely studied explanation of the arousal-love phenomenon, it has also been suggested that the reinforcement-affect model (discussed earlier) explains these various findings. It is proposed that the presence of an opposite-sex stranger is simply reinforcing — any subsequent attraction is thus based on the positive feelings elicited by that reinforcement (Kenrick, Cialdini, and Linder, 1979; Kenrick and Johnson, 1979). In one experiment, when subjects expected to receive an electric shock, the presence of a confederate was found to reduce their fear and to increase attraction toward a confederate (Riordan and Tedeschi, 1983). Whatever the ultimate explanation of the role of emotional arousal, it is clear that such arousal affects how one responds to potential love objects. The three-factor theory of passionate love is summarized in Figure 6.13.

Hatfield's (1983b) review of the literature suggests that men and women are very similar in what they hope to obtain from a relationship. Both sexes want love *and* sex; both want intimacy *and* the power to control what goes on in the relationship. Nevertheless, men seem to fall in love more easily than women, and women fall out of love more easily than men (Rubin, Peplau, and Hill, 1981).

FIGURE 6.13. According to the three-factor theory of passionate love, an individual is likely to fall in love and experience an intense emotional response if three conditions are present. (1) The person's culture must have provided information about the concept, including real and fictional models of loving couples. (2) The person must come into contact with someone who is perceived as an appropriate and desirable love object. (3) There must be some type of emotional arousal that is interpreted and labeled by the person as constituting "love." Passionate love, then, is believed to represent the blending of aspects of the present situation with past learning accompanied by a mislabeled state of arousal.

The three-factor theory of passionate love

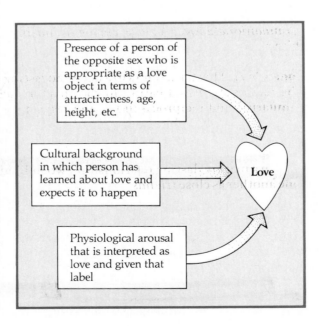

	Basic Love Styles	Sample Items Measuring Each Style
TABLE 6.1. Hendrick and Hendrick (1986) developed an attitude scale that identifies six different types of love. Individuals vary in their scores on the basis of such factors as sex, ethnic background, how many times they have been in love, and self-esteem.	1. Passionate love	My lover and I were attracted to each other immediately after we first met
		My lover and I became emotionally involved rather quickly
	2. Game-playing love	I have sometimes had to keep two of my lovers from finding out about each other
		I can get over love affairs pretty easily and quickly
	3. Friendship love	The best kind of love grows out of a long friendship
Love: Different meanings for different individuals		Love is really a deep friendship, not a mysterious, mystical emotion
	4. Logical love	It is best to love someone with a similar background
		An important factor in choosing a partner is whether or not he (she) will be a good parent
	5. Possessive love	When my lover doesn't pay attention to me, I feel sick all over
		I cannot relax if I suspect that my lover is with someone else
	6. Selfless love	I would rather suffer myself than let my lover suffer
		Whatever I own is my lover's to use as he (she) chooses

Companionate love: A close, caring friendship.   Despite the somewhat flimsy and often unrealistic basis of a passionate love affair, it is possible for a relationship to begin in that fashion and yet mature into **companionate love.** This term refers to a deep and lasting friendship that involves the factors discussed earlier in the chapter such as positive emotions, similarity, and reciprocal liking and respect. In addition, love involves *caring* about the other person (Steck et al., 1982). There are not many songs or movies about companionate love, but this seems to be the kind of emotional attachment that makes a lasting relationship possible.

In a mature, lasting relationship, two individuals must learn to enjoy one another as close *friends*. Each comes to place great value on the other, and both individuals are concerned about the other's happiness and welfare (Rubin, 1974). There is evidence indicating six different types of love. Hendrick and Hendrick (1986), building on the theoretical formulation of J. A. Lee, have developed a measure of these basic love styles. Each type is listed in Table 6.1, and sample items are shown to suggest the diverse attitudes that represent these approaches to love.

To learn some of the other factors involved in maintaining a positive interpersonal bond, see the **On the Applied Side** insert on page 212.

ON THE APPLIED SIDE

Maintaining a Positive Relationship: You Don't Send Me Flowers Anymore

When we are deeply involved in a close friendship or in a love affair, it is difficult to imagine that such warm feelings could change to indifference or dislike. Common experience, of course, tells us that it is not at all unusual for friendships to end (as suggested in the cartoon in Figure 6.14). We also know that lovers break up, all too often with considerable bitterness (Cimbalo, Faling, and Mousaw, 1976). Let's consider the problem in the context of a marriage.

Most of us would like to believe that if we fall in love, the eventual outcome will be a marriage in which we live happily ever after. Despite that rosy picture, the incidence of divorce is extremely high. In the United States a marriage is approximately as likely to end in divorce as to last through the couple's lifetime. A few years ago, advice columnist Ann Landers (1977) asked her readers, "If you had it to do over again, would you marry the person to whom you are now married?" During the next ten days, over 50,000 readers replied— 55 percent said "yes," and 45 percent said "no." Though there is much more research dealing with what leads to attraction, friendship, and love than there is on the reasons for marital failure, it is possible to take what little data we have and reach some plausible conclusions. Three general factors can be identified (Byrne and Murnen, 1987).

Often, two individuals in a long-term relationship discover they have too many areas of dissimilarity. We know from attraction research that similarity of attitudes, beliefs, values, personality, and behavioral characteristics plays an important role in causing two people to like one another. We know from research on passionate love that two people can be so overwhelmed by emotion that they fail to pay attention to such seemingly irrelevant details as the similarity between self and partner. A study of over two hundred college students who believed they were "in love" found that about half broke up the relationship within two years (Hill, Rubin, and Peplau, 1976).

FIGURE 6.14. No matter how positive a relationship may be, it is not uncommon for change to occur. Friends drift apart, lovers break up, and marriages fail. It is probably most realistic to think of relationships not as stable and unchanging units, but rather as fluid and dynamic interactions. In this cartoon, Amy is pleased to find that a particular friendship has lasted for several years. (Source: Register and Tribune Syndicate, Inc., July 12, 1985.)

As time passes, some friendships last and others deteriorate

Among the most common reasons they gave was the fact that they discovered they had different interests, backgrounds, sexual attitudes, intellectual ability, or views about marriage. In other words, love died when it became clear that the basic elements of a close relationship were missing.

Such problems could be avoided if individuals paid close attention to similarity factors early in the relationship. Some dissimilarity problems are more difficult to avoid, however. When one person changes and the other does not (in religious views, political beliefs, sexual attitudes, drinking habits, or whatever), similarity can turn into dissimilarity over a period of time (Levinger, 1980). Traditional role expectations still operate to affect different reactions to careers for men and women. For example, among couples with jobs equal in income and prestige, male commitment to a career causes no problems, but female commitment to a career causes unhappiness for both the husband and the wife (Nicola and Hawkes, 1986). Few individuals would be able to foresee these effects if their relationship was established early in their careers. There are also potential areas of dissimilarity in marriage that are difficult or impossible for a dating couple to predict — different attitudes about spending money versus saving it, disciplining children, or deciding who should clean the bathroom. When such differences are a vital part of the relationship (such as sexual preferences), dissimilarity easily leads to marital dissatisfaction (Byrne, Becker, and Przybyla, 1985).

In the study of college couples who broke up, Hill, Rubin, and Peplau (1976) also pinpointed a second general problem: *boredom*. The reasons for such a reaction have not been investigated in great detail (Skinner, 1986). Those who write about sex or about food frequently provide suggestions for seeking vari-

ety to add excitement to the bedroom or to the dining table. Beyond those two areas of life are hundreds of activities in which we can fall into potentially boring routines. On the basis of what we know about affect and attraction, it is not surprising that the negative aspects of feeling "in a rut" can be attributed to some failure of one's partner. We need to know a great deal more about why some couples succumb to boredom while others find ways to overcome it. Common sense suggests it should be helpful to be aware of the potential problem and to spend some effort seeking ways to avoid it. One couple may find it useful to expand their horizons by seeking new educational opportunities together or learning a new sport. Another couple may find that planning, engaging in, and viewing pictures of an annual family vacation provide new and different things to think about and talk about. Whatever the right solution for a given couple, it seems reasonable to suggest that doing the same things the same way day after day and year after year may well lead to monotony and unhappiness.

Finally, and perhaps most important of all, is the seeming *change in reciprocal evaluations* made by couples after a relationship is established, compared to an earlier stage in getting to know one another. The difference was suggested by the fictional presentation at the beginning of this chapter.

In what they say and do, two people dating and in the early stages of marriage tend to indicate to one another their positive feelings, ranging from liking to lust. As two people settle into the daily habits of a relationship, not only do many of these verbal and nonverbal niceties become less frequent, but negative evaluations begin to replace them. Both males and females often feel free in a close relationship to criticize, nag, complain, and find fault. Considering the powerful effects of positive and negative evaluations established in attraction research, it is not surprising that two people who find more negative than positive things to say find themselves less in love. Again, awareness of the problem and a conscious effort to avoid it would seem to be important in maintaining a positive marriage.

In each of the areas just discussed, it is proposed that a lasting union requires effort on the part of the two individuals. They each need to be realistic at the outset about the extent to which they are similar or dissimilar, and they need to talk about and try to deal with future areas of potential disagreement such as children, housework, and careers. Couples need to work at finding meaningful ways to avoid boredom and to bring zest and interest into their lives. And—two people who want to be together and stay together need to remind themselves frequently to be as nice as possible to one another. It may sound simple, or even simple-minded, but it is not. Such positive interpersonal behavior may be a central element in the success of a lifetime companionate love affair.

When relationships fail

Levinger (1980) describes relationships as passing through five possible stages: initial attraction, building a relationship, continuation, deterioration, and ending. Table 6.2 summarizes some of the factors operating at each stage. Much of the social psychological research on attraction over the past several decades has dealt with the first two stages. Currently, there is increased interest in pinpointing the factors that influence the remaining three stages. Most of this research deals with heterosexual relationships, but studies of homosexual couples suggest that identical variables are involved when one has a same-sex partner (Schullo and Alperson, 1984).

Attempting to continue a relationship: Jealousy and other pitfalls. One of the more common problems in a relationship is **jealousy**. When an individual perceives a rival for the affections of the one he or she loves, there is a threat that causes two kinds of suffering. An individual may lose the rewards the relationship offered, and there is also a lowering of self-esteem (Mathes, Adams, and Davies, 1985; White, 1981). The response is a consuming flood of unpleasant thoughts, feelings, and behaviors that we label as jealousy. Extreme jealousy involves anxiety, fear, pain, anger, and hopelessness along with physical symptoms such as a rapidly beating heart and the feeling of an empty stomach (Pines and Aronson, 1983). The rival may be real or imaginary, and the romantic attraction between the rival and one's partner may take place in the present, in the past, or even as a potential event in the future.

TABLE 6.2. Levinger (1980) proposes that relationships are divided into five stages, from initial attraction to a point at which they may end. At each stage are positive and negative factors that can cause the relationship to develop and maintain itself or to move toward dissolution.

The five stages of a relationship

Stage of Relationship	Positive Factors	Negative Factors
Initial Attraction	Propinquity and repeated exposure	Absence of propinquity and repeated exposure
	Positive emotions	Negative emotions
	High affiliative need and friendship motivation	Low affiliative need and friendship motivation
Building a Relationship	Equivalent physical attractiveness	Nonequivalent physical attractiveness
	Similarity of attitudes and other characteristics	Dissimilarity of attitudes and other characteristics
	Reciprocal positive evaluations	Reciprocal negative evaluations
Continuation	Seeking ways to maintain interest and variety	Falling into a rut and becoming bored
	Providing evidence of positive evaluation	Providing evidence of negative evaluation
	Absence of jealousy	Jealousy
	Perceived equity	Perceived inequity
	High level of mutual satisfaction	Low level of mutual satisfaction
Deterioration	Much time and effort invested in relationship	Little time and effort invested in relationship
	Work at improvement of relationship	Decide to end relationship
	Wait for improvement to occur	Wait for deterioration to continue
Ending	Existing relationship offers some rewards	A new life appears to be the only acceptable solution
	No alternative partners available	Alternative partners available
	Expect relationship to succeed	Expect relationship to fail
	Commitment to a continuing relationship	Lack of commitment to a continuing relationship

There are dramatic differences among individuals in the tendency to experience jealousy. In a mixed sample of adults, 54 percent described themselves as jealous people (Pines and Aronson, 1983). Some people are also more possessive than others in intimate relationships (Pinto and Hollandsworth, 1984). Those who are most jealous tend to feel inadequate, dependent, and excessively concerned about sexual exclusivity (White, 1981b). One determinant of the tendency to be jealous seems to be childhood experiences. The more a mother and father express feelings of jealousy, the more their offspring tend to react in that way when they become adults (Bringle and Williams, 1979).

Some people (about one in three college females and one in five males) deliberately attempt to make their partners jealous by their actions (White, 1980a). Students report that they talk about their attraction to someone else, openly flirt with others, go out with someone else, talk about former lovers, or simply make up stories about such matters. The reason for this behavior is to test the relationship, to make one's partner pay more attention, to get revenge, or to attempt to raise one's self-esteem. Obviously, those who try to induce jealousy are playing a dangerous game that can lead to deterioration of the relationship. Interestingly enough, when someone plans to engage in an extramarital affair, he or she is less likely to feel jealous about what the spouse does(Buunk, 1982).

An important aspect of any relationship is the extent to which each partner feels *equitably treated.* Equity exists, for example, when couples believe they are approximately equal in attractiveness, sociability, and intelligence. It is also important for partners to feel equally loved, equally desired sexually, and equally committed to the relationship. Equity also invokes such aspects of life as relative earnings, contributions to housework, and being easy to live with. Research has shown the importance of equity in the satisfaction of dating couples and in marital happiness and stability (Utne et al., 1984).

The deterioration and ending of a relationship.   Same-sex friendships often fade away simply because of physical separation, as when one of the individuals moves to another area (Rose, 1984). Relationships involving love are more painful to dissolve. Levinger (1980) proposes that deterioration begins when one or both partners comes to view conditions as less desirable than was previously the case.

The response to perceived deterioration can be either active or passive (Rusbult and Zembrodt, 1983). Actively, individuals can decide to end the relationship ("exit" behaviors) or to work at improvement ("voice" behaviors). Passively, one can wait for improvement to occur ("loyalty" behaviors) or for deterioration to continue ("neglect"). Voice and loyalty behaviors are judged to be constructive, while exit and neglect are destructive to the relationship. The contrasting possibilities are outlined in Figure 6.15. It is found that destructive behavior is the crucial element in causing distress in a relationship (Rusbult, Johnson, and Morrow, 1986).

Most investigators agree there are a variety of ways in which close relationships end. The process can be fairly simple, as when both partners agree that it is over:

> My lover was a married man who was visiting overnight on his way through Portland. We had a bad night, with a lot of unstated tension by both of us. On the way to the airport next day, we hardly spoke at all. When we did speak it wasn't concerning our relationship. We both knew that it was over and we would probably never see each other again (and that we were both relieved that it was over). (Baxter, 1984, p. 40).

In other instances, there is hostility, pain, and attempts to place the blame:

FIGURE 6.15. One analysis of deteriorating interpersonal relationships focuses on four different reactions, based on contrasting ways of dealing with the problem (Rusbult and Zembrodt, 1983). Once an individual perceives that a relationship is beginning to fail, he or she can respond either *actively* or *passively*. Within each of these possibilities, the person can make positive or negative assumptions about where the relationship is headed. On the positive side, it is possible to work actively in an attempt to improve the relationship or to wait passively for improvement to occur. Negatively, the person can actively end the relationship or passively wait for matters to get worse.

Reacting to a bad relationship: Active versus passive, positive versus negative

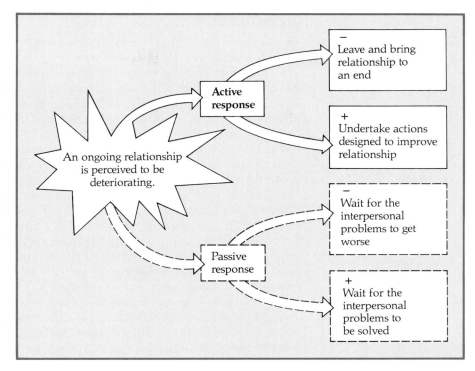

We had a most awful scene yelling and screaming at each other, and that's where the situation ended. We both wanted out, but were both angry with the other for causing the hurt. I wanted out because he was still seeing his former wife. He, of course, denied this, but said that he wanted out because I wasn't giving him enough breathing space—always accusing him of cheating when not with me (Baxter, 1984, p. 40).

Whether a break-up is long and painful or relatively rapid is found to depend on the amount of attraction the two individuals feel (Lee, 1984). Thus, a very loving relationship that fails leads to more unpleasantness, fear, and loneliness than one with weaker emotional bonds.

In any event, deterioration is likely to end in a breakup unless three factors are present. The relationship has to provide a high level of satisfaction; both partners must have already invested a great deal of time and effort; and alternative partners should not be readily available (Rusbult, 1980, 1983; Rusbult, Musante, and Soloman, 1982). Sometimes individuals expect a relationship to fail because they have observed the failure of other couples. Other times, a new life appears to be the only acceptable solution. This body of research leads us to conclude that love may strike an individual suddenly and effortlessly. Maintaining a relationship, in contrast, requires hard work over a long-term period by two committed individuals.

SUMMARY

Attraction is the evaluation of another person along a dimension ranging from love to hate.

Acquaintanceship with a stranger often begins when two people are brought together by such environmental factors as seating assignments in a classroom; **propinquity** leads to repeated exposure which leads to a positive emotional response. Attraction is strongly affected by emotions. One's feelings become *conditioned* to other people, forming the basis of liking or disliking. Initial contact between strangers is most probable if their respective affiliation motives are sufficiently strong, either in terms of traits or in terms of motivation elicited by external factors.

Once two individuals interact, other variables become important. **Physical attractiveness** plays a central role, especially when a romantic relationship is a possibility. There is also a consistently positive effect for various types of *similarity*, ranging from attitudes to personality characteristics. In an ongoing relationship, **reciprocity** becomes vital, in that each person wants and expects the other to express a positive evaluation in words and deeds from time to time.

The ultimate attraction response is love. Most familiar is **passionate love,** an intense emotional state that occurs when one is raised in a culture that stresses love, when an appropriate love object is present, and when some type of physiological arousal is attributed to love. **Companionate love** is a more stable and more lasting basis for a relationship, in that it involves a deep and caring friendship. Relationships often come to an end, and the reasons include jealousy, feelings of inequity, expectations of failure, lack of commitment, changes in one or both partners, and the presence of more desirable alternatives. The closer two individuals have been, the more painful and prolonged the breakup is likely to be. Maintaining a good relationship is a full-time job, one requiring more effort than falling in love in the first place.

GLOSSARY

affiliative need
The motive to seek interpersonal relationships and to form friendships.

attitude similarity
The degree to which two individuals share the same attitudes.

attraction
The degree to which we like other individuals.

balance
In Newcomb's theory, the pleasant state that exists when two people like each other and agree about some topic.

balance theory
A cognitive theory of interpersonal attraction. Attraction is assumed to be based on the relationships among cognitions about another person and about various objects or topics of communication.

companionate love
Love that rests on a firm base of friendship, common interests, mutual respect, and concern for the other person's happiness and welfare.

emotion
A physiological state of arousal associated with specific cognitive labels and appropriate behavior.

friendship motivation
The motive to establish warm and friendly interpersonal relationships.

imbalance
In Newcomb's theory, the unpleasant state that exists when two people like one another but disagree about some topic. Each is motivated to change some aspect of the interaction in order to achieve balance or nonbalance.

jealousy
The thoughts, feelings, and actions that are instigated by a real or imagined rival. Such a rival is a threat to the relationship and to one's self-esteem.

love
An emotional state involving attraction, sexual desire, and concern about the other person. It represents the most positive level of attraction.

matching hypothesis
The proposal that individuals with approximately equal social assets (such as physical attractiveness) will select one another as friends, lovers, spouses, and so on.

need compatibility
The proposal that, for at least some sets of needs, similarity should have a positive influence on attraction. For example, a highly sexed person would be expected to get along well with a highly sexed spouse, whereas an individual with low sex needs would prefer a spouse whose needs are equally low.

need complementarity
The proposal that, for at least some sets of needs, dissimilarity should have a positive influence on attraction. For example, a person with a need to dominate would be expected to get along well with a spouse who had a need to submit to domination.

need for affiliation
The motive to seek interpersonal relationships and to form friendships.

nonbalance
In Newcomb's theory, the indifferent state that exists when two people dislike one another and don't care whether they agree or disagree on various topics.

passionate love
An intense and often unrealistic emotional response to another person. It is interpreted by the individuals involved as "love."

physical attractiveness
The combination of facial features, bodily shape, and grooming that is accepted in a given culture at a given time as being that which is most pleasing.

propinquity
Physical proximity. As propinquity between two individuals increases, the probability of their interacting increases. Repeated interaction tends to lead to familiarity and acquaintanceship.

reinforcement-affect model
A theory proposing that all evaluations are based on positive and negative emotions. These evaluations are directed at whatever stimulus object is responsible for the emotion *and* at any other previously neutral stimulus that happens to be associated with the emotional arousal.

repeated exposure
The theory that repeated contact with any neutral or positive stimulus results in an increasingly positive evaluation.

FOR MORE INFORMATION

Berscheid, E. (1985). Interpersonal attraction. In G. Lindzey and E. Aronson (eds.), *Handbook of social psychology*, vol. 2. New York: Random House.
> This chapter is an up-to-date overview of the empirical research and theoretical formulations related to interpersonal attraction. Professor Berscheid has done extensive work in this field, and she brings an expert's knowledge to bear in summarizing this very large body of knowledge.

Duck, S., and Gilmour, R., eds. (1981–1984). *Personal relationships.* 5 vols. London: Academic Press.
> This is a series of five volumes, each consisting of chapters written by leading investigators in this field. Together, they provide an extensive review and summary of what is known about interpersonal relationships — from their earliest development to the difficulties of maintaining them. The five volumes cover the general topics: *Studying personal relationships* (1981), *Developing personal relationships* (1981), *Personal relationships in disorder* (1981), *Dissolving personal relationships* (1982), and *Repairing personal relationships* (1984).

Duck, S., and Perlman, D., eds. (1985). *Understanding personal relationships: An interdisciplinary approach.* London: Sage.
> This collection of chapters is designed to integrate the work on personal relationships from the fields of social psychology, sociology, clinical psychology, and family studies. This is an optimistic report on the progress being made in a rapidly growing field of social psychological interest.

Hatfield, E., and Walster, G. W. (1985). *A new look at love.* Lanham, MD: University Press of America.
> A well written, interesting, and comprehensive summary of current research and theory dealing with love. Both passionate and companionate love are described and discussed.

Hendrick, C., and Hendrick, S. (1983). *Liking, loving and relating.* Monterey, Cal.: Brooks/Cole.

> This text concentrates on all the topics dealt with in this chapter: interpersonal attraction, love, and personal relationships. Students interested in this area of social psychology will find much of interest in this comprehensive book.

CHAPTER 7

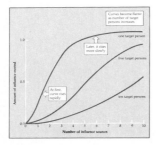

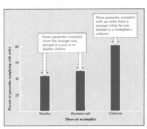

SOCIAL INFLUENCE:
Changing Others' Behavior

"Have you seen the year-end figures?" Chuck Carson asks Joan Ballinger as she enters the real-estate office where they both work.

"No, not yet," she replies, slumping into a chair near Chuck's desk. "But I'm sure there are no surprises. We both know who's going to come out on top — again."

"Well, no argument there," Chuck answers. "Penny's the big Number One, all right. But just look at her total: almost *four* million. Can you believe it? Even with the market this slow she's managed to sell more houses than last year. Whew! I wish I knew how she does it!"

"Me too, me too," Joan murmurs in reply. Then, stroking her chin, she continues. "But you know, I've been kind of watching her lately, to see just what makes her so good, and I've got a few ideas."

"Like what?" Chuck asks, sitting up straight in his chair, and showing keen interest in Joan's words.

"Well, it seems to be a lot of different things. For one, look at her strategy with new prospects. She starts by taking them to the most overpriced houses on her list — ones where the present owners are asking way too much. After that, everything else looks like a real bargain."

"Hmm," Chuck murmurs, "that makes a lot of sense. Why didn't *we* ever think of that?"

"Who knows; maybe if we did, *we'd* be on top around here instead of her. But that's just the start," Joan continues. "Her next move is to take them to the best houses around — ones way outside their price range. Then, when she finally gets around to houses they *can* afford, they seem downright cheap by comparison."

"Clever, very clever," Chuck comments. "That way she boosts them right up to their limit without wasting much time."

"Right. And then, at that point, she starts working on the status angle. She drops lots of hints to the effect that 'nice people like you' tend to live in certain neighborhoods — the ones where her top-priced houses are located, naturally."

"Naturally," Chuck says, shaking his head. "But don't forget something else: she's darn good with people — about the best I've ever seen. You know how she operates. She's free with the compliments, but never enough to overdo it. And she's great on doing favors for her clients. Remember the time she went to pick up that couple at the airport at 3:00 A.M.? After that, there was no way they could buy a house from anyone but her."

"I remember," Joan agrees, nodding her head. "But she doesn't stop there. She even does things for people *after* the sale. That's why she gets so much repeat business. Hmphh! She's actually sold *three* houses to the Valentes, and two houses to more people than I can remember. How can you win against someone like her?"

"You can't," Chuck exclaims, "but maybe, just maybe, you can learn to play the same kind of game. . . ."

AT ONE time or other, almost everyone has had the following daydream: somehow, we gain a special skill or power that permits us to exert total control over others. Through this power, we can get them to do, think, or feel anything we wish. This is a tantalizing fantasy, and for good reason. After all, if we possessed this ability, we could satisfy most of our desires instantly, and with very little effort. Unfortunately, of course, no magic formula for gaining such control exists. The people around us have minds of their own, and are willing to do our bidding only sometimes, and to a limited degree. Thus, the fantasy of exercising complete control over them must remain just that — an enticing but unattainable daydream.

While total control over others is beyond our grasp, however, there are many tactics we can use at least to move in this direction. In short, there are many procedures we can employ to exert **social influence** over others — to change their behavior, attitudes, or feelings in ways we desire (Cowan, Drinkard, and MacGavin, 1984; refer to Figure 7.1). Among the most important, common, and effective of these are **conformity, compliance,** and **obedience.**

Conformity occurs when individuals change their behavior in order to adhere to existing *social norms* — widely accepted rules indicating how people should behave in certain situations or under specific circumstances (Moscovici, 1985). Thus, it represents a crucial means through which groups, or even entire societies, mold the actions of their

FIGURE 7.1. As suggested by this cartoon, there are many different tactics for exerting influence over others. (Source: Reprinted with special permission of King Features Syndicate, Inc.)

Social influence in action: One example

members. A clear example of conformity is provided by the fact that most persons speak in a whisper when in libraries or hospitals, even if they usually prefer to converse in louder tones. They do so because both formal and informal rules indicate that this is the "correct" (appropriate) way to behave. As we will soon see, pressures toward conformity exist in many settings, and often exert profound effects upon social behavior.

In contrast, *compliance* represents a more direct or personal form of social influence. It takes place in situations where individuals alter their behavior in response to direct requests from others. Many techniques for enhancing compliance — for increasing the probability that target persons will say "yes" — exist, and when used with skill, these can prove very effective indeed. Finally, *obedience* occurs in situations where persons change their behavior in response to direct commands from others. Usually, the individuals who issue such orders have some means of enforcing submission to them: they hold *power* over those on the receiving end. Surprisingly, though, direct orders can frequently be effective in altering others' behavior even when the persons who employ them actually possess little or no authority over the recipients.

The remainder of this chapter focuses on the three major types of social influence described above. For each, we will consider why they seem to work — what makes them effective in changing others' behavior — as well as some of the factors that influence their success in this regard. In addition, we will touch upon their use in practical settings — how they are often applied by persons who hope to profit (either financially or socially) from getting others to say "yes."

CONFORMITY: *How Groups Exert Influence*

Have you ever found yourself in a situation where you felt that you stuck out like the proverbial sore thumb? If so, you have already had first-hand experience with pressures toward conformity. In such situations, you probably felt a strong desire to "get back into line" — to fit in with the other people around you. Such pressures toward conformity seem to stem from the fact that in many situations there are both spoken and unspoken rules indicating how we should or ought to behave. These are known as *social norms*, and can be quite precise and explicit. For example, governments often function through constitutions and written codes of law. Athletic contests are usually regulated by written rules. And signs along highways, in airports, and countless other public places often describe expected behavior in great detail.

In contrast, other norms are unspoken and implicit (e.g., Zuckerman, Miserandino, and Bernieri, 1983). For example, most of us obey such unwritten rules as "Don't stare at strangers on the street or in elevators," and "Don't come to parties or other social gatherings exactly on time." And we are often strongly influenced by current and rapidly changing standards of dress, speech, and personal style. Regardless of whether social norms are explicit or implicit, however, most are obeyed by most persons much of the time. For example, few people visit restaurants without leaving some sort of tip. Few drivers park in places reserved for handicapped motorists. And virtually everyone, regardless of political beliefs, stands when the national anthem is played at sports events and other public gatherings. At first glance, this strong tendency toward conformity—toward going along with society's expectations about how we should behave in various situations—may strike you as objectionable. After all, it does prevent us from "doing our own thing" on many occasions. Actually, though, there is a strong and eminently

FIGURE 7.2. When pressures to conform seem to serve no beneficial purpose, they can be objectionable.

Some social norms make little sense

rational basis for the existence of so much conformity: without it, we would quickly find ourselves in the midst of social chaos! For example, imagine what would happen outside movie theaters, at voting booths, and at supermarket checkout counters if people did not follow the simple rule, "Form a line and wait your turn." Similarly, consider the danger to both drivers and pedestrians if there were no clear and widely followed traffic regulations. Often, then, conformity serves a very useful function. But please note: this does not imply that it is *always* helpful. At times, norms governing individual behavior appear to have no obvious purpose — they simply exist. Why, to mention one instance, must meetings in many organizations start ten, twenty, or more minutes after their scheduled times? And why, to mention another, must both men and women often wear clothing that is ill-suited to prevailing weather (e.g., ties, jackets, and vests in summer, skirts and sheer nylon hosiery in winter)? It is in cases such as these, where norms governing behavior persist without offering any obvious practical benefits that some persons, at least, find them objectionable (see Figure 7.2).

While the existence of strong pressures toward conformity was recognized both within social psychology and outside it for many decades, it was not until the 1950s that this important process was subjected to systematic study. At that time, Asch (1951) conducted a series of revealing experiments that added much to our knowledge of this basic form of social influence. For a summary of his influential work, please refer to the **Focus** insert on pages 228–229.

Factors affecting conformity: Cohesiveness, group size, social support, and sex

Asch's research demonstrated the existence of powerful pressures toward conformity. However, even a moment's reflection indicates that conformity does not occur to the same degree in all settings or among all groups of persons. This fact, in turn, raises an intriguing question: what factors determine the extent to which individuals yield to conformity pressure? Several decades of research on this issue have generated a long list of variables that play a role in this regard. Among the most important of these appear to be (1) *cohesiveness* — degree of attraction to the influencing group, (2) group *size*, (3) the presence or absence of *social support*, and (4) the *sex* of the persons exposed to social pressure.

Cohesiveness and conformity: One reason why some groups are more influential than others. Imagine the following situation. In the past, you have considered yourself to be a political moderate, with a slight preference for liberal policies and Democratic candidates. Recently, though, you've noticed that most of your close friends are becoming more and more conservative, in true "Yuppie" fashion. Will your own views change? Perhaps. At the very least, you may refrain from contra-

FOCUS ON RESEARCH:
Classic Contributions

Studying Conformity: The Subject's Dilemma

Suppose, right before an important exam, you find that your answer to a homework problem is different from that obtained by three of your friends. Until you compared their results with yours, you were certain that you were correct. The problem worked out the way it was supposed to, and you carefully followed all the steps outlined by your instructor. So who's right? There's no time to find out, for at this moment the exam begins. Sure enough, one of the questions it contains relates to this very problem. Which answer should you enter — the one you obtained or the one reported by your friends? Unfortunately, life is filled with such dilemmas — instances in which we are torn between sticking to our own judgments or accepting those offered by others. What do most people do in such cases? In order to find out (and so to gain insight into the nature of conformity), Asch (1951) conducted a series of studies employing the following procedures.

Participants in these investigations were asked to respond to a series of simple perceptual problems (refer to Figure 7.3). In each, they indicated which of three comparison lines matched a standard line in length. Several other persons (usually six to eight) were also present during the session, but unknown to the subject, all were accomplices of the experimenter. On prearranged occasions (twelve out of eighteen problems), the accomplices offered answers that were clearly wrong (e.g., they unanimously stated that line *A* matched the standard line in Figure 7.3). Moreover, they gave their answers before the subject gave his. Thus, on such trials, subjects faced the same type of dilemma as the one described above: should they go along with the other persons present, or should they "stick to their guns" and provide what they felt were correct answers? You may be surprised to learn that in fact, participants in Asch's research showed strong tendencies to conform. Indeed, fully 76 percent of those tested in several studies went along with the group's false answers at least once. In contrast, only 5 percent of the subjects in a control group, who responded to the same perceptual problems but in the absence of any falsely-answering accomplices, made such errors. It is also important to note, though, that most subjects resisted conformity most of the time. As shown in Figure 7.4, almost 24 percent never conformed, and many others

FIGURE 7.3. One of the perceptual problems used by Asch in his classic research on conformity. Subjects' task was to indicate which of the three comparison lines (*A*, *B*, or *C*) matched the standard line in length.

Asch's line-judging task: An example

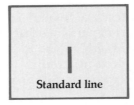

Standard line

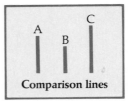

Comparison lines

FIGURE 7.4. While most subjects in Asch's research conformed at least once, a majority resisted group pressure on most occasions. For example, fully 58 percent conformed three times or less during the twelve critical trials (occasions when the accomplices made false judgments). (Source: Based on data from Asch, 1957.)

Asch's key results: Most persons conform, but only part of the time

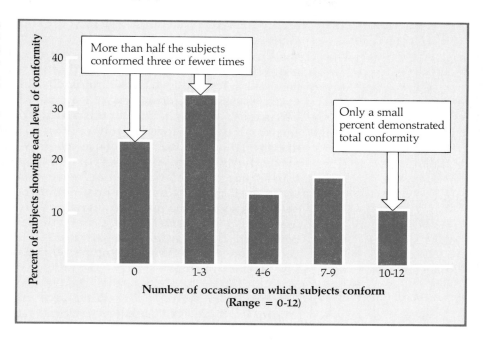

finding points to the importance of distinguishing between *public compliance* — doing or saying what others around us say or do, and *private acceptance* — actually coming to feel or think as they do. Often, it appears, we overtly adhere to social norms or yield to group pressure without changing our private views or interpretations of the social world (Maas and Clark, 1984). Thus, in Asch's research, and in many real-life situations as well, individuals may modify their overt actions so as to "get into line" with others, while at the same time maintaining their attitudes and personal views of reality intact. We will return to this distinction between public compliance and private acceptance below, in our discussion of the impact of small but committed minorities upon larger but perhaps less committed majorities.

yielded on only a few of the critical trials (trials on which the accomplices gave wrong answers). Yet, a large majority did conform to the accomplice's false answers at least part of the time. These results, and those obtained in many later studies (Tanford and Penrod, 1984), point to an unsettling conclusion: many persons find it less upsetting to publicly contradict the evidence of their own senses than to disagree openly with the unanimous judgments of other persons — even those of total strangers.

In subsequent research, Asch (1957) repeated the above procedures with one important change: instead of stating their answers out loud, subjects wrote them down on a piece of paper. As you might suspect, conformity dropped sharply under these conditions. This

dicting your friends when they express conservative political views. In short, you will experience considerable pressure to conform. Now, in contrast, imagine that you decide to take an art course in the evening, at a nearby community college. During class, several of the other people present make statements that suggest they hold extremely liberal views. Will their remarks have much impact upon you? Probably not. The reason for your different reactions in these two situations should be obvious. While you care strongly about the views of your close friends, you have much less interest in the opinions of the casual acquaintances in your class. Put another way, you have a much higher level of attraction or liking for your friends than for the virtual strangers. Thus, it is not at all surprising that the former group will exert a much stronger influence upon you than the latter. In social psychology, attraction toward a particular group to which we belong, or toward its individual members, is usually described by the term *cohesiveness*. And there is little doubt about the impact of this factor upon conformity: high levels of cohesiveness tend to produce much stronger pressures toward conformity than low levels of cohesiveness (e.g., Forsyth, 1983). Where conformity is concerned, therefore, all groups are definitely *not* equal. Ones high in cohesiveness are much more important in this regard than ones that are low on this dimension.

Conformity and group size: Why, with respect to social influence, "more" isn't always "better."   A second factor that exerts important effects upon our tendency to conform is the size of the influencing group. At first glance, you might guess that the greater the number of persons around us who act in some manner or who state some opinion, the greater our tendency to do the same. In fact, though, the relationship between group size and conformity is more complex. Studies designed to investigate this issue have often reported that conformity does increase with rising group size, but only up to a point. And, surprisingly, this point seems to occur quite rapidly. Conformity pressure, and the tendency to yield to it, seems to rise quickly up to about three or four group members (influence sources). Beyond this level, however, further increments in group size produce less and less additional effect (e.g., Gerard, Wilhelmy, and Conolley, 1968). One reason for this relationship may be as follows. As group size rises beyond three or four members, individuals exposed to social pressure may begin to suspect *collusion*. That is, they may conclude that group members are not expressing individual views or behaving in accordance with individual preferences. Rather, they are working together to exert influence (Wildman, 1977).

Regardless of the reason for the leveling-off of social influence, there is another complication in the picture. Groups do not always seek to exert their influence upon a single, hold-out member. On the contrary, conformity pressure may be directed to several persons rather than to only one. How does this factor enter the picture? One answer is provided by a formal model of social influence (the **social influence** or **SIM model**) proposed recently by Tanford and Penrod (1984). These investigators suggest that the function relating group size to conformity or social influence is *S*-shaped in form (refer to Figure 7.5). At first, each person added to the group (each additional source of influence) produces a larger increment in conformity pressure than the one before. Soon, however, this function levels off, so that each additional person adds *less* to the total amount of social influence than did the preceding ones. The SIM model also suggests that as the number of targets of social influence increases, the function relating group size to conformity becomes flatter in shape (see Figure 7.5). This, too, makes a great deal of sense. After all, even as a group increases in size, its impact upon several different members will be less than its impact upon a single hold-out. When Tanford and Penrod applied their model to the findings of many previous studies concerned with the impact of group size on conformity, they found that it predicted the results of these investigations with a high degree of accuracy. Thus, the SIM model appears to provide an excellent description of how social influence varies with both group size and the number of persons who are the target of conformity pressure.

The effects of support from others: Does having an ally help?   In Asch's research (and in many later studies of conformity) subjects were exposed

FIGURE 7.5. The SIM model predicts that at first, influence rises rapidly as group size increases. Soon, however, this function levels off, so that additional group members add less and less effect. The model also predicts that the curve relating group size to social influence becomes flatter as the number of targets rises. (Source: Based on suggestions by Tanford and Penrod, 1984.)

Group size, number of target persons, and social influence: The SIM model.

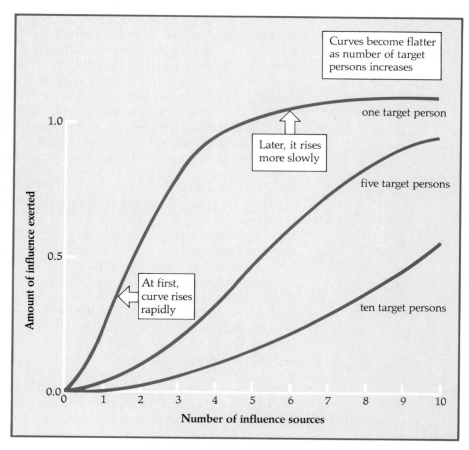

to social pressure from a unanimous group. All the other persons present seemed to hold views different from their own. Under such conditions, it is hardly surprising that many individuals yielded to social pressure. What would happen, though, if persons facing such pressure discovered that they had an *ally* — someone who shared their views, or at least failed to endorse the same position as the majority? Under such conditions, perhaps, conformity might be reduced. That this is actually so is indicated by the results of several different experiments (e.g., Allen and Levine, 1971; Morris and Miller, 1975). In these investigations, subjects provided with an ally or partner showed much less conformity than subjects not supplied with social support.

Perhaps the impressive effectiveness of such support in reducing conformity is best suggested by two additional facts. First, conformity is reduced even when the partner or ally is someone not competent in the present situation. For example, in one study involving visual judgments, conformity was reduced even by a partner who wore thick glasses and who could not even see the relevant stimuli (Allen and Levine, 1971). Second, it is not even crucial that the ally share the subject's views. Conformity is reduced even if this person merely differs from the other group members — breaks their united front, so to speak.

These and other findings suggest that almost any form of social support can be helpful from the point of view of resisting social pressure. As you might suspect, though, certain types are more effective than others. For example, it appears that support received early — before pressures toward conformity have grown — is more helpful than support received later, after such pressures are in place (Morris, Miller, and Spangenberg, 1977). Apparently, learning that someone else shares their views can help strengthen individuals' confidence in their own judgments and so enhances ability to resist group pressure as it develops. This fact has important implications for many real-life settings. If you ever find yourself in a situation in which pressures toward conformity are rising, and you feel that they should be resisted, try to speak out as quickly as possible. The sooner you do, the greater your chances of rallying others to your side and resisting the powerful impact of the majority.

Sex differences in conformity: A matter of status?   Many early experiments on conformity yielded a result that, from the perspective of the late 1980s, is somewhat unsettling: females seemed to be much more conforming than males (e.g., Crutchfield, 1955). This finding was consistent with then-prevailing views about the supposed characteristics of the two sexes (e.g., men are "tough" and women more yielding). Thus, this result was quickly accepted as true by many social psychologists. Indeed, for more than two decades the view that females are more susceptible to social influence than males went largely unchallenged. Beginning in the early 1970s, however, it was subjected to renewed examination. The results of this "second wave" of research were directly contrary to those of the first: no large or consistent differences between the sexes with respect to the tendency to conform were uncovered. Since these more recent studies are more sophisticated in both design and execution (e.g., Eagly and Carli, 1981), the conclusion they support would seem to be the correct one. But it is interesting to ask *why* the earlier experiments often found greater conformity on the part of females. The answer seems to lie in the type of materials employed in such research.

Briefly, in some of these investigations, the tasks or items presented to subjects tended to be more familiar to males than to females. Since individuals are usually more willing to yield to social influence from others when they are uncertain about how to behave than when they are more confident, it is hardly surprising that females demonstrated higher levels of conformity: after all, the dice were strongly loaded against them. That this factor was indeed responsible for the sex differences obtained in early research is indicated by the findings of an experiment carried out by Sistrunk and McDavid (1971). These researchers found that when females were less familiar with the items used than males, they did in fact show greater yielding to group pressure. However, when the tables were turned, so that the items used were less familiar to males, it was *they* who showed greater conformity. Clearly, then, in yielding to social pressure differences related to confidence or familiarity should *not* be attributed to basic and important differences between the two sexes.

In sum, it now seems clear that there are no important differences between males and females in terms of the tendency to conform. Yet, as you probably realize, the view that the sexes *do* differ in this respect continues to persist. Many persons still seem to believe that females are easier to "push around" or influence than males. Why is this the case? One possibility involves widespread beliefs about *status* and its relationship to both influenceability and sex. Consider the following points. First, many persons believe (and with some justification) that individuals low in status are somewhat easier to influence than are individuals high in status (e.g., Kipnis, 1984). Second, many also believe that, on average, females have lower status than males, both in society generally and in a wide range of work settings. Together, these beliefs lead to the assumption that females are often more conforming than males (refer to Figure 7.6).

FIGURE 7.6. The widespread — but false — belief that females are more susceptible to social influence than males seems to stem from the following factors: (1) many persons believe that low-status individuals are easier to influence than are high status persons, and (2) many also believe that females possess lower status than males. (Source: Based on suggestions by Kipnis, 1984, and Eagly and Wood, 1982.)

One explanation for the false belief that females are easier to influence than males

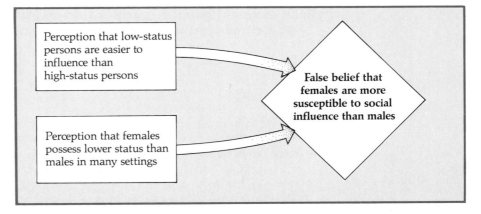

Support for this reasoning has been obtained in research carried out by Eagly and her colleagues. For example, in one study, Eagly and Wood (1982) asked men and women to read a brief story in which one employee of a business attempted to influence the views of another employee of the opposite sex. In half the cases the would-be influencer was male and the recipient was female; in the remainder, the reverse was true. In half of the stories, job titles were included, thus informing subjects of the status of the persons involved. In the remaining instances, information of this type was omitted. After reading the story, subjects were asked to indicate the extent to which the recipient would be influenced by the communicator. It was predicted that when no information on status was provided, subjects would tend to assume that females are lower in this regard than males. Thus, they would predict greater compliance by female recipients than by male recipients. When information on status was provided, however, this factor, rather than sex, would affect their judgments. Both predictions were confirmed. In the absence of any information about relative status, subjects predicted substantially greater yielding by females.

While these findings support the view that contrasting perceptions of the status of males and females contribute to the assumption that females are more conforming, it is important to note that similar results were not obtained in a follow-up study employing similar procedures (Steffen and Eagly, 1985). Here, when no information about the status of would-be influencers or their targets was provided, subjects did *not* assume that males were higher on this dimension. And, accordingly, they did not expect males to be more influential, and females to be more yielding. This difference between the results of the two investigations may stem from the fact that the persons mentioned in the stories in the latter study were described as working on the same task, and so appeared to be heavily interdependent; this was not the case in the experiment by Eagly and Wood (1982). However, as we noted in Chapter 5, it may also reflect continued progress on the part of females, especially in work settings. As women move into an increasing number of high-level jobs, the perception that they occupy only low rungs on the corporate or occupational ladder may be fading, along with other, related stereotypes (e.g., Peters et al., 1984). To the extent such changes continue, they may ultimately help to eliminate the widespread but false belief that females are more susceptible to social influence than males.

The bases of conformity: Why we often choose to "go along"

As we have just seen, many factors determine whether, and to what extent, conformity will occur. Yet, despite such variations, one fact is clear: such behavior is very common. To repeat a phrase we used before, most people conform to most norms most of the time. This, in turn, raises an important question: why is this so? Why do we usually choose to "go along" with the expectations of others, the rules established by society, or the norms of various groups to which we belong? As we're sure you can guess, there are no simple answers to this question. Many factors contribute to our strong tendency to conform. The most important of these, however, seem to involve two basic needs possessed by all human beings: the desire to be liked and the desire to be right (Insko, 1985).

The desire to be liked: Normative social influence.   How can we induce other persons to like us? This is one of the eternal puzzles of social life. As we saw in chapter 6, many strategies can prove effective in this regard. One of the most successful, though, is that of being as similar to others as possible. From our earliest days we learn that agreeing with the persons around us, and behaving much as they do, causes them to like us. Indeed, parents, teachers, friends, and others often heap praise and approval upon us for demonstrating such similarity. One important reason we conform, therefore, is simple: we have learned that doing so can yield the love and acceptance we so strongly desire. Conformity stemming from this source is known as **normative social influence,** since it involves altering our behavior to meet the expectations of others. And as you probably know from your own experience, it is extremely common.

The desire to be right: Informational social influence.   If you want to determine the dimensions of a room, you can measure them directly. Similarly, if you need to know the population of a particular city, you can look it up in an atlas. But how can you establish the "accuracy" of various political views or decide what kind of clothes are the most stylish and attractive? Here, there are no simple physical tests or handy reference sources to consult. Yet, you probably have just as strong a desire to be "right" about such matters as you do about questions relating to the physical world. The solution to this dilemma is obvious: in order to answer such questions, or at least to obtain information about them, we turn to other people. We use *their* opinions and *their* actions as guides for our own. This second important source of conformity is known as **informational social influence,** and is also a basic part of everyday life. In countless situations we choose to act and think like others because doing so assures us that we are "right" — or at least on the right track!

Together, these two factors — our strong desire to be liked (normative social influence) and our strong desire to be right (informational social influence) — go a long way toward assuring that conformity, not independence, will be our *modus operandi* (our standard manner of behaving). Indeed, given their powerful impact, it is hardly surprising that we choose to fit in with the crowd in most situations, much of the time.

Minority influence: Why the majority doesn't always rule

So far in this discussion, we have viewed conformity as a type of one-way street: the majority exerts influence and the minority helplessly knuckles under. In many cases, this is indeed the overall pattern. Yet we should also note that history is filled with events in which small but determined minorities have turned the tables on even overwhelming majorities and have *exerted* rather than yielded to social influence. For example, such giants of the scientific world as Galileo, Pasteur, and Freud faced large and virtually unanimous majorities who rejected their theories and views. Yet, over time, they won growing numbers of colleagues to their side, until ultimately their views prevailed. Similarly, in recent decades, initially small but resolute groups of reformers (e.g., environmentalists, persons seeking the elimination of racial and sexual prejudice) have often succeeded in altering even deeply entrenched attitudes and values. Such events suggest that minorities are not always powerless in the face of large and unified majorities. On the contrary, they can sometimes overcome the odds, and make *their* views prevail.

Direct evidence for the occurrence of such effects has been obtained in many different experiments (Maas and Clark, 1984; Moscovici, 1985). For example, in one well-conducted study, Bray, Johnson, and Chilstrom (1982) arranged for groups of six persons — four subjects and two accomplices — to discuss a series of problems of considerable interest to them (e.g., a plan to charge students for athletic tickets which had previously been free). During the discussion of each problem, the accomplices adopted a dissenting opinion, opposite to the one held by the four subjects. Later, after the discussions, subjects indicated their views on each issue. Results offered clear support for the occurrence of minority influence: subjects exposed to the dissenting views of the two accomplices did shift in the directions recommended by these persons, relative to subjects in a control condition who were never exposed to minority influence. These findings, and similar results reported in other studies (e.g., Moscovici and Faucheux, 1972), indicate that minorities can indeed affect the views of even much larger majorities. Additional research, however, suggests that such effects are more likely to occur under some conditions than others.

First, in order for a minority to be effective in influencing a majority, it is important that its members be consistent. If, instead, they "waffle," or oscillate back and forth between their own view and that of the majority, their impact will be lessened. Second, in order for a minority to affect a larger majority, such persons must avoid appearing rigid and dogmatic (Mugny, 1975). A minority that merely repeats the same position over and over again will often be less effective than one which demonstrates a degree of flexibility in its stance. Third, the general social context in which a minority operates is important. If a minority argues for a position that is consistent with current social trends (e.g., conservative views at a time of growing conservatism), its chances of influencing a majority are greater than if it argues for a position that is "out of phase" with such trends. Finally, it appears that *single minorities* — ones that differ from the majority only with respect to their beliefs or attitudes — are more effective in exerting influence than *double minorities* — ones that differ both in their attitudes and in their group membership. For example, in the United States members of a black radical group holding extreme political views would constitute a double minority; members of a white radical group holding similar views would represent a single minority.

In sum, it appears that under appropriate conditions committed, consistent minorities can indeed change the views of even much larger majorities. This fact, in turn, raises an important question: why is this the case? How, in short, can small numbers of persons not only resist pressure to get back "in line" from larger majorities, but actually turn the tables and serve as the source rather than as the mere recipient of social influence? One possible answer is provided by key aspects of attribution theory (Maas and Clark, 1984). As you may recall from our discussion of this topic in Chapter 2, we tend to view others' behavior as stemming from internal causes under conditions where (1) consensus is low (other persons don't act in the same way that they do), (2) consistency is high (the persons in question act in the same manner across time), and (3) distinctiveness is low (these persons act in the same manner in other situations). Clearly, these conditions apply very well to the actions of highly committed minorities. Such persons adopt an unpopular stand, maintain it consistently, and act in accordance with it in many different situations. The result: their actions are viewed as stemming from deep conviction and commitment. Little wonder, then, that their views are often taken seriously, and are at least considered with care by the majorities around them. In addition, of course, the *augmenting* principle comes into action: minorities adopt and maintain their unpopular views even in the face of strong pressure to give them up. Thus, the tendency of majority members to attribute their actions to conviction and commitment is further strengthened. (Refer to Figure 7.7 for a summary of these suggestions.)

FIGURE 7.7. Because minorities demonstrate low consensus, high consistency, and low distinctiveness, and also because they maintain unpopular views in the face of pressure to give them up, they are often perceived as possessing very strong convictions. This may account, at least in part, for their ability to exert influence upon much larger majorities.

The impact of minorities: One possible explanation

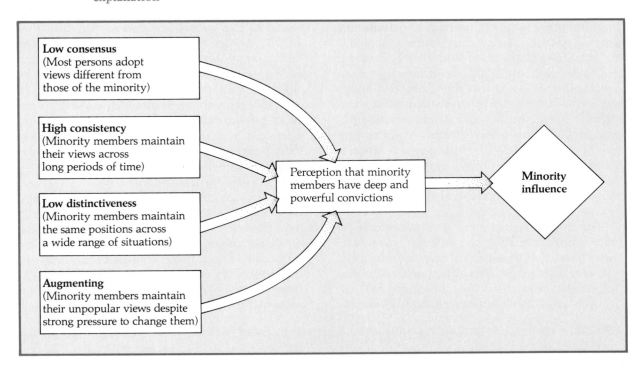

Low consensus
(Most persons adopt views different from those of the minority)

High consistency
(Minority members maintain their views across long periods of time)

Low distinctiveness
(Minority members maintain the same positions across a wide range of situations)

Augmenting
(Minority members maintain their unpopular views despite strong pressure to change them)

Perception that minority members have deep and powerful convictions

Minority influence

Minority and Majority Influence:
Two Processes or One?

That both majorities and minorities exert social influence is obvious. But how do they produce such effects? Two opposing views exist. According to one—the *single process* approach—both minorities and majorities exert social influence through the same basic process (Latané and Wolf, 1981). Briefly, the greater the number of influence sources (persons attempting to exert influence), the greater the influence produced. (Recall our discussion of the SIM model on pages 230–231.) In contrast, a second view—the *dual process* approach—suggests that minorities and majorities exert their impact in different ways (Moscovici, 1980). According to this view, majorities exert social influence because they control important material and psychological benefits that group members seek. Thus, they induce individuals to pay careful attention to what the majority is saying, and produce *public* influence—overt compliance with the majority's position. In contrast, minorities have an impact because, as noted above, they are perceived as being highly committed to their position. Because of this fact, they encourage individuals to consider the validity of their views quite carefully, and often produce *private* or latent influence. Which of these proposals is correct? While existing evidence is mixed—providing some support for both views—an experiment by Wolf (1985) seems more consistent with the single-process approach.

In this investigation, groups of four female students played the role of jurors, and considered a civil case involving an individual who was hurt while in another person's house. Before discussing this case, they met briefly to become acquainted, and rated their liking for one another. The experimenter then provided them with pre-arranged feedback indicating either that they liked one another very much (high cohesiveness) or that they disliked each other (low cohesiveness). After these procedures, subjects received information about the case, and were asked to indicate how much money should be awarded to the person who was hurt. It was at this point that social influence was introduced into the situation. Subjects next received a note from one of the other group members (designated as Juror C) indicating how much she thought should be paid in damages. In the *majority source* condition, this person's recommendation was lower than that of the subject, but in line with the recommendations of the other two group members (Jurors A and D). In the *minority source* condition, in contrast, this person's recommendation was lower than that of the subject, but also much lower than that of the other two group members. Thus, in the first condition the would-be influencer was part of a majority, while in the second she was in the minority. Finally, a third aspect of the study involved the *consistency* with which this other person (whose responses were actually simulated by the experimenter) maintained her position. In a *high-consistency* condition she stuck to the same position throughout, and expressed confidence in it. In the *low-consistency* condition she maintained the same position, but expressed some doubts about its accuracy.

The dual-process model outlined above suggests that the degree of influence exerted by a majority will depend mostly upon group dependence factors such as cohesiveness, while the degree of influence exerted by a minority will depend largely on factors relating to behavioral style, such as consistency. In contrast, the single-process model predicts that majorities will generally produce stronger in-

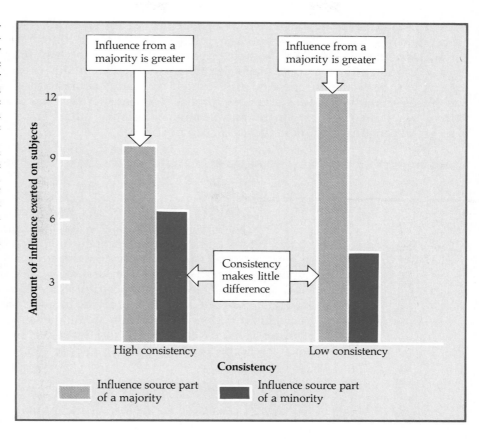

FIGURE 7.8. Consistent with the single-process view of minority influence, subjects were influenced to a greater extent by another person when she appeared to be part of a majority than when she appeared to be part of a minority. Further, contrary to the dual-process view, the consistency with which this person stuck to her position had little effect on her success in exerting influence. (Source: Based on data from Wolf, 1985.)

Minority influence: Evidence for the single-process view

fluence, and that if either cohesiveness or consistency plays a role in this process, the impact of these factors will be stronger in the case of majorities. As you can see from Figure 7.8, results offered support for the single-process view. Subjects were more strongly influenced by Juror C's recommendations when she was part of a clear majority than when she was a minority of one. In addition, as predicted by the single-process view, both majority and minority influence were enhanced by high group cohesiveness. Third, the impact of cohesiveness was indeed stronger in the case of a majority than in the case of a minority. And finally,

contrary to the dual-process approach, Juror C's degree of consistency failed to exert any appreciable effects upon her success in influencing subjects.

These findings, and those of related studies (e.g., Wolf and Latané, 1983), suggest that minorities and majorities exert their impact through the same basic process. However, before concluding, we should note that the manner in which these two potential sources of influence produce their effects may differ in at least two important ways. First, as mentioned earlier, majorities appear to be more effective in producing public compliance, while minorities are more successful in generating private acceptance—genuine change in underlying views (Maas and Clark, 1984). Second, minorities may induce other persons to consider more aspects of the issues in question, and to develop solutions they would otherwise probably overlook. In short, minorities may stimulate greater cognitive effort on the part of other group members (Nemeth, 1986). In this way, they may contribute to the development of better, more carefully reasoned decisions. To the extent this is actually the case, small but highly committed minorities can offer contributions to larger groups that far outweigh their limited numbers.

In sum, it appears that one reason committed minorities are often effective in influencing larger majorities is that they are perceived by these persons as passionately committed to their views. This gets the majority's attention. And then, assuming the conditions outlined above exist (e.g., the minority's position is consistent with current social trends), the stage is set for the few to influence the many. (Do minorities and majorities exert social influence in the same manner? Or are different processes involved? For a discussion of this intriguing question, please see the **Focus** insert that begins on page 238.)

COMPLIANCE: To Ask—Sometimes—Is to Receive

Requests from others are a basic part of social life. Friends ask for favors. Salespersons try to induce us to purchase their products. Lovers, spouses, and roommates ask us to change various aspects of our behavior. And politicians request our votes or financial support. We could continue almost indefinitely, for the list is practically endless. By now, though, you probably recognize the main point: attempts to gain compliance through direct requests are one of the most common, if not *the* most common, forms of social influence.

At first glance, this approach to changing others' behavior seems quite straightforward. And in its most basic form, it is: persons seeking compliance simply express their wishes, and hope they'll be granted. Often, though, attempts to gain compliance are much more subtle, and take the following form. Persons wishing to alter others' behavior do not present their requests "cold." Rather, they begin with preliminary steps or maneuvers designed to tip the balance in their favor — to enhance the likelihood that the targets of their requests will say "yes." Many different tactics are used for this purpose, and you have probably encountered most in your daily life. Among the most successful, though, are ones based on (1) **ingratiation**, (2) **reciprocity**, and (3) **multiple requests**.

Ingratiation: Liking as a key to influence

Earlier we noted that most people have a strong desire to be liked by others. While this motive probably stems from several different sources, one of the most important of these can be simply stated: we realize that if others like us, they are more willing to do things for us. That is, they are more likely to satisfy our wishes, help us with various tasks, and say "yes" to our requests. Recognition of this basic fact lies behind a common technique for gaining compliance: *ingratiation*. What this involves, in essence, is a strategy in which we first try to get others to like us, and then, after this has been accomplished, expose them to various requests (Jones, 1964). Several different procedures for enhancing our appeal to others in this fashion exist (Cialdini, 1985).

First, we can seek to accomplish this goal by improving our physical appearance; in general, attractive persons are liked much more than unattractive ones (Berscheid, 1985). Second, we can attempt to convince them that we are similar to them in some respect. This can involve demonstrating that we hold the same attitudes, that we have similar interests, or even that we possess the same traits (Byrne, 1971). Third, we can use a set of tactics best described by the phrase *other-enhancement* (Wortman and Linsenmeier, 1977). These all center around the goal of communicating a high degree of personal regard to the individuals we later wish to influence—convincing them that we like and care about *them*. Other-enhancement can involve complimenting such persons, hanging on their every word, or transmitting subtle nonverbal cues suggestive of positive feelings about them (see Figure 7.9). Fourth, we can engage in *impression management*, efforts to "put our best foot forward" and convince others that we possess many desirable traits (e.g., sincerity, intelligence, friendliness; refer to Chapter 2). Finally, we can sometimes gain others' liking merely by associating ourselves with positive events or even with people they already like. For example, we can "name-drop," thus indicating that we are linked to important persons.

FIGURE 7.9. *Other-enhancement* often takes the form of providing target persons with excessive and undeserved praise. (Source: Reprinted with special permission of King Features Syndicate, Inc.)

Ingratiation: A common tactic for gaining compliance

Direct evidence for the use of such tactics has recently been reported in an ingenious study by Godfrey, Jones, and Lord (1986). These researchers asked pairs of unacquainted male and female subjects to carry on two brief conversations with one another. Within each pair, one individual was asked to try to make the other person like him or her as much as possible. (Subjects in a control group were not given such instructions.) After the conversations were completed, subjects rated one another on a number of dimensions. In addition, videotapes of their conversations were carefully coded and analyzed by two trained raters. Results indicated that the subjects told to ingratiate themselves with their partners succeeded in this task: they were rated as more likable by these persons after the second conversation than after the first. In contrast, subjects in the control group failed to achieve such gains (refer to Figure 7.10). Further, some of the factors behind this success were apparent in the tapes. For example, the ingratiating subjects reduced the amount of time they spoke, and showed more agreement with their

FIGURE 7.10. Subjects instructed to make a stranger like them as much as possible succeeded at this task: their ratings of likability improved across two brief conversations with another person. In contrast, subjects not told to be ingratiating failed to achieve similar gains. (Source: Based on data from Godfrey, Jones, and Lord, 1986.)

Ingratiation: Direct evidence for its success

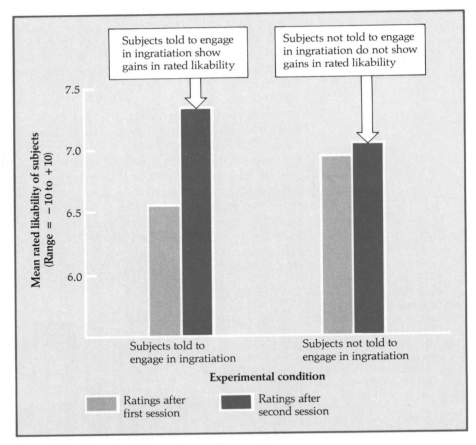

partners from the first to the second conversation. Again, control subjects failed to show such changes.

Through various tactics, then, we can increase others' liking for us, and so their willingness to say "yes" to later requests. Of course, as you probably already realize, all of these procedures can be overdone. If they are, the target persons may realize that we are simply trying to "butter them up," and the chances of later compliance may be reduced rather than increased. When ingratiation is used with skill, though, it can indeed serve as an effective entering wedge for gaining compliance from others.

Reciprocity: Taking more than you give

Have you ever received a gift you didn't want? If so, ask yourself this question: why did you object to getting it? The chances are good that your answer involves your recognition of the fact that it involved an unwanted obligation. Once you received the unwelcome gift, you probably felt that you had to reciprocate in some fashion — to return something to the giver. Your feelings in this regard reflect an important rule of social life: the **norm of reciprocity.** Briefly, this rule states that we should treat others the way they have treated us. Thus, if they have provided us with benefits or favors, we are obligated to return such treatment.

While reciprocity clearly plays a beneficial role in many forms of social interaction, it can also be pressed into service as a technique for gaining compliance. Specifically, persons wishing to influence others can begin by doing some small, unrequested favor for them. Once they do, the target persons are in their debt, and often have a more difficult time refusing later requests than would otherwise be the case (e.g., Regan, 1971). Moreover, this is true even when the favor requested in return is larger than the one initially offered by the user of this technique. A good example of such procedures in practical use is provided by members of the Hare Krishna sect, who regularly sought donations in airports and other public places during the 1970s (Cialdini, 1985). Such persons would walk up to unsuspecting pedestrians and hand them a flower. Since they were taken by surprise, many recipients accepted this small "gift" without hesitation (see Figure 7.11, page 244). Once they did, of course, they were "hooked": how could they now refuse to make a small donation to the group? Few persons were able to simply walk away, flower in hand, without offering reciprocation. Indeed, this strategy was so successful that it soon proved self-defeating: most individuals learned to head the other way as soon as they spotted Hare Krishna canvassers, in order to avoid their unwanted gifts. By now, the main point of this discussion should be clear: beware of unwanted and unsolicited favors. They may actually represent initial steps in a carefully planned campaign for gaining your compliance!

FIGURE 7.11.   Because of the *norm of reciprocity*, most persons feel obligated to return favors or benefits — even ones they didn't want or expect. This fact was used by Hare Krishna sect members to obtain donations from passersby in many public locations.

Reciprocity: Its use in gaining compliance

Multiple requests: Two steps to compliance

Often, when individuals seek compliance with their wishes, they do not limit their efforts to a single request. Rather, they employ a kind of two-step procedure designed to increase their chances of success. The rationale behind this strategy is simple: an initial request can serve as a kind of set-up for a second request — the one the influencer wanted all along. Thus, beginning with one request, which is refused, can weaken recipients' ability to resist so that they are more willing to comply with a second proposal. Several different techniques are used in this manner, but among the most common are the **foot-in-the-door**, the **door-in-the-face** (also known as the *rejection-then-retreat* tactic), and **low-balling.**

The foot-in-the-door: Small request first, large request second.   There is an old saying: "Give them an inch and they'll take a mile." What it refers to is the fact that individuals seeking compliance often begin with a small or trivial request. Then, once this is granted, they escalate to larger or more important ones. The use of this technique — often known as the *foot-in-the-door* approach — is common in many different settings. For example, door-to-door salespersons often start their pitch by asking potential customers to accept a free sample or even a brochure describing their products. Confidence artists frequently begin by asking potential "marks" to do something that seems totally safe and innocuous (e.g., help them find an address, hold a receipt or a safe deposit key for them). Only after these small requests are granted do they move on to requests that can cost their victims their entire life savings. Friends, co-workers, and lovers, too, often start with small requests they know we won't refuse, and only gradually increase the scope of their demands. In all such instances, the basic strategy is much the same: somehow induce another person to comply with a small initial request and thereby increase the chances that he or she will agree to a much larger one. Is this technique really successful? The findings of many different studies suggest that it is (Beaman et al., 1983).

For example, in perhaps the most famous study concerned with this topic (Freedman and Fraser, 1966), a number of homemakers were phoned by a male experimenter who identified himself as a member of a consumers' group. During this initial contact, he asked subjects to answer a few simple questions about the kinds of soap they used at home. Several days later, the same individual called again and made a much larger request: could he send a crew of five or six persons to the subject's home to conduct a thorough inventory of all the products he or she had on hand? It was explained that this survey would take about two hours, and that the crew would require freedom to search in all closets, cabinets, and drawers. As you can see, this was a truly huge request! In contrast, subjects in a one-contact control group were called only once, and were presented with the large, second request "cold." Results were dramatic: while only 22.2 percent of those in the one-contact condition agreed, 52.8 percent of those in the two-contact "foot-in-the-door" group complied. While results have not been as dramatic in many later studies (Beaman et al., 1983), existing evidence suggests that the foot-in-the-door tactic *is* effective in producing enhanced compliance in a wide range of settings, and in response to a wide range of requests — everything from signing a petition (Baron, 1973) through contributing to charity (Pliner et al., 1974) or placing a giant sign on one's front lawn (Freedman and Fraser, 1966). But how, precisely, does it operate? Why does agreeing to an initial, small request increase one's likelihood of saying "yes" to a later and much larger one? Additional evidence points to two possibilities.

First, it may be the case that once individuals agree to a small, initial request, they experience subtle shifts in their self-perceptions. Specifically, they come to see themselves as the kind of person who does that sort of thing — one who offers help to people who request it. Thus, when contacted again and presented with a much larger request, they agree in order to be consistent with their changed (and enhanced) self-image (Snyder and Cunningham, 1975). Indirect support for this view is provided by the fact that the foot-in-the-door effect is stronger or more consistent under conditions where strong external reasons for complying with the initial request are absent than under conditions where such reasons are present (e.g., DeJong and Musilli, 1982). Presumably, if external reasons for complying exist, individuals will attribute their helpfulness to these factors and will fail to experience shifts in self-perception. When such external justifications are absent, in contrast, they may attribute their initial compliance to internal causes, and so experience shifts in self-perception (refer to Figure 7.12).

Second, it is possible that after agreeing to a small request, individuals come to hold a more positive view of helping situations generally. That is, they now perceive such situations as less threatening or potentially unpleasant than would otherwise be the case. As a result, they are more willing to comply with later — and larger — requests (Rittle, 1981). This explanation, too, is supported by some research findings.

At present, it is not possible to make a clear choice between these two interpretations. Indeed, such a choice may be unnecessary, for both shifts in self-perception and changes in overall reactions to helping situations may contribute to the success of the foot-in-the-door tactic. Regardless of the precise mechanism responsible for impact of this procedure, however, there can be little doubt about its practical value in obtaining compliance. For example, in a study by Schwarzwald, Bizman, and Raz (1983) the proportion of citizens willing to make a donation to a charitable organization was raised more than 55 percent, and the size of their average donations more than 75 percent through use of the foot-in-the-door (i.e., by simply first asking potential donors to sign a petition favoring this charity). In view of such results, we can only conclude that the strategy of beginning with a small request and then shifting to a larger one can certainly be effective.

FIGURE 7.12. When individuals have strong external reasons for complying with a request from another person, they may attribute their compliance to these factors and not experience any shifts in self-perception. Then the foot-in-the-door tactic may fail (upper panel). In contrast, when external reasons for complying are absent, they may attribute their compliance to internal causes and experience such shifts in self-perception. Under these conditions, the foot-in-the-door tactic may succeed (lower panel).

The foot-in-the-door and shifts in self-perception

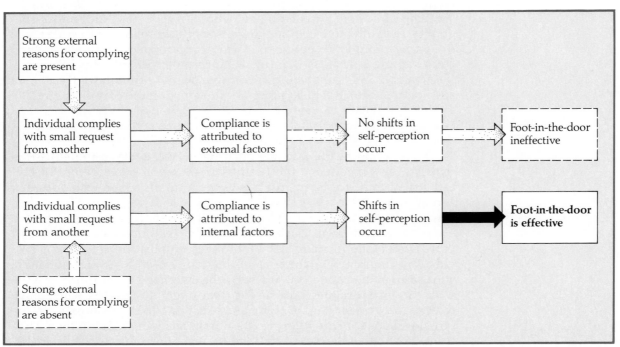

The door-in-the-face: Large request first, small request second.   While the technique of beginning with a small request and then shifting to a larger one seems quite useful, an opposite strategy, too, can often succeed. Here, persons seeking compliance start by asking for a very big favor—one the target is almost certain to refuse. Then, when refusal occurs, they shift to a smaller request—the favor they really wanted all along. This approach, known as the *door-in-the-face* or the *rejection-then-retreat* tactic, has been studied in several experiments, and also appears to be effective.

For example, in a well-known study on this tactic, Cialdini and his colleagues (Cialdini et al., 1975) stopped college students on the street and presented a huge request: would they serve as unpaid counselors for juvenile delinquents two hours a week for the next two years? As you might guess, none agreed to this proposal. When the experimenters then scaled down their request to a much smaller one—would they take a group of delinquents on a two-hour trip to the zoo—fully 50 percent agreed. In contrast, less than 17 percent of a control group agreed to this smaller request when it was presented alone, rather than after the first, giant request.

The use of this technique can also be observed in many real-life situations. For example, television writers who wish to get certain lines or scenes past the network censors often sprinkle words or situations they know the censors will want to cut throughout their scripts. Then, they can agree to the elimination of many of these, while still retaining the key lines they wanted all along (Cialdini, 1985). Similarly, the door-in-the-face is often used in politics, where groups or persons seeking funds for their own pet projects begin with requests for budgets far in excess of what they actually need. Then, when these are rejected by their opponents, they reduce their demands substantially, but still obtain adequate funding. Again we can ask, "Why does this two-step approach to gaining compliance succeed?" Two explanations have been proposed.

The first relates to the notion of *reciprocal concessions.* When individuals who start with a very large request back down to smaller ones, this may be viewed by the persons they hope to influence as important concessions on their part. The targets of this strategy may then feel obligated to make a matching concession themselves. After all, the requester has retreated in order to meet them halfway; how can they now refuse to do likewise? The result: they may become more willing to comply with the second, smaller request.

Another possibility involves concern over *self-presentation*— presenting ourselves in a favorable light to others (refer to our discussion in Chapter 2). If we refuse a large and unreasonable request from another person, this is justifiable, and our "image" probably won't suffer. If we then also refuse a much smaller request from the same source, though, we may appear unreasonable. Thus, we may often yield to the rejection-then-retreat tactic because we are afraid that failing to do so will cause us to look bad in the eyes of others. Support for this suggestion has been obtained by Pendleton and Batson (1979), who found that many persons felt they would indeed appear unfriendly and unreasonable if they re-fused modest requests for help from others.

We should note, by the way, that effective use of the door-in-the-face tactic requires considerable skill. If persons seeking to employ this pro-cedure begin with an initial set of demands that are so extreme as to seem unreasonable, the process may backfire and produce *less* compliance than merely presenting the requests they really want "cold" (Schwarz-wald, Raz, and Zvibel, 1979).

Low-balling: Changing the rules in midstream — and getting away with it.   If you should ever shop for a new car and be unlucky enough to fall into the hands of a dishonest dealer, you may encounter the following chain of events. First, the salesperson with whom you are dealing will make an extremely attractive offer: he or she will offer to sell the car you want at a price much lower than that quoted by the competition. In fact, the deal may be so good that you agree to accept it at once. As soon as you do, however, some complication will arise. The salesperson may sud-denly indicate that an expensive option you thought was included is *not* part of the offer. Or, she or he may return from the manager's office with the sad news that this person has refused to approve the deal as it stands. Then, in a key, final step, the salesperson will offer you another arrange-ment, less attractive than the one you eagerly accepted.

Common sense suggests that under these conditions, you should refuse to be "had" and should take your business elsewhere. But, sur-prisingly, this is not what usually happens. On the contrary, even though the deal now offered is less favorable than the initial one, many cus-tomers groan, sigh, and actually accept it. In short, they stick to their decision to make the purchase, even though the conditions that led them to make this choice no longer prevail. This technique of gaining compli-ance is known as *low-balling* or "throwing the low-ball," and is all too common. Further, it is not in any sense restricted to the world of busi-ness. Rather, it can be used for gaining compliance in many different settings. In essence, it operates as follows. First, a target person is in-duced to make a commitment to performing some behavior the would-be influencer wants him or her to perform. Then, the situation is changed so that some of the reasons behind the target person's decision (some of the inducements or rewards offered by the influencer) are removed. The low-ball succeeds if the target person sticks to his or her initial commit-ment despite these changes. (Please see Figure 7.13 for an amusing illus-tration of how the low-ball operates.)

Systematic evidence for the success of the low-ball procedure has been obtained in several intriguing studies (e.g., Burger and Petty, 1981; Cialdini et al., 1978). One of the most interesting of these is a field project carried out by Pallak, Cook, and Sullivan (1980). In this investi-gation, Iowa residents who heated their homes with natural gas were approached and told that if they managed to reduce the amount of fuel they consumed during the winter, their names would be listed in the newspaper in articles praising public-spirited citizens. Checks on the amount of gas they used during the next month indicated that this in-

FIGURE 7.13.   Persons using the low-ball technique to gain compliance first induce others to say "yes" by offering them very favorable terms. Later, they remove some of the promised benefits, but hope that the target persons will stick to their initial decision or commitment. (Source: Reprinted with special permission of King Features Syndicate, Inc.)

The low-ball procedure in operation

ducement was quite effective: they reduced the amount of gas they used by more than 12 percent. To see if they would stick to this initial commitment even though conditions were changed, subjects were then sent a letter indicating that the promised publicity would not be provided: their names would never appear in the newspaper. Common sense suggests that after receiving this news, participants would go back to their old energy-wasting ways; after all, one of the main reasons for adopting this behavior had been removed. In fact, this was not the case. On the contrary, they actually reduced their use of gas even further — by more than 15 percent! That these findings were not a mere fluke is suggested by the results of a follow-up study. Here, homeowners were promised favorable publicity for cutting their use of electricity during the summer (mainly, by reducing their use of air conditioning). Again, the promise of such public praise was effective: subjects decreased their electric consumption by almost 28 percent. And again, when the "deal" was changed, and they were told that such publicity would not be provided, they stuck to their initial commitment, actually reducing their use of electricity by almost 42 percent.

These results suggest that the low-ball technique can be a highly successful tactic for obtaining compliance. Apparently, once individuals become committed to a particular course of action, they are reluctant to change this commitment, even if the factors that led to its adoption are later altered. This may stem, in part, from the fact that once a commitment has been made, individuals quickly begin thinking up additional reasons that support it. In short, as Cialdini has noted, commitments, once made, tend to "grow their own legs" — they quickly generate additional support for their own acceptance. To the extent this is in fact the case, the widespread success of the low-ball technique is anything but surprising. (How can we manage to resist the many effective tactics for gaining compliance considered in this section? For some practical suggestions, please see the **Applied Side** insert on page 250.)

OBEDIENCE: Social Influence by Demand

What is the most direct technique one person can use to change the behavior of another? In one sense, at least, the answer is straightforward:

ON THE APPLIED SIDE

Techniques for Resisting Compliance

A basic principle of physics indicates that for every action, there is a reaction. Does the same formula apply to compliance? In short, are there effective rules we can follow in order to reduce the likelihood that we will yield to efforts at social influence from others? Fortunately, the answer is "yes." While no single procedure or set of procedures can guarantee immunity from such appeals, several steps can help us resist in many situations. Some of the most useful of these are outlined below.

(1) Regulating reciprocity: As we noted earlier, one effective technique for enhancing compliance involves the calculated use of reciprocity. Give someone a gift or do them a favor, it appears, and they become incapable of refusing requests for even much greater recompense at a later time. How can such tactics be resisted? One answer involves recognizing them for what they are. True, we *are* obligated by the norm of reciprocity to return genuine favors or benefits from others. But we are certainly *not* obligated to return such benefits if they are designed to manipulate or trick us. Thus, if you receive some unexpected benefit from another person, and this later turns out to be the entering wedge for gaining your compliance, simply remind yourself of this purpose. Once you do, any feelings of being obliged to reciprocate on your part may quickly vanish — along with the tendency to comply. (Incidentally, the same procedures can be used for resisting the door-in-the-face tactic. Reciprocity does not require that we match "concessions" by others who engage in such actions merely as a means of tricking us into compliance.)

(2) Limiting the effects of liking: In general, it is harder to say no to persons we like than to persons we dislike. How, then, can we protect ourselves against persons who are skillful at ingratiation — at getting us to like them before hitting us with various requests? According to Cialdini (1985), a noted expert on social influence, one useful defense involves being sensitive to such positive feelings. If, after a brief encounter with another person, we realize that we like them surprisingly well, a warning bell should sound in our mind. And if they are requesting our compliance in some manner, we should probably conclude that they are trying to turn our liking for them to their own advantage. At this point, we can defend ourselves by taking a step back from the situation, and separating our feelings for the would-be influencer from the decision or action they are trying to affect. After all, our liking for a stranger has little real bearing on buying a car, subscribing to a magazine, or related actions. With this distinction firmly in mind, we can decide whether to comply on the basis of rational considerations (e.g., the economic merits of the deal being offered), *not* the charm, friendliness, or attractiveness of the person involved.

(3) Slamming the door on the foot-in-the door: As we saw in Chapter 4, people have a strong desire to be consistent. And, as we noted above, this tendency often plays a role in compliance. Once we have agreed to a small request from another person, we may feel obliged to agree to larger ones in order to be consistent (with our new, improved self-image, if nothing else). Fortunately, this mechanism, too, can be resisted. Once again, the trick is in paying attention to your own feelings. If you find yourself in a situation where you feel compelled by your former actions to say yes again, pause and ask whether, in the absence of your former compliance, you would be likely to agree now. If the answer is no, then stop right there: refuse to be trapped into a

type of consistency that provides you with no benefits, and that may be prove costly in several respects.

(4) Dodging the low-ball: Once individuals make a decision and become committed to a specific course of action, they are reluctant to change their minds. This basic fact is well known to users of the low-ball. Indeed, they count on such reluctance to maintain compliance among their targets even after they remove the major reasons which led these persons to say yes in the first place. How can *this* effective tactic be resisted? Cialdini (1985) suggests that an important answer involves learning to separate the reasons behind initial commitments or decisions from ones we later generate ourselves. If you find yourself in a situation where another person has suddenly altered a prior agreement in a manner that's costly to you, ask yourself the following question: "Given current conditions, would I have agreed in the first place?" If the answer is no, try to identify the factors that are tempting you to remain in the deal or arrangement. The chances are good you will discover that they are ones of your own creation, and have little or nothing to do with the would-be influencer. At this point, it's probably time to back out; after all, why should you remain in a relationship that is so costly to you, but so beneficial to another?

simply ordering the target to do something. This approach is less common than either conformity pressure or compliance, but it is far from rare. Business executives often issue orders to their subordinates. Military officers shout commands that they expect to be followed at once. And parents, coaches, and umpires, to name just a few, seek to influence others in this manner. Obedience to the commands of such sources of authority is far from surprising; they usually possess some means of enforcing their directives (e.g., they can reward **obedience** and punish resistance). In short, they possess some form of *power* over the recipients of their directives. More surprising, though, is the fact that even persons lacking in such power can sometimes induce high levels of submission from others. Indeed, it appears that under some conditions even relatively powerless sources of authority can coerce others into engaging in actions they would not normally choose (e.g., Bushman, 1984). Perhaps the clearest evidence for the occurrence of such effects has been reported by Stanley Milgram in a series of famous and controversial experiments (Milgram, 1963, 1974).

Destructive obedience: Harm by demand

In these studies, Milgram wished to learn whether individuals would follow commands from an experimenter to inflict considerable pain and suffering on another person—a totally innocent stranger. To see if people would do this, he informed subjects that they were participating in a study of the effects of punishment on learning. Their task was that of delivering electric shocks to another person (actually an accomplice) each time he made an error in a simple learning task. These shocks were to be delivered by means of thirty switches on the equipment shown in Figure 7.13. Subjects were told to move to the next higher switch each time the learner made an error. Since the first switch supposedly delivered a shock of 15 volts, it was clear that if the learner made many errors, he would soon be receiving powerful jolts. Indeed, according to the labels on the equipment, the final shock would consist of 450 volts! In reality, of course, the accomplice (the learner) never received any shocks during the experiment. The only real shock ever used was a mild demonstration pulse from one button (number three) given to subjects to convince them that the equipment was real (refer to Figure 7.14).

During the session, the learner (following pre-arranged instructions) made many errors. Thus, subjects soon found themselves facing a dilemma. Should they continue punishing this person with what seemed to be increasingly painful shocks? Or should they refuse to go on? The experimenter pressured them to choose the former path, for whenever they hesitated or protested, he made one of a series of graded remarks. These began with "Please go on," escalated to "It is absolutely essential that you continue," and finally shifted to "You have no other choice, you *must* go on."

Since subjects were all volunteers and were paid, in advance, for their participation, you might predict that they would be quite resistant to these orders. Yet, in reality, fully *65 percent showed total obedience.* They proceeded through the entire shock series to the final 450-volt level (see Figure 7.15). In contrast, subjects in a control group who were not exposed to such commands generally used only very mild shocks during the session. Of course, as you might expect, many persons subjected to

FIGURE 7.14. The photo on the left shows the apparatus used by Milgram in his famous experiments on obedience. The photo on the right shows the experimenter (wearing a lab coat) and a subject attaching electrodes to the learner's (accomplice's) wrists. (Source: From the film *Obedience,* distributed by the New York University Film Library. Copyright 1965 by Stanley Milgram. Reprinted by permission of the copyright holder.)

Studying destructive obedience: The Milgram technique

 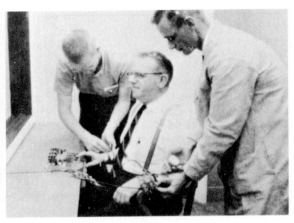

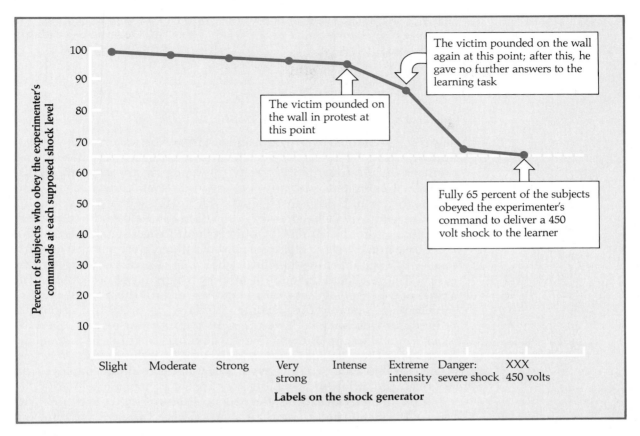

FIGURE 7.15. A surprisingly high proportion of the subjects in Milgram's research obeyed the experimenter's commands to deliver electric shocks of increasing strength to an innocent victim. Indeed, fully 65 percent demonstrated total obedience in this regard. (Source: Based on data from Milgram, 1963.)

Obedience in action: An unsettling demonstration

the experimenter's commands often protested and asked that the session be ended. When ordered to proceed, however, a majority yielded to social pressure, and continued to obey. Indeed, as you can see from Figure 7.14, they continued to do so even when the victim pounded on the wall as if in protest against the painful treatment he was receiving.

In further experiments Milgram (1965a, 1974) found that similar results could be obtained even under conditions that might be expected to reduce such obedience. For example, when the study was moved from its original location on the campus of Yale University to a rundown office building in a nearby city, subjects' level of obedience was virtually unchanged. Similarly, a large proportion continued to obey even when the accomplice complained about the painfulness of the shocks and begged to be released. Most surprising of all, many (about 30 percent) continued to obey even when this required that they grasp the victim's hand and force it down upon the shock plate! That these unsettling results were not due to special conditions present in Milgram's laboratory is indicated by the fact that similar findings were soon reported in studies conducted in several different countries (e.g., Jordan, West Germany, Australia) and with children as well as adults (e.g., Kilham and Mann, 1974; Shanab and Yahya, 1977). Thus, they seemed to be alarmingly general in scope.

Destructive obedience: Why does it occur?

The results obtained by Milgram and others are disturbing. The parallels between the behavior of subjects in these studies and atrocities against civilians during time of war or civil uprising are too clear to require additional comment. But why, precisely, do such effects occur? Why were subjects in these experiments—and many persons in tragic life situations outside the laboratory—so willing to yield to the commands of various authority figures? It would be comforting to conclude that this is the case because these sources of authority hold great power over those who obey, thus affording them little choice. In fact, this is not always the case. The experimenters in the studies by Milgram and others had little actual power over subjects; they could not reward them for obeying or punish them severely for resisting. Similarly, in many life situations, individuals who obey *do* have the right to protest or refuse, especially when ordered to commit acts that are obvious violations of human and legal rights. Yet, people often submit with little hesitation. What accounts for this strong willingness to accept influence from sources of real or imagined authority? Several factors appear to play a role.

First, in many situations, the persons in authority relieve those who obey of the responsibility for their own actions. "I was only carrying out orders," is the defense many offer after obeying harsh or cruel directives. In life situations, this transfer of responsibility may be implicit; in research on obedience, however, it was quite explicit. In Milgram's experiments, subjects were told, at the start, that the experimenter (the authority figure), not they, would be responsible for the victim's well-being. Little wonder, then, that they tended to obey.

Second, persons in authority often possess visible badges or signs of their status and power. These consist of special uniforms, insignia, titles, and related factors. Faced with such obvious reminders of who's in charge, most people find it difficult to resist. The powerful impact of such cues has been demonstrated recently by Bushman (1984). He arranged for pedestrians to be stopped on the streets of a large city, and ordered to give a dime to another individual who seemed to need it for a parking meter. In one condition, the person issuing this order was dressed as a firefighter; thus, he possessed a clear (although seemingly irrelevant) sign of authority. In a second condition, he was dressed as a business executive and so had high status, but no obvious authority. Finally, in a third condition he was dressed shabbily, in greasy coveralls and old work shoes. As you can probably guess, many more passersby obeyed this person's order to give a dime to a stranger when he wore a firefighter's uniform than in the other conditions (refer to Figure 7.16).

Further, when asked why they had complied or failed to comply with the accomplice's order, subjects in the three conditions offered contrasting answers. When the accomplice wore a uniform, many subjects indicated that they had complied simply because they had been told to—they demonstrated unquestioning obedience. In contrast, when the accomplice was dressed in shabby clothes, they reported that they had complied mainly because they wanted to help another person. In sum, it was clear that the possession of an outward badge of authority—even though it was totally irrelevant to the present situation—strongly affected both subjects' behavior and the motives behind it.

A third reason for obedience in many situations where the targets of such influence might resist involves its gradual nature. Often, commands are relatively small and innocuous at first. Only later do they increase in scope and come to require those who receive them to behave in dangerous or objectionable ways. For example, police or military personnel may at first be ordered to question, arrest, or threaten potential victims. Gradually, demands are increased to the point where they are commanded to beat, torture, or even kill unarmed civilians. In a similar manner, subjects in laboratory research on obedience were first required to deliver only mild and harmless shocks to the victim. Only as this

FIGURE 7.16. Passersby in a large city were more likely to obey a direct order from a stranger when he wore a uniform, and so seemed to possess authority, than when he was dressed in an ordinary suit or in very shabby clothing. This was true despite the fact that the uniform in question was totally irrelevant to the stranger's order. (Source: Based on data from Bushman, 1984.)

Outward signs of authority: Often, they are obeyed

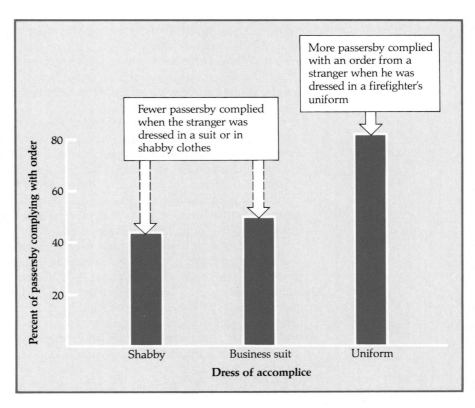

More passersby complied with an order from a stranger when he was dressed in a firefighter's uniform

Fewer passersby complied when the stranger was dressed in a suit or in shabby clothes

Percent of passersby complying with order

80

60

40

20

Shabby   Business suit   Uniform

Dress of accomplice

person continued to make repeated errors did the intensity of these "punishments" rise to harmful levels. Related to the above, of course, is the question of when subordinates should disobey. Where should they draw the line, so to speak? Unfortunately, since commands escalate in a gradual manner, there is no clear-cut point at which disobedience rather than obedience becomes more appropriate.

In sum, many different factors contribute to the high levels of obedience witnessed in laboratory studies and in a wide range of real-life contexts. Together, these factors merge into a powerful force — one that most persons find difficult to resist. Unfortunately, the consequences of this compelling form of social influence can be highly dangerous for countless innocent, defenseless victims.

Destructive obedience: Resisting its effects

Now that we have considered some of the factors responsible for our strong tendency to obey persons in authority, we can turn to a related — and crucial — question: how can this type of influence be resisted? Fortunately, several strategies seem effective in this regard.

First, individuals exposed to commands from authority figures can be reminded that they — not the authority person — are responsible for any harm produced. Under these conditions, we may expect sharp reductions in the tendency to obey, and the results of several studies suggest that this is actually the case (e.g., Hamilton, 1978; Kilham and Mann, 1974). When subjects in these investigations were informed that *they* would be responsible for the victim's safety, they showed much lower levels of obedience than when they were not provided with such information.

Second, the tendency to obey can be reduced by providing individuals with a sign that beyond some point, unquestioning submission to destructive commands is inappropriate. Evidence for such effects is provided by the results of several studies in which subjects have been exposed to *disobedient models* — other persons who refuse to obey an authority's commands. As you might guess, individuals exposed to such clear signs that obedience is inappropriate found it much easier to disobey, too (Milgram, 1965b; Powers and Geen, 1972).

Third, individuals may also find it easier to resist influence from sources of authority if they question the expertise and motives of such persons (Cialdini, 1985). Are they really in a better position to judge what is appropriate and what is inappropriate? What motives lie behind their commands — selfish gain or socially beneficial goals? By asking such questions, persons who might otherwise obey without hesitation may find support for independence rather than submission.

Finally, we might add that simply knowing about the power of authority figures to command blind obedience may be helpful in itself. Some research findings (e.g., Sherman, 1980) suggest that when individuals read about the findings of social psychological research, they become sensitized to the phenomena studied and to the effects described. They may then change their behavior to take account of this knowledge. With respect to obedience, there is some hope that knowing about this process may enhance individuals' ability to resist. To the extent this is the case, then even shocking or disturbing findings such as those reported by Milgram and others can have important social value; as they become public knowledge, they may contribute to desirable shifts in social behavior.

In sum, the power of authority figures to command obedience is certainly great. But it is definitely *not* irresistible. Under appropriate conditions it can be countered and reduced. We should hasten to add that in many cases, resisting such influence is not essential: the persons exercising authority do so appropriately, and for acceptable reasons. When we have grounds for suspecting that their commands are unjustified, stem from objectionable motives, and will produce harmful effects, however, our course of action is clear. In such cases, it is our *obligation*, as well as our right, to resist.

SUMMARY

Social influence involves efforts by one or more persons to alter the attitudes or behavior of one or more others. It takes many different forms, but among the most important of these are *conformity*, *compliance*, and *obedience*.

Conformity occurs when individuals change their attitudes or behavior in order to be consistent with *social norms* or the expectations of others. Conformity increases with *cohesiveness* — liking for the sources of such influence. It rises with the number of persons exerting influence, but only up to a point. Conformity is reduced by the presence of *social support* — one or more others who share the target person's views. Contrary to early findings, recent studies suggest that there are no significant differences between males and females in the tendency to conform.

Compliance occurs when individuals alter their behavior in response to direct requests from others. Many techniques exist that are designed to increase compliance — the likelihood that others will say yes. These include *ingratiation, reciprocity* (doing favors for others so that they will be obligated to return such benefits), and several procedures based on *multiple-requests* (e.g., the *foot-in-the-door*, the *door-in-the-face*, and *low-balling*). Although they are often effective, all these tactics for enhancing compliance can be resisted through appropriate counter-measures.

Obedience, the most direct form of social influence, occurs when one person orders one or more others to behave in some manner. Most individuals seem to have a strong tendency to obey the commands of those in authority, even when such persons actually have little power to enforce their directives. Fortunately, these tendencies toward obedience can be reduced in several ways (e.g., reminding the persons involved that they will be held responsible for their own actions; inducing them to question the expertise or motives of authority figures).

GLOSSARY

compliance
A form of social influence in which individuals change their behavior in response to direct requests from others.

conformity
A type of social influence in which individuals change their attitudes or behavior in order to adhere to the expectations of others or the norms of groups to which they belong.

door-in-the-face technique
A procedure for gaining compliance based on the strategy of beginning with a large request and then, when this is refused, retreating to a smaller request (the one actually desired all along).

foot-in-the-door technique
A procedure for gaining compliance based upon the strategy of beginning with a small request and then, when this is granted, escalating to a larger one.

informational social influence
Social influence based on our desire to be correct (i.e., to possess accurate perceptions of the social world). This often requires that we use others' actions and attitudes as guides for our own.

ingratiation
A technique for gaining compliance based on the strategy of first inducing target persons to like us, and only then making various requests.

low-ball technique
A form of social influence in which target persons are first convinced, through favorable conditions or other inducements, to perform some action desired by the would-be influencer. Then, these conditions are changed so as to be less beneficial. If the low-ball works, target persons will maintain their initial commitment even in the face of these alterations.

minority influence
Influence exerted by members of a minority over a larger majority.

normative social influence
Social influence based on our desire to be liked by other persons.

norm of reciprocity
The social norm indicating that we should return favors and other benefits provided by other persons. Because of this norm, we often feel obligated to reciprocate favors or gifts we never requested, and did not want.

obedience
A form of social influence in which one person orders one or more others to perform some action.

reciprocity
The basic social principle that we should treat others very much as they have treated us.

social influence
Efforts on the part of one or more persons to alter the behavior or attitudes of one or more others.

social influence (SIM) model
A general model of social influence designed to account for the impact of group size, number of targets, and several other factors upon the acceptance of influence in a wide range of settings.

multiple requests
Techniques for gaining compliance based on the use of more than one request. The foot-in-the-door and the door-in-the-face provide examples of this basic strategy.

FOR MORE INFORMATION

Cialdini, R. B. (1985). *Influence: Science and practice.* New York: Random House.

> A witty and insightful account of the major techniques human beings use to influence the persons around them. The book draws both on the findings of careful research and on informal observations made by the author in a wide range of practical settings (e.g., sales, public relations, fund-raising agencies, and the like). Without a doubt, this is the most readable and informative account of current knowledge about influence now available.

Forsyth, D. R. (1983). *An introduction to group dynamics.* Monterey, Cal.: Brooks/Cole.

> A solid overview of the complex but fascinating processes that take place within groups. The sections on conformity, obedience, and other forms of social influence are clearly written, and expand upon the coverage of these topics provided by the present chapter.

Milgram, S. (1974). *Obedience to authority.* New York: Harper.

> More than twelve years after it was written, this book is still the definitive work on obedience viewed as a social psychological process. The untimely demise of its author only adds to its value as a lasting contribution of our field to the comprehension of an important and all-too-common phenomenon.

CHAPTER 8

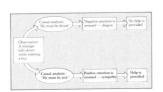

PROSOCIAL BEHAVIOR:
Helping, Intervening, and Resisting Temptation

The setting is a large supermarket near a college campus. Two students are standing in one of several checkout lines, waiting to pay for their purchases.

MARYANNE: No matter which line I pick, it always turns out to be the slow one.

JULIE: I know. The woman checking out now had a fistful of coupons, and now she's writing a check.

MARYANNE: Whatever happened to getting money at the bank and *then* going shopping?

At that moment, a young man who is also waiting in line looks around quickly, then reaches into the display racks to remove several packages of razor blades. He smoothly transfers these to his coat pocket and then just as quickly adds a few candy bars.

JULIE: (*shocked*) Did you see that?

MARYANNE: What?

JULIE: That guy is ripping off the store!

MARYANNE: Shh.

JULIE: What do you mean?

MARYANNE: Let's just stay out of it. I don't want any trouble.

JULIE: (*talking loudly*) Trouble? There's a thief stealing things right in front of your eyes. He's the one in trouble.

MARYANNE: Be quiet, or I'm going to get out of here and pretend I don't know you.

The young man is now looking back at them, frowning unpleasantly.

JULIE: Go, if that's what you want. I plan to tell the manager what's going on. Right is right.

MARYANNE: *Please* be careful. I just know something awful will happen.

JULIE: (*angrily*) Something awful happened already. Hold my place in line while I report this creep.

MARYANNE: (*whispering*) Don't look in his direction. He's staring at you.

JULIE: I hope he likes staring at the policeman who comes to get him.

MARYANNE: You're braver than I am. After all, it's just a few dollars worth of stuff.

JULIE: I wouldn't feel right if I just stood by and didn't do anything about it.

MARYANNE: Good luck. I admire what you are doing, but I'm moving to a different checkout line.

FIGURE 8.1. Though the members of a given culture tend to be in agreement about the ethically or morally "right" way to deal with most issues, their actual behavior may differ from those ideals. Such a contrast with respect to the responsibilities of fatherhood is suggested in this cartoon. (Source: Doonesbury, copyright, 1985, G. B. Trudeau. Reprinted with permission of Universal Press Syndicate. All rights reserved.

There is often a contrast between ethical ideals and actual behavior

JULIE AND Maryanne found themselves in a situation that forced them to deal with difficult questions of ethics and social responsibility. In this specific instance, behaving in the "right" way requires the expenditure of energy and the risk of retaliation. We frequently must either ignore a problem or engage in **prosocial behavior.** Prosocial acts have no obvious benefits (such as a material reward or social approval) for the person who carries them out and may involve some degree of sacrifice; such acts do, of course, benefit others. As will be discussed later, prosocial acts may have nonobvious benefits for the person performing them, for example, feeling good about oneself or being rewarded in the hereafter. Generally, those in a given culture are well aware of the "right" thing to do, though what is actually done may not conform to this ethical standard (as in the cartoon in Figure 8.1. In Chapter 10 we will discuss other sorts of helpful behavior, including *cooperation*, that involves people working together to reach a common goal.

Three quite different aspects of prosocial behavior have been of research interest. We will first examine what is involved when an individual is suddenly confronted with the possibility of *helping a stranger in distress*. Next, we will turn to the kind of problem faced by the two students in the checkout line who observed someone committing a crime. The decision to be made is whether to take steps that involve *deterring a wrongdoer.* The third type of prosocial behavior consists of making the decision to *resist temptation.* In addition, we will describe the way in which particular *motivations* play a role in altruistic behavior, the social psychological issues involved in intervening when *terrorists* take hostages, and one of the earliest experiments that focused on the behavioral differences between *cheaters and noncheaters.*

FACING AN EMERGENCY: *To Help or Not to Help a Stranger in Distress*

The following letter is based on an actual one written to a student newspaper describing an incident that occurred on a college campus:

> On Saturday night, as my friends and I were leaving the Student Union, we came across a student lying on a bench. At first glance, it seemed as if he were unconscious, but when we began to shake him and talk to him, he responded incoherently. It was cold, and he was not wearing a jacket. He was unable to move himself or open his eyes. We quickly called an ambulance, and he was taken to the medical center for emergency treatment.
>
> The reason we are writing is to point out that we observed several people passing by the immobile student, not bothering to see if he was hurt or in need of assistance. It seemed that people took the situation to be a normal occurrence—some drunken student. The problem is that he was alone and obviously in need of help. No one stopped. He could have been seriously ill, but it did not seem to matter to the Saturday night crowd.
>
> Those apathetic students who did not think twice about helping the man should be ashamed. Their behavior reinforced my beliefs about the severe lack of compassion and concern on this campus.

You have probably read of similar incidents in which bystanders failed to come to the aid of someone in need. In contrast, there are also quite different accounts of bystanders not only providing help to strangers in distress, but even risking their lives to do so. It is tempting to explain such events in terms of compassion versus indifference, but social psychological research indicates that quite different variables are of primary importance. Perhaps the most influential and most thoroughly studied factor that affects prosocial responding is whether the potential helper is alone or in the company of others. The fact that a lone bystander is more likely to help (and to provide help more quickly) than a bystander who is part of a group is known as the **bystander effect.**

The bystander effect: The greater the number of potential helpers, the less help

Actual incidents in which groups of people stood idly by, failing to help a stranger in distress, led Darley and Latané (1968) to hypothesize that helping behavior becomes less likely as group size increases. This proposal was first tested in an experiment in which each subject was led to believe there was only one other person carrying on a discussion through an intercom system, or two other subjects, or five others. Actually, there was only the real subject and the appropriate number of voices on tape recordings. After the discussion began, the stranger on one of the recordings gasped and seemed to be undergoing a seizure. How did the subjects respond? As predicted, the more fellow bystanders who appeared to be present, the less likely the subject was to try to provide help. Even when help *was* offered, the presence of others led to a delay. Those who were alone responded in less than a minute. When there were supposedly five bystanders, the subjects hesitated for three minutes before responding. This same general inhibiting effect of fellow bystanders has since been demonstrated repeatedly in laboratory experiments and in field settings (Latané and Darley, 1970). It should be noted that the bystander effect occurs in situations in which there is a degree of ambiguity as to what is going on and what should be done. In the cognitive model to be described next, you can see why ambiguity is important. If the problem and solution were very clear, the presence of bystanders would be irrelevant.

The presence of others clearly interferes with prosocial behavior, but *why* does this occur? Such situations can be conceptualized as confronting individuals with a series of decision steps, at each of which he or she must make choices that lead either to no help or to the next step in the series (as shown in Figure 8.2). At each stage of the process, specific variables operate to facilitate or to interfere with prosocial behavior. Two such variables have been studied extensively: diffused responsibility and fear of ridicule.

Whose "job" is it? Assuming responsibility.   At least one person has to assume responsibility in order for helping behavior to occur. When a

FIGURE 8.2. In the cognitive model of prosocial behavior formulated by Latané and Darley, the individual who is confronted by any emergency situation must go through a series of decision-making steps. At each point in the series, one decision leads to nonaltruistic behavior; the opposite decision takes the person one step closer to a helpful act. The person in need receives aid only if there is a "yes" decision at each of the five steps. (Source: Adapted from Byrne and Kelley, 1981.)

A cognitive model of prosocial behavior

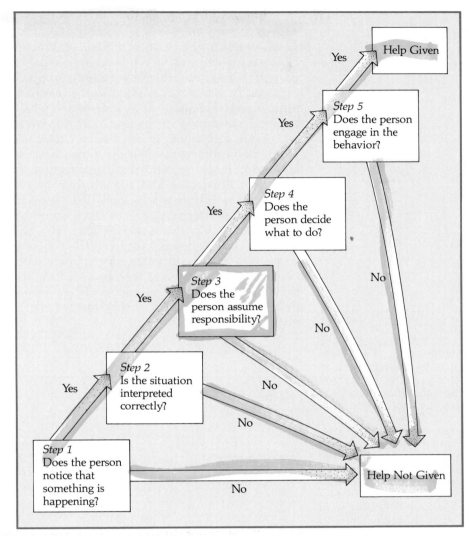

number of bystanders are present, each is potentially able to help. As a result, there is a **diffusion of responsibility.** When there is a recognized leader in the group to organize what is to be done, a group can easily be galvanized into action (Firestone, Lichtman, and Colamosca, 1975). Even without a leader, the actions of just one helpful individual tend to serve as a model for other bystanders, who follow his or her example (Morgan, 1978). Similarly, when social responsibility is clearly the normative belief of a group, the presence of others actually increases the probability of prosocial responding (Yinon et al., 1982). It is interesting to note that those who help after being exposed to very helpful models do not perceive themselves to be as altruistic as those who help spontaneously (Thomas, Batson, and Coke, 1981).

One of the reasons people may fail to help a stranger is that they simply do not know what to do or how to do it. That is one reason that the presence of a leader or other model is of crucial importance. It would also be logical to expect that when an individual has learned how to handle a particular problem, this new-found competence should result in an increase in prosocial responding. In a study of reactions to a stranger who seemed to be bleeding badly, individuals who had Red Cross first-aid and emergency training were more likely to provide efficient help than those who were untrained, as shown in Figure 8.3 (Shotland and Heinold, 1985). In another investigation, Pantin and Carver (1982) created a similar degree of competence by exposing female undergraduates to three films that illustrated first-aid information indicating how to deal with emergencies. Three weeks later these individuals took part in a seemingly unrelated experiment, as did a group of control subjects who had not seen the first-aid movies. Those who had not been exposed to the movies showed the familiar bystander effect in response to a "choking" stranger. Aid was provided more slowly when others were supposedly present. Among subjects who had seen the first-aid movies, in contrast, the presence of other bystanders did not inhibit their helpfulness. Thus, the competence induced by the films made it possible for them to assume responsibility.

FIGURE 8.3. The assumption of responsibility for helping in an emergency is much more probable if an individual has the expertise to help. When students were confronted with an "accident" that appeared to involve arterial bleeding, direct help was provided more often by those who had taken a Red Cross course dealing with first-aid and emergency care than by those who had not taken the course. Individuals who knew what to do (apply pressure to stop bleeding) were very likely to provide help, regardless of the presence or absence of fellow bystanders. (Source: Based on data from Shotland and Heinold, 1985.)

Training in emergency behavior leads to the assumption of responsibility

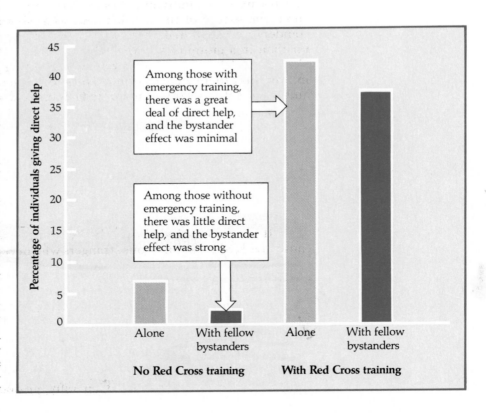

Among those with emergency training, there was a great deal of direct help, and the bystander effect was minimal

Among those without emergency training, there was little direct help, and the bystander effect was strong

Percentage of individuals giving direct help

Alone   With fellow bystanders

Alone   With fellow bystanders

No Red Cross training   **With Red Cross training**

It has been pointed out that there can be a special problem involved in assuming responsibility to provide help. What if you see an injured individual lying on the sidewalk, attempt to help him or her to stand up, and unintentionally cause further injury by doing this? It has been found that an increase in the number of bystanders results in the perception of increased responsibility for the helper causing accidental harm (Cacioppo, Petty, and Losch, 1986). Thus, the possibility that a prosocial act may cause more harm than good acts as an inhibitor, especially when others are present.

Avoiding potential ridicule.   Groups also inhibit prosocial acts because individuals are held back by their **fear of social blunders.** To respond to an emergency, a person must stop whatever he or she is doing in order to engage in some unusual, unexpected, out-of-the-ordinary behavior. Lone bystanders do just that, and without much hesitation. When several bystanders are present, the tendency is to wait for more information rather than to make a mistake and appear foolish. What if you misunderstood the situation? What if it was all a joke? Generally, people decide that it is better to "keep their cool" in order to avoid the possibility of being laughed at. Such social caution results in a lower probability of help being provided and in delays in helping.

In part, bystanders who are strangers to one another inhibit helpfulness because each individual hesitates to communicate with the others about the nature of the problem and what should be done. When bystanders are acquainted, there is much less inhibition of prosocial behavior than in a group of strangers (Latané and Rodin, 1969; Rutkowski, Gruder, and Romer, 1983). Even among strangers, there may be less inhibition if there were an opportunity to see one another in the future and to be able to explain potentially foolish actions. In a test of this proposition, Gottlieb and Carver (1980) used the intercom discussion task once again. When the choking fit occurred, some believed they were the single bystander, and others believed that four additional strangers were present. Half the subjects had been informed that they would never meet their fellow participants, and half expected to interact later in a face-to-face session. Helping was faster with a single bystander than with five apparent bystanders, while the expectation of a future interaction increased the speed with which help was offered (see Figure 8.4, page 268). It can be concluded that the bystander effect is strongest when those involved are anonymous strangers who never expect to meet again.

Calculating gains and losses: The rewards and punishments of helping

Though an individual's prosocial behavior may have no obvious benefits for him or her, many theorists assume that altruistic behavior occurs because it is, in fact, rewarding. Generally, prosocial acts make you feel

FIGURE 8.4.   The bystander effect is reduced considerably if the subject expects to interact with these strangers at a later time. The possibility of interaction provides the opportunity for the individual to explain away any blunders he or she may have made. In addition, knowing that one will see the strangers again is an incentive to act rather than to appear callous and uncaring. (Source: Based on data from Gottlieb and Carver, 1980.)

Reducing the bystander effect: Expecting future interactions with fellow bystanders

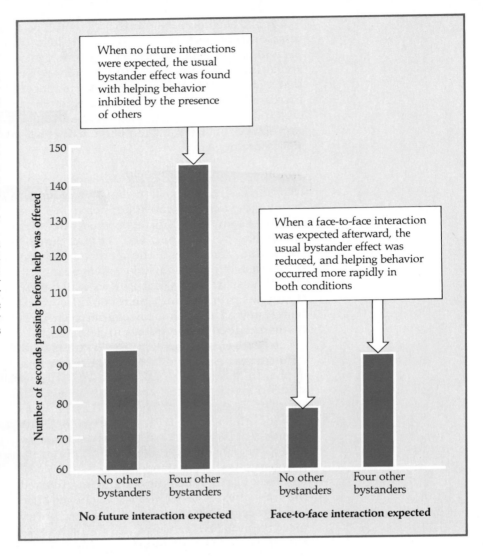

good about yourself. Interestingly enough, the more unpleasant or anxiety-evoking the prosocial act, the more rewarding it is to do, because a high level of drive is reduced by the behavior (Piliavin, Callero, and Evans, 1982). Why should helping others be a positive experience? One explanation is that altruism is a built-in response tendency that has survival value for the species (Cunningham, 1981). Cooperative behavior among related members of a species increases the odds of survival for the individual and for others who share common genes (Axelrod and Hamilton, 1981). Such reasoning leads to the conclusion that altruism is an integral part of human nature (Hoffman, 1981).

FOCUS ON RESEARCH:
The Cutting Edge

Males Helping Females: Altruism or Lust?

When altruism is viewed in terms of its reinforcement value, the motivation for helping behavior in any given situation can legitimately be raised. What rewards does the helper expect to receive or what punishments to avoid?

It is generally found that males are more likely to help females than vice versa (Latané and Dabbs, 1975). Does this mean that men are more altruistic than women? Because there is evidence that differences in one's level of moral development are related to whether or not helping occurs (Erkut, Jaquette, and Staub, 1981), sex differences in helping could be interpreted in such a way. Few social psychologists would agree with that conclusion. Among

many considerations, the fact that fifth- and sixth-grade females are more altruistic than boys of the same age (Shigetomi, Hartmann, and Gelfand, 1981) suggests that adult sex differences may have some other basis. For example, there is some evidence that, for males, morality is likely to be based on conceptions of justice, while females respond in terms of caring (Ford and Lowery, 1986; Gilligan, 1982). In certain situations, however, other explanations for male-female differences seem pertinent.

One such situation involves helping a motorist in distress (flat tire, stalled car, etc.), as shown in Figure 8.5; another is that of offering a ride to a hitchhiker. When the person in need of help is a female, passing cars are much more likely to stop than for a male or a male-female pair (Pomazal and Clore, 1973; West, Whit-

FIGURE 8.5. In investigations of helpfulness toward stranded motorists, it is consistently found that females are more likely to receive assistance than males, that their helper is most likely to be a male driving alone, and that attractive females receive more help than unattractive ones. Such findings have led some investigators to propose that the helpful males are motivated to a greater extent by romantic desires than by altruism.

Why do males help females, especially attractive ones?

FIGURE 8.6. In an experiment in which subjects were confronted by an opposite-sex stranger in need of help, altruistic behavior was examined as a function of previous exposure to an erotic videotape, a non-erotic video, or to no video. Female helpfulness was not affected by the video exposure. Male helpfulness, in contrast, was strongly affected. Almost all (90 percent) of the male subjects who had seen an erotic tape stopped to provide help to a female stranger. Thus, sexual arousal led males to behave altruistically toward females. (Source: Based on data from Przybyla, 1985.)

Motivation for altruism: Sexually aroused males help a female in distress

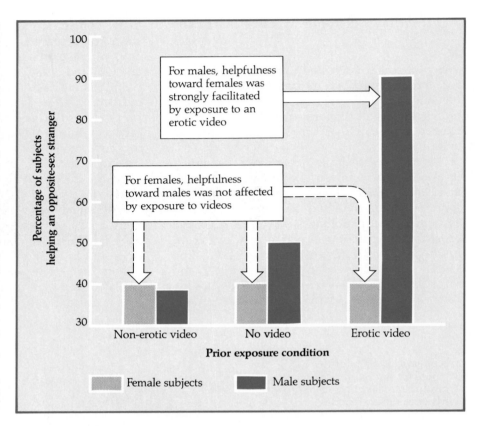

ney, and Schnedler, 1975; Snyder, Grether, and Keller, 1974). Those who stop are typically young males driving alone. Is it possible that they are motivated purely by the desire to be of assistance, or could sexual attraction play a role? The latter interpretation is supported by

Even without a biological basis, it can be argued that prosocial behavior often leads to rewards and hence can be learned as easily as any other behavior (Grusec and Redler, 1980). In some instances, prosocial acts result in punishment, so individuals can learn to *avoid* helping others. Research designed to test this **reinforcement theory of prosocial behavior** has shown that altruistic acts are strongly affected by whether previous acts of helping were rewarded or punished (McGovern, Ditzian, and Taylor, 1975; Moss and Page, 1972). Another way reinforcement plays a

the finding that aid is more likely to be offered to those who are physically attractive than to those who are unattractive (Benson, Karabenick, and Lerner, 1976; West and Brown, 1975).

In an attempt to test the role of sexual motives directly, Przybyla (1985) manipulated the sexual arousal of subjects to determine whether aroused individuals would be most likely to assist an opposite-sex stranger. In general, it is found that such arousal leads to positive interpersonal responses such as approaching and looking at members of the opposite sex and expressing feelings of love (Dermer and Pyszczynski, 1978; Griffitt, May, and Veitch, 1974).

In Przybyla's (1985) experiment, male and female undergraduates were exposed to a sexually explicit videotape, a nonsexual videotape, or to no video. Next, when the experiment was apparently over, each subject in leaving the laboratory area had to pass a confederate working at a table. Just as the subject passed, the confederate stood up and "accidentally" knocked a pile of questionnaires onto the floor. He or she said, "Oh, no!" and bent down to begin picking up the mess. Subjects were observed as to whether or not they provided any help and, for those who did so, how long they spent at the task.

As in the highway studies, sex influenced helping. Males spent much more time helping a female (over six minutes) than they spent helping a fellow male (about thirty seconds). Also, females were significantly less helpful than males.

The effect of being exposed to videotapes was the major focus of interest. Though both male and female subjects reported arousal in response to the erotic tape, only male helping behavior was affected — and only when the person in need was a female. As you can see in Figure 8.6, the greatest percentage of helping behavior occurred when males were sexually aroused and the person in need was a female. Further, it was found that the more arousal reported by the male, the more time he spent helping the female accomplice. When the papers were dropped by a male, arousal and duration of helping were unrelated. For female subjects, there was a trend such that greater sexual arousal was associated with *less* time spent in helping either male or female strangers.

One possible conclusion from such research is that male altruism toward females represents, at least in part, a desire to interact in a romantic way. Because females in our society are somewhat less likely to take the initiative in seeking out a male stranger, their "altruism" is unaffected by their sexual desires.

role in altruistic behavior is described in the **Focus** insert on page 269.

The function of rewards becomes more complex when we consider cognitive activity. Human beings respond not only to simple external pleasures and pains but also to a set of beliefs, values, and expectancies about the consequences of behavior (Clark, 1976; Darley and Batson, 1973). Piliavin and her colleagues (1981) suggest that the bystander who encounters an emergency must quickly weigh the positive and negative aspects of responding by using a kind of **bystander calculus.** If the costs (punishments) of providing help are greater than the benefits (rewards) of such behavior, the bystander is likely to pass the responsibility on to others, escape from the unpleasant situation, or misperceive what is going on (Kerber, 1984). In one test of this theoretical model, Batson and associates (1978) manipulated the costs of helping. A subject walking between buildings to an experiment was either hurrying to meet a deadline or had plenty of time; in addition, the subject had been told that participation either was vital or was not very important. On the way, each individual passed a stranger slumped down in a doorway. The higher the costs for stopping to help, the less likely an individual was to do so. Thus, the least helpful passersby were those with a deadline to meet who believed that their participation in the meeting was essential.

Emotions, attributions, and altruism

Positive emotional state.   It seems logical to assume that an individual in a positive mood would be more likely to behave in a helpful manner than one in a negative mood (Cunningham et al., 1980). A number of studies provide support for this proposition. Subjects who are made to feel more positively in a variety of ways (for example, succeeding at a task, finding money in a telephone coin return slot, or thinking of happy events in the past), are subsequently more helpful than control subjects who were not given a pleasant experience (Isen, Horn, and Rosenhan, 1973; Isen, Clark, and Schwartz, 1976; O'Malley and Andrews, 1983). People have even been found to be more helpful on a bright, sunny day than on a cloudy, rainy one (Cunningham, 1979). Despite these consistent results, other research has complicated the picture somewhat (Shaffer and Smith, 1985). Prosocial acts that involve potential embarrassment or danger are *less* likely to occur when subjects are in a positive mood (Forest et al., 1980; Rosenhan, Salovey, and Hargis, 1981). Individuals who feel very good seem to feel a sense of power. As a consequence, they feel free to refuse to provide help to a stranger.

Negative emotional state.   Negative feelings have an even less straightforward relationship to altruism. Research findings seem inconsistent in that they indicate that such emotions inhibit prosocial acts, facilitate such behavior, or have no effect at all (Barden et al., 1981; Shelton and Rogers, 1981). The crucial factor seems to be whether the negative mood causes the person to focus on his or her own needs and self-concerns; self-focus causes the individual to neglect others who may require help, unless the request for help is made highly salient (Mayer et al., 1985). When negative feelings are focused on the person who needs aid, thus arousing empathy, helpfulness increases (Thompson, Cowan, and Rosenhan, 1980; Thompson and Hoffman, 1980). In addition, it is found that when a person feels *personally responsible* for his or her negative mood, there is a greater willingness to help others (Rogers et al., 1982).

General arousal effects.   To complicate the picture further, Shaffer and Graziano (1983) found that *either* a positive or a negative mood facilitates helping when there are pleasant consequences; both types of mood inhibit helping when the consequences are unpleasant. One of the reasons for some of the seemingly inconsistent findings is that the ambiguity of the situation plays an important role. Sterling and Gaertner (1984) reported that general arousal — even arousal based on physical exercise — facilitates helping when the need for help is quite clear; such arousal inhibits helping when the emergency is ambiguous. These various findings dealing with the role of emotions are summarized in Figure 8.7.

FIGURE 8.7. The relationship between positive and negative emotional states and subsequent prosocial behavior has been found to be quite complex and strongly influenced by cognitive factors. Either type of emotion can lead to more helpfulness or to less, depending on the presence or absence of other variables, as indicated here.

Emotions and helping: Feelings play a complex role in altruism

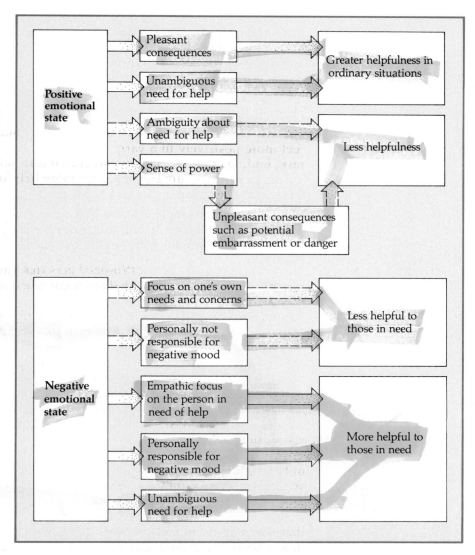

Attributions and altruism. One additional factor is involved in the relationship between emotions and helping. A potential helper must decide *why* another person is in need of assistance. Weiner (1980) suggests that we engage in a causal analysis that influences emotions and subsequent altruistic actions. The sequence is shown in Figure 8.8. We observe a person in need, make an attribution as to the cause of the problem, experience a positive or negative emotional reaction, and then provide help or fail to do so. If someone seems to be in trouble because of internal, controllable causes, such as taking drugs, we are likely to respond with disgust and walk away from the situation without bothering to do anything about it. In contrast, when the difficulty is caused by events beyond the victim's control, such as a mugging, we feel sympathetic and try to help (Meyer and Mulherin, 1980).

A somewhat different attributional approach has also been proposed (Brickman et al., 1982). Four common and quite different models of attribution about who is responsible for the problem and for the solution are outlined in Table 8.1. Different models are applied in different situations, and there are also differences among professional groups and among individuals in applying them. In education, the medical model is applied to children, the compensatory model to adolescents, and the moral model to college students. Two different models are applied to victims needing welfare aid. Either the medical or the enlightenment model is applied—both assume that someone other than the victim must solve the problem. The only difference is whether the victim is assumed to have been the cause of the difficulty. When a given problem is approached using a nontraditional model, interesting possibilities are raised. As one example, the enlightenment model is usually applied to criminals: it's their fault, and someone else has to do something about it. If the medical model were applied to criminals, there would be less

FIGURE 8.8. Weiner (1980) proposed that the observation of a person in need of help leads us to attempt to figure out the cause of the problem. If the cause seems to be internal and under the victim's control, we respond with negative feelings and decide not to be helpful. If the cause seems to be external and not under the person's control, our response is positive and prosocial acts are much more likely to occur.

A causal analysis of attributions, emotions, and likelihood of helping

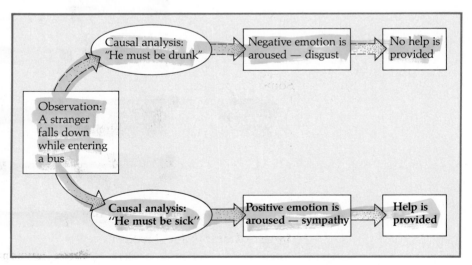

TABLE 8.1. An attribution approach to providing help has been proposed (Brickman et al., 1982) that deals with victim responsibility for his or her problem, victim responsibility for solving the problem, and the type of solution advocated. Four basic models are proposed, each with its own set of attributions.

Contrasting attribution models: Blame, responsibility, and solution

Model	Victim Responsible for Problem?	Victim Responsible for Solution?	What Does Victim Need?	Example
Moral	Yes	Yes	Motivation	A compulsive gambler is encouraged to focus attention on the monetary needs of his or her family, creating the desire to behave in a different way.
Compensatory	No	Yes	Power	An individual from a poor and undereducated family is taught the skills necessary to do well in school and to obtain meaningful employment.
Medical	No	No	Treatment	An alcoholic is given a drug that causes nausea and vomiting each time a drink is consumed.
Enlightenment	Yes	No	Discipline	An adolescent who vandalizes a school is made to work afternoons and weekends until the cost of the damage has been repaid.

interest in seeking appropriate punishment and more interest in developing some form of "treatment" effective in changing the undesirable behavior.

Who behaves in a prosocial way? Characteristics influencing altruism

Some people are more likely to be helpful than others, and research has found that community norms have a measureable effect on the altruism of those who reside there (Foss, 1983). Similarly, religious individuals are more likely to donate to someone in need than are those who are not religious (Yinon and Sharon, 1985). The altruism and honesty of children are also strongly affected by peer opinions (Berndt et al., 1984). Though the situation clearly plays a major role in determining how we respond (Kurtines, 1986), many investigators have focused on personality differences in helpfulness (Amato, 1985), as will be discussed below.

Stages of moral development.   The theoretical formulations of Kohlberg (1981) deal with stages of **moral development**. He describes how moral judgments change over a series of stages. These begin with the *preconventional level,* in which a young child tries to do the right thing simply to avoid punishment and, later, to obtain rewards. By middle childhood, the *conventional level* is reached; the individual tries to be a "good" boy or girl by rigidly adopting the rules of behavior provided by parents and others. In adolescence or adulthood, the *postconventional level* is attained (ideally), and the person is able to respond to moral values and adopt a set of ethical principles. Individuals generally progress through the levels as they grow older, but progress may be halted by the absence of appropriate models or the presence of various interfering factors. Though Kohlberg stresses that moral decisions rest on the development of the ability to reason logically, research by others suggests that practical reasoning (rather than logic) underlies morality (Haan, Weiss, and Johnson, 1982).

Moral growth is most likely to occur if the person is faced by moral dilemmas that involve cognitive dissonance (Rholes, Bailey, and McMillan, 1982). Presumably, the process of dissonance reduction is an impetus that helps the person move toward higher levels of moral reasoning. There is evidence that the higher one's level of moral development, the more likely one is to engage in helping behavior (Erkut et al., 1981). Depending on the specific behavior, there is generally a modest relationship between moral reasoning and moral actions (Morrison, Siegal, and Francis, 1984).

Fear of embarrassment.   Another personality dimension that has been related to helping behavior involves differences among individuals in their **fear of embarrassment.** McGovern (1976) predicted that those who score high on a measure of this fear would be less likely to help a stranger in distress than those low in this fear. That prediction was confirmed. In other research, it is found that the higher the masculinity of *both* males and females, the less likely an individual was to help a stranger in distress (Tice and Baumeister, 1985). One possible explanation is that extremely masculine subjects are the ones most likely to fear being embarrassed and losing their poise. Altruistic behavior clearly can be inhibited by a person's wish not to appear foolish in the eyes of others.

Need for approval.   The strong desire to win praise and acceptance from others is known as the **need for approval.** Generally, prosocial behavior tends to elicit approving responses from others. With respect to a charity request, subjects gave more money when others were watching than when no observer was present. Those high in need for approval gave more than those low in this need *only* when there were witnesses (Satow, 1975). Such findings suggest that, for many individuals, prosocial acts provide a way to win praise. For others, a different kind of motivation seems to underlie helpfulness. For example, those who hold strong religious values based on intrinsic motives tend to be helpful to others even when help is not requested (Batson and Gray, 1981).

FIGURE 8.9. Empathy is generally believed to play a crucial role in prosocial behavior. *Dispositional empathy* (a personality characteristic) leads one to perceive the world from the victim's perspective, thus facilitating *empathic arousal* (an emotional state). This state of arousal is unpleasant and serves to motivate the individual to provide assistance. The act of helping reduces the uncomfortable state of arousal.

Helping behavior as a function of empathy and empathic arousal

Empathy. A large body of research has dealt with **dispositional empathy** — the tendency to respond to the world from the perspective of others (Chlopan et al., 1985). When you are simply aware of another person's problem, you may feel *sympathy;* when you attempt to understand that person's subjective experience, *empathy* occurs (Wispé, 1986). In general, when we observe someone suffering, we feel either personal distress and self-concern or empathy for the victim. Only the feeling of empathy leads to an altruistic response (Batson et al., 1983). The theoretical role of empathy in helping (Coke, Batson, and McDavis, 1978) is outlined in Figure 8.9. To study the role of empathy in helping, Archer and his colleagues (1981) exposed subjects to a broadcast that indicated a person's need for help. Those subjects who volunteered the greatest amount of time to help the victim were high in dispositional empathy and had also received false feedback indicating they were aroused during the broadcast. Empathic individuals are also found to be more likely to watch the annual muscular dystrophy telethon and to contribute to it than are those who are non-empathic (Davis, 1983). It is important to note that those high in empathy are helpful even if no one (including the victim) knows about their actions (Fultz et al., 1986). The motivation clearly seems to be internal. Nevertheless, it can be argued that even the

Sociopathic

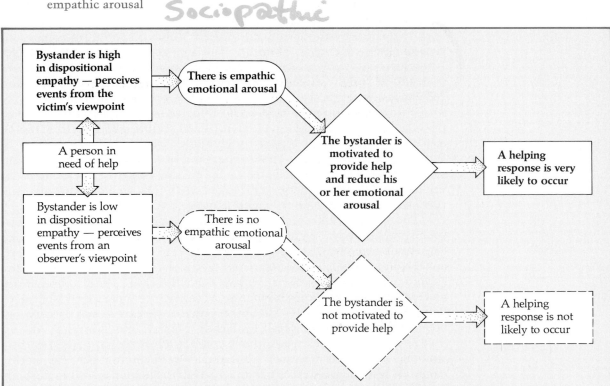

most altruistic behavior is based on selfish motives (Batson et al., 1986). That is, a person may simply be helpful because he or she wants to avoid shame and guilt.

Whatever the source of concern about helping others, empathic emotional arousal is less likely to occur among **sociopathic** individuals —those whose feelings are totally self-centered (Marks, Penner, and Stone, 1982). Empathic tendencies can be increased by telling subjects to try to imagine how the victim is feeling. Helping behavior increases when such instructions are given (Toi and Batson, 1982). Empathy and helping are also increased by information that indicates similarities between the victim and the observer (Batson et al., 1981), and this similarity effect even holds true for helping other nations by means of foreign aid (Taormina and Messick, 1983).

Reactions to being helped: Gratitude versus resentment

Though it may seem that anyone who *needs* help and receives it would be extremely grateful for such assistance, responses are more complicated than that. Even a simple "thank you" may be omitted unless the help is perceived as appropriate (Ventimiglia, 1982). Most people really do not like to ask for help (Broll, Gross, and Piliavin, 1974) and feel they will be viewed as less competent if they accept it (DePaulo and Fisher, 1980). In a sort of reverse bystander effect, as the number of potential helpers increases, help-seeking is inhibited (Williams and Williams, 1983). Also, internal versus external causes play a role in help-seeking. Help is more likely to be sought when the problem has an external source than when the cause is internal (La Morto-Corse and Carver, 1980). Being helped is uncomfortable, and the victim feels obligated to pay the helper back or to provide help to others (Gergen et al., 1975; Wilke and Lanzetta, 1982), and this discomfort is especially characteristic of individuals high in self-esteem (Nadler et al., 1986). There is also reason to believe that help from someone who is motivated by feelings of empathy is less threatening than help from someone motivated to do the "right" thing and thus feel good about himself or herself (Rosen et al., 1986).

Though people prefer to be helped by a friend or a stranger similar to themselves than by an enemy or a dissimilar stranger, such help is more threatening to one's self-esteem (DePaulo et al., 1981; Fisher, Harrison, and Nadler, 1978). This effect is greater if the help involves important skills such as intelligence or creativity (Nadler et al., 1983). Though the victim's self-esteem goes down, that of the helper increases (Fisher, DePaulo, and Nadler, 1981). The importance of threats to self-esteem has been explored in some detail by Fisher, Nadler, and Whitcher-Alagna (1982), and these investigators have come to a somewhat surprising conclusion. When self-esteem is threatened by receiving aid, the victim responds with negative feelings and dislikes the helper as well as the help itself, *but* these negative reactions motivate the person to seek self-help afterward. When self-esteem is not threatened, the victim has positive

Self Esteem

X

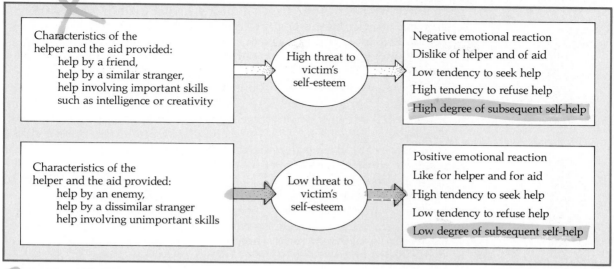

FIGURE 8.10. When aid is given to someone in need, several factors combine to bring about either a high or a low threat to the victim's self-esteem. The model presented here (Fisher, Nadler, and Whitcher-Alagna, 1982) indicates that high threat leads to a number of negative responses, plus one very positive consequence — the victim tends to engage in self-help on subsequent occasions. In contrast, low threat leads to positive responses plus one very negative consequence — the victim tends to avoid self-help subsequently.

A victim's reactions to receiving aid — threat, affect, and self-help

feelings and likes the helper and the aid, but subsequent self-help becomes unlikely. This series of reactions is outlined in the model presented in Figure 8.10.

One implication of such findings is that those who provide aid in the form of assistance to other nations, welfare for those in need, and the like, must face a curious choice. They might consider whether they want the recipient to feel happy and express gratitude though becoming dependent *or* to feel unhappy, ungrateful, and motivated to take personal responsibility in the future. Consistent with these research findings is some ancient Hindu advice to those who need help (quoted in Nadler et al., 1986): "The mind of the men who receive gifts is acted on by the mind of the giver, so the receiver is likely to become degenerate. Receiving gifts is prone to destroy the independence of mind and encourage slavishness. Therefore accept no gifts."

INTERVENING TO STOP A TRANSGRESSOR: A Difficult Prosocial Act

Helping a stranger in distress requires time, effort, and the decision to assume responsibility. Intervening to stop an ongoing act of crime or violence involves, in addition, the decision to cause harm to the wrongdoer and to risk the danger of possible retaliation. The costs of this type of prosocial behavior are potentially quite high. In one highly publicized incident, several bystanders who witnessed a group rape in a bar made no apparent effort to bring the crime to a halt: in New Bedford, Massachusetts, a woman was forced onto a pool table in Big Dan's Tavern and repeatedly raped by four men. The other patrons in the bar did nothing to stop the attack and did not even call the police to come to the woman's rescue. Still more chilling, two of the bystanders shouted encouragement to the rapists and actually helped them hold down their victim (*Newsweek*, March 28, 1983).

A major consideration in deciding whether or not to intervene is one's judgment as to who is to blame for causing harm (Fincham and Roberts, 1985). In studying reactions to a verbal and physical attack, Summers and Feldman (1984) presented undergraduates with a videotape of a male interacting angrily with a female about a dent his car received while she was using it. He becomes sufficiently angry that he slaps the female and shoves her around. Viewers were more likely to blame the woman for the incident if the two people were described as married than if they were supposed to be simply acquaintances. Males were more likely than females to blame the victim and to agree that husbands have a right to hit their wives. It seems reasonable to expect that any individual who holds violent, sexist views about males and females would not define such an attack as a wrongdoing and so would have no reason to intervene. Chapter 9 presents additional information about family violence. For a discussion of one of the most complex intervention situations of all, see the **Applied Side** insert on page 282.

The inhibiting effect of fellow bystanders

Just as in other emergency situations involving a stranger in need, witnesses to a crime have been found to be inhibited by the presence of additional bystanders. In one of the first investigations of this phenomenon, male undergraduates who were waiting to be interviewed witnessed a confederate steal forty dollars from a receptionist's desk (Latané and Darley, 1970). The subject was either the only person to witness the crime or was one of two bystanders. Most of the students did nothing to stop the theft, said nothing to the thief, and failed to report the incident to anyone. Nevertheless, more individuals reported the crime when they were alone than when there were two witnesses. In this and other studies of wrongdoing, the bystander effect is generally found. One inhibiting factor is the ambiguity in such situations. When the victim makes it clear that a theft has occurred, witnesses are more likely to act (DeJong, Marber, and Shaver, 1980).

Surprisingly, people are more likely to help when there is violence than in response to a simple theft. This fact is illustrated by the work of Schwartz and Gottlieb (1980). The experimenters created a situation in which subjects believed they were participating in a study of ESP. They watched a TV monitor depicting a confederate who was supposed to be sending mental images to another subject. The experimenter left the subject alone. After several minutes of observation, the subject saw a roughly dressed stranger enter the confederate's room and steal an expensive pocket calculator. A violent argument followed, and the stranger attacked the confederate. He threw him against the wall, punched him repeatedly in the stomach, knocked him to the floor, and left him doubled up in apparent pain from being kicked several times. Most of the subjects (89 percent) responded to the emergency, regardless of whether they thought they were the sole witness or were one of two observers. As the attacker was leaving, 33 percent went to aid the victim, 31 percent called the experimenter, and 25 percent rushed to try to confront the attacker. There was some evidence for the bystander effect in that subjects responded more quickly when they were alone than when they believed themselves to be one of two bystanders.

In studying responses to actual situations of danger, Huston and colleagues (1981) attempted to find out what personal factors differentiated those who intervened from those who did not. Individuals who had intervened in muggings, armed robberies, or bank holdups were interviewed and compared with a matched group of people who had failed to intervene in crimes. The major difference between the two groups was that those who intervened were found to be more competent to deal with such situations. As shown in Figure 8.11, those who did

FIGURE 8.11. When individuals who had intervened in actual instances of violent crime were compared with others who had failed to intervene, one major difference was the extent to which they had had emergency training. In addition to being well-trained to deal with these situations, those who intervened were found to be taller and heavier than noninterveners. In part, then, intervention behavior seems to be most likely among those who are physically able to deal with the problem and who have been trained to do so. (Source: Based on data from Huston et al., 1981.)

Intervening to stop violent crime: Competence based on training and physique

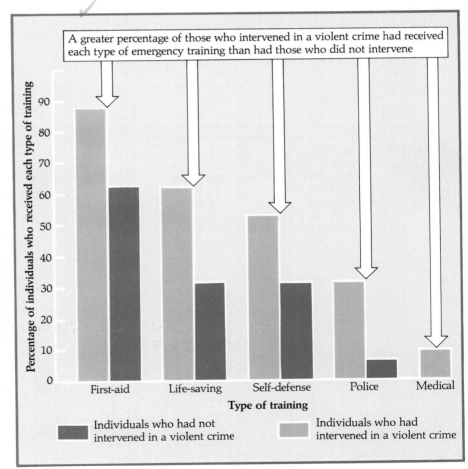

Responding to Terrorists: The Costs and Benefits of Intervening When Hostages Are Being Held

One of the most frightening and frustrating phenomena in recent years has been the increasingly frequent acts of political terrorism in which innocent citizens are held hostage (Netanyahu, 1986). Their release is often made contingent on the occurrence of some political action by one or more governments. In recent years, TV has shown us the occupation of buildings, airplanes, and even cruise ships. As the cartoon in Figure 8.12 suggests, there is a general conviction that television networks are sometimes overly eager in their attempts to use these tragic events as an exciting and popular topic to attract viewers. Regardless of the motivation involved, it also seems possible that such broadcasts play a role in influencing the subsequent behavior of at least some members of the audience.

Most of us are forced to sit by as helpless and powerless bystanders who watch the drama unfold. There is nothing that we can do even if we were willing to intervene and were convinced that we know precisely what to do. If, however, you did have the power and the responsibility to act, what should be done? There are three major possibilities for action, and each involves important social psychological principles. As is often the case, unfortunately, there are positive and negative aspects (costs and benefits) that accompany each possible response (Jenkins, 1983; Merari, 1985; Pruitt and Rubin, 1986).

FIGURE 8.12.   An all-too-familiar event throughout the world today is the news that innocent individuals have been taken hostage by terrorists. The terrorists, in turn, usually have demands ranging from publicity for their cause to the freeing of members of their group from prison. As this cartoon suggests, some observers believe the media have become an integral (and sometimes eager) part of the problem in that coverage of these dramas generates higher TV ratings, newspaper sales, and so forth. (Source: © 1985, Washington Post Writers Group, reprinted with permission.)

Covering the story of terrorists: Presenting news or generating ratings?

The most obvious and most emotionally satisfying response to hostage-taking is the use of force. As we will see in Chapter 9, most societies have responded to the problem of deterring violence by using some form of punishment. To strike back against terrorists with military power has all of the appeal of an action movie in which the strong hero punishes the evildoers and rescues the victims. An actual example of a successful rescue of this sort was the Israeli raid on the Entebbe airport in Uganda to rescue a group of hijacked airline passengers. The major drawback to this approach, of course, is that the victims may be killed deliberately by their captors or accidentally by their would-be rescuers. A military raid on a hijacked airliner in Malta by Egyptian commandoes resulted in a considerable loss of life among both terrorists and their hostages. An equally unsatisfying and frustrating outcome is the total failure of the rescue effort, as when an American military force attempted to rescue the embassy hostages in Teheran, but succeeded only in losing several of their own personnel.

The second major possibility is to assume that the lives of the hostages are all-important. In order to secure their release, the terrorists are given whatever they request that is within reason — the opportunity to spread their political message to an enormous audience, the release of prisoners belonging to their organization, the opportunity to escape unpunished, and, sometimes, money to fund their future operations. This approach is most likely to result in the release of the hostages, as was shown in the American response to the TWA hijackers who held the airline passengers in Beirut. Certainly from the viewpoint of the hostages or of their family and friends, this is the most desirable course of action. The negative features include the emotional frustration involved in giving in to the demands of those acting in a lawless and immoral fashion. More important, however, is the fact that unacceptable behavior has been strongly rewarded by the negotiators. Not only are the terrorists more likely to behave in a similar fashion in the future, but all *potential* terrorists who observe the drama are provided with a model for their own behavior (see Chapter 4). Thus, the rewards of violent behavior have been clearly demonstrated to all viewers.

The third possibility lies somewhere between the use of force and total capitulation to demands. Even though this seems to represent the most effective long-term solution, it is also the most difficult and, frankly, least likely to be implemented. With a total blackout on news reports, hostage-taking would be publicly ignored while communication with the terrorists could quietly take place (Rubin and Friedland, 1986). When the wrongdoers receive no publicity, they cannot act as models for others. Those in contact with the terrorists make it clear that the hostages must be released, and that any criminal acts (kidnapping, hijacking, piracy, murder, etc.) are subject to the ordinary legal punishments. If this procedure were practiced universally and consistently, the overall effect should be to discourage future attempts and thus to save the lives of untold numbers of individuals who might otherwise have been taken hostage.

It is obviously much easier to consider the pluses and minuses of each approach if you yourself are not facing death at the hands of a fanatic. Choosing the most effective alternative is also more difficult if you are a political leader who stands to gain or lose popularity on the basis of the public's perception of how well you responded to the emergency. Nevertheless, each of us would do well to consider the three alternatives and to decide which type of intervention is most consistent with our values and which type we expect to be most effective on the basis of what is known about human behavior.

something in response to a violent crime were much more likely than non-interveners to have been trained to deal with emergencies. Those who intervened were also taller and heavier and more likely to describe themselves as strong, aggressive, emotional, and principled. Altogether, response to violence seems more probable if the individual is physically able to handle the wrongdoer, emotionally predisposed to action, and has had the appropriate training.

Responding to shoplifters

At the beginning of this chapter, a fictional shoplifting scene was presented. In real life, the average person simply ignores such incidents, despite the fact that this particular crime costs us about ten billion dollars annually and is on the increase (Klentz and Beaman, 1981).

Field experiments have shown that the majority of shoppers will inform the management about a thief if a fellow shopper (an experimental confederate) simply reminds them that shoplifters should be reported (Bickman and Rosenbaum, 1977). In contrast, posters or mass media messages are not very effective. Such impersonal reminders influence *attitudes* about shoplifting and about reporting the thieves, but actual behavior doesn't change (Bickman and Green, 1977).

A program was developed by Klentz and Beaman (1981) to inform people about shoplifting and its costs. The most effective method to increase the number of individuals who intervene in shoplifting situations was the presentation of a lecture about how and why to report this crime *and* the reasons that bystanders are usually inhibited about taking action. An interesting question is whether those who simply read about intervention and nonintervention in books—such as this one—will behave differently in the future!

Responsibility and commitment: Basic elements in intervention behavior

In much of the research on prosocial behavior, it has been shown that people are most likely to be helpful to others if they feel *responsible* for providing aid. We noted, for example, that individuals are more likely to feel responsible if they are the sole observer of the problem, if they have been trained in dealing with emergencies, and if they are reminded of the right thing to do. Other research indicates that a male is more likely to confront someone who verbally attacks his partner (male or female) than to do so if a stranger or even if he himself is insulted (Meindl and Lerner, 1983). The individual seems to feel *responsible* for defending a partner who has been called a "jackass."

It is also possible to manipulate the feeling of responsibility in a direct fashion. Moriarty (1975) proposed that a **prior commitment** to be responsible should increase the probability of intervention behavior. On a crowded beach, a confederate selected individuals who were sitting alone as subjects. He placed his own blanket near that of the subject and turned his portable radio on. A few minutes later, he spoke to the subject and either asked for a match or (to create commitment) said, "Excuse me, I'm going to the boardwalk for a few minutes. Would you watch my things?" All of the subjects agreed to do so, thus committing themselves in advance as responsible bystanders. The confederate then walked away, and a second confederate came along, picked up the radio, and hurriedly walked away. What did the subjects do in response to this blatant theft of a stranger's radio? Of those subjects who had only been asked for a match, only 20 percent did anything about the stolen property. Among those who had been asked to be responsible, almost all (95 percent) took action! They stood up, ran after the thief, shouted at him, and even grabbed him to get back the radio. When people agree beforehand to take charge, they seem to do so with a vengeance.

The powerful effects of prior commitment have been shown under a variety of circumstances, such as watching a stranger's suitcase in an automat (Moriarty, 1975), a fellow student's belongings in a library (Shaffer, Rogel, and Hendrick, 1975), and a stranger's books in a classroom (Austin, 1979). With a slight nudge toward assuming responsibility, most people seem to respond to wrongdoing by taking appropriate action.

RESISTING TEMPTATION: Breaking the Rules to Secure Immediate Gains

We are constantly faced with choices between doing what we know is morally defensible versus taking the easy way out by cheating, lying, or stealing. It is very tempting to "cut corners" in order to gain some immediate reward. In a large-scale survey of over 24,000 respondents, surprisingly large percentages indicated that they had broken various rules of ethical conduct (Hassett, 1981). One out of four had cheated on an expense account, about 40 percent had driven while intoxicated, and almost two-thirds had stolen office supplies from their employers. In another investigation, nurses were found to "steal" an average of twenty-five minutes a week by taking longer breaks than were authorized (Jones, 1981). Even though a great many people obviously commit various illegal or immoral acts, a great many others are able to resist temptation. For social psychology, the question is whether we can identify the kind of situation that elicits each type of behavior or the kind of person who is likely to make one choice versus the other.

FOCUS ON RESEARCH:
Classic Contributions

Differences between Cheaters and Noncheaters: MacKinnon's Harvard Study

Though there are aspects of specific situations that make students more likely or less likely to cheat on examinations, within any given situation personality characteristics appear to be crucial factors. For example, those who cheat are low in the ability to delay gratification (Yates and Mischel, 1979), high in sociopathic tendencies (Lueger, 1980), high in need for approval (Millham, 1974), low in interpersonal trust (Rotter, 1980), high in chronic self-destructive tendencies (Kelley et al., 1985), low in adherence to the work ethic and in the desire to perform tasks industriously (Eisenberger and Shank, 1985), and high in the belief that transgressions are not automatically punished (Karniol, 1982). Altogether, cheaters are found to be emotionally and morally immature individuals who are not committed to hard work, are unable to give up immediate pleasures in order to obtain future goals, and who believe that they are likely to get away with breaking the rules.

One of the first investigations of the role of personality characteristics in cheating was conducted by MacKinnon (1933). This research was part of a large-scale, interdisciplinary study of personality by Murray (1938) and his colleagues at the Harvard Psychological Clinic.

In an experimental setting, male subjects were given a series of problems to solve. The solutions to the problems were contained in books placed on each subject's table, but they were only permitted to look at a few specified answers as they worked alone in the room. Though the subjects were unaware of the fact, the experimenter was able to observe their behavior. The subjects were almost evenly divided with respect to who did and who did not follow the rules about looking up answers — cheaters versus noncheaters.

The major interest was in identifying differences between these two groups. During the problem-solving activity, almost a third of the cheaters and none of the noncheaters overtly expressed anger toward the problems: "You bastard"; "These are the G — d — edest things I ever saw." One out of ten noncheaters ex-

FIGURE 8.13. The verbal and nonverbal behavior of those who cheat and those who are honest are found to differ. Cheaters respond to a difficult task with anger in their words and deeds while noncheaters respond with anxiety, nervous gestures, and guilt.

Cheaters versus noncheaters: Anger versus anxiety

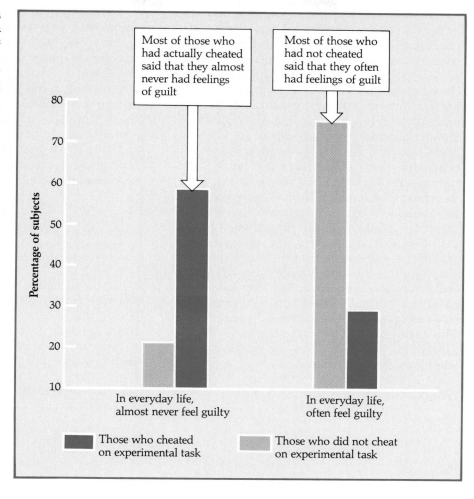

FIGURE 8.14. Feelings of guilt seem to play an important role in the inhibition of cheating. Those who cheated in an experimental situation reported that they almost never experience guilt, while three out of four non-cheaters said that they often feel guilty. (Source: Based on data from MacKinnon, 1933.)

Non-cheaters experience more everyday guilt than cheaters

Most of those who had actually cheated said that they almost never had feelings of guilt

Most of those who had not cheated said that they often had feelings of guilt

Percentage of subjects

In everyday life, almost never feel guilty

In everyday life, often feel guilty

Those who cheated on experimental task

Those who did not cheat on experimental task

pressed self-blame while none of the cheaters did so: "Jesus Christ, I must be dumb"; "I must be a nitwit." Those who resisted temptation were also more likely to make an overt attempt to solve the problem by verbalizing it or talking aloud about possible solutions.

Several types of nonverbal behavior also differentiated the two groups, as shown in Figure 8.13. Those who cheated were more likely to do something destructive or aggressive such as scuffling their feet, stamping on the floor, pacing around the room, kicking the leg of the table, or pounding their fists. Noncheaters were more likely to behave nervously rather than aggressively. They fidgeted, crossed and uncrossed their legs, hunched their shoulders, bit their nails, picked their noses, and played with their hair.

A few weeks after the experimental session, the subjects were asked if they had cheated. Those who had not broken the rules obviously said so. Those who did cheat tended to deny it or to admit cheating and add that they felt no guilt about their actions. The investigators wondered if this lack of guilt was a crucial variable, so they asked the noncheaters about a hypothetical act of cheating. These individuals indicated overwhelmingly (84 percent) that they would have felt guilty, conscience-stricken, ashamed, and so forth. Thus, the cheaters expressed little guilt while those who behaved correctly expressed guilt at just thinking about the possibility of such behavior. Given these findings, the experimenters asked the subjects a more general question about guilt: "Do you, in everyday life, often feel guilty about things which you have done or have not done?" The differences were again striking, as shown in Figure 8.14 (page 287). The most guilt was reported by those who did not cheat. Such feelings were relatively rare among those who cheated.

These dramatic differences in guilt and in verbal and nonverbal behaviors during the problem-solving task suggest very different dispositional responses to a challenging experience and to the temptation to cheat. All of us are frustrated and aroused when required to carry out a difficult task. Some of us become angry and seek an unethical solution to the problem, while others of us feel too anxious and guilty to break the rules. Freud (1930, p. 109) made a related observation about differences among people:

> The more righteous a man is, the stricter and more suspicious will his conscience be, so that ultimately it is precisely those people who have carried holiness farthest who reproach themselves with the deepest sinfulness. . . .

In the decades that followed MacKinnon's research, many other psychologists have assumed that cheating is a matter of personality. More recently, interest has also been directed at situational variables and their influence on such behavior.

What affects the commission of nonviolent crime?

Individuals seem to be most likely to engage in nonviolent crime if the potential benefits are high and if the probability of getting caught and the costs are both low. Lockard, Kirkevold, and Kalk (1980) found that fraud is a common illegal act because it fits those conditions. A more risky crime is the theft of property, and it is practiced primarily by young males. As individuals mature, their assessment of the costs and benefits change, and so older individuals (both males and females) are more likely to deceive a customer or lie about a product or service than to engage in thievery.

Tax evasion is an increasingly common white-collar crime. In the Hassett (1981) survey, 38 percent of those responding admitted to having cheated on their tax returns. Among U.S. taxpayers whose returns are audited by the Internal Revenue Service, 69 percent owe the government additional taxes. In a laboratory simulation involving the submission of tax returns, Friedland (1982) found that most subjects were willing to cheat but that this behavior decreased when the probability of being audited increased.

Temptation in the classroom: The easy, sleazy way out

Have you ever copied another person's answers on an exam or pretended that you wrote a term paper that was actually the work of someone else? Sadly enough, if your reply is "no," you are in the minority. Quite different surveys consistently find that about two-thirds of the population report having cheated in school at least once (Gallup, 1978; Hassett, 1981). Obviously, most of the time most students are honest when taking tests. When someone *does* decide to behave unethically by stealing a grade, he or she is totally wasting the time spent in school and unfairly lowering the grades of honest students. In the following sections we examine the research that identifies the characteristics of those who cheat, the situations that make cheating most likely to occur, and techniques that are used to discourage this behavior. You might first want to read about one of the earliest investigations that found differences between cheaters and noncheaters in the **Focus** insert on pages 286–288.

The influence of arousal on cheating

When there is a relatively low risk of getting caught, many people find it exciting to take a chance by violating the rules. There is an element of danger that "adds a thrill no different from a rock climber's thrill when he exposes himself to physical danger equally remote" (Scitovsky, 1980, p. 13).

There is another way in which excitement can facilitate unethical behavior. Lueger (1980) has proposed that any type of arousal is distracting and makes us less able to regulate our behavior. He presented adolescent boys with the opportunity to cheat on an intelligence test. Just before taking the test, they viewed either a relaxation film or an arousing one dealing with the effects of cigarette smoking. In the relaxed control condition, 43 percent cheated, while in the aroused group 70 percent cheated. This arousal effect probably accounts for the fact that warning students about the penalties for cheating just before they take an exam sometimes results in an *increase* in cheating (Heisler, 1974).

These various considerations lead to the prediction that any high-pressure school setting has the potential for adding to the cheating problem. The need to obtain high grades, competition with fellow students, and fear of academic failure all contribute to the students' level of arousal and hence to increased cheating.

Taking steps to reduce cheating

A common response to cheating (and to any other wrongdoing) is to increase the severity of punishment. This approach does not work very well because of the arousing effect just discussed and because few cheaters are detected. Only about one in five self-reported cheaters were ever caught (Gallup, 1978), and about the same number are worried about such risks (Norman and Harris, 1982).

Rather than increase the possible punishment, a different approach has been to raise the feelings of guilt about this behavior. Most people agree that cheating is wrong, and those who do cheat disapprove of the behavior as strongly as those who behave ethically (Hughes, 1981). Many schools have offered ethics courses in an attempt to influence the present and future behavior of students (Britell, 1981; Hechinger, 1980).

In a series of studies concentrating on this approach, Dienstbier and colleagues (1980) gave students a vocabulary test followed by reading materials dealing with moral behavior. Some read about morality as a response to fear of external punishment, while others read abut morality as a response to internally generated guilt. At this point, each student had the opportunity to cheat while correcting the vocabulary tests. Cheating was much lower in the internally oriented guilt condition than in the control group or in the externally oriented fear group. As in much of the research on prosocial behavior, people seem to behave best when they simply receive reminders about what they already know about moral behavior.

SUMMARY

Prosocial behavior refers to acts that have no obvious benefits for the individual engaging in them and may even involve risk or some degree of sacrifice. Such acts benefit others, and they are based on ethical standards of conduct.

When emergencies arise that involve a stranger in need of help, aid is less likely to be provided (or to be provided less quickly) as the number of bystanders increases: the **bystander effect.** Among the explanations for this effect are **diffusion of responsibility** and the **fear of social blunders.** Altruistic behavior also varies as a function of reward and punishment. In complex situations, individuals seem to weigh the potential costs and benefits of helping versus failing to help. Positive versus negative feelings affect altruism, but cognitive factors play an important intervening role. Several personality variables are associated with altruism; **empathy** has been the object of much research attention. Receiving aid can be very uncomfortable and threatening to self-esteem, but such a combination leads to a subsequent increase in self-help. Aid that is nonthreatening leads to a comfortable state of dependency.

When someone observes another person engaging in wrongdoing, intervention becomes less likely as the number of bystanders increases. Help is most likely to be provided by those who are competent to deal with the wrongdoer physically and/or to provide aid to the victim. Shoplifting is more often reported when individuals are reminded of the right thing to do or informed about the way in which responding is ordinarily inhibited. When a person makes a **prior commitment** to be responsible, the likelihood of taking action against a wrongdoer is greatly increased.

A great many people report engaging in a wide variety of unethical or illegal behaviors at one time or another. Nonviolent crimes, such as fraud or tax evasion, increase to the extent that there is a low risk of getting caught, a mild punishment, and potentially large gains. For students, cheating is one of the greatest temptations, and the majority of those surveyed report that they have cheated at least once. Cheating is associated with personality characteristics involving emotional and moral immaturity, the inability to make present sacrifices to gain future rewards, and the absence of guilt; in addition, emotional arousal also increases the incidence of cheating. Such behavior can be decreased by reminding students of their own values and of the guilt that is caused by not living up to those values.

GLOSSARY

bystander calculus
The process that is hypothesized to occur when a bystander to an emergency calculates the perceived costs and benefits of providing help compared to the perceived costs and benefits of not helping.

bystander effect
The fact that effective responses to an emergency are less likely to occur (and more likely to be delayed) as the number of bystanders increases.

diffusion of responsibility
The proposition that when there are multiple bystanders when an emergency occurs, the responsibility for taking action is shared among all the members of the group. As a result, each individual feels less responsible than if he or she were alone.

dispositional empathy
a personality characteristic that centers on the tendency to take the perspective of those who are unhappy, afraid, or otherwise in emotional difficulty. Individuals with this trait experience empathic emotional arousal when confronted by someone in need of help. This tendency to feel as the other person must feel leads to altruistic behavior.

fear of embarrassment
An extreme fear of saying or doing something that is inappropriate.

fear of social blunders
The dread of acting inappropriately or of making a foolish mistake witnessed by others. The desire to avoid ridicule inhibits effective responses to an emergency by members of a group.

moral development
The proposition that as we mature through stages of cognitive and social development, moral behavior is based on increasingly complex considerations.

need for approval
A personality characteristic that involves the desire to be accepted, liked, and thought well of by others.

prior commitment
An individual's agreement in advance to assume responsibility if trouble occurs. An example is committing oneself to protect the property of another person against theft.

prosocial behavior
Acts that have no obvious benefits for the person who carries them out and may involve risk or some degree of sacrifice. They benefit other people and are based on ethical standards.

reinforcement theory of prosocial behavior
The theoretical model that emphasizes the importance of rewards and punishments. Altruism is assumed to vary as a function of its intrinsic reinforcement value, the occurrence of external rewards and punishments, and the individual's expectations of future rewards and punishments as consequences of a given behavior.

sociopathic
A characteristic of behavior that involves self-centered motivation and the tendency to be unconcerned about the feelings of others.

FOR MORE INFORMATION

Berkowitz, M. W., and Oser, F., eds. (1985.) *Moral education: Theory and application.* Hillsdale, N.J.: Erlbaum.
>An up-to-date collection of chapters dealing with current research and theory centering on the process of moral education. This is an interdisciplinary contribution that attempts to integrate the approaches of psychology, philosophy, education, and organizational theory.

Eisenberg, N. (1985.) *Altruistic emotion, cognition, and behavior.* Hillsdale, N.J.: Erlbaum.
>Two of the crucial factors determining altruism — emotions and cognitions — are the central focus of this book. The specific topics include sympathy, conceptions of altruism, and moral decision making.

Piliavin, J. A., Dovidio, J. F., Gaertner, S. L., and Clark, R. D., III. (1981.) *Emergency intervention.* New York: Academic Press.
>This volume covers psychological research and theory dealing with the way bystanders become involved in the crises and emergencies of others. The emphasis is on the responsive bystander and the variables that affect his or her behavior. Included among the topics are the cost-benefit model, vicarious emotional arousal, the bystander effect, the contribution of personality characteristics, and cognition.

Rushton, J. P., and Sorrentino, R. M., eds. (1981.) *Altruism and helping behavior.* Hillsdale, N.J.: Erlbaum.
  This volume consists of a series of chapters by contributors who are actively involved in research on prosocial behavior. The topics include socialization processes, the effects of television, empathy, emotional variables, the role of education, the consequences of group size, and the reactions of those who receive help.

CHAPTER 9

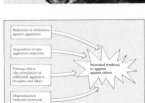

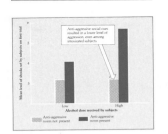

THEORETICAL PERSPECTIVES ON AGGRESSION: In Search of the
Roots of Violence

*Aggression as innate behavior • Aggression as an elicited drive: Motivation
to harm or injure others • Aggression as a reaction to aversive events: The
role of negative affect • Aggression as learned social behavior*

SOCIAL AND SITUATIONAL DETERMINANTS OF AGGRESSION:
External Causes of Violence

*Frustration: Thwarting as a potential cause of aggression • Direct provoca-
tion: When aggression breeds aggression • Exposure to media violence: The
effects of witnessing aggression • Heightened arousal and aggression: The
"energization" of violence*

AGGRESSION IN CLOSE RELATIONSHIPS: The Intimate Enemy

*The prevalence of aggression in close relationships: Who and where •
Some causes of aggression in close relationships*

INDIVIDUAL DETERMINANTS OF AGGRESSION

*Personality and aggression: The Type A behavior pattern • Sex differences in
aggression: Do they exist?*

THE PREVENTION AND CONTROL OF HUMAN AGGRESSION

*Punishment: An effective deterrent to aggression? • Catharsis: Does getting it
out of your system really help? • Other techniques for reducing aggression:
Nonaggressive models, training in social skills, and incompatible responses*

SPECIAL INSERTS

FOCUS ON RESEARCH: Classic Contributions — Studying human
aggression: A procedure for measuring hurt without harm

FOCUS ON RESEARCH: The Cutting Edge — Alcohol and aggression:
The dangerous drunk?

ON THE APPLIED SIDE — The art of constructive criticism

AGGRESSION:
Its Nature, Causes, and Control

Consolidated Products, Inc. has a problem, and it can be summarized in just two words: Fred Grayson. Fred is head of Consolidated's Consumer Products Division, and has considerable power in the company. Recently, he's been using his influence for just one purpose: to block a plan for reorganization proposed by Vic Slegal, another top executive in the firm. His opposition to the plan is something of a mystery, for Consolidated has been hard-hit by changing market conditions and desperately needs to modernize its operations. Yet all efforts to persuade him to change his mind have failed. Right now, Alicia Beyers, Fred's second-in-command, is trying to reason with her boss once again.

"Look, Fred," she begins, "I know you don't like Slegal's plan—heck, you've made that clear enough. What I don't understand is *why* you're so dead set against it. It really seems to make a lot of sense."

"Maybe to you," Fred replies firmly. "To me, it looks like a crock. I don't like it, I don't think it'll work, and I won't support it."

"But you know that we can't go on in the old way, right? We've lost market share, and we're in trouble from top to bottom. If we don't do *something* pretty soon, it will be too late. We'll find ourselves out of business, or the junior partner in a merger."

"What is this, some kind of holiday?" Fred asks, with obvious irritation. "Don't you have anything better to do than drive me nuts? I didn't hire you for *that*, you know."

"OK, OK," Alicia responds, somewhat shaken by Fred's reaction. "Don't get excited. But look, I've worked for you for what, three years now? And I've always felt you were one of the most level-headed and reasonable persons I've ever known. All I want is some hint as to *why* you're so negative on this plan."

Fred pauses for a moment, and then a strange gleam comes into his eye. "You really want to know?" he asks. "All right, I'll tell you. It's because Slegal is behind the whole thing."

"Slegal, what does he have to do with it?" Alicia asks with surprise.

"Everything," Fred answers grimly. "You probably don't know it, but we go back a long way — oh yes, a long, *long* way." (Fred says these last words with considerable bitterness.) "In fact, we worked together at Cutler, when we were both starting out. Real chums, that's what we were. I thought I could trust him like a brother. And then one day he sold me out; cut the ground right out from under me. It took me three years and two moves to get my career back on track. He was some friend, all right!"

Alicia is stunned. "But Fred," she mutters in confusion, "that must have been more than twenty years ago. You mean you're still holding a grudge after all this time?"

"You bet I am," Fred answers with conviction. "I vowed to get that dirty so-and-so back then, and I'll be darned if I'll miss an opportunity to pulverize him now."

"Even if it puts the whole company in jeopardy?"

"Right."

"And even if it tosses your own chances to be the next chairman right out the window?"

"Right again. I don't care who it hurts or how much it costs. I'm going to nail that rat if it's the last thing I do!"

TERRORISM, MURDER, war, child abuse, rape — at times it seems we are surrounded by an ever-rising tide of cruelty and violence (refer to Figure 9.1). **Aggression** — the intentional infliction of some type of harm upon others — is an all too common part of social life (Baron, 1977). And even if we are fortunate enough to avoid its more dramatic and violent forms, such as the ones listed above, we are almost certain to meet it, and perhaps to engage in it ourselves, in other contexts. Thus, it is a rare individual indeed whose feelings have never been hurt by harsh criticism or cutting remarks, who has not lost his or her temper when irritated by others, and who has not, like the character in our opening story, held a grudge and waited patiently for an opportunity to "repay" an enemy. Further, growing evidence suggests that it may be a rare person, too, who has not either witnessed or participated in some form of violence within his or her own family (Straus, Gelles, and Steinmetz, 1980). Given the harmful effects of aggression and its unsettling frequency, it is far from surprising that social psychologists have focused a great deal of attention on this topic. In the remainder of this chapter, we will summarize some of the key facts they have uncovered in such research.

We will begin by examining several different *theoretical perspectives* on aggression — contrasting views about the origins and nature of such behavior. Next, we will consider major *situational* causes of aggression — conditions in the social world around us that seem to stimulate or evoke such behavior. Third, we will turn to the occurrence of aggression in *close relationships* — violence between husband and wife,

FIGURE 9.1. Unfortunately, we seem to live in an increasingly violent world.

Aggression and violence: All too common facts of modern life

parent and child, and the members of dating couples. Here, we will consider both the frequency of such events and some of the factors responsible for their occurrence. Fourth, we will focus on various *personal* causes of aggression — characteristics and traits that seem to predispose certain persons toward aggressive encounters with others. Finally, we will examine various techniques for the prevention and control of human aggression. A number of these exist and, fortunately, several appear to be quite effective when used with skill and care.

THEORETICAL PERSPECTIVES ON AGGRESSION: In Search of the Roots of Violence

Why do human beings aggress? What makes them turn, with brutality unmatched by even the fiercest of predators, against their fellow human beings? Thoughtful persons have pondered such questions since ancient times, and interest in this topic certainly continues unabated in the 1980s. While many contrasting explanations for the paradox of human violence have been offered, most seem to fall into three basic categories. These suggest that aggression stems primarily from (1) innate urges or tendencies, (2) externally elicited drives to harm or injure others, or (3) existing social conditions coupled with previous learning experience.

Aggression as innate behavior

The oldest and probably best-known explanation for human aggression, **instinct theory,** suggests that human beings are somehow "programmed" for such behavior. The most famous early supporter of this view was Sigmund Freud, who held that aggression stems mainly from a powerful *death instinct* possessed by all human beings. According to Freud, this instinct is initially aimed at self-destruction but is soon redirected outward, toward others. Freud believed that the hostile impulses it generates increase over time and, if not released periodically, will soon reach high levels capable of producing dangerous acts of violence.

A related view of aggression has been proposed by Konrad Lorenz, a Nobel Prize-winning scientist. According to Lorenz (1966, 1974), aggression springs mainly from an inherited *fighting instinct* that humans share with many other species. Presumably, this instinct developed during the course of evolution because it yielded many benefits. For example, fighting serves to disperse populations over a wide area, thus ensuring maximum use of available natural resources. And since it is often closely related to mating, fighting also helps strengthen the genetic makeup of a species by assuring that only the strongest and most vigorous individuals manage to reproduce.

The theories proposed by Freud, Lorenz, and many others differ in important ways. However, all are similar in one basic respect: they are pessimistic about the possibility of preventing or controlling human aggression. After all, if aggression stems from built-in urges or tendencies, it can probably never be eliminated. At best, it can be channeled or controlled, so as to inflict the least possible harm. Since it is part of our essential human nature, though, we can never escape it entirely.

Aggression as an elicited drive: Motivation to harm or injure others

The idea that aggression is a built-in part of human nature is very popular even today. Indeed, if you asked your friends to express their own views on this issue, many would probably indicate support for this position. In contrast, most social psychologists reject the instinct approach. The main reason behind this rejection can be simply stated: to a surprising degree, instinct theories of aggression are *circular* in nature. They begin by noting that aggression is a common form of human behavior. On the basis of this observation, they reason that such behavior must stem from universal, built-in urges or tendencies. Finally, they use the high incidence of overt aggression as support for the presence of these instincts or impulses. As you can see, this is questionable logic! For this reason, and also because they object to the pessimism implied by instinct theories, many social psychologists have tended to favor an alternative view based on the suggestion that aggression stems mainly from an externally elicited *drive* to harm or injure others. This approach is reflected in several different **drive theories** of aggression (e.g., Berkowitz, 1978; Feshbach, 1984a). Such theories suggest that various external conditions (e.g., frustration, loss of face) serve to arouse a strong motive to engage in harm-producing behaviors. Such an aggressive drive, in turn, then leads to the performance of overt assaults against others. By far the most famous of these theories is the well known *frustration-aggression hypothesis*. According to this view (which we will examine in detail later), frustration leads to the arousal of a drive whose primary goal is that of harming some person or object. This drive, in turn, leads to attacks against various targets — especially the source of frustration.

Because they suggest that external conditions rather than innate tendencies are crucial, drive theories of aggression seem somewhat more optimistic about the possibility of preventing such behavior than do instinct theories. Since being frustrated or thwarted in various ways is an all too common part of everyday life, though, drive theories, too, seem to leave us facing continuous — and largely unavoidable — sources of aggressive impulses.

Aggression as a reaction to aversive events: The role of negative affect

Think back over occasions when you have behaved aggressively toward others. Now, try to remember how you felt at those times. The chances are good that you will recall feeling upset, irritated, or annoyed. In short, you probably experienced some type of *negative affect* in situations where you aggressed against others. This relationship between negative, unpleasant feelings and overt aggression has led to the formulation of a third theoretical perspective on aggression, sometimes described as the **cognitive neoassociationist** view (Berkowitz, 1984; Berkowitz and Heimer, 1987). Briefly, this theory suggests that exposure to aversive events (ones we prefer to avoid) generates negative affect (unpleasant feelings of annoyance, irritation, and anger). These reactions, in turn, automatically activate tendencies toward both aggression and flight (efforts to escape from the unpleasant situation), as well as associated physiological reactions and thoughts or memories related to such experiences.

FIGURE 9.2. According to the *cognitive neoassociationist* view, aversive experiences generate negative affect (feelings of annoyance, irritation, anger). These feelings, in turn, automatically activate tendencies toward both aggression and flight, as well as associated physiological reactions and related thoughts and memories. Whether aggression actually occurs depends, in part, on higher-order cognitive processes. (Source: Based on suggestions by Berkowitz and Heimer, 1987.)

Whether overt aggression then follows depends on several factors, such as higher levels of thought and cognitive processing. For example, if an individual has experienced some aversive event (e.g., physical pain, exposure to high temperatures, or other form of discomfort), she may be inclined to act aggressively. If she realizes that such behavior is inappropriate or disapproved of, however, she may actively restrain such tendencies (refer to Figure 9.2).

Because it offers a sophisticated framework for understanding how emotional and cognitive factors combine to influence human aggression, the neoassociationist view just described seems quite promising. Further, it is supported by the findings of a growing body of research (Berkowitz and Heimer, 1987). Like drive theories, though, it suggests we are constantly exposed to conditions resulting in strong instigations to aggression. As noted above, such instigations may be countered by higher-level thought and reasoning. Given the speed with which annoyed or irritated persons tend to "lash out" against others, however, there may often not be enough time for such rational processes to come into operation. Thus, the implications of this view, too, are somewhat unsettling where the prevention of human aggression is concerned.

Aggression and negative affect: The cognitive neoassociationist view

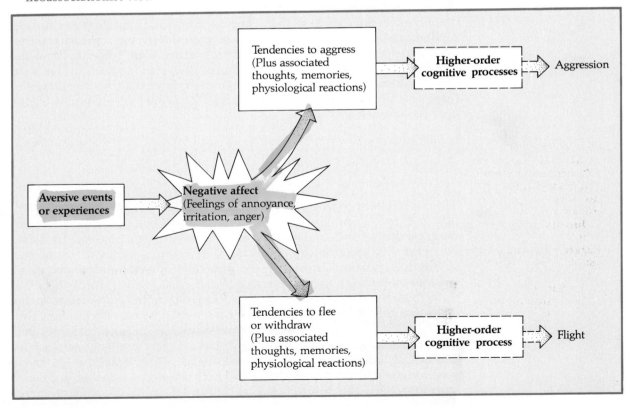

Aggression as learned social behavior

In recent years, a fourth theoretical perspective on human aggression — the **social learning view** — has gained increasing acceptance. Supporters of this view (Bandura, 1973; Baron, 1977; Berkowitz, 1984) emphasize the fact that aggression, dangerous and unsettling as it is, should be viewed primarily as a learned form of social behavior. In contrast to the central assumption of instinct theories, they argue that human beings are *not* born with a large array of aggressive responses at their disposal. Rather, they must learn these in much the same way that they learn other complex forms of behavior. Going further, supporters of this modern view suggest that if we are fully to understand the nature of aggression, we must possess information about three basic issues: (1) the manner in which such behavior is acquired, (2) the rewards and punishments that affect its current performance, and (3) the social and environmental factors that influence its occurrence in a given context. In contrast to other theories we have considered, then, the social learning view does *not* attribute aggression to one or a small number of factors. Rather, it suggests that the roots of such behavior are highly varied in scope and involve a complex interplay among these factors: aggressors' past experience (what aggressive behaviors have they previously acquired? what have they learned about the appropriateness of using such behaviors?); current conditions that promise either to reward or punish aggression; and a host of social, cognitive, and environmental variables that tend to either elicit or inhibit such actions (e.g., frustration, exposure to aggressive actions by others, aggressors' current moods and level of arousal; refer to Figure 9.3).

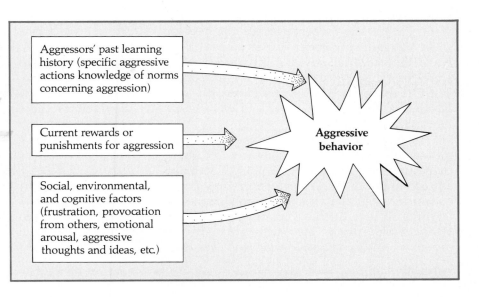

FIGURE 9.3. According to the *social learning view*, aggression stems from many different factors involving (1) the aggressor's past learning history; (2) current rewards or punishment for aggression; and (3) a host of social, environmental, and cognitive factors that either elicit or inhibit its performance.

Aggression: The social learning view

FOCUS ON RESEARCH:
Classic Contributions

Studying Human Aggression: A Procedure for Measuring Hurt without Harm

Researchers wishing to study human aggression in a systematic manner face a puzzling dilemma. On the one hand, they wish to investigate an especially dangerous form of behavior. On the other, they cannot permit any harm to persons participating in their research. How can this dilemma be resolved? For many years there seemed to be no ready answer. As a result, systematic research on aggression was restricted to studies of verbal rather than physical assaults, or to observation of aggressive actions in natural settings outside the laboratory. In the early 1960s, however, a simple but elegant solution emerged. This approach centered around the following strategy: why not attempt to convince research participants that they can physically harm another person when, in fact, they cannot? Under such conditions, their intentions to inflict pain or injury on others could be studied without any risk of actual harm to the supposed victim. Since aggression is usually defined as involving intentional harm to others, such procedures might well capture the essence, if not the precise form, of aggression in real-life situations. Several different variations on this basic approach were soon developed (e.g., Berkowitz, 1962). The one that gained widest use, however, was devised by Arnold Buss (1961). Briefly, Buss's method was as follows.

When subjects arrived for their appointments, they were told that they would be participating, along with another person (actually an accomplice of the experimenter), in a study concerned with the effects of punishment on learning. It was further explained that to investigate this topic, one of the two persons present would serve as a *teacher* and the other

as a *learner*. The teacher would present various materials to the learner, who would attempt to master them. On occasions when the learner made a correct response, the teacher would reward him by indicating that his response had been correct. Whenever the learner made an error, however, the teacher would "punish" this person by means of electric shock. These shocks would be delivered by means of a device similar to the one shown in Figure 9.4, (an apparatus that has come to be known in social psychology as the **aggression machine**), and could vary in strength from very mild to quite intense. (The higher the number on the button pushed by subjects, ostensibly, the stronger the shocks to the learner.) To convince subjects that the apparatus actually worked in this manner, mild sample shocks were then delivered to them from several of the buttons.

As you can probably guess, the subject was always chosen to serve as the teacher and the accomplice to serve as the learner. The accomplice then made a prearranged series of errors, thus providing subjects with several opportunities to deliver electric shocks. Since any shock, even the mildest one, would be sufficient to inform the learner that he had made an error, Buss argued that the strength of the shocks subjects actually chose to deliver provided a measure of aggression — their willingness to inflict harm or injury on the accomplice. (A second index of aggression was provided by the length of time subjects depressed each button — the duration of their assault against the victim.) Please note: *the accomplice never actually received any shocks during the study.* Rather, subjects were simply led to believe that shocks were delivered. Thus, it was possible to measure the willingness of one person to harm another in the absence of any real danger to participants.

With several modifications (e.g., subjects

FIGURE 9.4. Top: An *aggression machine* similar to the one used by Buss. Subjects are informed that they can deliver electric shocks (or some other type of aversive stimuli) to another person by pushing the buttons on this equipment. Bottom: An experimenter recording subjects' behavior. Two measures of aggression are often obtained: the strength and duration of the painful stimuli participants choose to deliver to their supposed victim. (Note: this person is an accomplice who never actually receives such stimuli.)

One technique for measuring physical aggression in the laboratory

are sometimes given the opportunity to "attack" the supposed victim by means of loud noise or uncomfortable levels of heat rather than electric shock) the procedures devised by Buss have been used to study many different aspects of aggression (Geen and Donnerstein, 1983). In fact, much of the information we present in the remainder of this chapter was obtained through their use. Before turning to the results of such research, therefore, we should consider one additional question: do these methods really work? Do they actually provide a valid means for studying human aggression under safe laboratory conditions? While there is far from total agreement on this point, the answer seems to be "yes."

First, the results of several different studies point to the usefulness of procedures based on Buss's technique. For example, it has been found that people with a prior history of violent behavior tend to inflict stronger levels of shock (or heat, or noise) upon victims than do persons without such a history (e.g., Gully and Dengerink, 1983; Wolfe and Baron, 1971). Second, as noted forcefully by Berkowitz and Donnerstein (1982), in order for laboratory studies of aggression to yield valid information it is *not* crucial that the situations they employ or the responses they measure closely resemble those outside the laboratory. Rather, what *is* crucial is that subjects believe that they can harm the supposed victim in some manner.

Since participants in studies employing the Buss procedure or similar methods generally accept this idea, the findings of such research can be viewed as valid in nature. At this point, we should hasten to add that despite these facts, the methods described above are far from perfect. They raise certain ethical issues, such as whether it is appropriate to place subjects in a situation where they believe, even temporarily, that they have harmed another person. And their continued use for almost three decades has tended to reduce their effectiveness; so many potential subjects have now heard about them that it is increasingly difficult to convince participants that they can in fact harm the victim. Taken together, though, existing evidence suggests that Buss's procedures yield at least a rough index of the central concept we wish to measure: the willingness of individuals to inflict harm — physical or otherwise — on another human being.

While the social learning view is more complex than the other perspectives on aggression we have considered, it offers two important advantages. First, it is more sophisticated, and therefore almost certainly more accurate, than earlier approaches. Second, it is much more optimistic about the possibility of preventing or controlling human aggression. After all, if such behavior is primarily learned, it should be open to direct modification and change. Because of these advantages, the social learning view has gained increasing support among social psychologists. Indeed, it is now by far the most widely accepted theoretical perspective on aggression in our field.

SOCIAL AND SITUATIONAL DETERMINANTS OF AGGRESSION: External Causes of Violence

Contrary to popular belief, aggression does *not* usually take place in a social or situational vacuum. While instances in which one person attacks one or several others totally at random do occur, they appear to be the exception, not the rule. Much more often, aggression springs from specific social or situational factors which pave the way for its occurrence and lead aggressors to choose specific victims. We will consider several of these factors here. Before doing so, however, we should consider another question about which you may already have begun to wonder: How can human aggression — especially physical aggression — be studied in a systematic manner without any danger to the persons involved? An ingenious and seemingly effective answer to this question was devised by Arnold Buss in the early 1960s (Buss, 1961). For a discussion of Buss's research, and the technique he devised for studying aggression, please see the **Focus** insert that begins on page 302.

Frustration: Thwarting as a potential cause of aggression

Suppose that you asked twenty people you know to name the most important single cause of aggression—how would they reply? Chances are good that a majority would answer "frustration." They would state that the most potent means of inducing human beings to aggress is thwarting their goals—somehow preventing them from getting what they want. Current, widespread acceptance of this view stems mainly from the well-known **frustration-aggression hypothesis** that we mentioned earlier. In its original form, this hypothesis made the following sweeping assertions: (1) frustration *always* leads to some form of aggression, and (2) aggression *always* stems from frustration (Dollard et al., 1939). In short, it held that frustrated persons always engage in some type of aggression and that all acts of aggression, in turn, result from frustration. Bold statements like these are always appealing; they are intellectually stimulating, if nothing else. But are they really accurate? Does frustration really play such an all-important role with respect to aggression? The answer is almost certainly "no." Both portions of the frustration-aggression hypothesis seem to be far too sweeping in scope.

First, it is now clear that frustrated individuals do *not* always respond with aggressive thoughts, words, or deeds. Rather, they show a wide variety of reactions, ranging from resignation and despair on the one hand, to attempts to overcome the source of their frustration on the other.

Second, it is also apparent that all aggression does *not* result from frustration. People aggress for many different reasons and in response to many different factors. For example, boxers hit and sometimes injure their opponents because it is their role to do so, or because they wish to win some valued prize, not because they are frustrated. Similarly, people wishing to get ahead in their careers sometimes use complex political maneuvers to eliminate rivals (by derailing *their* careers), in the total absence of frustration from such persons. In these and many other cases, aggression stems from factors other than frustration. To suggest that it is always the result of thwarting, then, is quite misleading.

In view of these considerations, few social psychologists now believe that frustration is the only, or even the single most important, cause of aggression. Instead, most believe that it is simply one of a host of different factors that can potentially lead to aggression (e.g., Berkowitz, 1978). Further, there is growing agreement that whether frustration will, indeed, produce such effects depends largely on two conditions: its intensity and its perceived legitimacy. Only when frustration is strong, and only when it is viewed as arbitrary or illegitimate, does it tend to increase the likelihood of later aggression. In contrast, when it is weak, or perceived as deserved and legitimate, it appears to have little impact upon subsequent aggression (e.g., Kulik and Brown, 1979; Worchel, 1974).

In sum, frustration is only one of many factors contributing to human aggression. Further, it is probably neither the most important nor the strongest of these variables. Thus, it does not seem to play the very central role in such behavior it was once assigned.

Direct provocation: When aggression breeds aggression

While frustration must be quite intense before it can elicit overt aggression, another factor—*direct verbal or physical provocation*—seems capable of producing such effects even when quite mild. Informal observation suggests that individuals often react very strongly to mild taunts, glancing blows, or other actions by others that they perceive as some sort of attack (refer to Figure 9.5). Moreover, when they do, they may begin a process of escalation in which stronger and stronger provocations are quickly exchanged, with dangerous consequences for both sides (Goldstein, Davis, and Herman, 1975).

Direct evidence for the strong impact of physical provocation on aggression has been obtained in many laboratory studies (e.g., Dengerink, Schnedler, and Covey, 1978; Ohbuchi and Ogura, 1984). In these experiments, individuals exposed to rising provocation from a stranger (usually in the form of ever-stronger electric shocks) have been found to respond to their attacker in kind. As provocation rises in intensity, so does their retaliation. Thus, most people seem to follow a general rule of *reciprocity* where aggression is concerned. Instead of "turning the other cheek" in response to provocation from others, they attempt to balance the scales, to return treatment as harsh (if not slightly harsher) than they have received themselves. Similar effects seem to occur with respect to verbal provocation as well. Here, too, individuals seem all too willing to respond aggressively to real or imagined slurs from others (e.g., Geen, 1968).

While reciprocity rather than forebearance seems to prevail where reactions to provocation are concerned, other evidence indicates that

FIGURE 9.5.   As shown here, many different actions can serve as provocations to aggression! (Source: Reprinted with special permission of King Features, Inc.)

Direct provocation: A powerful elicitor of aggression

this is not always the case. Several factors play a key role in determining whether, and to what extent, individuals choose to respond in kind to attacks from others, or to overlook such treatment. Among the most important of these are the perceived intentionality of such provocation, and certain characteristics of the persons from whom it stems.

Perceived intentionality and reactions to provocation: Accident or intention?   Imagine the following situation. You are talking to another person on the phone when, after a series of hissing and popping noises, the line goes dead. Will you react with anger and attempts to retaliate for your annoyance? Probably not, for it appears some technical problem broke the connection. In contrast, consider the same situation with one major change: the other person has clearly hung up on you. How will you respond now? The chances are good that you will grow angry, and take some steps to pay this individual back for her rude behavior. Your contrasting reactions in these two situations call attention to a crucial fact. Our response to apparent provocations from others is strongly mediated by our perceptions concerning the *intentionality* of these actions. If actions appear to be intentional — purposely enacted — we respond with anger and efforts to return such treatment. If, instead, they seem to be unintentional — the result of accident or factors beyond others' control — we are much less likely to lose our temper and behave aggressively. In short, our *attributions* concerning the causes behind provocative actions by others play a key role in determining just how we respond to such treatment.

Evidence for the importance of attributions in determining our response to provocation is provided by several experiments (e.g., Albert, 1981; Ferguson and Rule, 1983; Kremer and Stephens, 1983). For example, in one intriguing study on this topic, Johnson and Rule (1986) exposed male subjects to strong provocation from an accomplice, and then measured both their physiological reactions to such treatment and their later retaliation against this person. Half the subjects learned, prior to being provoked, that the accomplice was very upset over an unfairly low grade on a chemistry quiz; the remaining half received this information only after being angered. Results indicated that this information about *mitigating circumstances* had strong effects upon subjects' reactions. Those who received it before being provoked actually showed lower emotional upset (as measured by changes in heart rate) and lower retaliation against the accomplice (as indexed by the strength of bursts of noise they chose to deliver to him) than subjects who received such information only after being provoked. Clearly, then, subjects' interpretations of the *causes* behind the accomplice's attacks played an important role in determining their reactions to such treatment.

Additional and equally dramatic evidence for the importance of attributions in determining our reactions to provocation from others has been reported by Ohbuchi and Kambara (1985). These researchers arranged for female subjects to receive information suggesting that another person (actually a female accomplice) intended to deliver either mild or painfully strong electric shocks to them. Half the subjects then actually received the shocks intended by their opponent, while half received shocks opposite to those intended by this person. (If the opponent planned to deliver strong shocks, subjects received only mild ones, while if she planned to deliver weak shocks, they actually received strong ones.) Then, in a second phase of the study, subjects were given an opportunity to deliver shocks of varying strength to the accomplice.

If individuals respond mainly to the perceived intention behind others' provocative actions, it would be expected that those who learned that their opponent planned to give them strong shocks would direct stronger attacks against her than those who learned that their opponent intended to give them only weak shocks. Moreover, this would be the case regardless of the level of shocks they actually received. If, instead, individuals respond mainly to the actual level of provocation from others, then those who received strong shocks would react more aggressively, regardless of their opponent's intentions. As you can see from Figure 9.6, results offered clear support for the first of these two possibilities. Subjects who thought that their opponent planned to attack them

FIGURE 9.6.   When subjects learned that their opponent planned to expose them to strong shocks, they aggressed strongly in return. Moreover, this was true even if they received only weak attacks. Similarly, when subjects learned that their opponent planned to expose them to only weak shocks, they responded with weak attacks in return, even if they later actually received much stronger shocks. These findings suggest that our response to provocation from others depends, to a great degree, on the intentions behind such actions. (Source: Based on data from Ohbuchi and Kambara, 1985.)

Reactions to provocation: The role of perceived intentions

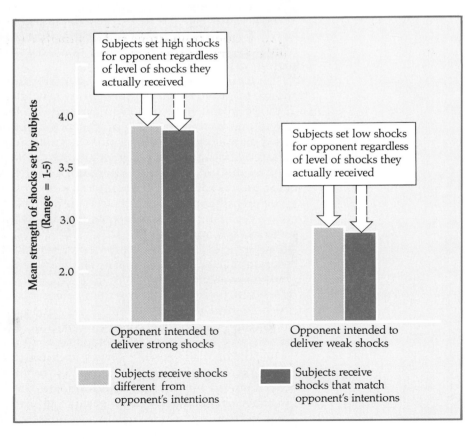

severely later directed much stronger attacks against her than those who thought she planned to assault them only weakly. Moreover — and this is the key point — this was true *regardless of the level of shocks subjects actually received.* These findings, and those of related studies, indicate that our reactions to provocation from others depend quite strongly on our understanding of the intentions behind their actions. Only when we view their annoying words or deeds as intentional do we respond in kind, according to the age-old principle of "an eye for an eye, and a tooth for a tooth."

Characteristics of the provoker: When beauty saves the day.   Suppose that while standing in line outside a movie theater, another person cuts in front of you. Further, imagine that this person is a young man well over six feet tall weighing at least two hundred pounds. How would you respond? Unless you are also quite large yourself, you might decide that in this case, it is best to bite your tongue and remain silent. In contrast, imagine that the person who provoked you in this manner was far less physically imposing (e.g., a woman about five feet tall, weighing under a hundred pounds). Here, you might well decide to protest loudly. Incidents such as this call attention to another factor that often determines our reactions to provocation from others: the characteristics of these persons. As you may expect, we are far less likely to respond aggressively to provocation from strong and seemingly dangerous individuals than to similar treatment from ones who appear less able to harm us. Similarly, males are generally less likely to retaliate against females than against other males (e.g., Hoppe, 1979). And, perhaps somewhat more surprising, we are less likely to respond aggressively to provocation from physically attractive than physically unattractive persons. This latter fact has been demonstrated clearly by Ohbuchi and Izutsu (1984). These researchers found that male subjects directed weaker attacks against a female accomplice who had previously provoked them very strongly when she was made up so as to look physically attractive than when she was made up to appear quite unattractive. These results suggest that as is the case in many other spheres of social life, persons blessed with an attractive appearance can "get away with murder" where provoking others is concerned. (Refer to our earlier comments in Chapter 6.)

Exposure to media violence: The effects of witnessing aggression

If there is one issue relating to human aggression that has gripped public attention in recent years, it is this: does continued exposure to filmed or televised violence cause an increase in similar behavior among viewers? Obviously, this is an important question, with serious social implications. It is not at all surprising, then, that it has been the subject of hundreds of research projects. The findings of these studies have been far from entirely consistent; given the complexity of the issue they have addressed, this is not surprising (Freedman, 1984). However, taken together, they point to the following conclusion: exposure to media violence may, in fact, be one factor contributing to the high level of violence in American society and elsewhere. Several different lines of research, conducted in very different ways, are consistent with this interpretation.

First, it is supported by many short-term laboratory studies. In the earliest of these investigations, young children watched either short films in which an adult model aggressed against an inflated toy clown (e.g., she sat on the clown and punched it repeatedly in the nose), or in which the same model behaved in a quiet and nonaggressive manner (Bandura, 1965; Bandura, Ross, and Ross, 1963). Later, the children were allowed to play freely in a room containing many toys, including several used by the model. Careful observation of their behavior in this setting revealed that those who had seen the model behave in an aggressive manner were much more likely to attack the plastic toy (known as a Bobo doll) than those who had not witnessed such behavior. These findings suggest that even very young children can acquire new ways of aggressing against others through exposure to filmed or televised violence. In subsequent laboratory studies, subjects viewed actual television programs or films, and were then given an opportunity to attack (supposedly) a real victim rather than an inflated toy (e.g., Liebert and Baron, 1972). Once again, results were the same: participants in such studies (both children and adults) who witnessed media violence later demonstrated higher levels of aggression than participants who were not exposed to such materials (Geen, 1978; Liebert, Sprafkin, and Davidson, 1982).

Additional, and in some ways more convincing, evidence for the aggression-enhancing impact of media violence is provided by a second group of studies using different methodology. In these *long-term field investigations*, different groups of subjects were exposed to contrasting amounts of media violence, and their overt levels of aggression in natural situations were then observed (e.g., Leyens et al., 1975; Parke et al., 1977). For example, in a study conducted by Leyens and his associates (Leyens et al., 1975) two groups of boys attending a private school in Belgium were exposed to contrasting sets of films. One group saw five violent movies, one each day, while the other group saw five nonviolent films presented in the same manner. When the boys' behavior was then observed as they went about their daily activities, an impact of media violence was obtained: those exposed to the violent movies showed an increase in several forms of aggression. That such results are not limited to children is suggested by the findings of several other studies (e.g., Loye, Gorney, and Steele, 1977). In what is perhaps the most surprising of these, Phillips (1983) found that the number of homicides in the United States rose significantly several days after the broadcast of championship heavyweight boxing matches. While it is difficult to interpret these results in a definitive manner, they do point to the possibility that exposure to highly publicized portrayals of aggression can have far-reaching social effects.

Finally, additional evidence for the impact of media violence is provided by several long-term *correlational studies* relating the amount of media violence watched by individuals as children to their rated levels of aggression several years — or even decades — later (e.g., Eron, 1982; Huesmann, 1982). Information on the first of these factors (amount of violence watched) is based on subjects' reports about the shows they watched plus violence ratings of these programs. Information about the second (their actual levels of aggression) is acquired from ratings of their behavior by classmates or teachers. The results of such investigations indicate that these two variables are in fact related: the more media violence individuals watch as children, the higher their rated levels of aggression later in life. Further, as would be expected, the strength of this relationship seems to increase somewhat with age (refer to Figure 9.7). Thus, there is some indication that the influence of media violence is cumulative: the more shows and programs of this type individuals watch over the years, the more likely they are to behave in an aggressive manner. At this point, we should insert a word of caution: while some studies demonstrate the kind of increase just described, others do not. Clearly, then, such results should be viewed as suggestive rather than conclusive (Freedman, 1984).

The impact of media violence: Why does it occur?   Together, the three groups of studies just described offer convincing support for the view that exposure to media violence can sometimes elicit similar actions on

FIGURE 9.7. The strength of the relationship between amount of media violence watched and overt aggression increases slightly with age. Interestingly, this trend is clearer among girls than among boys. (Source: Based on data from Huesmann, 1982.)

The effects of media violence: Evidence indicating that they are cumulative in nature

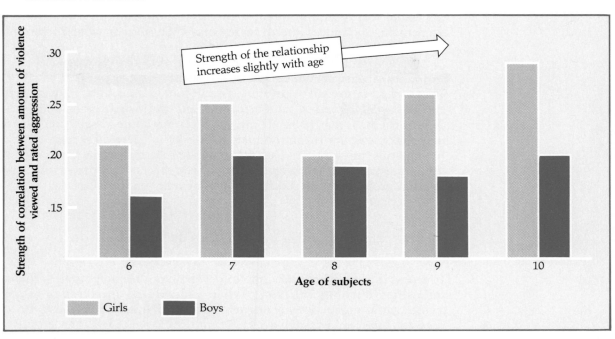

the part of viewers. Not all findings have been consistent with this conclusion (e.g., Feshbach and Singer, 1971; Freedman, 1984), but in general the weight of available evidence does seem to favor the existence of an aggression-stimulating impact of media violence. As we noted before, this is an important conclusion, with serious social implications. But *why*, precisely, do such effects occur? How does exposure to aggressive actions in films and television programs stimulate similar actions on the part of audience members? Four processes seem to be involved.

First, exposure to media violence seems to weaken the *inhibitions* of viewers against engaging in similar behavior. After watching many persons — including heroes and heroines — perform aggressive actions, some viewers seem to feel less restrained about performing such actions themselves. "After all," they seem to reason, "if *they* can do this, so can I."

Second, exposure to media violence may arm viewers with new techniques for attacking and harming others not previously at their disposal. And once these are acquired, it is only one further step to putting them into use when appropriate conditions arise (e.g., in the face of strong provocation from others).

Third, watching others engage in aggressive actions can exert strong effects upon viewers' cognitions (Berkowitz, 1984). For example, such materials can exert the type of *priming effect* discussed in Chapter 3: it can cause some audience members to have additional aggressive ideas and thoughts. Thus, following exposure to media violence, individuals may be more likely to perceive others in a negative or hostile light, or to interpret ambiguous actions by them as aggressive in nature. Similarly, such persons may raise their estimates of the frequency of aggression in the social world around them, seeing it as more common and so more acceptable. Such ideas and thoughts may then, in turn, foster overt aggression against others (e.g., Carver et al., 1983).

Finally, continued exposure to media violence may reduce emotional sensitivity to violence and its harmful consequences. In short, after watching countless murders, assaults, and fights, some viewers may become *desensitized* to such materials, and show little emotional reaction to them (Geen, 1981; Thomas, 1982). As you can see, such shifts may make it easier for individuals to engage in aggression themselves.

In sum, the impact of media violence seems to stem from several different sources (refer to Figure 9.8). Given this fact, it is hardly surprising that such effects are both far-reaching and general in scope.

Heightened arousal and aggression: The "energization" of violence

It is a well established principle in psychology that heightened arousal intensifies ongoing behavior. When individuals are physiologically aroused, the vigor of their current responses — whatever these are — tends to increase. Do such effects occur with respect to aggression? Re-

FIGURE 9.8.   The impact of media violence seems to stem primarily from the four processes shown here.

Media violence: Processes responsible for its effects

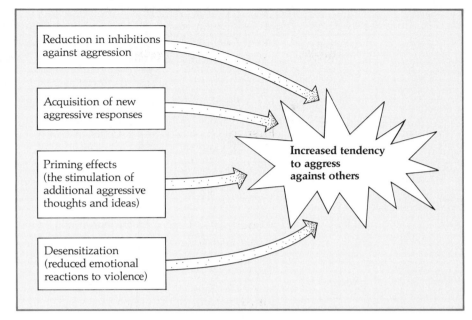

search evidence suggests that they do. Arousal stemming from such diverse sources as participation in competitive games (Christy, Gelfand, and Hartmann, 1971), vigorous exercise (Zillmann, 1983a), and even some types of music (Rogers and Ketcher, 1979) has been found to facilitate aggression in different experiments. One explanation for such effects now widely accepted by social psychologists is provided by the theory of **excitation transfer** (Zillmann, 1983a).

Briefly, this theory calls attention to the fact that physiological arousal dissipates slowly over time. As a result, some portion of such arousal may persist as individuals move from one situation to another. For example, a woman who is aroused by a near-miss in traffic may continue to be slightly aroused even many minutes later, as she interacts with a friend or acquaintance. Such residual excitement can then serve to intensify later emotional experiences—even ones totally unrelated to the initial cause of arousal. Thus, if the woman's friend now makes a cutting remark, she may react more strongly to this provocation than would be the case if such residual, carryover arousal were not present. Excitation transfer theory calls attention to the fact that such effects are most likely to occur when the persons involved are unaware of their residual arousal, or when they attribute it to events occurring in the present situation. Thus, the character in our example would be more likely to react strongly to provocation from her friend if she were unaware of the arousal persisting from her near-accident, and if she now attributed all of her emotional reactions to her friend's nasty remark. If, instead, she realized that part of her arousal stemmed from the prior

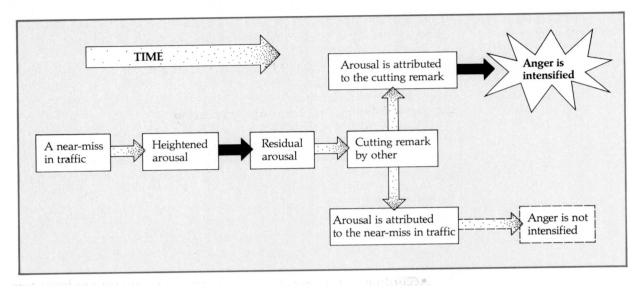

FIGURE 9.9. According-ing to *excitation transfer theory*, arousal occurring in one situation can persist and intensify emotional reactions in later, seemingly unrelated situations. For example, the arousal produced by a near-miss in traffic may persist, and later intensify angry reactions to a cutting remark by another person.

Such effects will only occur, however, if the residual (carryover) arousal is attributed to emotion-provoking events in the present situation (i.e., the nasty remark).

Excitation transfer: One explanation for the impact of heightened arousal on aggression

situation, she would be less likely to respond angrily to her friend's provocation (please refer to Figure 9.9).

The results of many studies offer support for predictions derived from excitation transfer theory (Zillmann, Katcher, and Milavsky, 1972; Zillmann, 1983a,b; Ramirez, Bryant, and Zillmann, 1983). For example, Beezley and her colleagues (Beezley et al., 1987) found that while large doses of amphetamine (a stimulant) increase physiological arousal, they do not significantly increase aggression, presumably because individuals attribute their arousal to this drug rather than to provocation or other factors relating to aggression. Thus, as Zillmann contends, heightened arousal does not necessarily—or automatically—facilitate assaults against others. Rather, such effects occur only under specific, limited conditions.

Sexual arousal and aggression: The fusion of love and hate? If arousal stemming from sources unrelated to aggression (e.g., physical exercise, competition) can sometimes enhance aggression, it seems reasonable to pose a related question: can sexual arousal, too, have such effects? Actually, it has often been proposed that these two aspects of behavior are closely linked. For example, Freud (1933) suggested that desires to hurt or be hurt by one's lover are a normal part of sexual relations. Similarly, Fromm (1956) proposed that any strong emotion—including desires to hurt or to be hurt—can readily blend with sexual desire. And more recently, Bardwick (1971) has argued that some women, at least, find moderate levels of pain sexually stimulating. (Needless to add, many persons disagree with this suggestion and find it objectionable.) These and similar comments by other authors imply that there is indeed an important link between sexual arousal and overt aggression. But is this really the case? Does this specific type of arousal actually affect our tendencies to aggress against others? Research findings indicate that this is actually so.

It appears that very mild levels of sexual arousal, such as those induced by exposure to pictures of attractive members of the opposite sex either nude or partially dressed, can reduce later aggression against persons who deliver some form of provocation (e.g., Baron, 1974, 1979; Baron and Bell, 1973; Ramirez, Bryant, and Zillmann, 1983). However, stronger levels of sexual arousal, such as those induced by reading highly erotic passages or by watching scenes of explicit lovemaking, can actually increase subsequent aggression (e.g., Jaffe et al., 1974; Zillmann, 1971, 1984.) In short, the relationship between sexual arousal and overt aggression appears to be curvilinear in form, with mild levels of arousal reducing aggression below that shown in the absence of any sexual arousal, and higher levels actually increasing aggression above this point. What accounts for this U-shaped function? A *two-component* model proposed by Zillmann (1984) offers one useful explanation.

According to this model, exposure to erotic stimuli produces two effects. First, it increases arousal among the persons involved. Second, it influences their current *affective state* — their positive and negative feelings. Whether sexual arousal will facilitate or inhibit subsequent aggression, then, depends on the overall pattern of such effects. Since mild erotic materials generate only weak levels of arousal, and since most people find them pleasant, it is not surprising that they often tend to reduce aggression; as we will note in more detail below, positive feelings often reduce tendencies to aggress against others. In contrast, more explicit forms of erotica generate stronger levels of arousal, coupled with negative feelings (many people find such materials repulsive or objectionable). The result: erotica of this kind may increase aggression. Evidence supporting this two-factor explanation has been obtained in several experiments (e.g., Ramirez, Bryant, and Zillmann, 1983; White, 1979). When subjects in these studies were exposed to erotic stimuli that induced low levels of arousal and positive feelings, their aggression was reduced. When, in contrast, they experienced high levels of arousal along with negative feelings, their subsequent aggression was increased.

In sum, it appears there is indeed a link between sexual arousal and aggression. However, the nature of this relationship is more complex than was at first suspected (Zillmann, 1984).

Sexual arousal and aggression: Further, disturbing findings. As we have just seen, existing evidence suggests that explicit forms of erotica, especially those that induce negative feelings among their audiences, can enhance overt aggression. Given the ready availability of such materials at the present time, these findings are somewhat disturbing. Unfortunately, the story does not stop there. Additional findings concerning the impact of erotic (or, some would say, *pornographic*) materials indicate that they may produce other negative effects as well.

First, consider the impact of what is known as **violent pornography**

—sexually explicit materials including scenes of rape, sado-masochism, and related acts of violence (much of it directed against women). Growing evidence suggests that exposure to such materials can (1) increase the willingness of males to aggress against females—something they are often reluctant to do; (2) increase the acceptance of false beliefs about rape (e.g., the myth that many women really want to be ravaged; Malamuth, 1984); (3) stimulate aggressive sexual fantasies (Malamuth, 1981); and (4) generate high levels of sexual arousal, at least among individuals who find the use of force in sexual relations to be arousing (Malamuth, Check, and Briere, 1986).

Second, it appears that unsettling effects can sometimes be produced even by repeated exposure to erotic materials most persons would find less objectionable: "standard" X-rated fare showing explicit scenes of lovemaking between consenting adults. Recent investigations suggest that regular viewing of such materials can exert negative effects upon both the attitudes and behavior of adults (Ceniti and Malamuth, 1984). Perhaps the clearest evidence for such effects has been reported by Zillmann and Bryant (1984).

These investigators arranged for male and female volunteers to watch a series of films in their laboratory. Six films lasting eight minutes each were shown during each of six weekly sessions. For one group of subjects (those in the *massive exposure* condition), all the films shown were erotic in nature: they depicted a wide range of explicit heterosexual behavior. For a second group (the *intermediate exposure* condition), half the films were erotic and half were non-erotic. Finally, subjects in a third, *no-exposure* group saw only non-erotic films. Several weeks after viewing the last of these films, subjects returned and completed several questionnaires. One of these asked them to estimate the percentage of individuals in the United States engaging in various sexual practices. Results indicated that those who had been exposed to a large dose of pornography (thirty-six erotic films) perceived several of these practices—especially ones many people find objectionable—to be more common than did other participants. For example, subjects in the massive exposure group reported that almost 15 percent of adults engage in sadomasochism; those in the no-exposure and intermediate exposure groups reported that only 8 percent of adults engage in such behavior.

A second questionnaire involved a fictitious rape case. After reading this case, subjects learned that the rapist had been convicted. They were then asked to recommend a sentence for him. As you can see from Figure 9.10, the more pornographic films subjects had witnessed, the more lenient they were in their treatment of the rapist. Moreover, this was true for females as well as males. Thus, it appeared that massive exposure to erotic materials led subjects to view this repugnant crime as somehow less serious and less deserving of punishment.

To conclude: mounting evidence suggests that the flood of X-rated books, films, and magazines released in recent years may be exerting adverse effects upon society. The word "may" should be emphasized, however, for the picture offered by existing evidence is far from clear

FIGURE 9.10. The more pornographic films subjects had previously watched, the shorter the sentences they recommended for a convicted rapist. Moreover, this was true for women as well as men. (Source: Based on data from Zillmann and Bryant, 1984.)

Repeated exposure to pornography: Some unsettling effects

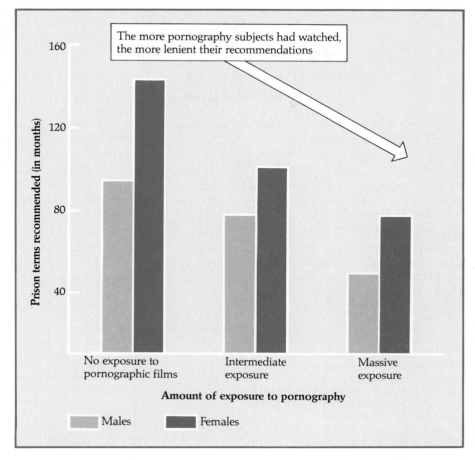

The more pornography subjects had watched, the more lenient their recommendations

(please refer to our discussion of this issue in Chapter 15). At present, there is some indication that explicit sexual materials can contribute, along with many other factors, to the occurrence of objectionable and dangerous forms of behavior. Whether there is sufficient evidence in this regard to call for regulation and control of such materials, though, remains largely a matter of personal judgment. (For discussion of another factor related to aggression that has also been the focus of both social concern and legislative attention, please see the **Focus** insert on page 318.)

AGGRESSION IN CLOSE RELATIONSHIPS: The Intimate Enemy

Were you ever spanked by your parents while a child? Did you ever see your mother strike your father, or your father hit your mother? Have you ever slapped, shoved, or kicked a person you were dating? If you an-

FOCUS ON RESEARCH:
The Cutting Edge

Alcohol and Aggression: The Dangerous Drunk?

Do people become more aggressive when they drink? It is widely believed that this is so. Indeed, many persons feel that bars and nightclubs are dangerous places to visit for just this reason, especially on Friday and Saturday nights. That alcohol consumption is indeed related to violence is suggested by the fact that almost 75 percent of the persons arrested for aggressive crimes (e.g., murder, assault, shootings, stabbings) are legally intoxicated at the time they are taken into custody (Shupe, 1954). Further, several laboratory studies, conducted under carefully controlled conditions,

also indicate that alcohol can contribute to the occurrence of overt aggression (Taylor and Leonard, 1983). In these experiments, subjects given substantial doses of alcohol — enough to make them legally intoxicated — have been found to respond more strongly to provocation than persons given drinks containing no alcohol, or doses so small they have no appreciable effect upon them (e.g., Bailey et al., 1983).

One possible explanation for the aggression-enhancing impact of alcohol is that this drug decreases individuals' restraints against such behavior by reducing their information-processing capacities. After consuming sufficient alcohol, drinkers may be unable to foresee the consequences of their actions, or to

FIGURE 9.11. Even when subjects had received a large dose of alcohol (enough to make them legally intoxicated), they still responded to social cues indicating that aggression was inappropriate. Thus, those who learned that most persons showed low levels of aggression in the experimental situation directed weaker attacks against their opponent than those who never received such information. (Source: Based on data from Jeavons and Taylor, 1985.)

Alcohol, aggression and social cues

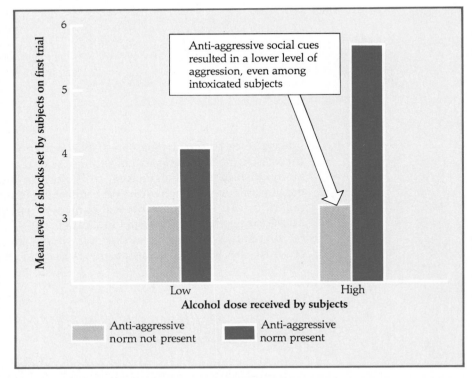

evaluate their appropriateness (Zeichner and Pihl, 1980). If this is the case, it may be difficult, if not impossible, to control aggression by intoxicated persons. Fortunately, this suggestion does not appear to be correct. On the contrary, recent findings reported by Jeavons and Taylor (1985) suggest that even intoxicated individuals remain sensitive to social cues, and can inhibit their aggression when these suggest that such actions are inappropriate.

In this study, male subjects consumed either a large or a small dose of alcohol. Then they competed in a reaction time task with another person (who was actually fictitious). In this task, the slower player on each trial received a shock from his opponent. Thus, subjects' willingness to aggress against the fictitious opponent could be assessed in terms of the strength of the shocks they set for this individual (from 1 to 10). To provide provocation, subjects were made to "lose" on half the trials, and received shocks on those occasions. In order to determine if the aggression-provoking effects of alcohol could be reduced by ap-

propriate social information, half the subjects in both the low- and high-dose groups received information suggesting that most people tended to make use of relatively mild shocks. (This was the *norm* condition.) The remainder never received such information (the *no norm* group). Results were clear: among subjects given a large dose of alcohol, the presence of the anti-aggressive norm substantially reduced aggression. Among subjects given a very small dose, in contrast, this norm had little effect. (These individuals demonstrated a uniformly low level of aggression; refer to Figure 9.11.)

Apparently, then, intoxicated persons are *not* inevitably programmed for aggression. Under appropriate conditions, they can show considerable restraint even in the face of strong provocation. The implications of these findings for legal proceedings seem clear: defenses based on the suggestion that persons accused of violent crimes consumed so much alcohol that they didn't know what they were doing are suspect at best.

swered "yes" to one or even to several of these questions, don't be alarmed: you have lots of company. Indeed, it appears that aggression between parents and children, brothers and sisters, husbands and wives, and dating couples is anything but rare (e.g., Laner, 1983; Straus, Gelles, and Steinmetz, 1980). In this section we first examine the prevalence of such violence — how common it is, and where it tends to occur. Then we will consider some of the factors that play a role in its occurrence.

The prevalence of aggression in close relationships: Who and where

Given the deep love and affection existing between the members of most families, common sense suggests that violence should be rare among

FIGURE 9.12. Many married couples report having engaged in acts of violence against their spouse at some point during their marriage. (Source: Based on data from Straus, Gelles, and Steinmetz, 1980.)

Husband-wife violence: More common than you might expect

such persons. However, a large-scale survey conducted by Straus, Gelles, and Steinmetz (1980) suggests that, in this case, common sense is wrong —dangerously wrong. After studying over two thousand families chosen to be representatives of the total population of the United States, these investigators reached the following, sad conclusion: violence is an integral part of family life. A few statistics tell the story.

First, consider aggression between husbands and wives. When asked if they had directed any one of eight violent acts toward their spouse during the past year, fully 16 percent of the participants in the survey answered "yes." Further, this number rose to fully 28 percent when the entire marriage (not just the preceding year) was considered. As you can see from Figure 9.12, the acts in question were not trivial ones; sizable proportions of married couples reported having slapped, kicked, or thrown something at one another. Interestingly, there appeared to be little difference between men and women: both sexes reported carrying out assaults against their spouse with approximately equal frequency. As you might guess, though, they reported using certain violent acts with

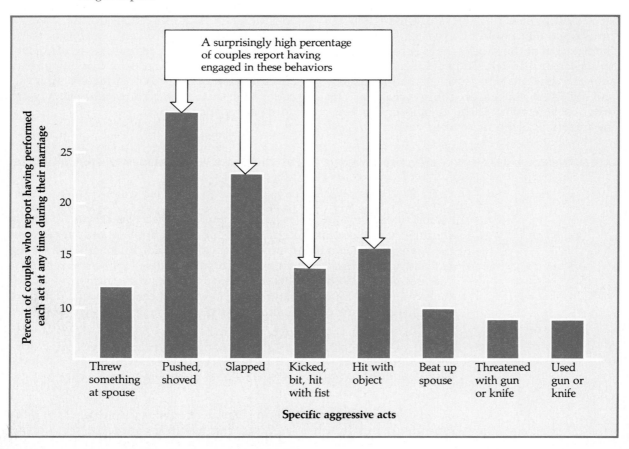

contrasting frequency (e.g., wives reported being more likely to throw things, or to hit their spouse with various objects; husbands reported being more likely to push or slap their partner). In any case, these data lend support to the view that for many persons, a marriage license is perceived as a "hitting license."

That married couples engage in acts of violence with a high frequency is unsettling. Perhaps even more disturbing, though, is the fact that parents often turn their rage upon victims much less able to defend themselves: their children. Data gathered by Straus, Gelles, and Steinmetz (1980) indicate that almost three-quarters of parents report having used some form of physical aggression on their offspring at some point during their childhood. And again, these assaults are not uniformly mild in nature. Seventy-one percent mention using slaps or spankings, while 20 percent admit to striking their children with an object. On the basis of these findings, Straus and his colleagues estimate that approximately 2.3 million youngsters have been beaten by their parents at one time or another, and that perhaps over one million have been threatened with a knife or a gun!

At this point, we should add that the alarming rates of violence we have just described are not restricted to families. They also seem to occur in close relationships outside this context. This fact is clearly demonstrated by a study conducted by Sigelman, Berry, and Wiles (1984). These researchers asked more than five hundred college students whether they had ever performed or received any of the eight violent acts listed in Figure 9.12 within the context of a heterosexual relationship. More than 50 percent of both sexes reported that they had used one or more of these actions themselves, and slightly more men than women (58.9 percent versus 47.8 percent) indicated that they had been on the receiving end of such assaults. Only in one respect did the sexes differ substantially: men reported having perpetrated sexual violence (using physical force to engage in sexual activity against their partner's will) more frequently than women (11.8 percent versus 1.8 percent).

In sum, existing evidence provides another and more chilling meaning to the phrase, "You always hurt the one you love." Violence, it appears, is a much more common aspect of close and intimate relationships than most of us care to admit.

Some causes of aggression in close relationships

The statistics outlined above are unsettling, and paint a disturbing picture of life in many American families. By themselves, however, they do not explain *why* violence is so common in families and in other intimate relationships. As you might guess, the origins of such behavior are complex, and involve many different factors. Several of the most important of these are described below.

Suppose that you grew up in a family where your mother and father often engaged in acts of physical violence against one another. Further, imagine that they also hit you whenever they lost their temper. Do you think that you might be likely to engage in similar actions yourself with respect to your own spouse, children, or lovers? Apparently, the answer is "yes." Existing evidence indicates that all too often, violence does beget violence. Persons who witnessed physical aggression between their parents are more likely to become violent husbands or wives than ones never exposed to such assaults. Individuals who were physically punished as children are more likely to abuse their own youngsters than ones who were not disciplined in this manner. And persons exposed to both types of family violence are more than three times as likely to engage in similar behavior themselves than persons raised in environments where such assaults were absent (Straus, Gelles, and Steinmetz, 1980). In sum, it appears that a propensity toward family violence is passed on from generation to generation in a repetitive cycle.

A second major cause of family violence is stress. Families experiencing high levels of stress are more likely to be the scene of violent behavior than families fortunate enough to avoid such conditions. Among the factors important in this respect are family size (the greater the number of dependent children at home, the greater the likelihood of family violence), economic problems (e.g., loss of a job, inability to pay debts), the death of a close friend or relative, unwanted pregnancy, and difficulties with in-laws. The more events of this type experienced by individuals, the more likely they are to abuse their spouse or children.

A third factor closely linked to family violence involves the division of power within families, and the manner in which they reach decisions. Families in which power is shared between husbands and wives, and in which decisions are reached democratically (through discussion among members) are much less likely to experience serious forms of violence than ones in which most power is concentrated in the hands of either the husband or wife, and in which this power-holder makes most of the decisions. Apparently, sharing and participation promote the resolution of the conflicts that are unavoidable when people live together, and so serve as a buffer against the development of violent modes of behavior.

To conclude: violence in close relationships stems from a host of different factors. Fortunately, many — if not all — of these seem open to at least a degree of modification. Thus, the repetitive cycle of such aggression *can* be broken. However, this can only be accomplished through active, concrete steps. Simply assuming that people who love one another will rarely become involved in violent encounters is a serious error, and one that can place large numbers of persons at unnecessary risk.

INDIVIDUAL DETERMINANTS OF AGGRESSION

Do you know any persons who, because of "low boiling point," seem to become involved in more than their share of aggressive encounters? Similarly, can you recall others who seem to lack a temper, and almost never behave aggressively no matter how strongly they are provoked? In all probability, you are acquainted with individuals of both types. The reason for this is clear: individuals differ greatly in terms of their propensity toward aggression. Some demonstrate high levels of aggression, while others are much less likely to engage in such behavior. Recognition of this basic fact has led social psychologists to conduct research designed to identify those traits and characteristics contributing to such differences. Many such factors — often described as **individual determinants of aggression** — have been identified. Here, though, we will focus on two of the most important: the **Type A behavior pattern** and differences between the sexes.

Personality and aggression: The Type A behavior pattern

In recent years, a great deal of attention has been focused on what has come to be known as the *Type A behavior pattern* (Glass, 1977; Matthews, 1982). One reason for this interest is as follows: persons showing this pattern are more than twice as likely as others to suffer serious heart attacks! The key characteristics possessed by such persons (known as *Type As*) are excessive competitiveness (Type As want to win all the time, in every situation), exaggerated time urgency (they are always in a hurry and never relax), and a high level of hostility and aggression (Glass, 1977). Clearly, this pattern should be related to overt aggression. That is, Type As should become involved in aggressive encounters more frequently than persons who do not share their traits (usually labeled *Type Bs*). The results of several experiments indicate that this is indeed the case (Baron, Russell, and Arms, 1985; Carver and Glass, 1978). Perhaps the most revealing of these investigations is one reported by Strube and his colleagues (Strube et al., 1984).

In this investigation, male subjects previously identified through their responses to a questionnaire as being Type A or Type B were either frustrated (by being unable to complete a difficult puzzle in the allotted time) or not frustrated; they were then provided with an opportunity to deliver rewards or fines to another person (who was actually an accomplice). Rewards were to be administered when the accomplice made correct responses on a learning task, and fines when he made errors. Half the participants were led to believe that their partner (the accomplice) would know how large the rewards and fines were (the *full-feedback* condition). In contrast, the remainder were informed that this person would know only how large the rewards were; he would *not* receive information about the size of the fines *(partial feedback)*. Strube and his coworkers reasoned that if subjects chose to deliver large fines to the accomplice in this latter condition, they would be demonstrating *hostile aggression:* after all, since the accomplice would have no knowledge of the size of the fines he was receiving, there was no way in which large ones could improve his performance relative to small ones. Thus, if subjects chose to employ

FIGURE 9.13. Following frustration, Type As showed higher levels of *hostile aggression* than Type Bs. They chose to deliver larger fines to the victim when he made errors in a learning task under conditions where large fines could be of no benefit to his performance (i.e., when the learner received no information on the size of the fines he was receiving). (Source: Based on data from Strube et al., 1984.)

Type As: More likely to engage in hostile aggression

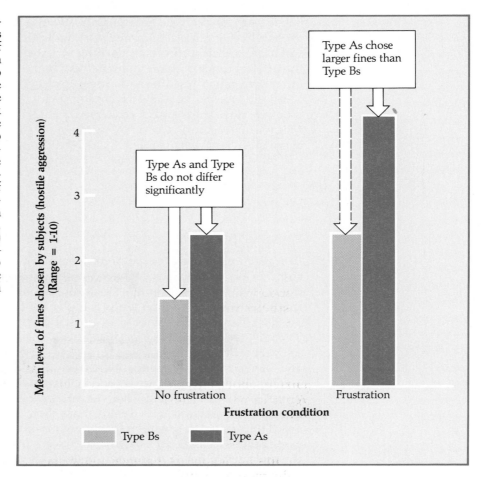

large fines, this would be indicative of a desire on their part to harm the learner. In contrast, if subjects chose to deliver large fines in the full-feedback condition, this would constitute *instrumental aggression:* subjects might be fining the accomplice in order to help him attain better task performance. As you can probably guess, Strube and his associates predicted that Type As would engage in more hostile aggression than Type Bs. As shown in Figure 9.13, this was actually the case. In the partial-feedback condition, Type As exposed to frustration did use stronger fines than Type Bs. In the absence of frustration, however, the two groups did not differ.

Additional findings confirm these results. For example, Type As seem to be likelier than Type Bs to engage in such actions as child abuse. Indeed, fully 75 percent of a group of women under treatment for child abuse were found to be Type As. In contrast, only 50 percent of those in a non-abusive control group fit into this category (Strube et al., 1984). Such findings suggest that the greater propensity of Type As to engage in hostile aggression has practical implications of a very serious nature.

Sex differences in aggression: Do they exist?

Are males more aggressive than females? Folklore suggests this is the case. And crime statistics do reveal that males are more likely than females to be arrested for violent acts. Does this mean that large and consistent sex differences in the tendency to aggress actually exist? Systematic research on this issue presents something of a mixed picture.

After carefully reviewing all existing evidence on this issue, Eagly and Steffen (1986) reached the conclusion that males do indeed appear to be somewhat more aggressive than females. However, the size of this difference seemed to be small. Moreover, it appeared to be greater in some contexts than others. For example, this sex difference was more pronounced in studies involving physical aggression against others than in studies involving non-physical forms of aggression (e.g., verbal assaults, rating others negatively along some dimension). Similarly, it was larger in situations where aggression seemed to be required rather than freely chosen. In addition, males and females appeared to differ somewhat in their attitudes toward aggression. Males indicated less guilt or anxiety about engaging in such behavior than females, while females reported greater concern over the possibility that aggressing against others might pose a threat to their own safety (e.g., if the victim chose to retaliate). Finally, Eagly and Steffen (1986) found that both sexes directed slightly more aggression against male targets than female ones.

In sum, it appears that men and women do differ to a degree in their willingness to handle interpersonal relations through aggression. The next question, then, is obvious: what is the source of such differences? Are men somehow "programmed" for violence to a greater degree than women? Or are these differences largely the result of contrasting gender roles — the cultural beliefs that men should be tough, hard, and aggressive, while women should be kind, caring, and cautious (i.e., avoid exposing themselves to danger)? As Eagly and Steffen (1986) note, little evidence on this issue currently exists. However, given the fact that many other supposedly "innate" differences between the sexes have been found, on close examination, to stem primarily from contrasting sex roles and socialization practices for boys and girls (refer to our discussion in Chapter 5), it seems likely that this one, too, rests largely on such foundations. To the extent this is the case, sex differences in aggression will be a "sometime thing," occurring under some conditions but not others. Further, they may well decrease somewhat in the years ahead, as traditional stereotypes of "masculinity" and "femininity" continue to weaken.

THE PREVENTION AND CONTROL OF HUMAN AGGRESSION

Can aggression be prevented? Or are we doomed to repeat an endless cycle of violence and cruelty until, perhaps, it brings about our own demise as a species? While some are pessimistic on this score, we are not. In our view, effective, workable techniques for reducing human aggression already exist and can be put to practical use (Baron, 1983). In this final section, we will summarize several of these techniques and call attention to some of their basic strengths and weaknesses.

Punishment: An effective deterrent to aggression?

FIGURE 9.14. Does punishment or the threat of punishment serve as an effective deterrent to aggression? Most societies assume that it does, and have established severe penalties for acts of violence.

Punishment: The penalty for violence in most societies

Throughout history, most societies have used **punishment** as a primary means of deterring human violence. Thus, they have established harsh punishments for such crimes as murder, rape, and assault (refer to Figure 9.14). Are such tactics actually effective? In one sense, of course, they are. If persons convicted of violent crimes are imprisoned or executed, they will obviously be unable to repeat these actions in the future. But what about the issue of deterrence: will punishment prevent such persons from repeating their aggressive actions, and will it discourage others from engaging in the same forms of behavior? Here, the pendulum of scientific opinion has swung back and forth across the decades. At

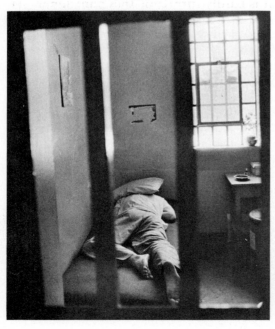

present, though, there seem to be firm grounds for concluding that if used in an appropriate manner, punishment *can* be effective as a deterrent to future violence.

First, growing evidence suggests that punishment can exert a powerful and lasting effect upon behavior if it is administered under certain conditions (Bower and Hilgard, 1981). These include: (1) *immediate delivery* — punishment must follow objectionable behavior as soon as possible, (2) *severity* — it must be of sufficient magnitude to be aversive to the recipient, and (3) *high probability* — it must follow undesirable behavior on almost every occasion when it occurs. Second, it is a well established fact that individuals are often strongly affected by observing the outcomes of others. If they witness other persons being rewarded for some activity, their tendency to engage in it themselves is increased. In contrast, if they observe others being punished for some behavior, they may refrain from similar actions (e.g., Bandura, 1977). Thus, there is a scientific basis for asserting that if potential aggressors witness the punishments received by former perpetrators, they may be reluctant to engage in similar actions themselves.

Unfortunately, of course, the conditions just described rarely prevail when punishment is used to deter human aggression. In many societies, the delivery of punishment for aggressive acts does *not* take place in accordance with the three principles listed above. The interval between the performance of a violent crime and punishment for it is often very long. The magnitude of punishment delivered varies greatly, being harsh in some localities and lenient in others. And the probability of being apprehended and punished for a given act of violence is very slight indeed. In view of these facts, it is hardly surprising that punishment has been viewed, by many, as quite ineffective in deterring violent crime. The dice, so to speak, are heavily loaded against it. Similarly, most persons have little opportunity to witness the punishments administered to those convicted of violent crimes. Thus, there is little chance for such treatment to influence the future behavior of potential aggressors. In sum, the fact that punishment does not currently seem to be effective in deterring human violence by no means implies that punishment itself is ineffective. Rather, it appears that this procedure is simply being used in ways that virtually guarantee its failure. If these conditions were changed, we believe, the potential impact of punishment might well be enhanced. And then, the health, safety, and well-being of countless innocent victims might also be better assured.

Catharsis: Does getting it out of your system really help?

Imagine that one day, your boss criticizes you harshly for something that was not your fault. After she leaves, you are so angry that you slam your fist down on your desk over and over again. Will this behavior make you feel better? And will it reduce your desire to "get even" with your boss in some manner? According to the **catharsis hypothesis**, it might. This view suggests that when angry individuals "blow off steam" through vigorous but nonharmful actions, they will experience (1) reductions in their level of arousal, and (2) lowered tendencies to engage in overt acts of aggression. Both of these suggestions have enjoyed widespread acceptance for many years. Surprisingly, though, neither is strongly supported by existing research evidence (Feshbach, 1984a).

First, with respect to the view that the emotional tension stemming from frustration or provocation can be reduced through participation in nonaggressive activities, results have been mixed. Performing physically exhausting activities does seem to reduce such arousal in some cases (Zillmann, 1979). However, such effects are temporary, and the best means of attaining them appears to be that of attacking the source of one's anger (Hokanson, Burgess, and Cohen, 1963). Obviously, this is not an effective tactic for reducing harmful aggression!

Turning to the suggestion that the performance of "safe" aggressive actions reduces the likelihood of more harmful forms of aggression, the picture is even more discouraging. Research on this topic indicates that overt aggression is *not* reduced by (1) watching scenes of filmed or televised violence (Geen, 1978), (2) attacking inanimate objects (Mallick and McCandless, 1966), or (3) aggressing verbally against others. Indeed, there is some evidence that aggression may actually be increased by each of these conditions.

Contrary to popular belief, then, catharsis does not appear to be a general or highly effective means for reducing overt aggression. While participating in exhausting, nonaggressive activities may produce temporary reductions in emotional arousal, and so in the tendency to aggress, such arousal may quickly be regenerated when individuals encounter or simply think about the persons who previously angered them. Thus, the potential benefits of catharsis have probably been overemphasized in the past.

Other techniques for reducing aggression: Nonaggressive models, training in social skills, and incompatible responses

While punishment and catharsis have probably received most attention as potential tactics for controlling human aggression, additional procedures have been suggested—and carefully investigated—in recent years (Baron, 1983). Initial results with respect to several of these have been promising, so they are worthy of brief mention here.

Exposure to nonaggressive models: The contagion of restraint.   If exposure to aggressive actions by others in films or on TV can increase aggression among viewers, it seems only reasonable to expect that parallel—but opposite—effects may result from exposure to persons who demonstrate or urge restraint in the face of provocation—*nonaggressive*

ON THE APPLIED SIDE

The Art of Constructive Criticism

"Sticks and stones may break my bones, but words will never harm me." Almost everyone repeats this phrase as a child, but if ever a proverb was wrong, this is it. Words *do* hurt, and hurt badly. Moreover, they often do so unnecessarily. The reason for this is simple: most persons do not know how to criticize others effectively (Weisinger and Lobsenz, 1981). They seem to believe that in order to be effective, criticism must be biting, harsh, and hostile. Thus, when criticizing others they engage in such actions as shaming the target person — humiliating this individual in some manner, blaming him or her for what went wrong, reminding this person of previous warnings ("I told you so"), and couching their criticism in angry, emotional tones. Needless to say, the reaction of most individuals to such treatment is far from positive. Indeed, they view it as a signal to make endless excuses, ignore the criticizer, or get angry and retaliate in kind. Under such conditions, the probability of any beneficial change in their behavior is close to zero.

Are there any ways of avoiding these pitfalls? In short, are there steps we can follow to assure that our criticism of others is *constructive* rather than *destructive* in its effects? A growing body of evidence (Hughes, 1974; Larson, 1986; Weisinger and Lobsenz, 1981) suggests there are. Among the most important are these.

First, when criticizing others, make your comments specific. Statements such as, "Can't you do *anything* right?" or, "How dumb can you get?" may be satisfying to the critic, but they don't transmit any practical information to the person being criticized. It is much more useful to describe precisely what needs to be done, and what should be changed. Second, always be sure that the behavior you are criticizing can in fact be altered. If it can't, save your breath: all you'll accomplish is upsetting or angering the recipient. Third, consider the manner in which you communicate your criticism. Try to speak in a calm tone, and avoid ordering the other person to "shape up." A calm approach is more likely to produce change instead of resistance. Fourth, offer incentives for change. Describe the benefits that the recipient can obtain by acting on your suggestions. Finally, reserve your criticisms for an appropriate time and place. For example, it is unwise to criticize others publicly, so that they "lose face." Similarly, it is usually a waste of time to engage in criticism when the recipients are tired, irritable, or under stress. Waiting for a calmer moment is often good strategy.

By following these principles, you can turn criticism from a source of anger or humiliation into a valuable form of feedback and a stimulus to desirable change. In short, you can succeed in maximizing its benefits, while minimizing its potential costs.

---

models. That this is so is suggested by the findings of several experiments (e.g., Baron, 1972; Donnerstein and Donnerstein, 1976). In these studies, persons exposed to the actions of nonaggressive models later demonstrated lower levels of aggression than persons not exposed to such models. Moreover, this was the case even when they had previously been strongly provoked. Such findings suggest that it may be useful to plant nonaggressive models in tense and threatening situations; their presence may well serve to tip the balance away from violence.

Training in social skills: Learning to get along with others.   One major reason why many persons become involved in aggressive encounters is disturbingly simple: they are sorely lacking in social skills that would enable them to avoid such difficulties (refer to Figure 9.15). For example, they are unable to communicate their wishes to others, have an abrasive style of self-expression, and are insensitive to cues that reveal others' emotional states. As a result, they experience severe and repeated frustration (after all, no one can figure out what they want!), and they say or do things that unnecessarily anger persons around them. Growing evidence suggests that persons lacking in such skills account for a high proportion of the violence occurring in most societies (Toch, 1980, 1985). To the extent this is true, equipping such individuals with the skills they so badly lack may go a long way toward reducing the prevalence of aggression. (For discussion of one social skill in which nearly everyone needs improvement, please see the **Applied Side** insert on page 329.)

Incompatible responses: Empathy, humor, and mild sexual arousal.   A final technique for reducing aggression we will mention rests upon the following basic principle: it is impossible to engage in two **incompatible responses** or experience two incompatible emotional states at the same time. Applying this idea to aggression, it seems possible that such behav-

FIGURE 9.15. Individuals lacking in basic social skills often experience more than their fair share of aggressive encounters. (Source: Drawing by Lorenz; ©1980 by The New Yorker Magazine, Inc.)

Social skills: One reason why they're essential

"Please forgive Edgar. He has no verbal skills."

ior can be reduced through the induction, among potential aggressors, of feelings or responses incompatible with aggression or the emotion of anger. That this is indeed the case is indicated by a growing body of research evidence. When angry individuals are induced to experience emotional states incompatible with anger or overt aggression, such as *empathy, humor, or mild sexual arousal*, they do show reduced levels of aggression (Baron, 1971, 1983; Ramirez, Bryant, and Zillmann, 1983). This finding suggests that getting angry individuals "off the aggressive track," so to speak, may often be an effective means for preventing overt violence. People in a pleasant or happy frame of mind, it appears, are simply not prime candidates for performing acts of violence.

SUMMARY

Aggression involves the intentional infliction of harm or injury upon others. Although it has often been attributed to instincts or other innate tendencies, most social psychologists view it as a learned form of behavior, affected by many social, environmental, and cognitive factors.

Among the social and situational causes of aggression are *frustration*, direct *provocation* from others (especially when it appears to be intended), and exposure to *media violence.* Aggression can also be enhanced by *heightened arousal.* Sexual arousal and aggression appeared to be linked, in that exposure to certain forms of erotic materials (ones that induce high levels of arousal and negative feelings or that contain sexual violence) can increase subsequent aggression. High doses of *alcohol*, too, appear to facilitate aggressive actions.

A great deal of violence takes place in *close relationships* (within families and between dating couples). The high incidence of such aggression stems from many factors, including exposure to violence in one's own family while a child, and high current levels of stress.

Aggression is also affected by many tactics or characteristics possessed by individuals. Type As are more aggressive than Type Bs. In addition, there is one indication that males are more aggressive than females.

Several techniques for the control of human aggression exist. These include *punishment, catharsis, exposure to nonaggressive models*, and training in basic *social skills* (e.g., knowing how to criticize others constructively). In addition, aggression can often be reduced through the induction of responses or emotional states incompatible with such behavior (e.g., empathy, humor, mild sexual arousal).

GLOSSARY

aggression
Behavior directed toward the goal of harming or injuring another living being who is motivated to avoid such treatment.

aggression machine
Apparatus used to measure physical aggression under safe laboratory condition.

catharsis hypothesis
The suggestion that providing angry persons with an opportunity to behave in vigorous but nonharmful ways will reduce both (1) their level of emotional arousal, and (2) their tendency to aggress against others.

cognitive neoassociationist view
An explanation for the occurrence of human aggression suggesting that aversive events generate negative affect. Such affect, in turn, activates tendencies toward both aggression and flight. Which of these actions then follows depends, in part, on higher levels of cognitive processing.

drive theories of aggression
Theories that view aggression as stemming from particular external conditions serving to arouse the motive to harm or injure others. The most famous of these is the frustration-aggression hypothesis.

excitation transfer
A theory that explains the impact of heightened arousal upon aggression. According to this view, arousal occurring in one situation can persist and intensify emotional reactions occurring in later situations.

family violence
Aggression between husbands and wives, parents and children, or siblings.

frustration-aggression hypothesis
A view suggesting that frustration is a very powerful elicitor of aggression.

individual determinants of aggression
Characteristics possessed by individuals (e.g., personality traits) that predispose them toward either low or high levels of aggression.

incompatible responses
Responses or emotional states incompatible with anger and acts of overt aggression.

instinct theory
The view that aggression stems primarily from innate urges and tendencies.

punishment
Procedures in which aversive consequences are delivered to individuals each time they perform certain actions. Under appropriate circumstances, punishment can be an effective deterrent to human aggression.

social learning view
A modern perspective that views aggression as a learned form of social behavior.

Type A behavior pattern
A cluster of characteristics that appear to adversely affect the health of persons who possess them. Among the most important of these traits are excessive competitiveness, time urgency, and aggressiveness.

violent pornography
Highly explicit erotic materials in which one or more of the persons shown engage in acts of violence against one or more others. Often, the victims in such materials are females.

FOR MORE INFORMATION

Baron, R. A. (1977). *Human aggression.* New York: Plenum.
> An overview of major research findings concerning human aggression. Separate chapters examine the social, environmental, and personal determinants of such behavior. Techniques for preventing or controlling aggression are also discussed.

Geen, R. G., and Donnerstein, E., eds. (1983). *Aggression: Theoretical and empirical reviews.* New York: Academic Press.
> A collection of chapters dealing with many different aspects of aggression. Each was prepared by an expert on such behavior, so all are thorough and informative.

Liebert, R. M., Sprafkin, J. N., and Davidson, E. S. (1982). *The early window: Effects of television on children and youth,* 2nd ed. New York: Pergamon.
> A clearly written review of research concerned with the behavioral impact of television. The effects of TV viewing on aggression and several other forms of behavior are discussed in an easy-to-follow style.

Zillmann, D. (1984). *Connections between sex and aggression.* Hillsdale, N.J.: Erlbaum.
> A thorough examination of one of the most intriguing relationships ever studied by psychologists: that between sexual arousal and aggression. Potential bases for such a link in neurophysiology, motivation, emotion, and even cognition are discussed, and a wealth of fascinating findings are described. If you would like to know more about this topic, you could not choose a better source.

CHAPTER 10

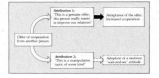

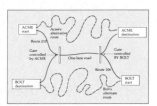

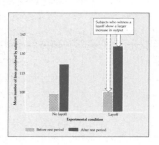

COOPERATION AND COMPETITION: Working with — Or
Against — Others

*Cooperation from others: Do we reciprocate or exploit? • Attribution and
social exchange: Reacting to others' motives • Groups versus individuals:
Which is more cooperative? • Personal orientation and cooperation:
Cooperators, competitors, individualists, and equalizers*

BARGAINING: The Give-and-Take Road to Resolving
Interpersonal Conflict

*Overall strategy in bargaining: Is it better to be "tough" or
conciliatory? • Framing: Focus on gains versus focus on losses • Other
factors affecting bargaining: Negotiator experience, power, confidence, and
constraints • When bargaining fails: Other tactics for resolving
interpersonal conflict*

PERCEIVED FAIRNESS IN SOCIAL EXCHANGE: In Search of Equity

*Judgments of fairness in social exchange: Equity and inequity • Equality and
relative needs: Alternative standards for judging fairness • Procedural
justice: It's not just what you get that counts — How you get it matters,
too • Reactions to unfairness: Tactics for dealing with injustice*

SPECIAL INSERTS

FOCUS ON RESEARCH: Classic Contributions — Communication
and cooperation: Some benefits, some costs
FOCUS ON RESEARCH: The Cutting Edge — Reducing costly
conflicts: An interpersonal approach
ON THE APPLIED SIDE — Comparable worth: Equity in the
world of work

SOCIAL EXCHANGE:
Coming to Terms
with Others

It's an old but sad story. Because of their growing concern over corruption in local politics, three diverse groups of citizens (the Junior Chamber of Commerce, a coalition of many of the town's churches, and an alliance of pro-environment groups) joined forces to turn the incumbents out of office. After a hard-fought campaign, they were successful: city hall is now under their control. But this, it seems, was the *start*, not the end, of the reformers' problems. Try as they may, they cannot seem to agree on a uniform plan of action. The current meeting of the town council illustrates their plight.

"Look, I don't know why you're being so unreasonable," Pam Fletcher remarks to Ben Clayton. "After all, it was *our* group that put us over the top. Without the support of the business community, none of us would be sitting here now. So it's only right that our issues get first priority."

"*You* put us over the top? Who are you kidding?" is Ben's angry reply. "Humph! It's *my* supporters who made the difference. What nerve! Why don't you go back to your real estate office and let people who know something make the decisions."

Pam's angry reply is already on her lips when she is interrupted by Tom Pilkowski, the new mayor. "People, people, please! I'm so *tired* of all this bickering. We didn't break our backs winning the election just to jump down each others' throats. Can't we do anything but fight?"

"OK, OK," Pam answers, "but it's just that he's being so *unfair*. After all, it really *was* our group that turned this thing around, so it's only right that our development plans get top priority."

"Just where do you get your ideas, anyway?" Ben asks angrily. "All you did was pay for a few ads in the paper and kick in a few bucks. It was my people who really got out there and rang doorbells;

we got the voters concerned, not you. so, we're not even going to consider your miserable plans for paving over the whole county till we get some action on that river. I mean, it's so bad you can smell it miles away—"

At this point Tom bangs his gavel on the table. "Enough! Enough! I know that everyone here thinks that they were responsible for winning the election; that's just human nature, I guess. But that's all beside the point now. We're here, and that's what really matters. Besides, I do know this: unless we're willing to compromise, we'll never get anywhere. In fact, the people out there may get so tired of hearing us squabble, they'll be glad to have old Mayor Stirm and his gang back in office! So come on, let's get down to business. No one's going to get everything they want; we don't have unlimited resources. But if we put our heads together and act in a reasonable manner, we all ought to be able to get *something*."

UNLESS YOU, too, are active in local politics, we doubt that you've ever been involved in a situation precisely like this one. Yet, we're sure that you *have* had direct experience with several of the processes it involves. Like the people in this incident, you've probably *cooperated* with others to reach some common goal, or *competed* against them to attain ones of your own. Similarly, you have probably *bargained* or *negotiated* with others over various issues and experienced *conflict* with them if your efforts at reaching agreement failed. Finally, like Pam and Ben, you've probably sometimes felt you were not being treated fairly by others — you were not getting what you deserved in your dealings with them.

All of these processes occur in the context of **social exchange** — social relationships in which we provide others with something, and expect to receive something back in return. The *something* traded, of course, can vary greatly (refer to Figure 10.1). In economic relationships, such as those between buyers and sellers or employees and employers, it centers around items and services having direct economic value. In lasting social relationships such as those between friends, lovers, or relatives, it often involves less tangible factors such as approval, loyalty, or love (Foa, 1976). And in many contexts, it encompasses the exchange of *status* (signs of esteem and value) or *information* (advice, opinions, instructions; Brinberg and Castell, 1982). Regardless of the precise nature of the *resources* traded or the context in which such exchange takes place, however, each of the processes mentioned above can come into play. It is on these central aspects of social interaction that we will focus in the present chapter. Specifically, we begin by examining **cooperation** and **competition** — patterns of behavior many experts view as constituting opposite poles on a single dimension. Next, we turn to **bargaining** and other techniques for resolving interpersonal conflict. Finally, we consider the question of how individuals decide whether they are being treated fairly or unfairly in social relationships, and the effects these perceptions of **equity** or **inequity** have on their later behavior.

COOPERATION AND COMPETITION: *Working with — Or Against — Others*

As we noted in our discussion of prosocial behavior (see Chapter 8), individuals sometimes offer aid to others without expecting anything in return. While such one-way assistance does occur very frequently, it is far less common than another pattern — one in which two or more persons work together or coordinate their actions so that the outcomes of each are enhanced. Such mutual, two-way assistance is known as *cooperation* and represents an important form of social exchange.

As you probably know from your own experience, cooperation involves individuals or groups working together to attain shared goals. Given the obvious benefits yielded by cooperation, this is far from surprising. In fact, you might at first assume that it will develop any time two or more persons seek the same goal. While this seems reasonable, there is an important reason why it can't be so: *often the goals sought simply can't be shared.* To mention just a few examples, it is usually impossible for athletes competing in the same Olympic event to share

FIGURE 10.1. As shown here, almost anything can be traded in *social exchange.* (Source: Drawing by Booth; ©1977 by The New Yorker Magazine, Inc.)

Social exchange: The range of what's traded is great

BOOTH.

"I'm going to send you down the hall to see Dr. Hunseth. And please tell Dr. Hunseth it's his turn to send one of his patients to me."

first prize, for several persons seeking the same job or promotion all to attain it, or for two would-be lovers to gain the affections of the same individual at the same time. In these and many other cases, cooperation is impossible, and an alternate form of behavior—*competition*—develops instead. Here, each person strives to maximize his or her own outcomes, often at the expense of others. Because many attractive goals are sought by more persons than can actually hope to achieve them, competition, too, is a common form of social interaction.

As we have just seen, the choice between cooperation and competition is often an obvious one; indeed, there may really be no choice at all. In others, however, the persons or groups involved may find that they do have some room to maneuver. They can choose either to work with others, toward mutually desired goals, or against them, for their own gain. This fact brings us to the central question we wish to address: what conditions serve to tip the balance toward one or the other of these patterns? Several factors that play a role in this respect are described below.

reciprocally

Cooperation from others: Do we reciprocate or exploit?

Throughout our lives, we are urged to follow the Golden Rule: do unto others as you would have them do unto you. Despite such recommendations, however, many of our interactions with other persons seem, instead, to be governed by the principle of **reciprocity**. We often behave toward others as they have acted toward us, *not* as we ourselves prefer to be treated. As we have noted in previous chapters, this tendency toward reciprocity is quite general in scope. Indeed, it applies to behaviors and reactions as varied as liking or disliking for others, helping, and aggression (please refer to chapters 6, 8, and 9). Given this high degree of generality, it is not surprising to learn that reciprocity applies to social exchange, too. Research findings indicate that when others treat us in a highly competitive manner, we usually respond in kind (e.g., Rosenbaum, 1980). When they adopt a more conciliatory or cooperative strategy, we tend to match *this* pattern (Black and Higbee, 1973). And when they offer very high levels of cooperation, we sometimes respond with high levels of trust and coordination ourselves (Kuhlman and Marshello, 1975). The word "sometimes" should be emphasized, though, for it appears that this will be the case only under certain conditions. If one person offers a high level of trust or cooperation to another, but also makes it clear that such behavior will continue only if it is returned, cooperation may well be enhanced. In contrast, if total trust or cooperation is offered without any clear requirement that it be reciprocated, a sharply different pattern may emerge. The recipients of such *noncontingent cooperation* may be strongly tempted to take advantage of those offering it. To the extent they do, they may respond to the cooperation they receive with exploitation. That such temptation can be hard to resist

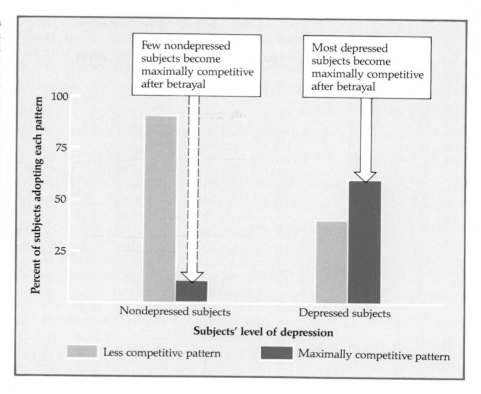

is suggested by the fact that in one well-known study (Shure, Meeker, and Hansford, 1965) fully 129 of 143 participants responded to total cooperation from an opponent with exploitation.

We should add that while reciprocity is ordinarily the guiding principle for most persons where the choice between cooperation and competition is concerned, important individual differences in this tendency also exist. For example, the results of a recent study by Haley and Strickland (1986) suggest that depressed persons, who hold negative views about themselves and the world around them, tend to react more strongly to betrayal (competition from others when they expect cooperation) than persons who are not depressed. In this study, the subject's partner (an accomplice) first promised to cooperate, but then actually behaved in a competitive manner — one that would maximize her own rewards at the expense of the subject. Fully 60 percent of depressed persons (ones who had previously scored high on a measure of depression) responded to such betrayal by shifting to a maximally competitive pattern in future dealings with the accomplice. In contrast, only a small proportion of nondepressed persons did so (refer to Figure 10.2). Apparently, being betrayed by another person serves to activate depressed individual's negative views (schemas) about themselves and others, and so maximizes their tendencies to reciprocate harsh treatment.

Such individual differences aside, the tendency to treat others as they have treated us seems very strong where cooperation is concerned. In sum, you can usually count on getting back what you yourself have previously "dished out" in your dealings with others.

Attribution and social exchange: Reacting to others' motives

Imagine that at some point in the future you work for a large company. One of your fellow employees is a direct rival, and you often compete with her for promotions, raises, and other benefits. One day, she visits you in your office and makes a surprising proposal: from now on, you should stop competing and join forces. How would you respond? Probably with a great deal of caution! Before deciding what to do, you'd want to know something about the motives behind her behavior. Is she sincere? Or is this merely part of some complex political maneuver, designed to cut the ground right out from under your feet? Until you are confident that you know the answer, you'd probably be reluctant to proceed.

This situation illustrates a key fact about cooperation and competition: in choosing between these contrasting patterns, we are often strongly affected by more than the overt actions of others. Frequently, we also pay careful attention to their motives and intentions. Thus, in the example described above, you may decide to cooperate with your rival if you felt that she had "seen the light" and sincerely believed that you'd do better by joining forces. However, if you concluded that she was simply "setting you up for the kill" in some way, you'd decline her offer, and also probably redouble your guard (refer to Figure 10.3). In short, our

FIGURE 10.3. Whether we choose to cooperate or compete with others depends, to an important degree, upon our *attributions*—our beliefs about the causes behind their behavior. Thus, as shown here, if you interpreted an offer of cooperation from another person as genuine, you might well reciprocate. If, instead, you viewed it as some kind of manipulative tactic, you'd probably adopt a cautious "wait-and-see" approach.

Attributions: Their important role in social exchange

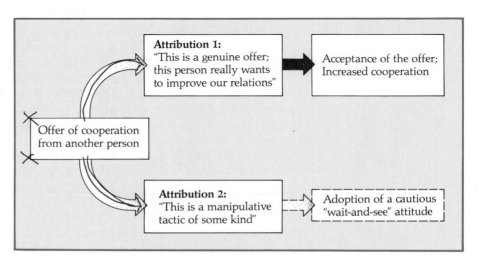

attributions about others, and about the causes behind their behavior, often play a key role in both cooperation and competition.

Direct evidence for the impact of attributions on these aspects of social exchange is provided by the results of several different studies (e.g., Brickman, Becker, and Castle, 1979; Enzle, Hansen, and Lowe, 1975). Briefly, these studies suggest that if we view others' behavior as stemming from a genuine desire to cooperate with us to gain mutual benefits, we may choose to cooperate with *them*. However, if we interpret their actions as stemming from a desire to manipulate or exploit us, we may spurn any overtures of cooperation and react competitively instead. And please note: in reaching such decisions, our attributions about the motives behind others' actions often seem to be crucial; their actual behavior appears to be of less importance.

In a sense, the finding that our interpretations of others' behavior play a key role in our decision to cooperate or compete with them is far from surprising. As we have noted at several points in this book, attributions often shape our interactions with other persons (see chapters 2 and 9). Somewhat more surprising, however, is the fact that on some occasions, this relationship can be reversed. That is, *our* own tendencies to cooperate or compete with others can influence our attributions about them. For example, if we behave cooperatively toward another person, we may come to view him or her as cooperative and expect such behavior in return. Similarly, if we behave competitively toward another, we may view that person as competitive, and expect him or her to act in this manner. In short, our own tendencies to cooperate or compete may influence our perceptions of the persons around us and our expectations concerning their behavior (Messé and Sivacek, 1979).

One factor that that may account for this tendency is the **false consensus effect.** This refers to the fact that we often view our own behavior as typical — as similar to that of most other persons (Ross, 1977; Van der Pligt, 1984). This belief can then lead us to expect that others will behave very much as we do in a wide range of situations, including ones involving cooperation and competition. Regardless of the precise basis for the impact of our own behavior upon our perceptions of others, though, one fact is clear: attributions can exert powerful effects upon situations involving social exchange. In deciding whether to cooperate or compete with others, we do not simply respond to their overt actions. Rather, we often pay careful attention to the motives and intentions that lie behind this behavior. For this reason, the occurrence of both cooperation and competition often involves far more than at first meets the eye.

Groups versus individuals: Which is more cooperative?

As we have already noted, cooperation between two persons can be difficult to attain. Each may be uncertain as to the other's motives, with the result that both choose a cautious approach or strategy. If such difficulties exist when only two individuals are involved, it stands to reason that establishing cooperation among larger numbers of persons may be even more complex. In fact, this appears to be the case (e.g., Fox and Guyer, 1978). As the number of persons participating in a social exchange rises, the level of cooperation among them frequently drops. Several factors probably contribute to this disturbing pattern. For example, the greater the number of persons present, the greater the likelihood that at least one will behave in an exploitative, selfish manner. Since such actions will be reciprocated, competition quickly spreads throughout the group. Second, as the number of persons involved rises, the probability that they will divide into separate groups or units also increases. As it does, the type of in-group/out-group processes described in Chapter 5 may take hold and reduce the likelihood of cooperation. Specifically, the persons belonging to each of these groups may become more concerned with outstripping the other group than with maximizing their own outcomes (e.g., Tafjel, 1982). To the extent they do, the chances of mutual cooperation can be sharply reduced. That such processes actually occur, and block cooperation in situations involving several persons, is clearly indicated by a study conducted by McCallum and her colleagues (McCallum et al., 1985). In this investigation, male and female subjects played one of two games either as individuals (playing against a single opponent) or as two-person teams (playing against another two-person team). Both games were structured so that participants could either choose to cooperate or to compete with their opponents. However, in one of the games (the *prisoner's dilemma game*), choosing to compete both increased subjects' outcomes and reduced those of their opponents. In the other (the *mutual-fate-control game*), choosing to compete merely reduced the outcomes of subjects' opponents; it had no impact whatsoever on the size of their own winnings. (In both games, subjects played for points which represented cents. Further, they were told they could keep all the money they won.)

Results were clear: when subjects played as two-person groups, they showed lower levels of cooperation than when they played as individuals. That is, they made fewer cooperative choices and won less money in the former condition than in the latter (see Figure 10.4). Further—and here is the surprising point—this was true in both types of game. Since competitive choices in the mutual-fate-control game reduced their opponents' winnings but did not simultaneously increase subjects' own rewards, it seems clear that when they adopted this strategy, participants were primarily concerned with maximizing their *relative advantage*—doing better than their opponent. And since groups made such choices more often than individuals, it is reasonable to suggest that such motivation lay behind their lower level of cooperation.

In sum, it appears that one important reason why groups are less cooperative than individuals involves the basic nature of groups themselves—their strong tendency to perceive nonmembers as "outsiders" who must be defeated, or at least surpassed. The practical implications of these findings for anyone wishing to promote cooperation among large

FIGURE 10.4. Groups of two persons made fewer cooperative choices in two different games than individuals. In one of these games (the mutual-fate-control game), competitive choices reduced their opponents' winnings, but did not affect subjects' own outcomes. These findings suggest that when playing as groups, subjects' primary concern was to surpass their opponent, *not* to maximize their own gains. (Source: Based on data from McCallum et al., 1985.)

Evidence that groups are less cooperative than individuals

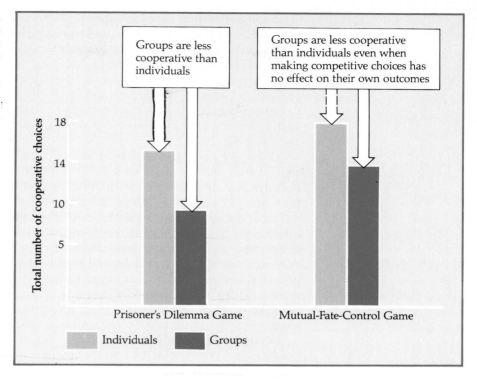

numbers of persons seem clear: simply dividing such persons into several groups or units will probably *not* do the trick. In fact, this strategy, which is often used to promote cooperation in organizations and other applied settings, may actually boomerang, and promote competition rather than cooperation (e.g., Komorita and Lapworth, 1982). A better approach may be that of arranging conditions so that <u>pairs of individuals, rather than groups,</u> can work together or coordinate their actions. And if this is not feasible, then steps should be taken to "defuse" the kind of intergroup competition described above (e.g., by establishing <u>*superordinate goals for all to seek*</u>; refer to our discussion in Chapter 5). Through these and related tactics, cooperation *can* be attained, even when large numbers of persons are involved. However, as the evidence we have reviewed suggests, the task is far from easy, and requires careful thought and planning.

Personal orientation and cooperation: Cooperators, competitors, individualists, and equalizers

Think back over the many persons you have known. Can you remember several whose major goal in life seemed to be that of doing better than others — surpassing them in every task? Similarly, can you recall others who preferred to cooperate — to work closely with the persons around them, and to minimize any differences between their outcomes? You probably have little difficulty in bringing examples of both types to mind, for individuals differ greatly in their tendencies to cooperate and compete. Actually, systematic research on such differences indicates that most persons fall into one of four distinct categories in this respect, each reflecting a contrasting perspective toward social exchange (Derlega and Grzelak, 1982).

First are **competitors**. These are persons whose primary motive is that of maximizing their own gains relative to others. In other words, they are mainly concerned with doing better than the people with whom they must deal. As a result of this orientation, they will even settle for negative outcomes, as long as these are more favorable than those of their opponents. Second, there are **cooperators**. Such individuals are primarily concerned with maximizing both their own gains and those of others (i.e., joint profits). They want all participants in a social exchange to obtain positive outcomes, and are unhappy unless such results are obtained. Third, there are **individualists**. These are persons whose major concern is simply maximizing their own gains. Usually, they have little interest in the outcomes of others, and do not care whether they do better or worse than themselves. Their major focus is firmly on doing as well as possible in every social exchange. Finally, some individuals can be described as **equalizers**. Their major goal is minimizing the differences between their own outcomes and those of others. In short, they adhere closely to the principle of "share and share alike" and attempt to assure that they and everyone else receive about the same results.

At this point, we should note that while many persons seem to fall into one or the other of these major categories, many demonstrate a mixture of two or more perspectives. For example, some seem to combine an individualistic orientation with a competitive one: they want to do as well as they can but are also interested in surpassing others. Similarly, others combine an individualistic orientation with a desire for equality: they want to do as well as they can, but don't want their outcomes to get *too* far out of line with those of others.

By now, you may be wondering about the following question: just how common are each of these patterns? Are there more competitors or cooperators? Do the mixed patterns outnumber the "pure" ones? Revealing information on these issues is provided by an intriguing study conducted by Knight and Dubro (1984).

These investigators had both male and female subjects complete a task designed to measure the personal orientations toward social exchange outlined above. Briefly, subjects were asked to rate the desirability of each of forty-nine pairs of outcomes in which they and another person would receive some money. (For example, one division was 0 cents to the subject and 6 cents to their partner; another was 6 cents to them and 0 cents to this stranger.) Subjects' ratings of each of these divisions were then subjected to careful statistical analysis. Results indicated that almost all individuals fell into one of the six categories described above (cooperators, competitors, individualists, equalizers, the two mixed patterns). Further, certain differences between males and females also emerged. As shown in Figure 10.5, more males than females were classified as competitors. However, more females than males were cooperators or equalizers. Needless to add, the origins of such differences are probably highly complex, and can only be clarified through a great deal of further research.

Not surprisingly, persons adopting different perspectives toward social exchange tend to behave quite differently in their dealings with others (Kuhlman and Marshello, 1975). Competitors frequently attempt to exploit opponents, while cooperators usually seek to work together with them to maximize joint gains. Individualists, in contrast, tend to adopt whatever strategy will maximize their own outcomes in a given situation: they are true pragmatists where social exchange is concerned. Finally, persons with a mixed orientation are somewhat harder to predict; they may vacillate, or they may adopt intermediate levels of coordination. Such differences are definitely worth considering from a practical point of view. For example, if you ever find yourself in a situation where you must choose a subordinate from among several potential

FIGURE 10.5. Most persons seem to possess one of six different orientations toward social exchange. However, males and females appear to differ to some degree in this respect. For example, a competitive orientation is more common among males than among females, while a cooperative orientation is more common among females than males. (Source: Based on data from Knight and Dubro, 1984.)

Personal orientations toward social exchange

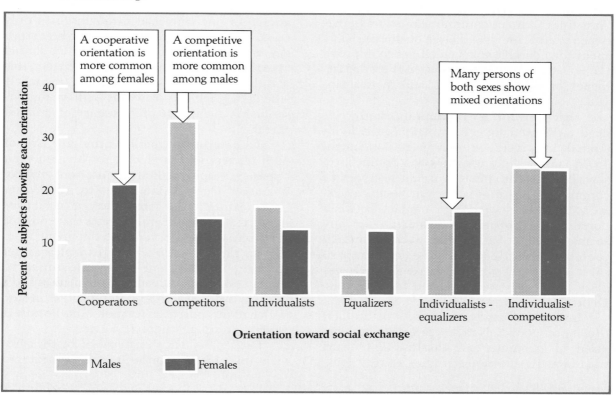

FOCUS ON RESEARCH:
Classic Contributions

Communication and Cooperation: Some Benefits, Some Costs

In many situations where cooperation could potentially develop but does not, its absence is blamed on a "failure to communicate." It is suggested that better or more frequent contact between the persons or groups involved might have facilitated coordination. Is this suggestion correct? In one sense, the answer is "yes." Some forms of communication *do* seem to increase the likelihood of cooperation in many contexts. For example, an open exchange of views may convince all persons involved that working together is the best strategy. Similarly, unless some minimal level of communication exists, close coordination of various activities may be impossible. On the basis of such reasoning, powerful nations have established "hot lines" (direct communication links) between their leaders, and large businesses have spent considerable sums on efforts to improve the flow of information between their departments or divisions (Peters and Waterman, 1982).

That some forms of communication do indeed facilitate cooperation has been demonstrated in several studies (e.g., Wichman, 1970). Other findings, however, point to a sharply different conclusion: not all types of communication produce these beneficial effects. Indeed, one type of contact between potential cooperators — **threats** — actually seems to reduce rather than enhance mutual coordination. Evidence for the occurrence of such effects was first provided almost three decades ago by two insightful investigators, Deutsch and Krauss (1960).

In order to study the effects of implicit threats on cooperation, these researchers devised an ingenious task that has since been used in many additional studies. In this situation, generally known as the *trucking game,* pairs of subjects were asked to imagine that they were in charge of two companies. The task faced by each was that of moving some merchandise from one point to another. Their profits in the game (which were only imaginary) would be determined by the speed with which they accomplished this task. On each trial, both players started with sixty cents, and "operating expenses" were deducted from this amount at the rate of one cent per second, until one or both players reached their goal. As you can see from Figure 10.6, each player (called Acme and Bolt) could follow either a short, direct route to the goal or a longer, alternate route. Since winnings would be determined by the amount of time needed to arrive at these spots, the direct route was clearly the preferred one. Unfortunately, though, it involved a stretch of one-lane road through which only one truck at a time could pass. The best strategy, then, was cooperation: the players should take turns in using the short route. In fact, this was the pattern that emerged most frequently when the game was played as we have just described it — without the presence of implicit threats.

To determine whether providing one or both players with a chance to threaten their opponent would facilitate or interfere with cooperation, Deutsch and Krauss then added another feature to the game. They gave subjects in two experimental groups gates that could be closed at will to prevent the opponent from moving through the one-lane road (please refer to Figure 10.6). In one group, the *unilateral threat* condition, only one of the players had a gate. In a second, the *bilateral-threat* group, both had this potential weapon. (In a no-threat control group, neither had a gate.)

Please note: the threats posed by the gates were only *implicit* ones. It was not required

FIGURE 10.6. In the game shown here, subjects had the task of moving from their start positions to their respective destinations. The shortest route involved a one-lane road over which only one player at a time could pass. Note the presence of gates, which could be used by one or both players to implicitly threaten their opponent, and actually to block his or her progress. (Source: Adapted from Deutsch and Krauss, 1960.)

The Deutsch and Krauss trucking game

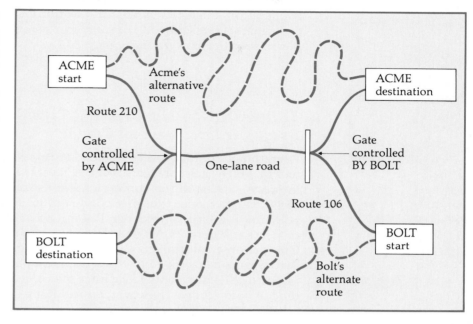

that persons possessing them actually use them. Thus, if subjects were willing to trust their partners, cooperative behavior could still develop. If each player assumed that persons possessing gates would use them, though, cooperation might be prevented as each sought to strike first. In reality, this is precisely what happened. Possession of a gate by either player led to considerable conflict and larger losses for both persons. Moreover, losses were greater under conditions where both players had gates than where only one possessed this option. In the bilateral threat group, both players typically slammed their gates shut at the start of each trial and then sat idly by as their profits continued to shrink. In sum, providing subjects with an implicit means of threatening their opponent sharply reduced the occurrence of cooperation in this situation.

Needless to add, the trucking game designed by Deutsch and Krauss is somewhat restrictive in nature. In many life situations, persons who may potentially cooperate can communicate with one another more directly and fully than participants in this classic study. However, growing evidence suggests that, often, even face-to-face communication fails to increase the likelihood of cooperation (e.g., Stech and McClintock, 1981). One reason for this is as follows: in many cases, individuals view such contacts as an opportunity for intimidating or manipulating their opponents. As a result, they employ threats, icy stares, and similar tactics with a surprisingly high frequency. To the extent that such conditions prevail, of course, even prolonged and direct communication may fail to enhance cooperation.

candidates, it would probably be wise to select one with a cooperative orientation. While competitors may give the impression of being more dedicated to success, their desire to surpass others may also carry hidden costs. Indeed, the job they may be after, ultimately, may be your own! (Is cooperation enhanced by communication between persons seeking to coordinate their behavior? For some surprising information on this issue, please see the **Focus** insert on page 346.)

BARGAINING: The Give-and-Take Road to Resolving Interpersonal Conflict

Regrettably, **conflict** — direct confrontations between groups or individuals in which each side fears that the other is about to frustrate its major interests — is an all-too-common part of social life (Blake and Mouton, 1984). Further, once it begins, conflict often acquires an unsettling, self-perpetuating nature (Brockner, Rubin, and Lang, 1981). Each side comes to feel that it must "win" in order to justify costs it has already incurred! One possible solution to conflict, of course, lies in the use of force. Participants can seek to overpower their opponents, and so succeed in imposing their own will. Since force may breed counterforce, and people tend to hold grudges, however, efforts along these lines are often totally self-defeating. Even if one side *does* succeed in achieving total victory, the seeds of future conflict will probably flourish in the discontent and anger of the defeated (refer to Figure 10.7).

It is for these reasons that individuals and groups often turn to another means for resolving their conflicts: the process of **bargaining.** In this form of social exchange, the parties involved (or their representatives) engage in a mutual trading of offers, counteroffers, and — it is hoped — concessions. If the process succeeds, an arrangement acceptable to both sides may be reached, and further conflict avoided. If it fails, however, discussions may be abandoned, and other, less desirable approaches adopted. Two key questions relating to bargaining, then, are these: (1) what factors influence the chances of its success? and (2) what factors or conditions determine the outcomes of each participant? It is on these issues that we will focus in the following discussion.

Overall strategy in bargaining: Is it better to be "tough" or conciliatory?

Suppose you were about to bargain with another person over some item or issue (e.g., the price of a used car; how to divide various household chores). What would be the best way to proceed? Two sharply contrasting strategies come readily to mind. In the first, you would adopt a very "tough" and inflexible stance. You'd begin with an extreme offer (e.g.,

FIGURE 10.7.   At the
end of World War I (top
photo), the victorious
allies imposed harsh
terms on Germany, their
defeated opponent.
Many historians believe
that through this action
they planted the seeds
for an even more
destructive conflict —
World War II (bottom
photo).

Total victory in a
conflict: Often, it's
self-defeating

suggest a very high price for the car if you were the seller, or a very low
one if you were the buyer), and would make few (and quite small) concessions to your opponent.

The second strategy, in contrast, involves a much more conciliatory
approach. Here, you'd start with a moderate offer (one quite close to the
point at which you felt agreement could be reached). And you would
offer frequent and generous concessions to your opponent as your dis-

cussions proceeded. Which of these approaches would be best? The answer, of course, depends on whose perspective — yours or your opponent's — we adopt. From the standpoint of your opponent, the second, conciliatory strategy would be preferable; it would practically guarantee a favorable outcome to this person. From *your* perspective, in contrast, the first, "tough" stance may be better. A large number of studies concerned with this issue suggest that persons adopting a "tough" stance (an extreme initial offer coupled with few concessions to their opponent) usually obtain better results than those who choose a more conciliatory stance (e.g., Chertkoff and Conley, 1967; Lawler and MacMurray, 1980; Yukl, 1974). For example, they obtain higher prices for various items when acting as a seller and pay lower prices for them when acting as a buyer when they follow a "tough" strategy. Such effects seem to stem from the impact of this type of strategy upon opponents' aspirations. Faced with an inflexible adversary, many persons conclude that they probably can't do as well in the exchange as they had initially hoped. As a result, their willingness to grant concessions increases — and so do the results obtained by their opponent.

While a "tough" strategy does seem to be effective in many cases, it is important to note that this is not always the case. As you can probably guess, this approach runs the real risk of angering the persons exposed to it. Then, they may adopt a similar inflexible strategy themselves, or may even break off the negotiations altogether. Recent evidence reported by Shelom, Walker, and Esser (1985) indicates that such effects are most likely to occur in situations where persons on the receiving end of a "tough" strategy have alternatives at their disposal — where they can go elsewhere for better terms than those offered by their harsh adversary.

In this experiment, female subjects bargained with three different dealers over the price of a new car. These dealers (who were simulated by the experimenter) adopted three contrasting strategies. One showed the uniformly "tough" approach we have been discussing. This person began by demanding the full list price for the car, and made no concessions until the subject had offered one. From then on, the dealer made concessions only half as large as the ones offered by subjects. The second dealer also began by demanding the full list price for the car. However, this individual then matched all concessions made by the subject (e.g., if the subject raised her offer $100, the dealer lowered the price by an equal amount). Finally, the third dealer adopted a more conciliatory strategy, beginning with a request for less than the list price of the car, and then continuing to match all concessions offered by subjects. Subjects were told that after an initial exchange with each dealer, they were free to bargain with any ones they wished. Bargaining then continued until agreement was reached, or until subjects decided to break off their negotiations with all the dealers.

Results were consistent in revealing the advantages offered by a conciliatory strategy in this type of situation. As you can see from Figure 10.8, subjects strongly preferred to deal with the conciliatory opponent (they made more offers to this individual than to the other two com-

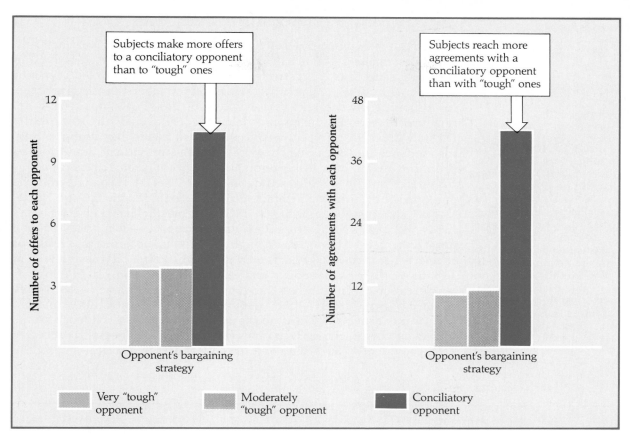

FIGURE 10.8. When given a choice among several bargaining opponents, subjects strongly preferred one who adopted a conciliatory style. They made more offers to this person, and were more likely to reach agreement with him. (Source: Based on data from Shelom, Walker, and Esser, 1985.)

The benefits of a conciliatory bargaining style

bined). Further, they also made more concessions to this individual, and were more likely to reach agreement with him. Perhaps more surprising, even the dealers themselves seemed to profit from the use of a conciliatory approach. Although the "tough" dealers earned more on each completed deal than the "soft" one, this latter individual actually earned more per customer contact. That is, since he was much more successful in closing deals and actually selling the car, he earned more per unit of sales effort than did the others.

In sum, it appears that both "tough" and conciliatory bargaining strategies offer benefits. A "tough" approach is more likely to wring concessions from one's opponents in situations where they feel that they have no alternative to dealing with its user. However, a conciliatory or "soft" approach may yield more favorable outcomes to both sides in situations where bargainers do have such alternatives (when they can potentially make a deal with any of several different partners). Clearly, then, choosing an overall strategy is a complex task — one that bargainers should consider with care before proceeding.

Framing: Focus on gains versus focus on losses

There is an old saying to the effect that "optimists see a glass as half full, while pessimists see it as half empty." These different perspectives, in turn, are assumed to exert strong effects on the behavior of both types of persons. Optimists, presumably, are confident "doers," willing to strive for difficult goals and take reasonable risks. Pessimists, in contrast, are much more anxious, and adopt a defensive, passive posture toward life. Do such differences in perspective also play a role in bargaining? Growing evidence indicates that they do. Whether individuals tend to focus primarily on potential losses or on potential gains seems to exert powerful effects on the strategies they adopt in a social exchange, and the outcomes they ultimately obtain (e.g., Bazerman, Magliozzi, and Neale, 1985; Kahnemann and Tversky, 1982). In particular, when bargainers focus primarily on the losses they may experience — when they adopt a **negative frame** — they often dig in their heels and become quite resistant to making concessions. This is only reasonable; after all, they view such actions on their part as costly and unappealing. In contrast, when such persons focus primarily on the gains they may achieve — when they adopt a **positive frame** — they demonstrate greater flexibility, and are usually more successful in attaining an agreement. Clear evidence for the impact of these perspectives upon the bargaining process has recently been provided by Bazerman and his colleagues, in a series of carefully

FIGURE 10.9. When subjects focused on the potential gains in a bargaining situation (i.e., when they adopted a *positive frame*), they made larger concessions to their opponent but earned more money for their companies than when they focused on potential losses (i.e., when they adopted a *negative frame*). (Source: Based on data from Neale and Bazerman, 1985.)

The impact of framing on bargaining

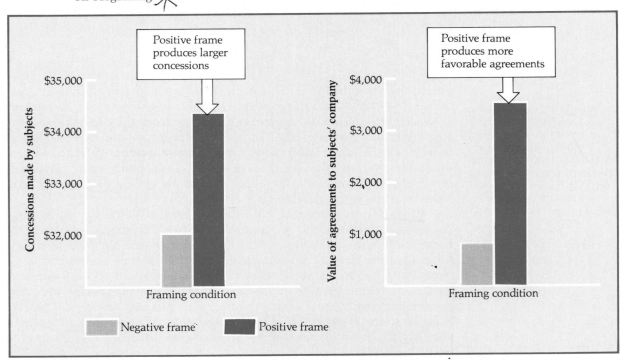

conducted studies. For example, in one of these investigations (Neale and Bazerman, 1985), male and female subjects played the role of management negotiators, and bargained with a union representative (actually a trained accomplice) over several issues (vacation pay, medical plan, wages, paid sick days). Half of the subjects received instructions designed to induce a *negative frame:* they were told to view all concessions by the company as involving serious financial losses, and urged to minimize such costs. The others received instructions designed to induce a *positive frame:* they were told that any concessions they managed to wring from the union would result in important gains for the company, and were instructed to concentrate on maximizing such outcomes. Bargaining continued for twenty minutes, and if no agreement was reached, subjects were asked to submit a final offer that would be given to an arbitrator.

As you can see from Figure 10.9, results offered strong support for the benefits of positive framing. Subjects induced to adopt this perspective made larger concessions to their opponent, resolved more of the issues under discussion, and obtained settlements more favorable to the company than those induced to adopt a negative frame. These findings suggest that the manner in which individuals approach a bargaining situation can be crucial; indeed, such perspectives or frames-of-reference may sometimes be more important, from the point of view of attaining a final settlement, than the objective factors (costs and benefits) involved. As Neale and Bazerman (1985) note, training negotiators to be aware of such effects can enhance their effectiveness in many contexts, and perhaps give them an important strategic advantage over their opponents.

Other factors affecting bargaining: Negotiator experience, power, confidence, and constraints

While the overall "style" adopted by negotiators and the extent to which they focus on either gains or losses both exert important effects upon the outcomes of bargaining, this form of social exchange is also affected by several other factors. First, as you might expect, bargainers tend to become better at uncovering *integrative solutions* — ones maximally beneficial to both sides — as they gain increasing experience in negotiations (Bazerman, Magliozzi, and Neale, 1985; Pruitt, 1983). Thus, in this case, practice *does* seem to make perfect (or at least better!). Second, negotiations often seem to proceed more smoothly and more efficiently when the persons taking part in them have considerable power in the groups or organizations they represent (Jackson and King, 1983). Apparently, when negotiators are relatively powerless, and have to consult with their superiors at every step, their flexibility is hampered, and opportunities for desirable agreements may be missed. Third, and perhaps somewhat more surprising, bargaining is more successful when negotiators are not overly optimistic about the chances of reaching an agreement (Neale and

Bazerman, 1985). Many individuals seem to approach bargaining with inflated expectations about the possibility of inducing their opponents to accept their offers. As a result, they resist making concessions, and so impede the entire process. For this reason, training negotiators to avoid such overconfidence can be a definite "plus." Finally, bargaining tends to yield more positive outcomes when participants operate under constraints that prevent them from accepting only minimally beneficial results (Bazerman, Magliozzi, and Neale, 1985). In short, both sides tend to do best when they set out to achieve challenging but realistic goals with respect to joint outcomes.

As even this brief summary suggests, bargaining is a highly complex process. Thus, there can be no simple answer to the question: "How can its success be assured?" Given the important role played by this form of social exchange in the lives of individuals, the functioning of organizations, and the affairs of nations, however, efforts to understand it as fully as possible seem to be well worthwhile.

When bargaining fails: Other tactics for resolving interpersonal conflict

When bargaining succeeds, it yields highly beneficial results. A settlement acceptable to both sides is obtained and conflict is reduced, if not totally resolved. Unfortunately, though, attempts at negotiation often fail (refer to Figure 10.10). Despite their best efforts, two sides may deadlock and be unable to reach an acceptable compromise. As a result, bitter strikes, tragic wars, and painful personal disputes continue long past the point at which either side has any hope of recouping past losses. Is there any way out of such dilemmas (often described as *entrapping conflicts*)? In short, are there alternative means of resolving conflicts, once negotiations have stalled? Fortunately, the answer is "yes." Several tactics useful in getting discussions back on track or otherwise bringing costly conflicts to a halt exist. Among the most effective of these are adoption of a *problem-solving approach or strategy*, and several types of *third-party intervention.*

Adoption of a problem-solving strategy: In search of integrative agreements. The ideal outcome of any negotiation is an *integrative solution* — one in which both sides obtain the maximum potential benefit (Pruitt, 1983). The essence of such solutions is clearly illustrated by the following situation. Two cooks working in the same kitchen both need a whole orange for different recipes they are preparing — one for juice, the other for peel. What should they do? If your answer is "Cut the orange in half," you have proposed a reasonable compromise, but *not* an integrative solution. If they follow this plan, neither will have enough of what they need. A better strategy, then, would be to share the orange, one taking all the peel and the other all the juice. How can such agreements be obtained,

FIGURE 10.10. Despite the best efforts of the persons or groups involved, bargaining often fails. (Source: Drawing by Ed Fisher; ©1978 by the New Yorker Magazine, Inc.)

Bargaining: The outcome is never assured

"I suppose this means the usual communiqué: 'A full and frank exchange of views.'"

especially after bargaining has reached an impasse? According to Pruitt and his colleagues, one answer lies in getting both sides to adopt a *problem-solving orientation* to their relations (Pruitt, 1983). Within such an orientation, participants view the exchange not as a "win or lose" situation in which they must defeat their opponent or be defeated, but as as a *solvable problem* — one in which their task is finding an agreement advantageous to both. According to Pruitt, adoption of a problem-solving orientation encourages bargainers to engage in an open exchange of information, to be more flexible, and to make concessions when these seem appropriate. In short, it facilitates negotiations in several ways, and paves the way toward attainment of integrative solutions.

Fortunately, research by Pruitt and others indicates that bargainers can often be induced to adopt a problem-solving orientation, especially when the potential benefits offered by such an approach are clearly specified (Pruitt, 1981, 1983). Thus, efforts to encourage this orientation may prove useful in a wide range of conflict situations.

FOCUS ON RESEARCH:
The Cutting Edge

Reducing Costly Conflicts: An Interpersonal Approach

When feelings run high, it is often observed, reason flies right out the window. Thus, when the parties to a dispute are angry, resentful, or otherwise upset, it frequently becomes more difficult for them to move toward an agreement. Given this fact, it seems possible that tactics which either reduce or prevent such reactions may prove useful in resolving many costly conflicts. Evidence that this is the case has been reported in several recent studies (e.g., Baron, 1984; Kabanoff, 1985). As an example of this research, and the approach to conflict resolution it suggests, we will consider an investigation by Baron (1985).

The basic idea behind this investigation was simple: when faced with another person who behaves in a conflict-inducing manner, most individuals try to understand why their opponent has chosen this course of action. In short, they formulate *attributions* concerning the reasons behind this person's decision to thwart their goals or interests. Such attributions, in turn, may strongly affect their own behavior toward their opponent. If they conclude that this individual has voluntarily chosen to thwart their interests because he is competitive by nature, they may grow angry and respond in kind. Then, the chances of a mutually acceptable agreement will be reduced. In contrast, if they conclude that he is acting in a conflict-inducing manner largely because of external factors (e.g., instructions to do so from the group he represents), they will be less likely to become angry, and the chances of an agreement may be higher.

In order to examine these suggestions, Baron had male and female subjects play the role of an executive representing a department in a large organization and discuss the division of $1,000,000 in surplus funds with another person representing a different department. In reality, this individual was an accomplice, specially trained to behave in a conflict-inducing manner. Specifically, the accomplice demanded fully $800,000 for his or her own department, and made only two small concessions (of $50,000 each) during the session. While the accomplice behaved in the same unreasonable manner in all conditions, this person made remarks suggesting contrasting causes for such behavior in various experimental groups. In one condition (*internal-competitive*) these comments suggested that the accomplice was simply a combative type, who had voluntarily chosen to adopt a "tough" position (e.g., "I always like to come out on top, so I'm not changing my offer"). In a second condition (*external*), the remarks suggested the accomplice was simply following instructions from his or her department to do as well as possible in the exchange ("They're counting on me to do as well as I can"). Finally, in a third group (*sincere belief*), the accomplice's remarks indicated that this person sincerely believed his or her department to be more deserving of the funds ("I really feel that my department is more important to the company, and needs the money more"). (In a fourth *control* group, no information about the causes behind the accomplice's behavior was provided.)

After the conclusion of the bargaining session, subjects completed questionnaires designed to assess their reactions to the accomplice, and their plans for handling future conflicts with this person. It was predicted that they would react in a more favorable and conciliatory manner to the accomplice when his or her actions seemed to stem from external than internal causes. However, as you can see from Figure 10.11, this was not the case. Instead,

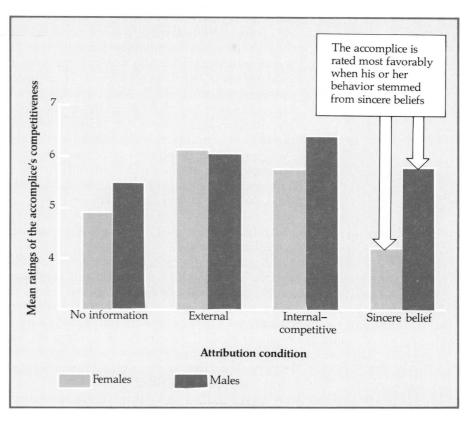

FIGURE 10.11. Both male and female subjects rated an accomplice who behaved in a conflict-inducing manner more favorably (i.e., as being less competitive) when this person's behavior appeared to stem from sincere beliefs than when it derived from external causes or the accomplice's competitive nature. (Source: Based on data from Baron, 1985.)

Attributions and the reduction of interpersonal conflict

subjects responded most positively when the accomplice's actions seemed to derive from sincere beliefs about the value of his or her department. Specifically, participants made larger concessions to the accomplice, rated this person more favorably, and reported stronger intentions to collaborate with him or her in the future in this condition than in the others. Subsequent research (Baron, 1986) suggests that these unexpected findings derived from two factors. First, subjects had very positive reactions to apparent sincerity on the part of the accomplice. Second, they viewed statements to the effect that he or she was "just following orders" and *had* to behave in a con-

flict-inducing manner with suspicion. This is hardly surprising; most persons have heard others quite insincerely make such remarks as "I wish I could do otherwise, but my hands are tied . . ."

Regardless of the precise mechanisms involved, however, these findings, plus those of other studies (e.g., Kabanoff, 1985) indicate that efforts to reduce anger, resentment, and other negative reactions among the parties to a conflict can have highly beneficial results. Indeed, they suggest that, often, eliminating the negative feelings that accompany conflict can go a long way toward eliminating this costly process itself.

Third-party intervention: Mediation and arbitration. Another technique that can be effective in resolving persistent, costly conflicts involves intervention by a third, neutral party. Such intervention can take the form of **mediation**, in which the outside agent merely suggests the terms of an agreement and these can then be accepted or rejected by the two sides. Alternatively, it can involve **arbitration**. Here, the parties to the dispute agree, in advance, to accept the terms proposed by the arbitrator, whatever these may be. Both mediation and arbitration are widely used to settle disputes in cases where direct bargaining between the opposing sides has failed. And a considerable body of evidence indicates that it can be quite effective in this respect (Rubin, 1980). As you probably already suspect, however, third-party intervention is more effective under some conditions than others.

First, mediation tends to be more successful when mediators have some control over the future outcomes of the disputants than when they lack such influence (Hamilton, Swap, and Rubin, 1981). The reason for this seems obvious: when mediators can "sweeten the deal" by offering both sides something concrete for accepting their recommendations, their influence is likely to be greater than when they cannot offer such inducements.

Second, mediation is more likely to yield positive outcomes when the conflict between the opposing sides is large and costly than when it is small and unimportant (Hiltrop and Rubin, 1982). This is the case because when conflicts are costly, the persons or groups involved are reluctant to make concessions: doing so may cause them to *lose face,* to appear weak or foolish to others. It is precisely under such conditions that mediators can be of great assistance, since concessions in response to the recommendations of an ostensibly neutral third party do not incur the loss of face just described.

In sum, third-party intervention can often prove very helpful. As is the case with any technique designed to influence complex social relations, however, it must be carefully adapted to the specific situation in question. (While many conflicts between individuals stem from opposing interests or goals, others seem to derive from more personal factors — grudges, misunderstandings, and the like. How can conflicts of this type be resolved? For some suggestions, see the **Focus** insert on page 356.)

PERCEIVED FAIRNESS IN SOCIAL EXCHANGE: In Search of Equity

Have you ever taken part in a social exchange that you felt was unfair? Probably, your answer is "yes." Experiences of this type are simply too common a part of social life for your answer to be otherwise. In most cases, such feelings of unfairness center around the belief that we have somehow been shortchanged — that we have received less (or given more) than is fair. For example, we conclude that we have done more for another person than he or she has done for us, or that we have received less praise, recognition, or pay for some job than we deserve. In other instances (far fewer, it appears), feelings of unfairness may stem from the belief that we have actually gotten more than we should — that we have taken unfair advantage of others (Adams, 1965; Leventhal, 1976). Regardless of which of these reactions is involved, it is the perception of *unfairness* that is crucial, for as you may expect, individuals do not sit idly by, twiddling their thumbs, in such cases. Once they conclude that they have been treated unfairly, they often take active steps to rectify the situation. We will consider several potential means of dealing with such unfairness below. Before turning to such reactions, however, we will address an even more basic question: what factors or conditions, precisely, lead individuals to conclude that they have been treated unfairly? Several decades of research on this topic suggest that the process involved is quite complex (e.g., Greenberg, 1982; Walster, Walster, and Berscheid, 1978). In essence, though, it includes the following steps.

First, we examine the outcomes received by all parties to the exchange. Next, we compare these to one of several abstract *rules* or *standards* that we use for judging fairness in such contexts. The closer the match between the actual outcomes we observe and the pattern suggested by our rule, the more likely we are to view the situation as fair. While this might sound relatively simple, such judgments are complicated by two facts: (1) several rules of this type exist, and (2) we tend to apply them under somewhat different conditions. It is to these contrasting standards for judging social fairness that we turn next.

Judgments of fairness in social exchange: Equity and inequity

Suppose that you and several other persons work on a joint task. One of your partners puts a great deal of effort into the project, and brings a considerable level of skill to it. Another has absolutely no past experience with such tasks, and generally coasts along, doing the minimum she can get away with. You fall somewhere in between these persons on both dimensions. Now, imagine that the project is successful, and there are rewards to divide among you. Who should get the largest share? And who should get the smallest? The answer probably strikes you as obvious: the person who contributed most should get the biggest "piece of the pie," while the one who contributed least should receive the smallest share. The reason the situation seems so simple is that you already have a good working knowledge of one basic rule for evaluating fairness in social exchange: **distributive justice** or **equity.** According to this rule, fairness exists when persons who have made large contributions receive relatively large outcomes (rewards), those who have made small contributions receive small outcomes, and so on. In contrast, fairness is not per-

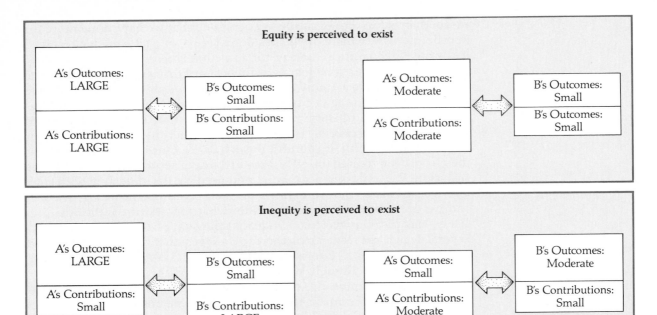

FIGURE 10.12. *Equity* is perceived to exist in a social exchange when persons who have made large contributions receive large outcomes, those who have made small contributions receive small outcomes, and so on (upper panel). Inequity is perceived to exist when contributions and outcomes do not "balance" in this manner (lower panel).

Equity and inequity in social exchange

ceived to exist when individuals who have made large contributions receive small outcomes, or when those who have made small contributions receive large ones (refer to Figure 10.12). In this context, the term "outcomes" refers to all benefits an individual obtains from a social exchange — anything from money and other tangible rewards on the one hand through love, special "perks," and status on the other. Similarly, the term "contributions" refers to everything a person brings to a social exchange — charm, experience, effort, specific goods or services, and so on.

Please note that for equity to exist, it is *not* necessary for all persons involved in an exchange relationship to receive the same outcomes or make the same contributions. Rather, what *is* crucial is that the *ratios* of these factors be in balance, as shown in Figure 10.12. Also note that both equity and inequity exist primarily in the eye of the beholder. Each individual makes his or her own judgments about the relative size of the outcomes and contributions of each party to the exchange. Thus, one may see fairness where another perceives gross unfairness, and vice versa. Needless to add, such differences in perspective are responsible for a great many conflicts and disputes. This is especially likely in cases where the *egocentric* (or *self-serving*) *bias* operates. As you may recall, this refers to our tendencies to attribute good outcomes or results to internal causes (our own sterling characteristics), but bad or unfavorable ones to external causes (factors beyond our control, others' shortcomings). When it operates in the context of social exchange, this bias leads us to conclude that we have contributed more than we really have, and so deserve a larger share of available rewards, than an outside observer might suggest. Needless to say, such perceptions on the part of several persons involved in an exchange can lead to a great deal of friction between them. After all, each magnifies his or her own contribution, and so expects more favorable outcomes (e.g., Messick and Sentis, 1979).

A second, and closely related, type of bias involves the fact that in general, we are much more sensitive to inequity when it operates to our disadvantage (*underpayment inequity*) than when it operates to our benefit (*overpayment inequity*). Receiving even slightly less than we feel we deserve may cause us to experience strong feelings of unfairness. In contrast, receiving even considerably more may have little impact upon us; we simply take such unexpected benefits in stride! Interestingly, our thresholds for both types of inequity seem to depend, to an important degree, upon their source. We are considerably more tolerant of underpayment inequity (receiving less than we deserve) when it involves another person than when it involves a large, impersonal organization. Specifically, we react more strongly when an organization rather than another person tries to cheat us. In contrast, we are *more* tolerant of overpayment inequity (getting more than we deserve) when it involves an organization rather than another person (Greenberg, 1986). In other words, we find it more acceptable to take advantage of an impersonal entity than a real human being.

In sum, judgments of fairness in social exchange often rest upon the rule of equity or distributive justice. Only when the benefits received by participants are in balance with their contributions is the situation perceived as fair. (For a discussion of recent efforts to apply this basic rule in work settings, please see the **Applied Side** insert on page 362.)

Equality and relative needs: Alternative standards for judging fairness

While equity seems to be the most important rule we follow in judging the fairness of exchange relations, it is not the only standard in this respect. Two others — **equality** and **relative needs** — are also sometimes applied.

The first simply implies that all participants to an exchange should receive equal outcomes; any departure from this pattern is unfair, and should be avoided. As you probably know from your own experience, the equality rule is less common, in actual use, than equity. However, it *is* adopted under certain circumstances. First, it is often followed when individuals believe that their outcomes on a task have been determined by chance or other factors beyond their control (e.g., Greenberg, 1980).

Comparable Worth: Equity in the World of Work

A secretary is paid less than a truck driver. A janitor earns more money than an accounts clerk. A gardener receives higher wages than a cook (refer to Figure 10.13). Are these differences unfair? Or do they merely reflect the fact that truck drivers, janitors, and gardeners work harder — or have more skills — than secretaries, accounts clerks, and cooks? As you can readily see, these are complex questions with no simple answers. Yet, basic principles of fairness require that they be addressed. One way of doing so is through adherence to the principle of **comparable worth**. What this requires, in essence, is that jobs involving approximately equal levels of effort, skill, and commitment should receive equal wages and other benefits.

At first glance, this principle seems so reasonable, and so consistent with the rule of distributive justice considered above, that you may wonder why it has been the focus of so much controversy in recent years. The answer is as follows: while almost everyone agrees that the principle behind comparable worth is correct, it is not yet clear just how it should be applied. In order to determine whether two jobs deserve equal pay, it is first necessary to decide whether they involve equal levels of effort, skill, or difficulty. And while this might sound like an easy task, it has actually turned out to be extremely difficult (Burgess, 1984). Several different techniques for conducting such *job evaluations* have been proposed and put to use, but none seems entirely satisfactory. For example, in *point systems*, a committee representing different levels and groups within an organization is formed, and is asked to assign points to various jobs, according to how much of various *compensable factors* (e.g., effort, skill) they require. Jobs assigned equal numbers of points should then receive equal wages. Another method makes use of *guide charts.* Here, individuals compare various jobs by trying to identify their location on charts representing different levels of key compensable factors (know-how, problem solving, accountability). The relative worth of each job — and the pay it should command — is then determined from its position on the chart.

While these and several other approaches seem reasonable, and offer certain advantages, existing evidence casts doubt upon their ability to effectively establish comparable worth. For example, in one recent study (Madigan, 1985) it was found that several popular methods for evaluating jobs yielded very different results. A job classified at one level by a particular method was often classified at other grades or levels by other methods. Until such difficulties are resolved, efforts to establish comparable worth will remain controversial. However, given the devastating impact of feelings of inequity upon both morale and performance of the employees involved, there is little doubt that concern with this important form of fairness will continue in the years ahead, for practical as well as ethical reasons.

This makes good sense, for if outcomes are unrelated to effort or ability, the fairest way of dividing rewards may be that of distributing them equally among all persons involved. Second, it is sometimes applied when individuals must work together, and fear that following the dic-

FIGURE 10.13. Should the persons performing these diverse jobs receive the same pay? The answer depends on whether the jobs require equal levels of effort or skill and whether they are equally difficult.

Comparable worth: Applying equity to the world of work

tates of equity will prove disruptive (Elliott and Meeker, 1984). In such cases, the persons involved may feel that matching rewards to contributions in a precise manner will stir up more problems than it solves, and so opt for an equal distribution. Third, equality is often followed in situations where individuals wish to maintain good relations with others, or make a good impression on them (Greenberg, 1983). Finally, equality, not equity, is actually the preferred standard for judging or establishing fairness in some cultures. For example, Chinese subjects view an equal division of rewards among friends as more fair than one based on the principle of equity (Leung and Bond, 1984).

The second rule mentioned above — *relative needs* — suggests that outcomes in a social exchange should be distributed according to the current needs of the participants. Those in greatest need should receive the largest share, while those with less need should receive smaller portions. While this standard for judging fairness seems to be applied less frequently than either equity or equality, it *is* used in some situations. For example, the rule of relative needs is often followed at times of accident or disaster, so that those most in need of aid receive it first. In addition, recent findings suggest that important cultural differences exist with respect to this standard, too. An investigation conducted by Murphy-Berman and her colleagues (Murphy-Berman et al., 1984) provides clear evidence on this topic.

In this study, male and female students in both the United States and India were asked to indicate how either a bonus or a cut in pay should be divided between two employees. One of these persons was described as having average work performance but a poor financial situation and serious illness in his or her family. Thus, this person was relatively low in merit, but high in need. The other employee was described as having excellent work performance, and a good financial situation; this individual was high in merit, but relatively low in need. Results indicated the existence of interesting differences in the reactions of the Indian and American subjects. Indian participants tended to favor the needy person; they preferred to divide the bonus or cut in pay in accordance with current needs. In contrast, Americans seemed to prefer a division based on equity, or at least one in accordance with equality; they suggested giving more of the bonus or less of the pay cut to the worker with outstanding performance. In addition, it was found that subjects in both countries showed a greater tendency to favor the needy person when a cutback in pay rather than a bonus was involved. Apparently, they were concerned about discouraging this poor performer still further by reducing his or her pay.

At this point, we should note that these alternate rules for dividing (allocating) available rewards are *not* mutually exclusive. In fact, it appears that they often operate concurrently. In deciding how much to assign to each group member, we take all available information into account — members' relative contributions, level of need, and current group morale. This process is illustrated by a recent study conducted by Elliott and Meeker (1986). These investigators asked subjects to divide $1,000 among five persons who had worked together on a research project. Before making this allocation, they received information concerning the relative contribution to the project of each person, and his or her level of financial need. Four of these individuals were about equal on

TABLE 10.1. When asked to divide $1,000 among five persons who had worked together on a research project, subjects took account both of relative contributions and of current needs. Thus, they gave more to Person B (the one who was markedly different from the others) when he was a high rather than a low contributor, and more when his need was high than when it was low. (Source: Based on data from Elliott and Meeker, 1986.)

	Low	High
Contribution	176.30	226.18
Need	188.51	214.01

Allocating rewards; Adopting multiple rules

both dimensions, while the fifth (Person B) was much higher or lower than the others. As you can see from Table 10.1, subjects seemed to pay careful attention to both contributions and needs in making their allocations. They gave more to Person B when he was a high contributor rather than a low one, and more when his need was high than when it was low. Thus, subjects were influenced by considerations of both equity and need in reaching their decisions.

To conclude: it appears that our judgments concerning the fairness of any social exchange can rest upon any of several different rules. For this reason, the same division of outcomes among participants can appear to be fair or unfair, depending on which rule — or combination of rules — we apply.

Procedural justice: It's not just what you get that counts — How you get it matters, too

So far, we've concentrated on *distributive justice* — the rules individuals use in deciding whether their outcomes in a social exchange are fair. At this point, we should note that there is another aspect of the process that is crucial, too. Not only do we care about the outcomes we receive; the way in which these allocations were determined is also important to us. In short, we care about **procedural justice** — the fairness of the steps taken in dividing available rewards (Thibaut and Walker, 1975; Walker and Lind, 1984).

That concern with procedural justice is high is indicated by a growing body of research evidence. For example, in one recent study, Barrett-Howard and Tyler (1986) asked subjects to read scenarios describing different allocation decisions involving one decision maker and two recipients of available rewards. After reading these stories, they rated the importance of eight different criteria that might be used in selecting an allocation process. Included were distributive justice (rewards should be assigned in accordance with relative contributions), procedural justice (fairness of the steps taken to divide the rewards), speed (there should be a quick decision), and feasibility (the procedure should be practical). Results indicated that procedural justice was rated as the most important of all these factors, even slightly higher than distributive justice.

The findings reported by Barrett-Howard and Tyler (1986), plus those of related research projects, call attention to an important fact: in judging the fairness of any social exchange, we are concerned with more than just the actual outcomes we receive. Not only do we want to get our "fair share"; we want to feel that the procedures through which the decision was reached are reasonable, too.

Reactions to unfairness: Tactics for dealing with injustice

As we're sure you already know from your own experience, feelings of inequity — of being treated unfairly — are quite unpleasant. Indeed, they are something few people can tolerate for long. How, then, do we cope with such reactions? What steps or strategies do we use to restore fairness — or at least escape from the negative feelings generated by perceptions of unfairness? Several different tactics seem useful.

Alterations in contributions.   First, individuals who conclude that they have been treated unfairly often attempt to cope with such feelings by *altering their contributions* to the exchange in question. Thus, if they believe that they have received less than they deserve, they may reduce the contributions they provide. For example, an employee who feels underpaid may reduce his or her effort, arrive late and leave early, or refuse to perform any activities not clearly in his or her job description. Evidence for such effects has been obtained in many studies (e.g., Greenberg, 1982). For example, in one well known investigation, Pritchard, Dunnette, and Jorgenson (1972) found that individuals led to believe that they were being underpaid reduced their output on a tedious record-keeping task, relative to persons led to believe that they were fairly compensated.

Correspondingly, if individuals feel that they have received *more* than they deserve, they may actually increase the magnitude or scope of their contributions. They may work harder, put out more effort, or provide more to others than they were supplying before. While you may find such reactions surprising (why, after all, should individuals offer more than they have to in a social exchange?) growing evidence indicates that they do occur. Perhaps the most intriguing findings in this regard are ones reported recently by Brockner, Davy, and Carter (1986).

These researchers reasoned that when some individuals working in a particular company are laid off from their jobs, those remaining — the *survivors* — may experience feelings of inequity. The reason for this is simple: they continue to enjoy the benefits of working, while their former co-workers do not. Moreover, such feelings would be most likely to occur under conditions where the layoffs occurred in a seemingly arbitrary or random manner. How would survivors then attempt to cope with their feelings of inequity? According to Brockner and his colleagues, perhaps by working harder. Thus, they predicted that after random layoffs, remaining employees would demonstrate an increase in performance.

In order to test this hypothesis, male and female subjects worked on a proofreading task in one room, while a female accomplice worked on a similar task in a separate location. Midway through the session, there was a brief rest period, and during this interval, subjects were exposed to one of two events. In the *layoff condition*, the experimenter explained that because of a scheduling problem one of the two persons present would have to leave without receiving the promised compensation (extra course credit). A rigged drawing was then held, with the accomplice always losing. In the *no-layoff condition*, no mention of a scheduling problem was made, and the accomplice and the subject were simply ushered to their separate rooms once again when the rest period ended. The subject then worked on the proofreading task once more.

As noted above, it was predicted that individuals exposed to the random layoff would work harder than those not exposed to this event. Results (illustrated in Figure 10.14) offered clear support for this prediction. Subjects who had witnessed the layoff did in fact show a much larger increase in productivity after the rest period than those in the no-layoff (control) condition. Moreover, and also consistent with predic-

FIGURE 10.14. Subjects who witnessed a co-worker being fired increased their output after this event more than subjects who did not witness such a layoff. In this way, they were able to reduce feelings of inequity stemming from the fact that they had retained their job while their partner had not. (Source: Based on data from Brockner, Davy, and Carter, 1986.)

Increasing contributions on the job: One technique for dealing with feelings of inequity

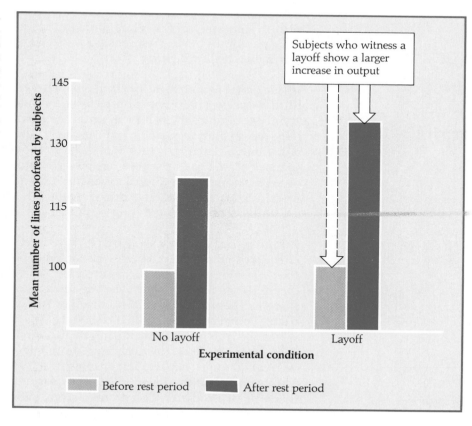

tions based on equity theory, subjects in the layoff condition reported feeling luckier and more guilty on a postexperimental questionnaire than did those in the control group. It is hard to imagine a more convincing demonstration of the fact that individuals who feel overrewarded will sometimes attempt to deal with such inequity by increasing the contributions they provide.

Alterations in outcomes.   A second major strategy for eliminating feelings of unfairness involves attempts by the persons involved to *alter their outcomes* in an exchange. If such individuals feel that they are receiving less than they deserve, they can attempt to obtain a larger share of available rewards. Thus, workers who feel underpaid often seek to gain increased benefits through strikes and related actions. Similarly, persons who feel that they are not getting what they deserve from friends, spouses, or co-workers often complain or take other actions to correct the situation and "balance the scales" (for example, they may request more affection, specific favors, and so on; Walster, Walster, and Traupmann, 1978).

On the other hand, persons who feel that they are getting more than they feel is fair may occasionally seek to lower their share of current benefits. The word *occasionally* should be emphasized, however; as we noted earlier, most people seem to be far less sensitive to overpayments than to underpayments. Thus, in many cases the question of adjusting their outcomes never arises; as far as they are concerned, they are only getting what they deserve!

Withdrawal from a relationship: An effective, but drastic solution.   A third strategy sometimes adopted by individuals experiencing inequity is simply withdrawing from the unfair relationship altogether. Thus, if they feel exploited in their job they may resign and seek employment elsewhere. Similarly, if they feel they are providing much more to their spouse or lover than they are receiving in return, they may seek divorce or separation. While such actions are certainly effective, they are also drastic. Thus, they usually occur only in cases where feelings of inequity are both pronounced and long-standing.

Psychological strategies.   Finally, persons experiencing feelings of unfairness often attempt to deal with such reactions through *psychological strategies*. Here, they make no attempt to alter the actual conditions of the exchange. Rather, they alter their beliefs or perceptions about it. For example, persons who find themselves receiving the "short end of the stick" sometimes rationalize this state of affairs by convincing themselves that the persons exploiting them actually *deserve* more than they do — after all, aren't they brighter, more talented, of noble birth, and so on? As you might expect, persons low in self-esteem seem more likely to adopt this tactic than people who possess more positive feelings about themselves (Brockner, Davy, and Carter, 1986).

In an even more bizarre manner, the victims of inequitable treatment may conclude that they are actually *benefitting* from their current situation. After all, a little suffering is good for the soul! Perhaps the most unsettling type of distortion that occurs in such situations, however, involves a tendency by persons receiving more than they deserve to derogate or devalue those receiving unfair treatment—a phenomenon known as **victim derogation.** Such persons often conclude that the victims of their unfair tactics somehow deserve the treatment they are receiving; if not, why would they receive it? Such effects were noted by Brockner and his colleagues (1986) in a study described earlier. Subjects in that experiment reported more negative feelings about the accomplice when she was fired than when she remained in the job.

In sum, individuals attempt to cope with feelings of inequity in many different ways, and some of these are more reasonable—and effective—than others. Regardless of the specific tactics they employ, though, two facts are clear: (1) most persons react negatively to unfair treatment at the hands of others, and (2) when such unfairness occurs, in the context of social exchange, they take active steps to deal with its presence.

SUMMARY

Social exchange occurs when individuals trade or exchange something (anything from love and affection through goods, information, or services) with others. Two important patterns that can develop in exchange are *cooperation* and *competition.* Individuals are more likely to choose cooperation when they receive similar treatment from others, when they act individually rather than as part of a group, and when they possess a cooperative rather than a competitive personal orientation.

In order to resolve interpersonal *conflict,* individuals often turn to **bargaining.** Research findings indicate that adoption of a "tough" bargaining strategy (an extreme initial offer coupled with few concessions to one's opponent) frequently yields positive results to those who use it. However, when opponents have alternatives (other parties with whom to bargain), a conciliatory approach may be preferrable. Bargaining is more likely to be successful when participants adopt a *positive frame of reference* (focus on potential gains rather than potential losses), when they have considerable power in the groups they represent, and when they operate in the context of *constraints* (minimum outcomes they can accept).

When bargaining fails, other tactics for resolving conflict can be used. These include adoption of a *problem-solving* orientation, and *third-party intervention* (mediation or arbitration). In cases where disputes stem from personal factors (e.g., grudges, misunderstandings), an *interpersonal approach* to resolving conflicts may prove useful.

Individuals evaluate the fairness of social exchange by means of several abstract rules or standards. The most important of these, **equity,** suggests that an exchange is fair if participants' outcomes reflect their relative contributions. Another, *equality*, indicates that an exchange is fair if all participants receive similar outcomes. A third rule, *relative needs*, suggests that outcomes should be distributed in accordance with participants' needs. When individuals conclude that an exchange has been unfair, they often take active steps to counter such reactions. Among the tactics they employ are (1) altering the size of their contributions, (2) altering the magnitude of their outcomes, (3) withdrawing from the relationship, or (4) changing their perceptions of it.

GLOSSARY

arbitration
A form of third-party intervention in bargaining in which recommendations of the person intervening are binding upon the parties involved.

bargaining
A form of social exchange in which individuals trade offers and counteroffers in an attempt to reach an agreement acceptable to both sides.

comparable worth
The principle that jobs requiring equal levels of effort, training, or skill should receive equal pay.

competition
A form of social exchange in which individuals attempt to maximize their own outcomes, often at the expense of others.

competitors
Individuals whose main concern in social exchange is that of surpassing their opponent.

conflict
Direct confrontations between individuals or groups in which one or both sides perceives that the other has thwarted or soon will thwart its major interests.

cooperation
A form of social exchange in which two or more persons coordinate their behavior in order to reach a shared goal.

cooperators
Individuals whose main concern in social exchange is maximizing joint outcomes.

equality rule
A standard for judging or establishing fairness in social exchange which suggests that all participants should receive equal outcomes.

equalizers
Individuals whose main concern in social exchange is that of assuring that all participants receive about the same outcomes.

equity (distributive justice)
A rule for judging fairness in social exchange suggesting that the outcomes received by all participants should be proportional to their contributions.

false consensus effect
The belief (often false) that other persons think and feel very much as we do.

individualists
Persons whose chief concern in social exchange is maximizing their own outcomes.

inequity
Refers to the negative feelings experienced by participants in a social exchange who perceive that the outcomes received by individuals are not proportional to their contributions.

mediation
A form of third-party intervention in bargaining in which a neutral person recommends a compromise agreement.

negative frame
A tendency on the part of bargainers to focus upon potential costs in the situation.

positive frame
A tendency on the part of bargainers to focus on potential gains in the situation.

procedural justice
The fairness of the procedures or steps used to allocate available rewards to various members of a group.

reciprocity
The basic rule of social life suggesting that we should treat others much as they have treated us.

relative needs
A rule for judging fairness in social exchange suggesting that participants in an exchange should receive a share of available rewards reflecting their current needs.

social exchange
A form of social interaction in which participants exchange something of value. What they exchange can range from specific goods or services through information, love, and approval.

threats
A form of communication in which one individual informs another that negative actions will follow if the recipient of the threat does (or does not) behave in some manner.

victim derogation
The tendency for persons who take unfair advantage of others to view negatively the victims of their exploitation (i.e., as somehow *deserving* such treatment).

FOR MORE INFORMATION

Bazerman, M. H., and Lewicki, R. J., eds. (1983). *Negotiation in organizations.* Beverly Hills: Sage.

> A collection of chapters dealing with the process of bargaining in applied contexts. If you'd like to know more about how this key aspect of social exchange actually occurs, this is an excellent source to consult.

Blake, R. R., and Mouton, J. S. (1984). *Solving costly organizational conflicts.* San Francisco: Jossey-Bass.

> A clearly written discussion of the causes of conflict (especially within organizations), and of techniques that may prove useful in resolving such disputes. The authors are experts on these topics, and bring many years of both research and practical experience to bear upon them in this book.

Greenberg, J., and Cohen, R. L., eds. (1982). *Equity and justice in social behavior.* New York: Academic Press.

> An excellent review of research findings concerning equity and perceived justice. The chapters can be somewhat complex (they were written primarily for a professional audience), but a great deal of intriguing information is presented.

Lewicki, R. J., and Litterer, J. A. (1985). *Negotiation.* Homewood, Ill.: Richard D. Irwin.

> A clear, concise, and well written summary of current knowledge concerning the process of negotiation. Basic aspects of this form of social exchange (e.g., communication, persuasion, the personality traits of negotiators) as well as practical tactics for increasing its success are described. All in all, a useful and timely book.

CHAPTER 11

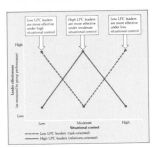

GROUPS AND INDIVIDUAL BEHAVIOR: The Consequences of Belonging

"How could we ever have been so stupid?" Rick Olson, a top official in the state organization of a major political party murmurs. "It's as though we set out to wreck everything we've been working for over the past ten years."

"Yeah, you can say that again," Terri Caruso agrees. "We should have seen this mess coming a mile away. Just listen to these headlines" (and with this remark, she begins to read from a stack of newspapers): "Candidate Linked to Organized Crime"; "Would-Be Gov on the Take . . ."

"Stop, please stop!" Rick exclaims with a look of pain. "I can't stand any more; it's been going on for days now. We're finished for this election, that's for sure; not much we can do except try to minimize the damage. We've had problems before, and we'll have them again. I can live with that. But what I *can't* understand is how we ever got into this fix in the first place. We all knew that nominating Leeds was risky. There were all those rumors floating about. What made us go ahead and do it?"

"I don't know," Terri answers, shaking her head. "I can remember that meeting like it was yesterday. Several people expressed reservations about him at the start, and most of us knew they made sense, but did that stop the Lucky Leeds bandwagon? No way! We made like they didn't exist."

"That's right. The problems were there, but we just didn't seem to give them any weight. Maybe the turning point was when Lila Carson endorsed him. You know how influential *she* is around here."

"Yeah, old money and that sort of thing," Terri agrees. "She sure swung a lot of people over to his camp. But you know, thinking it over, the whole thing is kind of spooky. I mean, the more we discussed him, the stronger his support seemed to get. It was almost as though we convinced ourselves that he couldn't lose!"

At this comment, Rick emits an audible groan. "You're so right! It *was* like that. And when any questions about his past came up, there seemed to be ten good reasons for ignoring them, or for thinking that they didn't count. Yeah, it was strange, all right."

"Well, whatever the reason, we've got a real disaster on our hands now. The top of the ticket is a goner. All we can do now is try to isolate the problem, and save what we can at the local level." Then, with a weak attempt at a smile, she continues: "Well, at least we know one thing: if the party can survive this, it can probably survive anything. So look at it this way: we're so low right now there's only one way we can go from here. We'll bounce back; it'll take time, but eventually, we'll do it . . . "

WHAT HAPPENED in this situation? What led this experienced group of political "king-makers" to go so badly off the deep end and nominate a candidate who dragged them all down to electoral ruin? As the characters involved realize, there is no clear or simple answer. Individually, most members of this decision-making group recognized the dangers of nominating the person in question. Yet, when they discussed this course of action together, something seemed to happen: they lost sight of the many warning signs visible to most of them and "accentuated the positive"— they overestimated the potential benefits associated with this candidate.

The "something" to which we just referred is often described, in social psychology, by the phrase **group influence** (McGrath, 1984). It refers to the fact that when we are part of a group—when we work together with other persons to reach common goals—our behavior is often quite different from what it is under other circumstances. You are probably familiar with this phenomenon yourself. For example, you realize that your actions may be quite different when you are in the presence of other persons (especially ones with whom you have an ongoing relationship) than when you are alone. Similarly, you know that when you joined various groups (e.g., neighborhood play groups, fraternities or sororities, unions, churches), you were expected to behave and think in certain ways—ones endorsed by these groups. Groups, in short, often exert powerful effects upon their members. And since most individuals join many different groups during their lives, such effects play an important role in many contexts, and involve a wide range of social behavior. It is on this topic, therefore, that we focus in the present chapter. Specifically, our discussion of group influence—the consequences of belonging—will proceed as follows.

First, we will consider the basic nature of groups—just what they

FIGURE 11.1. Which of these photos show "true" groups? Most social psychologists would agree that only the top photo shows a group.

Group versus aggregates

are, and how they function. Next, we will turn to the impact of groups upon *task performance* — how being part of a group affects the performance of individuals (**social facilitation**), and the question of whether groups or individuals are more efficient in completing various tasks. Third, we will consider **decision making** in groups, examining the process through which group decisions are made, their nature, and several forces that tend to distort or bias their outcome. Finally, because groups often exert their strongest influence upon their members through the actions of *leaders*, we will conclude with a discussion of the important process of **leadership**.

GROUPS: *Their Nature and Operation*

Look at the photos in Figure 11.1 (page 377). All show several persons. Does this mean that all also illustrate social groups? The answer is a firm and definite "no." In order to be considered members of a group, the persons involved must meet certain criteria. First, they must be involved in some kind of social interaction with one another, or at least possess the potential for such interaction; just being in the same place at the same time is not sufficient. Second, they must be *interdependent* in some manner. What happens to one must affect what happens to the others in at least some respect. Third, their relationship must be relatively *stable* — it must persist across an appreciable period of time. A brief conversation between two passersby does not make them a group; only if they continue to interact in some stable, structured way is this term appropriate. Fourth, they must share at least some common *goals*. Groups, in short, form for a reason. If such rationale is lacking, we may question whether the persons involved actually constitute a social group. Finally, the persons involved must perceive themselves as belonging to a group. They must recognize the special relationship among them, and realize that they are similar and interdependent in important ways. Only to the extent these criteria are met can a collection of two or more persons be considered a group. In sum, our formal definition of the term **group** is as follows: *groups consist of two or more persons engaged in social interaction who have some stable, structured relationship with one another, are interdependent, share common goals, and perceive that they are, in fact, part of a group.*

Applying this definition to the photos in Figure 11.1 (page 377), you can see that only the persons in the top picture qualify as a group. Those in the other photos are mere collections or aggregates of individuals; they are *not* true social groups.

How groups function: *Roles, norms, and cohesiveness*

Earlier, we noted that groups often exert powerful effects on their members. Given the definition of groups just offered, this is hardly surprising. Since persons belonging to a given group share common goals, interact with one another, and are interdependent, it is only reasonable to expect that they will influence one another in important ways. Such *group influence* will serve as the focus of the remainder of this chapter.

Before turning to specific instances of this process, however, it makes sense to consider a more general issue: how, precisely, do groups exert such effects? A complete answer to this question involves many different processes, including several we have examined earlier in this book (e.g., conformity, persuasion, interpersonal attraction). However, there is general agreement that three aspects of groups are most important in this regard: **roles, norms, and cohesiveness** (Forsyth, 1983).

Roles: Differentiation within groups.   Think of one group you have belonged to — anything from Scouts through an association related to your occupation or college major. Once you have a specific group firmly in mind, consider the following question: Did everyone in it act in the same way or perform the same functions? In all probability, your answer is "no." On the contrary, a considerable degree of *differentiation* may well have existed. Specific persons worked at different tasks and were expected to accomplish different things for the group. In short, they played different *roles* within this context. Often such roles are assigned in a relatively formal manner. Thus, specific persons may be chosen by a group to serve as its leader, secretary, treasurer, and so on. In other cases, individuals simply drift into various roles on the basis of their interests and skills, in the absence of any formal assignment to them. Whatever the mechanism involved, however, once individuals assume specific roles within a group, they are expected, by other group members, to behave in certain ways. Such *role expectations* can be very powerful, and frequently they constitute an important way in which groups exert strong effects upon their members.

Norms: The rules of the game.   We have already considered a second factor responsible for the powerful impact of groups upon their members: *norms.* As you may recall from our discussion of conformity in Chapter 7, norms are rules — implicit or explicit — established by various groups to regulate the behavior of their members. Thus, they tell group members how to behave, or how *not* to behave, in various situations (Sorrels and Kelley, 1984). Since most groups insist upon adherence to their norms as a basic requirement for membership, it is hardly surprising that individuals wishing to join or remain in specific groups generally follow these "rules of the game." If they do not, they may soon find themselves on the outside looking in!

Cohesiveness: The effects of wanting to belong.   Consider two groups: in the first, members like one another very much, strongly desire the goals their group is seeking, and feel that they could not possibly find another group that better fills their needs. In the second, members dislike one another and get along poorly, do not share common goals, and are actively seeking alternative groups that might offer them a better deal. Which would exert stronger effects upon its members? The answer is obvious: the first. The reason for this difference, too, is obvious: *cohe-*

siveness is much higher in the first group than in the second. As you can probably tell from this example, cohesiveness refers to all of the forces, both positive and negative, that cause individuals to remain in a group. On the positive side are such factors as attraction among members, a good match between individual needs and the group's goals, and high costs associated with leaving. On the negative side are low attraction among members, a poor match between individual needs and group goals, and low costs of withdrawing and seeking membership in other groups. At first glance you might assume that high cohesiveness is always a "plus" where groups are concerned, and usually this is so. However, there are a few cases in which high cohesiveness can actually get in the way and interfere with effective performance. For example, groups high in cohesiveness may spend so much time in pleasant social interaction that their level of output suffers. Similarly, recent findings indicate that high cohesiveness can interfere with performance in industrial settings

FIGURE 11.2. Groups often influence their members through the operation of three factors: *roles, norms,* and *cohesiveness.* The basic nature of each of these important elements of group functioning is illustrated here.

Roles, norms, and cohesiveness: Three important aspects of groups

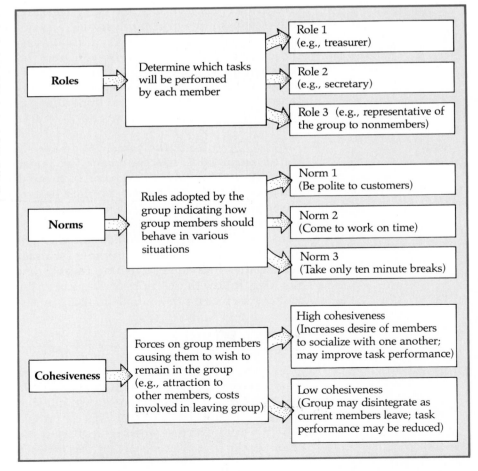

when group members feel that their efforts are not supported by management (Schriesheim, 1980). Under such conditions, cohesive groups may decide to pursue their own self-interest, while ignoring the larger goals of their organization or company. In general, though, a high level of cohesiveness—*esprit de corps*, if you will—has beneficial effects on group performance, and also magnifies the impact of groups upon their members. (For a summary of the effects of roles, norms, and cohesiveness, please refer to Figure 11.2).

GROUPS AND TASK PERFORMANCE: *The Benefits—and Costs—of Working with Others*

According to a famous poem, "No man is an Island; No man stands alone" (read "person" for "man," of course). While these words may not apply equally to all spheres of life, they certainly seem accurate where work is concerned. Human beings rarely perform their jobs or carry out other important tasks entirely on their own. More frequently, they work with others, or at least in their presence. A key question concerning groups, therefore, is this: what impact, if any, do they exert upon task performance? In order to answer this question, it is necessary for us to consider two separate but related issues: (1) what are the effects of the mere presence of others on individual performance (in other words, do individuals perform differently in front of an audience than when alone)? and (2) how efficient are groups, relative to individuals, in performing various tasks?

Social facilitation: Performance in the presence of others

Imagine that as part of your job, you must make a speech in front of a large audience. You have several weeks to prepare, so you write the speech and then practice it at home in the evening and on weekends. Time passes, and the moment of truth arrives. You are introduced, and begin your speech. How will you do? Will you stumble over your words and perform more poorly in front of a live audience than when you were alone? Or will the presence of these people actually spur you on to greater heights of eloquence? Early research concerned with this issue yielded confusing results (Triplett, 1898). Sometimes performance was *improved* by the presence of an audience. In other situations, though, the opposite was true. How could this puzzle be solved? One intriguing answer was offered by Zajonc (1965) in what has come to be known as the **drive theory of social facilitation.**

The drive theory of social facilitation: Other persons as a source of arousal. Before describing Zajonc's theory, we should make one point clear. The term *social facilitation*, as used in social psychology, refers to *any* effects on performance stemming from the presence of others. Thus, it includes decrements as well as improvements in task performance.

The basic idea behind Zajonc's theory can be simply stated: the presence of others produces increments in our level of motivation or arousal. As you can readily see, this suggestion agrees with informal experience. Often, the presence of other persons—especially in the form of an audience—*does* cause us to experience signs of heightened arousal (e.g., feelings of tension or excitement). But how do such increments in arousal then affect our performance? According to Zajonc, the answer involves two basic facts.

First, it is a well established fact in psychology that increments in arousal enhance the performance of *dominant responses*—the ones an individual is most likely to perform in a given situation. (An example: your tendency to smile at others when they smile at you.) Thus, when arousal increases, our tendency to perform strong, dominant responses increases, too. Second, such dominant responses can be either correct or incorrect for any task we are currently performing.

When these two facts are combined with the suggestion that the presence of others is arousing, two predictions follow: (1) the presence of others will facilitate performance when an individual's dominant responses in a given context are correct ones; (2) the presence of others will actually impair performance when a person's dominant responses in the situation are incorrect. (Please refer to Figure 11.3.) Stated in slightly different terms, the presence of others will facilitate the performance of strong, well-learned responses, but may interfere with the performance of new and as yet unmastered forms of behavior.

Early studies designed to test these predictions generally yielded positive results (e.g., Matlin and Zajonc, 1968; Zajonc and Sales, 1966). That is, individuals were in fact more likely to emit dominant responses when in the presence of others than when alone, and performance on various tasks was then either enhanced or impaired, depending on whether these responses represented correct responses or errors (Geen and Gange, 1977). Further, additional findings offered support for the view that the presence of others is indeed arousing; subjects showed higher levels of physiological arousal when in the presence of others than when they were alone (e.g., Martens, 1969).

Additional research, however, soon raised an important question: does social facilitation stem from the mere physical presence of others, as Zajonc's theory suggests? Or do other factors (e.g., concern over their possible evaluations) also play a role? Support for the latter possibility was provided by the findings of several intriguing studies. For example, Cottrell and his colleagues (1968) had subjects perform a task involving the emission of previously learned responses under one of three conditions: (1) while alone in the room, (2) in the presence of two other persons who wore blindfolds, and (3) in the presence of two other persons who expressed interest in watching their behavior and who actually did so. Results indicated that social facilitation (an increase in subjects' ten-

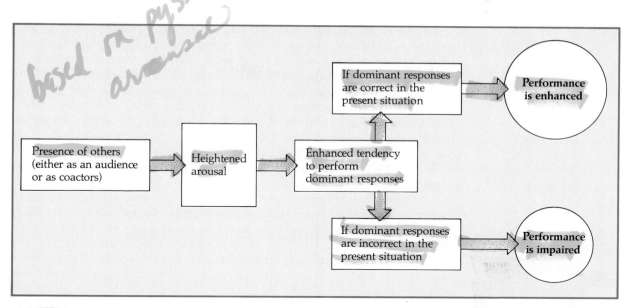

based on pyskal arousal

FIGURE 11.3. According to the *drive theory* of social facilitation, the presence of others increases our level of motivation or arousal. This increased arousal, in turn, enhances the performance of dominant responses (our strongest responses in a given situation). If these are correct, performance is enhanced. If they are incorrect, performance is reduced.

The drive theory of social facilitation: A summary

dencies to emit dominant responses) occurred only under the last condition — when members of the audience could observe and evaluate subjects' performance.

These and related findings (e.g., Bond, 1982; Bray and Sugarman, 1980) led some researchers to propose that social facilitation actually derives either from **evaluation apprehension** — concern over being judged by others, or related concerns over *self-presentation* — looking good in front of others (Carver and Scheier, 1981). Thus, it may be these factors, not the mere physical presence of others, that are crucial in determining the impact of an audience or coactors upon task performance.

At first glance, such suggestions seem quite reasonable. After all, most of us *are* concerned with the impressions we make on others, and care about their evaluation of us. Further, such concerns might indeed be motivating or arousing in many situations. However, we must note that other evidence points to the conclusion that social facilitation effects can sometimes occur even in situations where these factors do not seem to play a role (e.g., Markus, 1978). For example, many animals appear to be affected in the same manner as human beings by the presence of an audience or coactors (e.g., Rajecki, Kidd, and Ivins, 1976). Indeed, even roaches show an increased tendency to perform dominant responses when in the presence of an audience of other roaches (Zajonc, Heingartner, and Herman, 1969)! Since it makes little sense to assume that animals or insects share our concerns about "looking good" to each other, it appears that social facilitation can occur quite apart from the impact of such factors.

A potential resolution: The distraction-conflict model.   Taken as a whole, the findings described above seem to leave us facing a dilemma. Does social facilitation stem from mere physical presence, evaluation apprehension, concerns over self-presentation, or other factors? At present, no conclusive answer exists. One possibility—supported by some recent findings—is that all (or at least several) of these variables play a role (Sanders, 1984b). Another is provided by the **distraction-conflict theory,** developed jointly by Baron, Sanders, and Moore (e.g., R. S. Baron, 1986; Sanders, 1983; Sanders, Baron, and Moore, 1978).

Like the other explanations of social facilitation we have already considered, this theory assumes that the impact of audiences and coactors on task performance stems from heightened arousal. In contrast to earlier views, however, it suggests that such arousal stems from conflict between two tendencies on the part of organisms performing various tasks: (1) the tendency to pay attention to the task at hand, and (2) the tendency to direct attention to an audience or coactors. The conflict produced by these competing tendencies leads to increments in motivation or arousal. These, in turn, enhance the tendency to perform dominant responses, and either increase or decrease performance, depending on whether such responses are correct or constitute errors (refer to Figure 11.4).

Growing evidence offers support for this theory. For example, various sources of distraction (even nonsocial ones such as flashing lights) do seem to produce increments in arousal, as the theory suggests (Sanders, 1983). Second, audiences seem to produce social facilitation effects (e.g., increased vigor in performing simple responses) only when directing attention to them conflicts in some way with task demands (Groff, Baron, and Moore, 1983). When paying attention to audience

FIGURE 11.4.   The *distraction-conflict theory* of social facilitation suggests that the presence of others induces competing tendencies to (1) pay attention to these persons, and (2) pay attention to the task being performed. The conflict generated by these competing tendencies results in heightened arousal, which then produces social facilitation.

The distraction-conflict theory of social facilitation

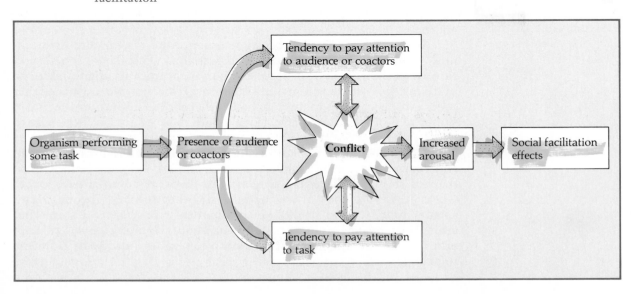

members does not conflict with task performance, social facilitation fails to occur. Third, individuals report experiencing greater degrees of distraction when they perform various tasks in front of an audience than when they perform such tasks alone (Baron, Moore, and Sanders, 1978). Fourth, when individuals have little reason to pay attention to others present on the scene (e.g., these persons are performing a different task), social facilitation fails to occur. When, in contrast, they have strong reasons for directing attention to others (e.g., these persons are performing the same task as themselves), social facilitation effects appear (Sanders, 1983).

We should hasten to add that not all findings have been consistent with predictions derived from distraction-conflict theory (e.g., Berger et al., 1982). However, most existing evidence provides support for its usefulness. In addition, distraction-conflict theory offers two important advantages not provided by any of the competing views. First, since animals as well as people can experience the type of conflict shown in Figure 11.4, it explains why social facilitation occurs in many different species — even the lowly roach! Second, with certain modifications (R. S. Baron, 1986) distraction-conflict theory can explain the occurrence of social facilitation without reference to the notion of arousal. The reasoning is as follows. The presence of an audience (or coactors) threatens the persons involved with information overload — they have more things demanding their attention than they can readily handle. As a result, they focus their attention primarily on those cues most central to the task at hand. Such focused attention may then enhance performance on simple tasks, but can reduce performance on complex ones, which usually require attention to a wide range of stimuli. In short, a modified form of distraction-conflict theory can explain social facilitation effects in terms of our limited information-processing capacity.

To conclude: while the theory proposed by Baron, Sanders, and Moore may not offer a final answer to the persistent puzzle of social facilitation, it seems quite promising in this respect. In any case, it has added substantially to our understanding of what many social psychologists consider to be the simplest type of group effect.

Groups and task performance: Do "many hands" really "make light the work"?

Earlier, we noted that most work is performed in group settings; individuals rarely perform their jobs (or other important tasks) entirely alone. The reason behind this reliance on groups is obvious: there is a strong and general belief that people working together can accomplish more than people working alone. As we saw in our discussion of cooperation (Chapter 10), this is often the case. By coordinating their efforts, groups of persons *can* often attain goals that none of them could hope to reach alone. But does this necessarily imply that groups are always, or even usually, more productive than individuals? The answer, it turns out, is fairly complex. Working in groups does indeed offer certain advantages. For example, it allows individuals to pool their knowledge and skills. Similarly, it allows for an efficient division of labor, so that specific persons perform those tasks for which they are best equipped. On the other hand, though, group settings exact certain costs. As we mentioned earlier, when cohesiveness is high, members may spend a lot of time engaging in pleasant — but nonproductive — social interaction. Further, pressures to adhere to existing norms and "do things the way we've always done them" may interfere with the development of new and better procedures for completing essential tasks. In short, group settings offer a mixed bag of potential pluses and minuses where performance is concerned. Perhaps the most important single factor determining whether groups or individuals are more efficient, however, involves the type of task being performed. Thus, it is to this topic that we turn next.

Type of task and group performance.   A useful framework for understanding the different types of tasks performed by groups has been proposed by Steiner (1972, 1976). According to this approach, most tasks can be viewed as falling into one of three different categories.

First, there are **additive tasks.** These are ones in which the contributions of each member are combined into a single group product. For example, when several persons combine their strength to lift a heavy load, or when several carry petitions door-to-door to get the required number of signatures, the tasks being performed are additive. Obviously, coordination is crucial in such efforts; it would make little sense for the people trying to lift the load to exert their effort at different times, or for different canvassers to visit the same potential signers. Only if such coordination exists will there be anything to "add" in determining the group's final output.

Second, there are **conjunctive tasks.** Here, the group's final product is determined by its "weakest link" — by the poorest performing member. A clear example of this type of task is provided by the efforts of a group of acrobats who build a "human pyramid" as part of their act. Obviously, the height to which this pyramid can rise is determined by the strength of the weakest member of the team. At the point where this person cannot support additional weight, the whole structure will collapse.

Finally, there are **disjunctive tasks.** Here, too, the group's product (and hence its success) is determined by a single member. However in this case, it is the best or most competent person who sets the limit. For example, consider a group of scientists faced with a complex problem relating to their research. The group can adopt only one solution or approach at a time, so its success will reflect the quality of the best idea or solution proposed by any of its members. (A word of caution: as we will see below, the best solution or course of action is not always recognized as such. If it is not, group performance will be below this level.)

Now to return to our basic question: how do groups and individuals compare with respect to each of these types of tasks? A general answer is as follows. On additive tasks, groups usually outperform individuals, *provided that:* (1) the type of coordination mentioned above exists, and (2) a phenomenon known as **social loafing**, in which individual members decide to take it easy and let others do the work, does not develop. (Please see the **Focus** insert on page 388 for a discussion of social loafing.) Unfortunately, existing evidence suggests that in many cases, coordination among group members is difficult to attain. Individuals seem to distract one another and get in each other's way, with the overall result that groups actually produce *less* than equivalent numbers of individuals working alone (e.g., Wood, Polek, and Aiken, 1985). The situation is even less favorable to groups in the case of conjunctive tasks, where overall performance is determined by the weakest member. Here, individuals usually tend to surpass groups in both output and quality. Finally, with respect to disjunctive tasks, groups tend to have an edge, provided they possess at least some competent, talented members, *and* provided such persons are successful in getting their ideas or solutions accepted (Laughlin, 1980). A summary of these proposals is offered in Figure 11.5; please review it carefully before reading further.

FIGURE 11.5. Groups often surpass individuals in the performance of *additive* tasks. The same pattern exists for *disjunctive* tasks, provided that groups possess at least some competent members. Individuals often surpass groups in the performance of *conjunctive* tasks, however.

Task performance: Do groups or individuals have the edge?

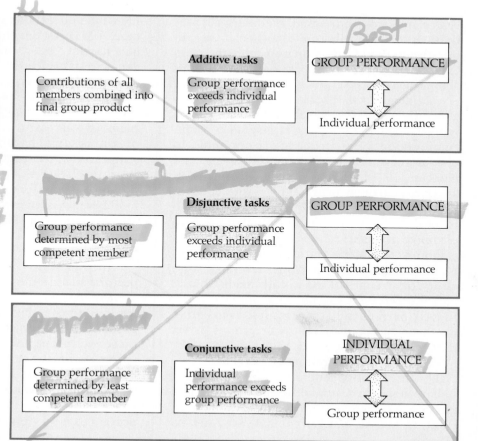

FOCUS ON RESEARCH:
The Cutting Edge

Social Loafing: "Passing the Buck" When Part of a Group

Have you ever watched a group of workers struggle to move a heavy piece of equipment or a large piece of furniture? If so, consider the following question: do you think all the persons involved were exerting equal effort? If you answered "yes," think again: the temptation to "take it easy" and let others do most of the work is quite strong in such cases. After all, no one can directly measure each person's output. Thus, by grunting and groaning realistically, each participant can convince the others that she or he is working as hard as possible. Further, the larger the group, and therefore the easier it is for individual members to pass their responsibilities on to others (refer to our discussion of *diffusion of responsibility* in Chapter 8), the stronger such tendencies should be.

Evidence for precisely such effects—generally known as **social loafing**—has been reported by Latané and his colleagues in a continuing series of experiments. For example, in one of these studies (Latané, Williams, and Harkins, 1979), groups of male students were asked to clap or cheer as loudly as they could at specific times, supposedly so that the experimenter could determine how much noise people make in social settings. Subjects engaged in clapping and cheering either alone or in groups of two, four, or six persons. Findings were clear: the strength of the sounds made by each person decreased sharply as group size rose. Indeed, participants produced less than half as much noise when members of groups of six than when working alone.

Additional research suggests that such social loafing is quite general in scope, occurring in both sexes, in several different cultures, and under a wide range of work conditions (e.g., Harkins, Latané, and Williams, 1980; Harkins

and Petty, 1982; Weiner, Latané, and Pandey, 1981). Needless to add, such findings are somewhat discouraging. In essence, they suggest that many persons will "goof off" when working with others. And since groups perform many key tasks in society, this tendency has important practical implications. Is social loafing, then, an unavoidable part of group task performance? Or can something be done to lessen its impact? Fortunately, growing evidence points to the latter conclusion. In particular, two simple strategies appear to be effective in reducing its occurrence.

First, tendencies toward social loafing can practically be stopped "cold" by making the output or effort of each participant readily identifiable (e.g., Williams, Harkins, and Latané, 1981). Under these conditions, individuals cannot "hide" in the group, so the tendency to sit back and let others do the work for them virtually disappears.

Second, social loafing can be sharply reduced by increasing group members' commitment to successful task performance. Here, pressures toward working hard should offset temptations to engage in social loafing. Moreover, the larger the group, the stronger such pressures should be. Thus, output per group member may actually *increase* rather than decrease as group size rises. Convincing evidence for such effects has been reported by Zaccaro (1984).

In this study, male and female subjects performed a simple construction task: making as many paper "moon tents" as possible in fifteen minutes. Subjects performed this task in groups of two or groups of four. Within each of these conditions half of the participants (those in the high task-attactiveness group) were exposed to information designed to increase their commitment to high performance. They were told that the study dealt with a very important topic — the causes of recent declines in

FIGURE 11.6. When subjects' commitment to good performance was enhanced by procedures designed to increase task attractiveness, their tendency to engage in social loafing was reduced. Thus, performance was not lower in groups of four than in groups of two. When task attractiveness was low, in contrast, social loafing did occur. (Source: Based on data from Zaccaro, 1984.)

Enhanced task attractiveness: One technique for combating social loafing

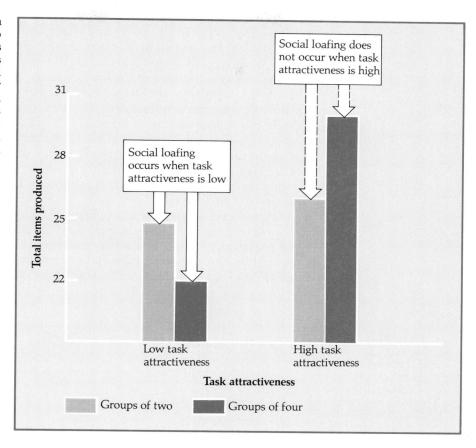

productivity among American workers. In addition, they were informed that the highest scoring groups would receive a bonus (additional credit) for their work. In contrast, the remaining subjects (those in the low task-attractiveness group) were not given similar information or inducements.

As you can see from Figure 11.6, results offered support for the view that increasing individuals' commitment to good performance could eliminate social loafing. While performance dropped as group size increased in the low task-attractiveness condition, it actually rose in the high task-attractiveness group.

Here, output per member was higher in groups of four than in groups of two. (Please note: this pattern is precisely opposite to that which would be expected on the basis of social loafing.)

In sum, it appears that social loafing *can* be overcome, and by relatively straightforward procedures. Thus, it is not an unavoidable "side effect" of performance in group settings. Given that much of the work in all modern societies is currently carried out by committees, work groups, and teams, these findings are comforting, to say the least.

DECISION MAKING BY GROUPS: *How It Takes Place, the Outcomes It Yields, and the Pitfalls It Faces*

Groups are called upon to perform a wide range of tasks — everything from conducting delicate surgical operations through harvesting the nation's crops. One of the most important activities they perform, however, is making *decisions.* Governments, large corporations, military units, and virtually all other social entities entrust their key decisions to groups. As a result, most of the laws, policies, and business practices that affect our daily lives (or shape the future course of society) are determined by committees, boards of directors, and similar groups — *not* by single individuals (refer to Figure 11.7). The rationale behind this approach is clear: most persons believe that groups, by pooling the expertise of their members, can often reach better decisions than individuals. Moreover, it is also assumed that because of the give-and-take that occurs during their deliberations, groups are less likely than individuals to "go off the deep end."

Are these assumptions accurate? Do groups actually make better (i.e., more accurate) decisions than individuals? In their efforts to answer this practical question, researchers concerned with group decisions have focused on three major topics: (1) how, precisely, do groups reach their decisions — what is this process really like? (2) do decisions reached by

FIGURE 11.7. As shown here, groups are called upon to make a very wide range of decisions! (Source: Drawing by Frascino; ©1981 The New Yorker Magazine, Inc.)

Decision making: A major function of groups

"All in favor of summoning the powers of darkness say 'Aye.'"

groups differ in any way from those reached by individuals? and (3) what accounts for the fact that groups occasionally make totally disastrous decisions — ones so bad they are hard to explain?

How groups reach decisions: social decision schemes and social transition schemes

When groups first begin to discuss some issue, their members rarely voice unanimous agreement. Rather, they support a wide range of views and favor competing courses of action. After some period of discussion, however, a decision is usually reached. Of course, this is not always the case; juries do become "hung," and other decision-making groups, too, may deadlock. In most cases, though, *some* decision is ultimately reached. Is there any way of predicting this final outcome? In short, can we predict the decision a group is likely to reach from information about the views initially held by its members? Growing evidence suggests that we can (e.g., Davis, 1980; Kerr and MacCoun, 1985).

In particular, it appears that the final decision reached by a group can often be predicted with a high degree of accuracy by means of relatively simple rules known as **social decision schemes.** These rules relate the initial distribution of member views or preferences to the group's final decision, and are quite straightforward. For example, one — the *major-ity-wins scheme* — suggests that, in many cases, the group will opt for whatever position is initially supported by a majority of its members. According to this rule, discussion serves mainly to confirm or strengthen the most popular view. In contrast, a second decision scheme — the *truth-wins rule* — suggests that the correct solution or decision will ulti-mately come to predominate, as its virtue is recognized by growing num-bers of members. A third decision scheme, adopted by many juries, is the *two-thirds majority rule.* Here, juries tend to convict defendants if two-thirds of the jurors initially favor this decision. However, if this crucial majority is not reached, the likelihood that the jury will be "hung" is quite high (Davis et al., 1984). Finally, some groups seem to adopt the *first-shift rule.* That is, they tend, ultimately, to adopt a decision consist-ent with the direction of the first shift in opinion shown by any member.

Surprising as it may seem, the results of many studies indicate that these simple rules are often quite successful in predicting even complex group decisions. Indeed, in recent studies, they have been successful in this regard up to 80 percent of the time (e.g., Kerr, 1981). Of course, different rules seem to be more successful under some conditions than others. Thus, the majority-wins scheme seems best in situations involv-ing *judgmental tasks* — ones that are largely a matter of opinion, and for which no objectively correct decision exists. In contrast, the truth-wins rule seems best in predicting group decisions with respect to *intellective tasks* — ones for which there is a correct decision. But given that the final decisions reached by groups can often be predicted, another and perhaps even more basic question remains: how, precisely, are such outcomes reached? How do groups actually move toward final agreement? This is a complex question; yet recent investigations have begun to shed considerable light even on this matter (e.g., Vinokur et al., 1985). One basic strategy in such research has been to focus on **social transition schemes** —rules indicating how groups move through different patterns of member views or positions en route to their final decisions (e.g., Kerr, 1982; Penrod and Hastie, 1980). As an example of such research, and of the intriguing results it has yielded, we will consider a recent study by Kerr and MacCoun (1985).

In this experiment, groups of either three, six, or twelve subjects (all males or all females) played the role of jurors, and discussed nine separate armed robbery cases described to them in one-page summaries. During their deliberations, subjects could indicate their personal verdict preferences (guilty or not guilty) by pressing one of two buttons on a panel before them. They were free to change their views at any time, and discussion of each case continued for ten minutes. If they were not able to reach a unanimous verdict within this period, they were to consider themselves as "hung," and should proceed to the next case.

Results were complex, but provide intriguing insights into the process through which groups reach decisions. First, as you might suspect, the proportion of the mock juries that became "hung" increased with group size. While 45 percent of the twelve-person groups deadlocked, only 28 percent and 9 percent of the six and three-person groups reached an impasse. This suggests that it is indeed easier for small than large groups to attain unanimous agreement. Second, and again as you would probably predict, large groups took longer to reach decisions than small ones. Thus, while three-person groups required less than three minutes, on average, to come to their decisions, six- and twelve-person groups required approximately twice as long in this respect. Third, and most important, the manner in which the groups moved through various patterns of member views en route to their decisions was also affected by their size. In particular, as shown by Figure 11.8, a two-thirds majority in favor of conviction was much more successful in producing shifts in this direction among the remaining hold-outs in groups of three than in groups of six or twelve. This latter finding suggests that reducing the size of decision-making groups (and especially juries) below six may increase the likelihood of a "majority wins" process developing. In other words, in some cases, it may substantially reduce the chances that a group will give full consideration to all possible courses of action. Needless to say, this possibility has important implications for group decisions in many different contexts.

To conclude: research on social transition schemes and related topics suggests that the process by which groups move toward agreement is complex. Final group decisions are affected by where the group has been (i.e., previous patterns of views held by its members), how long it has been deliberating, its size, and many other factors. Yet, the process is far

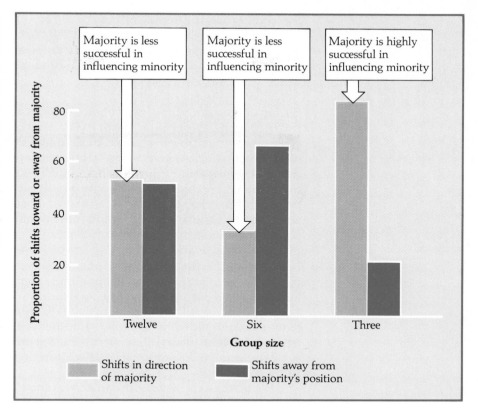

FIGURE 11.8. The process through which groups reach decisions appears to be strongly affected by group size. As shown here, a two-thirds majority in favor of conviction was much more successful in winning over the minority to this view in groups of three than in groups of either six or twelve. (Source: Based on data from Kerr and MacCoun, 1985.)

Group size and the decision making process

from random. On the contrary, it appears to be quite orderly. Thus, while groups may not always arrive at the best or most accurate decisions, the road they travel to them, at least, seems to be predictable.

The nature of group decisions: Moderation or polarization?

Suppose that one day, the premier of the Soviet Union presents a dramatic plan for immediate nuclear disarmament to the President of the United States. (We can dream, can't we?) How would the President react: would he or she take the plan under advisement and reach a decision about its acceptance alone? Or would the President confer with a group of close advisers before responding to the offer? As you can readily guess, the second course of action is much more likely. Governments — even those headed by dictators — rarely make important decisions without deliberation by *some* high-level group. As we noted earlier, an important reason behind this strategy is the widespread belief that groups are much less likely than individuals to make serious errors — to reach rash decisions, or go straight "off the deep end." Is this really the case? Are groups really better at making decisions — or at least more conservative in this regard — than individuals? Research conducted by social psychologists offers some surprising answers.

Group versus individual decisions: A shift toward risk or a shift toward polarization? More than twenty years ago, a graduate student named James Stoner decided to examine this question in his master's thesis. In order to do so, he asked college students to play the role of advisers to imaginary persons supposedly facing the task of deciding between risky but attractive courses of action, and conservative but less attractive ones (Stoner, 1961). For example, in one of these situations, a fictitious character had to choose between a low-paying but secure job, and a higher-paying but less secure one (refer to Table 11.1 for other examples of such *choice-dilemma* questions).

During the first phase of Stoner's study, each subject made recommendations about these situations alone. Then, they met in small groups and discussed each problem until a unanimous agreement was reached. In accordance with the comments above, Stoner expected that the decisions recommended by groups would be more conservative than those offered by their individual members. Surprisingly, however, just the opposite occurred. Groups actually recommended riskier decisions than individuals.

While the size of this difference was small, it had important implications. After all, if groups do indeed make riskier decisions than individuals, the strategy of entrusting important choices to committees, juries, and so on may be in error. In fact, it may be downright dangerous! Impressed by such implications, many researchers focused their attention on this effect, which soon came to be known as the **risky shift** (e.g., Burnstein, 1983; Lamm and Myers, 1978). Many of the experiments they conducted seemed to confirm Stoner's initial findings: they, too, noted a shift toward risk within decision-making groups. In contrast, though, other studies failed to confirm such changes. Indeed, in a few cases, group discussion actually seemed to produce shifts toward *caution* rather than risk (e.g., Knox and Safford, 1976). How could this be? How could group discussion produce both shifts toward caution and shifts toward risk? Gradually, a compelling explanation emerged. What had at first seemed to be a shift toward risk was actually a more general phenomenon — a *shift toward polarization.* Group discussion, it appeared, led individual members to become more extreme — *not* simply more risky or more cautious. Thus, if they were mildly in favor of a particular course of action prior to the group discussion, they came to favor it even more strongly after these deliberations. And if they were mildly opposed to some action prior to the group discussion, they came to oppose it more strongly after the exchange of views. The shifts induced by group discussion, then, are quite general in scope. They represent shifts in the direction of greater extremity, hence the label **group**

TABLE 11.1 These items are similar to the ones used by Stoner (and many other researchers) to compare individual and group decisions. Subjects answer each item twice: once alone, and then again after engaging in group discussion. (Source: Adapted from Kogan and Wallach, 1964.)

Choice-dilemma items

1. Ms. F is currently a college senior who is very eager to pursue graduate study in chemistry leading to the Doctor of Philosophy degree. She has been accepted by University X and University Y. University X has a world-wide reputation for excellence in chemistry. While a degree from University X would signify that she is outstanding in this field, the standards are so very rigorous that only a fraction of the candidates actually receive the degree. University Y, on the other hand, has a lower reputation in chemistry, but almost everyone admitted is awarded the Doctor of Philosophy degree, though the degree has much less prestige than that from University X.

Imagine that you are advising Ms. F. Listed below are several probabilities or chances that Ms. F would be awarded a degree at University X, with the greater prestige. Please check the *lowest* probability that you would consider acceptable to make it worthwhile for Ms. F to enroll in University X rather than University Y.

_____ The chances are 9 in 10 that Ms. F would receive a degree from University X.
_____ The chances are 7 in 10 that Ms. F would receive a degree from University X.
_____ The chances are 5 in 10 that Ms. F would receive a degree from University X.
_____ The chances are 3 in 10 that Ms. F would receive a degree from University X.
_____ The chances are 1 in 10 that Ms. F would receive a degree from University X.
_____ Place a check here if you think Ms. F should *not* enroll in University X, no matter what the probabilities.

2. Mr. A, an electrical engineer, who is married and has one child, has been working for a large electronics corporation since graduating from college five years ago. He is assured of a lifetime job with a modest, though adequate, salary, and good pension benefits upon retirement. On the other hand, it is very unlikely that his salary will increase much before he retires. While attending a convention, Mr. A is offered a job with a small, newly founded company that has a highly uncertain future. The new job would pay more to start and would offer the possibility of a share in the partnership if the company survived the competition with larger firms.

Imagine that you are advising Mr. A. Listed below are several probabilities or chances of the new company's proving financially sound. Please check the *lowest* probability that you would consider acceptable to make it worthwhile for Mr. A to take the new job.

_____ The chances are 1 in 10 that the company will prove financially sound.
_____ The chances are 3 in 10 that the company will prove financially sound.
_____ The chances are 5 in 10 that the company will prove financially sound.
_____ The chances are 7 in 10 that the company will prove financially sound.
_____ The chances are 9 in 10 that the company will prove financially sound.
_____ Place a check here if you think Mr. A should *not* take the new job, no matter what the probabilities.

polarization. (The basic nature of this process is illustrated in Figure 11.9, page 396.)

As we noted earlier, the tendency for groups to become increasingly extreme in their views over time has important—and unsettling— implications (recall the opening story to this chapter). Thus, it is not surprising that this phenomenon has been the subject of a considerable amount of research (e.g., Burnstein, 1983). But why, precisely, does it occur? What factors account for the development of group polarization? It is to this question that we turn next.

FIGURE 11.9. After taking part in a group discussion, group members often shift to views that are more extreme (in the same general direction) than the ones they held initially. Such shifts are known as group polarization effects.

Group polarization: Its basic nature

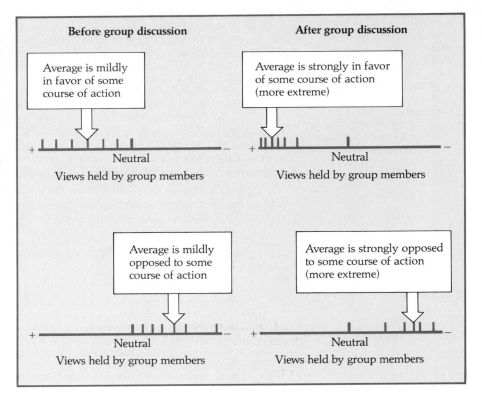

Group polarization: Why does it occur? While several different explanations for group polarization have been proposed, two have received most attention. These are known as the *social comparison* and *persuasive arguments* views.

The social comparison approach suggests that prior to group discussion, most individuals assume that they hold "better" views than the other members. That is, they assume that their views are more extreme, in the "right" or valued directions, than those of the people around them. Since it is obviously impossible for everyone to be above average in this respect, many group members soon experience a rude awakening: they learn that their own views are not nearly as extreme (in positive, valued directions) as they at first believed. Because most persons wish to maintain a positive self-image, and attempt to do so by comparing themselves favorably with others (through *social comparison*), this puts pressure upon them to shift to more extreme positions. As they do, the group as a whole moves in this direction, and the polarization effect develops (e.g., Goethals and Zanna, 1979; Sanders and Baron, 1977).

This explanation for group polarization is supported by several interesting findings. For example, individuals do tend to perceive themselves as being more extreme, in the "right" direction, than others (e.g.,

Wallach and Wing, 1968). Similarly, shifts toward extremity seem to occur in the total absence of group discussion, when individuals simply learn that their views are not as far above average as they initially assumed (Myers et al., 1980). However, some evidence appears to be inconsistent with the social comparison view. Specifically, individuals sometimes recommend more extreme or risky decisions for strangers than for themselves (Laughlin and Earley, 1982). This does not seem to agree with the notion that most persons wish to appear above average in boldness or related traits.

The persuasive arguments view offers a contrasting explanation for the occurrence of polarization. It contends that during group discussion, individual members present arguments that support their own views. Since some of these arguments, at least, will be ones not previously considered by other members, the persons hearing them for the first time may be persuaded to alter their views in these directions. Thus, over time the group will shift toward the point of view that is supported by the largest number of convincing arguments. In sum, the view that predominated at the start will enjoy stronger and stronger support, and polarization will develop (Vinokur and Burnstein, 1974).

This explanation, too, is supported by several research findings. First, it has been found that most arguments presented during group discussions do in fact support the initial views of most group members (Vinkour and Burnstein, 1974). Second, it appears that the greater the number and persuasiveness of the arguments favoring a particular point of view, the greater the shift in its direction as a result of group discussion (Ebbesen and Bowers, 1974). Clear evidence along these lines has recently been provided by Hinsz and Davis (1984). These researchers had individuals or groups of four persons read either eight or twenty-four arguments supporting either risky or cautious courses of action in connection with choice-dilemma items of the type shown in Table 11.1 (page 395). The persuasiveness of the arguments was also varied, so for some subjects within either the small or large number condition persuasiveness was high, while for others, it was low. In accordance with the persuasive arguments view, polarization was affected by both of these factors. Specifically, it was greater when the number of arguments was large than when it was small, and greater when the arguments presented were highly persuasive than when they were less persuasive. We should add, however, that other results do not support the accuracy of this interpretation. For example, polarization effects seem to occur even with respect to simple perceptual judgments. In such cases, arguments and persuasion should play little part (Baron and Roper, 1976).

Taking all available evidence into account, therefore, a clear choice between these two theories does not seem possible. In fact, such a choice may be unnecessary. Both social comparison *and* the exchange of information among individuals may play a role in the occurrence of group polarization. Moreover, an additional process may enter the picture. When individuals feel they are part of a group — even a temporary and unimportant one — the process of *social categorization* or *social identi-*

fication, which we discussed in Chapter 5, may swing into action. This, in turn, may lead them to perceive the group's position as more extreme than it really is. The result: they experience self-generated pressure to conform to this inaccurate view, with the result that the group itself shifts toward greater extremity (Mackie, 1986). Regardless of the precise basis for group polarization, though, it has important implications. The occurrence of polarization may lead many decision-making groups to shift toward positions that are more and more extreme — and more and more dangerous. In this context, it is interesting to speculate about the potential role of such shifts in disastrous decisions by political or military groups who should, by all accounts, have known better (e.g., the decision by President Lyndon Johnson and his advisers to escalate American involvement in Vietnam or the decision by the Nazi high command to invade the Soviet Union during World War II). Did group polarization play a role in these events? At present, it is difficult to say. But evidence gathered in many separate experiments suggests this possibility is at least worth considering.

Decision making by groups: Some special problems

As we have just pointed out, the tendency of many decision-making groups to drift toward polarization can interfere with their ability to make accurate or effective choices. Unfortunately, this is not the only process that can develop during the course of group activities and produce such effects. Several others, too, can lead decision-making groups into disastrous courses of action. We will consider two of these here: **groupthink** and the inability of group members to *pool their unshared information.*

Groupthink: Why groups sometimes lose contact with reality.   Common sense seems to suggest that a high level of cohesiveness among group members is a good thing. After all, if members like one another very much, and feel deeply committed to the group, its performance should be enhanced, right? In fact, this reasoning can be wrong — dead wrong. When a high level of cohesiveness is coupled with several other conditions (e.g., sealing-off of the group from outside information or influences; the presence of a dynamic, influential leader), an unsettling process known as **groupthink** may be set in operation (Janis, 1982). *Groupthink* is characterized by several trends, all of which severely hamper the decision-making capacity of a group. For example, when groupthink develops, group members begin to see themselves as invulnerable — they believe that they simply *can't* make mistakes! Second, they engage in collective rationalization, discrediting or ignoring any information counter to the group's current thinking. Third, pressure toward conformity becomes intense, so that few, if any members, are willing to challenge the group's position, or dissent from it in any way.

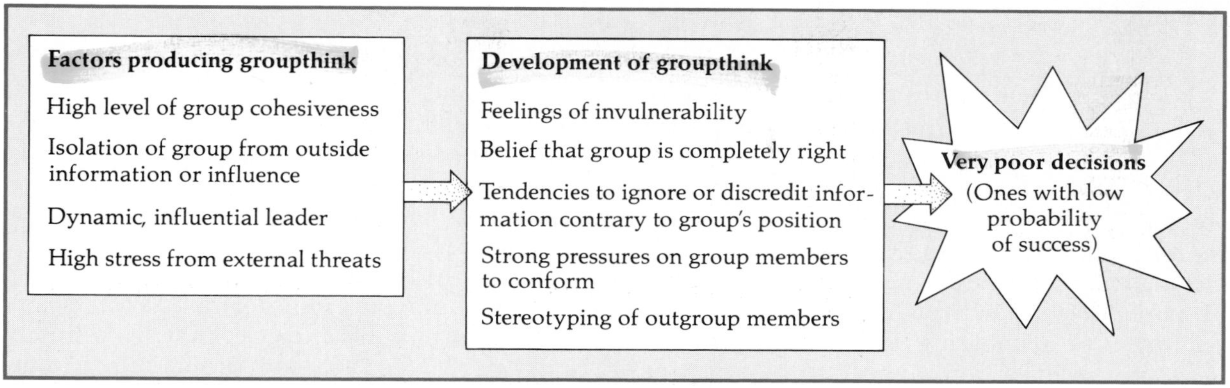

Factors producing groupthink	Development of groupthink	Very poor decisions

Factors producing groupthink

High level of group cohesiveness

Isolation of group from outside information or influence

Dynamic, influential leader

High stress from external threats

Development of groupthink

Feelings of invulnerability

Belief that group is completely right

Tendencies to ignore or discredit information contrary to group's position

Strong pressures on group members to conform

Stereotyping of outgroup members

Very poor decisions
(Ones with low probability of success)

FIGURE 11.10. When groups are highly cohesive, are isolated from outside influence, and have a dynamic, persuasive leader, *groupthink* may develop. That is, group members may come to feel they are invulnerable and are completely right in their views. This may lead them to place greater pressure on members to conform, and can result in very poor decisions.

Groupthink: An overview

The result of these and related tendencies is that the groups experiencing them (and groupthink) often head straight over the edge: they adopt extremely poor decisions, and then convince themselves, more and more firmly, that these are correct ones. (Please refer to Figure 11.10 for a summary of the causes, nature, and effects of groupthink.)

Unfortunately, groupthink does not seem to be a rare or unusual event. On the contrary, since many important decision-making groups enjoy high cohesiveness, face stressful situations in which rapid decisions are necessary, and are directed by strong, dynamic leaders, it is a real danger in many contexts. Along with tendencies toward polarization, it helps explain why seemingly intelligent, rational groups of people sometimes reach decisions that are catastrophic in every respect. (Can groupthink be prevented? Please see the **Applied Side** insert on page 400 for some encouraging information on this issue.)

The inability of groups to exchange unshared information: Biased sampling in group discussion. One of the major advantages often attributed to decision-making groups is their ability to pool the resources of their individual members. It is assumed that since each member brings a unique pattern of skills and knowledge to the task at hand, the group's final decision will benefit from the pooling of these intellectual resources. While this is a comforting belief, it has recently been called into serious question by Stasser and Titus (1985).

These researchers suggest that when groups meet to consider various problems and reach important decisions, their discussions are often biased in ways that tend to reduce the potential benefits described above. First, such groups tend to discuss *shared* rather than *unshared* information. This is because shared information is more likely to be introduced by one or several members than unshared information. Second, their discussion is biased in favor of the current preferences of group members. Since each is likely to present information that supports his or her views, initial preferences are intensified, not corrected, by the give-

ON THE APPLIED SIDE

Overcoming Groupthink: The Nominal Group Technique

Given the dangers inherent in groupthink, it seems important to develop techniques for countering this process. Have any procedures for accomplishing this goal been uncovered? Fortunately, the answer is "yes." Several procedures for combating the development of groupthink exist, and appear to be effective (e.g., Ulshak, Nathanson, and Gillan, 1981). Perhaps the most practical of these is the **nominal group technique** (NGT).

In NGT, small groups of individuals meet to propose and discuss various solutions to current problems. Although they meet in a face-to-face manner, they do *not* operate in a manner typical of decision-making groups. Specifically, they do not try to attain a group consensus. Rather, they simply express their individual preferences for each proposed solution. The process is as follows.

First, the persons present identify the problem to be considered. Next, each member considers the problem alone, and writes down his or her ideas about its solution. In a third step, each individual presents his or her ideas to the group; these are entered by the group's leader on a large chart visible to all. After all ideas have been presented, the group discusses each one in turn, in order both to clarify its content and to evaluate its potential for success. Finally, each individual privately rank-orders the various solutions. The one that receives the highest rank (when all members' scores are combined) is then adopted as the group's decision. (Refer to Figure 11.11 for a summary of these procedures.)

The nominal group technique offers several important advantages. First, it is highly efficient. Indeed, it can often help groups reach solutions to highly complex problems in a matter of only a few hours. Second, it discourages the strong tendencies to conform that play a key role in the development of groupthink. Third, it encourages members to consider *all* potential solutions — not just the ones initially favored by most members or by the group's leader. Finally, by permitting different members to voice contrasting opinions, it helps prevent the illusions of unanimity and invulnerability from which decision-making groups often suffer.

That NGT can be effective in countering groupthink is supported by the findings of several experiments. For example, in one such study, Van de Ven and Delbecq (1974) had seven-member groups work on the problem of clearly defining the requirements of a specific job (dormitory counselor). Subjects carried out this task either in accordance with the nominal group technique, or under ordinary group con-

and-take of group discussion. The final outcome, then, is *not* a sharing of information among group members, so that all obtain a more complete and accurate picture of the situation than was true initially. Rather, it is an intensification of initial preferences or views.

Stasser and Titus (1985) have recently obtained direct support for these disturbing processes in a well-conducted study. In this experiment, male and female students met in four-person groups to decide which of three imaginary candidates for student body president was best. Subjects received short profiles of each candidate prior to their discussion. In one condition (*shared information*), all group members received identical

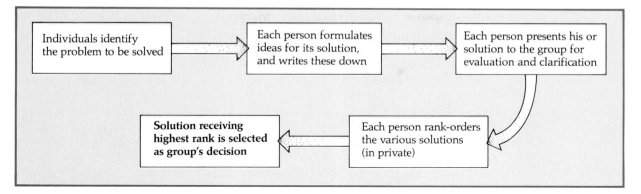

FIGURE 11.11. The *nominal group technique*, summarized here, appears to be an effective means for combating the development of groupthink.

The nominal group technique: One means for avoiding groupthink

ditions. Results indicated that they made better judgments and were more satisfied with their work when using NGT than when simply interacting in the usual group manner. This is not to imply, of course, that NGT is a perfect means for combating groupthink. It is not applicable to some situations (e.g., ones in which groups must make decisions concerning extremely complex issues), and it may be difficult to implement in cases where groups have a long history of prior interaction and a well established leader who is reluctant to surrender any portion of her or his authority. In many cases, though, NGT does seem to be a useful tactic — one whose potential benefits should not be overlooked.

information about each candidate. In two others, each member received only partial information about the candidates. Thus, some of the information each person had was shared, and some was unshared. In one of these groups (*unshared/consensus*), positive information about Candidate A (e.g., he held popular positions on important local issues) and negative information about Candidate B (e.g., this person held unpopular positions on local issues) was unshared in such a way as to bias the group in favor of Candidate B. Each subject received only one-fourth of the positive information about A but all of the negative information about him. In contrast, each received all of the positive information about B, but only one-fourth of the negative information about him. In a third condition (*unshared/conflict*), two members of each group received information biased in favor of Candidate B, and two received information biased in favor of Candidate C. It is important to note that in fact, the total pattern of information provided favored Candidate A. Thus, if group members actually shared the information at their disposal (pooled their resources), they should come to prefer this individual as a result of group discussion. If the types of bias outlined above operate, however, this would not be the case. Instead, groups would tend to make their decisions on the basis of biased, unshared information, and prefer Candidates B and C.

As you can see from Figure 11.12, results offered strong support for the later prediction. Following group discussion, subjects in the shared-information condition did come to prefer Candidate A more strongly. However, those in the unshared/consensus-condition actually showed increased support for Candidate B (who possessed fewer positive characteristics than Candidate A). And subjects in the unshared/conflict group

FIGURE 11.12. When group members shared all relevant information about various candidates for student body president, group discussion enhanced their initial preference for the most qualified person (Candidate A). When each person possessed only part of this information and it was distributed in a way that favored Candidates B or C, however, group discussion did *not* correct these errors. Instead, it enhanced preferences for these less qualified persons. These findings suggest that groups do not engage in an unbiased pooling of unshared information held by their individual members. (Source: Based on data from Stasser and Titus, 1985.)

Pooling of unshared information in groups

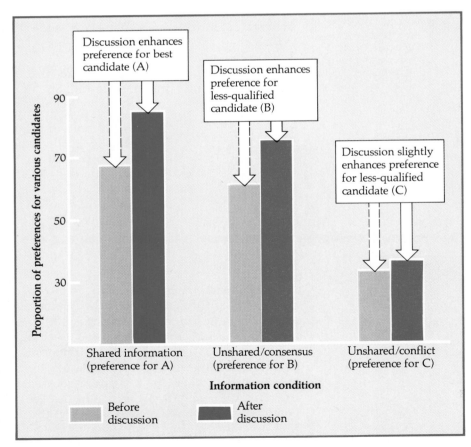

more or less stuck to their initial preferences for both Candidates B and C.

As Stasser and Titus note, these findings cast doubt upon the ability of groups to profit from an unbiased exchange of information among their members. On the contrary, when persons participating in a group discussion do not possess the same information, they appear to concentrate on the "facts" they *do* have in common, while paying scant attention to other, equally important knowledge they do not share. As a result, group discussion may fail to fill the gaps in members' grasp of the entire situation; indeed, it may actually tend to perpetuate such errors. An important task for all decision-making groups, therefore, is that of protecting against such outcomes.

LEADERSHIP: *Influence within Groups*

At different times during your life, you have belonged to many groups. Think back over some of these now. For each, can you recall one member who was more influential than the others? In all likelihood you can, for almost every group contains one person who wields more power than all the rest. Such individuals are usually labeled **leaders;** the process through which they exert influence over others and guide group activities is known as **leadership.**

As you probably already realize, the impact of leaders upon the groups they direct can be profound. Such persons often strongly affect the attitudes, behavior, and even perceptions of their followers. Indeed, in extreme cases they may induce subordinates to accept views that make little sense to others, or to engage in actions they would otherwise never perform (refer to Figure 11.13). Because of such effects, our discussion of

FIGURE 11.13. Leaders often exert powerful effects upon their followers. A dramatic illustration of this fact was provided several years ago by the mass suicide of members of one religious cult when ordered to do so by their leader.

Leaders: Often, their impact upon followers is profound

groups and their impact upon individuals would be incomplete without attention to this topic. In this final section, therefore, we turn to the nature and impact of leadership. In particular, we will consider two important questions: (1) who becomes a leader — why do some persons but not others rise to positions of power and authority? and (2) what factors determine a leader's success once he or she has assumed this role?

Are leaders born or made? The role of traits, situations, and followers

Are some persons born to lead? Common sense seems to suggest that this is so. Great leaders of the past such as Queen Elizabeth I, Alexander the Great, and George Washington do seem to differ from most persons in several ways. And even leaders lacking such worldwide fame seem different from their followers in certain respects. Top executives, many politicians, and sports stars often seem to possess a special "aura" that sets them apart from other persons. On the basis of such observations, early researchers interested in leadership formulated a view known as the **great person theory.** According to this approach, great leaders possess key traits that distinguish them from most other persons. Further, these traits remain stable across time and across groups, so that all great leaders share the same characteristics, regardless of where and when they live.

These are intriguing suggestions, and ones that seem to fit well with our own experience. However, they have *not* been strongly confirmed. Decades of active research failed to yield a short, agreed-upon list of key traits shared by all leaders (Geier, 1969). A few consistent findings emerged (e.g., leaders tend to be slightly taller and brighter than their followers), but these were hardly dramatic in scope. Indeed, so disappointing were overall results that most researchers came to the following conclusion: leaders simply do not differ from followers in clear and consistent ways.

While this conclusion is still accepted today, we should note a recent reawakening of interest in the possibility that leaders and followers *do* differ in some respects. Several types of evidence have contributed to this trend. First, research suggests that persons possessing certain patterns of motives (e.g., a high need for power plus a high degree of self-control) are more successful as managers (leaders in business settings) than persons not possessing this pattern (e.g., McClelland and Boyatzis, 1982). Second, political leaders do appear to differ from nonleaders in several respects (e.g., they are higher in self-confidence and dominance; Costantini and Craik, 1980). Third, it appears that individuals possessing certain traits — especially the ability to adapt to changing conditions — do rise to leadership in a wide range of different settings (Kenney and Zaccaro, 1984). For example, in several recent studies (Fleischer and Chertkoff, 1986; Nyquist and Spence, 1986), individuals high in dominance were chosen to be the leaders of small groups by other members much more frequently than persons low in dominance (over 70 percent of the time in groups where all participants were of the same sex).

Together, such findings suggest that certain traits *can* play a role in determining who becomes a leader, at least in some contexts, and to some extent. But they certainly do *not* suggest that all leaders share key traits, or that possession of these is required for leadership at all times and in all places. Thus, the conclusion noted above, that leaders do not differ from followers in clear and easily recognized ways, remains valid.

At this point, you may be a bit puzzled. If leadership is not largely a function of the traits of leaders, what, precisely does it involve? One answer is provided by the **situational approach** to leadership. Central to this view (which replaced the great person theory several decades ago) is recognition of the fact that different situations often call for different types of leaders. For example, a football team may require a leader who is aggressive, competitive, and tough — as well as skilled in the game. In contrast, a negotiating team attempting to conclude a delicate international agreement may need a leader who is calm, persuasive, and charming. Thus, according to the situational approach, full understanding of who becomes a leader involves careful attention *both* to the traits of potential leaders and to situational constraints (e.g., the tasks being performed, resources available, etc.; Bass, 1981). Selection of a leader, then, should involve a process of *matching* — one in which an individual whose particular mix of skills and characteristics is closely aligned with the requirements of the current situation.

Because it took account of many factors largely ignored by the great person theory, the situational approach represented an important advance over this earlier view. However, it, too, suffered from a major drawback: it devoted little or no attention to the role and impact of *followers.* Largely because of this weakness, it has recently been replaced by a third, and even more sophisticated, perspective: the **transactional approach.**

This view — which is currently accepted, in one form or another, by most social psychologists — recognizes an essential fact: while leaders certainly exert influence upon their followers, these persons, in turn, frequently exert reciprocal influence upon leaders (Hollander, 1978). Indeed, leaders are often strongly affected by their followers' attitudes, preferences, perceptions, and values. This makes eminent good sense; after all, leaders who pay little attention to the wishes of the persons they lead may soon find themselves without a following. Thus, if they are wise, they are keenly interested in feedback from other group members, and take this into account in planning future actions (refer to Figure 11.14 on page 406).

Support for the accuracy of the transactional view has been obtained in several recent experiments (e.g., Price and Garland, 1981; Sims and Manz, 1984). Such studies indicate that leaders do indeed respond to the wishes and perceptions of their followers. Indeed, they may even shift leadership style to take account of follower characteristics (Scandura and Graen, 1984).

FIGURE 11.14. In order to be effective, leaders must pay careful attention to the views and preferences of their followers. Thus, they often seek feedback from these persons. (Source: Drawing by Chas. Addams; ©1982 The New Yorker Magazine, Inc.)

Feedback from followers: A key ingredient in leader effectiveness

"Would you say Attila is doing an excellent job, a good job, a fair job, or a poor job?"

To conclude: because it emphasizes the social nature of leadership and directs attention to the complex interaction among leaders, situations, and followers, the transactional approach provides a more complex answer to the question, "Who becomes a leader?" than earlier views. Such complexity is well justified, however, for it also offers a more complete account of the leadership process. And obtaining such understanding, after all, is what science (and the field of social psychology) is all about.

Leader effectiveness: A contingency approach

All leaders are definitely *not* equal. Some are effective and contribute to high levels of performance and morale on the part of their followers, while others are much less successful in these respects. Why is this the case? What factors determine leaders' degree of success in directing their groups? This has been a central issue in much research concerned with leadership. Indeed, most of the major theories dealing with this process address the issue of leader effectiveness in one manner or another (e.g., House and Baetz, 1979; Vroom and Yetton, 1973). As an example of this work, we will consider an important theory proposed by Fiedler (e.g., Fiedler, 1978; Fiedler and Garcia, 1987).

Fiedler labels his model the **contingency theory,** and this term is certainly appropriate, for its central assumption is this: a leader's contribution to successful performance by his or her group is determined both by the leader's traits and by various features of the situation in which the group operates. To fully understand leader effectiveness, both types of factors must be considered.

With respect to characteristics possessed by leaders, Fiedler identifies *esteem for least preferred co-worker* (LPC, for short) as most important. This refers to a leader's tendency to evaluate the person with whom she or he finds it most difficult to work either favorably or unfavorably. Leaders who perceive this person in negative terms (low LPC leaders) seem primarily concerned with attaining successful task performance. In contrast, those who perceive their least preferred coworker in a positive light *(high LPC leaders)* seem mainly concerned with establishing good relations with their subordinates. Which of these types of leaders is more effective? Fiedler's answer is: it depends. And what it depends upon is several situational factors.

Specifically, Fiedler suggests that whether low LPC or high LPC leaders are more effective depends on the degree to which the situation is favorable to the leader, or provides this person with *control* over other group members. This, in turn, is determined largely by three factors: (1) the nature of the leader's *relations with group members* (the extent to which she enjoys their support and loyalty), (2) the degree of *structure* in the task being performed (the extent to which task goals and roles are clearly defined), and (3) the leader's *position power* (his or her ability to enforce compliance by subordinates). Combining these three factors, the leader's situational control can range from very high (positive relations with group members, a highly structured task, high position power) to very low (negative relations, an unstructured task, low position power).

Now, to return to the central question: when are different types of leaders most effective? Fiedler proposes that low LPC leaders (ones who are task-oriented) are superior to high LPC leaders (ones who are people-oriented) when situational control is either low or high. In contrast, high LPC leaders have an edge when situational control falls within the moderate range (refer to Figure 11.15, page 408). The reasoning behind these predictions is as follows.

Under conditions of *low* situational control, groups need considerable guidance and direction to accomplish their tasks. Since low LPC leaders are more likely to provide such structure than high LPC leaders, they will usually be superior in such cases. Similarly, low LPC leaders also have an edge in situations that offer the leader a *high* degree of situational control. Here, low LPC leaders realize that conditions are good, and often adopt a relaxed "hands-off" style—one that is appreciated by their followers. In contrast, high LPC leaders, feeling that they already enjoy good relations with their subordinates, may shift their attention to task performance. Their efforts at providing guidance may

FIGURE 11.15. According to a theory proposed by Fielder, low LPC leaders (ones who are primarily task-oriented) are more effective than high LPC leaders (ones who are primarily people-oriented) under very favorable and very unfavorable conditions (high or low situational control). In contrast, the opposite is true under moderately favorable or unfavorable conditions (moderate situational control).

The contingency model of leader effectiveness

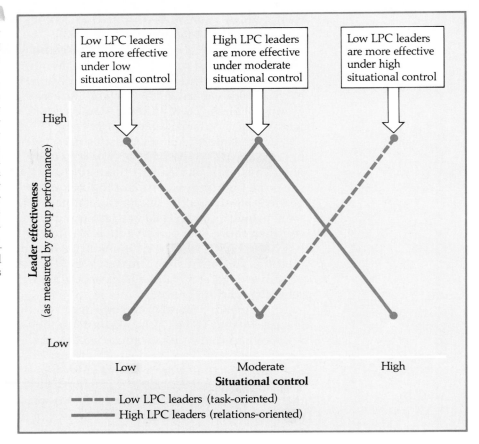

then be perceived as needless meddling by their followers, and can, in fact, interfere with group performance. Turning to situations offering the leader *moderate* control, conditions are mixed, and attention to good interpersonal relations is often needed. High LPC leaders, with their interest in people, often have an important advantage in such cases. In contrast, low LPC leaders, who continue to focus on task performance, may adopt an autocratic, directive style, and so induce negative reactions among subordinates.

To repeat: Fiedler's theory predicts that low LPC (task-oriented) leaders will be more effective than high LPC (relations-oriented) leaders under conditions of either low or high situational control. In contrast, high LPC leaders will have the edge under conditions where such control is moderate.

Contingency theory: Its current status.   Because it directs attention to characteristics of leaders, situational factors, and even the reactions of subordinates, Fiedler's theory is fully consistent with the modern, transactional approach described above. Where any scientific theory is con-

does intellectw ability

cerned, though, the ultimate question must be: how does it fare when put to actual test? For the contingency theory, the answer appears to be "moderately well." One review of more than 170 studies undertaken to test various aspects of Fiedler's framework indicates that most obtained positive results (Strube and Garcia, 1981). For example, consider a recent study by Chemers and his colleagues (1985). These investigators reasoned that leaders who were "out of match" with the conditions in their groups (i.e., low LPC leaders who enjoyed moderate control, or high LPC leaders who had high or low degrees of control) would experience greater job-related stress than leaders whose personal style matched these conditions (i.e., low LPC leaders with high or low control, high LPC leaders with moderate control). To test this hypothesis, they had administrators at a large university complete questionnaires designed to measure their degree of situational control, their standing in terms of LPC, and the level of job stress they experienced. As you can see from Figure 11.16, results offered support for the initial predictions. Leaders whose personal style did not match the level of situational control they enjoyed (according to Fiedler's theory) did report greater stress than ones whose personal style matched this factor.

At this point, we should note that not all findings have been consistent with the theory. In fact, a recent review suggests that while labora-

FIGURE 11.16. When leaders' style did not match their level of situational control, they experienced higher levels of stress than when such matching existed. These findings provide support for Fiedler's contingency theory of leader effectiveness. (Source: Based on data from Chemers et al., 1985.)

The match between leader style and situational control: An important determinant of work-related stress

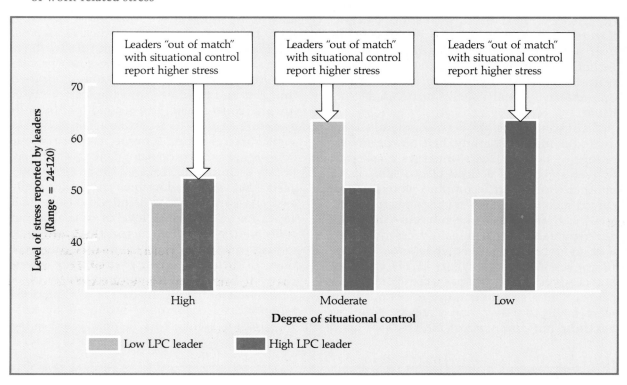

FOCUS ON RESEARCH:
Classic Contributions

Deindividuation: Groups as Releasers of Impulsive Behavior

Have you ever attended a football or baseball game at which members of the crowd shouted obscenities or threw things at referees? Have you ever gone to a party where, after things "warmed up," many persons present began acting in unusual ways (e.g., saying ridiculous things, throwing food at one another)? If so, you are already acquainted with another potential effect of groups on individuals: their ability to weaken restraints against wild, impulsive actions.

This process, known as **deindividuation,** was first studied systematically by Zimbardo (1970). He proposed that deindividuation stems from certain social conditions (e.g., feelings of anonymity, diffusion of responsibility) and that as it develops, the persons involved experience important internal shifts, such as lowered self-awareness and reduced concern over others' reactions to their behavior. Together, such effects then weaken individuals' restraints against engaging in various forms of impulsive — and usually prohibited — behavior.

To study this process, Zimbardo conducted an ingenious study. In this experiment, groups of four college women were asked to deliver apparently painful electric shocks to another woman (an accomplice who never received such treatment). In one condition many steps were taken to make subjects feel totally anonymous. Each participant dressed in a lab coat and face hood immediately upon arriving for the session (refer to Figure 11.17), the room was dimly lit, and no names were ever used. In contrast, in a second condition, several steps were taken to assure that subjects would be anything *but* anonymous. No coats or hood

were used, the laboratory was brightly lit, and all participants wore large name tags. In accordance with his theory, Zimbardo reasoned that deindividuation would be more likely to develop under conditions of anonymity and that as a result, subjects would feel less restrained against shocking the innocent victim in the first condition just described. Results provided clear support for this prediction: participants did use shocks of much longer duration when they felt anonymous than when they felt they were readily identifiable.

While Zimbardo's research offered results consistent with his theory of deindividuation, we should note that subsequent studies by other investigators (Diener, 1980; Prentice-Dunn and Rogers, 1982, 1983; Prentice-Dunn and Spivey, 1986) paint a somewhat different picture of this process. This research suggests that the key to understanding deindividuation may lie in shifts in *self-awareness.* Actually, there are two distinct types of such awareness, and these seem to play different roles with respect to deindividuation. The first, *private self-awareness*, refers to attention to our own thoughts and feelings — our tendency to look inward, so to speak. The second, *public self-awareness*, refers to attention to ourselves as social objects — for example, concern about how we appear to others. Evidence gathered by Prentice-Dunn and Rogers (1982, 1983) suggests that only reductions in private self-awareness are related to deindividuation. Such shifts, induced by a high level of arousal, group cohesiveness, and other factors that cause individuals to focus their attention outward rather than on themselves, contribute to the occurrence of impulsive behavior by generating a deindividuated state. In contrast, reductions in public self-awareness, produced by anonymity or related factors, do not operate in the

FIGURE 11.17. Dressed in this manner, subjects in a famous study conducted by Zimbardo (1970) were totally anonymous. Zimbardo suggested this might enhance the occurrence of deindividuation, and so increase participants' later willingness to harm an innocent victim. These predictions were confirmed. (Source: From Zimbardo, 1970, p. 267. Reprinted by permission.)

Deindividuation: Conditions that enhance its occurrence

same manner. They, too, can generate unrestrained, impulsive behavior. However, they do so by causing individuals to realize that they will not be held accountable for their actions; deindividuation plays no role in such instances.

In sum, deindividuation appears to be largely a matter of private self-awareness.

Conditions that prevent individuals from focusing their attention on their own attitudes, values, and feelings can induce an internal state that may cause them to behave in ways they would never consider when alone. Clearly, this is yet another way in which groups exert powerful effects upon their members.

tory studies have tended to support Fiedler's view, field investigations (ones carried out with existing groups operating in a wide range of contexts) have not been as favorable in this respect (Peters, Hartke, and Pohlmann, 1985). Indeed, such investigations have sometimes yielded results contrary to what contingency theory would predict.

Taking all existing evidence into account, therefore, it appears that contingency theory can benefit from further development and refinement. At the same time, though, there is little doubt that it has added much to our understanding of leadership and leader effectiveness. In these respects, it certainly represents a major contribution, well worth considering.

Do leader abilities count? Cognitive resource theory.   Before concluding our discussion of leadership, we will consider one additional issue that has received growing attention in recent years: do the intelligence and other cognitive abilities of leaders affect their success in this role? At first glance, the answer seems obvious. After all, how could the intelligence of leaders *fail* to matter in this regard? Surprisingly, though, research on this relationship has yielded relatively weak results (e.g., Bass, 1981). Leader intelligence *is* related to various measures of leader effectiveness, but only weakly (correlations in the range of .20 to .30). How can this puzzling finding be explained? A theory devised by Fiedler and Garcia (1987) offers one potential answer.

According to this view, known as **cognitive resource theory,** whether leaders' intellectual abilities affect the success of their groups depends on several factors. First, this relationship depends on the extent to which leaders are directive — give concrete instructions and orders to their followers. When leaders are highly directive, their intellectual abilities will be important, for the higher these are, the better the plans, decisions, and strategies they communicate to their followers. When leaders are not directive, however, their intelligence will matter to a much lesser degree. After all, even the most brilliant plans and decisions can have little impact if they are not communicated to subordinates! Second, the link between leader intellectual abilities and group performance is strongly mediated by stress. When this factor is low, leaders will focus primarily on task-related issues, and their intellectual abilities will be closely linked to group performance. When, instead, stress within a group is high, leaders' attention may be diverted to matters not directly linked to task performance. Under such conditions, their intelligence and other intellectual abilities will have little chance to influence group performance. In such cases, leaders' experience with the tasks at hand, and perhaps their social skills, will be more important in this regard.

Considerable evidence gathered by Fiedler and his colleagues offers support for the accuracy of these suggestions (Fiedler and Garcia, 1987). For example, in one study, Army infantry squad leaders (Fiedler and Leister, 1977) reported on the level of stress they experienced with their supervisors. In addition, a measure of their intelligence (from Army records) and ratings of their performance (provided by their superiors) were also obtained. When these factors were correlated, a clear pattern of findings emerged. Under conditions of low stress, the squad leaders' intelligence was significantly correlated with their performance. Under conditions of high stress, however, this relationship totally vanished (refer to Table 11.2).

TABLE 11.2 Under conditions of low stress, squad leaders' intelligence was significantly related to ratings of their performance by their supervisors. However, as stress increased, the strength of this relationship dropped, so that there was no apparent link between leader intelligence and performance when stress was high. (Source: Based on data from Fiedler and Leister, 1977.)

Leader intelligence and leader performance: The mediating role of stress

Correlation between Leader Intelligence and Leader Performance under Three Levels of Stress

Low	Moderate	High
.43	.27	−.01

In sum, it appears that leaders' intellectual abilities do matter — do affect the performance of the groups they head — but only under certain conditions. Thus, as is true in many other spheres of life, high intelligence, in and of itself, is no guarantee of success where leadership is concerned. Other factors will often determine when, and to what extent, it contributes to effectiveness in this important role. (For discussion of another process through which groups sometimes affect their members, please see the **Focus** insert on page 410.)

SUMMARY

A **group** consists of individuals who share common goals, are somehow interdependent, have a stable relationship, and recognize the group's existence. Individuals are often strongly affected by group membership. Such effects often take place through the influence of *roles*, *norms*, and *cohesiveness.*

In **social facilitation,** the presence of others (or concern over "looking good" in front of them) affects individuals' performance on various tasks. Groups sometimes outperform individuals and sometimes fail to equal individual performance. The type of task being performed *(additive, conjunctive,* or *disjunctive)* is crucial in determining which pattern emerges.

Groups make many key decisions. Often, these can be predicted by *social decision schemes* — simple rules relating the initial distribution of members' views to the final outcome. The manner in which groups move toward agreement can be described by *social transition schemes,* which indicate the likelihood that group members will shift from one pattern of views to another. As a result of their deliberations, groups often demonstrate **group polarization.** That is, they shift toward more and more extreme positions. Decision-making groups are also subject to **groupthink** — a dangerous process in which group members perceive themselves as invulnerable, and refuse to consider information contrary to their current views. An additional problem faced by decision-making groups is their apparent inability to pool unshared information.

Leaders are those members of a group who exert the most influence. At one time it was assumed that individuals rise to positions of leadership because they possess special traits (the *great person theory*). Now it is realized that leadership stems from a complex interplay between leader characteristics, situational requirements, and follower preferences and perceptions (the *transactional view*). Many factors play a role in leader effectiveness. According to the *contingency theory* proposed by Fiedler, the most important of these involve a leader's personal style (whether mainly task or relationship-oriented) and the degree of situational control enjoyed by the leader.

GLOSSARY

additive tasks
Tasks for which group productivity represents the sum of individual member efforts.

cohesiveness
All the forces (both positive and negative) that cause individuals to maintain their membership in specific groups. These include attraction to other group members and a close match between individuals' needs and the goals and activities of the group.

conjunctive tasks
Tasks for which group productivity is determined by the effort or ability of the weakest member.

contingency theory of leader effectiveness
A theory suggesting that leader effectiveness is determined both by characteristics of leaders and by several situational factors.

decision making
The process through which groups identify problems and attain solutions to them.

deindividuation
A psychological state characterized by reduced self-awareness and major shifts in perception. It is encouraged by certain external conditions (e.g., anonymity) and enhances the performance of wild, impulsive forms of behavior.

disjunctive tasks
Tasks for which group performance is determined by the most competent or skilled member.

distraction-conflict theory of social facilitation
An explanation for the occurrence of social facilitation effects. According to this view, the presence of others induces conflict between the tendencies to pay attention to these persons and to the task in hand. Such conflict increases arousal and produces social facilitation.

drive theory of social facilitation
A theory suggesting that the mere presence of others is arousing and increases the tendency to perform dominant responses.

evaluation apprehension
Concern over being evaluated by others. Such concern may increase arousal and may play an important role in social facilitation.

great person theory of leadership
A theory suggesting that all great leaders share key traits that equip them for positions of power and authority.

group influence
The impact of groups upon their members.

group polarization
The tendency of group members to shift toward more extreme positions than those they held initially, as a function of group discussion.

groups
Two or more persons who interact with one another, share common goals, are

interdependent, and recognize the existence of these relationships between them.

groupthink
The tendency of members of highly cohesive groups led by dynamic leaders to adhere to shared views so strongly that they totally ignore external information inconsistent with these views.

leaders
Those individuals in groups who exert the greatest influence on others.

leadership
The process through which leaders exert their impact upon other members.

nominal group technique
A technique for combating tendencies toward groupthink.

norms
Rules within a group indicating how its members should behave in various situations.

risky shift
The tendency for individuals to recommend riskier courses of action following group discussion than was true prior to such interaction.

roles
Rules or understandings about the tasks persons occupying certain positions within a group are expected to perform.

situational approach to leadership
The view that those members of a group most likely to become leaders are those who can best help it to reach its major goals.

social decision schemes
Rules relating the initial distribution of member views to final group decisions.

social facilitation
Effects upon performance resulting from the presence of others.

social loafing
The tendency of individuals performing a task to exert less effort on it when they work together with others than when they work alone.

social transition schemes
Models describing the process through which groups move through different patterns of member views until they reach agreement or some decision.

transactional approach to leadership
An approach suggesting that leadership involves a complex social relationship between leaders and followers in which each exerts influence upon the other.

FOR MORE INFORMATION

Diener, E. (1980). Deindividuation: The absence of self-awareness and self-regulation in group members. In P. B. Paulus (ed.), *The psychology of group influence*. Hillsdale, N.J.: Erlbaum.

> An insightful discussion of the nature of deindividuation by a researcher who has studied this topic for more than a decade.

Fiedler, F. E., and Garcia, J. E. (1987). *Leadership: Cognitive resources and performance.* New York: Wiley.

> This book presents a thoughtful, well written, and comprehensive overview of what we currently know about the complex process of leadership. Several topics that have only recently been studied in a systematic manner (e.g., the relationship between leaders' intelligence and group performance) are considered in detail. All in all, a valuable source to consult if you'd like to know more about this important group process.

Forsyth, D. R. (1983). *An introduction to group dynamics.* Monterey, Cal.: Brooks/Cole.

> This excellent text examines many aspects of group functioning. The discussions of deindividuation, group performance, and conformity are especially interesting.

Pruitt, D. G., and Rubin, J. Z. (1986). *Social conflict.* San Francisco: Random House.

> A succinct and well written overview of the psychological factors and processes that play a role in social conflict. The discussions of escalating or entrapping conflicts, and techniques for resolving ongoing disputes, are especially insightful.

Wright, G., ed. (1985). *Behavioral decision making.* New York: Plenum.

> A thorough examination of many aspects of decision making by groups. The approach taken is multidisciplinary, with scholars from several different fields (e.g., psychology, management science, sociology, political science) contributing chapters.

CHAPTER 12

THE URBAN ENVIRONMENT AND SOCIAL BEHAVIOR

Adaptation to urban stimulation • Cities aren't all bad • Stimulation and affect in the city

ENVIRONMENTAL STRESS

The hazards of a noisy environment • Temperature and weather as environmental stressors • Temperature and aggression • Air pollution • Effects of negative ions

THE INTERPERSONAL ENVIRONMENT

Personal space • "Space invaders": Intrusions into personal space • Territorial behavior • Territorial dominance • Other effects of territoriality • Territory and architectural design

CROWDING: The Effects of Too Many People and Too Little Space

Early evidence • A social psychological look at crowding • Long-term effects of crowding • Avoiding the effects of crowding

ENVIRONMENTAL INFLUENCES ON SOCIAL BEHAVIOR

The setting is the patio of a suburban house, looking out into a back yard that contains two very small trees and a vegetable garden beside the back fence. Two individuals, husband and wife, are sipping iced tea. The man, Bill, has just come home from work.

PAM: Honey, Arlene called this morning. She and Dave have extra tickets for the Pavorotti recital. I've been wanting to see him perform live for years.

BILL: *(sighing)* Tonight? I'm just too tired even to think about it.

PAM: Oh. You know that Dave promised to stop kidding you about our garden. The first year of back to the soil is hard for anyone — he believes you.

BILL: That's comforting, but no, it really isn't that. My problem is that I spent almost an hour fighting my way out of the city in that damned traffic. Now you want me to turn around and go all the way back.

PAM: Don't be such a grouch. Rush hour is over now. Besides, there wouldn't be a problem if we lived downtown like Arlene and Dave do.

BILL: Oh no. Here we go again! Pam, we are not moving back to the city and that's that. My garden may look like an old age home for wounded vegetables, but it's *my* land, *my* territory. I really love having space to live in. Dave misses that, being in a condo where people can't really call anything their own. That's the real reason he has to make fun of me all the time.

PAM: Come on, Billy Whiskers. That's pretty Freudian for an

accountant. Besides, the vegetables aren't wounded—they're resting in peace. Dave and Arlene can get better stuff in their little neighborhood groceries than we'll ever be able to grow.

BILL: Maybe, but that's not the point. How many times do I have to remind you why we moved to the suburbs in the first place? We were fed up with all the problems of city life.

PAM: Yes, yes. You never knew when someone was going to sneak up on you in a dark alley and force you to listen to Luciano Pavorotti.

BILL: Let's be serious for a minute. Think—I mean really try to remember being surrounded by all that noise. There were crowds, no sunset, no stars. . . .

PAM: You be serious. You haven't gone outside to look at the stars in months.

BILL: Yeah, but I can if I want to, and I like knowing that.

PAM: And what about the excitement? Stars are nice once in a while, but lots of times it's just too quiet around here. For all I know, the vegetables died of boredom. I just miss that feeling of—well, you never know what might happen. I felt so full of life.

BILL: You're still full of something. *(She hits him with a fly swatter.)* Ow! That hurt. Speaking of fighting, that's something we do a lot less of. We were always at each other's throats, and no wonder. That oppressive heat that wouldn't quit, even at night. And you couldn't turn around without a stranger staring you in the face. It really put me on edge.

PAM: Talk about *my* memory. What about the community spirit we had in the city? All that tradition—it was our neighborhood against the world. Ever since we moved here, it's been hard to get a sense of belonging. Even the vegetables are rootless.

BILL: *(groaning)* That's your third vegetable joke. You're getting as bad as Dave. On the other hand, Pam, I must admit that you have a much better sense of humor since we moved out here.

PAM: "Pam," huh? You used to call me "hot stuff."

BILL: Well, everything was hot in the city. But even the suburbs can generate some warmth. *(He intercepts the fly swatter and kisses her gently.)*

PAM: OK, Mr. Wide Open Spaces. I'll tell Arlene we can't make it. Life in the boonies has not completely dulled your finer points.

THIS BRIEF interaction touches on a number of important aspects of the way the physical environment affects our lives. Most of us are aware that our surroundings can make us miserable when either the physical or the interpersonal environment is undesirable in some way. In contrast, our surroundings can be a major source of pleasure when they make life seem exciting and well worth living. In recent years, social psychologists have been strongly involved in determining just how we react to the positive and negative aspects of the environment.

Environmental psychology is the field that deals with the interaction between the physical world and human behavior (Holahan, 1986). Originally, research attention focused on questions about our reactions to the physical presence of other people as a function of how many there are, how far away they are located, who they are. With a growing recognition in the 1960s and 1970s of such problems as a steadily increasing world population, overcrowding, and air pollution and noise in urban settings, the interest in environmental psychology intensified. Quite often, research in this field is conducted as a cooperative venture in which social psychologists, architects, urban planners, and many others play a role (Sommer, 1980). The goal is to understand the way in which the physical and social environment affects behavior and to use this knowledge to bring about environmental improvement.

In this chapter, we discuss four areas of environmental psychology. First, we will examine the way *urban environments* influence social behavior. Then we will look at some specific aspects of the environment, beginning with the physical causes of *environmental stress* such as noise, air pollution, and the weather. In the third section, dealing with the *interpersonal environment,* we describe work on personal space, territory, and reactions to intrusions. In the final section, we discuss *crowding* — the effects of too many people in too little space. Attention will also be given to three special topics: a classic experiment on the *effect of noise,* recent findings about people's long-term reactions to the *technological threat* of the nuclear accident at Three-Mile Island, and the effects of *crowding in prison.*

THE URBAN ENVIRONMENT AND SOCIAL BEHAVIOR

As suggested at the beginning of this chapter, people have conflicting attitudes about cities. Opinion polls indicate that many people have quite negative views of city life, but nevertheless the population of metropolitan areas continues to increase. At the present time, the United States is witnessing a population shift in which people are moving back to the city and away from the suburbs (Logan and Molotch, 1986). How does urban life affect human social behavior? Why does the urban setting sometimes have positive effects and at other times have negative effects? We will try to answer these questions in the following sections.

Adaptation to urban stimulation

In a key sense, cities present an overload of information — sights, sounds, and the presence of large numbers of people (Milgram, 1970). **Stimulus overload** theory proposes that urban dwellers learn to screen out stimuli that are not directly relevant to them in order to cope with the

FIGURE 12.1. Behavior of various kinds is affected by where people live. It is consistently found that those living in small towns are more likely to help a stranger than are residents of large cities.

People in small towns are more helpful than those in large cities

overload. One method of adapting is to develop norms of noninvolvement. One consequence is that urbanites should be less helpful to others in need and that they should be less friendly toward strangers. Fairly strong stereotypes about unhelpful, unfriendly city dwellers and friendly, helpful small-town residents are common, as documented in survey studies (Krupat and Guild, 1980; Schneider and Mockus, 1974; see Figure 12.1.)

A number of experiments have been carried out to test the proposition that under some conditions people living in cities differ in friendliness and helpfulness compared to those living in small communities (Korte, 1980, 1981; Milgram, 1970). A recent large-scale research program by Amato (1983) studied several helping acts in a sample of fifty-five cities and towns in Australia. Some of the helping behaviors that were investigated included (1) picking up fallen envelopes, (2) giving a donation to charity, (3) writing down your favorite color for a student project, (4) correcting inaccurate directions which were overheard, and (5) helping a stranger (actually a confederate) who collapsed on the sidewalk. The results consistently showed that population size was negatively related to four of the helping measures. Only picking up a dropped envelope was unrelated to community size. Amato concluded that helping rates are generally lower in larger urban areas, but that the nature of the helping act may be important. Picking up the fallen envelope may have been different from the other acts because the need for assistance was seen as very low, and because no help was directly requested.

There is also evidence that people in cities are less friendly toward strangers than are people in underpopulated areas. Fewer city dwellers will reciprocate the friendly handshake of a stranger than will those in small towns (Milgram, 1977), and commuters in a downtown terminal are less likely to make eye contact with a stranger than they are in a suburban train station (McCauley, Coleman, and DeFusco, 1977). Results of this sort suggest that city life may bring about a certain style of interpersonal behavior, perhaps in response to stimulus overload.

Cities aren't all bad

Despite the negative aspect of reacting to strangers in a city, there are no differences in the quantity or quality of close social ties between those living in urban and small-town settings (Fischer, 1982; Glenn and Hill, 1977; McCauley and Taylor, 1976). Newcomers to cities usually take longer to form friendships than those who are newcomers to less populated areas (Franck, 1980), but in a few months there are an equal number of social ties in the two locations. In fact, city life may provide more opportunities for informal contact and assistance because a greater number of people are accessible (Verbrugge and Taylor, 1985). In cities, the extent to which people help those they know seems to be as high as or higher than in suburban areas. Imig (1985) found that when families experienced unemployment, money problems, and similar threats, there was more disruption in family relationships among rural than among urban families. One reason for this may be that rural families limit their support networks to a few primary ties, while urban families have many more social outlets that can diffuse stress. Also, urban areas are more likely than suburban and rural ones to have professional social service agencies that take care of people who need help.

Stimulation and affect in the city

The concept of cognitive overload emphasizes the negative effects of stimulation, but many people enjoy environments that are highly stimulating. Indeed, a great many individuals are attracted to city life for its wide range of social and environmental activities. In contrast, it is easy to describe life away from metropolitan areas as boring and unexciting: "Nothing ever happens here." It may be most appropriate to assume that people prefer environments that provide an optimal level of arousal — not too much stimulation and not too little (Fisher, Bell, and Baum, 1984; Geller, 1980; Wohlwill and Kohn, 1973).

Some investigators suggest that the effects of the environment are best considered in terms of how exciting or dull the surroundings are *and* of how pleasant or unpleasant they may be (Mehrabian and Russell, 1974; Russell, Ward, and Pratt, 1981). They propose that complex, arousing, pleasant environments should lead to friendly, affiliative behavior toward strangers. In contrast, arousing, unpleasant places should inhibit friendly behavior. Amato and McInnes (1983) tested this hypothesis in a field study by first classifying twelve diverse city settings in terms of their pleasantness and their arousing qualities. For example, a downtown pedestrian shopping mall was rated pleasant and arousing, while a downtown construction site was unpleasant and arousing. In each of these various settings, individuals who were walking along were given a friendly greeting by a male or a female investigator. The degree to which each subject made eye contact, smiled, nodded, or spoke was noted. When this sort of friendly, affiliative behavior was compared across the four types of environmental settings, the results were as predicted. Arousing positive environments were characterized by more friendly interpersonal behavior than arousing negative environments (see Figure 12.2).

Findings of this sort suggest that even a friendly response to strangers may not be absent just because one lives in an urban environment. Instead, it depends on how pleasant and how stimulating the setting is. Such findings indicate that it may be fruitful to look more carefully at the different components of the environment and how each affects behavior. We will next look at some very specific aspects of the physical environment and the way they can be stressful.

ENVIRONMENTAL STRESS

Stress occurs in any situation in which the individual perceives an external threat. When threat is perceived, and the individual attempts to cope with it and adapt, feelings of fear, anxiety, or anger are generated (Lazarus and Folkman, 1984). There is the feeling of being overwhelmed by events beyond one's control. Some forms of environmental stress involve **cataclysmic phenomena,** such as natural disasters like floods and earth-

FIGURE 12.2.
Friendly, affiliative responses to a friendly stranger are affected by two aspects of urban environments — pleasantness and stimulation. In unpleasant settings, stimulating, physiologically arousing conditions lead to less friendly responses than is true for unarousing conditions. In pleasant settings, the reverse is true — stimulating, physiologically arousing conditions lead to *more* friendly responses than unarousing ones. (Source: Based on data from Amato and McInnes, 1983.)

Friendliness in the city: Environmental pleasantness and stimulating conditions

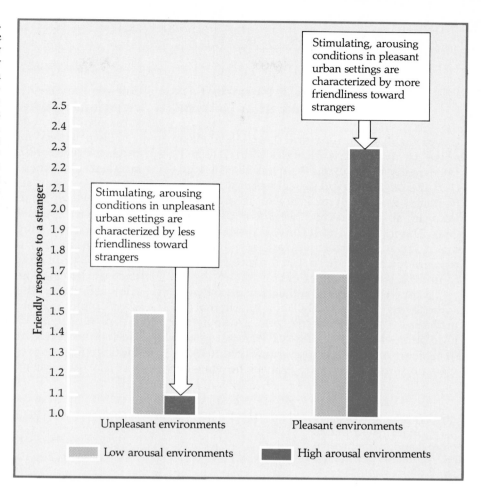

quakes or technological disasters such as the dumping of toxic wastes at Love Canal. Still other stressors may not be very dramatic. They can occur over long periods of time and may be beyond the individual's control (Evans, 1981). Included here are such unpleasant aspects of the environment as polluted air and hot, humid weather. One source of stress, **noise,** was the subject of one of the first important experiments in environmental psychology. This work is described in the **Focus** insert on page 426.

The hazards of a noisy environment

A jet take-off at 200 feet is approximately 120 decibels, and such noise is generally considered intolerable if continued for an extended period of

FOCUS ON RESEARCH:
Classic Contributions

The Effects of Noise on Task Performance: Immediate or Delayed?

It is probably obvious to you that high levels of noise can interfere with one's ability to perform many tasks (Broadbent, 1958). In addition, the psychological properties of noise may be just as important as, if not more important than, its absolute level. Two social psychologists, David Glass and Jerome E. Singer (1972) made some significant discoveries about the psychological factors that can make exposure to noise a stressful experience.

In one experiment, subjects were asked to solve some simple verbal and mathematical problems. While working, one group heard loud bursts of noise regularly for a few seconds of each minute. A second group was exposed to the same amount of noise, but the bursts were delivered for varying lengths of time at unpredictable intervals. A third group worked on the same problems with no background noise.

Surprisingly, all three groups performed at the same level of skill. If the investigators had stopped there, they might well have concluded that noise has no effect on performance. There was, however, a second phase of the experiment. In this part, the noise was shut off for all subjects while they worked on a demanding proofreading task and some difficult puzzles. When Glass and Singer examined the performance of the three groups in this second phase, they found that the group exposed to the unpredictable noise made more proofreading errors (see Figure 12.3) and gave up on the puzzles sooner than subjects exposed to the predictable noise or to no noise at all.

The investigators proposed that exposure

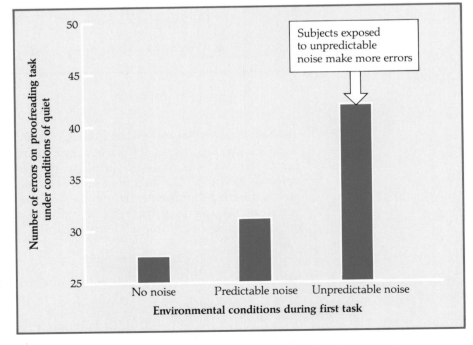

FIGURE 12.3. Subjects working on simple verbal and mathematical problems did equally well under conditions of quiet, predictable noise, or unpredictable noise. Afterward, however, when all subjects worked under quiet conditions, those who had earlier experienced the unpredictable noise made the greatest number of errors on a proofreading task. (Source: Based on data from Glass and Singer, 1972.)

Exposure to unpredictable noise: Some disturbing aftereffects

to unpredictable noise leads to the feeling that one is not in control — that one is helpless to change the situation. These feelings of helplessness then lead to frustration, less effort being expended, and consequently to poorer subsequent performance. To test the helplessness hypothesis, another experimental condition was created. Subjects were again exposed to unpredictable noise, but they were also provided with a button that could be pressed if they wanted the noise to cease. The experimenters asked the subjects *not* to use the button, but they could do so if they wished. Even though none of the subjects used the button, their performance on the tasks in phase two was as good as that of the predictable noise and no noise groups. These results strongly suggest that the perception of control determines whether noise is stressful.

Though these experiments concerned the short-term effects of noise in a laboratory, a follow-up field study explored the long-term effects of exposure to noise (Cohen, Glass, and Singer, 1973). It was hypothesized that chronic exposure to traffic noise may impair the intellectual performance of children. The investigators studied children living in a high-rise apartment complex situated over a busy highway in New York City. Sound readings showed that noise levels were higher on lower floors. The prediction, then, was that children on the lower floors would show intellectual deficits compared to those on higher floors away from the traffic. The children's reading achievement and ability to make auditory speech sounds were measured. As predicted, even after controlling for such variables as social class and air pollution, children who lived on lower floors read less well and had poorer auditory discrimination than those living on higher floors.

This work helped to focus interest on environmental sources of stress and also pointed to novel ways of studying such phenomena in the laboratory and in real-world settings.

time. Nevertheless, rock groups playing in a concert commonly produce the same level of noise for hours. It seems that people enjoy high levels of noise under certain circumstances. Whether enjoyable or not, it must be noted that hearing loss can result when people are repeatedly exposed to high decibel levels (Lebo and Oliphant, 1968).

Health and noise. In addition to hearing loss, exposure to high noise levels at industrial plants or in neighborhoods near airports has been associated with general health problems and elevated blood pressure (Cohen et al., 1981; Cohen and Weinstein, 1981; Peterson et al., 1981), higher rates of admission to mental hospitals (Meecham and Smith, 1977), and increased risk of death from strokes (Dellinger, 1979). These effects are believed to be the result of the arousing and stressful effects of chronic high noise levels. It should be pointed out that these data are correlational in nature. Thus, it is possible that high illness rates are the result of noise or of other factors associated with noise.

The Los Angeles Noise Project (Cohen et al., 1980, 1981, 1986) studied children who lived and went to school close to an airport, where there was a flight overhead approximately once every two and a half minutes. Compared to children attending a quiet school, the noise-impacted children had higher blood pressure levels.

Behavioral effectiveness.   In examining the effects of noise on schoolchildren, Cohen and his colleagues also found that in a school located near an airport, children have lower math achievement scores and perform less well on a puzzle-solving task than those in quiet schools. The longer the children attend a noisy school, the slower they are at solving problems.

This inefficiency in response to noise also affects adults in their everyday lives (Smith and Stansfeld, 1986). Those exposed to high levels of aircraft noise report making more errors of various types than those not exposed to such noise. For example, people in noisy environments are more likely to say that they confuse left and right when giving directions, fail to see items they are seeking in a supermarket, forget appointments, can't remember something that's "on the tip of my tongue," and frequently drop things. It seems that regular exposure to noise is disruptive in many ways.

Social effects.   If noise is arousing and stressful, it should come as no surprise that it influences social behavior. Consistent with this expectation, people are found to be less likely to provide help to a stranger in a noisy environment unless the need is great (Mathews and Canon, 1975; Page, 1977), neighbors have fewer informal social interactions in noisy neighborhoods (Appleyard and Lintell, 1972), and people in noisy conditions are more likely to be aggressive if provoked (Donnerstein and Wilson, 1976; Konecni, 1975). Noise also causes people to focus their attention on a constricted portion of their environment; this may lead to more extreme and premature judgments about other people (Siegel and Steele, 1980).

Temperature and weather as environmental stressors

Mark Twain noted, "Everybody talks about the weather, but nobody does anything about it." More recently, social psychologists have been learning how important weather can be in affecting human behavior.

According to the reinforcement-affect model of attraction (discussed in Chapter 6), we should expect a decrease in liking toward strangers when we experience unpleasant environmental conditions. In fact, several laboratory studies have demonstrated that we like strangers less when we are in a hot, humid room than when the temperature is comfortable (Griffitt, 1970). If, however, the stranger has recently complimented or insulted us, our feelings of like or dislike are virtually unaffected by temperature (Bell and Baron, 1974, 1976). This suggests that high temperatures can influence attraction, but that effect can be "wiped out" by the other person's positive or negative behavior toward us.

Temperature also affects helping behavior. Subjects exposed to very warm conditions in the laboratory are subsequently less likely to help others even when there are comfortable conditions where the help is needed (Page, 1978). In a field study, Cunningham (1979) found that pedestrians were more willing to be interviewed as temperature rose during winter months, but were less likely to be cooperative when the temperature rose during summer months. These findings suggest that helping may be inhibited at either extreme of the temperature continuum. It is also possible that people are simply more helpful on nice days. In the winter that means a relatively warm day, while in the summer that means a relatively cool day.

This simple relationship between temperature and helping is complicated by the fact that high levels of helping can be observed during cold, harsh winters. Possibly this occurs because people accept the norm of helpfulness when conditions are really threatening (Bennet et al., 1983; Fisher, Bell, and Baum, 1984). It is one thing to agree to respond to an interviewer when the thermometer is hovering around zero and quite another to help a motorist stuck in the snow at the same temperature level.

Temperature and aggression

A story in the June 13, 1982, edition of the *New York Times* was titled, "When tempers are short and topics are hot, it's June in Miami." The story concerned a homicide in which one neighbor killed another. The killing was precipitated by a minor argument that turned out to be deadly on an extremely hot day. The general proposition that uncomfortably hot temperatures increase interpersonal aggression has become part of our folk wisdom. Just consider such expressions as "hot under the collar" and "tempers flaring." The U.S. Riot Commission noted the strong possibility that hot temperatures may have contributed to the large number of civil disorders that occurred in the 1960s.

Initial studies of the relationship between heat and aggression appeared to contradict the folk wisdom. Instead, it was found that aggression increases as the temperature rises, but only up to a certain point. Beyond this level, aggression actually drops (Baron, 1972; Baron and Bell, 1975, 1976; Baron and Ransberger, 1978). The explanation was that moderately hot temperatures cause annoyance and anger, while very hot temperatures are so unpleasant that the individual is motivated to escape and seek comfort rather than to aggress.

As interesting as that model may be, the bulk of recent evidence shows a positive relationship between temperature and interpersonal

FIGURE 12.4. There is a relationship between temperature and aggressive crimes such as murder and rape. The daily rate of these crimes is higher on hot days than on cool days. The figures shown here are for Houston, Texas. (Source: Based on data from Anderson and Anderson, 1984.)

As temperature increases, aggressive crimes occur more frequently

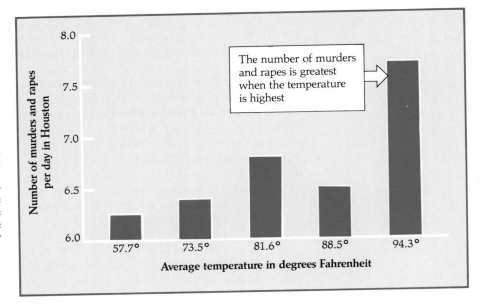

The number of murders and rapes is greatest when the temperature is highest

aggression (Cotton, 1986; DeFronzo, 1984; Harries and Stadler, 1983; Rotton and Frey, 1985b). In one recent study, Anderson and Anderson (1984) examined the relationship between the number of aggressive crimes (murder and rape) and the ambient temperature recorded over a two-year period in two large American cities. The results for one of these locations, Houston, are shown in Figure 12.4. As you can see, acts of criminal violence increased in frequency as the temperature rose. In Phoenix, Arizona, a field experiment revealed that horn honking in response to a car blocking the road at a green light increased as the temperature increased over a series of spring and summer days (Kenrick and MacFarlane, 1986). Of course, it is possible that in areas such as Houston and Phoenix the residents have adapted to fairly hot temperatures. If so, *extremely high* temperatures would be required to bring about an opposite (escape) effect. This remains a question for future research.

Air pollution

Exhaust gases from automobiles and airborne particles from industrial wastes have been identified as sources of numerous health problems. The Clean Air Act has led to some improvement of the situation in the United States, but there is a continuing debate between those who want to clean up the environment and those who think that alarmists are exaggerating the problem and standing in the way of profit and progress (see Figure 12.5).

Though there are data linking pollution to physical and psychiatric health problems (Blot et al., 1975; Briere, Downs, and Spansley, 1983; *Los Angeles Times*, September 20, 1981; Mendlesohn and Orcutt, 1979; Rotton and Frey, 1985b), people tend to adapt to pollution psychologically. That is, over time they tend not to notice polluted air or to identify it as a problem (Evans, Jacobs, and Frager, 1982). For this reason, newcomers to a city such as Los Angeles focus on smog as a major problem, but long-term residents rank smog low on the list of community problems.

One form of personal pollution that has received attention recently is cigarette smoke. Of course, the risks of lung cancer and emphysema are well known to smokers (see Chapter 13). There is an additional problem that is raised for nonsmokers, however. Passive smoking (which occurs when a nonsmoker breathes the air filled with the smoke of others) may also be a serious health risk. For example, nonsmoking wives of heavy smokers have a higher rate of lung cancer than nonsmoking wives of nonsmokers (*Washington Post*, July 28, 1985). Beyond the health risks, nonsmokers tend to dislike cigarette smoke and react negatively when confronted by those who smoke (Bleda and Sandman, 1977), and they will withdraw from such interactions (Bleda and Bleda, 1978) or act in a hostile manner (Zillmann, Baron, and Tamborini, 1981). In a related vein, subjects exposed to foul-smelling chemicals tend to report more negative moods and express less liking for strangers (Rotton et al., 1979).

Rotton and Frey (1985b) examined the relationship between family disturbances reported to the police in a Midwestern city and atmospheric ozone levels over a two-year period. Ozone is a form of smog made up of

FIGURE 12.5. Air pollution has become a matter of widespread concern. There is considerable debate, however, between those who want a pure environment and those who feel that the general problem is overstated and that the costs of environmental purity are too high. Are industrial productivity and economic prosperity incompatible with a clean environment? This cartoon suggests that they are. (Source: Drawing by Joe Mirachi, ©1985 The New Yorker Magazine, Inc.)

Air pollution: Does clean air cost too much?

"Where there's smoke, there's money."

automobile emissions and industrial waste. The results indicated that there were more family disturbances when ozone levels were high than when they were low. The investigators reasoned that pollution elicits a negative emotional state, and this, in turn, lowers the threshold for aggressive behavior. Altogether, it appears that polluted air not only has negative effects on health, but this environmental stressor also has negative emotional and behavioral effects.

Effects of negative ions

As a result of lightning, wind, and other weather conditions, molecules in the air are often split into positively and negatively charged particles called *ions.* It has been proposed that the degree of **atmospheric electricity** (as indicated by the number of positive and negative ions in a particular location) may affect social behavior. There are archival data indicating that suicides, industrial accidents, and some types of crime increase in frequency as the level of ions in the atmosphere increases (Muecher and Ungeheuer, 1961; Sulman et al., 1974). There are also indications that elevated ionization results in negative mood shifts.

To study these effects in the laboratory, experimenters have employed special equipment which can generate high levels of atmospheric electricity. One hypothesis tested in recent research is that negative ions may bring about heightened activation, enhancing whatever tendencies are dominant for an individual in a given situation. Consistent with this proposition, exposure to high levels of negative ions increases the aggressivity of Type A individuals, presumably because they possess relatively strong aggressive tendencies in the first place (Baron, Russell, and Arms, 1985).

Another experiment (Baron, 1987) tested the hypothesis that a high level of negative ions would exert effects on interpersonal attraction. It was predicted that under conditions that ordinarily generate liking for a stranger (a high level of attitude similarity), negative ions should enhance that reaction and hence increase liking. In contrast, under conditions that tend to produce dislike for a stranger (low level of attitude similarity), negative ions should intensify dislike. In an experiment, college students learned that a stranger held attitudes either highly similar or highly dissimilar to their own. They received this information under conditions of either high or low levels of negative ions. As Figure 12.6 indicates, the hypothesis was confirmed. Negative ions enhanced the perceived friendliness of the stranger in the high attraction condition but had a negative effect on this response in the low attraction condition.

These results are interesting because they add still another environmental factor with important implications for social behavior. One reason this is significant is that in recent years several companies have actively promoted negative ion generators to enhance mood and psychological well-being among employees in offices, factories, and other work

FIGURE 12.6.   As you would expect from research on interpersonal attraction, strangers with similar attitudes are perceived as more friendly than strangers with dissimilar attitudes. The presence of negative ions in the surrounding atmosphere enhances these differences — a similar stranger is perceived as even *more* friendly and a dissimilar stranger as even *less* friendly — than under more neutral atmospheric conditions. (Source: Based on data from Baron, 1987.)

Negative ions: Enhancing social perception

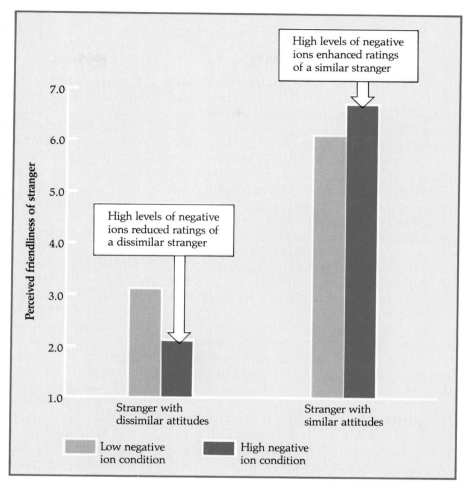

settings. The experiments described above suggest, however, that high levels of negative ions may yield harmful as well as beneficial effects, depending on each individual's dominant tendencies in a particular situation.

Our focus in the present section has been on environmental stressors that are relatively familiar, especially in urban settings. Beyond these factors, there is another source of environmental stress that is more dramatic and more frightening. We are increasingly familiar with the threat of technological disaster such as the dumping of toxic wastes and the possibility of accidents at nuclear power plants. Psychologists have been extremely interested in determining how people adapt to this new source of danger. Please see the **Focus** insert on page 434 for a discussion of work on the psychological impact of the Three-Mile Island nuclear accident on the people who lived near this plant.

FOCUS ON RESEARCH:
The Cutting Edge

Three-Mile Island and Stress

In March 1979 there was a malfunction at the Three-Mile Island nuclear power plant in Pennsylvania. The core of one of the two reactors located there was accidentally exposed by a drop in the level of coolant water, and this resulted in the collection of a great deal of contaminated water and radioactive gas being trapped in the reactor building. Both the contaminated water and gas became potential sources of radiation exposure. Besides, gas occasionally leaked from the containment building into the atmosphere throughout the year following the accident. Only with considerable time, money, and expense has the reactor at Three-Mile Island been cleaned up. Even now, plant operators have not been permitted to start the reactor again, in part because of concerns about the perceived safety of the facility on the part of local residents and environmentalists.

Experts agree that levels of radiation exposure were too low to have harmful physical effects, but local residents continue to express fears and concerns about the present radiation and about the possibility of another accident. Their apprehension is not completely unfounded. In December 1985 the second reactor, which previously had presented no problems, had a small radioactive leak. Given all of this, what are the psychological effects of the chronic uncertainty felt by local residents? These individuals have been the focus of studies, sponsored by the Nuclear Regulatory Agency and the State of Pennsylvania, designed to ascertain the environmental and psychological impact of these past events and possible future dangers.

In one of these studies (Baum, Gatchel, and Schaeffer, 1983), conducted three years after the accident, subjects were asked to describe any recent physical symptoms, to perform a challenging task, to provide urine specimens to assess physiological arousal, and to indicates their feelings of depression and anxiety. A group of randomly selected Three-Mile Island residents were compared to three other groups of individuals similar in age, social class, and the like. These other groups consisted of individuals living eighty miles away from the nuclear plant, some living near a fossil-fuel plant that presented no risk of catastrophe, and residents living near a nuclear power plant that had not had any accidents.

As shown in Figure 12.7, the Three-Mile Island residents were found to have more physical symptoms (such as digestive problems, headaches) and higher levels of anxiety and physiological arousal than the other three groups. They also performed less well on a stress-sensitive task. Because these data were collected three years after the accident, it appears that stress reactions are relatively long-lasting.

An additional finding was that people living near Three-Mile Island reported more problems about maintaining control over their lives. They were more likely to say that they didn't care about what they did, and it didn't matter whether they had a choice or not. In addition, the greater this reported perception of lack of control, the more physical symptoms they had (Davidson, Baum, and Collins, 1982). These results provide evidence that the nuclear accident left many local residents feeling helpless. As was discussed earlier in the chapter, a perceived loss of control was an important factor in the behavioral effects of noise.

These studies are continuing, and the health and psychological responses of those living near Three-Mile Island are regularly monitored (Hartsough and Savitsky, 1984). In the meanwhile, what data are available suggest

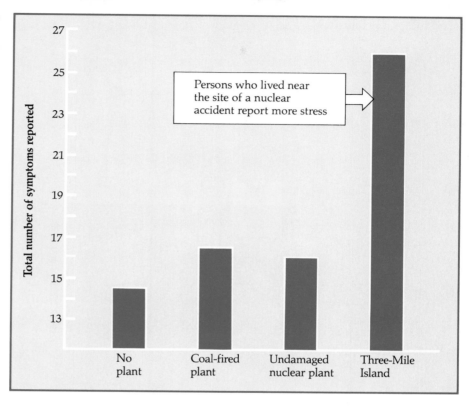

FIGURE 12.7. Anxiety and physical symptoms caused by stress were found among local residents of Three-Mile Island three years after a nuclear accident. Comparable subjects who did not live near the site showed much lower levels of stress-related symptoms. (Source: Based on data from Baum, Gatchel, and Schaeffer, 1983.)

The lasting effects of living near the site of a nuclear accident

Persons who lived near the site of a nuclear accident report more stress

Total number of symptoms reported

No plant · Coal-fired plant · Undamaged nuclear plant · Three-Mile Island

that the stress and uncertainty of living in the vicinity of a technological disaster has had and continues to have negative consequences. The Chernobyl nuclear disaster in the Soviet Union on April 26, 1986, had widespread negative consequences far beyond the Kiev area — in Eastern Europe, Scandinavia, and beyond. This explosion and its aftermath serve to remind us that no one is totally protected from such accidents. We are very likely to have similar events in the future, so it is important that we learn as much as possible about the aftereffects and also about possible ways to reduce their psychological and physical impact.

THE INTERPERSONAL ENVIRONMENT

We turn now from the problems created by certain aspects of our physical surroundings to those that are the result of the people around us. Our reactions to the interpersonal environment are clearly of great importance in our everyday lives.

FIGURE 12.8. Females generally interact with one another at closer distances than do males.

Sex differences in using personal space

Personal space

There is an area immediately surrounding each of us that we treat as an integral part of ourselves. This area is referred to as one's *personal space.* Typically, this area extends around us on all sides, but it usually is larger in front of us than at our backs or sides.

Effects of sex and culture.   Intrusions into one's personal space can be aversive or not, depending on the identity of the intruder. Ashton, Shaw, and Worsham (1980) asked pairs of friends and pairs of strangers to stand at various distances and report how they felt. Both males and females felt more comfortable when an opposite-sex friend stood relatively close (50 centimeters) rather than a stranger. As depicted in Figure 12.8, there are also sex differences in the closeness of interactions. Females interact at closer distances than males, especially in same-sex interactions (Heshka and Nelson, 1972). Females place more distance between themselves and an opposite-sex stranger than do males (Rüstemli, 1986). Males also tend to be more concerned about invasions from the front while females respond more negatively to invasions from the side (Fisher and Byrne, 1975).

Much of the research attention paid to personal space was initiated by the work of an anthropologist, Edward T. Hall (1966). He became interested in **proxemics** (the study of interpersonal distance) as a result of his cross-cultural investigations. He observed that people in North America, Great Britain, and Scandinavia prefer greater space between one another than do people in the Middle East, France, and Greece. These different norms about personal space frequently create problems. Visitors to foreign countries who are unaware of the norms may become upset when they feel "cornered" by someone from a country where close interactions are customary.

Cultural differences in the distances considered appropriate are apparently the result of socialization. Observations of young children show that they play at very close distances and touch each other frequently (Burgess, 1981). By the fourth grade (about age ten), children space themselves at greater distances and make less physical contact (Aiello and Aiello, 1974; Price and Dabbs, 1974; Shea, 1981). Pagan and Aiello (1982) observed the same-sex interactions of Puerto Rican children growing up either in New York City or in Puerto Rico. Native Puerto Ricans generally adopt closer interpersonal distances than North Americans. Figure 12.9 shows that, as in previous studies, interaction distances

FIGURE 12.9. The distance individuals place between themselves when they interact generally increases from childhood to adulthood. In addition, interpersonal distance is affected by cultural factors. In a study of Puerto Rican youngsters, both effects are observed. (Source: Based on data from Pagan and Aiello, 1982.)

Personal space is affected by age and by culture

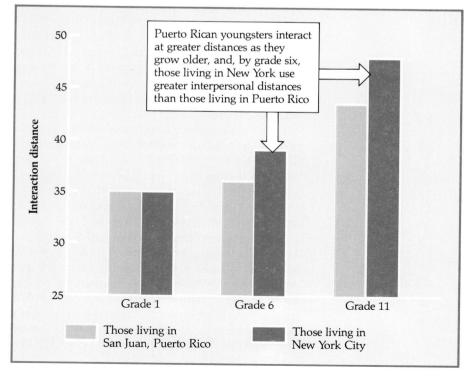

Puerto Rican youngsters interact at greater distances as they grow older, and, by grade six, those living in New York use greater interpersonal distances than those living in Puerto Rico

Those living in San Juan, Puerto Rico

Those living in New York City

increased for children in higher grades. Also, there is a divergence based on where the children grew up. Those living in New York learned to keep greater space between themselves than did Puerto Rican children living in San Juan. These results demonstrate the joint impact of cultural pressures and age norms.

Situational effects on personal space.   Hall also pointed out that our personal space needs change according to the situation. He observed that North Americans interact at one of four distances, depending on the nature of the parties interacting and the content of the communication. **Intimate distance,** which is zero to one and a half feet, is the distance appropriate for such acts as lovemaking and fighting. **Personal distance** is from one and one-half feet to four feet and is used in everyday interactions among friends and acquaintances. **Social distance** is from four to twelve feet and is the distance maintained in conducting business interactions and other impersonal relationships. Over twelve feet is **public distance,** which is usually used in formal settings as when a speaker addresses an audience.

Studies have shown that interactions are uncomfortable when conducted at an inappropriate distance. For example, Albert and Dabbs (1970) had college students listen to a persuasive message presented by an experimenter who sat either two, five, or fifteen feet away. Since this is a business type of interaction, the appropriate distance should be five feet, according to Hall's analysis. After the message was completed, subjects were asked some questions about the message and the communicator. Subjects recalled more information, judged the communicator to be more expert, and paid more attention when they were sitting five feet apart than at either of the two inappropriate distances. A more recent study (Scott, 1984) showed that people prefer to sit closer when talking about intimate subjects (such as a sex problem) than when discussing impersonal topics (such as restaurants). They also sit closer to persons with whom they are personally very friendly, especially when discussing intimate topics.

The special interaction zones serve a number of functions. First, they provide a kind of "buffer zone" for protection. Second, they help to prevent sensory overload — standing too close to another individual may result in feeling his or her heat, smelling the other person's body, and the like (Nesbett and Steven, 1974). Third, spatial zones allow people to regulate and maintain control over desired levels of privacy and intimacy (Altman, 1975; Argyle and Dean, 1965; Patterson, 1976).

The control function of personal space is illustrated by a study with Type A coronary-prone individuals. Those fitting this description are believed to have a high need for control over the social and physical environment (Glass, 1977). Strube and Werner (1984) predicted that if Type As have a strong need for control, they should desire larger personal spaces for themselves. To test this hypothesis, subjects were asked to assume the role of salesperson or of a customer in a simulated sales interaction. They could select the personal space that they preferred for the interaction. Type As chose a larger personal space than did Type Bs. Also, when Type As played the role of customer, where there is greater perceived threat to one's control, they wanted the greatest amount of space.

"Space invaders": Intrusions into personal space

What happens when people invade our personal space? Your first thought may be that an intrusion would be a negative experience. This seems to be the case, at least with respect to strangers. Konecni et al. (1975) had same-sex confederates stand either one, two, five, or ten feet from subjects who were standing on the sidewalk waiting to cross the street. The results showed that the closer the stranger stood, the faster the person crossed the street. In a subsequent study (Smith and Knowles, 1979), this procedure was repeated; in addition, subjects were interviewed about their perceptions of the "invader." Strangers who stood close were described as more rude, aggressive, and hostile than those who stood at a greater distance.

If one cannot leave the scene, there is a tendency to respond to a spatial intrusion by avoiding eye contact or by changing body orientation away from the intruder (Patterson, 1973; Sundstrom and Sundstrom, 1977). This sort of behavior is easily observed on a crowded elevator.

Spatial intrusions usually produce increases in physiological arousal, as shown in a field study by Middlemist, Knowles, and Matter (1976). In a men's room, confederates used a urinal that was either next to one used by a subject or two urinals away. The closer the confederate, the more time was required by the subject to begin urinating and the faster the act was completed — two physiological indicators of stress.

Thus far, we have focused on spatial intrusion as a negative experience, but it need not always be the case. In other chapters, you have seen how feelings of anger, happiness, or love may develop on the basis of the cognitive label that the individual places on his or her arousal. Though a stranger sitting close by may evoke negative feelings, the same "intrusion" by a close friend or lover is likely to result in positive feelings. Even a friendly stranger can reverse the usual effects of personal space invasion. Storms and Thomas (1977) had a male experimenter sit either six inches or thirty inches from a male college student. Half of these subjects were treated in a friendly manner and given positive feedback. The other half were treated in an unfriendly manner and given negative feedback. Subjects liked best the friendly experimenter who interacted at six inches and least liked the unfriendly experimenter who interacted at that distance. Other studies show that children react positively to an "intruding" adult if that person provides assistance (Cowen, Weissberg, and Lotyczewski, 1982). If one adult asks a favor of another, a close distance is also positive (Baron, 1978; Willis and Hamm, 1980).

These studies suggest that spatial invasions lead to physiological arousal. Whether the arousal is experienced as positive or negative depends on the way in which the situation and the arousal are labeled.

Territorial behavior

Personal space controls how closely we interact with others and is a flexible, invisible boundary. It can be contrasted with **territory,** which is an area that is staked out and defended (**territorial behavior**). Animals typically mark off their territories by leaving their scent around the perimeter by urinating or defecating. Humans use a different approach —they employ signs, fences, and other kinds of "markers" (Sommer, 1969).

Though both humans and animals have typical territorial behaviors, there are differences not only in what is done but why (Sundstrom and Altman, 1974). Animals control territories to protect food sources, shelter, mating, and nesting. They generally use one territory for a continuous period. In contrast, humans use a number of territories, some only temporarily, and will release their space to others when they are finished. Also, animal behavior is largely determined by biological factors, while humans are also influenced by social and cultural determinants.

Territories serve two principal functions for humans. They help to regulate privacy and to maintain control (Altman, 1975). Humans appear to have three kinds of territory. A **primary territory** is owned and used by an individual or a group for an extended period of time. Homes and apartments are examples of primary territories. Because people view these spaces as "theirs," they feel more safe and comfortable when there. By the same token, people are highly distressed when a primary territory is intruded upon by uninvited strangers (Taylor and Stough, 1978).

There are individual differences in the degree to which people mark off their territory. Those homeowners who erect signs, fences, and hedges or have doormats with their initials are found to respond to their doorbells more quickly than those without such markers (Edney, 1972). It is suggested that territorial people are more concerned about having their privacy invaded and want to intercept potential intruders as quickly as possible (see Figure 12.10).

A **secondary territory** is a space that is used regularly but is shared with others. An example would be the seat you occupy regularly in your social psychology class or one's usual place in church. At other times of the day, different people are likely to occupy these same spaces. Have you ever walked into a class and found someone else sitting in your usual seat? You might feel annoyed, but you realize that you do not have exclusive rights to that territory. Generally, of course, norms develop about the "rights" to secondary territories. Thus, classmates tend to honor your territory just as you honor theirs.

Public territories are spaces like public waiting rooms at airports or

FIGURE 12.10. People feel uncomfortable when their primary territory is invaded by uninvited strangers, so they take special precautions to assure control. This cartoon depicts a rather extreme example of territorial behavior. (Source: Drawing by Koren; © 1984 by The New Yorker Magazine, Inc.)

Keeping invaders away from one's territory

bus stations that can only be occupied temporarily and are available on a first-come, first-served basis. Nevertheless, public territories may be defended. For example, players in a game arcade establish temporary possession of a given machine by touching it when a potential intruder approaches (Werner, Brown, and Damron, 1981). Personal belongings can serve as territorial markers that indicate the space should be saved. For example, you might leave your coat or a book to save "your" space in a library (Sommer and Becker, 1969). Studies of different kinds of markers used in public libraries reveal that people are more likely to honor the marker, and not invade the space, the more personal the item used — for example, a sports coat rather than a newspaper (Sommer, 1969; Sommer and Becker, 1969), as long as alternative space is available. The limited control one has over public territories probably accounts for the fact that people report feeling least safe and in control when they are in this type of territory (Taylor and Stough, 1978).

The importance of territory and privacy may well be overlooked by those who design space for others (Duffy et al., 1986). In nursing homes, designers and administrators tend to prefer arrangements that encourage social interaction. In contrast, the residents of nursing homes prefer designs that enhance privacy.

Territorial dominance

Both animals and humans tend to assume dominance over intruders or strangers when they are in their own territory. For example, a chicken is more likely to peck a strange bird when in its home cage than in a stranger's cage (Rajecki et al., 1981). This has been termed the **prior**

FIGURE 12.11. Studies of various sports indicate that home teams are more likely to win than are the visitors. Territorial factors favor those playing on their own court or field.

The home team has an advantage over a visiting team

residence effect or, more popularly, the *home field advantage*. People are more successful at a competitive task when the setting is their own room than when the setting is someone else's room (Martindale, 1971) and are more likely to dominate the conversation (Taylor and Lanni, 1981).

One of the most interesting manifestations of the home field advantage is in competitive sports (see Figure 12.11). For some time, it has been recognized that, for some sports, teams tend to do better at home than when they are "away." For example, the outcomes of major league baseball, professional football, professional hockey, and college basketball games reliably find the home team is more often the winner (Hirt and Kimble, 1981; Schwartz and Barsky, 1977). Territorial dominance has been offered as one plausible explanation. Home players may feel more in control and less inhibited on their own turf. You may remember from the discussion in Chapter 3 that home teams do not always have the advantage. During championship competition, home teams actually tend to perform below their proven ability — they choke (Baumeister and Steinhilber, 1984.)

Other effects of territoriality

Perceptions of territoriality are related to fears about crime, especially among vulnerable individuals such as the elderly (Patterson, 1978). In one study, Normoyle and Lavrakas (1984) interviewed a sample of elderly women living in Chicago with respect to their fear of crime, perceptions of control, and territoriality. Women who viewed their experiences as predictable and controllable were more likely to assume a territorial stance with respect to their homes and community. They say such things as, "I have tried to arrange my home so that other people would know it belongs to me." In addition, those who expressed greater territoriality were less fearful of crime. One implication of these findings is that encouraging people to display territorial markers may enhance their feelings of security (Pollock and Patterson, 1980).

Territoriality also plays a role within the family. For example, family members tend to agree on the territorial attributes of different rooms (Sebba and Churchman, 1983). Some areas belong to an individual, such as one parent's study or a particular child's room. Other rooms are perceived as belonging to the entire family, such as the kitchen. Even in that instance, one person may be perceived as having primary jurisdiction over it.

Family relationships may also be influenced by whether family members spend significant portions of time on family "turf." Raviv and Palgi (1985) found that if children in an Israeli kibbutz sleep in the primary territory of their parents rather than in a communal room, family members tend to perceive their relationships as more cohesive.

FIGURE 12.12. Shared, partitioned offices provide less privacy than conventional offices. Shared space is also associated with a low level of satisfaction and efficiency.

Office designs and territoriality: Privacy, satisfaction, and efficiency

Territory and architectural design

As mentioned earlier, territories serve to regulate privacy and control. These needs may not be well served by a recent trend to structure offices such that large spaces are subdivided with partitions of varying heights to create individual and small group work areas (see Figure 12.12). One supposed benefit of this design is enhanced communication. Studies

show, however, that employees in such offices — compared to those in traditional private offices — tend to be dissatisfied, and their work efficiency suffers (Oldham and Brass, 1979; Sundstrom et al., 1982).

Becker and colleagues (1983) studied the effects of large subdivided offices and conventional offices on faculty work patterns and faculty-student interactions at three colleges. Faculty were surveyed about office conditions and office behavior. Students were asked about when they wished to meet with faculty and how comfortable they felt at such meetings. As in past work, the large shared offices were less liked than traditional ones, particularly because of lack of privacy and the difficulty in concentrating. Students also felt less comfortable about dropping in without an appointment, believed they were given insufficient time, and indicated that they received less useful feedback about their work and progress. As in the nursing home research described earlier, these results suggest that the most comfortable architectural designs are those that provide an opportunity for privacy.

CROWDING: The Effects of Too Many People and Too Little Space

Some years ago the television program *Star Trek* had an episode about a planet that was so overcrowded its leaders tried to introduce a fatal disease so that portions of the population would die off, making life more bearable for the survivors. The idea that crowding has negative effects on social behavior and health is an old one. Is it correct?

Early evidence

Some early experiments with rats, first conducted over two decades ago (Calhoun, 1962, 1971), provided evidence of extremely negative consequences of overcrowding. Even though the animals were well fed and had plenty of water, those in a densely packed environment reacted in a variety of negative ways, ranging from aggression to cannibalism or physical illness. Later studies with animals found similar effects (Anderson et al., 1977; Chapman, Masterpasqua, and Lore, 1976; Massey and Vanderbergh, 1980).

Does overcrowding have the same effects among humans? Early sociological research examined the association between population density (number of people per square mile) and indicators of crime and both physical and psychiatric illness. There appeared to be a positive correlation between population density and social problems, but the research was flawed by a confounding variable (Zlutnick and Altman, 1972): overpopulated areas also tend to be lowest in average income and educational opportunities. Thus, crime and illness may be the result of poverty rather than overcrowding per se (Booth, 1975). When both income level and population are taken into account (Galle, Gove, and McPherson, 1972), no relationship is found between community size and social problems.

Why do animals show strong negative effects in conditions of high population density, while humans do not? One explanation is that animals are biologically programmed to respond to overcrowding (Calhoun, 1971). In contrast, humans are influenced by social and cognitive factors that might moderate the effects of densely packed areas. Also, humans can find ways to escape from most overcrowded environments, at least for brief periods. In the animal studies, the subjects did not have such an option.

A social psychological look at crowding

There are situations in which people react negatively to too many people or to too little space. For example, high density tends to have negative effects when it interferes with our goals (Schopler and Stockdale, 1977), provides information overload (Cohen, 1978; Milgram, 1970; Saegert, 1978), or prevents us from predicting future events or controlling significant outcomes (Baron and Rodin, 1978; Baum and Valins, 1979; Schmidt and Keating, 1979).

An important distinction is made between **density** and **crowding** (Paulus, 1980; Stokols, 1972). *Density* refers to the actual number of people in a given space, while *crowding* refers to a negative psychological response. Imagine that you are in a densely packed elevator that stops at every floor. You are likely to consider this a "crowded" situation and label it as aversive. On the other hand, imagine a similarly densely packed crowd at a Bruce Springsteen concert. The identical high level of density may be labeled as exciting and pleasurable. In other words, the absolute number of people does not always correspond to one's emotional reactions.

It has been proposed that the feeling of crowding occurs when the individual feels aroused and attributes the arousal to spatial restrictions (Worchel and Teddle, 1976). This hypothesis was tested in an experiment by Worchel and Brown (1984) in which the situation was manipulated so as to provide plausible alternative explanations for the subjects' arousal. Small groups of subjects watched a film under conditions where their interpersonal seating distances were appropriate or inappropriately close. There were four different kinds of films — three were arousing (humorous, aggressive, or sexual) and one was unarousing. Each subject saw only one film. It was predicted that subjects in the inappropriate distance condition would attribute their arousal to the film if it was an arousing one, so they should not feel crowded. With the unarousing film,

FIGURE 12.13.
Inappropriately close interpersonal distances are stressful and physiologically arousing. Under neutral conditions, this arousal leads the individual to perceive himself or herself as crowded. When the arousal can be attributed to some other source, such as an arousing movie, interpersonal closeness is less likely to be perceived as crowdedness. (Source: Based on data from Worchel and Brown, 1984.)

Perceived crowding: The mediating role of attributions

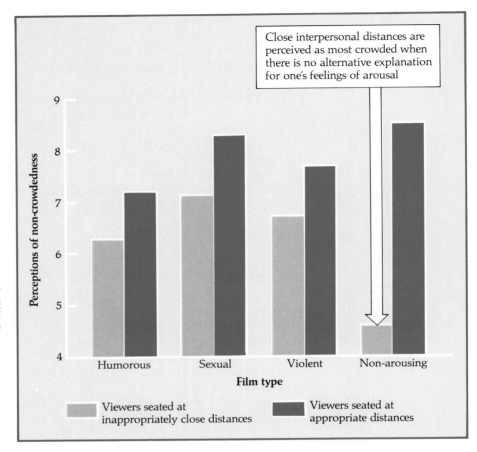

the arousal would be attributed to the interpersonal conditions, and feelings of crowdedness should result. As shown in Figure 12.13, the results supported the hypothesis. Whether a person felt crowded or not depended on the perceived source of the arousal.

The effect of crowding may also be influenced by the kind of density involved. It is useful to distinguish between **social density** and **spatial density** (Baum and Valins, 1977; Paulus, 1980). Social density increases as the number of people in a given space increases; an example would be an apartment on an ordinary evening versus the evening of a large party. Spatial density increases as the amount of space for a given number of people decreases; an example would be a group waiting in the lobby of a large building versus the same group after they entered a small elevator. In general, high levels of social or spatial density have negative effects on a wide range of behaviors. Social density appears to have stronger effects — such as negative affective states, especially among males (Ross et al., 1973); physiological arousal (Aiello, Epstein, and Karlin, 1975; Evans,

1979; Saegert, 1978; Singer, Lundberg, and Frankenhaeuser, 1978); and less attraction toward strangers (Griffitt and Veitch, 1971; Zuckerman, Schmitz, and Yosha, 1977). High density also impairs individual performance on complex tasks (Paulus et al., 1976) but has little effect on simple tasks (Freedman, Klevansky, and Ehrlich, 1971).

Long-term effects of crowding

Most laboratory studies can only examine short-term exposure to crowding. To find out what happens over a longer period of time, it is necessary to identify situations in which individuals are exposed to such conditions in their everyday lives. One obvious setting for long-term conditions of crowdedness is the home. Research by environmental designer Marjorie Inman indicates that a crucial element in creating stress is the number of bathrooms available (Meer, 1986). Even in uncrowded homes, those with only one bathroom reported more stress than those with two or more.

Another such crowded setting is a student dormitory. It is here that the stronger effects of social density than of spatial density become clear. Studies show that dorm residents living in three-person rooms that were built for two are less satisfied with their roommates, feel more crowded, and express greater dissatisfaction with their residential living situation than do students in two-person-occupied rooms (Baron et al., 1976; Gormley and Aiello, 1982). Those in "triples" also have lower grade-point averages than "doubles" (Karlin, Rosen, and Epstein, 1979).

Students living in suite-style dorms are found to react differently from those living in long-corridor dorms. Though residents in each type of arrangement had equivalent square footage of living space available, those in corridor dorms felt more crowded, had more desire to avoid others, and reported having less control over their social interaction than those in suites (Baum and Valins, 1977). The difference appears to be attributable to differences in social density.

The feeling of stress and loss of control among corridor residents tended to increase as the semester progressed, but this did not happen among suite residents. Corridor residents were also more likely to give up in a laboratory game situation than were suite residents, and this behavior increased the longer they remained in the stressful living arrangement (Baum and Gatchel, 1981). Altogether, these results suggest that lack of control over social interactions increased feelings of helplessness as well as other negative reactions. Of course, college students can typically find ways to alter their living arrangements, but some cannot. What are the effects of chronic exposure to crowding where alternatives are *not* available? To learn more about this issue, please see the **Applied Side** insert on page 448.

ON THE APPLIED SIDE

Crowding in Prisons: Cruel and Unusual Punishment?

From 1975 to 1980 the number of prison inmates in the United States increased 94 percent, reflecting both a growth in the total population and changes in the sentences handed down (National Institute of Justice, 1980). Several prisoners have instituted law suits based on the argument that crowding constitutes cruel and unusual punishment (*Ruiz* v. *Estelle*, 1980). Others have also expressed concern that prison crowding may have serious negative consequences. What do we know about the actual effects of crowding in prisons?

Consider some archival data collated from prison records (Cox, Paulus, and McCain, 1984). One general pattern across states and institutions is that as the population of the prison increases, so does the death rate and the number of disciplinary infractions. In one institution the population doubled but the rate of serious infractions increased sixfold. In that same prison the suicide rate increased threefold.

FIGURE 12.14.
Perceived crowdedness was consistently higher among prisoners assigned to large, open dormitories than among those assigned to single cells. (Source: Based on data from Cox, Paulus, and McCain, 1984.)

Perceived crowding in prisons

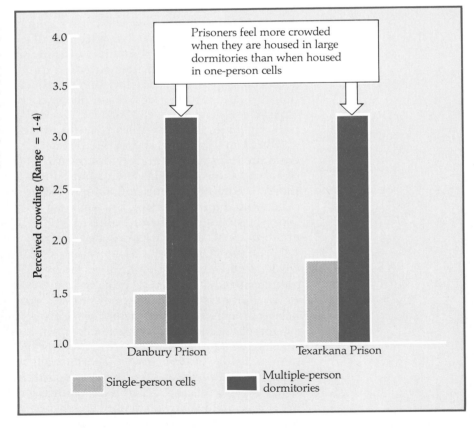

One question is whether social density and spatial density each contribute to prison problems. Looking at illness complaints, Cox and his colleagues found little difference based on size of cells (spatial density). Inmates living in single or double housing units reported comparable amounts of illness (Paulus and McCain, 1983).

In contrast, comparison of housing units varying in number of inmates, while controlling for amount of space (social density), revealed important differences. Across various types of prison cells, the more inmates housed together, the higher the illness rate and the higher were the ratings of perceived crowding.

Figure 12.14 shows the ratings of crowdedness for singles and dormitories by inmates in two different prisons.

McCain et al. (1985, p. 1155) observed that "if exposure to increased risk of illness, death, psychopathology, and violence does at some level constitute cruel and unusual punishment then our data are pertinent." In the next few years, information collected by social psychologists and environmental psychologists will be used in court cases brought by prison inmates and others. It will be interesting to see if housing standards are changed as a result of this environmental research.

Avoiding the effects of crowding

If it is the perception of loss of control that leads to negative reactions to overcrowding, then perhaps this perception can be altered. Consistent with that idea, when subjects are informed beforehand as to the details of a situation and what to expect, they report less aversive reactions (Baum, Fisher, and Solomon, 1981; Fisher and Baum, 1980). Even subtle indicators of perceived control may make a difference. For example, in a densely packed elevator, subjects who were standing by the control panel felt less crowded and perceived the elevator as larger than did those standing away from the panel (Rodin, Solomon, and Metcalf, 1979).

Of course, a more obvious way to avoid negative effects is to alter the environment. Sometimes relatively simple changes can be effective. For example, dorm residents report more liking where there are bunk beds rather than twin beds (Rohner, 1974). This appears to be because the bunk bed arrangement provides more room to move about and ensures that one's roommate is out of sight at night. A more radical change was instituted in another study. A long corridor dorm was divided into two shorter hallways by constructing a wall. In this altered setting, privacy increased, feelings of crowding decreased, and fewer social problems were reported (Baum and Davis, 1980). Still another study (McCain et al.,

1985) found that a 43 percent reduction in enrollment in a junior high school (while maintaining the same faculty-student ratio) improved attitudes about school and grades, and there was also less faculty absenteeism. This reduction in the size of the total population had clear benefits for students and faculty alike.

The sampling of the work in environmental psychology presented in this chapter provides ample evidence of the impact of our physical and interpersonal surroundings on many aspects of behavior.

SUMMARY

Environmental psychology is the field that deals with the interaction between the physical world and human behavior. Among the concerns of the field are the effects on human behavior of the urban environment and of such environmental stressors as noise and air pollution, the influences of the interpersonal environment, and overcrowding.

People adapt to the **stimulus overload** of city life by developing norms of noninvolvement with respect to strangers. The way people interact is, however, also a function of the pleasantness and arousing qualities of the urban setting.

Various events in the physical environment are a cause of stress, and research has documented negative effects. Repeated exposure to **noise** can have serious consequences for academic performance, health, and social behaviors. Excessive heat can decrease some forms of positive social behavior and increase interpersonal aggression. Air pollution can cause serious health problems and can increase aggressive behavior. **Atmospheric electricity** does not have uniformly positive or negative effects, but it does facilitate whatever behavioral tendency is dominant in a given situation.

Each of us treats the area surrounding our bodies as a zone of personal space, and any invasion of this zone elicits an emotional reaction, including fear, anger, and attraction. The size of one's personal space varies with culture, sex, the relationship between individuals, and the nature of the interaction. **Territorial behavior** involves staking out and defending some particular space. One interesting phenomenon is that animals and humans are more dominant and generally more effective on their home territory.

The number of people in a given area can sometimes have significant effects on social and individual behavior. Both population **density** and the subjective perception of **crowding** have been investigated. A situation is perceived as crowded when the individual feels aroused and attributes the arousal to spatial restrictions. In general, negative effects are more likely to occur as the result of too many people rather than too little space.

GLOSSARY

atmospheric electricity
The number of positive and negative ions in the atmosphere. High levels of negative ions enhance an individual's dominant behavioral tendencies in any given situation.

cataclysmic phenomena
Stressful events such as war or natural disaster that are widely shared within a society.

crowding
The perception that too many people are occupying a given space. This subjective evaluation of one's surroundings is stressful.

density
An objective physical condition that is defined by the number of people occupying a particular space of a given size.

environmental psychology
The field that deals with the interaction between the physical world and human behavior.

intimate distance
In Hall's system, the appropriate interpersonal distance for affectionate interactions, contact sports, and aggression.

noise
Technically, a sound composed of many nonharmonious frequencies. Subjectively, an unpleasant sound—especially if it is loud, unpredictable, and uncontrollable.

personal distance
The zone around each individual into which most people are not supposed to trespass.

primary territory
In Altman's system, space that is used regularly on a long-term basis as an essential part of a person's everyday activities.

prior residence effect
The "home-field advantage" that both human beings and other animals usually have when they are on their home territory. It involves both dominance and general effectiveness in interacting with others.

proxemics
The study of the distance people place between and among themselves in various kinds of interactions.

public distance
In Hall's system, the appropriate interpersonal distance for formal contacts between a speaker and an audience.

public territory
In Altman's system, a space that is occupied only temporarily and is available to whoever gets there first.

secondary territory
In Altman's system, a space that is used regularly by specific people on a limited basis.

social density
This type of density increases as the number of individuals in a given space increases.

social distance
In Hall's system, the appropriate interpersonal distance for impersonal and business-like contacts.

spatial density
This type of density increases as the amount of space for a given number of individuals decreases.

stimulus overload
A phenomenon that may occur in urban environments in which an individual receives too much stimulus information to be able to process it efficiently.

stress
A response to an external threat that involves fear, anxiety, and anger.

territorial behavior
A variety of actions in which people engage to stake out and defend portions of the environment against intrusion.

territory
An area that an individual or a group occupies exclusively and defends against any intruders.

FOR MORE INFORMATION

Altman, I., and Werner, C. M., eds. (1985). *Home environments.* New York: Plenum.
> A collection of original chapters on psychological, social, and behavioral aspects of the home environment. Among the topics discussed are the role of the home in familial relationships and the meaning of home in relation to societal forces.

Fisher, C. S. (1984). *The urban experience.* New York: Harcourt Brace Jovanovich.
> This is a highly readable review of research on the many aspects of life in large cities.

Fisher, J. D., Bell, P. A., and Baum, A. (1984). *Environmental psychology*, 2nd ed. New York: Holt, Rinehart, and Winston.
> An excellent coverage of the field of environmental psychology by three individuals who are active contributors to research in this area.

Holahan, C. J. (1982). *Environmental psychology.* New York: Random House.
> This text is geared to advanced undergraduates and gives particular attention to the view that people actively shape and adapt to their surroundings.

Stokols, D., and Altman, I. (1986). *Handbook of environmental psychology.* New York: Wiley.

This volume consists of a series of chapters on the major topics of environmental psychology, each written by scientists who are actively involved in research, theory, and application in this area.

CHAPTER 13

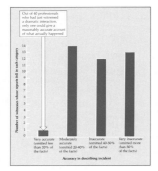

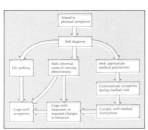

APPLYING SOCIAL PSYCHOLOGY

The scene is an apartment in a medium-size city. A young husband bursts happily through the door into the living room with some exciting news for his wife.

EVAN: (*shouting*) Christy! Christy! Where are you? Come in here if you want to be in the presence of a rising star in the executive training program.

CHRISTY: (*from another room*) Wait a minute, Evan. I'm almost finished with my presentation for tomorrow's sales meeting.

EVAN: (*a little miffed*) Too bad. I had planned to share this bottle of champagne with you while I gave you some pretty important news.

CHRISTY: (*entering with a pad of papers in her hand*) Why didn't you say so? I could use a reward after working for the past four hours.

EVAN: Now pay attention. This is a quiz, and you have only one guess.

CHRISTY: (*sitting down on a throw cushion*) I hope you give hints.

EVAN: No hints. Guess which handsome, intelligent, modest trainee at Ludlow Products just received a $100 monthly raise, starting in January?

CHRISTY: (*standing*) I can't imagine. I was going to guess that it was you, but the adjective "modest" ruled that out. (*Kissing him*) I'm really proud of you. Besides, we can use the money.

EVAN: This is only the beginning. Let's get the corkscrew, and I'll let you in on some of my *modest* plans. (*The telephone rings.*)

EVAN: (*picking up the receiver*) Hello . . . Oh, it's you,

Norman . . . (*frowning in mock dismay*) No, no, you're not interrupting anything.

CHRISTY: Tell him you're busy having an emergency appendectomy. He likes unpleasant news.

EVAN: What can I do for you, Norm? . . . Yes, you heard it right. One hundred a month . . . (*a startled look*) No, no one told me. Congratulations. I'm sure you deserve it. Well, Christy is calling me to give her a hand with something or other. Why don't we have lunch tomorrow? Bye.

CHRISTY: Don't tell me that your favorite and mine, good old Norm, got a raise, too.

EVAN: (*shoulders slumping*) You guessed it. I've done a great job all year while Norm barely hung on by his dirty fingernails. I'm not sure he could name our main products at Ludlow.

CHRISTY: (*giving him a hug*) Never mind, Ev. Let's just forget Norman. You had a wonderful year, got a good raise, and are about to drink champagne with a sensuous artist.

EVAN: (*taking off his coat and tie and going into the bedroom*) Thanks, Chris, but maybe some other time. I just don't feel like it right now.

IN THIS scene, elation about a raise turns into distress about the same raise given to someone who is perceived as undeserving. It appears that social psychological factors (perceptions of *equity*, as discussed in Chapter 10) were operating. As we have suggested throughout this book, social psychology does not begin and end in the laboratory. Nevertheless, when it is proposed that psychology can be applied to "real world" problems, one of two reactions is frequently heard. Some think of psychological research as isolated from everyday concerns and irrelevant to them, while others assume that applied psychology only involves psychotherapy with disturbed clients (Altmaier and Meyer, 1985). After reading the previous twelve chapters, you know that neither perception is accurate.

Instead, basic research in social psychology leads rather naturally to application. Quite often, social psychologists wear two hats — one is that of the scientist who constructs theories based on empirical research, and the other is the hat of the behavioral engineer who uses this basic knowledge to solve practical problems outside the laboratory (Carroll, 1982). A sampling of some recent applied research appears in Table 13.1.

Social psychologists exhibited an interest in application almost as soon as the field was established. For example, in 1899 William James pointed out how psychological findings could be utilized to improve education. That tradition has continued, and many social psychologists devote their primary professional efforts to solving societal problems (Kiesler, 1985; Spielberger and Stenmark, 1985). Social psychology is useful in providing data relevant to issues as diverse as the improvement

TABLE 13.1 The findings of social psychologists have been applied to a wide variety of problems, as this brief sample indicates.

The broad applications of social psychological knowledge

Questions to Which Applied Psychological Research Supplied Answers	Reference
Is accurate knowledge about one's family history of heart disease relevant in motivating preventive behavior?	Hastrup et al., 1985
What are the causes of work overload among police dispatchers?	Kirmeyer, 1984
How much public support is there for legislation to control handguns?	Tyler and Lavrakas, 1983
Do attitudes toward seat belt usage predict who will buckle up?	Wittenbraker and Gibbs, 1983
Is the rate of drug use among adolescents affected by whether the individual lives at home versus away?	Bachman et al., 1984
Do newspaper crime stories increase the general fear of crime?	Heath, 1984
Is it helpful to change attitudes about oneself in order to initiate weight loss?	Weinberg et al., 1984
Are IQ tests unfair when used in schools to classify those who are not middle-class whites?	Talarico, 1985

of day care for children and the evaluation of affirmative action policies (Shotland and Mark, 1985).

An increasing emphasis on applied activity is reflected in the occupational shift of social psychologists away from academia and into applied settings. In the 1980s, a smaller proportion of new Ph.D.s in social psychology are entering university positions (33 percent) than was true just a few years ago when 50 percent did so (Stapp and Fulcher, 1984). The majority of new social psychologists are now employed in hospitals, government agencies, business organizations, and other nonacademic institutions.

In this general context, we define **applied social psychology** as the utilization of social psychological principles and research methods in real-world settings in the attempt to solve social problems (Rodin, 1985). The scope of this activity is sufficiently broad that only a small portion can be covered in the present chapter. First, we will describe the role of social psychology in the *legal system*, one of the earliest settings for applied research. Next, we will turn to *health psychology* and the role of applied research in every aspect of health care from preventive medicine to coping with illness. Then we will examine the importance of psychology in the work setting as we discuss *organizational behavior*.

THE SOCIAL PSYCHOLOGY OF THE LEGAL SYSTEM

Our legal system is designed to yield objective, unbiased decisions based on a set of rules and procedures. Research in the field of **forensic psychol-**

FIGURE 13.1. Though our legal system is designed to produce objective and fair judgments, research shows that psychological factors act to interfere with objectivity and fairness at each step of the process. In this example, the emotions of the jurors appear to have been involved in their verdict of guilty. (Source: Drawing by Modell; ©1985 The New Yorker Magazine, Inc.)

Emotions in the courtroom: One of many sources of bias

"We find the defendant guilty as all getout."

ogy indicates that human beings do not always conform to such idealistic principles, as suggested by the cartoon in Figure 13.1. Whenever people interact, their behavior and their judgments are affected by factors such as attitudes, cognitions, and emotions. We will describe how these variables affect the major participants in the courtroom — witnesses, judges, attorneys, and defendants.

Before examining the current psychological research on behavior in the legal system, we will look at one of the earliest attempts to conduct applied research in this area. In solving crimes and in prosecuting criminals, the testimony of eyewitnesses is frequently crucial, and the accuracy of these witnesses is a matter of some importance. At the turn of the century, Hugo Munsterberg began investigating such questions, initiating a line of research that has continued to the present day. This early work is described in the **Focus** insert on page 459.

Eyewitness testimony: The whole truth and nothing but the truth

Anyone who has witnessed a crime, an accident, or any kind of event that is important in a trial swears to tell the truth about what he or she has seen or heard. Unfortunately, we have known for some time that even

FOCUS ON RESEARCH:
Classic Contributions

The Accuracy of Eyewitnesses to a Crime

Early research on memory and the effect of emotions on perception convinced Munsterberg (1907) that the same kinds of distortions and inaccuracies that are found among laboratory subjects would be characteristic of actual witnesses testifying in criminal trials. His book, *On the Witness Stand: Essays on Psychology and Crime*, presented data indicating numerous instances in which eyewitnesses to the same event contradicted one another and presented testimony that was inconsistent with known facts. He also found that witnesses strongly believed they were reporting the absolute truth.

Witnesses often must provide such details as the number of people present at a given place or are asked to estimate how much time elapsed between two events, and Munsterberg tested such behavior in his psychological laboratory. His subjects at Harvard were unable to agree about even the simplest phenomena, such as the number of spots on a card that had been presented or the number of seconds elapsing between two signals. When shown a pointer moving at a constant speed, some reported that it was as slow as a crawling snail while others said that the speed approximated that of an express train. The investigator concluded that if disagreement and inaccuracy were common among very bright university students in a psychological laboratory, there should be even greater difficulty among random citizens who found themselves suddenly exposed to an emotionally arousing event such as a robbery or an accident.

Munsterberg was one of the earliest investigators to point out that people have a tendency to reconstruct events in ways that do not match what actually occurred. He proposed that emotions strongly affect the memories of witnesses so that accounts of "what happened" were often greatly distorted by fear, anxiety, and anger. One of his field experiments resembles the social psychological deception studies that were carried out many decades later. During a scientific meeting, there was a sudden interruption from a street carnival going on outside. The doors opened and a clown in bright costume rushed in excitedly, followed by a black man carrying a revolver. They shouted at one another, one fell down and the other jumped on him, a shot was fired, and both quickly left. All of this occurred in less than half a minute. The gentleman conducting the meeting was the only one who knew that it was a staged event, and he requested those present to write down exactly what had happened, because it would undoubtedly be "requested by the police for use in court."

As shown in Figure 13.2 (page 460), there was a high percentage of omissions in the forty reports handed in. Only one eyewitness could be considered to have described the scene with any accuracy. The remainder omitted major segments of the "crime." Munsterberg pointed out that these witnesses were bright, well educated individuals from the fields of psychology, medicine, and the law. These seemingly reliable observers not only omitted a lot, but they also made a surprising number of totally false statements. For example, the black man actually wore no hat but was "seen" in a derby, a top hat, and so forth. He was described as wearing a red suit, a brown one, a striped one, a jacket, and shirtsleeves—in fact, he wore white trousers, a black jacket, and a red tie. In studying the written descriptions, the investigator concluded that the majority of

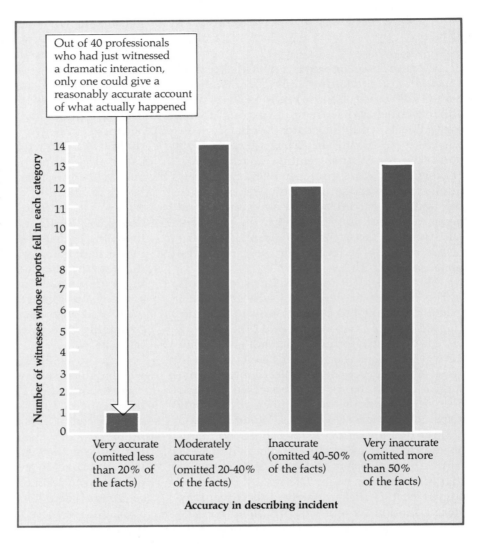

FIGURE 13.2. Beginning with the earliest research designed to investigate the accuracy of eyewitnesses, it was found that omissions and distortions frequently occur. In a field study of a staged event, forty professionals observed a brief interaction, but only one could be described as giving an accurate report. (Source: Based on data from Munsterberg, 1907.)

The inaccuracy of eyewitnesses

observers omitted or falsified about half of what had just happened before their eyes.

As in current research, there was an effort to find ways to increase the accuracy of eyewitness testimony. Munsterberg devised a physiological instrument to detect lying, and he investigated the use of hypnosis as a way to

ensure accuracy among witnesses. Both lie detection and hypnosis are the focus of current research efforts in this field (e.g., Sanders and Simmons, 1983; Spiegel, 1985; Zuckerman, Driver, and Koestner, 1982).

Because he believed that not only witnesses but also judges and jurors were subject to the effects of persuasion and suggestibility, Munsterberg warned that hypnosis could also be used to distort the truth rather than to uncover it. As one example, he recounted the story of a London trial in which a criminal hypnotist was able to catch the eye of those on the witness stand and cause them to alter their testimony so that they were speaking nonsense. This dangerous defendant was even described as putting the judge under his influence so that the magistrate suddenly confessed that he himself was the criminal.

Though the description of the hypnotized witnesses and judge may be taken with a grain of salt, it is interesting to find that some of the psychological issues observed and investigated in courtroom research eighty years ago are much the same as those of concern to applied social psychologists today.

the most honest and well-meaning citizen may be extremely inaccurate when testifying (Shepherd, Ellis, and Davies, 1983). Even the ability to point out the guilty individual among others in a line-up (see Figure 13.3) is notoriously inadequate. In one experiment, for example, subjects were shown a televised film of a mock crime and afterward asked to identify the culprit in a line-up (Buckhout, 1980). Only 14.1 percent selected the correct person as the criminal, a figure no greater than would be expected by chance.

You may think that such findings are restricted to artificial laboratory settings and that people witnessing real crimes would do a better job. Sadly enough, accuracy is no better for a real than for a staged event

FIGURE 13.3. Witnesses are often asked to identify the individual who committed a crime by selecting that person from a group assembled in a line-up. Such identifications are often quite inaccurate, but there are some procedures that improve witness performance.

Identifying the guilty person in a line-up

(Murray and Wells, 1983). The U.S. Supreme Court has ruled that eye-witnesses who expressed certainty about their testimony could be considered more credible than those who were uncertain. Once again, research brings us the discouraging news that there is no relationship between certainty and accuracy (Wells and Murray, 1983).

Given the consistent inaccuracy of eyewitness testimony, you might conclude that jurors have learned to ignore this type of evidence. Research by Leippe (1985) suggests instead that such testimony has a striking effect on verdicts. In a mock trial situation, all aspects of the evidence in a case of robbery were held constant, but the victim and a bystander either agreed that the defendant committed the crime or one of them said he was "not the man." When both individuals identified the defendant as the robber, 70 percent of the jurors decided he was guilty. When one of the witnesses failed to identify the defendant, only 12.5 percent of the jurors gave a guilty verdict. Clearly, such testimony has a strong impact on judicial decisions.

Because correct identification of a criminal depends on accurately perceiving and then remembering the person's appearance, wrongdoers often attempt to alter how they look before appearing in a line-up (Brigham, 1982). Even without such deliberate attempts to confuse witnesses, there are other factors that can interfere with the process. For example, witnesses seem to pay more attention to clothing than to height, weight, facial features, and the like. Sanders (1984) demonstrated how this bias operates by having an innocent volunteer wear the same eyeglasses and T-shirt the suspect had worn during a videotaped crime. Otherwise, the person was very dissimilar in appearance to the one who committed the crime. Nevertheless, the innocent volunteer was identified as the wrongdoer to a greater extent than was the actual criminal.

It is obviously very important to attempt to overcome the problem of inaccurate witnesses. Because there are individual differences in the tendency to pay attention to the behavior and appearance of others, one possibility is to devise procedures to identify accurate and inaccurate eyewitnesses (Hosch and Platz, 1984). Another approach is to provide witnesses with practice and to sensitize them to the dangers of making incorrect decisions. This "training" of witnesses is accomplished by using a blank line-up before the actual identification must be made (Wells, 1984). Witnesses are shown a line-up composed entirely of innocent volunteers. Those who discover that they have incorrectly identified one of these persons as the suspect are much more accurate when presented with the actual line-up containing the suspect. This pretreatment seems to act as a learning experience that sharpens the witness's memory for the crucial characteristics of the suspect.

The biasing influence of attorneys and of the judge

A trial is shaped in many ways by the behavior of the opposing attorneys and of the judge. Attorneys decide who will testify, what questions will be asked, and how the total case is to be summarized for the jury. The judge presides over the scene, rules on the admissibility of evidence, explains the case and the law to the jury, and imposes a sentence on those who are found guilty. These various acts each serve to influence the decision of the jurors, as has been shown in applied social research.

The attorney: Advocate or foe—and for whom?   Lawyers obviously play a crucial role in the courtroom. For example, the opening statement by a defense attorney tends to have a more favorable effect on jurors the earlier it is presented in the trial (Wells, Wrightsman, and Miene, 1985). Such statements are least influential when the attorney waits until after the prosecutor has presented a statement along with evidence against the defendant. In addition, questions asked by lawyers can be worded in such a way as to influence the witnesses' responses. In one experiment, subjects watched an automobile accident on videotape. Afterward, those who were asked whether two cars "smashed" when they collided testified about a more serious accident than was true of other witnesses asked whether the two cars "bumped" (Loftus, 1980). When asked about the cars that *smashed,* the witnesses reported seeing broken glass, but those questioned about cars that *bumped* did not.

What is asked not only influences the witness but also the perceptions of the jury. When questioning their own witnesses, attorneys tend to ask for direct information such as, "Tell me what happened on the afternoon of September 20th." During cross-examination, witnesses for the other side tend to be asked closed questions such as, "You left the door open, didn't you?" (McGaughey and Stiles, 1983). Jurors perceive the witness as less competent and less credible when closed questions are asked.

Though most trials are based on assigning opposing attorneys as adversaries, it is possible to arrange the situation so that lawyers on each side are working to discover the truth rather than attempting to win. Experiments with these two different ways of conducting a trial suggest that a nonadversarial system may be more fair to the accused than is the usual trial (Sheppard and Vidmar, 1980). Subjects were shown a tape recording and photographs of a fight in a bar. A week later, the witnesses were questioned by either adversarial or nonadversarial attorneys about what they had seen. Those in the nonadversary condition produced the most accurate descriptions of the fight, while the adversarial attorneys succeeded in obtaining testimony that was biased toward either the plaintiff or the defendant. Such research has led some to question the fairness of the present legal system (Greenberg and Ruback, 1982).

The judge: An impartial referee?   Judges as well as lawyers can behave in ways that affect the outcome of a trial. For example, during a trial the judge rules as to whether jurors may consider certain evidence — it may be admissible or inadmissible. The effect of such rulings was studied by Carretta and Moreland (1983). College students served as jurors in a trial in which the defendant was charged with murdering a store owner. Some

FIGURE 13.4. In an experimental mock trial situation, when the judge ruled that wiretapped evidence was admissible, a guilty verdict was less likely when the evidence favored the defense. When the evidence favored the prosecution's case, a ruling that it was admissible meant a guilty verdict was much more likely. (Source: Based on data from Carretta and Moreland, 1983.)

Effect of judge's ruling as to admissibility of crucial evidence

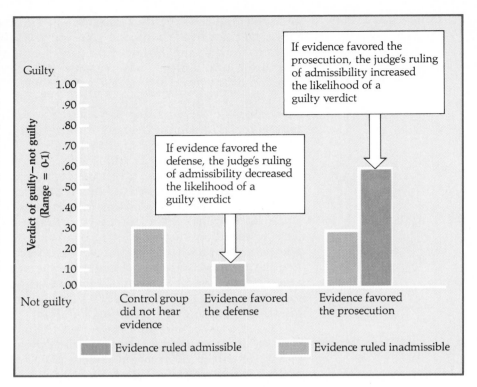

of the crucial evidence was obtained by means of wiretapping a telephone conversation. In this conversation, some jurors heard the defendant admit he had extra money that presumably was stolen during the murder; this information obviously favored the prosecution's case. Other jurors heard the same conversation conducted by a clerk in the store — evidence that favored the defendant. Half of the jurors were exposed to a judge who ruled that the evidence was admissible. The remaining jurors were told that it was inadmissible. As shown in Figure 13.4, compared to a control group that did not hear the telephone conversation, the defendant was seen as less guilty when the evidence favored him, especially when it was ruled admissible. The opposite verdict was most likely when the admissible evidence favored the prosecution. It seems that a ruling of admissibility intensifies the impact of evidence.

Because judges have the final word in explaining the meaning of evidence to the jury, they can also influence the outcome at that point in the trial. For example, when judges attack the credibility of key witnesses on one side or the other, the final verdict can be affected (Cavoukian and Doob, 1980). Though these various problems could be solved by having totally objective and unbiased judges presiding over trials, it is difficult to imagine how anyone could truly fit that description.

In a much more subtle way, a judge is found to convey his or her attitudes about a defendant through tone of voice (Goleman, 1986). In a study of actual trials, when judges were aware of a defendant's past felonies (and the jurors were not), the final instructions to the jury were lacking in warmth, tolerance, and patience. Even though jurors were unaware of any biases held by the judges, the verdicts in these instances were twice as likely to be "guilty" as those for other defendants who had no felonies on their records.

Defendants and jurors: Fairness and unfairness once again

When you read about research involving prejudice, attraction, attributions, and so forth, you might keep in mind that these variables are also operating in the courtroom. Though race, attitude similarity, attractiveness, and related factors have nothing to do with the merits of a given case, research shows that they nevertheless affect the outcome of both real and simulated trials.

The defendants: Are they treated equally?   A clear example of a powerful but supposedly irrelevant characteristic is the physical attractiveness of the person on trial. Attractive defendants tend to be acquitted more often than unattractive ones (Michelini and Snodgrass, 1980), and, when found guilty, they receive lighter sentences (Stewart, 1980). Juries not only respond positively to an attractive victim, but they also are more sympathetic to an attractive defendant (Kerr, 1978a). Because attorneys are aware of such biases, they often advise clients to go to great lengths to improve their appearance. Since the idea of a trial as a beauty contest is not a very appealing one, various suggestions have been made as to how to overcome these effects. Attractiveness has been found to be less powerful if a sufficient amount of factual information is presented to the jury (Baumeister and Darley, 1982), if the judge explicitly reminds the jury of the basis on which the verdict should be reached (Weiten, 1980), and if the jury is presented with transcripts of the testimony rather than being directly exposed to those who testify (Kaplan and Miller, 1978).

The race of a defendant is also found to affect the verdict that is reached (see Figure 13.5, page 466). Though many factors may play a role in affecting responses to blacks versus whites in the courtroom (prejudice, social class, differential crime rates, etc.), the outcome is nevertheless one in which black defendants in the United States are at a disadvantage. Blacks are more likely to be convicted and more likely to receive a prison sentence than whites (Stewart, 1980). The race of the victim also plays a role. In the United States, criminals who kill white victims have an 11.1 percent chance of receiving a death sentence, while those who kill a black have only a 4.5 chance of such a sentence (Henderson and Taylor, 1985).

Jurors and their biases.   One influence on the decisions of juries is the crime itself; another is the punishment for that crime. In effect, jurors may differ with the law about the seriousness of a given crime and about

FIGURE 13.5. Judgments made in the courtroom depend in part on factors irrelevant to the legal case, such as the defendant's race and the jurors' racial prejudice. In the interest of fairness, every possible effort must be made to reduce or totally eliminate these biasing effects.

Race and racial prejudice in the courtroom

the appropriateness of a given punishment. When cases involve unpopular laws, such as Prohibition in the 1920s or anti-marijuana laws today, jurors tend to vote for acquittal. Decisions are also based on the severity of the punishment. Though many individuals seem to feel that crime can be discouraged by passing increasingly harsh laws, research shows that the more severe the prescribed punishment, the less likely jurors are to vote for conviction (Kerr, 1978b).

Personality differences also affect the decisions of jurors. For example, jurors high in **authoritarianism** (see Chapter 14) tend to be biased against a defendant accused of causing harm to an authority figure such as a police officer (Mitchell, 1979). Those on the opposite end of this dimension (**egalitarianism**) have the opposite bias and tend to make harsh judgments when the roles are reversed and a police officer is on trial.

An even more serious problem is the fact that in murder cases in states having the death penalty, juries are ordinarily selected so as to eliminate anyone who is opposed to that punishment. The jurors in such cases are termed "death-qualified." This creates a problem because psychological research has consistently shown that death-qualified jurors are also more likely to convict a defendant than are jurors who oppose the death penalty (Turkington, 1986). The U. S. Supreme Court has decided that a defendant can have a fair trial even when the jury is composed of individuals with a set of beliefs that are known to be associated with decisions favoring the prosecution. One counterproposal to eliminate this bias is to let the guilt or innocence of accused murderers be decided by juries that are *not* death-qualified. Afterward, decisions about how to punish the guilty could be made by jurors who accept that particular law.

There are also procedural variables that affect the decisions of jurors.

After hearing all of the evidence in a murder trial, members of the jury are asked to consider the harshest verdict first—murder in the first degree. If they cannot agree on this, they must consider second degree murder, then voluntary manslaughter, and finally involuntary manslaughter. Research by Greenberg, Williams, and O'Brien (1986) indicates that this procedure leads to harsher verdicts than if the order is reversed, beginning with the most lenient verdict. Because some sort of bias is created by either order, perhaps the only fair solution would be to require jurors to consider different possible verdicts in random order with respect to harshness.

In summary, applied research on the legal system provides convincing evidence that psychological factors influence witnesses, jurors, and responses to defendants, attorneys, and judges. One conclusion is that additional effort is needed to make our legal system as fair and objective as we wish it to be.

HEALTH PSYCHOLOGY: *The Social-Psychological Aspects of Health Care*

It is generally accepted that health and illness involve more than simply physical factors. We know, for example, that some personality variables predispose an individual to having certain illnesses and that the behavior of physicians can influence the course of recovery (Krantz, Grunberg, and Baum, 1985). Not only do psychological variables affect one's physical well being, but an increase in physical fitness results in an improvement in psychological characteristics such as creativity (Gondola, 1985). **Health psychology** is the field that studies the psychological processes that affect the prevention and treatment of physical illness (Rogers, 1983). Table 13.2 presents a few recent examples of research demonstrat-

	Some Recent Findings in Health Psychology	Reference
	Psychological stress brings about negative physiological changes	Auerback et al., 1983
	Learned health habits can be beneficial to one's health but they can also be harmful	Holmes et al., 1983
	Personality traits predispose individuals to develop specific illnesses	Krantz and Glass, 1984
	How an individual copes with illness may be as important as how he or she copes with the health care system	DiMatteo and Friedman, 1982
	Those who smoke cigarettes are also more likely to be users of alcohol and coffee than are nonsmokers	Carmady et al., 1985
	Patients who are well adjusted to their illness have relatively ineffective cancer-fighting physiological responses. Reactions such as anger are associated with more effective control of cancer spread.	Levy et al., 1985

TABLE 13.2 Applied psychological research has provided a great deal of information of importance in health care. A sampling of recent findings is presented here.

Some research findings in health psychology

ing the role of psychological variables in the health process. Because health psychology is increasingly important, several graduate training programs with this emphasis have been developed (Olbrisch et al., 1985). We now examine some of the ways in which social psychological research is relevant to medical issues.

Behavior that helps prevent illness

It is obvious that preventing illness is preferable to treating illness. The question is how to achieve such a goal. Do we rely on teaching children about health care as early as possible? Is it helpful to mount massive health campaigns targeted at adults who have already learned many unhealthful habits (Koop, 1983)? In either instance, the greatest challenge is to motivate people to act in their own best interest.

Personality variables and effective preventive behavior.   Any health program must deal with individual differences in the willingness to follow medical advice (Kirscht, 1983). Analysis of the problem led to the development of the **health belief model.** In essence, an individual's beliefs about health and the threat of illness are used to predict his or her health-related behavior.

One such model was proposed by Weinstein (1984), who found that college students hold unrealistically optimistic beliefs about their health risks. For example, students tend to feel that they themselves are unlikely ever to suffer a heart attack or to have a drinking problem, while other students are perceived as having much higher risks for those outcomes. Though students assume correctly that such factors as family history may have some effect on their risk for a given illness, they ignore their own health practices that could affect the same illness. For example, they saw no relationship between their risk of a heart attack and how much they exercised, consumed red meat, smoked, or ate high cholesterol foods such as eggs.

These findings may suggest lack of knowledge on the part of students, but that is not the case. In one study, college students, high school teachers, and licensed nurses rank-ordered several activities as to how health-protective they were (Turk, Rudy, and Salovey, 1984). It was found that the knowledge of the students was surprisingly similar to that of the teachers and nurses. So, basic information about health seems to be widespread, but the problem lies in applying it to oneself.

One important element is the expectation that the preventive health practices will actually pay off, and the belief that one's efforts will accomplish the goal. The latter belief involves **self-efficacy** (Bandura, 1977), a concept that will also be discussed in Chapter 14. The way expectancies and beliefs influence health behavior was shown in one study of older adults who had chronic lung disease. Some patients were given specific information about how to carry out an exercise program and others were not (Kaplan, Atkins, and Reinsch, 1984). Those who were told in detail what to do exercised more, and their increased feelings of efficacy seemed to underly the behavior. In a similar way, women who expressed high self-efficacy with respect to the birth process were able to tolerate the pain of labor for a longer period without medication than those low in self-efficacy (Manning and Wright, 1983). Still other research shows that feelings of efficacy among cancer patients are associated with lower levels of anxiety and fewer side effects in response to chemotherapy (van Komen and Redd, 1985).

Preventing cigarette smoking before it starts.   The evidence linking cigarette smoking and such diseases as lung cancer is now well established, and most people are aware of the dangers of smoking (Eiser, 1983). Those who argue in favor of smoking despite the potential harm tend to stress such positive consequences as tension reduction, peer acceptance, and weight reduction (Chassin et al., 1984b; Fishbein, 1982). Giving up the use of an addictive substance is difficult, even when one firmly decides to quit (Eiser and van der Pligt, 1986; Shiffman, 1984). As important as it is to help smokers give up the habit, it is even more important to prevent the behavior from ever starting.

One strategy is to attempt to identify those who may be most likely to start smoking—children and adolescents. As distressing as it may seem, about one out of three third-grade students surveyed in one study reported having tried cigarettes (Hirschman, Leventhal, and Glynn, 1984). Those who continued to smoke after trying it were identified as being influenced by their peers (for example, having friends who smoked) and as feeling helpless when confronted by any failure experience. A study of fifteen-year-olds in Britain also found that friends had a powerful influence, as did parents who expressed little objection to the habit (Eiser and van der Pligt, 1984). Presumably, the more information children and adolescents receive about the harmful effects of smoking (see Figure 13.6, page 470), the better able they are to resist the effects of peers, parents, and the feeling of helplessness.

In one prevention study, Canadian sixth-graders were selected as subjects on the basis of posing a high risk for becoming adult smokers (Best et al., 1984). These young people either had powerful models for smoking behavior (parents, siblings, friends), or they were already smoking at least occasionally. The experimental group attended sessions that included information on the negative effects of smoking, training in skills designed to resist social influence, and encouragement to make public decisions not to smoke. A control group took part in a health education program that omitted any consideration of smoking. The effectiveness of the program was evaluated after two and a half years had passed. While 25 percent of the control group stopped smoking, 43 percent of those in the experimental group did so (Evans, Raines, and Hanselka, 1984). This and other research suggests that the most effective aspects of the prevention program consisted of learning how to resist pressure to smoke and in receiving information about its effects; public

FIGURE 13.6. As the big bad wolf has discovered, cigarette smoking can cause coughing, shortness of breath, and decreased physical stamina. It is assumed that the more children and adolescents are exposed to information about the harmful effects of smoking, the less likely they will be to become smokers. (Source: Reprinted by permission: Tribune Media Services.)

Some harmful effects of smoking

commitment does not seem to be very important (McCaul et al., 1983; Murray et al., 1984).

The anatomy of an illness episode

Almost all of us become ill from time to time. Though you may not think of psychological factors having much to do with your response to illness, Figure 13.7 outlines a series of decisions and behavioral differences that affect the outcome of such an episode. We will examine some of the research dealing with these differential responses.

Attending to physical symptoms: Does optimism help? As you might guess from the earlier discussion of college students and expectancies about heart attacks and alcoholism, there is an unrealistic degree of optimism in this population about how susceptible they are to illness (Weinstein, 1983). Students are more likely to believe that they could develop an infectious disease — such as a cold — than a disorder that depends on their own behavior — such as drug addiction (Weinstein, 1984).

Research indicates that this optimism is associated with experiencing fewer physical symptoms of disease (Scheier and Carver, 1985). For example, those who agreed with statements such as "Every cloud has a silver lining" reported fewer symptoms during the subsequent month than those who disagreed. Optimism has a negative side, also. Those who feel invulnerable to illness tend to avoid engaging in appropriate preventive behavior—for example, immunization against influenza (Cummings et al., 1979).

Imagining one's potential illnesses.   It has been proposed that we are most likely to imagine and apply to ourselves those symptoms that are easiest to remember (Sherman et al., 1985). In one experiment, students were given information about symptoms that were easy to remember and imagine—muscle aches, headaches, and low energy level. Other symptoms were much more difficult—a vague sense of disorientation and a malfunctioning nervous system. The subjects rated the easy symptoms much more likely to happen to them than the difficult ones.

It seems likely that preventive health programs would do well to describe all relevant symptoms in concrete ways that are easy to recall.

Diagnosing your symptoms.   Until such time as a person decides that symptoms indicate illness, he or she obviously will do nothing about seeking help. It appears that most people use a common-sense model of self-diagnosis (Leventhal and Nerenz, 1983). For example, a sore throat may be interpreted as a symptom of an oncoming cold. This label leads the individual to attempt to detect other symptoms (runny nose, fatigue, etc.) that past experience indicates should accompany that diagnosis. If

FIGURE 13.7.   During an illness episode, the individual is faced with several choice points. Self-diagnosis of physical symptoms precedes whatever action is taken, ranging from doing nothing to seeking medical advice and treatment. Regardless of the person's decision about taking action, he or she must cope with the symptoms. In addition, any formal or informal cures require coping with the treatment process.

The anatomy of an illness episode

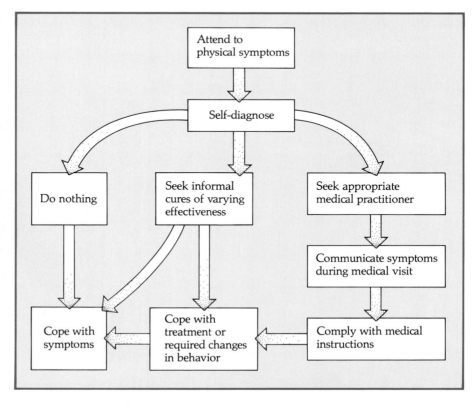

FOCUS ON RESEARCH:
The Cutting Edge

Behavior as a Contributor to Physical Illness and a Response to It

Whether or not we become ill at a particular time is, in part, dependent on the way we respond to stress. The effect of external events on internal physiological states is currently the focus of attention in research on **psychoneuroimmunology**. This has been described as "a new area of study that attempts to formalize concepts previously accepted only by faith healers and grandmothers" (Schindler, 1985).

One of the links between psychological responses and illness lies in the release of *stress hormones* (Axelrod and Reisine, 1984). One study examined graduate students in the process of defending their doctoral dissertations in oral examinations. Such individuals showed a threefold increase in adrenalin production during the weeks before and after the exams (Johansson et al., 1983). If the immune system is negatively affected by the presence of this hormone, it is clear why illness is more likely to occur during stressful periods of one's life. It can be argued that, in human history, adrenaline production was once a helpful reaction to stress because the hormone helped us respond actively by fighting or running for safety. Today, social stress — such as undergoing a job interview — does not require us to attack or to flee, and the production of stress hormones only does us harm (see Figure 13.8).

Research consistently shows that immunity to disease is reduced by exposure to certain situations and that there are individual differences in perceiving a given situation as a source of stress. For example, male prisoners who have a strong need for power and control respond to the prison environment with the greatest amount of stress and the least immunity to disease (McClelland, Alexander, and Marks, 1982). Because being in prison acts to thwart the exercise of power and the ability to control events, these individuals experience

FIGURE 13.8. Stress leads to the overproduction of hormones such as adrenalin. When the appropriate response to danger is physical activity (for example, fighting or running away), adrenalin is helpful. When the appropriate response is to remain in the situation and engage in acceptable interpersonal behavior, adrenalin tends to have an adverse effect on the body's immune system and therefore on the development of illness.

Stress: Adrenalin can decrease immunity to disease

stress and begin to manufacture lower levels of a chemical substance known as *immunoglobulin A*. When this occurs, illnesses such as upper respiratory infections show an increase. Once again, the psychological response has physiological effects which, in turn, affect health.

A familiar sort of stress that is found to affect the immune system is the loss of or separation from a loved one. The death of your parent or of your child, divorce or separation, or the geographical relocation of a close friend are followed by a reduction in immunity to disease (Laudenslager and Reite, 1984). In a similar way, chronic, uncontrollable stress, such as the serious illness of a spouse or the strains of an unhappy marriage, can eventually result in immunity reduction.

Sadly enough, there is another source of stress that is an integral part of the disease process. Once a person becomes seriously ill, feelings of helplessness and hopelessness often increase. These reactions then make one even less resistant to disease. For example, cancer is serious enough, but the patient's depressed reaction to that diagnosis acts to make the physical situation even worse, thus interfering with recovery (Goldberg and Tull, 1984). Not only is illness a source of stress, but having to be hospitalized adds to the problem; the patient is forced into a situation in which he or she is relatively powerless (Peterson and Raps, 1984).

Stress need not have such negative effects if the individual can learn to respond physically in a less self-defeating way. For example, relaxation training among elderly adults has been found to increase immunity when their health records are compared with those of untreated control subjects (Keicolt-Glaser et al., 1985). Thus, the effect of our thoughts and our emotions on physiological responses and health need not be negative. We can be taught to overcome the usual effects and to use psychological responses to our advantage.

the initial self-diagnosis is incorrect, the entire labeling process may lead the individual to ignore incompatible information and thus to avoid necessary medical treatment.

Without appropriate information or personal experience with a given set of symptoms, the common-sense model can lead to serious health-related mistakes (Routh and Ernest, 1984). For example, a person who experiences a stomachache and vomiting may decide the problem is simply an intestinal virus that will soon go away. If the actual problem is something more serious, such as a diseased appendix, the organ may burst before medical help is sought. In a similar way, a person's own incorrect beliefs about a serious illness such as hypertension can lead to the avoidance of treatment altogether or to the failure to take medication (Meyer, Leventhal, and Gutman, 1985). Because there are no obvious symptoms of this disorder, the patient may decide the problem no longer exists. Beyond the decision-making process, psychological factors are found to influence the development of illness in other ways, as described in the **Focus** insert on page 472.

Perceived control and distress.   There is a basic human need to control events in one's life (Dembroski, MacDougall, and Musante, 1984). It is found that both psychological well-being and physical health benefit when an individual has **perceived control** over what happens. As was pointed out in Chapter 12, those who believe they have control over aversive stimuli, such as shock or loud noises, experience less stress and greater tolerance for the unpleasantness than those who believe they are helpless in the situation (Gatchel and Proctor, 1976; Staub, Tursky, and Schwartz, 1971). A low sense of control results in chronic depression (Martin et al., 1984). It is also true that a change in mood leads to changes in perceived control. For example, when a positive mood is induced, experimental subjects believe they have increased control over events (Alloy, Abramson, and Viscusi, 1981). In everyday life, uncontrollable distressing occurrences such as the loss of a job are followed by a greater likelihood of admission to a psychiatric hospital, suicide, and death from natural causes (Liem and Raymono, 1982). Even minor everyday hassles (for example, equipment that doesn't work or rude remarks by others) that are beyond one's control have negative effects on health (Zarski, 1984).

With physical illness, perceived control is also important. People tend to explain their own illnesses in terms of either internal or external causes (Lau and Hartman, 1983). External causes are perceived as beyond one's control; if someone with a contagious disease coughs in your face, you are likely to catch the disease through no fault of your own. Internal causes tend to involve not taking proper care of oneself, and the person feels responsible for the resulting disorder. Individuals who perceive internal causes seem to feel more responsibility concerning preventive behavior, self-diagnosis, and restoration of health. Even with an illness as serious as breast cancer, those who believe in their ability to control the course of the illness function more effectively during treatment (Taylor Lichtman, and Wood, 1984). Those who have accidents at work return to the job sooner and with more positive feelings if they perceive that they caused the accident and hence can prevent its happening again (Brewin, 1984). A person who focuses on external causes tends to be relatively pessimistic about maintaining good health, and such beliefs are associated with childhood experiences with illness or death when helplessness was a realistic perception of the child's role (Lau, 1982b).

The desire for control is generally adaptive, but it can be sufficiently strong that it interferes with the efficient use of the medical system (Wallston et al., 1984). For example, some of those who use community medical services are characterized as the "worried well" because they visit the agencies frequently and inappropriately (Wagner and Curran, 1984). Such individuals overestimate the seriousness of minor symptoms and seek unneeded medical help.

Responding to one's self-diagnosis.   Once an individual decides on the nature and cause of a given symptom or set of symptoms, his or her subsequent behavior may help or hinder recovery. Those who are characterized by the personality trait of **chronic self-destructiveness** tend to respond by avoiding potentially helpful activities (for example, seeking medical help) and by continuing to engage in potentially harmful acts (for example, smoking; Kelley et al., 1985). Self-destructive individuals tend to place the blame for their difficulties on external causes, and they are low in self-control (Kelley and Musialowski, 1986b).

Interacting with medical personnel and undergoing treatment

As shown on the model (Figure 13.7, page 471), once a person decides to seek treatment, it is necessary to undergo the frightening experience of visiting a physician and facing the possibility of painful procedures and a threatening diagnosis.

Doctor-patient interactions.   Because of the anxiety and fear associated with medical visits, patients often forget to mention crucial symptoms and neglect to ask important questions; the result is dissatisfaction with the experience. This general problem can be overcome, in part. In one experimental intervention, Roter (1984) asked patients to spend ten min-

FIGURE 13.9.   Patients who are instructed to develop a list of questions before seeing a physician ask more questions during the visit than those who are not instructed to develop a list. Both medical and nonmedical questions were asked in greater numbers. For example, patients with lists asked such varied things as "Are there any side effects with this prescription?" and "How are your children?" (Source: Based on data from Roter, 1984.)

Helping patients learn to ask questions

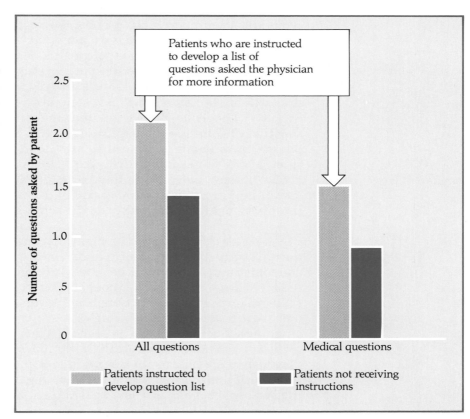

utes with a health educator before seeing the physician. The purpose was to identify the patient's areas of concern and to generate a list of questions to ask. As Figure 13.9 (page 475) shows, this procedure resulted in an increase in the number of questions directed toward the physician.

The behavior of physicians is also of importance. For example, why are some physicians perceived as more comforting and having a better "bedside manner" than others? Part of the answer lies in the nonverbal behavior of the doctor. This behavior was manipulated in one experiment in which physicians were instructed to lean forward in interacting with some patients and not with others, fold their arms or not, and so forth (Harrigan and Rosenthal, 1983). The most positive evaluations from patients came when the physicians simultaneously leaned forward, did not fold their arms, and nodded their heads. It should be fairly easy to teach medical students to behave in such a way as to generate positive and comfortable feelings among their patients.

Compliance with medical instructions.   Following a formal medical diagnosis, appropriate treatment often includes the recommendation to change some aspects of the patient's usual behavior, taking prescribed drugs, and/or undergoing surgical procedures. Whether or not the patient actually does any of these things depends in part on the person's beliefs about them. Those who feel an exercise program will work are more likely to undertake it (Dishman, 1982). Those who believe they would be able to detect the presence of an abnormal growth are more likely to engage in breast self-examination (Alagna and Reddy, 1984). Again, efficacy is an important element in adaptive behavior.

Though the physician writes a prescription and directs the patient to follow certain instructions, there is actually a very good chance that the drug will not be taken or will be taken incorrectly (Haynes, Taylor, and Sackett, 1979). Following instructions about prescribed drugs is in part a function of information, and patients need to know more than either physicians or pharmacists tend to provide (Keown, Slovic, and Lichenstein, 1984). For example, the typical patient is much more concerned about "minor" side effects than are professionals and may decide to discontinue treatment when unexpected symptoms appear. The more information provided to patients, the better their compliance.

Coping with treatment.   With many diagnostic and therapeutic procedures, the patient must undergo interventions that are intrusive, painful, and sometimes dangerous. The process of **coping** with such events refers to the behavior, feelings, and thoughts that make it possible to tolerate or even master the threat (Hartsough and Myers, 1985). Early in an illness, one of the best short-term strategies is to avoid thinking about or doing anything about the problem (Suls and Fletcher, 1985). Stress is decreased if you don't admit that you are ill. As the illness progresses, however, it is obviously preferable to pay attention to it and to seek treatment.

The ability to cope is influenced by important variables present in the person's everyday life and in the treatment procedure itself. It has been found that social support from a network of friends is helpful in the coping process (Fleming, Baum, and Singer, 1984; Folkman, 1984). We benefit from having concerned friends who encourage us to return to good health (Rook and Dooley, 1985). With respect to the treatment itself, distress and fear are in part a function of not knowing what is going to happen, how much pain is involved, and how long the process will last. Even small children can cope with procedures that hurt if they know enough about what is going on (Jay et al., 1983).

It becomes clear from even a brief sampling of health psychology that psychological factors are involved in every aspect of health from preventive behavior to dealing with illness and its treatment. We will now turn from social psychological concerns with health to concerns with occupations and what happens on the job.

THE WORK SETTING: Organizational Behavior

As you might guess from earlier descriptions of social psychological research dealing with matters such as bargaining (Chapter 10) and leadership (Chapter 11), the applications of our field to behavior in organizations are widespread. A large portion of the lives of many adults is spent working at a job outside of the home, within organizations (see Figure 13.10). Thus, the study of **organizational behavior** has broad conse-

FIGURE 13.10. Because most adults spend a large portion of their waking lives at work, it is important to know as much as possible about the factors that influence the motivation of employees, satisfaction with a given job, productivity, and all other aspects of behavior within an organization.

On-the-job behavior: A major part of many lives

ON THE APPLIED SIDE

How Can Management Motivate Employees to Work?

In any organization, a primary requirement of those in charge is to interact with employees in such a way as to reach the work goals and to get the job done as effectively as possible. This same issue must be faced whether the organization is a manufacturing plant, a military unit, a fast-food franchise, or a university. Offhand, the question of how to motivate workers may seem to be a simple one, but quite different answers have been proposed at various times. In part, your initial response to the question tends to be based on how you conceptualize human behavior (Altman, Valenzi, and Hodgetts, 1985). Before reading about the three major behavioral theories of management, you may find it helpful to stop and consider your own current beliefs about why people work, what role a job plays in one's life, and how employees might best be treated.

In the United States following the Civil War, the increasing industrialization of society led to new problems of management. One answer was **classical management** theory which focused on the way to maximize productivity and hence to maximize profits. The guiding philosophy assumed that the primary motivation for work was money, in that money was required to buy food, clothing, shelter, and so forth. Given the basic need for money, workers could be treated however management wished. An authoritarian atmosphere was assumed to be the most appropriate one; managers were to set goals, give orders, and treat employees more or less as children who would not know what to do without explicit directions from superiors.

By the 1920s the realization had begun to grow that workers were human beings who had needs beyond decent wages. The result was a humanizing and extension of classical theory that became known as **human relations theory**. While still accepting the motivating power of money, human relations advocates felt that other factors were equally important, for example, the opportunity for social interaction with fellow workers. Rather than simply issuing orders from the top down, managers were expected to solicit ideas and suggestions from those who worked for them. It was deemed important to provide opportunities for workers to voice complaints to a sympathetic management that was at least willing to hear what they had to say. Instead of a model involving a stern father who dealt with incompetent children, the new theory of management was more like that of a kindly parent who was responsible for the welfare of immature adolescents.

Currently, a third theory of management —**human resources theory**—has wide support. Managers are not described as having to *control* employees (either blatantly or subtly) but as acting to *facilitate* their job performance. This approach recognizes the fact that various needs can be fulfilled (or frustrated) in the work setting (see Figure 13.11). Beyond an adequate salary and the desire to socialize, people also want to achieve, to be respected, to have a sense of responsibility and freedom, to have some control over what happens at work, and to feel secure in their occupation (Wexley and Yukl, 1984). To meet such needs, managers are encouraged to foster creativity, autonomy, and communication. From this theoretical perspective, employees are regarded as adults whose activities are facilitated by the actions of management.

Among the other emphases of human resource theory is a belief in the importance of empirical research. Regardless of one's personal philosophy about a given issue or procedure, a more important question is, "What do the data indicate?" A second emphasis is on the

FIGURE 13.11. In the *human resources theory* of management, it is recognized that individuals working in an organization have multiple needs that can be met on the job under appropriate conditions. Shown here are six key needs and examples of ways that each can be met within an organization. (Source: Based on material in Wexley and Yukl, 1984.)

Needs that can be gratified (or frustrated) in the work setting

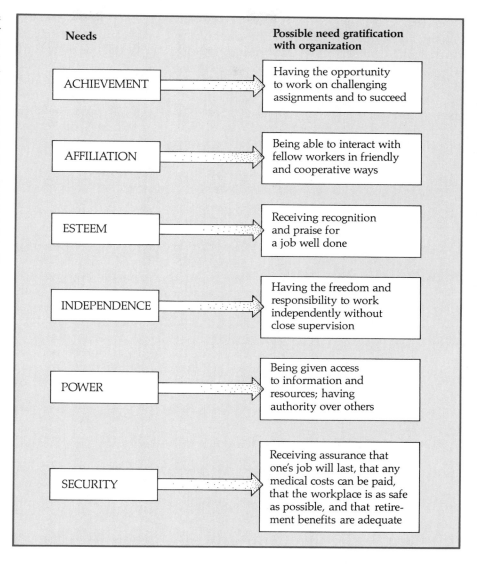

Needs	Possible need gratification with organization
ACHIEVEMENT	Having the opportunity to work on challenging assignments and to succeed
AFFILIATION	Being able to interact with fellow workers in friendly and cooperative ways
ESTEEM	Receiving recognition and praise for a job well done
INDEPENDENCE	Having the freedom and responsibility to work independently without close supervision
POWER	Being given access to information and resources; having authority over others
SECURITY	Receiving assurance that one's job will last, that any medical costs can be paid, that the workplace is as safe as possible, and that retirement benefits are adequate

importance of combining all that is known into a theoretical framework that provides both a concept of management and a guide for applied research. The final emphasis of this theory of management is on the importance of a **systems approach.** A system is a unit consist- ing of interacting parts. One aspect of a system is the individual who enters an organization with certain skills, needs, and traits. There is also a formal organizational structure with specified divisions, departments, and the like. In addition, an informal organization operates to control the behavior of fellow workers by setting norms and procedures. The goals of the formal and informal organizations may or may not coincide. For example, pressure can be brought by other workers against an individual who works "too fast" and as a result makes others appear inefficient. These three elements interact to yield a unique *fusion* that operates within a specific physical environment. Thus, the sort of variables discussed in Chapter 12 provide a context for individual-organization interactions.

When an organization is conceptualized as a system in this fashion, it follows that any research or any plan of action must consider the total system rather than an isolated part of it. It also becomes clear that motivating workers and achieving high levels of productivity are difficult and somewhat complex goals.

quences for both employees and employers (Baron, 1986b). This field seeks to understand and predict human behavior in organizational settings by means of the scientific study of individuals, groups, and the structure and function of organizations. Application in this setting often raises questions about values, and the needs and beliefs of the workers may well conflict with those of their employers (Hackman, Lawler, and Porter, 1983). In such cases, the organizational psychologist must be acutely aware of the implications of each research finding and of any recommendations to which it leads. (Several issues relevant to such values are raised in the **Applied Side** insert on page 478.)

Achieving job satisfaction and assessing its effects

A prospective employee's first contact with an organization occurs during the job interview. At that point, the employer desires to hire the employee most suitable for a particular position in that specific organization.

Selecting the right employee.   The better the fit between employee and job, the greater will be that person's eventual job satisfaction and productivity (Hunter and Schmidt, 1983). As you might expect from the research on attraction (Chapter 6), the interpersonal decision to hire or not can be on the basis of liking rather than on logical grounds related to job suitability. For example, the applicant's physical attractiveness (Cash and Kilcullen, 1985; Jackson, 1983) and the interviewer's mood (R.A. Baron, 1986a) are irrelevant factors that have been found to affect hiring decisions.

In other instances, job-relevant characteristics do have an effect on which individuals are given jobs. For example, those who are most skilled at interpersonal communication are more likely to obtain high-level managerial positions than those who do not communicate well (Sypher and Sypher, 1983).

Increasing job satisfaction.   It is generally accepted that **job satisfaction** is beneficial to the worker and perhaps to the organization. As you might suspect, perceptions of one's work as stressful or rewarding depend, in part, on actual job conditions (LaRocco, 1985). Satisfaction with work may not necessarily increase productivity (Musialowski, 1986; Nelkin and Brown, 1984), but it is nevertheless widely accepted that job satisfaction should ideally be maximized (Lawler, 1982). A general finding is that satisfaction is greater when employees possess an adequate amount of information about such matters as promotion policies and the way their performance is rated (Penley, 1982).

One possibility for increasing satisfaction is to make jobs more interesting by introducing variety into routine tasks and by giving the worker more control over what he or she does on the job. Such changes are known as **job enlargement**. A widely known example of this approach was carried out in Sweden's Volvo plant. Both labor and management responded positively to job enlargement, and the quality of the product improved — however, overall productivity *decreased* (Gyllenhammar, 1977).

Another attempt to increase satisfaction is through the use of flexible time schedules (**flexitime**). It is found that having greater freedom in deciding when to work leads to a decrease in absenteeism, but job satisfaction is not necessarily improved (Narayanan and Nath, 1982).

Beyond the details of the job itself, satisfaction is positively related to the extent to which the individual feels **organizational commitment** (Coombs, 1979). An employee is committed to an organization to the extent that he or she feels involved, loyal, and able to identify with the company. Commitment increases when workers are high in the need to achieve and when they are given some degree of responsibility. Because of the success of Japanese firms in generating such commitment, many American firms have been trying to adopt their techniques. Thus, Japanese practices such as providing job security and encouraging identification (using company songs, wearing identifiable clothing or insignia, etc.) are being imported into the United States (Kupferberg, 1980).

One employee-participation procedure widely practiced in Japan that is now being applied elsewhere is the concept of *quality circles* (Lawler and Mohrman, 1985). The idea was actually brought to Japan after World War II by an American, H. Edwards Deming. Individuals who are engaged in similar work in an organization meet voluntarily once a week to discuss problems on the job and to suggest solutions (Marks, 1986). The basic assumption is that a person who performs a given job is best able to identify problems and to correct them. In addition to the general benefits provided by coming up with useful solutions, employees are said to become more motivated in their work and more committed to the organization.

The relationship between satisfaction on the job and one's personal life is fairly direct (Koch et al., 1982). For example, job satisfaction seems to lead to slightly increased feelings of general contentment (Near et al., 1983). In addition, those who are happily married indicate they like their jobs better than do those who are single (Bersoff and Crosby, 1984). It seems logical to expect that any satisfactions or dissatisfactions involving either one's work or one's home life would necessarily have an effect on the other.

Performance appraisal: Attributions and interventions

In the discussion of attribution theory in Chapter 2, we pointed out that people tend to explain the behavior of others in terms of external and internal causes. These same processes operate when another person's job performance is being evaluated. We will examine some of the factors affecting such judgments and some of the techniques used in the attempt to improve performance.

Judging how well a job is done.   An obvious element influencing evaluations is how well an individual actually performs a task. For example, business managers tend to give the largest salary increases to those whose objective performances are best (Alexander and Barrett, 1982). No one finds fault with this kind of criterion. The problem arises when subjective variables, such as attributions, come into play.

For example, the evaluator who has not had first-hand experience with the job in question may give undue credit to the employee who performs well and place undue blame on those who are having difficulty (Mitchell and Kalb, 1982). In general, a supervisor's blame for poor performance tends to rest on attributions about the worker (skill, motivation) rather than on the role of situational determinants of performance (Gioia and Sims, 1985). Heerwagen, Beach, and Mitchell (1985) have shown that it is possible to alter attributions by stressing the importance of situational factors.

It is also found that there is a tendency to reward hard work and effort to a greater extent than skill (Knowlton and Mitchell, 1980). An employee is evaluated more highly if he or she is perceived as expending a lot of energy on the job than if perceived as being talented and taking it easy.

Focusing on the individual versus the task.   In most organizations, performance is rated periodically — perhaps once or twice a year. Theoretically, this means that the evaluator must pay attention to performance during the intervening time period, judge that performance, and remember it accurately when performance appraisal is required. In actual practice, appraisal is usually not a very salient issue most of the time, and anything that interferes with attention or memory will make the appraisal less accurate and less fair.

FIGURE 13.12.   When supervisors are periodically asked to rate the performance of employees, their evaluations are often based on general impressions of the individuals involved rather than on the quality of the work performed. When they are first required to recall how well each individual carried out specific jobs, their evaluations tend accurately to reflect differences in performance, especially good performance versus that which is average or poor. (Source: Based on data from Williams, 1986.)

Performance appraisal: Recall as an aid in making accurate evaluations

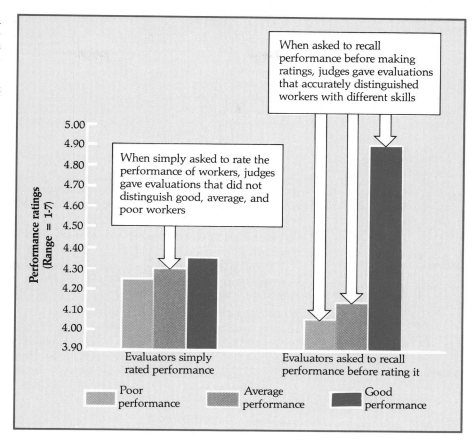

When asked to recall performance before making ratings, judges gave evaluations that accurately distinguished workers with different skills

When simply asked to rate the performance of workers, judges gave evaluations that did not distinguish good, average, and poor workers

Performance ratings (Range = 1-7)

Evaluators simply rated performance

Evaluators asked to recall performance before rating it

Poor performance   Average performance   Good performance

A major source of interference is the general tendency to focus on individuals rather than on performance itself (Williams, 1986). Thus, without specific instructions to do otherwise, raters tend to form impressions of each individual to be rated. They then rate job performance in large part on the basis of how much the worker is liked or on the person's general performance rather than on how well a given task is actually performed.

In an experimental investigation of the evaluation process, Williams found that job appraisal is improved if evaluators are told in advance that they will later be rating performance. Even if the ratings are not anticipated, evaluators do better if they are instructed to *recall* the details of performance prior to making the ratings. The experimenter created videotapes in which a series of jobs (sanding, sawing, hammering, etc.) were done very well, with average skill, or very poorly. Evaluators either were asked to rate the workers, or they were asked first to recall how well each specific task had been done. As shown in Figure 13.12, the ratings reflected objective performance differences when recall was requested first, but good, average, and poor workers were not differentiated when the judges were not given the recall request. Having to focus on performance rather than on people seems to lead evaluators to deal with the appraisal task more systematically and rationally than would otherwise be the case.

Increasing productivity

The traditional way to motivate employees to work harder is through the promise of higher pay. There is often an incentive plan whereby appropriate compensation is increased after performance improves in a specified way (Caldwell, O'Reilly, and Morris, 1983; O'Malley, 1983). A key word here is "appropriate," because a salary increase that is perceived as either unjustified or inadequate can be extremely disruptive and counterproductive.

Productivity can be enhanced when employees receive increased information about their jobs (Katzell and Guzzo, 1983). Thus, it is helpful to provide improved training with respect to job requirements, instructions about how to set realistic goals for performance, and training in decision making. At a more general level, performance is improved when the worker possesses practical knowledge about how best to succeed in his or her career. Such information has been termed *tacit knowledge* (Wagner and Sternberg, 1985). These "rules of the game" are usually not openly expressed, but they have practical implications about how to succeed. In occupations as different as college professor and bank manager, the importance of tacit knowledge has been shown. It is beneficial in either field to know how to manage oneself (for example, arranging a daily schedule) and how to promote one's career (for example, awareness of which colleagues to ask for advice). Successful professionals possess this tacit knowledge to a greater extent than unsuccessful ones. Presumably, with the appropriate educational efforts, tacit knowledge could be more widely held.

When organizations reach out to each of us: Consumer behavior

A somewhat specialized aspect of applied social psychology deals with the behavior of individuals as they react to advertising, product information, packaging, brand names, and all the other elements involved in marketing products and services. **Consumer psychology** is the field that deals with the factors affecting consumer behavior (Bettman, 1986).

One focus is on how we weigh information in making an economic decision (Jaccard, Brinberg, and Ackerman, 1986). In buying a car, for example, you learn the price, the gas mileage, and perhaps the past repair records of cars made by that firm. You may pay attention to styling, color, and various options that are available. Some of these variables are more important in determining your final decision than others, and people differ in the amount of weight they assign to each. There is also the problem of having too much information. For example, with prescription drugs, it can be useful to have detailed data about contents and possible side effects, but too much information may produce overload and lead us to ignore it entirely (Hoyer and Jacoby, 1983; Jacoby, 1984).

Advertising is of great concern to consumer psychologists in that millions are spent daily to persuade us to spend our money in specific ways. Among the variables found useful in getting our attention are size of the ad, the use of color, and any content that makes a given message memorable. In one experiment, the relative value of pictures versus words was compared (Childers and Houston, 1984). Subjects instructed to pay attention to the visual material remembered the name of the product better than those instructed to attend to the words. It also appears that whether you like or dislike an ad is not as important as whether you remember the product. Many people hate the "ring around the collar" commercials — but they remember that Wisk gets shirts clean.

This brief introduction to the application of social psychology to organizational and consumer behavior suggests once again that psychological factors are vital in every aspect of our lives. It is, in fact, difficult to imagine any human endeavor in which the findings of social psychology would be irrelevant and inapplicable. We hope you agree that the findings of social psychological research are widely generalizable and potentially useful to us all.

SUMMARY

Applied social psychology is the use of social-psychological research and practice in real-world settings as an attempt to solve a variety of social problems.

The field of **forensic psychology** serves to link psychology with the legal process. Beginning early in this century, research on eyewitness testimony has documented the inaccuracy of witnesses in their testimony, though some procedures have been developed to increase the validity of such information. Attorneys and judges have considerable influence on the way witnesses respond, whether such witnesses are perceived as credible, and on the jury's verdict. Many characteristics of the defendant (behavior, physical attractiveness, race, likeability, etc.) affect a jury's decisions. In addition, jurors respond partly on the basis of their personality traits, their beliefs, and their attitudes about the crime in question.

Health psychology refers to the application of psychological research to health problems. Interest is focused on preventive health behavior (involving diet, exercise, smoking, etc.), reactions to illness and treatment, psychological factors influencing immunity to disease, and the way in which self-diagnosis affects subsequent behavior. Interactions between patients and medical practitioners can be improved by teaching patients what questions to ask and by training practitioners in communication.

The study of **organizational behavior** involves what people do in organizational settings. Several theories of management have evolved over the decades, and today there is general acceptance of **human resources theory** that stresses the facilitation of job performance, meeting the varied needs of employees, basing decisions on empirical research data, and the use of a **systems approach. Job satisfaction** is not always positively related to productivity, but it has various benefits for both employers and employees. Among the techniques developed in this regard are flexible work schedules, introducing variety into the tasks that are performed, and an emphasis on equitable treatment. Performance appraisal is crucial within an organization, and it is important to improve the process by eliminating irrelevant psychological influences. Work in **consumer psychology** concentrates on the responses of consumers to products and services, the effects of advertising, and the way product information is processed.

GLOSSARY

applied social psychology
Social psychological research and practice in real-world settings directed toward the understanding of human social behavior and the attempted solution of social problems.

authoritarianism
The personality dimension that ranges from the authoritarian to the egalitarian extremes. Authoritarians are characterized by adherence to conventional values, submission to a strong leader, aggression toward those who deviate, and a concern with power.

chronic self-destructiveness
The tendency to avoid doing things that would be expected to result in beneficial outcomes for the individual, while choosing to engage in acts that are harmful.

classical management theory
The organizational theory (now outdated) that emphasizes productivity and profit. Workers are assumed to be motivated primarily by the need for money.

consumer psychology
The study of the psychological factors influencing the behaviors and attitudes of consumers of products and services.

coping
Those things a person does, feels, or thinks in order to master, tolerate, or decrease the negative effects of a threatening situation.

egalitarianism

The opposite personality extreme from authoritarianism. It is characterized by a democratic approach to the role of leaders, tolerance for deviant ideas, disinterest in power, and a concern for the free expression of ideas and feelings.

flexitime

The policy that permits employees to arrange their work schedules at hours convenient to them while maintaining the same total number of working hours

forensic psychology

The study of the relationship between psychology and the law. This includes eyewitness reliability, and factors involving attorneys, judges, defendants, victims, and jurors.

health belief model

A set of beliefs and expectancies applied to health and the threat of illness.

health psychology

The study and practice of the psychological aspects of the prevention and treatment of physical illness.

human relations theory

The organizational theory that recognizes the importance of social needs in addition to the need for income. Workers are encouraged to communicate ideas, suggestions, and complaints.

human resources theory

The organizational theory that stresses the importance of being able to satisfy multiple needs in the work setting. The role of managers is to facilitate job performance rather than to give orders about what to do and how to do it. This approach also includes reliance on empirical research and an integrated theoretical emphasis that includes a systems approach.

job enlargement

The practice of expanding the content of a job so as to include an increased number of different and varied tasks for each worker.

job satisfaction

The extent to which a worker is content with his or her position in an organization, the work conditions, compensation, and general treatment relative to others in the organization.

organizational behavior

The study of human behavior in organizational settings. The focus includes individual processes, group processes, and organizational structure and function.

organizational commitment

The extent to which an individual feels loyal to the organization for which he or she works and feels identified and involved with it.

perceived control

The extent to which an individual believes that he or she is able to influence the course of events.

psychoneuroimmunology

The study of the way our responses to external events affects internal physiological states which influence immunity to illness.

self-efficacy
How well an individual believes he or she can do in carrying out a given task
or activity.

systems approach
A theoretical analysis of organizational structure that focuses on the
interaction and fusion of the individual, formal organization, and informal
organization within a specific environmental context.

FOR MORE INFORMATION

Altmaier, E. M., Delworth, U., and Hanson, G. R., eds. (1983). *Helping
students manage stress: New directions for student services.* No. 21. San
Francisco: Jossey-Bass.

> This manual describes techniques to be used for the reduction of stress
> experienced by students on college campuses. It evaluates each technique
> on the basis of research findings dealing with the causes and effects of
> stress.

Altmaier, E. M., and Meyer, M. E., eds. (1985). *Applied specialties in
psychology.* New York: Random House.

> This textbook spans the range of psychological applications to individual
> health, consumer behavior, business settings, and the courtroom. The
> chapters are written by experts representing each of the specific areas
> covered.

Baron, R. A. (1986). *Behavior in organizations: Understanding and managing
the human side of work,* 2nd ed. Boston: Allyn and Bacon.

> A comprehensive and up-to-date introduction to the field of
> organizational behavior. It describes how basic psychological principles
> —such as learning, personality, perception, attitudes, and motivation—
> are relevant to behavior in the organizational setting. Also covered are
> the work-related aspects of stress, communication, decision making,
> group behavior, leadership, and various aspects of organizational
> structure and functioning.

Hine, F. R., Carson, R. C., Maddox, G. L., Thompson, R. J., Jr., and Williams,
R. B., Jr. (1983). *Introduction to behavioral science in medicine.* New York:
Springer-Verlag.

> The broad scope of the field of health psychology is presented in this
> text. It includes sections on the psychological contributions to illness and
> the interactions of patients with the health care system.

CHAPTER 14

PERSONALITY TRAITS: Characteristic Behavior across Situations
Personality and behavior: How useful is the trait concept? • Identifying personality traits • Constructing a personality measure • Determining if a new test is reliable and valid

TYPE A CORONARY-PRONE PERSONALITY: Aggressiveness, Working under Pressure, Achievement
The Type A behavior pattern and its development • Behavioral differences: Type A versus Type B individuals

LOCUS OF CONTROL: Assigning Responsibility for Life's Outcomes
How we obtain rewards and avoid punishments • Behavioral differences: Internals versus externals

LONELINESS: An Unmet Need for Social Contact
Assessing loneliness • Lonely children and lonely adults • The behavior of those who are lonely and how it can be changed

PERSONALITY:
Individual Differences in
Social Behavior

*The setting is a small study room in a college dormitory. A student —
Tom — is pacing back and forth rapidly, periodically glancing at the
door and at his watch. Under his breath, he talks disgustedly to himself.*

   TOM: It's ten minutes after four. . . . Why can't he ever be on
time? . . . I've got a hundred other things I need to be doing.

   *Door opens and another student — Howard — comes in, eating an
ice cream cone.*

   TOM: *(sarcastically)* You didn't have to rush on my account.
You're only twelve minutes late.

   HOWARD: Am I? My watch stopped running last week, and I
haven't gotten around to fixing it.

   TOM: That's sick. How can you function without knowing what
time it is?

   HOWARD: Someone like you is usually around to tell me.

   TOM: *(sitting down, leaning forward expectantly)* Cute. Could
we get to this week's math assignment? As usual, we were supposed to
work on twenty problems each and then exchange answers. You know
that this study arrangement is the prof's idea, not mine. I'd rather
work by myself.

   HOWARD: *(looking out the window)* Wait until I finish my cone.
You know, there's a nice view of the campus center from here.

   TOM: Good lord! Would you *please* sit down so we can get this
over with?

   HOWARD: *(taking a chair)* I'll sit down, but . . .

TOM: *(interrupting)* You haven't gotten the work done. I knew it. I just knew it.

HOWARD: I did five of them last night, but then some of the guys came by, and we went out for a couple of beers.

TOM: I worked on my problems for three solid hours last Sunday afternoon and then went to the library to make a copy for you. I can't believe this.

HOWARD: It'll be all right. I'm sure old Jensen will give us an extension.

TOM: I don't want an extension. *(gathering up his books and papers, heading for the door)* You can do whatever you bloody please, but I'm handing in my work today and requesting a new work partner for the future — preferably someone from this planet.

HOWARD: *(unruffled)* No sweat, man. I'll just go with the flow.

TOM: *(as he leaves)* I really don't care where you flow.

THESE TWO individuals have become acutely aware of the fact that different people can react in very different ways to the same social situation. One is impatient, driven by the demands of the task, and eager to do his own work quickly and well. The other is easy-going, relaxed about time pressures, and more concerned about other matters than about the quality of his work. We'll discuss these characteristics shortly when we describe *Type A* and *Type B* personalities.

Such differences among individuals are the result of many possible influences, including those present at birth, as suggested in the cartoon in Figure 14.1. From that point on, experiential factors become of critical importance. From earliest infancy, we are each affected by our interactions with our particular families and friends and by the demands of a specific culture, social class, race, religion, and many other factors. The end result is that each of us responds in characteristic ways to many situations. We can be described as having a series of relatively lasting dispositions that are known as **personality traits**. Despite the major role played by situational factors in determining behavior, variations among individuals are often associated with particular traits.

In this chapter, we will take a look at a small sample of such personality variables and the ways they affect social behavior. Specifically, we will focus attention on current controversies about the *conceptualization of traits*. Then, we will describe how they are measured, with *authoritarianism* serving as an example. Next, we will describe research on several personality dimensions that have been of special interest to social psychologists, including *Type A coronary-prone behavior, locus of control,* and *loneliness.* We will also deal with the way investigators have gone about the *identification of traits*, the role of the personality disposition known as *self-monitoring* in predicting *dating behavior*, and the societal influences on *need for achievement in females.*

FIGURE 14.1. The origins of the kinds of individual differences in behavior that we label *personality* include genetic factors, events that occur during gestation, and all of the environmental influences that affect us after we are born. Despite this cartoon, it seems unlikely that we are born with differential tendencies to worry. (Source: Drawing by Chas. Addams; © 1984 The New Yorker Magazine, Inc.)

One possible origin for personality differences

PERSONALITY TRAITS: *Characteristic Behavior across Situations*

As was discussed in Chapter 1, *social psychology* is defined as the scientific field that seeks to comprehend the nature and causes of individual behavior in social situations.

Traditionally, this meant that social psychologists studied the effects of specific classes of stimulus events on human behavior. A closely related field, *personality psychology*, has tended to focus attention on the ways in which people with different traits differ in their responses to a given stimulus. From the point of view of the individual, **personality** is defined as the combination of the relatively enduring traits that influence behavior in a variety of situations. *Personality variables* represent what the individual brings to the situation, while *social variables* are contained in the situation itself. These two fields of psychology are not in conflict. They both seek to predict human behavior, but they represent contrasting approaches to that goal.

The value and even the existence of personality variables has periodically been a matter of controversy, and we will present a brief overview of the issues that have been raised.

Personality and behavior: How useful is the trait concept?

The earliest view of personality included the assumption that people could be expected to behave consistently from situation to situation and from year to year. A woman who is the life of the party with her close friends is believed to be equally amusing at her office. A quarrelsome little boy is assumed to grow up to be a quarrelsome man. William James (1950) proposed that, by the age of thirty, a person's tendencies were "set like plaster," never to change.

This general view of behavior led to the development of numerous personality tests in the first half of this century. It follows that if behavior is determined by personality, the ability to measure personality would permit us to predict behavior. The first tests were *global measures* that were designed to assess as much as possible about an individual's basic personality. These measures ranged from *projective tests* that used ambiguous stimuli, such as ink blots (Rorschach, 1921) and drawings (Morgan and Murray, 1938), to *objective tests* that asked for agree-disagree or true-false responses to a series of statements (Hathaway and McKinley, 1940). The general idea was an appealing one. Personality assessment has been viewed as a potentially powerful tool for predicting behavior across situations.

Doubts about personality traits: Situational factors as overwhelmingly important determinants of behavior. Personality tests were widely used in clinical settings as diagnostic tools and in various organizations as personnel selection devices. They also became the focus of a great deal of psychological research. The fact that these instruments were not impressive as predictors of behavior led some critics to express doubts about the utility of the trait concept itself. For example, Rotter (1954) reviewed the work done with such measures and was forced to conclude that, "The very best techniques we have are of doubtful validity for predicting the specific behavior of any person in a particular situation."

Though it was possible to argue that the solution lay in constructing better tests, a more revolutionary suggestion was made by one of Rotter's former students, Walter Mischel (1968, 1977). He argued that any system built on traits was inherently inadequate because behavior is simply not very consistent across situations or from one time period to another. Others raised the possibility that the widespread belief in behavioral consistency was only an illusion (Schweder, 1975). There are counterarguments to these criticisms. The evidence for situational stability is better if large rather than small samples of behavior are studied (Epstein, 1979) and if many different situations are sampled (Moskowitz, 1982). Stability over time is greater in adulthood than during childhood or adolescence (McCrae and Costa, 1984). Some have argued, nevertheless, that the trait model needs to be replaced by a totally new conceptualization (Burke, Kraut, and Dworkin, 1984; Hyland, 1985). One example is a model of individual differences based on conscious experience rather than on external behavior (Singer, 1984).

One implication of the "situational revolution" among personality psychologists was the possibility that the traditional social psychological approach had been correct all along — research attention might best be focused on the situation and not on traits (Snyder and Ickes, 1985). At the same time that these considerations were being raised in the field of personality, social psychologists were discovering that the situation *alone* is no more powerful in predicting behavior than are traits alone (Funder and Ozer, 1983). One solution for both fields was to attempt an integrated approach (Kenrick, 1986).

Integrating social and personality psychology.   Probably the most reasonable conclusion about the trait-situation controversy is that both sides were partially correct (Feshbach, 1984b). The best prediction of behavior would be expected to occur when we pay attention to *both* influences and their interaction simultaneously (Malloy and Kenny, 1986). Figure 14.2 (pages 496–497) indicates how this is done. When social psychologists wish to include traits in their conceptualizations, how can they decide which traits may be important in which situations? A few guidelines have been formulated.

(1) THE MORE NARROW AND LIMITED THE TRAIT, THE BETTER BEHAVIORAL PREDICTOR IT IS LIKELY TO BE.   In Chapter 4 it was pointed out that narrow attitudes are better predictors of behavior than broad ones. An analogous rule hold true for personality traits. Instead of relying on very broad characteristics, attention is increasingly paid to relatively specific and circumscribed aspects of personality. For example, a wide-ranging concept such as sociability tends to be less helpful in predicting social behavior than a narrow characteristic such as dating anxiety. The more specific the trait, the more consistent the behavior across relevant situations. Thus, some specific consistencies can be identified even if the more general rule is that people respond differentially across situations (Mischel, 1985).

(2) PEOPLE DIFFER WITH RESPECT TO THE TRAITS ON WHICH THEY ARE CONSISTENT.   Rather than seeking universal consistency across all characteristics, Kenrick and Stringfield (1980) suggest that consistency-inconsistency varies. To test this hypothesis, they asked subjects to select traits on which they were most and least consistent from situation to situation. For the highly consistent traits for a given person, there was good agreement among parents, friends, and self as to how the individual behaved.

FIGURE 14.2.   To an increasing extent, personality and social research combine the traditional emphasis of personality psychology on dispositional traits with the traditional social psychological emphasis on the effect of situational (or stimulus) variables. The result is an improved ability to predict behavior because *both* situational and personality factors are considered simultaneously.

Behavior is determined by traits and by situational factors

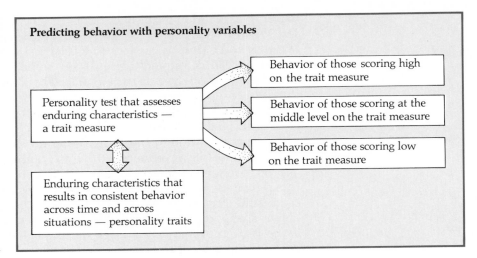

For traits on which an individual said he or she was inconsistent, parents, friends, and relatives reported very different kinds of behavior.

It is also found that people differ in how predictable they are from situation to situation, in part because they differ in their perceptions of how similar these situations are (Klirs and Revelle, 1986). For example, if you perceive a conversation with your parents as very much like a conversation with your friends, you are likely to behave in about the same way in these two situations. If someone else perceives these as very different kinds of interaction, he or she may behave quite differently in the two situations.

(3) THE LESS POWERFUL THE SITUATIONAL INFLUENCES, THE GREATER IS THE ROLE PLAYED BY PERSONALITY TRAITS.   Monson et al. (1982) proposed a simple yet important rule for deciding when traits are and are not useful for predicting behavior in a specific situation. When a situational variable is a powerful one (such as attitude similarity in determining attraction, Chapter 6), it is difficult to find traits that improve one's ability to predict behavior. With behavior that seems to be only weakly influenced by the situation (such as classroom cheating, Chapter 8), several traits are found to be valuable predictors.

(4) PEOPLE MAY CHOOSE TO BE IN THE KINDS OF SITUATIONS THAT BEST FIT THEIR PERSONALITIES.   In experiments, we usually place subjects in particular situations and assess their responses. Staats and Burns (1982) have shown that approach-avoidance responses to a given situation occur as a function of personality factors. Diener, Larsen, and Emmons (1984) propose that in real life we often have the power to select where we spend our time — which situations we approach and which we avoid. They found, for example, that extroverted people are more likely to seek recreation in a social setting than in solitude. Analogously, energetic people select a

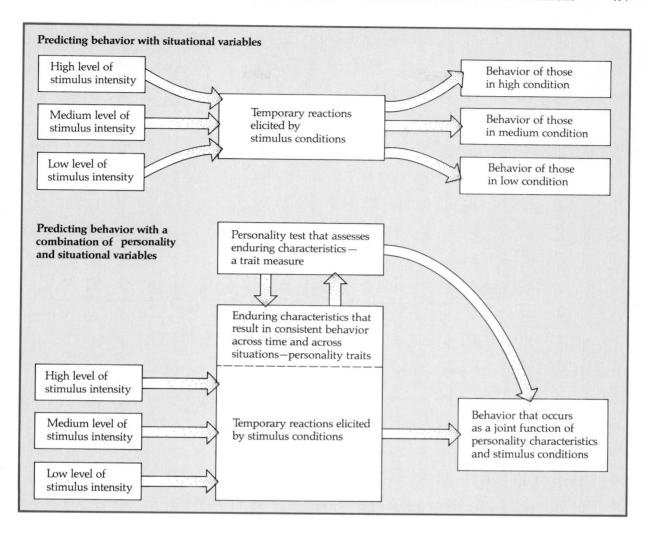

Predicting behavior with situational variables

High level of stimulus intensity

Medium level of stimulus intensity

Low level of stimulus intensity

Temporary reactions elicited by stimulus conditions

Behavior of those in high condition

Behavior of those in medium condition

Behavior of those in low condition

Predicting behavior with a combination of personality and situational variables

Personality test that assesses enduring characteristics— a trait measure

Enduring characteristics that result in consistent behavior across time and across situations—personality traits

High level of stimulus intensity

Medium level of stimulus intensity

Low level of stimulus intensity

Temporary reactions elicited by stimulus conditions

Behavior that occurs as a joint function of personality characteristics and stimulus conditions

FIGURE 14.2 (cont.)

setting where energetic behavior can occur (Gormly, 1983). In such research, it is shown that personality traits play a role in influencing behavior, but that would not be obvious to an investigator unless a free choice of situations were permitted.

(5) WHEN PERSONALITY TEST ITEMS INCLUDE A SITUATIONAL CONTEXT, THEY ARE MORE LIKELY TO PREDICT BEHAVIOR IN SPECIFIC SITUATIONS.   It was pointed out by Gergen, Hepburn, and Fisher (1986) that the typical test item is stated in a way that leaves out any situational context. For example, how would you respond to the item, "I am a loving person"— agree or disagree? It would obviously help to know whether the question refers to specific conditions such as on a date or in military combat and to specific targets such as toward a member of the opposite sex or toward

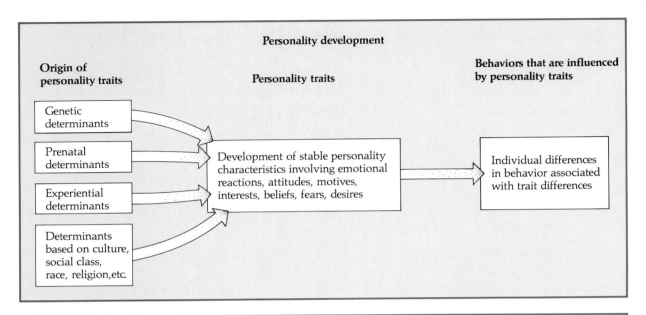

Personality development

Origin of personality traits

Genetic determinants

Prenatal determinants

Experiential determinants

Determinants based on culture, social class, race, religion, etc.

Personality traits

Development of stable personality characteristics involving emotional reactions, attitudes, motives, interests, beliefs, fears, desires

Behaviors that are influenced by personality traits

Individual differences in behavior associated with trait differences

FIGURE 14.3. Whatever the origin of personality characteristics in heredity or in experience, it is necessary to develop measuring instruments that tap individual differences. Test scores are assumed to reflect relatively stable dispositions, and test responses contribute to the prediction of behavior.

Using personality tests to tap stable dispositions

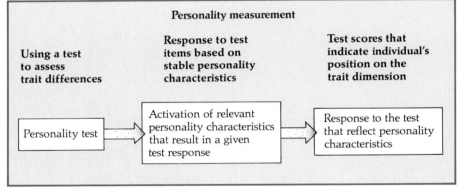

Personality measurement

Using a test to assess trait differences

Personality test

Response to test items based on stable personality characteristics

Activation of relevant personality characteristics that result in a given test response

Test scores that indicate individual's position on the trait dimension

Response to the test that reflect personality characteristics

reptiles. To the extent that tests are designed to include the specification of situations, they should become much more useful as predictors of behavior (Byrne and Kelley, 1981).

In summary, the debates about personality versus the situation seem to have led to better conceptualizations of the way the two classes of variables operate and how they can be integrated as predictors of behavior (Peele, 1984). We will now turn to the way that personality variables are measured and how they are used in research.

Identifying personality traits

How do psychologists identify the traits on which people differ? Actually, the origin of most of the traits studied by psychologists can be traced to general assumptions common to our culture. Long before there was a science of behavior, people observed that human beings tend to differ in various aspects of their behavior. Some were more shy than others. Some were more honest than others. Some were more self-confident than others, and so forth. It has been shown in various studies that we tend to describe one another in terms of traits, and this tendency actually increases as a relationship becomes closer (Hampson, 1983).

These observations found their way into our language, and thousands of such trait terms were identified in a classic study by Allport and Odbert (1936) that is described in the **Focus** insert on page 500. Rather than attempting to measure every possible trait, psychologists have tended to identify a single trait that is of interest for a given type of research and then to construct a measuring instrument to assess the characteristic. The general assumptions underlying personality development and measurement are outlined in Figure 14.3.

Constructing a personality measure

Once one has identified a potential trait that seems to be of theoretical relevance to a given realm of behavior, the next step is to construct an appropriate measuring device. An example of how one such measure was developed and subsequently evaluated provides a general idea of how the process works.

In the 1930s and 1940s, fascist ideology was gaining adherents in many parts of the world, with Nazi Germany being the most obvious and most powerful center of such beliefs. The results of this political movement included World War II and the deliberate murder of millions of men, women, and children in death camps. Shortly after the Axis powers were defeated, a group of psychologists began working on the problem of how to predict what persons would be attracted to totalitarian political movements and a fascist way of life (see Figure 14.4).

FIGURE 14.4. Adherence to a totalitarian political ideology is one of the characteristics that the personality variable of *authoritarianism* was assumed to include. The *F Scale* was designed to predict who would be most susceptible to this type of political appeal.

Authoritarianism: Politics and personality

FOCUS ON RESEARCH:
Classic Contributions

How Many Traits Are There? The Psycho-lexical Study of Allport and Odbert

In 1936 Gordon W. Allport at Harvard and Henry S. Odbert at Dartmouth suggested that personality psychologists need some guidance when they seek to identify and name behavioral traits. They felt that past work had been haphazard and that there should be a logical way to conceptualize the total array of human traits.

Their solution was a unique one in that they found all traits for which there are words in the English language, as provided by Webster's unabridged dictionary. They produced a list of 17,953 terms, or 4.5 percent of the total English vocabulary. (This list was later condensed to 171 traits.) It was pointed out that each term constitutes a cultural record of informal behavioral observations. In other words, if the adjective "flexible" appears in our language, this means that particular types of individual differences in behavior were repeatedly noticed and that a word was eventually created to label these differences. The authors describe the process as follows (Allport and Odbert, 1936, pp. 1–2):

. . . men experience a desire to represent by name such mental processes or dispositions of their fellows as can be determined by observation or by inference. There is a demand for depicting personality as accurately and as faithfully as possible, for with a suitable term, corresponding to authentic psychological dispositions, the ability to understand and to control one's fellows is greatly enhanced. There is then reason to suppose that trait-names are not entirely arbitrary, that they are to some extent self-correcting, for there is little to gain by preserving through names erroneous beliefs in merely fictitious or fabulous entities.

The implication for psychologists is that they may wish to take advantage of hundreds of years of common-sense behavioral observations and investigate these traits that have been identified in everyday life. If a given personality variable is in our language, we may hypothesize that individual differences in this disposition are important in predicting behavior. If so, it would be necessary to construct a test to measure the trait in question.

Considering some of the current controversies in the field, we may take comfort in discovering that they are not new issues. Allport and Odbert noted that some psychologists feel traits do not exist, and there are only situation-specific habits. In contrast, trait psychologists proposed that more complex units of characteristic behavior could and should be included in any attempt to develop psychological prediction.

To attempt to measure the proposed personality trait of authoritarianism, the first step was to create test items that seemed to represent the kinds of attitudes, beliefs, and values held by fascists and potential fascists (Adorno et al., 1950). The test was built by giving these preliminary items to large numbers of people and statistically examining the extent to which each item measured a common construct. Items that did not correlate with the total body of items were either rewritten for a second try or discarded altogether. Several such item analyses resulted in a widely used

TABLE 14.1. A few of the trait names identified by Allport and Odbert (1936). Some have found their way into personality research, and some have not.	Traits That Have Been Measured and Widely Used in Psychological Research	Traits That Have Not Yet Played a Major Role in Psychological Research
Trait names: Only a portion have been studied	altruistic	affected
	bashful	banal
	compulsive	contrary
	dependent	depraved
	expressive	effusive
	fearful	fickle
	guilty	gossipy
	honest	hopeless
	industrious	indiscreet
	jealous	jovial
	masochistic	morbid
	nervous	neighborly
	open-minded	oafish
	prejudiced	pithy
	repressive	rude
	self-approving	shallow
	ultraconservative	unctuous
	virile	vapid
	zealous	zany

Now that almost half a century has passed, it is interesting to look over their massive list of terms and to note that some of them have played a prominent role in our theories and empirical studies, while others have yet to catch the research attention of psychologists. A sampling of both types is presented in Table 14.1. You can conceptualize the first column as a sampling from the history of our field and the second column as a possible blueprint for future test construction and social-personality research. For anyone who is interested, there are thousands of potential traits waiting for the right investigator to come along.

personality test, the **F Scale**, with *F* standing for *fascism*. Among the items making up this measure are such typical ones as:

- ✓ What the youth need most is strict discipline, rugged determination, and the will to work and fight for family and country.

- ✓ Obedience and respect for authority are the most important virtues children should learn.

Determining if a new test is reliable and valid

After a measure has been constructed, two types of evaluation are necessary. A good test is one that has acceptable **reliability** and **validity.**

Reliability refers to the *consistency* with which the instrument measures whatever variable it was designed to assess. The term "reliability" includes the concept of internal consistency (all of the items measure the same construct), consistency over time, and consistency of scoring. These different aspects of reliability are described in Figure 14.5. With respect to the F Scale, many studies have established that it is a reliable measuring device.

FIGURE 14.5. All useful tests must be reliable and valid. Reliability refers to consistency of measurement and validity to accuracy of measurement. Each of these concepts involves more than one aspect, and questions as to a test's evaluation cannot be answered thoroughly without dealing with each aspect.

The multiple aspects of reliability and validity

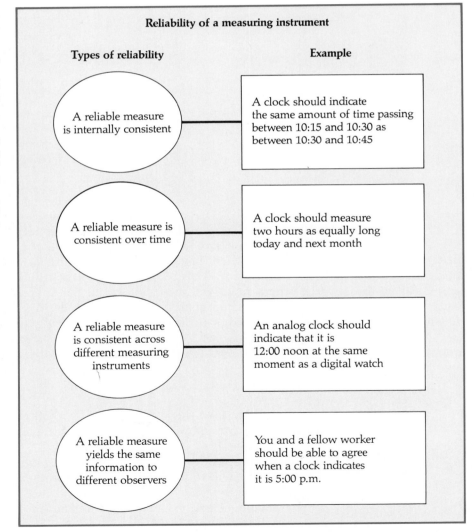

Reliability of a measuring instrument

Types of reliability

Example

A reliable measure is internally consistent

A clock should indicate the same amount of time passing between 10:15 and 10:30 as between 10:30 and 10:45

A reliable measure is consistent over time

A clock should measure two hours as equally long today and next month

A reliable measure is consistent across different measuring instruments

An analog clock should indicate that it is 12:00 noon at the same moment as a digital watch

A reliable measure yields the same information to different observers

You and a fellow worker should be able to agree when a clock indicates it is 5:00 p.m.

Validity is usually defined as the extent to which a test measures what it was designed to measure. For example, a measure of college aptitude is valid to the extent that scores on the test accurately predict grades in college. The better the prediction, the greater the validity. For personality tests, there is no single criterion analogous to college grades and no simple way of designating validity.

Instead of a single basic validity coefficient, personality tests must be evaluated with respect to **construct validity.** This refers to a series of relationships established in research that link scores on the test with other theoretically relevant responses. For example, there is no simple index of authoritarianism to serve as a criterion of the F Scale, so its

FIGURE 14.5 (cont.)

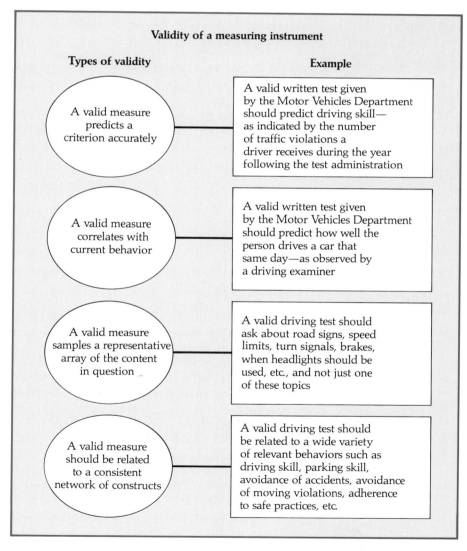

construct validity is based on *all* of the research that has employed this measure and that has related it to other variables. For example, those with high scores are consistently found to vote for the most conservative political candidates in elections (Byrne and Przybyla, 1980), to be conformist and self-protective rather than conscientious (Browning, 1983), to be influenced as jurors more by a defendant's character than by judicial instructions in recommending punishment (Mitchell and Byrne, 1982), to believe what they are told by TV newscasters and newspaper columnists (Levy, 1979), and to obey when an authority figure orders them to administer punishment to a stranger (Elms and Milgram, 1966).

In other words, these and hundreds of other studies provide good evidence for the construct validity of the test. This statement means simply that scores on the F Scale have been found to be related to many different behaviors in a manner consistent with the concept of authoritarianism.

It should be noted that some psychologists (for example, Eysenck, 1986) feel that this trait-by-trait approach to understanding personality is a mistake. They propose that we first establish what the basic traits are (by means of techniques such as factor analysis) and then investigate personality as a unified entity. For others (Duke, 1986), the solution to the same problem is to take an interdisciplinary approach in cooperation with sociology, anthropology, biology, and other areas. As reasonable as these approaches appear to be, the field is still characterized by research focused on a variety of single traits of interest to specific groups of investigators.

TYPE A CORONARY-PRONE PERSONALITY: *Aggressiveness, Working under Pressure, Achievement*

Medical research indicates that the risk of cardiovascular disorders increases as a function of genetic predispositions plus such physical factors as age, the level of serum cholesterol, blood pressure, and cigarette smoking (Krantz, Grunberg, and Baum, 1985). In addition, personality factors are found to play a role in heart disease. That possibility was first raised two thousand years ago when Celsus proposed that fear, anger, and other emotional states tend to excite the pulse. In 1868 a German physician observed that those who are prone to coronary problems are apt to speak in a loud voice and to behave as (in today's terminology) workaholics (Dembroski and MacDougall, 1982).

Despite centuries of this type of casual observation concerning psychological links to coronary disease, systematic investigation did not get underway until the 1950s when Friedman and Rosenman (1959) described the **Type A** coronary-prone behavior pattern. As suggested in the cartoon in Figure 14.6, it was demonstrated that individuals who are

FIGURE 14.6. The Type A coronary-prone individual is characterized by a behavioral style that involves high work standards, time urgency, impatience, and a tendency to express interpersonal hostility. The young lady in this cartoon may deny fitting the Type A pattern, but her behavior is clearly consistent with coronary-proneness. (Source: *Sally Forth* by Greg Howard © News America Syndicate, 1985. Permission of News America Syndicate.)

The Type A individual: Perfectionistic, impatient, and hard to get along with

hardworking, aggressive, always in a hurry, and the like, were more likely to develop coronary problems than were those labeled **Type B.** The latter individuals are easy-going, sociable, and relaxed (Glass, 1983). When a person develops symptoms of heart trouble (such as chest pains), those who are Type As tend to belittle the amount of discomfort and to wait longer than Type Bs to decide that they are ill and need help (Matthews et al., 1983). Though much of the original research was confined to male subjects, the same relationships hold true for females (Haynes, Feinleib, and Kannel, 1980).

Psychological research on the Type A – Type B dimension has broadened beyond concerns with health into such areas as personality development, occupational behavior, and interpersonal relationships.

The Type A behavior pattern and its development

The original method for assessing this personality entity was by means of a special interview. Most of the psychological research has used a self-report test, the **Jenkins Activity Survey** (Jenkins et al., 1979).

Among the basic characteristics of those on the Type A end of the dimension are a focus on competition and the feeling that there is never enough time to get things done. Other people are a problem in that they usually interfere with one's work, take up time, and, as a result, cause the Type A individual to become impatient and irritable (Rosenman and Friedman, 1974). The pressing need for success leads to a preference for working alone when under pressure (Dembroski and MacDougall, 1978) and to become angry when anything or anyone gets in the way (Carver and Glass, 1978). When the Type A individual *denies* feelings of irritability, the cardiovascular response to a difficult task is greater than when the individual is aware of the angry feelings (Smith, Houston, and Stucky, 1984). Smith and Brehm (1981a) found that Type As want to do things perfectly, and they do not tend to avoid their responsibilities. One consequence of such a pattern of behavior is sleep problems (Hicks et al., 1980) and another is elevated blood pressure when stressed (English and Baker, 1983).

Time is a matter of special importance to Type As (Strube and Lott, 1984), and they tend to arrive early for appointments and to feel irritated when others are late (Gastorf, 1980). Those who are Type As work more quickly than Type Bs, get more done, and perceive that time is passing by more quickly (Yarnold and Grimm, 1982). In social situations, Type As feel uncomfortable and have a sense of insecurity (Jenkins et al., 1977). At the opposite extreme, Type Bs are careless about time and get along well with other people (Glass, 1977). Some of the basic behavioral tendencies of those at the Type A end of the dimension are summarized in Table 14.2.

To date, only a modest amount of research has dealt with the factors determining how Type A and Type B characteristics develop. It is found, for example, that Type A individuals were raised in families in which high — though ambiguous — standards were set. The mother pushes her child to do well and then to do even better (Matthews, 1977; Matthews, Glass, and Richins, 1977). The child's response is to work hard, strive for success, and try to reach many different goals in order to maintain parental approval. The developing Type A individual thus learns to set high personal goals beginning in childhood (Matthews and Siegel, 1983).

Strube and Ota (1982) proposed that pressure-oriented parent-child interactions were more likely to occur for first-born children than for those who are later-born. Generally, expectations are greatest and most unrealistic for the first child. Besides, as additional children are born, there is simply less time for parents to push them toward achievement. In any event, the investigators did find the relationship they predicted. Among college students, those who were first-born obtained higher Type A scores than did the later-born. Further, for both males and females, the

TABLE 14.2.   Those on the Type A end of the coronary-prone dimension can be identified by their everyday behavior. The calm, unhurried Type B individual is characterized by the absence of these indicators. (Source: Based on information in Brody, 1980.)

The behavior of those who are Type A coronary-prone

Typical Behavioral Characteristics of Type A Individuals

Doing more than one thing at a time.

Scheduling more and more activities and having less time to spend on each one.

Ignoring one's surroundings unless they are relevant to what one is doing.

Urging others to hurry up and finish what they are saying.

Becoming irritated when slow cars block traffic or when one has to wait in line.

Believing that you can get a thing done right only by doing it yourself.

Gesturing a lot while talking.

Tapping fingers or jiggling one's legs nervously.

Speaking explosively and using obscenities a lot.

Having to be on time.

Finding it difficult to sit with nothing to do.

Playing to win at every game, even with children.

Measuring success in terms of quantity.

Nodding one's head, clenching fist, or pounding table when talking.

Becoming impatient when watching others carry out a task.

Blinking eyes rapidly or lifting eyebrows for emphasis.

larger the family, the stronger the relationship between birth order and Type A behavior.

Other investigators have identified similar parental pressures in situations as diverse as Little League baseball and programs for gifted children. Children are taught that it is all-important to win and that academic achievement requires being at the top of one's class. Parents sometimes assume that a child must be Number One in whatever he or she undertakes (Brody, 1980). This type of parent-child interaction seems to contribute to the development of Type A characteristics.

It is also possible that some aspects of Type A behavior are attributable to the situation. For example, you might expect Type A reactions to occur more frequently in demanding occupations that put a premium on speed, competition, quantifiable output, and deadlines. Morell and Katkin (1982) compared the scores of female professionals with the scores of homemakers and found the former group much higher in Type A characteristics. The higher the job status, the greater is the incidence of Type A behavior. The authors speculated that as women have more and more opportunities to pursue high-level goals in education and in their careers, they will also catch up to men in the development of coronary heart disease. It is equally possible, of course, that those women with Type A characteristics find themselves motivated to enter demanding professions and to work toward higher occupational status. If so, personality variables can be seen to lead the individual to certain situations rather than the trait developing *because* of the situation (Smith and Anderson, 1986).

Behavioral differences: Type A versus Type B individuals

The realms of Type A – Type B behavioral differences receiving the most attention have been task-related behavior, productivity and success on the job, and interpersonal relationships.

Responding to the challenge of a task. Many aspects of the work situation are found to elicit quite different responses from those who fall at different points on the A – B dimension. One example is deadlines. Type As work hard with or without an explicit deadline, but they feel pressured when a specific time is set for completing a task. Type Bs, in contrast, expend extra effort only when a deadline is set (Burnham, Pennebaker, and Glass, 1975).

Those who are Type A tend to focus attention on the task at hand and to ignore any distractions that might interfere with finishing the job (Matthews and Brunson, 1979). Those who are Type A are more responsive to positive incentives to perform well (Blumenthal et al., 1980), and they complain less about hard work (Weidner and Matthews, 1978). Given multiple tasks and interruptions, Type Bs do not perform well, while Type As actually get more done under such difficult conditions

(Fazio et al., 1981). These performance differences are in part a function of the tendency of Type As to focus on the essential aspects of a task while ignoring anything that is trivial (Humphries, Carver, and Neumann, 1983; Stern, Harris, and Elverum, 1981).

As you might expect, the hard work and concentration of the Type A individual is associated with potentially damaging psychophysiological reactions (Houston, 1983). Type As are found to seek challenging activities (Ortega and Pipal, 1984), and, in responding to challenges, the Type A person shows an increase in cardiovascular activity (Goldband, 1980; Jorgensen and Houston, 1981; Pittner, Houston, and Spiridigliossi, 1983). Work-related stress, such as dealing with a very difficult task, leads to an increase in blood pressure and the type of changes in blood content that are associated with cardiovascular disease (Glass et al., 1980; Holmes, McGilley, and Houston, 1984). It seems to be a combination of a high-stress job (such as being an administrator) and the possession of Type A characteristics that makes cardiovascular difficulties most likely to occur (Rhodewalt et al., 1984).

There is a general tendency for the Type A person to want to maintain control of each situation (Rhodewalt and Davison, 1983). When faced with an uncontrollable task, Type As respond with frustration and anger (Levine and Moore, 1979). Those who are Type A desire control so badly that they refuse to give it up even to avoid an undesirable consequence (Miller, Lack, and Asroff, 1985). This tendency was shown in an experiment that employed a reaction-time task. Either a confederate or the actual subject was supposed to react quickly when a signal was received. Only one of them was "in control" as the individual performing the task. Both received a blast of aversive noise if the one in control did not react quickly enough, and the trained confederate was better at this task than the untrained subject. As shown in Figure 14.7, when given a choice, Type As tended to elect to retain control more often than Type Bs, even though control meant they were more likely to be punished by the unpleasant noise.

Even when Type As and Type Bs do not differ in how much control they are able to exert, others perceive Type As as exerting more control (Strube et al., 1986). The authors suggest that the coronary-prone individuals have a more active, dynamic style, and this leads observers to see them as more competent and more in control than is actually true. In contrast, the relaxed Type Bs don't receive enough credit for their competence and control.

Because they strive for high goals, Type As say they failed even if their work is good (Snow, 1978). Type As are also more apt to fear failure than are Type Bs (Gastorf and Teevan, 1980). When presented with a series of unsolvable problems on which they cannot succeed, Type As decline in the ability to work effectively. They then are angry at both themselves and at the situation (Brunson and Matthews, 1981). In response to the same frustration, Type Bs continue to use effective problem-solving strategies, and they blame failure on the task, on the experimenter, and on chance. In general, Type As see themselves as the cause of

FIGURE 14.7. Those who are Type A have the strong desire to control all aspects of a situation. Given a task in which the speed with which one of two people reacted was the determinant of whether or not an unpleasant noise would be heard, Type As preferred to retain control even though the other person was better able to prevent the punishment. (Source: Based on data from Miller, Lack, and Asroff, 1985.)

A Type A individual would rather "do it myself"

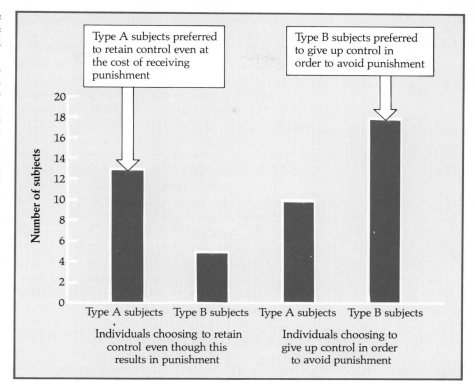

negative outcomes, while Type Bs blame the external situation (Rhodewalt, 1984). It seems that lack of success is much harder on Type As than on Type Bs.

Productivity on the job: Type As and success in academia.   It is obvious that many aspects of the Type A pattern of behavior are less desirable than those of Type Bs. The Type A person is often unpleasant in dealing with fellow workers, interpersonal relationships suffer, and there is increased risk of developing coronary heart disease (Cooper, Detre, and Weiss, 1981). The health factor in particular has led to the development of therapy programs designed to reduce the level of Type A tendencies (Kasl, 1980; Kiesling, 1983; Suinn, 1982).

In fairness, one should also consider the other side of the coin. If the Type A individual works hard, tries to do his or her best, and puts forth extra effort, it seems reasonable to expect some measure of occupational success to be associated with this personality dimension. If so, we should recognize that behavioral changes that lower the health risk might be accompanied by a decrease in work productivity (Lenfant and Schweizer, 1985).

Though the effect of personality on work quantity and quality may vary across occupations, in one field the results have been as expected.

For male social psychologists, it was found that as Type A characteristics increase, work quantity and quality increase (Matthews et al., 1980). Those on the Type A end of the personality dimension publish more research and their research is more often cited by fellow psychologists than is true for Type Bs.

Because that research was limited to males in a specific field, Taylor et al. (1984) undertook a study of both males and females in academia who worked in a variety of different disciplines. They also measured success at this type of work in several different ways.

Faculty members in university departments as diverse as botany, English, engineering, and psychology were surveyed. Both males and females at each academic rank were included. In addition to measuring Type A–Type B characteristics and assessing job performance, the investigators also assessed **self-efficacy** (Bandura, 1977). Self-efficacy is defined as how well an individual believes he or she can deal with a given task.

It was found that males and females did not differ and that Type A scores were associated with academic success. It was, by the way, the job involvement aspects of this trait that predicted how well an individual did in academia, *not* competitiveness or impatience.

A sophisticated statistical analysis makes it possible to describe just how a series of variables are interrelated. The way Type A and the other variables affect productivity, citations, and the person's rank and salary are shown in Figure 14.8. You can see that Type A scores directly predict feelings of self-efficacy, the tendency to set goals for oneself, and the tendency to engage in multiple projects at the same time. Those high in Type A were found to be most likely to have their work cited by others, and Type A in combination with others factors was related to productivity and the person's rank and salary. In the "publish or perish" world of research-oriented universities, it pays to work hard on research, set goals, and engage in many projects at once.

Clearly, those who are identified as Type As tend to perform better than those who are Type Bs. Taylor and her colleagues pointed out that in other occupations, involving less freedom to set one's own goals and level of work activity, this personality measure is not a very good predictor of performance (Locke et al., 1981). In these more structured occupational settings, the situation can be powerful enough to outweigh individual differences. In contrast, in a situation such as that faced by university faculty, personality factors can be very important.

Interpersonal relationships of Type As and Bs.   The general description of Type A individuals provides cues to suggest that interpersonal interactions might be a source of difficulty. Keep in mind that Type As are upset by anything that interferes with their work, they want to outperform others, and they need to control the situation. As was discussed in Chapter 9, hostility is quite characteristic of Type As. This combination of tendencies leads them to be competitive in interactions and to want to know about others so as to predict their responses (Gotay, 1981; Smith

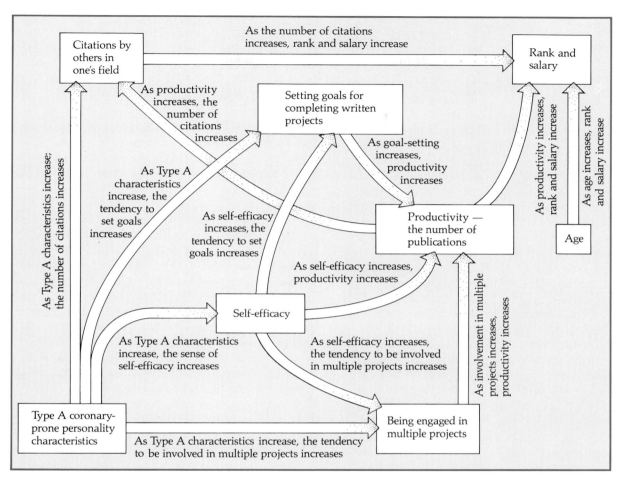

FIGURE 14.8. Among research-oriented faculty members in a university setting, differences in Type A personality characteristics play a role, along with other variables, in influencing success in terms of productivity, being cited by those in the field, and the individual's rank and salary. (Source: Based on data from Taylor et al., 1984.)

Type A behavior as a factor in academic success

and Brehm, 1981b). For both males and females, Type A characteristics are associated with masculinity (DeGregorio and Carver, 1980).

A very special interpersonal setting is marriage. Here, husbands and wives must interact repeatedly with respect to household activities, social relationships, sexual behavior, and so forth. How might Type A and Type B patterns affect these interactions? Becker and Byrne (1984) sought to answer that question by asking couples to respond to surveys that dealt with their daily activities. Compared with Type B males, those who were Type A reported less communication with their wives, more time spent in work-related activities at home, and less frequent, less time-consuming marital sex. Type A females indicate that they relax less frequently and for a shorter period of time than those who are Type B. Subsequent research has shown that the poorest marital adjustment occurs in couples in which the husband is Type A and the wife Type B (Blaney et al., 1986). With respect to sexual adjustment specifically, it is

FOCUS ON RESEARCH:
The Cutting Edge

The Role of Self-Monitoring in Dating Relationships

The concept of **self** has a long history in personality psychology. It is usually defined as the array of attitudes, judgments, and values a person holds with respect to his or her behavior, ability, appearance, and general worth. Because people differ in the way they evaluate themselves, differences in characteristics such as *self-esteem* have often been treated as a personality dimension (Byrne and Kelley, 1981). For many theorists — Carl Rogers, for example — the self-concept is viewed as the most important aspect of one's total personality (Lynch, Norem-Hebeisen, and Gergen, 1981).

Besides differences in our self-conceptions, another aspect of the self is related to personality. We are able to reflect on ourselves — on who we are and what we should do in any given situation (Schlenker, 1982). A special aspect of this general tendency toward self-reflection has been identified as **self-monitoring** (Gangestad and Snyder, 1985; Snyder and Ickes, 1985). Those who are high in self-monitoring tend to regulate their behavior on the basis of the situation. They pay a great deal of attention to what is socially appropriate in a given interaction and behave accordingly. On the **Self-Monitoring Scale,** a test designed to measure this personality dimension, those who score high endorse items such as:

- When I am uncertain how to act in social situations, I look to the behavior of others for cues.
- In different situations and with different people, I often act like very different persons.

In contrast, low self-monitors tend to regulate their behavior on the basis of internal factors. On the Self-Monitoring Scale, they agree with such statements as:

- My behavior is usually an expression of my true inner feelings, attitudes, and beliefs.
- I would not change my opinions (or the way I do things) to please someone else or to win their favor.

An interesting difference between those high and low in this dimension is found in the words they use in casual conversations (Ickes, Reidhead, and Patterson, 1986). Low self-monitors are more likely than highs to speak in the first person (I, me, my, etc.), while high self-monitors are more likely than lows to speak in the third person (he, she, they, etc.). Presumably, those who score high are most concerned about what others do and how they react, while low self-monitors concentrate on their own behavior and reactions.

One of the early interests in this dimension was with respect to an issue discussed earlier in this chapter: the extent to which behavior is consistent across situations and across time. As you might expect from the description just given, low self-monitors are much more consistent than high self-monitors (Shaffer, Smith, and Tomarelli, 1982; Snyder and Monson, 1975). You could say that those low on this dimension behave according to trait theory, while those who are high self-monitors behave according to situational theory.

In other research on this personality dimension, high self-monitors (compared to lows) show less correspondence between private attitudes and public behaviors (Zanna and Olson, 1982) and between self-ratings and ratings by their acquaintances (Tunnell, 1980). In choosing friends as partners for a specific activity, high self-monitors based their choices

FIGURE 14.9. Individuals high and low in *self-monitoring behavior* tend to respond quite differently to opposite-sex partners. Low self-monitors express more commitment and prefer to be with their partners, regardless of the activity involved. High self-monitors are much less committed to being with a particular partner. These differences are also reflected in their actual dating behavior and are of potential importance in predicting marital stability. (Source: Based on data from Snyder and Simpson, 1984.)

Low self-monitors feel committed to their dating partners, but high self-monitors do not

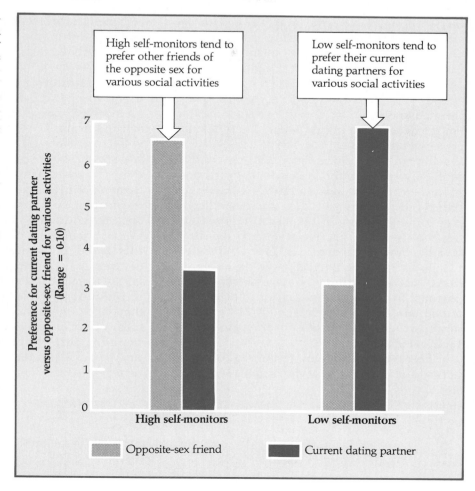

High self-monitors tend to prefer other friends of the opposite sex for various social activities

Low self-monitors tend to prefer their current dating partners for various social activities

Preference for current dating partner versus opposite-sex friend for various activities (Range = 0-10)

High self-monitors   Low self-monitors

▨ Opposite-sex friend   ▰ Current dating partner

on how well the person can carry out the activity, while low self-monitors chose on the basis of how much they like the person (Snyder, Gangestad, and Simpson, 1983).

More recently Snyder and Simpson (1984) have extended work on self-monitoring to behavior in dating relationships. It was generally expected that high self-monitors would find it relatively easy to go from one partner to an-other, based on the activity to be performed and the skills of the other person. Low self-monitors should be more likely to stick with their current partner, no matter what the activity or skills involved. In a series of studies, male and female undergraduates were each asked various details about his or her current dating partner, other friends of the opposite sex, the activities they engaged in on dates, and the skills of the various individuals with respect to the various activities.

When presented with choices of specific people and specific activities, high self-monitors tend to choose to be with opposite-sex friends who were good at the activity in question. Low self-monitors preferred their regular dating partner, no matter what. These results are shown in Figure 14.9, page 513.

One implication of these findings is a difference in commitment based on this personality dimension. Low self-monitors would seem to feel more committed to their partner than is true for high self-monitors. Because this study dealt only with relatively casual activities (sailing, bowling, tennis, etc.), a second study, using different undergraduates as subjects, asked about willingness to change dating partners in favor of some other opposite-sex friend. High self-monitors tended to prefer a new partner, while low self-monitors chose their current partner.

These quite different responses to members of the opposite sex were also found to be reflected in the actual dating behavior of high and low self-monitors. Those high on this dimension dated nearly twice as many different partners in the previous year as did those low in self-monitoring. Consistently, low self-monitors reported dating their current partner for nearly twice as long as was true for high self-monitors.

Such data suggest that the interpersonal relationships of high and low self-monitors are quite different. Those high on this dimension enter a dating relationship with a lack of commitment and a willingness to change partners. Such individuals find it easy to terminate a relationship in order to start a new one. Though this line of research has not yet been extended to married couples, Snyder and Simpson (1984) raise the interesting possibility that low self-monitors may be more committed to their marriages and that such unions may be longer lasting than in the case of high self-monitors. If these hypotheses are confirmed, the effect of this personality trait on marital success may turn out to be of considerable importance.

female Type A behavior that is associated with marital difficulties (Becker, 1984).

It appears that the hard-driving, work-oriented style of Type As that is evident in the outside world also plays a major role in their homelife. Other personality variables also affect interpersonal behavior and the relationship between males and females. For an example of a dimension that is quite important in this respect, see the **Focus** insert on page 512 to learn about the role of *self-monitoring.*

LOCUS OF CONTROL: Assigning Responsibility for Life's Outcomes

One of the basic personality characteristics that influences behavior involves one's assumptions about responsibility for good and bad events. A person who believes that he or she is able to act so as to maximize the possibility of good outcomes and to minimize the possibility of bad outcomes is said to have **internal locus of control**. The opposite assumption about one's ability to control events is that individuals are helpless and at the mercy of luck, fate, and other uncontrollable outside forces — **external locus of control.** Individual differences in this respect were proposed by Julian Rotter as constituting the dimension of **locus of control** (Rotter and Hochreich, 1975). We will outline the theory underlying this concept and describe some of the research based on differences in locus of control.

internal v external

How we obtain rewards and avoid punishments

In Rotter's personality theory, behavior occurs as a function of a person's *expectancy* that the behavior will result in reinforcement and the *value* he or she places on any particular reinforcement. It is assumed that people act so as to maximize highly valued rewards and to minimize extremely distasteful punishments.

Besides the expectancies and values that operate in a specific situation, Rotter proposes that each of us acquires a general set of beliefs about life and the cause of our rewards and punishments. On the basis of childhood experiences and observations, each person comes to a conclusion about the extent to which good versus bad outcomes are controlled by his or her own actions or by uncontrollable outside forces (Phares, 1978). At the internal extreme of this belief system is the assumption that skill, hard work, foresight, and taking responsibility will pay off. At the external extreme, the person assumes that events are determined by chance and other unknown factors.

To measure generalized expectancies, several different locus of control tests have been constructed for adults, and others have been developed for children (Lefcourt, 1982). The instrument Rotter (1966) developed is known as the **I-E Scale.** Those taking the test must choose between two alternatives on each item. Two sample items provide an idea of the test's content. In each instance, you are supposed to select the alternative you believe to be more true:

(1) _____ a. Many of the unhappy things in people's lives are partly due to bad luck.
_____ b. People's misfortunes result from the mistakes they make.
(2) _____ a. In the case of the well-prepared student there is rarely such a thing as an unfair test.
_____ b. Many times exam questions tend to be so unrelated to course work that studying is really useless.

Responses to a series of such items yield a locus of control score. Differences along this dimension have been related to behavior in a variety of social situations, and we will now summarize some of these findings.

Behavioral differences: Internals versus externals

As with most personality dimensions, one of the basic questions about locus of control is the way differences develop. Why are some people on the internal extreme and others on the external extreme of this dimension?

Developing expectancies about control.   Research on this trait indicates that those with an internal orientation were raised by mothers who expected them to behave independently at an early age and who did not try to control every aspect of their offspring's behavior (Chance, 1965). Parents of internals tend to baby them and to be protective, affectionate, and approving (Katkovsky, Crandall, and Good, 1967). In general, parents of internals expect a lot of their children and also offer a great deal of affectionate involvement. It should be stressed that internals develop not simply as the result of being spoiled and overindulged. Rather, the child learns that reinforcements depend on what he or she does (Crandall, 1973). The major lesson to be learned is that reinforcements are *contingent* on behavior.

At the other extreme, externals seem to experience more rejection, hostile control, and criticism (Davis and Phares, 1969). Long after infancy and childhood, externally oriented college students describe their parents as having been restrictive (Johnson and Kilmann, 1975). Altogether, it appears that an external orientation develops in response to overcontrolling, critical parents.

The original theory was that maladjustment should be associated with either extreme of this personality dimension. One could be maladjusted by assuming total helplessness and feeling no sense of responsibility for events. Equally maladjusted is someone who feels totally in control of life's events (Lefcourt, 1982). The research to date has shown, however, that internality is a more positive asset than externality. Among school children, for example, those who are external are neurotic, impulsive, and hyperactive (Linn and Hodge, 1982; Raine, Roger, and Venables, 1982). In a study that included samples from the United States, India, and Hong Kong, it was consistently found that externally oriented individuals were also characterized by self-destructive behaviors such as drinking, smoking, and driving unsafely (Kelley et al., 1986). Those high in externality are also found to be depressed (Burger, 1984).

Responding to interpersonal situations.   Differences in locus of control are related to behavior in competitive situations. Competitive demands lead those with an external orientation to give up. Internals outperform externals when competition is involved, but they do not differ in a cooperative situation (Nowicki, 1982). When there is pressure to conform, externals are more likely to do so than internals (Crowne and Liverant, 1963). Internals not only fail to conform, but they resist the influence of experimenters and attempt to behave in ways contrary to what is expected (Lefcourt, 1982). Generally, internals seem to be less inclined

FIGURE 14.10. In school there are dramatic differences between those who are internals and those who are externals. Internals assume that hard work in school pays off both at the time and in the future. Externals see no relationship between expending effort in school and what happens later in their lives.

Internals versus externals in school: Eager participation versus seeming irrelevance

than externals to submit in an unquestioning manner either to fellow members of a group or to a person in charge.

In their social interactions, internals take steps to control the outcome. For example, internally oriented college females use more cosmetics than externals (Cash, Rissi, and Chapman, 1985). Even in sexual relationships, internality for both males and females is associated with more frequent and more satisfying interactions with the opposite sex (Catania, McDermott, and Wood, 1984).

Most of the research dealing with school performance and achievement indicates that internality is positively related to success (Bar-Tal and Bar-Zohar, 1977; Findley and Cooper, 1983; see Figure 14.10). For females, at least, high levels of cognitive development are characteristic of internals (Shute, Howard, and Steyartt, 1984). Sadly enough, the academic difficulties faced by racial minorities and other disadvantaged groups are made worse by locus of control factors. In the United States, externality is common among nonwhites, and this orientation leads to a perception of school as a hopeless exercise in futility (Lefcourt, 1982). The effects of locus of control are felt throughout the educational process, including postdoctoral work. Among graduate students studied over a five-year period, internals were found more likely to complete their requirements and obtain a Ph.D. than were externals (Otten, 1977).

At work, it would seem that pay increases act as an obvious incentive to work harder and to be more satisfied with one's job. That is not quite true, and locus of control is one of the complicating factors. Earn (1982) placed college students in an experimental situation that required them to solve a series of simple puzzles. Some were paid nothing for the task, some received $2.50, and a third group was given $5.00. When asked afterward to rate how much they liked the work, internals and externals responded quite differently, as shown in Figure 14.11. The higher the pay, the more positive the internally oriented students were about the

FIGURE 14.11. When internally and externally oriented students engaged in a task for either no money, $2.50, or $5.00, their liking for the task was a function of the amount of pay and of locus of control. For internals, liking increased as the pay increased. For externals, liking decreased as the pay increased. (Source: Based on data from Earn, 1982.)

Internals and externals react differently to being paid for their work

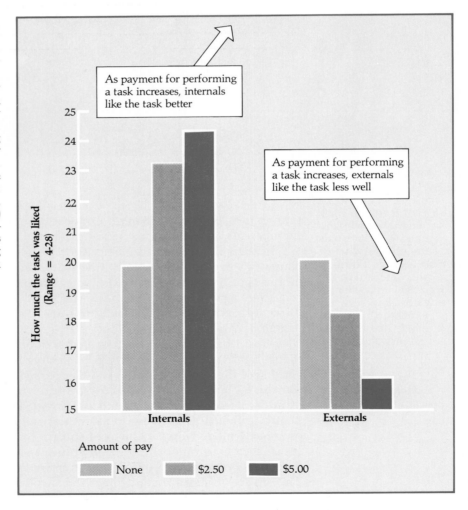

As payment for performing a task increases, internals like the task better

As payment for performing a task increases, externals like the task less well

task, but the reverse was true for those with an external orientation. In addition, the amount of time spent working when the experimenter was out of the room increased with pay level for internals and decreased with pay level for externals. The author suggested that internals interpret the rewards as indicating how competent they are. In contrast, externals regard extra rewards as an indication that the task must be unpleasant — otherwise why would someone pay them to do it? In actual work settings, it is hypothesized that internals work harder and are more satisfied with their occupation.

Factors bringing about changes in locus of control. As with most personality traits, locus of control is relatively stable over time (Wolfle and Robertshaw, 1982). Under the appropriate conditions, however, change can occur. Some changes are the result of everyday life events. Aging is a factor for all of us. In childhood, internality increases with age (Penk, 1969). This is a realistic assessment of events, because as time passes young people are able to exert more and more control over what happens to them. In adulthood, jobs that involve the ability to exert control have the same effect. Administrators show increases in internality the longer they spend in such positions (Harvey, 1971).

In the opposite direction, extremely disrupting life events result in a shift toward externality. For example, women who are physically abused by their husbands are more external than non-battered women (Cheney and Bleker, 1982). The longer a woman remains in an abusive situation, the higher she scores in the external direction. Divorce also pushes women toward externality, but they later return to their pre-divorce level (Doherty, 1983). Finally, old age is characterized by externality (Lumpkin, 1986). The combination of health problems, retirement, offspring growing up and leaving home, and declining social involvement leaves the individual feeling less and less in control of life events.

When there is a deliberate attempt to bring about personality change, it is to increase internality because that is viewed as the better adjusted alternative. In one school experiment, for example, teachers were instructed to encourage children to develop internal control expectancies by means of reinforcement manipulations. Measures of locus of control before and after this procedure indicated an increase in internality (Reimanis, 1971). Similar changes in college students were brought about by specially designed counseling sessions. The students became more internal, and they also did such things as renting a new apartment, changing majors, and seeking feedback from their instructors.

This research suggests that both children and adults can be taught to perceive themselves as active, hopeful participants in their lives rather than as helpless pawns. To the extent each of us is able to control our life, it is obviously to our advantage to do so.

Personality characteristics do not develop in a vacuum, and societal pressures are important as suggested in the **Applied Side** insert on page 520.

ON THE APPLIED SIDE

Personality and Societal Influences: The Achievement Needs of Females

Since the early 1950s psychologists have been interested in a complex personality dimension known as **need for achievement.** Achievement need is conceptualized as a learned motive to strive for success and excellence, and it is measured by examining the content of fantasies created by subjects responding to a series of pictures (McClelland et al., 1949). A large body of research has provided evidence that need for achievement scores can be used to predict school grades, the willingness to take reasonable risks in order to succeed at a task, ability to delay gratification, and an interest in and success at a business career (Byrne and Kelley, 1981).

One curious factor has characterized this research from the beginning. The findings are based almost entirely on male subjects, and attempts to predict the achievement behavior of females have repeatedly met with failure. It seems that one of the reasons for sex differences in this personality attribute is that society discourages female achievement. Despite massive changes in female consciousness, the women's liberation movement, and legal battles to ensure equality of opportunity, females still face psychological obstacles that are sometimes subtle and sometimes blatant. One reason for sex differences in achievement need is that females receive two conflicting messages about what it means to succeed, while males receive only one (Elder and MacInnis, 1983). For some females, behavior is directed toward success in terms of dating, courtship, marriage, and having offspring. For others, the path is more like that of males — education and a career. Of great potential importance is which message is being emphasized by society.

The tendency to discourage female achievement begins with our earliest exposure to fairy tales and children's books in which males are shown in active roles while females act as passive admirers or as victims to be rescued (McArthur and Eisen, 1976; Phelps, 1981; Scott and Feldman-Summers, 1979). For adults in the 1980s we might think that such issues are primarily of historical interest. In fact, movies and magazines continue to exploit females as sex objects, valued primarily for their appearance, and television seems to be an even more pervasive source of sex stereotyping (see Figure 14.12).

For example, it is consistently found that on prime-time TV, women who are portrayed as working outside the home tend to be single, divorced, or widowed, while working men are much more likely to be shown as happily married (Weigel and Loomis, 1981). In other words, males can have a career *and* a happy home life, but females must make a choice.

One particularly upsetting type of televised message is the commercial. Typically, females are shown to be concerned with how the wash smells, the kitchen floor shines, and how her husband likes the new dish she has prepared.

In one very interesting experiment, a series of such traditional male-superior commercials were presented to female college students, and other females were shown specially prepared ones in which the roles of males and females were reversed (Jennings, Geils, and Brown, 1980). You might not think that a small sample of this new type of commercial would have any effect on behavior after a lifetime of viewing the usual content. Surprisingly, the students who saw the nontraditional commercials were found to be less conforming in a laboratory experiment, and they behaved more self-confidently when giving a speech.

If the media manage to present and reinforce undesirable sex role stereotypes, we might conclude that it is important to find

FIGURE 14.12. Our ideas about males and females and the possibility of reaching achievement-oriented goals are shaped in part by the books we read, the movies we see, and the television we watch. To an alarming degree, females are depicted in stereotypical ways in a world built on male achievement.

Women in advertisements: One barrier to female achievement?

ways to change these presentations. The overall goal would be to increase the number of achieving females. This does not mean that every female should become an astronaut—any more than every male should become an entrepreneur. It does mean that personality traits can be strongly influenced by what we read, see, and hear and that there is no reason to encourage particular characteristics in one sex rather than the other.

LONELINESS: An Unmet Need for Social Contact

One personality variable that is of particular interest to social psychologists is **loneliness.** An individual is lonely if he or she desires close interpersonal relationships but is unable to establish them (Peplau and Perlman, 1982). No matter how many people surround you at school, at work, or wherever, it is possible to feel isolated and friendless. Such considerations recently have led to the construction of a test to measure loneliness, to the study of its development, and to investigations of the ways lonely and nonlonely people differ in their social interactions.

Assessing loneliness

Russell, Peplau, and Cutrona (1980) constructed the **UCLA Loneliness Scale** to measure individual differences in this characteristic. The first step was to gather an initial sample of items dealing with the experience of loneliness. After going through item analysis procedures, the final test consists of twenty statements, some expressing feelings of being lonely and some worded the opposite way (Russell, 1982). Subjects respond to each item on a four-point scale ranging from never to often. Examples of the items are:

- I feel left out.
- I have a lot in common with the people around me.

Once the test's reliability was established, studies were conducted that dealt with the relationship between scores on this instrument and other behavior. For example, college students attending a clinic dealing with social problems scored much higher than a sample of nonclinic students. Those who obtain high loneliness scores also report feeling depressed, anxious, dissatisfied, unhappy, and shy (Russell, 1982). Those who are lonely say they feel self-conscious in public, are socially anxious, and express low self-esteem (Jones, Freeman, and Goswick, 1981). These relationships are found to hold true for senior citizens as well as for college students (Perlman, Gerson, and Spinner, 1978).

Construct validity for this measure is also provided by its relation to several specific behaviors. Those who are most lonely, compared to those who are least lonely, report spending more time by themselves each day, more often eating dinner alone, and spending more weekends without companionship. Consistently, those high in loneliness engage in fewer social activities and are likely not to be dating (Russell, Peplau, and Cutrona, 1980). It may seem obvious that those who are lonely would report having fewer friends, but this is not always so. Those scoring high on the scale name as many friends (including "close friends") as those with low scores (Williams and Solano, 1983). Their friendships, however, are at a lower level of intimacy and are often not reciprocated.

Given these basic reliability and validity data about the construct, investigators have begun seeking the origins of this personality characteristic. Why are some people more lonely than others?

Lonely children and lonely adults

Most of us had some experiences of loneliness as we grow up. This is especially true if one's family has moved from one location to another or if events such as illness caused enforced periods of solitude. These unpleasant episodes are usually overcome, however, and do not seem to be the major cause of adult loneliness.

Later interpersonal problems are much more likely among those who never learned appropriate social skills during childhood (Rubin, 1982). There is no very systematic instruction for any of us about how to make and keep friends, how to provide interpersonal reinforcements, how to deal with disagreements, or how to become sensitive to the feelings of others (Putallaz and Gottman, 1981; Rubin, 1980). Some individuals happen to have good role models for these behaviors in their families, and others probably stumble on appropriate ways to deal with others by accident. It is usually at some point when we are away from our parents in day care, nursery school, or kindergarten that we first have to develop and practice appropriate social behavior (Rubin, 1982). For those who never quite get the knack of dealing with others, the most usual responses are to become aggressive or to withdraw into loneliness.

We need to be reminded of the sharp distinction between being alone and feeling lonely. Some children are quite able to make friends and to interact with them smoothly and yet prefer to spend a lot of time in solitary activities. There is nothing wrong with preferring to avoid companionship at times in order to pursue a hobby, read, listen to music, or just to engage in thought. It is only when a child is alone and unhappy that parents should become concerned about their offspring (Suedfeld, 1982).

Despite the problems of childhood, it is in adolescence that loneliness can reach a peak (Brennan, 1982). During this period we begin to separate from our parents, seek close relationships outside of the home, and begin to assume personal responsibility for our actions (see Figure 14.13). One common result is a feeling of loneliness and alienation from parents, teachers, and others (Brennan and Auslander, 1979). Adolescents who are most lonely possess poor social skills and lack interest in other people (Brennan, 1982). These same characteristics are typical of college students who are chronically lonely (Cutrona, 1982).

FIGURE 14.13. Though loneliness can occur at any age, adolescence is a particularly vulnerable time because friendships and opposite-sex relationships become of vital importance. Those without the necessary social skills tend to feel lonely and unhappy.

Adolescence: A danger period for loneliness

The behavior of those who are lonely and how it can be changed

In studies of children, adolescents, and adults, it seems clear that certain kinds of social behavior contribute to the individual's inability to form close relationships. The ability to deal with others in a social setting has been found to differ for those high and low in loneliness. In one experiment, subjects had to interact with a stranger during a brief period. Those high in loneliness were much less skillful in such a situation than those low on this dimension (Jones, Hobbs, and Hockenbury, 1982). Those who are lonely were observed to refer to the other person less, to be less inclined to follow up on topics introduced by the stranger, and to ask fewer questions. In general, they simply paid less attention to the person with whom they were interacting. This lack of interest (or lack of ability even to pretend interest) seems to be a major reason for social rejection.

Because of past failures in social situations, lonely individuals have a high expectation of failure when dealing with others. They expect others not to like them, even when this is untrue (Jones, Freeman, and Goswick, 1981). Interpersonal evaluations, even positive ones, can be painful if you are anxious about social interactions (Arkin and Appelman, 1983). Besides not showing interest in others, those who are lonely also disclose less about themselves both in the laboratory and in real life (Berg and Peplau, 1982; Solano, Batten, and Parish, 1982). The self disclosures of those who are lonely tend to be inappropriate — too intimate with those of the same sex and too unrevealing to members of the opposite sex. Altogether, lonely individuals give evidence of inadequate interpersonal skills. They unintentionally drive away potential friends by showing disinterest, expressing negative expectancies, and engaging in inappropriate levels of self-disclosure.

Among the effects of these interpersonal deficits is the tendency to be cynical about other people, to feel pessimistic about life, and to express an external locus of control (Jones, 1982). Their views of the opposite sex seem designed to maximize failure. Lonely individuals are less likely to believe in love as a basis for marriage and more likely to expect that their own marriages will end in divorce (Jones, Hansson, and Smith, 1980).

Unless there is some outside intervention, loneliness tends to persist from year to year. When asked, those who are lonely say that their condition will not change, and one solution is wish-fulfilling fantasy (Revenson, 1981). Other "solutions" are absorption in work and overconsumption of alcohol and drugs (Paloutzian and Ellison, 1979). The coping strategies used by the lonely serve to maintain isolation and even to make it worse. What can be done to change such behavior?

One of the more successful intervention techniques is the use of **cognitive therapy** to bring about a change in the way the lonely person thinks about himself or herself in social situations (Young, 1982). There is an attempt in therapy to make the person's thoughts, actions, and emotions very explicit. Once a male is able to verbalize, for example, that his self-concept is low because he is dull and boring, it is possible to explore the validity of that assumption and also the belief that everyone must be lively and witty to make friends. Once a female describes her social fears as based on the assumption that others are sitting in judgment and waiting for her to make a fool of herself, these cognitions can be discussed and potentially altered.

In addition to changing cognitive beliefs and assumptions, it is useful to teach social skills to those lonely individuals who never quite learned how to deal with others (Rook and Peplau, 1982). With **social skills training,** clients observe successful models, practice interpersonal behavior, observe their performance on videotape, and even carry out "homework assignments" (see Figure 14.14). Those who are lonely fear rejection so much that they fail to take social risks, such as initiating relationships or introducing themselves to new neighbors (Schultz and Moore, 1984). One can, of course, *learn* to do these things. It may seem odd at first, but it can be extremely useful simply to receive instructions

FIGURE 14.14. Social skills training involves specialized instruction in the basic elements of meeting and dealing with other people. Those who lack such skills tend to interact with others in such a way as to invite rejection and thus cause loneliness.

Overcoming loneliness by learning social skills

about such ordinary matters as how to begin a conversation, how to speak comfortably on the telephone, how to give compliments and receive them, and even how to look more attractive with changes in hair style, clothing, or make-up.

During a period as brief as a couple of months, some seemingly miraculous changes can be brought about (Rook and Peplau, 1982). Loneliness, then, is not a hopeless condition that must be endured. Once an individual thinks about social situations in a different way, learns different ways of interacting with others, and makes changes in his or her appearance, it is possible to eliminate extreme feelings of loneliness.

SUMMARY

Relatively stable individual differences in behavior are known as personality **traits**. **Personality** is defined as the combination of enduring characteristics possessed by an individual. The traditional assumption of personality psychology was that behavior depended primarily on the operation of stable internal characteristics. Disappointment with the predictive power of personality tests led some psychologists to emphasize situational variables as an alternative. Increasingly, trait and situational approaches are treated in an integrated fashion. Most of the traits of interest to psychologists were first observed long before there was a science of behavior. Tests often grow out of observation and theory. A useful test must have acceptable **reliability** and **validity**.

The hardworking, aggressive individual who is always in a hurry is identified as having a **Type A** coronary-prone behavior pattern. Type As differ from those who are Type B in the kinds of demands that are placed on them in childhood and in their approach to work. Type As handle demanding situations well and ignore distractions. Though there are physiological penalties for this hard work, there is also evidence that they achieve success. Interpersonally, the Type A pattern leads to difficulties in that such individuals become impatient and irritated with others.

According to Rotter, people develop a generalized expectancy involving **internal** versus **external locus of control**. We begin to learn such expectancies early in life. Internally oriented individuals do well in competitive situations, resist conformity pressures and social influence, and attempt to control their physical and social environments. Expectancies can be changed by life events and by specific intervention procedures. Personality characteristics can be strongly influenced by societal factors such as television, and sex differences in **need for achievement** represent one example of such influences.

Loneliness refers to an individual's subjective perception that he or she lacks close interpersonal relationships. Those who are lonely are depressed and anxious, self-conscious in social situations, and shy. Loneliness often begins in childhood when an individual fails to learn appropriate social skills. It can intensify in adolescence, and the general social ineffectiveness of the lonely person leads to cynicism and pessimism. The most successful techniques for reducing loneliness consist of **cognitive therapy** and **social skills training**.

GLOSSARY

authoritarianism
The personality dimension that ranges from the authoritarian personality to the egalitarian personality. Authoritarians are characterized by adherence to conventional values, submission to a strong leader, aggression toward those who deviate, and having a concern for power.

cognitive therapy
Psychotherapy in which the emphasis is on altering the client's maladaptive thought processes.

construct validity
The series of relationships established between scores on a personality test and other theoretically relevant responses.

external locus of control
The generalized belief that reinforcements are controlled by external factors, such as luck, over which the individual has no influence.

F Scale
The Fascist Scale, a personality test that was constructed to measure the trait of authoritarianism.

I-E Scale
A personality test that measures locus of control and identifies where individuals fall along the internal-external dimension.

internal locus of control
The generalized belief that reinforcements are controlled by oneself through the functioning of such factors as ability and effort.

Jenkins Activity Survey
A personality test that measures coronary-prone behavior (Type A) and its opposite (Type B).

locus of control
The generalized expectancy as to where the control for one's reinforcements lies—either in uncontrollable outside forces or in one's own actions.

loneliness
The personality dimension that involves the subjective experience of isolation. The individual feels unhappy and cut off from close personal relationships.

need for achievement
A learned motive to strive for success and excellence.

personality
The combination of those relatively enduring characteristics of an individual that are expressed in a variety of situations.

reliability
The consistency with which a measuring instrument assesses a variable.

self
The array of attitudes, judgments, and values a person holds with respect to his or her behavior, ability, appearance, and general worth.

self-efficacy
How well an individual believes he or she can do in performing a given task.

self-monitoring
A personality dimension that ranges from the tendency to regulate one's behavior on the basis of the situation (high self-monitors) to the tendency to regulate one's behavior on the basis of internal factors (low self-monitors).

Self-Monitoring Scale
The test devised by Snyder to measure individual differences in self-monitoring.

social skills training
A therapeutic intervention technique that concentrates on teaching individuals what to do and say in interpersonal interactions.

trait
A behavioral dimension or personality characteristic involving differences among individuals.

Type A
Those individuals at the extreme of a personality dimension involving coronary-prone behavior, characterized by a hardworking, aggressive, time-pressured lifestyle.

Type B
Those individuals at the low-risk extreme of the coronary-prone dimension. They are easygoing and relaxed, unconcerned about time pressures, and unlikely to develop cardiovascular disease.

UCLA Loneliness Scale
The personality test that assesses the extent to which an individual experiences loneliness.

validity
The extent to which a test is related to or able to predict relevant behavior.

FOR MORE INFORMATION

Aronoff, J., and Wilson, J. P. (1985). *Personality in the social process.* Hillsdale, N.J.: Erlbaum.

> This important text is based on the assumption that our behavior is a function both of enduring dispositions and of situational demands. This integrative approach is applied to such diverse areas as social perception, information processing, interpersonal attraction, negotiating behavior, and group functioning.

Babladelis, G. (1984). *The study of personality: Issues and resolutions.* New York: Holt, Rinehart & Winston.

>   This basic personality text takes the point of view that personality is not a separate area of psychology but rather is linked with all other areas. The discussion includes the determinants of individual differences, the extent to which we are characterized by consistency versus change, and the role of theory and measurement.

Lefcourt, H. M. (1982). *Locus of control: Current trends in theory and research,* 2nd ed. Hillsdale, N. J.: Erlbaum.

>   An up-to-date review of the theory underlying the concept of locus of control and of the several decades of research involving internality and externality. Specific topics include the measurement of this construct, developmental studies, the correlates of the internal-external dimension, and the way one's orientation can change.

Peplau, L. A., and Perlman, D. (1982). *Loneliness: A sourcebook of current theory, research, and therapy.* New York: Wiley.

>   Numerous contributors provide an extensive examination of the personality variable of loneliness. Topics range from its origins in childhood to intervention techniques designed to change it. A unique feature is a comprehensive bibliography of all of the loneliness research conducted between 1932 and 1981.

Surwit, R. S., Williams, R. B., Jr., and Shapiro, D. (1982). *Behavioral approaches to cardiovascular disease.* New York: Academic Press.

>   This book contains a great deal of basic information about coronary heart disease ranging from physiology to behavior therapy. Though the authors do not conclude the evidence is totally convincing, they suggest that behavioral factors play an important role at every stage of coronary dysfunction.

CHAPTER 15

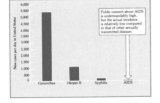

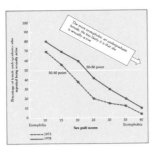

VARIATIONS IN SEXUAL ATTITUDES AND BEHAVIOR: From Repression to Revolution (and Back Again?)

Differences among societies • Changes in sexual permissiveness within the United States • Attitudinal changes • Changes in behavior

THE EFFECTS OF EROTIC IMAGES on Motives, Attitudes, and Behavior

The motivational effects of sexual images • Attitudinal effects of erotica • Do erotic images affect behavior? • Erotica and sex crimes: The ultimate danger

POSITIVE AND NEGATIVE SEXUAL ATTITUDES: Erotophilia and Erotophobia

Measuring sexual attitudes and their development • Sexual responsiveness: The effect of sexual attitudes • Other sex-related behaviors: Learning, health, and the prevention of unwanted pregnancies

---

SPECIAL INSERTS

FOCUS ON RESEARCH: Classic Contributions — Studying actual sexual behavior: The laboratory findings of Masters and Johnson

FOCUS ON RESEARCH: The Cutting Edge — Anxiety and sexual arousal: Interference or enhancement?

ON THE APPLIED SIDE — Pornography: Is it a problem? If so, what should be done about it?

HUMAN SEXUALITY:
The Most Intimate Social Behavior

The scene is a radio talk show, and the host has brought up the topic of bookstores, movie theaters, and video rental outlets that specialize in explicit sexual material.

HOST: A story in last night's paper was the impetus for my introducing the topic of sex this morning. The challenger in the mayoral race in the upcoming election proposed that all of these X-rated businesses be closed down and run out of our fair city. I'm quoting Mr. Stevens who said, "It's not a matter of censorship any more, it's a matter of public health and safety. I ask my opponent to let the voters know whether he's in favor of deadly diseases and sex crimes or whether he's for healthy bodies and streets that are safe for women and children to walk on." That's pretty strong stuff, listeners, and you can call 851-2250 to let us know what you think. Let's take our first call at WKUP talk radio, where your ideas count. Good morning.

CALLER 1: Is this the radio station?

HOST: The last time I looked at the sign on the door, that's what it said.

CALLER 1: Good. I just want to say that Stevens is the first politician around here in years who has made any sense. Those sink holes of filth should be burned to the ground. People go in those places and get vile ideas about what to do with every which part of their bodies. They spread diseases throughout the community. I don't mind if they crawl someplace and die, but they'll give it to the rest of us first.

HOST: And you think pornography is the basic problem?

CALLER 1: I know it is. When I was a young man, people went about their business with clean thoughts. You could read a good book without exposing yourself to every barnyard word some yahoo wants to stick in your face. Young people were innocent and had a good time, and there was no reason to be ashamed to take your mother to the movies. There were perfectly nice words like "gay" that didn't refer to perverts. All this slime has got to stop somewhere.

HOST: Well, I thank you for your opinion. Let's see what others have to say. Good morning, you're on WKUP talk radio.

CALLER 2: I'm glad you got that old fool off the air before my blood pressure shot through the roof.

HOST: I have the feeling you disagree with some of his sentiments.

CALLER 2: I disagree with *everything* he said. Let me tell you first that I'm married and the mother of two darling preschoolers. I'm not in favor of disease or sex crimes, and nobody in their right mind favors such things. There *are* a lot of people in favor of storm trooper tactics—starting with censorship and attempting to control the morality of others.

HOST: Do you think it's possible society has gone too far in its tolerance and permissiveness?

CALLER 2: Of course not! People talk as if sex were invented about twenty years ago. Did you ever read about bisexuality in ancient Greece, see the erotic drawings and statuary in Pompeii, or study the practice of child prostitution in Victorian England? Every sexual act and every sex crime have been known throughout the world since the dawn of history. The only difference from time to time and place to place is the extent to which people are free to talk about these things and free to depict them in their artistic creations. Besides, no one is forced to read words they don't want to read or to see pictures they don't want to see.

HOST: Thanks for calling. You and our first caller might get together sometime and have a lively conversation.

CALLER 2: He would think I'm an evil sinner, and I know he's a Nazi.

HOST: Well, it takes all kinds. 'Bye now. Before I get to the next caller, we'll listen to a message from the good folks down at Butler's Garage.

THE ATTITUDES and beliefs expressed on this imaginary show are common ones, and they deal with only one aspect of the importance of **sexuality** in our social interactions. Psychological research on this topic has increased at a rapid rate, beginning in the 1970s. In this chapter, we will present some of the highlights of recent work. First, we will outline the revolutionary *changes in sexuality* that have occurred in recent decades. The crucial role of fantasy in human sexual behavior will be described as we look at the *effects of erotic images on motivation and behavior*. The role of *individual differences in sexual attitudes* will also be summarized. In addition, there will be special coverage of the classic research on sexual behavior conducted by *Masters and Johnson*, a description of research on the *effects of anxiety on sexual arousal*, and a discussion of current views on the effects of pornography.

VARIATIONS IN SEXUAL ATTITUDES AND BEHAVIOR: From Repression to Revolution (and Back Again?)

One of the striking aspects of sexual behavior is the fact that it varies dramatically across cultures and across generations. The physical expression of this biological need is strongly influenced by the attitudes and beliefs that prevail at a given time and in a given place. What people do, how frequently they do it, with whom, at what age, and their emotional reactions to sexuality are determined much more by psychosocial factors than biological ones.

Changes in what people do sexually and in their attitudes about various aspects of sexuality have been common over the centuries. There are periodic shifts between permissiveness and restrictiveness, and no one has successfully identified the reasons for these sometimes abrupt changes. In the present century, much of Western Civilization has undergone what has been termed a **sexual revolution**. The move toward greater sexual freedom and tolerance first was noted following World War I and gained steadily in strength until the late 1970s. Though it is a bit too soon to be certain, there is increasing evidence that the 1980s are witnessing the beginning of a reverse movement (see Figure 15.1, page 534). We examine some of the evidence dealing with both types of change in the present section.

Differences among societies

The work of anthropologists has added a special dimension to our understanding of human sexuality. As Gregersen (1986) points out, most people believe that their own culture is superior to that of others and that basic human nature is represented by the activities of those like themselves. When cross-cultural comparisons are made, it becomes obvious that much of what we do and believe must be based on learning, because other human beings act and believe quite differently than ourselves (Ford and Beach, 1951; Malinowski, 1929; Mead, 1969). In the sexual realm, anthropologists have provided a large body of evidence that almost every aspect of sexual behavior is based on culturally supplied norms rather than on biologically determined imperatives. For example, the most common position for intercourse among several South American Indian

FIGURE 15.1. At the present time in our society it is possible to find numerous signs of the permissive changes brought about by the sexual revolution as well as indications of a possible backlash or "counterrevolution."

Changes in sexual attitudes: Alternation between permissiveness and restrictiveness

groups is that of mammalian rear entry; throughout the Pacific islands the male kneels and the female lies on her back ("Oceanic" position); while in Europe and the Western Hemisphere the "missionary" position is the norm (Davenport, 1978; Gregersen, 1982).

In recent years, increasing interest has been directed at behavior in highly developed societies. For example, the most dramatic changes toward greater sexual permissiveness and experimentation centered primarily in Western Europe, led by the Scandinavian countries, followed by the United States and Japan (Christensen, 1969; Leo, 1983; Perlman et al., 1978; Sigusch and Schmidt, 1973). Within the United States the behavior of blacks and whites is found to be strikingly similar (Fisher, 1980b; Robinson and Calhoun, 1983). In other contemporary societies such as the USSR (Orinova, 1981) and the People's Republic of China (Butterfield, 1980) the response to nudity, erotic books and movies, pre-marital sex, and so forth, is much more restrictive than our own. Still other nations, such as Colombia, report sexual patterns that resemble those of the United States several decades ago. For example, unmarried males there are much more sexually active (93.9 percent) than females (38.3 percent) (Alzate, 1984).

Changes in sexual permissiveness within the United States

Anyone who has viewed an X-rated movie (or even a non-explicit R-rated movie) might find it difficult to believe that a novel such as *Ulysses* by James Joyce was the focus of censorship battles in U. S. courts from 1914 to 1933. In 1953, *Playboy* magazine was inaugurated with a relatively modest photograph of an unclothed Marilyn Monroe. During the next three decades, there was a slow, steady increase in explicitness (ranging from pubic hair that was not airbrushed to gynecological close-ups). Male nudes were shown in *Playgirl* and *Cosmopolitan*, and interacting female nudes or male-female couples became common in many mass circulation magazines. By the 1960s legal threats to the publication of sexual words or to the presentation of visual sexual images had largely disappeared or were ineffective. A fine line was drawn between publications such as *Penthouse* and hard-core *pornography* involving pictorial explicitness. Pornography was not illegal, but there are generally restrictions about its public display and its sale to minors.

Movies have been considered potentially dangerous sources of sexual influence almost from the beginning. Strict censorship in the United States began in 1934, shortly after the development of "talkies." A production code was drawn up to specify what could and could not be said and shown. The duration of a kiss, for example, was precisely limited. Two people could not occupy the same bed, even to converse, unless there was at least one foot touching the floor. Twin beds became very popular during that period, because that is what was shown in the typical movie bedroom. By 1968 the old rules seemed increasingly unrealistic, and a rating system was introduced to restrict audiences by age rather than to place any restrictions on movie content. The proportion of G-rated movies (all ages admitted) dropped from 41 percent in 1968 to 3 percent in 1980 (Yagoda, 1980). Audiences are found to stay away from "wholesome" family movies, so moviemakers add some mild violence or sexual references to earn a rating of PG (parental guidance suggested), PG-13 (those under age thirteen need parental consent), or R (those seventeen or under must be accompanied by an adult). The final rating, X, means that one has to be eighteen years of age or older to attend, and there are no restrictions on what is depicted. Though one may think of

FOCUS ON RESEARCH:
Classic Contributions

Studying Actual Sexual Behavior: The Laboratory Findings of Masters and Johnson

Societal changes in attitudes about sexuality appear to have had highly visible effects on the scientific community. Scientists do not operate in a vacuum, and they are affected by the same legal, religious, and ethical concerns as everyone else in the community. The history of sex research reflects the kind of shifts in restrictiveness and permissiveness that we have described for the culture as a whole.

At the end of the last century and the beginning of the present one, the study of human sexuality was limited to a medical focus on "abnormal" practices (Ellis, 1899; Krafft-Ebing, 1886). Freud (1905) represented this same tradition but went on to shock the civilized world by emphasizing the importance of sex in *everyone's* developmental history. During the first few decades of this century, survey studies were undertaken to examine the details of what ordinary people did and did not do sexually (Davis, 1929; Hamilton, 1929; Terman et al., 1938). This work reached the general public's consciousness only in mid-century with the publication of the findings of Alfred Kinsey and his colleagues (Kinsey, Pomeroy, and Martin, 1948; Kinsey et al., 1953).

Among social psychologists, interest in sexual behavior was almost nonexistent, except for a small number of investigators who exposed subjects to mild stimuli such as photographs of the opposite sex or various musical selections. The subsequent fantasy productions of the subjects (on the TAT) were then examined for possible changes in amount of sexual content (Beardslee and Fogelson, 1958; Clark, 1952).

Over this entire array of research covering several decades, the actual behavior in question was not studied—investigators only dealt with verbal reports about past behavior or with verbal fantasies. An exception was John B. Watson (1929) who made the case for psychological research in this area quite a while before society was prepared to accept it. He went even further by carrying out a short-lived physiological study of his sexual interactions with a female graduate student (Magoun, 1981), quickly ending both his marriage and his academic career. There were plans at the Kinsey Institute for an ethically defensible laboratory study of sexual behavior, but that plan was never activated (Pomeroy, 1972).

Not until the 1960s was the climate appropriate for such research. William Masters, a physician, and Virginia Johnson, a psychologist, began a series of observational studies in which male and female adults engaged in sexual activity while being observed and physiologically monitored (Masters and Johnson, 1960, 1962, 1963, 1966). Though they began by using prostitutes as subjects, the investigators soon turned to the staff of their university-hospital complex in St. Louis, couples with sexual problems, and a variety of other volunteers. As they themselves made clear, this subject sample was by no means representative of the general population. Their initial reports were based almost exclusively on white, upper socioeconomic level, well educated residents of a large city. Perhaps more importantly, their subjects were those who were willing to engage in non-private masturbation, intercourse, and other acts.

Despite the sampling problems and subsequent criticisms of their work (Zilbergeld and Evans, 1980), it should be emphasized that

TABLE 15.1.
The pioneering work of Masters and Johnson in studying the sexual behavior of laboratory volunteers provided information of a type never before available. The psychological implications of many of their findings went far beyond the physiological and anatomical details of their observations.

Sex research and some of its implications

Finding	Implications
Both males and females go through a sexual response cycle that consists of a rapid excitement phase, a plateau phase, orgasm, and a resolution phase.	Many of our beliefs about the differences between the sexes were shown to be false. Many of the sex differences that we observe were now believed to be based on learning rather than on genetic differences.
Males experience a refractory period following orgasm, during which they are unresponsive to additional stimulation. Females remain responsive to stimulation and can thus experience subsequent sexual response cycles.	The idea that women have the potential to experience multiple orgasms resulted in a reversal of the traditional perception of sex differences in sexual power. Suddenly, males were described as having limited sexual stamina, while many females were clearly able to "outperform" them.
Female sexual excitement is primarily elicited by clitoral stimulation rather than by vaginal stimulation. Later work with gay females provided data consistent with this conclusion (Masters and Johnson, 1979).	For females, the greatest sexual pleasure and the greatest likelihood of orgasm is based not on intercourse but on other types of activity such as manual, oral, or vibratory stimulation.

these studies provided us for the first time with a body of new and basic knowledge about human sexual responses. In addition, the findings influenced both scientists and the general public in their conceptualizations of human sexuality. Three of the most important of these influences are summarized in Table 15.1. These findings and their implications clearly fit in well with what was happening sexually and politically in the general society, including the role of women.

Following these pioneering efforts, Masters and Johnson went on to investigate a variety of sexual phenomena including dysfunctions, homosexuality, and the effects of aging. Other investigators, including a large number of social and clinical psychologists, have benefitted from the Masters and Johnson example. Today, it is not at all unusual in university laboratories to conduct experiments using direct physiological measures of male and female sexual excitement. Without the groundbreaking that took place in St Louis, such work might well have been impossible. It is also of interest to reflect that this kind of research was unthinkable at the beginning of the century, thinkable but impossible over the next half-century, shocking in the 1960s, and a regular occurrence today. Once again, we can see that *change* characterizes almost everything related to human sexual behavior.

X-rated films as primarily shown in theaters frequented by a small male audience, the development of videotape recorders and the availability of video rentals has created a new mixed-sex audience who watch explicit sexual movies at home. In fact, the number of X-rated theaters in the United States is decreasing — down from a high of 800 in 1983 to fewer than 500 today (*Sex News*, 1985). Beyond books, magazines, and movies, a similar increase in permissiveness can be traced in the theater, on television, and especially in contemporary music (Heard, 1985).

A survey of individuals ranging in age from thirteen to thirty-nine indicates that exposure to sexually oriented R-rated materials has become essentially universal in our culture for both males and females (Bryant, 1985). Even underage junior high school students report having seen an average of 6.3 sexy R-rated films, and the mean age of first exposure was twelve and a half years. Totally explicit, X-rated magazines and films had been seen by the majority of the respondents. The age when an individual first sees such material seems to be dropping rapidly. Adults report first viewing an explicit movie at age eighteen; high school students at seventeen; and junior high students at fifteen. It appears there has been a dramatic change in this type of "sex education," presumably in part as a function of the availability of sexual publications, sexual material on cable TV, and the increasing presence of sexual videotapes in the home. Scientific activity is not isolated from the rest of culture, and the **Focus** insert on page 536 traces some of the changes in sex research that paralleled the changes in our society's permissiveness.

Attitudinal changes

Though no one is able to document whether changes in sexual attitudes preceded or followed cultural changes, it is well documented that both kinds of changes have occurred.

Between the post-war studies of Kinsey and more recent survey studies (Hunt, 1974) there were large shifts in American attitudes about sex. Up until the 1980s, at least, the shifts were consistently in the direction of increased willingness to tolerate the sexual practices of others. People gradually accepted the view that their neighbors' private activities were not a matter for public concern.

One way to demonstrate the attitudinal changes from generation to generation is to compare the attitudes of different age groups about various topics. In addition, there is evidence that amount of education, especially at the college level, is positively associated with permissive attitudes. Glenn and Weaver (1979) examined data from nationwide surveys involving several thousand subjects. Among the questions were items dealing with premarital sexual relations (see Figure 15.2). At each age level, permissiveness increases as educational level increases. The greatest change, however, was found to be across generations. Between the oldest and youngest subjects in the study, acceptance of premarital intercourse more than doubled. Beginning about 1980, however, attitude surveys began to show a shift in the opposite direction. For example, there has been an increase in the belief that sex before marriage is immoral (Robinson and Jedlicka, 1983). In studies of undergraduate females, Gerrard (1986) found a steady increase in negative attitudes about sex from the mid-1970s to the mid-1980s.

FIGURE 15.2. Survey research indicates that permissive attitudes about such activities as premarital sexual activity are more likely to be held by those with the most education. The effect across generations is more striking, with younger individuals expressing much more permissive attitudes than older ones. (Source: Based on data from Glenn and Weaver, 1979.)

Changes in behavior

The decades over which there were increases in the permissiveness of sexual attitudes were also a period of profound changes in sexual behavior. Perhaps the most remarkable change is that males and females are now much more similar in their sexual behavior than was the case in previous eras (Phillis and Gromko, 1985). During the first part of the twentieth century, the age of first coitus dropped steadily each decade among Czechoslovak women (Raboch and Bartak, 1980). In a similar

Sexually permissive attitudes: The effects of education and age

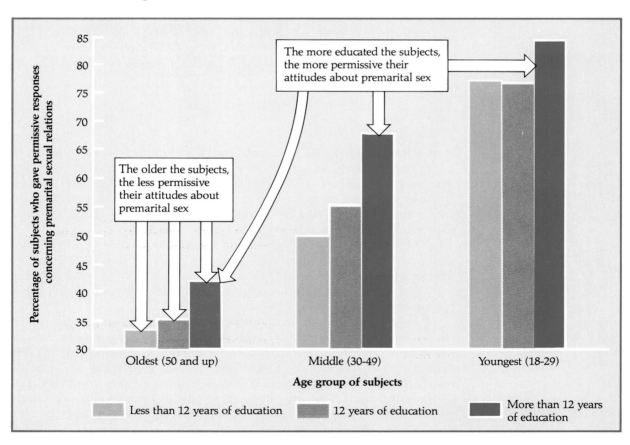

FIGURE 15.3.   Research on the sexual behavior of West German students indicates a striking increase in the incidence of premarital sexual activity even during the relatively brief time period from 1966 to 1981. As has been found in other nations in Europe and North America, the greatest change over time is among females. (Source: Based on data from Clement, Schmidt, and Kruse, 1984.)

Increases in premarital sex among males and females

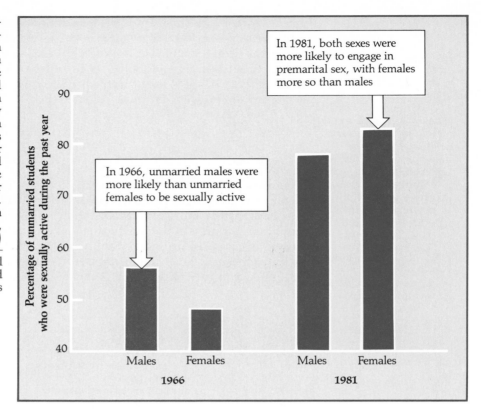

way, each age group of Americans has been more likely to engage in premarital sex than the previous one, with the greatest changes occurring among females (Reed and Weinberg, 1984). A study of unmarried West German students, summarized in Figure 15.3, indicates a striking increase in sexual activity in the brief period between 1966 and 1981 (Clement, Schmidt, and Kruse, 1984).

Though the data may suggest the attainment of newfound freedom and carefree sex, some studies indicate negative reactions. College women, for example, often report guilt and anxiety about becoming involved in intimate relationships for the first time and about being exploited by males (Weis, 1983).

Those individuals (both males and females) most likely to have intercourse at very young ages are found to be independent, to place a low value on academic achievement, to be relatively nonreligious, to feel distant from their parents, and to use alcohol, marijuana, and various illicit drugs (Jessor et al., 1983). Further, those who become sexually active before age fifteen are not likely to perceive sex and love as closely related (Rosen, Herskovitz, and Stack, 1982). It is also found that the younger an individual is when engaging in intercourse for the first time, the less likely he or she is to use any method of contraception (Cvetko-vitch and Grote, 1983).

Beyond premarital sex, generational changes are also found with respect to increases in the *frequency* of engaging in most sexual acts including intercourse, masturbation, and oral sex (Downey, 1980). Interestingly, there has been little or no change over the years in the incidence of homosexuality.

In addition to generational changes, there is also a degree of misperception across generations brought about, in part, by the difficulty parents and their offspring have in communicating about sex. It is generally agreed that parents respond to their children's sexuality with varying degrees of anxiety and conflict, as suggested by the cartoon in Figure 15.4. Perhaps more surprising is the discomfort felt by college-age offspring in thinking about their own parents as being sexually active. Across a series of studies, it has consistently been found that males and females underestimate the frequency of parental lovemaking by at least 50 percent (Murnen and Allgeier, 1986; Pocs and Godow, 1977; Zeiss, 1982).

One of the negative — and frightening — aspects of increased sexual experimentation has been the increase in the incidence of **sexually transmitted disease.** Both gonorrhea and syphilis are at record highs, but the 1980s has seen the rise of two as-yet-incurable diseases. So far, **genital herpes** has struck over 20,000,000 Americans (Felman et al., 1983). It involves painful blisters in the area of sexual contact, accompanied by itching, fever, and headaches. Though not usually serious, herpes can on occasion result in meningitis, and it *is* extremely dangerous to newborn infants whose mothers have the disease. Even more frightening is the advent of **Acquired Immune Deficiency Syndrome (AIDS).** This condition is known to be transmitted by semen or by blood, and it has been most prevalent among gays, but is by no means restricted to this group. AIDS is fatal, and half of those so diagnosed have already died. The annual death rate in the United States has increased from 118 in 1981 to 16,000 in 1986. In the social realm, fear of these diseases appears to be one reason for a decline in the incidence of casual sexual interactions of both heterosexuals and homosexuals. A comparison of the incidence of these diseases with the more familiar ones of gonorrhea and syphilis is

FIGURE 15.4. In addition to changes in sexual attitudes and behavior across generations, parents and their offspring find it difficult to communicate about sex. Most people do not want to think of their parents as being sexually active, and most parents (as suggested here) are uncomfortable when confronted by the sexuality of their sons and daughters. (Source: Copyright, 1985, Universal Press Syndicate. Reprinted with permission. All rights reserved.)

Parent-child sexual communication: Anxiety on both sides

542   Chapter 15   Human Sexuality: The Most Intimate Social Behavior

FIGURE 15.5. The fear of sexually transmitted disease is beginning to have a major effect on attitudes about casual sexual encounters. Though many people seem to assume that gonorrhea and syphilis are no longer problems, their incidence remains high. With both diseases, the major problems involve the reluctance of individuals to seek prompt treatment and basic changes in the disease organisms that produce penicillin-resistent strains. Most current interest is focused on the as-yet-incurable herpes II and AIDS. The later disease is especially frightening because it is fatal. (Source: Based on 1984 data from the Center for Disease Control, December 7, 1985.)

Sexually transmitted diseases: A source of fear

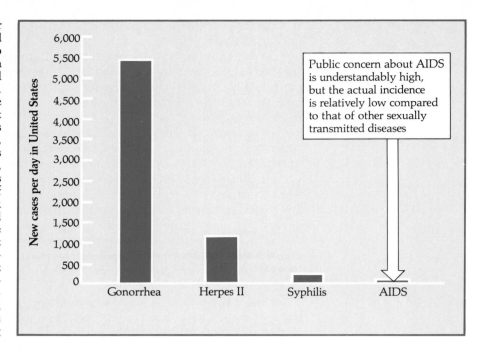

presented in Figure 15.5. With respect to AIDS, it should be noted that the number of cases per year is increasing rapidly. The Center for Disease Control estimates the number of new cases of AIDS in the United States in 1986 to be 44 — more than three times that for 1984.

It is widely believed that a combination of health considerations and a widespread shift toward conservative values is bringing about a reverse in sexual permissiveness. Despite an avalanche of books and articles indicating that the sexual revolution has faded (Frank, 1983), that Americans favor monogamy and are sexually conservative (Brody, 1983; Goleman, 1985), that marriage is making a comeback (Leo, 1985), and that celibacy is the new sexual fad (Brown, 1980; Lee, 1980), data indicating actual changes in behavior are just now becoming available. There are several recent indications that a reversal in permissive sexuality may be beginning. Data from the U. S. Census show that the number of cohabiting unmarried couples declined in 1985 after at least fifteen years of steady increases (Beckwith, 1985). A study of patients at a sexual disease center in Denver revealed a drop in the number of sexual partners as a function of learning about AIDS (McQuay, 1985). Heterosexual men averaged a decreased from 2.1 to 1.6 partners a month, heterosexual women dropped from 1.7 to 1.5, and gay men showed the greatest decline — from 4.7 to 2.1 partners. In a national poll, one out of five single individuals reports a change in sexual practices resulting from fear of AIDS (Schulte, 1986). Perhaps the most convincing data documenting the earlier increase in premarital sexual activity followed by a more recent reversal are provided by Gerrard (1986). Three time samples are

FIGURE 15.6. Surveys of undergraduate females during the past decade show an increase in the percentage of those who were sexually active during the 1970s and a decrease in the 1980s. (Source: Based on data from Gerrard, 1986.)

Changes in sexual activity: A reverse in the revolution?

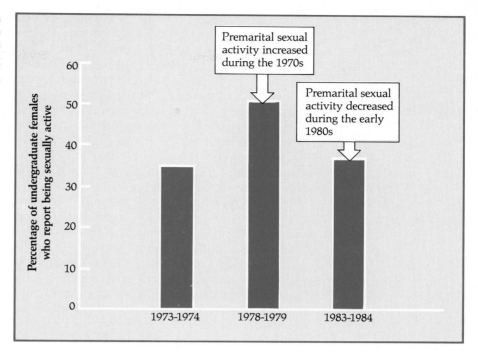

presented in Figure 15.6, and it can be seen that the percentage of sexually active female undergraduates increased during the 1970s and decreased to an equal degree by the mid-1980s. Only time will tell whether we are witnessing a temporary phenomenon or the beginning of a genuine reversal in behavioral trends.

THE EFFECTS OF EROTIC IMAGES on Motives, Attitudes, and Behavior

Among human beings, some of the most powerful variables affecting sexual behavior are not physiological but psychological. Within limits, we apparently respond less to hormone levels than to erotic fantasies (Kelley, 1986).

The motivational effects of sexual images

Much of our behavior is influenced by both internal and external sexual images in the form of pictures and words, and these images have a major impact on what we desire, how we evaluate our behavior, and on what we actually do.

Internal images.   Perhaps the earliest historical awareness of the power of erotic imagery was directed at the existence of sexual dreams that resulted in physiological arousal, often to the point of orgasm, in both males and females (Money, 1985). During the Dark Ages and continuing through the time of the Inquisition, such mysterious and powerful nocturnal events were explained as possession by demons. In fact, having a sexually exciting dream was considered proof that the individual engaged in witchcraft. When we are awake, such fantasies occur voluntarily. By the eighteenth century, the demon theory had given way to the degeneracy theory of Swiss physician Simon André Tissot. The general idea was that any lustful thoughts while one was awake led to sexual dreams, and that both were evil because loss of bodily fluids caused the body and its organs to lose the power to function.

If one omits the involvement of demons and assumptions about evil and degeneration, some of the general points made by these early conceptualizations have a germ of truth. That is, sexual thoughts do, in fact, lead to sexual arousal and to sexual dreams (Byrne and Lamberth, 1971). It is now known that many individuals have learned to control their sexual thoughts while masturbating or engaging in intercourse in order to enhance their pleasure (Sue, 1979), to delay or to speed up the occurrence of orgasm (Przybyla, Byrne, and Kelley, 1983), and to increase the probability of being orgasmic (Davidson and Hoffman, 1986; Lentz and Zeiss, 1984).

External images.   Despite the commonality of internal sex fantasies, more research interest has been concentrated on the role of the external fantasies to which we are exposed in books, magazines, movies, and so forth (Yaffe and Nelson, 1982). The fact that these images ordinarily cause an individual to become sexually excited (both subjectively and physically) is now well documented (Kelley and Byrne, 1983). All of the bodily changes recorded in the Masters and Johnson laboratory are found to occur in response to erotic passages, tapes, slides, and movies — there is congestion of the blood supply in the genital area that leads to a swelling and reddening of the tissue, accompanied by an increase in temperature and the secretion of lubricatory fluids.

One characteristic of current research is its close attention to the specific content of erotic stimuli. For example, for both sexes the depiction of dominant behavior appears to be more arousing than scenarios involving true equality (Garcia et al., 1984; Kelley et al., 1983). When the script goes beyond domination into violence and coercion, what are the effects? Women who are asked to create their own fantasies are much more aroused and have more positive feelings about scenes of an "erotic rape" than about scenes of a realistic rape (Bond and Mosher, 1986). Similar differences are found when the two types of external fantasies are presented. In one such experiment (Stock, 1985), female subjects were presented with one of several audiotapes containing a description of mutually consenting sex, a depiction of rape that emphasized the victim's fear, pain, and negative emotions, neutral nonsexual material, or a typical pornographic depiction of rape in which the female is overpowered by the rapist and then finds herself extremely aroused by the enjoyable experience. Sexual arousal, as measured subjectively and physiologically, was greatest in response to the pornographic version of rape. In addition, in a later exposure to a description of a realistically presented rape, those who had been exposed to the mythical rape scene were more sexually aroused and expressed more positive feelings than the subjects in the other conditions. The possibility was raised that the commonness of pornographic rape portrayals places females in conflict — they find such rape themes arousing but this does not fit their beliefs about sexual coercion.

The process through which external sexual images lead to arousal seems to involve cognitive activity in that the external stimuli are translated into internal images in which the viewer is an active participant in the scene. The arousal that follows is in response to one's own personal fantasy version of the external presentation. How might one investigate the functioning of this internal cognitive activity? Geer and Fuhr (1976) devised an ingenious procedure. They asked male subjects to listen to an erotic story and *at the same time* to engage in nonsexual cognitive tasks that should interfere with any internal fantasy activity. This was accomplished through the use of a *dichotic listening task* in which earphones delivered a stimulus (an erotic story) to one ear and a different stimulus (random numbers) to the other ear. It was found that the more complex the task the subjects had to perform with the numbers, the less sexually aroused they were in response to the story. Just listening to the numbers did not interfere with arousal, adding each pair of numbers interfered some, and classifying each pair as either odd or even and as either above or below 50 interfered a great deal. In each instance, the subjects *heard* the story and knew what it was about, but those who had complex cognitive tasks to perform were too occupied to be able to process the story and create a personal fantasy. In extending this work to visual stimuli, Przybyla and Byrne (1984) found a striking sex difference. For males, complex cognitive activity interfered with arousal in response to auditory erotica but not in response to visual stimuli. For females, cognition decreased arousal in response to both types of erotica. One possibility is that males are basically much more responsive than females to visual images of sex and much more resistent to interference (Money, 1985). Consistent with this possibility is the finding that women find rock music more romantic if shown without sexual video images while men find the music more romantic when accompanied by such images (Zillmann and Mundorf, 1986). Another variable that affects how people respond to erotic images — anxiety — is examined in the **Focus** insert on page 546.

Attitudinal effects of erotica

While much concern about the effects and possible effects of erotic fantasies centers on overt behavior such as sexual coercion, there is also increased interest in the way such material may shape and change atti-

FOCUS ON RESEARCH:
The Cutting Edge

Anxiety and Sexual Arousal: Interference or Enhancement?

Though the arousal of nonsexual emotions such as anger is found to have no effect on sexual arousal (Kelley et al., 1983), what about anxiety or fear? Might these emotions lead to less responsiveness to erotic stimuli or to greater responsiveness? Strangely enough, there is contradictory anecdotal and clinical evidence suggesting that negative emotions should interfere with sexual responsiveness and other evidence that such emotions should enhance response. Sex therapists have suggested that general anxieties about sex and specific fears about performance tend to prevent normal sexual functioning. In contrast, there is the suggestion that sexual excitement is greatest when there is an element of danger — for example, the fear of getting caught when having illicit sex.

In laboratory studies of response to erotic films, there is consistent support for the proposition that anxiety *increases* sexual arousal. In the first experimental tests of this relationship, it was found that when females (Hoon, Wincze, and Hoon, 1977) or males (Wolchik et al., 1980) view an anxiety-producing film such

FIGURE 15.7. Anxiety can have either an inhibiting or an enhancing effect on sexual arousal. When male subjects watching an erotic movie were periodically given visual feedback about their state of physical arousal, those who were sexually dysfunctional responded differently than those who were not. The arousal of the dysfunctional group *decreased* while that of the normal group *increased*, compared to the control condition. (Source: Based on data from Abrahamson, 1985.)

Anxiety arousal can increase or decrease sexual arousal

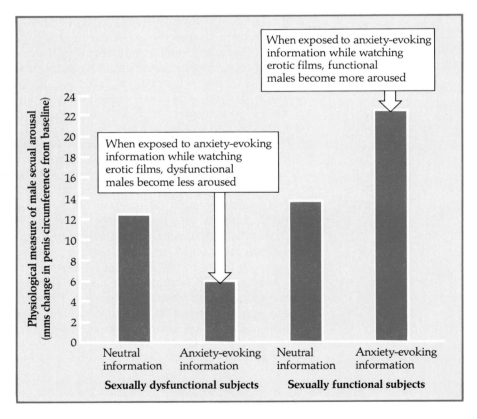

as the depiction of automobile accidents, their arousal to an erotic film shown afterward is greater than if they first saw a neutral film. It was suggested that the subjects may have just felt relieved when the unpleasant movie ended, and, thus, relief was responsible for the arousal effect. To test that possibility, Barlow, Sakheim, and Beck (1983) examined what happens when anxiety is created *during* exposure to erotica. Males were shown explicit films under neutral conditions and under conditions in which a light signal indicated that an electric shock was about to be delivered. Just as in the unpleasant movie studies, sexual arousal was greater in the anxiety condition than in the neutral condition.

The question of why anxiety was not found to interfere with sexual responsivity in the laboratory remained puzzling until Abrahamson (1985) utilized an anxiety-arousing condition specifically designed to elicit fears about sexual performance. Using sexually functional and dysfunctional males, the experimenter exposed them to erotic and neutral films. To create performance-related anxiety, subjects were given live visual feedback at various times during the movies to indicate the degree to which they were physically aroused. This condition was compared to a neutral task in which the movies were interrupted to make judgments about the length of a line. As may be seen in Figure 15.7, the functionals and dysfunctionals responded very differently to the anxiety-evoking task. Specifically, the sexually dysfunctional subjects became *less* aroused in response to the threatening stimulus, while the normally functioning subjects became *more* aroused. It thus appears that both hypotheses about the effect of anxiety were correct. Anxiety — specifically performance anxiety — causes some individuals to have difficulty in responding sexually. The same kind of anxiety (as well as anxiety aroused by quite different stimuli) has the opposite effect on those without sexual problems — it enhances sexual arousal. In the latter instance, Zillmann's theory of excitation transfer (discussed in Chapter 9) provides a convincing explanation.

tudes. It was noted in Chapter 9 that exposure to violent **pornography** can bring about attitudinal changes, such as the acceptance of false statements about rape. It was also pointed out that exposure to massive amounts of nonviolent, explicit sexual movies leads to more lenient attitudes about punishing rapists. There are other effects, as well.

If the typical X-rated movie is examined, it quickly becomes apparent that such concepts as love, commitment, marriage, and family are absent. Instead, casual sex between strangers is presented as normative behavior. This same concentration on non-relationship sex is also found to be characteristic of the mass media (Abramson and Mechanic, 1983). To determine the attitudinal effects of such themes, Bryant (1985) exposed college students to three hours of nonviolent, explicit sexual films every day for five days. Others watched nonsexual situation comedies such as *Benson, Different Strokes*, and *Family Ties* for the same amount of time. Three days after the concentrated viewing experience, all subjects were shown brief television clips of sexual and nonsexual crimes, transgressions, indiscretions, or improprieties. For example, they saw a scene from *Hotel* in which a wife enters her husband's hotel room and slips into bed to surprise him. To *her* surprise, he and his homosexual lover emerge dripping wet from the shower. Subjects who had previously been exposed to fifteen hours of pornography found such sexual behavior to be *less morally bad* than did the control subjects, and they felt that the victim had been *less severely wronged.* Similar findings were reported with respect to written descriptions of moral impropriety, such as an adult male seducing a twelve-year-old girl and a husband having an extramarital affair. It was concluded that the amoral (or immoral) values of pornography can affect how the viewer judges morality in everyday life.

Other research has found that those males who report the greatest amount of exposure to violent sexual stimuli hold relatively traditional attitudes about women and tend to express pro-rape beliefs such as "women cause rape through their appearance or behavior" (Garcia, 1986). Interestingly enough, exposure to violent pornography also produces more negative, stereotypic attitudes about men (Kelley, 1985a).

Do erotic images affect behavior?

The rationale for campaigns against pornography and the enactment of censorship laws are generally based on the assumption that external erotic images affect not only attitudes, arousal, and internal fantasies but also undesirable overt behavior (Wills, 1977). When the first Commission on Obscenity and Pornography was appointed in the late 1960s, it was discovered that despite centuries of censorship, almost nothing was known about the relationship between erotic images and subsequent behavior. The body of research supported by the commission appeared in 1971, and the general conclusion was that the effects of erotica were temporary, nonspecific, and not a matter of great concern. In the years since that report was issued, a great deal of additional research has been conducted. Now considerably more is known, and the conclusions are more complex—and more controversial. Partly in response to this growing body of information, Attorney General Meese appointed a new Commission on Pornography in 1985 to study what is now known and to make recommendations to the nation. We will present the highlights of this recent work.

The question to be answered by psychological research is whether exposure to erotica has any influence on interpersonal behavior and on the nature and frequency of subsequent sexual activity.

Effects of erotica on interpersonal behavior.   When individuals become sexually aroused, their evaluations of the opposite sex and their interpersonal behavior are altered in ways you might expect. For example, males who have been aroused by erotica perceive females as more physically attractive and sexually responsive than do unaroused males (Stephan, Berscheid, and Walster, 1971). Similarly, sexual arousal leads males to respond to their female partners with expressions of love (Dermer and Pyszczynski, 1978). In fact, both positive *and* negative responses to relevant cues are affected by arousal. Exposure to erotica leads males and females to perceive a good-looking stranger of the opposite sex as more attractive and desirable as a date; when the stranger is unattractive, however, aroused subjects perceive him or her as *less* attractive (Istvan, Griffitt, and Weidner, 1983). This intensifying effect of arousal is shown in Figure 15.8.

In addition to affecting feelings and judgments about the opposite sex, arousal by erotica also affects overt behavior. Individuals who are aroused and who feel positively about being aroused spend more time looking at an opposite sex stranger and sit closer to that individual than

FIGURE 15.8. Sexual arousal serves to intensify evaluations of the opposite sex. Both males and females who have been shown erotica tend to rate an attractive stranger as *more* attractive and an unattractive stranger as *less* attractive. (Source: Based on data from Istvan, Griffitt, and Weidner, 1983.)

Attractiveness ratings are intensified when individuals are sexually aroused

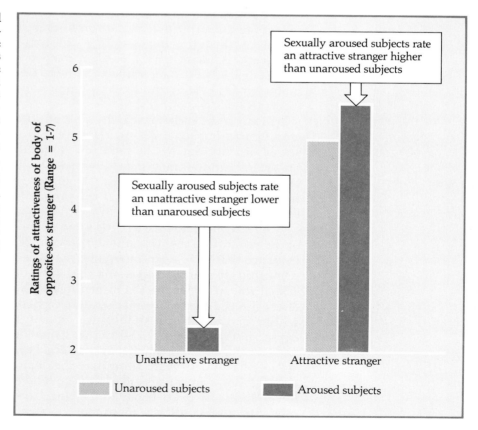

do nonaroused subjects. Those to whom arousal is a negative experience tend to avoid looking at or sitting near someone of the opposite sex (Griffitt, May, and Veitch, 1974).

There is another aspect of exposure to explicit sexual images, and that is the tendency to compare one's partner and one's sexual activity to that depicted on the screen. In an experiment that involved exposure to explicit hour-long videotapes once a week for six weeks, male and female subjects (compared to a control group) were less satisfied with their partner's physical appearance and sexual performance (Zillmann and Bryant, 1986). Whether such a contrast leads to negative interactions or to a break-up of relationships is a question that needs to be explored in future research.

Erotica as an activator of sexual acts and a model for behavior.   Since it is well established that internal and external erotic images induce sexual excitement, it seems reasonable to expect that those who are excited by such stimuli would be more likely to seek sexual gratification than those who had not been exposed to such stimulation. Research is consistent with that expectation. Even with soft-core erotic romances, females who read them have sexual intercourse twice as often as those who do not (Coles and Shamp, 1984). When college students were asked to write sexual fantasies during a twenty-minute period, they engaged in more sexual acts the following week than did subjects who did not create such fantasies (Eisenman, 1982). Further, women who create sexual fantasies while engaged in sex are found to be more physiologically responsive to fantasy and to erotic stimuli than women who do not fantasize (Stock and Geer, 1982).

Much of the earlier research on the effects of erotica found that those who view arousing slides or films are more likely to engage in some sexual activity during the next few hours than individuals who view nonsexual stimulus material (Amoroso et al., 1971). Cattell, Kawash, and De Young (1972) also found that the more aroused an individual was in response to erotica, the greater the probability of having sexual inter-course afterward.

Such research indicated little or no relationship between the content of the erotica and the subsequent behavior. Because there is considerable evidence that people tend to model the behavior shown in films and on television, it seemed surprising that such effects were not evident in sexual research. Among the difficulties with establishing the modeling effect are the fact that most sexual activity requires an available and willing partner, the possibility that anxiety may inhibit specific sexual expression, and the probability that behavioral change may require re-peated exposure to the model over a period of time. A viewer of an erotic act in a film might want to imitate the depicted behavior, might think about doing so over a period of time, and might form an intention to act long before any overt behavioral changes could be observed. To study modeling effects, then, experimenters must take into account anxiety reduction, planning of future activity, and the availability of an appropriate partner.

The effect of erotica on anxiety about the depicted behavior and on future plans to engage in that behavior was investigated by Wishnoff (1978). His subjects were undergraduate females who had never engaged in intercourse and who reported high levels of anxiety. They were shown one of three fifteen-minute videotapes: explicit sex, nonexplicit sex, or nonsex scenes. After viewing the tapes, sexual anxiety was lowest among those who had seen the explicit sexual material and highest among those watching the nonsex presentation. The subjects were also asked about their plans to engage in sex in the near future. Asked about twelve sexual acts (from breast fondling to intercourse), those who saw the explicit film expected to engage in eleven of them. The figures for intercourse are quite startling. *All* of those in the explicit sex condition expected to have intercourse for the first time very soon, while only 15 percent of those in the other two groups had such plans. We don't know whether such expectations were carried out, and the availability of a suitable partner is obviously one of the prerequisites. Other research has controlled for the availability factor by studying the effects of a masturbation film on the subsequent masturbatory activity of those who watched it. Heiby and Becker (1980) found that female subjects engaged in autosexual activity more frequently after viewing a filmed model engage in that behavior.

Other recent research (Bryant, 1985) has surveyed young adolescents and adults to determine the effects of their first contact with X-rated films and magazines. Males reported overwhelmingly that seeing such material made sex seem more appealing. Females were divided more or less evenly as to whether they reacted in that way, and were much more likely than males to report disgust and revulsion. Of greater potential importance is the effect of sexually explicit erotica on their desire to imitate the depicted behavior and on their actual modeling activity. As may be seen in Figure 15.9 (page 552), the effects on the *desire* for imitation are greater than the effects on *actual* imitative behavior. Two-thirds of the males wanted to copy what they had seen, as did almost half the females. In general, the younger the subject, the greater the desire for imitation. Further, one-quarter of the males and 15 percent of the females actually did carry out the activity they had viewed. This imitative reaction was greatest among high school students.

Other research utilized adult females ranging in age from eighteen to their late fifties and asked about receiving requests from males to imitate erotic scenes (Russell and Trocki, 1985). It was found that 10 to 15 percent of these individuals reported feeling upset by requests from boyfriends or husbands to enact the content of pornographic films or stories. Furthermore, 38 percent of the victims of wife rape indicated having this experience.

At the present time, a fair summary of what is known seems to be that exposure to filmed models engaged in explicit sexual acts affects viewers' behavior in that sexual anxiety is reduced, plans to imitate the

FIGURE 15.9. For various reasons, individuals do not necessarily rush out to imitate whatever pornographic scenes they see or read about. People report overwhelmingly, however, that they *want* to imitate whatever sexual activity they are first exposed to in X-rated material. In addition, surprisingly large numbers of individuals actually carry out their imitative desires — 25 percent of the males and 15 percent of the females. (Source: Based on data from Bryant, 1985.)

Modeling X-rated activity: Desire to imitate and actual imitation

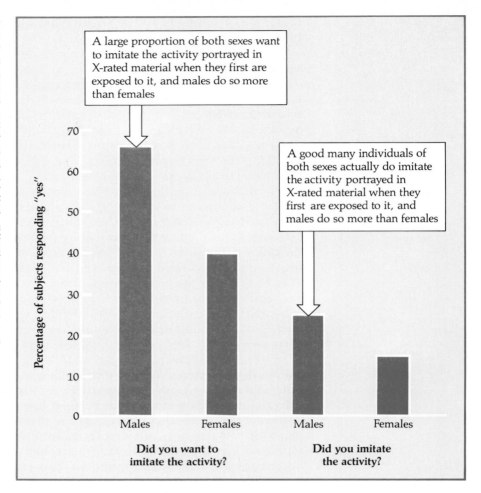

A large proportion of both sexes want to imitate the activity portrayed in X-rated material when they first are exposed to it, and males do so more than females

A good many individuals of both sexes actually do imitate the activity portrayed in X-rated material when they first are exposed to it, and males do so more than females

Percentage of subjects responding "yes"

Males   Females   Males   Females

Did you want to imitate the activity?

Did you imitate the activity?

models are increased, and (when availability is taken into account) the frequency of the depicted behavior is increased.

Erotica and sex crimes: The ultimate danger

You may be pleased or alarmed to find that viewing films about masturbation or intercourse seems to increase the probability of copying those activities. What if the erotic content and the subsequent behavior were the commission of sex crimes such as rape? Presumably, almost all of us would agree that this effect would pose a very real danger to society. It might be noted that almost all sexual crimes are committed by males, and that the victims are almost always females. What is known about the role of erotic stimuli in rape behavior? Five types of data are relevant in attempting to answer this question.

Studies of sex criminals.   Males convicted of sex crimes have been compared with other kinds of criminals and with noncriminals. You may be surprised to learn that sex offenders are found to have had *less* contact with erotic stimuli (including magazines such as *Playboy*) during their adolescence than is true of non-offenders (Goldstein, Kant, and Hartman, 1974). Those who commit sex crimes report childhood experiences involving sexual repression and sexually restrictive parents. Nevertheless, if one looks at specifically childhood experiences (ages six to ten), 30 percent of the rapists had been exposed to explicit pornography compared to only 2 percent of the non-offenders. Thus, the timing of exposure may be critical.

More recently, Marshall and Barbaree (1984) proposed that sex offenders are people who are especially vulnerable to the influence of pornography. A group of rapists and child molesters were compared with noncriminal males matched on the basis of age, intelligence, and socioeconomic status (Marshall, 1985). The offenders were much more likely than normals to utilize fantasies involving rape. It was found that 53 percent of the child molesters and 33 percent of the rapists reported looking at pornography as part of their preparation for committing a criminal act.

Sexually aggressive males in the non-criminal population.   Though the term "sex criminals" refers to those who have broken the law, been apprehended, indicted, tried, and convicted, sexual aggression is characteristic of a much wider segment of the male population. Studies of college women (Kanin and Parcell, 1977) and college men (Mosher and Anderson, 1986; Rapoport and Burkhart, 1984) suggest that forced sex is a common occurrence in this population.

Sexually aggressive males appear to be those who are aroused by fantasies of violence and rape whether the scenes are created by others (Malamuth, 1986) or in their own imagination (Greendlinger and Byrne, 1986). It is not known whether these males are aroused by sexual violence because of greater exposure to such images or whether some other events in their lives have predisposed them to react positively to this theme.

Whatever the origin of their behavior, there is clearly a rather large subgroup of males in the population who aggress against women sexually and who enjoy internal and external fantasies of violent sex. These individuals are also characterized by a tendency to accept violence in general but especially against women, to value dominance, and to express a macho attitude that includes callousness about sex and a positive reaction to danger (Malamuth, 1986; Malamuth, Check, and Briere, 1986; Mosher and Anderson, 1986; Smeaton and Byrne, 1986). For this group of males, there is an association between violent sexual imagery and unacceptable sexual behavior.

Effects of legalizing pornography.   A very different type of study involves examining the incidence of sex crimes in a given society before and after changes in that society's permissiveness about pornography. Denmark provided a convenient test of any proposed pornography-crime link when the Danish Parliament in 1969 legalized the sale of sexual materials to anyone over the age of sixteen (Kutchinsky, 1985). If explicit sexual material evokes criminal behavior, there should have been a dramatic rise in the number of sex crimes after the law was changed. Instead, the number of rape cases remained the same, and there was a marked decrease in child molestation and homosexual offenses. This decline continued over the next several years (Green, 1985).

In a similar way, when West Germany legalized pornography in 1973, rape showed no change, but the total number of sex crimes decreased by 11 percent over the next seven years. Sex offenses against children under age six decreased by 60 percent (Green, 1985). The British experience with the publication of sexually explicit magazines, beginning in 1974, led to no increase in crimes of sexual violence. Finally, it should be noted that in Japan the most common theme of pornography is rape, but the rate of that crime is one-sixteenth of that in the United States (Abramson and Hayashi, 1984).

Comparisons within a given society.   Other relevant research involves a correlational study of different geographical areas with respect to pornography and the commission of sex crimes. L. Baron (1985) compared the fifty states of the United States with respect to the circulation of eight sexually oriented magazines (*Playboy, Penthouse, Hustler*, etc.) and the incidence of rape in each state. It was found that the greater the circulation of these magazines, the more rapes. He cautioned that this correlation does not necessarily indicate a causal relationship. Further, the incidence of rape was more highly correlated with the number of divorced men, economic inequality, and urbanization than with erotic magazine circulation (L. Baron and Straus, 1984).

Doubts about cause and effect are also raised by the fact that the availability of explicit sexual materials in adult theaters and bookstores is unrelated to rates of reported rape (Green, 1985). Interestingly enough, rape *is* related to the circulation of masculine "outdoor" publications such as *Field and Stream* and *Guns and Ammo* (Scott, 1985). The latter finding is consistent with the research discussed previously identifying aggressiveness and macho attitudes as key factors in predicting sexually coercive behavior among males.

Laboratory research on violent pornography.   The experiments that were described in Chapter 9 are also relevant. When investigators utilize violent erotica in experiments, negative effects are found — including an increase in male aggression against females. Malamuth and Donnerstein (1984) conclude on the basis of a series of such investigations that themes of sexual violence reduce inhibitory anxiety and thus make aggression more acceptable and more likely to occur. The same effect is found when males are shown nonviolent erotica with a permissive female confederate who says such things as "that looks like fun" and "I'd like to try that" (Leonard and Taylor, 1983). Again, the explanation is that permissiveness reduces inhibitions for otherwise unacceptable behavior. Such laboratory effects have not been tied specifically to the commission of sexual crimes, but they are sufficiently disturbing to constitute a warning signal with respect to erotica.

Most of those conducting the aggression experiments have emphasized that the critical element is *violence* rather than sex. With that in mind, it is important to identify the major sources of violent fantasies to which the general population is exposed. It should be noted that only 5 percent of the films produced in the U.S. over the last couple of decades were rated X. The remainder were rated G (13 percent), PG (36 percent), PG-13 (1 percent), and R (45 percent) (Blake 1986). In comparing the content of movies on the basis of their ratings, Scott (1985) found considerably fewer violent acts per X-rated movie than in those rated G, PG, and R (see Figure 15.10). Consistent with that finding is a survey of pornographic magazines in an adult bookstore in Times Square. Only 6 percent of them dealt with such themes as sadomasochism or bondage (Winick, 1985). If violent content does in fact lead to interpersonal aggression, our concern needs to have a broader focus than simply the problem of violent pornography.

The amount of non-sexual violence in popular films is easy to overlook unless you focus on specific examples, such as *Cobra* starring Sylvester Stallone, a 1986 hit movie. Denby (1986, p. 130) provides a graphic description of the content of this non-sexual presentation:

> Over and over, we see this mauler smash the windows of a car to get at an
> innocent woman, and then carve her up with his knife. This knife, photo-

FIGURE 15.10. Though there is understandably much concern about the possible effects of violent pornography, two facts are sometimes not considered. As these data show, there tends to be much more violence in standard commercial movies rated G, PG, and R than in X-rated pornographic films. (Source: Based on data from Scott, 1985.)

Violence: Pornographic versus nonpornographic

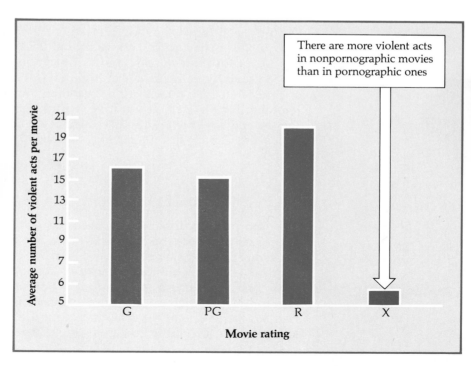

There are more violent acts in nonpornographic movies than in pornographic ones

graphed in close-up as lovingly as an erect penis in a porno short, has a long, curved blade and a studded handle that glistens in the light. We get to see quite a lot of it in the murder scenes, which are thoroughly disgusting, with heavy emphasis on the terrified helplessness of the women strapped into their cars and screaming, screaming, with no one to help them.

Research indicates that males enjoy such films most when they are with a female who responds with distress (Zillmann et al., 1986). Females enjoy them most when accompanied by a masterful male. One might guess that these reactions are relevant to the subsequent behavior, possibly even the sexual behavior, of the viewers.

Given contradictory research findings about the effects of explicit sexual presentations, what can you conclude about the effects of erotica on negative behavior? If you find that question difficult, rest assured that behavioral scientists are as uncertain as you are. (To get an overview of the current controversies surrounding the implications of our current knowledge, turn to the **Applied Side** insert on page 558. In that same section is a discussion of what might be done about certain types of erotica if negative effects were established.)

POSITIVE AND NEGATIVE SEXUAL ATTITUDES:
Erotophilia and Erotophobia

Because sexuality is a topic that elicits very strong emotional reactions — both positive and negative — what each of us learns about sex is often more influenced by attitudes than by neutral, objective facts (Hudson, Murphy, and Nurius, 1983). Instead, what we learn about sexual anatomy, sexual behavior, and sexual morality is often associated with varying degrees of anxiety, fear, guilt, curiosity, joy, and interest. Depending on one's family, religion, and culture, each of us falls at some point along a dimension that ranges from extremely positive attitudes about sex (**erotophilia**) to extremely negative attitudes (**erotophobia**). We will examine the way in which individual differences along this dimension influence a great many of our sexual responses.

Measuring sexual attitudes and their development

The two primary instruments used to assess positive versus negative sexual attitudes are the **Sex Guilt Scale** (Mosher, 1968) and the **Sexual Opinion Survey** (Fisher et al., 1986). Both measures present subjects with a series of statements about diverse aspects of sexuality such as pornography, homosexuality, prostitution, and the like. Subjects respond in a way that indicates positive or negative evaluations. We will describe studies that have used one or the other measuring device to classify individuals as relatively erotophilic (low in sex guilt) or relatively erotophobic (high in sex guilt). Basically, extreme erotophiles respond to many aspects of sex with positive emotions, and sexual cues act as reinforcers and elicit approach responses (Kelley, 1985c). Extreme erotophobes respond to sexuality with negative emotions, and sexual cues act as punishments and elicit avoidance responses (Griffitt and Kaiser, 1978; O'Grady, 1982).

On the basis of several different investigations, it seems clear that erotophobia is most likely to develop in a family background that encompasses conservative values, a religious orientation and regular church attendance, and avoidance of sex as a topic of conversation (Byrne, 1983; Gerrard, 1980). Erotophobic parents are found to provide less sexual information and to be less likely than erotophilic ones to give frank answers when their children ask questions about sex (Lemery, 1983; Yarber and Whitehill, 1981). In response to questions such as, "Where do babies come from?" erotophobic parents are likely to say that they will discuss that "when you are older." Because spouses are found to be quite similar in their sexual attitudes (Byrne, Becker, and Przybyla, 1986; Fisher and Gray, 1983), a child's parents are likely to be quite consistent in the way they react to and communicate about sexual matters.

The effect of broader cultural influences on sexual attitudes has been shown by Abramson and Imai-Marquez (1982) in a comparison of Japanese-Americans who were first-, second-, or third-generation residents of the United States. It was assumed that the American culture is more permissive than the Japanese in defining what is sexually appropriate. If a society shapes its members sexually (Abramson, 1982), it would follow that as a family's exposure to this permissive culture increased, erotophobia would decrease. That hypothesis was confirmed. From first- to third-generation individuals there were lower and lower levels of erotophobia.

Sexual responsiveness: The influence of sexual attitudes

As might be expected, individual differences in sexual attitudes are related to differences in many sex-related activities. In general, the more erotophobic the test score, the more likely the individual is to respond to sexual cues with negative emotions and to avoid situations and activities that have sexual components.

For example, erotophobic subjects are less responsive to sexual films than are those who are erotophilic, and such films elicit feelings of disgust, anxiety, and fear (Mosher and O'Grady, 1979). This negative response is greatest in response to images of same-sex activity (Kelley, 1985d). Given free choice as to how long to look at explicit sexual slides, male and female erotophiles chose longer viewing times than erotophobes and recalled the content of the pictures more accurately (Becker and Byrne, 1985).

Internal fantasies are also affected by sexual attitudes. The higher an

ON THE APPLIED SIDE

Pornography: Is It a Problem? If So, What Should Be Done about It?

Established in 1985, the Attorney General's Commission on Pornography held a series of hearings in six American cities. Social psychologists and others were invited to present their latest findings and any conclusions they might have drawn from the research data. As with any scientific enterprise, the data are a matter of public record, and many of the relevant studies have been described in this chapter. The conclusions that one reaches on the basis of such data are, however, amazingly varied.

The wide range of opinions falls into three categories. Pornography is perceived as a positive factor in society, as something relatively innocuous and irrelevant, or as a serious threat. The following quotes provide a flavor of these different views:

Positive. "The availability of portrayals of a forbidden activity, accompanied by autoerotic activity, may provide an outlet for antisocial impulses" (Green, 1985).

Neutral. "The conclusion is very clear that pornography is not a danger — neither to persons, neither to society, neither to children, nor to adults. It doesn't lead to sex offenses; it doesn't lead to sexual deviations" (Kutchinsky, quoted in Hefner, 1986, p. 59).

Negative. "[P]ornography is an attack on the family and on our social fabric. Pornography libels our society and can incite it to violent acts against its members. It is treason against the American family and treason against our society. Treason has no First Amendment rights" (Fagin, 1985, p. 31).

Many psychologists feel there are serious limitations in our present knowledge and additional work is required to establish the links, if any, between particular erotic content and specific undesirable behavior (Kelley, 1985b; Malamuth, 1985; Stock, 1985). If such links were verified and if consensus were reached with respect to the dangers, what solutions would then be appropriate? Three proposals have received the most attention.

Censorship is the most common suggestion. The call for censorship is frequently heard, and pressures on public schools to ban books, films, and magazines in school libraries is increasing (Hilts, 1981). The term "censor" suggests the workings of a totalitarian society in which bureaucrats with scissors and rubber stamps approve and disapprove all material to be distributed to the public. Sometimes, however, the process is sufficiently subtle that the consumer does not even know that censorship has occurred. If you had read the Doonesbury cartoon shown in Figure 15.11 in various newspapers back in 1977, you would have seen one person in bed answering the telephone. In other papers, you would have seen two (unmarried) people sharing a bed. Only if you saw both versions would you have been aware of censorship.

The arguments against censorship are fairly simple. It violates constitutional guarantees of free speech; it gives decision-making power and control to an elite group; and it has been shown repeatedly to be ineffective.

The second approach is to apply *warning labels* to pornography in the way that analogous messages are placed on cigarette packages. Presumably, educational efforts plus these reminders motivate consumers to avoid the product. It has been demonstrated, however, that the labels may enhance rather than discourage the appeal (Kelley, 1985b; Kelley and Musialowski, 1986a) and that cigarette sales in the United States increased steadily for two decades following the introduction of the Surgeon General's warning.

The third approach involves *consciousness raising* of audiences, writers, producers, directors, photographers, publishers, and any-

FIGURE 15.11. Censorship can take many forms, but perhaps the most disturbing kind is sufficiently subtle that it is difficult to know that it is taking place. This is an example from *Doonesbury* that ran in many newspapers. The version at the top was altered to protect readers from knowing that an unmarried male and female share the same bed. The version at the bottom is the way cartoonist Garry Trudeau intended it to appear. (Source: *Doonesbury*, Copyright, 1977, G. B. Trudeau. Reprinted with permission of Universal Press Syndicate, All rights reserved.)

Doonesbury censored

one else involved in the production and use of popular fantasies (Byrne, 1985). If we agree that the presentation of ethnic minorities in a stereotyped, demeaning, and degrading fashion is both morally wrong and potentially detrimental to society, we neither produce nor serve as audiences for such imagery. Such changes *have* occurred in this century, and they did so without the imposition of new laws and penalties. If we could in a similar way agree on the unacceptability of portraying violence (sexual or otherwise), or of women as sex objects, or of sex as a dehumanized exercise, the result would be a voluntary revolution in what we tolerate as entertainment.

individual's erotophilia score, the more explicit their fantasies (Walker, 1983). Positive sexual attitudes are associated with positively-toned fantasies and positive emotions (Kelley, 1985e). In responding to self-created fantasies, those with negative sexual attitudes have relatively low levels of arousal (Green and Mosher, 1985). In a similar way, when asked to draw nude figures, erotophobic subjects create less sexually explicit and detailed drawings than do those who are erotophilic (Przybyla,

FIGURE 15.12. Individuals with erotophobic attitudes tend to avoid many aspects of sexuality compared to those with erotophilic attitudes. In this example, you can see that the figures drawn by erotophilic subjects (top row) are much more explicit and detailed than those drawn by erotophobic subjects. Figures drawn by male subjects are at left; those by females are at right. (Source: Based on material from Przybyla, Byrne, and Allgeier, 1986.)

Erotophiles and erotophobes: Differences in drawing nude figures

Byrne, and Allgeier, 1986), as shown in Figure 15.12. On the basis of such findings, it seems reasonable to conclude that those with negative sexual attitudes tend to avoid sex-related cues in their everyday lives as well as in the laboratory.

In interpersonal interactions, erotophobic males administer less "pleasure" (a mild electric stimulation presumably conducted through the other person's chair seat) to a female confederate on the Brock Pleasure Machine than do erotophilic males (Janda et al., 1981). It also follows that this personality dimension should be related to overt sexual behavior. Research data confirm this expectation. For example, erotophilic undergraduates are more sexually experienced, interact with more sexual partners, and engage in more frequent autosexual acts than erotophobic ones (Fisher, 1984). Even among older individuals (aged twenty-seven to seventy-three), erotophobia is associated with a lower level of sexual activity (DiVasto, Pathak, and Fishburn, 1981).

In general, the greater the erotophobia, the lower the probability of engaging in premarital sex (Gerrard, 1980; Gerrard and Gibbons, 1982). This relationship is sufficiently strong that it is possible to predict the probability of female college students' current sexual activity on the basis of test scores. Comparing samples obtained at two points in time, Gerrard (1982) found that the higher the erotophobia score, the less likely a student was to be sexually active, as shown in Figure 15.13. It can also be seen that the same relationship held true in each of the two years sampled, despite the fact that the percentage of sexually active females increased from 35 to 51 percent of the population over the five-year span. To be in the least sexually active half of the female students, an individual had to be more erotophobic in 1978 than in 1973. That is, as the norms for premarital sex shifted in a permissive direction during that time span, a more negative sexual attitude was required to resist the pressure to engage in this behavior.

Other sex-related behaviors: Learning, health, and the prevention of unwanted pregnancies

Beyond the direct influence of erotophobia-erotophilia on emotional reactions to explicit sexual images and acts, these attitudes are found to generalize to many different activities that are related to sexuality. Once again, the general finding is that such attitudes consistently predict the tendency to approach or to avoid anything and everything related to sex.

FIGURE 15.13. Female university students show a strong relationship between sexual attitudes and sexual activity. The more erotophobic their test scores, the lower the probability of their engaging in intercourse. The same trend held at two different time periods (1973 and 1978), but a larger proportion of the 1978 sample were sexually active. (Source: Based on data from Gerrard, 1982.)

Sexual attitudes as predictors of sexual behavior

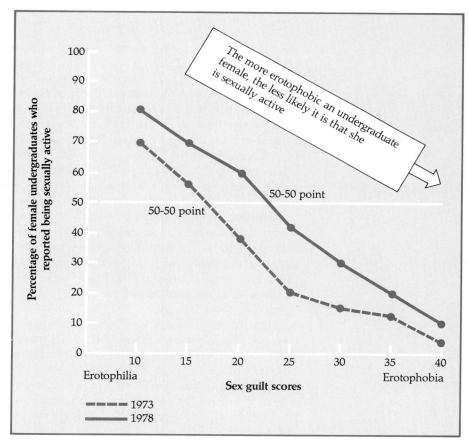

Learning and education. Sexual stimuli should act as punishers for erotophobes and as rewards for erotophiles. In a learning task, Griffitt and Kaiser (1978) found precisely that effect. It is as if sexual words and pictures are analogous to electric shock if one is erotophobic and analogous to candy if one is erotophilic. These reactions influence both learning and teaching. A survey of health teachers revealed that as erotophobia increased, the instructor was more likely to omit anxiety-evoking topics such as birth control or abortion from his or her course (Yarber and McCabe, 1985).

Such findings suggest that erotophobic attitudes would interfere with an individual's ability to deal with educational topics that involve sexual content. That hypothesis has been confirmed in a laboratory experiment and in college classes. When subjects were presented with a twenty-minute taped lecture on sterilization and abortion, erotophobics remembered less of the content when tested immediately afterward than did erotophilics (Schwartz, 1973). In a human sexuality class, Fisher (1980a) found that erotophilic students outperformed erotophobic ones on examinations even though their performance in nonsex courses was equal. It seems clear that with sexual topics, negative sexual attitudes interfere with comprehension, retention, and performance.

Sex-related health care. Most of us feel somewhat reluctant to visit a doctor's office and find it easy enough to postpone or avoid taking the proper steps to maintain good health. When the problem involves any aspect of one's sexual anatomy or functioning, erotophobic attitudes would be expected to increase these avoidance tendencies. A study of several hundred women confirmed this expectation. Erotophobic females reported they obtained gynecological examinations less frequently than did erotophilic females. Even frequency of self-examination for breast cancer shows those same erotophobe-erotophile differences (Fisher, Byrne, and White, 1983). Erotophobic individuals are also less likely to engage in preventive behavior with respect to sexually transmitted diseases (Yarber and Fisher, 1983).

Many aspects of behavior during pregnancy and following childbirth are found to be related to sexual attitudes (Fisher and Gray, 1983). Sexual activity is more restricted for erotophobic couples, as one might expect. In addition, erotophilic fathers are more likely to choose to be in the delivery room during childbirth, and erotophilic mothers are more likely to breastfeed their infants.

Contraceptive behavior. One of the more consistent findings of the past decade is that the majority of sexually active teenagers in the United States either use no method of contraception or use contraception inconsistently (Alan Guttmacher Institute, 1981). The consequence is approximately one million teenage pregnancies annually (see Figure 15.14). These unwanted conceptions result in abortions (46 percent), out-of-wedlock births (26 percent), and hasty, primarily unsuccessful marriages (13 percent). The remainder end in miscarriages. According to the U. S.

FIGURE 15.14. The increased permissiveness that characterized the sexual revolution had as one negative consequence a rapid rise in teenage pregnancies. In the United States alone, there are over one million unwanted pregnancies among young people each year.

Teenage sex, teenage pregnancy, and teenage parents

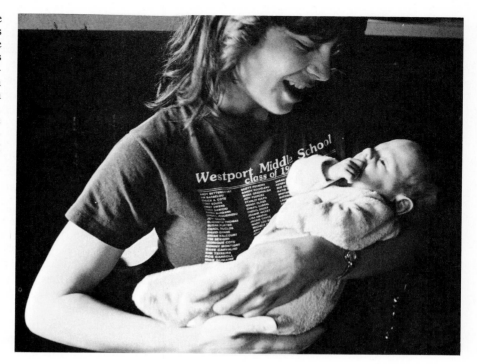

Census Bureau, in some locations (for example, Washington, D.C.), abortions now outnumber births. Also, in some subgroups of the population (for example, young American blacks), almost 80 percent of births occur among unmarried females, and 70 percent of the black poor live in homes headed by a female (*Mending broken families*, 1986). Among whites the illegitimacy rate is about 20 percent.

Why would a teenage couple risk unwanted parenthood by engaging in intercourse without contraceptive protection? A common assumption is that the individuals were not sufficiently knowledgeable about conception and how to prevent it. That is undoubtedly true in some instances (Allgeier, 1983), but research on erotophobia suggests a quite different explanation. Those individuals who have the most negative attitudes about sexuality would be expected to avoid every aspect of the contraceptive process — from acknowledging their sexual plans to obtaining and using the necessary services and procedures (Byrne, 1983).

One argument against the "lack of knowledge" hypothesis is that bright and well informed college students are as contraceptively careless as much younger, less bright, and less well informed teenagers. Even older, presumably more mature individuals behave in a similar way. A survey of single women in their twenties indicates that one in six regularly engages in intercourse without using contraceptives (King, 1986). Attitudes about sex seem to play a major role in such maladaptive behavior, at least among college students. For both male and female undergraduates, as erotophobia increases, individuals are less likely to utilize the contraceptive services of a student health center (Fisher et al., 1979), less likely to use contraceptives (Fisher, 1984), and less likely to use effective forms of contraception (Gerrard, 1982). As might be expected, erotophobic female students who are sexually active are more likely to conceive than are erotophilic ones (Gerrard, 1977). An interesting side effect of decreased sexual activity among today's undergraduates is that those who *are* sexually active in the 1980s are more likely to use effective contraceptive methods than was true in the late 1970s (Gerrard, 1986). It is suggested that when the level of premarital sex is high, even those with negative attitudes participate and that they are relatively less likely to use contraceptives. When the level of premarital sex is low, only those with positive attitudes and adaptive contraceptive practices are likely to be sexually active.

On the basis of such research, it has been suggested that teenage behavior could be altered by means of procedures designed to reduce negative reactions to sexual cues. A program designed by Gerrard, McCann, and Geis (1982) tested two different methods for changing the contraceptive behavior of college women. All of the subjects were sexually active, unmarried, and using either ineffective contraceptive techniques or no contraception at all. The investigators compared an informational approach with one combining information with an examination of erroneous ideas about contraception based on negative attitudes and beliefs. A control group received no treatment. The focus on information led to changes in contraceptive behavior, but the combination of information and cognitive restructuring produced the greatest change. It seems accurate to conclude that it is possible to bring about significant improvement in the contraceptive practices of those who do not wish to conceive offspring.

SUMMARY

Twentieth century changes in sexual attitudes and practices have been characterized as a **sexual revolution**. The changes include increased legal tolerance for sexual content in books, magazines, and movies. These societal changes were accompanied by increasingly permissive attitudes and by increases in the frequency and variety of sexual activity. Scientific research was also influenced by these changes, and beginning in the late 1960s we started to learn more about human sexuality than ever before. There is some evidence that a reversal in permissiveness is now underway.

Fantasies that are either self-created or presented in external images are found to elicit physiological arousal. The effects of explicit erotica are a matter of considerable importance. Fantasy-based arousal affects interpersonal behavior and perception, and it results in the increased likelihood of sexual activity. Modeling of the behavior presented in erotica occurs, but the process is somewhat complicated. Concerns about

pornography, especially when violence is the theme, have a long history, but research on the behavioral effects has only been conducted during the past fifteen years. Research with convicted sex criminals, comparisons between and within societies, and laboratory experiments have yielded a large and not totally consistent body of findings. Research is continuing, and there are conflicting views about whether some types of erotica have a detrimental effect on society.

Attitudes about sexuality fall along a positive-negative dimension that ranges from **erotophilia** to **erotophobia.** Negative attitudes are most likely to develop in families that are conservative and religious and in which the topic of sex is neglected and ignored. The more erotophobic an individual, the more he or she is likely to avoid and to respond negatively to sexual stimuli including erotica, self-created fantasies, and sexual interactions. In addition, negative sexual attitudes interfere with acquiring and imparting knowledge about sexuality, engaging in important health-related practices, and utilizing effective methods of contraception. The latter behavior can be changed by means of intervention procedures that include both information and efforts to bring about attitude change.

GLOSSARY

Acquired Immune Deficiency Syndrome (AIDS)
This is an extremely serious, fatal disease that is not yet curable. The AIDS virus has been found in the blood and in semen and can be transmitted through sexual contact, infected needles, and by means of blood transfusion.

erotophilia
The positive and relatively permissive end of a personality dimension that involves attitudes about a variety of sexual topics.

erotophobia
The negative and relatively restrictive end of a personality dimension that involves attitudes about a variety of sexual topics.

genital herpes
A sexually transmitted disease that is caused by a virus and for which no cure is yet available. It is dangerous to the victim's life only in rare instances, but it is extremely dangerous to the newborn infant of a female victim.

pornography
Originally, pornography meant writing by or about prostitutes. The word came to mean any material whose primary function was to arouse sexual thoughts and bring about sexual excitement. It is often designated as "soft-core" (erotic material that is not totally explicit) and "hard-core" (erotic material that is totally explicit).

Sex Guilt Scale
The personality test that assesses the tendency to punish oneself with anxiety whenever sexual standards are violated in thought or deed. High sex guilt is associated with erotophobic attitudes and low sex guilt with erotophilic attitudes.

sexuality
All aspects of sexual functioning ranging from physiological processes and anatomical structures to the fantasies, attitudes, beliefs, emotions, and activities involving sexual matters.

sexually transmitted disease
Diseases such as gonorrhea, syphilis, AIDS, and genital herpes that are transmitted from person to person primarily by means of sexual contact.

Sexual Opinion Survey
The personality test that assesses positive and negative attitudes about various sexual topics. High scores indicate erotophilic attitudes, while low scores indicate erotophobic attitudes.

sexual response cycle
The phases of physiological activity described by Masters and Johnson as excitement, plateau, orgasm, and resolution.

sexual revolution
This term is usually applied to the changes in the first three-fourths of the twentieth century in many societies toward greater sexual permissiveness and tolerance accompanied by increases in the frequency and variety of sexual activities.

FOR MORE INFORMATION

Byrne, D., and Kelley, K., eds. (1986). *Alternative approaches to the study of sexual behavior.* Hillsdale, N.J.: Erlbaum.

> This is a collection of original theoretical contributions from the fields of anthropology, sociology, and psychology. The authors focus on conceptual and methodological differences that arise when different perspectives are brought to bear on the same phenomena. The importance of both genetic and experiential factors is emphasized, and there is some attempt to integrate these diverse ways of seeking to understand sexual behavior.

Griffitt, W., and Hatfield, E. (1985). *Human sexual behavior.* Glenview, Ill.: Scott, Foresman.

> A basic introduction to the study of human sexuality written by two well known social psychologists. The text includes coverage of sex research, basic physiological and anatomical information, gender identities and gender roles, sexual behavior, sexual problems, and the interpersonal and social aspects of sexuality.

Malamuth, N. M., and Donnerstein, E., eds. (1984). *Pornography and sexual aggression.* New York: Academic Press.

> An up-to-date collection of original chapters dealing with one of the most important and controversial topics in the field — the role of pornography in eliciting sexually coercive and violent behavior. Chapters focus on such topics as violence against women, massive exposure effects, cross-cultural comparisons, and the legal implications of current research findings.

Zillmann, D. (1984). *Connections between sex and aggression.* Hillsdale, N.J.: Erlbaum.

> A scholarly examination of the proposed association between sexual and aggressive impulses and behaviors. Ranging from historical accounts to descriptions of research involving animals, neuroanatomy, and physiological processes, the chapters lead up to a description of emotion transfer theory and human behavioral studies.

BIBLIOGRAPHY

Abbott, A. R., and Sebastian, R. J. (1981). Physical attractiveness and expectations of success. *Personality and Social Psychology Bulletin, 7*, 481–486.

Abramson, D. J. (1985). *The effects of two types of distracting tasks on sexual arousal in sexually functional and dysfunctional males.* Unpublished doctoral dissertation, State University of New York at Albany.

Abramson, P. R. (1982). *The sexual system: A theory of human sexual behavior.* San Francisco: Academic Press.

Abramson, P. R., and Hayashi, H. (1984). Pornography in Japan: Cross-cultural and theoretical considerations. In N. M. Malamuth and E. Donnerstein (eds.), *Pornography and sexual aggression* (New York: Academic Press, pp. 173–183.

Abramson, P. R., and Imai-Marquez, J. (1982). The Japanese-American: A cross-cultural, cross-sectional study of sex guilt. *Journal of Research in Personality, 16*, 227–237.

Abramson, P. R., and Mechanic, M. G. (1983). Sex and the media: Three decades of best-selling books and major motion pictures. *Archives of Sexual Behavior, 12*, 185–206.

Adams, G. R. (1977). Physical attractiveness research: Toward a developmental social psychology of beauty. *Human Development, 20*, 217–239.

Adams, J. S. (1965). Inequity in social exchange. In L. Berkowitz (ed.), *Advances in experimental social psychology*, vol. 2. New York: Academic Press.

Adorno, T. W., Frenkel-Brunswick, E., Levinson, D. J., and Sanford, R. N. (1950). *The authoritarian personality.* New York: Harper & Row.

Aguero, J. E., Bloch, L., and Byrne, D. (1984). The relationships among sexual beliefs, attitudes, experience, and homophobia. *Journal of Homosexuality, 10*, 95–107.

Aiello, J. R., and Aiello, T. DeC. (1974). The development of personal space: Proxemic behavior of children 6 through 16. *Human Ecology, 2*, 177–179.

Aiello, J. R., Epstein, Y. M., and Karlin, R. A. (1975). Effects of crowding on electrodermal activity. *Sociological Symposium, 14*, 43–57.

Ajzen, I., and Fishbein, M. (1977). Attitude-behavior relations: A theoretical analysis and review of empirical research. *Psychological Bulletin, 84*, 888–918.

Alagna, F. J., Whitcher, S. J., and Fisher, J. D. (1979). Evaluative reactions to interpersonal touch in a counseling interview. *Journal of Counseling Psychology, 26*, 465–472.

Alagna, S. W., and Reddy, D. M. (1984). Predictors of proficient technique and successful lesion detection in breast self-examination. *Health Psychology, 3*, 113–127.

Alan Guttmacher Institute. (1981). *Teenage pregnancy: The problem that hasn't gone away.* New York: Alan Guttmacher Institute.

Albert, R. D. (1981). Effects of a victim's attributions on retaliation and transmittion of aggression. Unpublished manuscript, University of Illinois.

Albert, S., and Dabbs, J. M., Jr. (1970). Physical distance and persuasion. *Journal of Personality and Social Psychology, 15*, 265–270.

Alexander, R. A., and Barrett, G. U. (1982). Equitable salary increase judgments based upon merit and nonmerit considerations: A cross-national comparison. *International Review of Applied Psychology, 31*, 443–454.

Allen, V. L., and Levine, J. M. (1971). Social support and conformity: The role of independent assessment of reality. *Journal of Experimental Social Psychology, 4*, 48–58.

Allgeier, A. R. (1983). Informational barriers to contraception. In D. Byrne and W. A. Fisher (eds.), *Adolescents, sex, and contraception.* Hillsdale, NJ: Erlbaum.

Alloy, L. B. (1986). *Cognitive processes in depression.* New York: Guilford.

Alloy, L. B., and Abramson, L. Y. (1979). Judgments of contingency in depressed and nondepressed students: Sadder but wiser? *Journal of Experimental Psychology: General, 108*, 441–485.

Alloy, L. B., Abramson, L. Y., and Viscusi, D. (1981). Induced mood and the illusion of control. *Journal of Personality and Social Psychology, 41*, 1129–1140.

Allport, F. H. (1924). *Social psychology.* Boston: Houghton Mifflin.

Allport, G. W. (1935). Attitudes. In C. Murchison (ed.), *Handbook of social psychology.* Worcester, MA: Clark University Press.

Allport, G. W. (1985). The historical background of social psychology. In G. Lindzey and E. Aronson (eds.), *Handbook of social psychology.* New York: Random House.

Allport, G. W., and Odbert, H. S. (1936). Trait-names: A psycholexical study. *Psychological Monographs, 47* (211).

Allyn, J., and Festinger, L. (1961). The effectiveness of unanticipated persuasive communications. *Journal of Abnormal and Social Psychology, 62*, 35–40.

Altmaier, E. M., & Meyer, M. E. (eds.) (1985). *Applied specialties in psychology.* New York: Random House.

Altman, I. (1975). *The environment and social behavior.* Monterey, CA: Brooks/Cole.

Altman, S., Valenzi, E., and Hodgetts, R. M. (1985). *Organizational behavior: Theory and practice.* New York: Academic Press.

Alzate, H. (1984). Sexual behavior of unmarried Colombian university students: A five-year follow-up. *Archives of Sexual Behavior, 13*, 121–132.

Amabile, T. M. (1983). Brilliant but cruel: Perceptions of negative evaluators. *Journal of Experimental Social Psychology, 19*, 146–156.

Amato, P. R. (1983). Helping behavior in urban and rural environments: Field studies based on a taxonomic organization of helping episodes. *Journal of Personality and Social Psychology, 45*, 571–586.

———. (1985). An investigation of planned helping behavior. *Journal of Research in Personality, 19*, 232–252.

Amato, P. R., and McInness, I. R. (1983). Affiliative behavior in diverse environments: A consideration of pleasantness, information rate, and the arousal-eliciting quality of settings. *Basic and Applied Social Psychology, 4*, 109–122.

Amoroso, D. M., Brown, M., Pruesse, M., Ware, E. E., and Pilkey, D. W. (1971). An investigation of behavioral, psychological, and physiological reactions to pornographic stimuli. In *Technical report of the Commission on Obscenity and Pornography,* vol. 8. Washington, DC: U. S. Government Printing Office.

Andersen, S. M. (1984). Self-knowledge and social influence. II. The diagnosticity of cognitive/affective and behavioral data. *Journal of Personality and Social Psychology, 46*, 294–307.

Andersen, S. M., and Bem, S. L. (1981). Sex typing and androgyny in dyadic interaction: Individual differences in responsiveness to physical attractiveness. *Journal of Personality and Social Psychology, 41*, 74–86.

Andersen, S. M., and Ross, L. (1984). Self-knowledge and social inference: I. The impact of cognitive/affective and behavioral data. *Journal of Personality and Social Psychology, 46*, 280–293.

Anderson, C. A., and Anderson, D. C. (1984). Ambient temperature and violent crime: Tests of the linear and curvilinear hypothesis. *Journal of Personality and Social Psychology, 46*, 91–97.

Anderson, C. A., Lepper, M. R., and Ross, L. (1980). Perseverance of social theories: The role of explanation in the persistence of discredited information. *Journal of Personality and Social Psychology, 39*, 1037–1049.

Anderson, C. A., New, B. L., and Speer, J. R. (1985). Argument availability as a mediator of social theory perseverance. *Social Cognition, 3.*

Anderson, C. A., and Scheler, E. S. (1986). Effects of explanation and counterexplanation of the development and use of social theories. *Journal of Personality and Social Psychology, 50*, 24–34.

Anderson, T. W., Erwin, N., Flynn, D., Lewis, L., and Erwin, J. (1977). Effects of short-term crowding on aggression in captive groups of pigtail monkeys. *Aggressive Behavior, 3*, 33–46.

Antill, J. K. (1983). Sex role complementarity versus similarity in married couples. *Journal of Personality and Social Psychology, 45*, 145–155.

Appleyard, D., and Lintell, M. (1972). The environmental quality of city streets: The residents' viewpoint. *Journal of the American Institute of Planners, 38*, 84–101.

Archer, R. L., Diaz-Loving, R., Gollwitzer, P. M., Davis, M. H., and Foushee, H. C. (1981). The role of dispositional empathy and social evaluation in the empathic mediation of helping. *Journal of Personality and Social Psychology, 40*, 786–796.

Argyle, M., and Dean, J. (1965). Eye contact, distance and affiliation. *Sociometry, 28*, 289–304.

Arkin, R. M., and Appelman, A. J. (1983). Social anxiety

and receptivity to interpersonal evaluation. *Motivation and Emotion*, 7, 11–18.

Arkin, R. M., Gleason, J. M., and Johnston, S. (1976). Effects of perceived choice, expected outcome, and observed outcome of an action of the causal attributions of actors. *Journal of Experimental Social Psychology*, 12, 151–158.

Aronson, E., Bridgeman, D. L., and Geffner, R. (1978). Interdependent interactions and prosocial behavior. *Journal of Research and Development in Education*, 12, 16–27.

Aronson, E., and Mills, J. (1959). The effect of severity of initiation on liking for a group. *Journal of Abnormal and Social Psychology*, 59, 177–181.

Asch, S. E. (1951). Effects of group pressure upon the modification and distortion of judgment. In H. Guetzkow (ed.), *Groups, leadership, and men.* Pittsburgh: Carnegie.

———. (1957, April). An experimental investigation of group influence. In *Symposium on preventive and social psychiatry*, 15–17. Walter Reed Army Institute of Research, Washington, DC: U. S. Government Printing Office.

Ashton, N. L., Shaw, M. E., and Worsham, A. P. (1980). Affective reactions to interpersonal distances by friends and strangers. *Bulletin of the Psychonomic Society*. 15, 306–308.

Auerbach, S. M., Martelli, M. F., and Mercuri, L. G. (1983). Anxiety, information, interpersonal impacts, and adjustment to a stressful healthcare situation. *Journal of Personality and Social Psychology*, 44, 1284–1296.

Austin, W. (1979). Sex differences in bystander intervention in a theft. *Journal of Personality and Social Psychology*, 37, 2110–2120.

Averill, J. R., and Boothroyd, P. (1977). On falling in love in conformance with the romantic ideal. *Motivation and Emotion*, 1, 235–247.

Axelrod, J., and Reisine, T. D. (1984). Stress hormones: their interaction and regulation. *Science*, 224, 452–459.

Axelrod, R., and Hamilton, W. D. (1981). The evolution of cooperation. *Science*, 211, 1390–1396.

Bachman, J. A., O'Malley, P. N., and Johnston, L. D. (1984). Drug use among young adults: the impacts of role status and social environment. *Journal of Personality and Social Psychology*, 47, 629–645.

Bailey, D. S., Leonard, K. E., Cranston, J. W., and Taylor, S. P. (1983). Effects of alcohol and self-awareness on human physical aggression. *Personality and Social Psychology Bulletin*, 9, 289–295.

Bandura, A. (1965). Influence of models' reinforcement contingencies on the acquisition of imitative responses. *Journal of Personality and Social Psychology*, 1, 589–595.

———. (1973). *Aggression: A social learning analysis.* Englewood Cliffs, NJ: Prentice-Hall.

———. (1977). *Social learning theory.* Englewood Cliffs, NJ: Prentice-Hall.

———. (1986). *Social foundations of thought and action.* Englewood Cliffs, NJ: Prentice-Hall.

Bandura, A., Ross, D., and Ross, S. (1963). Imitation of film-mediated aggressive models. *Journal of Abnormal and Social Psychology*, 66, 3–11.

Barden, R. D., Garber, J., Duncan, S. W., and Masters, J. C. (1981). Cumulative effects of induced affective states in children: Accentuation, inoculation, and remediation. *Journal of Personality and Social Psychology*, 40, 750–760.

Bardwick, J. M. (1971). *Psychology of women: A study of bio-cultural conflicts.* New York: Harper & Row.

Barlow, D. H., Sakheim, D. K., and Beck, J. G. (1983). Anxiety increases sexual arousal. *Journal of Abnormal Psychology*, 92, 49–54.

Baron, L. (1985, September). *Toward an integrated theory of rape.* Paper presented at the U. S. Justice Department Hearings, Houston.

Baron, L., and Straus, M. A. (1984). Sexual stratification, pornography, and rape in the United States. In N. M. Malamuth and E. Donnerstein (eds.), *Pornography and sexual aggression.* New York: Academic Press pp. 186–209.

Baron, R. A. (1971). Magnitude of victim's pain cues and level of prior anger arousal as determinants of adult aggressive behavior. *Journal of Personality and Social Psychology*, 17, 236–243.

———. (1972). Aggression as a function of ambient temperature and prior anger arousal. *Journal of Personality and Social Psychology*, 21, 183–189.

———. (1972). Reducing the influence of an aggressive model: The restraining effects of peer censure. *Journal of Experimental Social Psychology*, 8, 266–275.

———. (1973). The "foot-in-the-door" phenomenon: Mediating effects of size of first request and sex of requester. *Bulletin of the Psychonomic Society*, 2, 113–114.

———. (1974). The aggression-inhibiting influence of heightened sexual arousal. *Journal of Personality and Social Psychology*, 29, 117–124.

———. (1977). *Human aggression.* New York: Plenum.

———. (1978). Invasions of personal space and helping: Mediating effects of invader's apparent need. *Journal of Experimental Social Psychology*, 14, 304–312.

———. (1979). Heightened sexual arousal and physical aggression: An extension to females. *Journal of Applied Social Psychology*, 9, 103–114.

———. (1981). The "costs of deception" revisited: An openly optimistic rejoinder. *IRB: A Review of Human Subjects Research*, 3, 8–10.

———. (1983a). *Behavior in organizations.* Boston: Allyn and Bacon.

———. (1983b). The control of human aggression: An optimistic perspective. *Journal of Social and Clinical Psychology*, 1, 97–119.

———. (1984). Reducing organizational conflict: An incompatible response approach. *Journal of Applied Psychology*, 69, 272–279.

———. (1985c). Reducing organizational conflict: The role of attributions. *Journal of Applied Psychology, 70,* 434–441.

———. (1986a). Interviewer's moods and reactions to job applicants: The influence of affective states on applied social judgments. Unpublished manuscript, Purdue University.

———. (1986b). *Behavior in organizations: Understanding and managing the human side of work,* 2nd edition. Boston: Allyn and Bacon.

———. (1986c). Self-presentation in job interviews: When there can be "too much of a good thing." *Journal of Applied Social Psychology.*

———. (1987a). Effects of negative air ions on interpersonal attraction: Evidence for intensification. *Journal of Personality and Social Psychology,* in press.

———. (1987b). Interviewer's moods and reactions to job applicants: The influence of affective states on applied social judgments. *Journal of Applied Social Psychology, 16,* 16–28.

Baron, R. A., and Bell, P. A. (1973). Effects of heightened sexual arousal on physical aggression. *Proceedings of the 81st Annual Convention of the American Psychological Association,* 171–172.

———. (1975). Aggression and heat: Mediating effects of prior provocation and exposure to an aggressive model. *Journal of Personality and Social Psychology, 31,* 825–832.

———. (1976). Aggression and heat: The influence of ambient temperature, negative affect, and a cooling drink on physical aggression. *Journal of Personality and Social Psychology, 33,* 245–255.

Baron, R. A., and Ransberger, V. M. (1978). Ambient temperature and the occurrence of collective violence: The "long hot summer" revisited. *Journal of Personality and Social Psychology, 36,* 351–360.

Baron, R. A., Russell, G. W., and Arms, R. L. (1985). Negative ions and behavior: Impact on mood, memory, and aggression among Type A and Type B persons. *Journal of Personality and Social Psychology, 48,* 746–754.

Baron, R. M., Mandel, D. R., Adams, C. A., and Griffen, L. M. (1976). Effects of social density in university residential environments. *Journal of Personality and Social Psychology, 34,* 434–446.

Baron, R. M., and Rodin, J. (1978). Personal control as a mediator of crowding. In A. Baum, J. E. Singer, and S. Valins (eds.). *Advances in environmental psychology,* vol. 1. Hillsdale, NJ.

Baron, R. S. (1986). Distraction-conflict theory: Progress and problems. In L. Berkowitz (ed.), *Advances in experimental social psychology,* (Vol. 20). New York: Academic Press.

Baron, R. S., and Moore, D., and Sanders, G. S. (1978). Distraction as a source of drive in social facilitation research. *Journal of Personality and Social Psychology, 36,* 816–824.

Baron, R. S., and Roper, G. (1976). Reaffirmation of social comparison views of choice shifts: Averaging and extremity effects in an autokinetic situation. *Journal of Personality and Social Psychology, 33,* 521–530.

Barrett-Howard and Tyler, T. R. (1986). Procedural justice as a criterion in allocation decisions. *Journal of Personality and Social Psychology, 50,* 296–304.

Bar-Tal, D., and Bar-Zohar, Y. (1977). The relationship between perception of locus of control and academic achievement. *Contemporary Educational Psychology, 2,* 181–199.

Bartol, K. M., and Butterfield, D. A. (1976). Sex effects in evaluating leaders. *Journal of Applied Psychology, 61,* 446–454.

Bass, B. M. (1981). *Stogdill's handbook of leadership: A survey of theory and research.* New York: Free Press.

Batson, C. D., Bolen, M. H., Cross, J. A., and Neuringer-Benefiel, H. E. (1986). Where is the altruism in the altruistic personality? *Journal of Personality and Social Psychology, 50,* 212–220.

Batson, C. D., Cochran, P. J., Biederman, M. F., Blosser, J. L., Ryan, M. J., and Vogt, B. (1978). Failure to help when in a hurry: Callousness or conflict? *Personality and Social Psychology Bulletin, 4,* 97–101.

Batson, C. D., Duncan, B. D., Ackerman, P., Buckley, T., and Birch, K. (1981). Is empathic emotion a source of altruistic motivation? *Journal of Personality and Social Psychology, 40,* 290–302.

Batson, C. D., and Gray, R. A. (1981). Religious orientation and helping behavior: Responding to one's own or to the victim's needs? *Journal of Personality and Social Psychology, 40,* 511–520.

Batson, C. D., O'Quin, K., Fultz, J., and Vanderplas, M. (1983). Influence of self-reported distress and empathy on egoistic versus altruistic motivation to help. *Journal of Personality and Social Psychology, 45,* 706–718.

Baum, A., and Davis, G. E. (1982). Reducing the stress of high-density living: An architectural intervention. *Journal of Personality and Social Psychology, 38,* 471–481.

Baum, A., Fisher, J. D., and Solomon, S. K. (1981). Type of information, familiarity, and the reduction of crowding stress. *Journal of Personality and Social Psychology, 40,* 11–23.

Baum, A. and Gatchel, R. J. (1981). Cognitive determinants of response to uncontrollable events: Development of reactance and learned helplessness. *Journal of Personality and Social Psychology, 40,* 1078–1089.

Baum, A., Gatchel, R. J., and Schaeffer, M. A. (1983). Emotional, behavioral, and physiological effects of chronic stress at Three Mile Island. *Journal of Consulting and Clinical Psychology, 51,* 565–572.

Baum, A., and Valins, S. (1977). *Architecture and social behavior: Psychological studies of social density.* Hillsdale, NJ: Erlbaum.

Baum, A., and Valins, S. (1979). Architectural mediation of residential density and control: Crowding and the regulation of social contact. In L. Berkowitz (ed.), *Ad-*

vances in experimental social psychology, vol. 12. New York: Academic Press.

Baumeister, R. F. (1984). Choking under pressure: Self-consciousness and paradoxical effects of incentives on skillful performance. *Journal of Personality and Social Psychology, 46*, 610–620.

———. (1985). The championship choke. *Psychology Today, 19* (4:April), pp. 48–52.

———. (1986). *Identity*. New York: Oxford University Press.

Baumeister, R. F., and Covington, M. V. (1985). Self-esteem, persuasion, and retrospective distortion of initial attitudes. *Electronic Social Psychology, 1*, 1–22.

———. (1986). Self-esteem, persuasion, and retrospective distortion of initial attitudes. *Electronic Social Psychology*.

Baumeister, R. F., and Darley, J. M. (1982). Reducing the biasing effect of perpetrator attractiveness in jury simulation. *Personality and Social Psychology Bulletin, 8*, 286–292.

Baumeister, R. F., Hamilton, J. C., and Tice, D. M. (1985). Public versus private expectancy of success: Confidence booster or performance pressure? *Journal of Personality and Social Psychology, 48*, 1447–1457.

Baumeister, R. F., and Steinhilber, A. (1984). Paradoxical effects of supportive audiences on performance under pressure: The home field disadvantage in sports championships. *Journal of Personality and Social Psychology, 47*, 85–93.

Baumeister, R. F., and Tice, D. M. (1984). Role of self-presentation and choice in cognitive dissonance under forced compliance: Necessary or sufficient causes? *Journal of Personality and Social Psychology, 46*, 5–13.

Baumgardner, A. H., Heppner, P. P., and Arkin, R. M. (1986). Role of causal attribution in personal problem solving. *Journal of Personality and Social Psychology, 50*, 636–643.

Baumrind, D. (1979). The costs of deception. *IRB: A Review of Human Subjects Research, 6*, 1–4.

Baxter, L. A. (1984). Trajectories of relationship disengagement. *Journal of Social and Personal Relationships, 1*, 29–48.

Bazerman, M. H., Magliozzi, T., and Neale, M. A. (1985). Integrative bargaining in a competitive market. *Organizational Behavior and Human Decision Processes, 3*, 294–313.

Beaman, A. L., Cole, C. M., Preston, M., Klentz, B., and Steblay, N. M. (1983). Fifteen years of foot-in-the-door research: A meta-analysis. *Personality and Social Psychology Bulletin, 9*, 181–196.

Beardslee, D. C., and Fogelson, R. (1958). Sex differences in sexual imagery aroused by musical stimulation. In J. W. Atkinson (ed.), *Motives in fantasy, action, and society* (pp. 132–142). Princeton: D. Van Nostrand.

Beck, S. B., Ward-Hull, C. I., and McLear, P. M. (1976). Variables related to women's somatic preferences of the male and female body. *Journal of Personality and Social Psychology, 34*, 1200–1210.

Becker, F. D., Gield, B., Gaylin, K., and Sayer, S. (1983). Office design in a community college: Effect on work and communication patterns. *Environment and Behavior, 15*, 699–726.

Becker, M. A. (1984). *Type A coronary-prone behavior and sexual interactions of 56 married couples*. Unpublished doctoral dissertation, State University of New York at Albany.

Becker, M. A., and Byrne, D. (1984). Type A behavior and daily activities of young married couples. *Journal of Applied Social Psychology, 14*, 82–88.

———. (1985). Self-regulated exposure to erotica, recall errors, and subjective reactions as a function of erotophobia and Type A coronary-prone behavior. *Journal of Personality and Social Psychology, 48*, 228–235.

Beckwith, D. (1985). Solo Americans. *Time, 126*(22), p. 41.

Beezley, D., Gantner, A. B., Bailey, D. S., and Taylor, S. P. (in press). Amphetamines and human physical aggression. *Journal of Research in Personality*.

Bell, P. A., and Baron, R. A. (1974). Environmental influences on attraction: Effects of heat, attitude similarity, and personal evaluations. *Bulletin of the Psychonomic Society, 4*, 479–481.

———. (1976). Aggression and heat: The mediating role of negative affect. *Journal of Applied Social Psychology, 6*, 18–30.

Bem, D. J. (1972). Self-perception theory. In L. Berkowitz (ed.), *Advances in experimental social psychology*, vol. 6. New York: Academic Press.

Bem, D. J., and McConnell, H. K. (1970). Testing the self-perception explanation of dissonance phenomena: On the salience of premanipulation attitudes. *Journal of Personality and Social Psychology, 14*, 23–31.

Bennet, R., Rafferty, J. M., Canivez, G. L., and Smith, J. M. (1983). The effects of cold temperature on altruism and aggression. Paper presented at the Midwestern Psychological Association meeting, Chicago.

Benson, P. L., Karabenick, S. A., and Lerner, R. M. (1976). Pretty pleases: The effects of physical attractiveness, race, and sex on receiving help. *Journal of Experimental Social Psychology, 12*, 409–415.

Berg, J. H. (1984). Development of friendship between roommates. *Journal of Personality and Social Psychology, 46*, 346–356.

Berg, J. H., and Peplau, L. A. (1982). Loneliness: The relationship of self-disclosure and androgyny. *Personality and Social Psychology Bulletin, 8*, 624–630.

Berger, S. M., Carli, L. C., Garcia, R., and Brady, J. J., Jr. (1982). Audience effects in anticipatory learning: A comparison of drive and practice-inhibition analyses. *Journal of Personality and Social Psychology, 42*, 378–386.

Berkowitz, L. (1962). *Aggression: A social psychological analysis*. New York: McGraw-Hill.

———. (1978). Whatever happened to the frustration-aggression hypothesis? *American Behavioral Scientist, 8*, 691–708.

———. (1984). Some effects of thoughts on anti- and prosocial influences of media events: A cognitive-neoassociation analysis. *Psychological Bulletin, 95,* 410–427.

Berkowitz, L., and Donnerstein, E. (1982). External validity is more than skin deep: Some answers to criticisms of laboratory experiments. *American Psychologist, 37,* 245–257.

Berkowitz, L., and Heimer, K. (1987). Aversive events and negative priming in the formation of feelings. Unpublished manuscript, University of Wisconsin.

Berndt, T. J., McCartney, K., Caparulo, B. K., and Moore, A. M. (1984). The effects of group discussions on children's moral decisions. *Social Cognition, 2,* 343–359.

Bernstein, W. M., Stephenson, B. O., Snyder, M. L., and Wicklund, R. A. (1983). Causal ambiguity and heterosexual affiliation. *Journal of Experimental Social Psychology, 19,* 78–92.

Berscheid, E. (1985). Interpersonal attraction. In G. Lindzey and E. Aronson (eds.), *Handbook of social psychology,* 3rd ed. New York: Random House.

Berscheid, E., Dion, K., Walster, E., and Walster, G. W. (1971). Physical attractiveness and dating choice: A test of the matching hypothesis. *Journal of Experimental Social Psychology, 7,* 173–189.

Bersoff, D., and Crosby, F. (1984). Job satisfaction and family status. *Personality and Social Psychology Bulletin, 10,* 79–83.

Best, J. A., Flag, B. R., Towson, S. M. J., Ryan, K. B., Perry, C. L., Brown, K. S., Kersell, M. W., and Avernas, J. R. (1984). Smoking prevention and the concept of risk. *Journal of Applied Social Psychology, 14,* 257–273.

Bettman, J. R. (1986). Consumer psychology. In M. R. Rosenzweig and L. W. Porter (eds.), *Annual review of psychology,* vol. 37 (pp. 257–289). Palo Alto, CA: Annual Reviews Inc.

Bickman, L., and Green, S. K. (1977). Situational cues and crime reporting: Do signs make a difference? *Journal of Applied Social Psychology, 7,* 1–18.

Bickman, L., and Rosenbaum, D. P. (1977). Crime reporting as a function of bystander encouragement, surveillance, and credibility. *Journal of Personality and Social Psychology, 35,* 577–586.

Bierley, M. M. (1985). Prejudice toward contemporary outgroups as a generalized attitude. *Journal of Applied Social Psychology, 15,* 189–199.

Black, T. E., and Higbee, K. L. (1973). Effects of power, threat, and sex on exploitation. *Journal of Personality and Social Psychology, 27,* 382–388.

Blake, R. R. (1986). The classified cinema: Rating of new feature films. *Albany Times Union,* July 24, p. C-1.

Blake, R. R., and Mouton, J. S. (1979). Intergroup problem solving in organizations: From theory to practice. In W. G. Austin and S. Worchel (eds.), *The social psychology of intergroup relations.* Monterey, CA: Brooks/Cole.

———. (1984). *Solving costly organizational conflicts.* San Francisco: Jossey-Bass.

Blaney, N. T., Brown, P., and Blaney, P. H. (1986). Type A, marital adjustment, and life stress. *Journal of Behavioral Medicine.*

Blankenship, V., Hnat, S. M., Hess, T. G., and Brown, D. R. (1984). Reciprocal interaction and similarity of personality attributes. *Journal of Social and Personal Relationships, 1,* 415–432.

Bleda, P. R., and Bleda, S. (1978). Effects of sex and smoking on reactions to spatial invasion at a shopping mall. *Journal of Social Psychology, 104,* 311–312.

Bleda, P. R., and Sandman, P. H. (1977). In smoke's way: Socioemotional reactions to another's smoking. *Journal of Applied Psychology, 62,* 452–458.

Blocker, T. J., and Koski, P. R. (1984). Household income, electricity use, and rate-structure preferences. *Environment and Behavior, 16,* 551–572.

Blot, W. J., Brinton, L. A., Fraumeni, J. F., Jr., and Stone, B. J. (1975). Cancer mortality in U. S. countries with petroleum industries. *Science, 198,* 51–53.

Blumenthal, J. A., McKee, D. C., Haney, T., and Williams, R. B. (1980). Task incentives, Type A behavior pattern, and verbal problem solving performance. *Journal of Applied Social Psychology, 10,* 101–114.

Bodenhausen, G. V., and Wyer, R. S. (1985). Effects of stereotypes of decision making and information-processing strategies. *Journal of Personality and Social Psychology, 48,* 267–282.

Bond, C. F. (1982). Social facilitation: A self-presentational view. *Journal of Personality and Social Psychology, 42,* 1042–1050.

Bond, S. B., & Mosher, D. L. (1986). Guided imagery of rape: Fantasy, reality, and the willing victim myth. *Journal of Sex Research, 22,* 162–183.

Booth, A. (1976). *Urban crowding and its consequences.* New York: Praeger.

Bordens, K. S., and Horowitz, I. A. (1983). Information processing in joined and severed trials. *Journal of Applied Social Psychology, 13,* 351–370.

Bower, G. H., & Hilgard, E. R. (1981). *Theories of learning* (5th edition). Englewood Cliffs, NJ: Prentice-Hall.

Brauer, D. V., and DePaulo, B. M. (1980). Similarities between friends in their understanding of nonverbal cues. *Journal of Nonverbal Behavior, 5,* 64–68.

Bray, R. M., Johnson, D., & Chilstrom, J. T., Jr. (1982). Social influence by group members with minority opinions: A comparison of Hollander and Moscovici. *Journal of Personality and Social Psychology, 43,* 78–88.

Bray, R. M., & Sugarman, R. (1980). Social facilitation among interaction groups: Evidence for the evaluation-apprehension hypothesis. *Personality and Social Psychology Bulletin, 6,* 137–142.

Breckler, S. J. (1984). Empirical validation of affect, behavior, and cognition as distinct components of attitude. *Journal of Personality and Social Psychology, 47,* 1191–1205.

Brehm, J. W. (1966). *A theory of psychological reactance.* New York: Academic Press.

Brennan, T. (1982). Loneliness at adolescence. In L. A. Peplau and D. Perlman (eds.), *Loneliness: A sourcebook of current theory, research, and therapy.* New York: Wiley.

Brennan, T., and Auslander, N. (1979). *Adolescent loneliness: An exploratory study of social and psychological predispositions and theory*, vol. 1. Prepared for the National Institute of Mental Health, Juvenile Problems Division, Grant No. R01-MH 289 12-01, Behavioral Research Institute.

Brewin, C. R. (1984). Attributions for industrial accidents: Their relationship to rehabilitation outcome. *Journal of Social and Clinical Psychology, 2*, 156–164.

Brickman, P., Becker, L. J., and Castle, S. (1979). Making trust easier and harder through two forms of sequential interaction. *Journal of Personality and Social Psychology, 37*, 515–521.

Brickman, P., Rabinowitz, V. C., Karuza, J., Jr., Coates, D., Cohn, E., and Kidder, L. (1982). Models of helping and coping. *American Psychologist, 37*, 368–384.

Briere, J., Downes, A., and Spensley, J. (1983). Summer in the city: Urban weather conditions and psychiatric emergency-room visits. *Journal of Abnormal Psychology, 92*, 77–80.

Brigham, J. C. (1980). Limiting conditions of the "physical attractiveness stereotype": Attributions about divorce. *Journal of Research in Personality, 14*, 365–375.

Brinberg, D., and Castell, P. (1982). A resource exchange theory approach to interpersonal interactions: A test of Foa's theory. *Journal of Personality and Social Psychology, 43*, 260–269.

Bringle, R. G., and Williams, L. J. (1979). Parental-offspring similarity on jealousy and related personality dimensions. *Motivation and Emotion, 3*, 265–286.

Britell, J. K. (1981, April 26). Ethics courses are making slow inroads. *New York Times* Education Section, p. 44.

Broadbent, D. (1958). *Perception and communication*. Oxford: Pergamon.

Brockner, J., Davy, J., and Carter, C. (1986). Layoffs, self-esteem, and survivor guilt: Motivational, affective, and attitudinal consequences. *Academy of Management Journal 29*, 373–384.

Brockner, J., and Guare, J. (1983). Improving the performance of low self-esteem individuals: An attributional approach. *Academy of Management Journal, 26*, 642–656.

Brockner, J., Rubin, J. Z., and Lang, E. (1981). Face-saving and entrapment. *Journal of Experimental Social Psychology, 17*, 68–79.

Brody, J. E. (1980, October 22). Rushing your life away with "Type A" behavior. *New York Times*, pp. C-1, C-12.

———. (1983, October 4). Relations: Americans on conservative side. *Albany Times Union*, A-1, A-8.

Broll, L., Gross, A. E., and Piliavin, I. (1974). Effects of offered and requested help on help seeking and reactions to being helped. *Journal of Applied Social Psychology, 4*, 244–258.

Broome, B. J. (1983). The attraction paradigm revisited. Response to dissimilar others. *Human Communication Research, 10*, 137–151.

Brown, G. (1980). *Why more men and women are abstaining from sex—and enjoying it*. New York: McGraw-Hill.

Browning, D. L. (1983). Aspects of authoritarian attitudes in ego development. *Journal of Personality and Social Psychology, 45*, 137–144.

Buunk, A. (1982). Anticipated sexual jealousy: Its relationship to self-esteem, dependency, and reciprocity. *Personality and Social Psychology Bulletin, 8*, 310–316.

Brunson, B. I., and Matthews, K. A. (1981). The Type A coronary-prone behavior pattern and reactions to uncontrollable stress: An analysis of performance strategies, affect and attributions during failure. *Journal of Personality and Social Psychology, 40*, 906–918.

Bryant, F. B., and Veroff, J. (1982). The structure of psychological well-being: A sociohistorical analysis. *Journal of Personality and Social Psychology, 43*, 653–673.

Bryant, J. (1985, September). *Testimony on the effects of pornography: Research findings*. Paper presented at the U. S. Justice Department Hearings, Houston.

Buck, R. (1984). *The communication of emotion*. New York: Guilford Press.

Buckhout, R. Nearly 2,000 witnesses can be wrong. *Bulletin of the Psychonomic Society, 16*, 307–310.

Burke, P. A., Kraut, R. E., and Dworkin, R. H. (1984). Traits, consistency, and self-schemata: What do our methods measure? *Journal of Personality and Social Psychology, 47*, 568–579.

Burger, J. M. (1984). Desire of control, locus of control, and proneness to depression. *Journal of Personality, 52*, 71–89.

Burger, J. M., and Petty, R. E. (1981). The low-ball compliance technique: Task or person commitment? *Journal of Personality and Social Psychology, 40*, 492–500.

Burgess, J. W. (1981). Development of social spacing in normal and mentally retarded children. *Journal of Nonverbal behavior, 6*, 89–95.

Burgess, L. R. (1984). *Wage and salary administration*. Columbus: Charles E. Merrill.

Burnham, M. A., Pennebaker, J. W., and Glass, D. C. (1975). Time consciousness, achievement striving, and the Type A coronary-prone behavior pattern. *Journal of Abnormal Psychology, 84*, 76–79.

Burnstein, E. (1983). Persuasion as argument processing. In M. Brandstatter, J. H. Davis, and G. Stocker-Kreichgauer (eds.). *Group decision processes*. London: Academic Press.

Bushman, B. J. (1984). Perceived symbols of authority and their influence on compliance. *Journal of Applied Social Psychology, 14*, 501–508.

Buss, A. H. (1961). *The psychology of aggression*. New York: Wiley.

Butterfield, F. (1980, January 13). Love and sex in China. *New York Times Magazine*, 15–17, 43–44, 46–49.

Byrne, D. (1971). *The attraction paradigm*. New York: Academic Press.

———. (1983a). The antecedents, correlates, and consequents of erotophobia-erotophilia. In C. M. Davis (ed.),

Challenges in sexual science (pp. 53–75). Philadelphia: Society for the Scientific Study of Sex.

———. (1983b). Sex without contraception. In D. Byrne and W. A. Fisher (eds.), *Adolescents, sex, and contraception* (pp. 3–31). Hillsdale, NJ: Erlbaum.

———. (1985, September). *External and internal imagery as determinants of sexual and aggressive behavior.* Paper presented at the U. S. Justice Department Hearings, Houston.

Byrne, D., Becker, M. A., and Przybyla, D. P. J. (1985). *Similarity of sexual attitudes as a determinant of attraction, marital compatibility, and sexual dysfunction.* Unpublished manuscript, State University of New York at Albany.

———. (1986). *Sexual attitudes, attraction, and marital compatibility.* Manuscript submitted for publication.

Byrne, D., Clore, G. L., and Smeaton, G. (1986). The attraction hypothesis: Do similar attitudes affect anything? *Journal of Personality and Social Psychology.*

Byrne, D., Ervin, C. R., and Lamberth, J. (1970). Continuity between the experimental study of attraction and real life computer dating. *Journal of Personality and Social Psychology, 16,* 157–165.

Byrne, D., and Kelley, K. (1981). *An introduction to personality* (3rd ed.). Englewood Cliffs, NJ: Prentice-Hall.

Byrne, D., and Lamberth, J. (1971). The effect of erotic stimuli on sex arousal, evaluative responses, and subsequent behavior. In *Technical report of the Commission on Obscenity and Pornography,* vol. 8. Washington, DC: U. S. Government Printing Office.

Byrne, D., and Murnen, S. (1987). Maintaining loving relationships. In R. J. Sternberg and M. L. Barnes (eds.), *The anatomy of love.* New Haven: Yale University Press.

Byrne, D., and Nelson, D. (1965). Attraction as a linear function of proportion of positive reinforcements. *Journal of Personality and Social Psychology, 1,* 659–663.

Byrne, D., and Przybyla, D. P. J. (1980). Authoritarianism and political preferences in 1980. *Bulletin of the Psychonomic Society, 16,* 471–472.

Cacioppo, J. T., and Petty, R. E. (1981). Effects of extent of thought on the pleasantness of P-O-X triads: Evidence for three judgmental tendencies in evaluating social situations. *Journal of Personality and Social Psychology, 40,* 1000–1009.

Cacioppo, J. T., Petty, R. E., and Losch, M. E. (1986). Attributions of responsibility for helping and doing harm: Evidence for confusion of responsibility. *Journal of Personality and Social Psychology, 50,* 100–105.

Caldwell, D. F., O'Reilly, C. A., III, and Morris, J. H. (1983). Responses to an organizational reward: A field test of the sufficiency of justification hypothesis. *Journal of Personality and Social Psychology, 44,* 506–514.

Calhoun, J. B. (1962). Population density and social pathology. *Scientific American, 206,* 139–148.

———. (1971). Space and the strategy of life. In A. H. Esser (ed.), *Environment and behavior: The use of space by animals and men.* New York: Plenum.

Campbell, J. D. (1986). Similarity and uniqueness: The effects of attribute type, relevance, and individual differences in self-esteem and depression. *Journal of Personality and Social Psychology, 50,* 281–294.

Caplow, T., and Forman, R. (1950). Neighborhood interaction in a homogeneous community. *American Sociological Review, 15,* 357–366.

Carlson, R. (1984). What's social about social psychology? Where's the person in personality research? *Journal of Personality and Social Psychology, 47,* 104–1309.

Carmody, T. P., Brischetto, C. S., Matarazzo, J. D., O'Donnell, R. P., and Connor, W. E. (1985). Co-occurrent use of cigarettes, alcohol, and coffee in healthy, community-living men and women. *Health Psychology, 4,* 323–335.

Carretta, T. R., and Moreland, R. L. (1983). The direct and indirect effects of inadmissable evidence, *Journal of Applied Social Psychology, 13,* 291–309.

Carroll, J. S. (1982). What is this thing called "Applied Social Psychology"? *Contemporary Psychology, 27,* 772–773.

Carver, C. S., Antoni, M., and Scheier, M. F. (1985). Self-consciousness and self-assessment. *Journal of Personality and Social Psychology, 48,* 117–124.

Carver, C. S., Ganellen, R., Froming, W., and Chambers, W. (1983). Modeling: An analysis in terms of category accessibility. *Journal of Experimental Social Psychology, 19,* 403–421.

Carver, C. S., and Glass, D. C. (1978). Coronary-prone behavior pattern and interpersonal aggression. *Journal of Personality and Social Psychology, 36,* 361–366.

Carver, C. S., and Scheier, M. F. (1981). *Attention and self-regulation: A control-theory approach to human behavior.* New York: Springer-Verlag.

———. (1981). The self-attention-induced feedback loop and social facilitation. *Journal of Experimental Social Psychology, 17,* 545–568.

———. (1982). Control theory: A useful conceptual framework for personality-social, clinical, and health psychology. *Psychological Bulletin, 92,* 111–135.

Cash, T. F., and Derlega, V. J. (1978). The matching hypothesis: Physical attractiveness among same-sexed friends. *Personality and Social Psychology Bulletin, 4,* 240–243.

Cash, T. F., and Kilcullen, R. N. (1985). The age of the beholder: Susceptibility to sexism and beautyism in the evaluation of managerial applicants. *Journal of Applied Social Psychology, 15,* 591–605.

Cash, T. F., Rissi, J., and Chapman, R. (1985). Not just another pretty face: Sex roles, locus of control, and cosmetics use. *Personality and Social Psychology Bulletin, 11,* 246–257.

Catania, J. A., McDermott, L. J., and Wood, J. A. (1984). Assessment of locus of control: Situational specificity in the sexual context. *Journal of Sex Research, 20,* 310–324.

Cattell, R. B., Kawash, G. F., and De Young, G. E. (1972). Validation of objective measures of ergic tension: Response of the sex erg to visual stimulation. *Journal of Experimental Research in Personality, 1,* 103–114.

Cavoukian, A., and Doob, A. N. (1980). The effects of a judge's charge and subsequent recharge on judgments of guilt. *Basic and Applied Social Psychology, 1,* 103–114.

Ceniti, J., and Malamuth, N. M. (1984). Effects of repeated exposure to sexually violent or nonviolent stimuli on sexual arousal to rape and nonrape depictions. *Behavior Research Therapy, 2,* 535–548.

Chacko, T. I. (1982). Women and equal employment opportunity: Some unintended effects. *Journal of Applied Psychology, 67,* 119–123.

Chance, J. E. (1965). *Internal control of reinforcements and the school learning process.* Paper presented at the meeting of the Society for Research in Child Development, Minneapolis.

Chapman, L. J., and Chapman, J. (1982). Test results are what you think they are. In D. Kahneman, P. Slovic, and A. Tversky (eds.) *Judgment under uncertainty: Heuristics and biases* (pp. 239–248). New York: Cambridge University Press.

Chapman, R., Masterpasqua, F., and Lore, R. (1976). The effects of crowding during pregnancy on offspring emotional and sexual behavior in rats. *Bulletin of the Psychonomic Society, 7,* 475–477.

Chassin, L., Presson, C. C., Sherman, S. J., Corty, E., and Olshavsky, R. W. (1984a). Predicting the onset of cigarette smoking in adolescents: A longitudinal study. *Journal of Applied Social Psychology, 14,* 224–243.

——. (1984b). Self-images and cigarette-smoking in adolescence. *Personality and Social Psychology Bulletin, 7,* 670–676.

Chemers, M. M., Hays, R. B., Rhodeawlt, F., and Wysocki, J. (1985). A person-environment analysis of job stress: A contingency model explanation. *Journal of Personality and Social Psychology, 49,* 628–635.

Cheney, A. B., and Bleker, E. G. (1982, August). *Internal-external locus of control and repression-sensitization in battered women.* Paper presented at the meeting of the American Psychological Association, Washington, DC.

Chertkoff, J. M., and Conley, M. (1967). Opening offer and frequency of concession as bargaining strategies. *Journal of Personality and Social Psychology, 7,* 181–185.

Chidester, T. R. (1986). Problems in the study of interracial interaction: Pseudo-interracial dyad paradigm. *Journal of Personality and Social Psychology, 50,* 74–79.

Childers, T. L., and Houston, M. J. (1984). Conditions for a picture-superiority effect on consumer memory. *Journal of Consumer Research, 11,* 643–654.

Chlopan, B. E., McCain, M. L., Carbonell, J. L., and Hagen, R. L. (1985). Empathy: Review of available measures. *Journal of Personality and Social Psychology, 48,* 635–653.

Christensen, H. T. (1969). Normative theory derived from cross-cultural family research. *Journal of Marriage and the Family, 31,* 209–222.

Christy, P. R., Gelfand, D. M., and Hartmann, D. P. (1971). Effects of competition-induced frustration on two classes of modeled behavior. *Developmental Psychology, 5,* 104–111.

Cialdini, R. B. (1985). *Influence: Science and Practice.* Glenview, Il: Scott, Foresman.

Cialdini, R. B., Cacioppo, J. T., Bassett, R., and Miller, J. A. (1978). Low-ball procedure for producing compliance: Commitment then cost. *Journal of Personality and Social Psychology, 36,* 463–476.

Cialdini, R. B., and Petty, R. (1979). Anticipatory opinion effects. In R. Petty, T. Ostrom, and T. Brock (eds.), *Cognitive responses in persuasion.* Hillsdale, NJ: Erlbaum.

Cialdini, R. B., Vincent, J. E., Lewis, S. K., Catalan, J., Wheeler, D., and Darby, B. L. (1975). Reciprocal concessions procedure for inducing compliance: The door-in-the-face technique. *Journal of Personality and Social Psychology, 31,* 206–215.

Cimbalo, R. S., Faling, V., and Mousaw, P. (1976). The course of love: A cross-sectional design. *Psychological Reports, 38,* 1292–1294.

Clark, R. A. (1952). The projective measurement of experimentally induced levels of sexual motivation. *Journal of Experimental Psychology, 44,* 391–399.

Clark, R. D., III. (1976). On the Piliavin and Piliavin model of helping behavior: Costs are in the eye of the beholder. *Journal of Applied Social Psychology, 6,* 322–328.

Clement, U., Schmidt, G., and Kruse, M. (1984). Changes in sex differences in sexual behavior: A replication of a study on West German students (1966–1981). *Archives of Sexual Behavior, 13,* 99–120.

Clore, G. L., and Byrne, D. (1974). A reinforcement-affect model of attraction. In T. L. Huston (ed.), *Foundations of interpersonal attraction* (pp. 143–170). New York: Academic Press.

Clore, G. L., Wiggins, N. H., and Itkin, S. (1975). Gain and loss in attraction: Attributions from nonverbal behavior. *Journal of Personality and Social Psychology, 31,* 706–712.

Cohen, C. E. (1981). Person categories and social perception: Testing some boundaries of the processing effects of prior knowledge. *Journal of Personality and Social Psychology, 40,* 441–452.

Cohen, S. (1978). Environmental load and the allocation of attention. In A. Baum, J. E. Singer, and S. Valins (eds.), *Advances in environmental psychology,* vol. 1. Hillsdale, NJ: Erlbaum.

Cohen, S., Evans, G. W., Krantz, D. S., and Stokols, D. (1980). Physiological, motivational, and cognitive effects of aircraft noise on children. *American Psychologist, 35,* 231–243.

Cohen, S., Evans, G. W., Krantz, D. S., Stokols, D., and Kelly, S. (1981). Aircraft noise and children: Longitudinal and cross-sectional evidence on adaptation to noise and the effectiveness of noise abatement. *Journal of Personality and Social Psychology, 40,* 331–345.

Cohen, S., Evans, G. W., Stokols, D., and Krantz, D. (1986). *Behavior, health and environmental stress.* New York: Plenum.

Cohen, S., Glass, D. C., and Singer, J. E. (1973). Apartment noise, auditory discrimination, and reading ability in children. *Journal of Experimental Social Psychology, 9,* 407–422.

Cohen, S., and Weinstein, N. (1980). Nonauditory effects of noise on behavior and health. *Journal of Social Issues, 37,* 36–70.

Coke, J. S., Batson, C. D., and McDavis, K. (1978). Empathic mediation of helping: A two-stage model. *Journal of Personality and Social Psychology, 36,* 752–766.

Coles, C. D., and Shamp, M. J. (1984). Some sexual, personality, and demographic characteristics of women readers of erotic romances. *Archives of Sexual Behavior, 13,* 187–209.

Conway, M., and Ross, M. (1984). Getting what you want by revising what you had. *Journal of Personality and Social Psychology, 47,* 738–748.

Cook, S. W. (1984a). Cooperative interaction in multiethnic contexts. In N. Miller and M. Brewer (eds.), *Groups in contact: The psychology of desegregation* (pp. 155–185). New York: Academic Press.

———. (1948b). The 1954 social science statement and school desegregation: A reply to Gerard. *American Psychologist, 39,* 819–832.

———. (1985). Experimenting on social issues: The case of school desegregation. *American Psychologist, 40,* 452–460.

Coombs, L. C. (1979). The measurement of commitment to work. *Journal of Population, 2,* 203–223.

Cooper, J., and Fazio, R. H. (1984). A new look at dissonance theory. In L. Berkowitz (ed.), *Advances in experimental social psychology,* vol. 17, (pp. 229–266). New York: Academic Press.

Cooper, J., Zanna, M. P., and Taves. P. A. (1978). Arousal as a necessary condition for attitude change following induced compliance. *Journal of Personality and Social Psychology, 36,* 1101–1106.

Cooper, T., Detre, T., and Weiss, S. M. (1981). Coronary-prone behavior and coronary heart disease: A critical review. *Circulation, 63,* 1199–1215.

Costantini, E., and Craik, K. H. (1980). Personality and politicians: California party leaders, 1960–1976. *Journal of Personality and Social Psychology, 38,* 641–66.1.

Cotton, J. L. (1986). Ambient temperature and violent crime. *Journal of Applied Social Psychology.*

Cottrell, N. B., Wack, D. L., Sekerak, G. J., and Rittle, R. H. (1968). Social facilitation of dominant responses by the presence of an audience and the mere presence of others. *Journal of Personality and Social Psychology, 9,* 245–250.

Cowan, G., Drinkard, J., and MacGavin, L. (1984). The effects of target, age, and gender on use of power strate-gies. *Journal of Personality and Social Psychology, 47,* 1391–1398.

Cowen, E. L., Weissberg, R. P., and Lotyczewski, B. S. (1982). Physical contact in helping interactions with young children. *Journal of Consulting and Clinical Psychology, 50,* 219–225.

Cox, V. C., Paulus, P. B., and McCain, G. (1984). Prison crowding research: The relevance for prison housing standards and a general approach regarding crowding phenomena. *American Psychologist, 39,* 1148–1160.

Crandall, V. C. (1973). *Differences in parental antecedents of internal-external control in children and in young adulthood.* Paper presented at the meeting of the American Psychological Association, Montreal.

Crosby, F. (1982). *Relative deprivation and working women.* New York: Oxford University Press.

Crouse, B. B., and Mehrabian, A. (1977). Affiliation of opposite-sexed strangers. *Journal of Research in Personality, 11,* 38–47.

Crowne, D. P., and Liverant, S. (1963). Conformity under varying conditions of personal commitment. *Journal of Abnormal and Social Psychology, 66,* 547–555.

Croyle, R., and Cooper, J. (1983). Dissonance arousal: Physiological evidence. *Journal of Personality and Social Psychology, 45,* 782–791.

Crusco, A. H., and Wetzel, C. G. (1984). The midas touch: The effects of interpersonal touch on restaurant tipping. *Personality and Social Psychology Bulletin, 10,* 512–517.

Crutchfield, R. A. (1955). Conformity and character. *American Psychologist, 10,* 191–198.

Cummings, K. M., Jette, A., Brock, B. M., and Haefner, D. P. (1979). Psychosocial determinants of immunization behavior in a Swine Influenza campaign. *Medical Care, 17,* 639–649.

Cunningham, M. R. (1979). Weather, mood, and helping behavior: Quasi experiments with the sunshine Samaritan. *Journal of Personality and Social Psychology, 37,* 1947–1956.

———. (1981). Sociobiology as a supplementary paradigm for social psychological research. In L. Wheeler (ed.), *Review of personality and social psychology,* vol. 2. Beverly Hills, CA: Sage.

Cunningham, M. R., Steinberg, J., and Grev, R. (1980). Wanting to and having to help: Separate motivations for positive mood and guilt induced helping. *Journal of Personality and Social Psychology, 38,* 181–192.

Cutrona, C. E. (1982). Transition to college: Loneliness and the process of social adjustment. In L. A. Peplau and D. Perlman (eds.), *Loneliness: A sourcebook of current theory, research, and therapy.* New York: Wiley.

Cvetkovich, G., and Grote, B. (1983). Adolescent development and teenage fertility. In D. Byrne and W. A. Fisher (eds.), *Adolescents, sex, and contraception.* Hillsdale, NJ: Erlbaum.

Daher, D. M., and Banikiotes, P. G. (1976). Interpersonal attraction and rewarding aspects of disclosure content and level. *Journal of Personality and Social Psychology*, 33, 492–496.

Darley, J. M., and Batson, C. D. (1973). "From Jerusalem to Jericho": A study of situational and dispositional variables in helping behavior. *Journal of Personality and Social Psychology*, 27, 100–108.

Darley, J. M., and Gross, P. (1983). A hypothesis-confirming bias in labeling effects. *Journal of Personality and Social Psychology*, 44, 20–33.

Darley, J. M., and Latané, B. (1968). Bystander intervention in emergencies: Diffusion of responsibility. *Journal of Personality and Social Psychology*, 8, 377–383.

Davenport, W. H. (1978). Sex in cross-cultural perspective. In F. A. Beach (eds.), *Human sexuality in four perspectives*. Baltimore: Johns Hopkins Press.

Davidson, J. K., Sr., and Hoffman, L. E. (1986). Sexual fantasies and sexual satisfaction: An empirical analysis of erotic thought. *Journal of Sex Research*, 22, 184–205.

Davidson, L. M., Baum, A., and Collins, D. (1982). Stress and control-related problems at Three Mile Island. *Journal of Applied Social Psychology*, 12, 349–359.

Davis, J. H. (1980). Group decisions and procedural justice. In M. Fishbein (ed.), *Progress in social psychology*. Hillsdale, NJ: Erlbaum.

Davis, J. H., Tindale, R. S., Nagao, D. H., Hinsz, V. B., and Robertson, B. (1984). Order effects in multiple decisions by groups: A demonstration with mock juries and trial procedures. *Journal of Personality and Social Psychology*, 47, 1003–1012.

Davis, K. B. (1929). *Factors in the sex life of 2,200 women*. New York: Harper & Row.

Davis, M. H. (1983). Empathic concern and the muscular dystrophy telethon: Empathy as a multidimensional construct. *Personality and Social Psychology Bulletin*, 9, 223–229.

Davis, W. L., and Phares, E. J. (1969). Parental antecedents of internal-external control of reinforcement. *Psychological Reports*, 24, 427–436.

Deaux, K. (1982). *Sex as a social category: Evidence for gender stereotypes*. Invited address, American Psychological Association, Washington, DC.

Deaux, K., and Lewis, L. L. (in press). The structure of gender stereotypes: Interrelationships among components and gender label. *Journal of Personality and Social Psychology*.

Deci, E. L. (1975). *Intrinsic motivation*. New York: Plenum.

DeFronzo, J. (1984). Climate and crime: Tests of an FBI assumption. *Environment and Behavior*, 16, 185–210.

DeGregorio, E., and Carver, C. S. (1980). Type A behavior pattern, sex role orientation, and psychological adjustment. *Journal of Personality and Social Psychology*, 39, 286–293.

DeJong, W., Marber, S., and Shaver, R. (1980). Crime intervention: The role of a victim's behavior in reducing situational ambiguity. *Personality and Social Psychology Bulletin*, 6, 113–118.

DeJong, W., and Musilli, L. (1982). External pressure to comply: Handicapped versus nonhandicapped requesters and the foot-in-the-door phenomenon. *Personality and Social Psychology Bulletin*, 8, 522–527.

Dellinger, R. W. (1979). Jet roar: Health problems take off near airports. *Human Behavior*, 8, 50–51.

Dembroski, T. M., and MacDougall, J. M. (1978). Stress effects on affiliation preferences among subjects possessing the Type A coronary-prone behavior pattern. *Journal of Personality and Social Psychology*, 36, 23–33.

———. (1982). Coronary-prone behavior, social psychophysiology, and coronary heart disease. In J. R. Eiser (eds.), *Social psychology and behavioral medicine*. New York: Wiley.

Dembroski, T. M., MacDougall, J. M., and Musante, L. (1984). Desirability of control versus locus of control: Relationship to paralinguistics in the Type A interview. *Health Psychology*, 3, 15–26.

Denby, D. (1986). Poison. *New York*, 19 (23), pp. 130–131.

Dengerink, H. A., Schnedler, R. W., and Covey, M. K. (1978). Role of avoidance in aggressive responses to attack and no attack. *Journal of Personality and Social Psychology*, 36, 1044–1053.

DePaulo, B. M., Brown, P. L., Ishii, S., and Fisher, J. D. (1981). Help that works: The effects of aid on subsequent task performance. *Journal of Personality and Social Psychology*, 41, 478–487.

DePaulo, B. M., and Fisher, J. D. (1980). The costs of asking for help. *Basic and Applied Social Psychology*, 1, 23–35.

DePaulo, B. M., Stone, J. L., and Lassiter, G. D. (1985a). Deceiving and detecting deceit. In B. R. Schlenker (ed.), *The self and social life* (pp. 323–370). New York: McGraw-Hill.

———. (1985). Deceiving and detecting deceit. In B. R. Schlenker (ed.), *The self and social life*. (pp. 323–370). New York: McGraw-Hill.

———. (1985c). Telling ingratiating lies: Effects of target sex and target attractiveness on verbal and nonverbal deceptive success. *Journal of Personality and Social Psychology*, 48, 1191–1203.

Derlega, V. J., and Grzelak, J. (eds.). (1982). *Cooperation and helping behavior: Theories and research*. New York: Academic Press.

Dermer, M., and Pyszczynski, T. A. (1978). Effects of erotica upon men's loving and liking responses for women they love. *Journal of Personality and Social Psychology*, 36, 1302–1309.

Deutsch, M., and Krauss, R. M. (1960). The effect of threat upon interpersonal bargaining. *Journal of Abnormal and Social Psychology*, 61, 181–189.

Diener, E. (1980). Deindividuation: The absence of self-awareness and self-regulation in group members. In P. B. Paulus (ed.), *The psychology of group influence*. Hillsdale, NJ: Erlbaum.

Diener, E., Larsen, R. J., and Emmons, R. A. (1984). Person

X situation interactions: Choice of situations and congruence response models. *Journal of Personality and Social Psychology, 47,* 580–592.

Dienstbier, R. A., Kahle, L. R., Willis, K. A., and Tunnell, G. B. (1980). The impact of moral theories on cheating: Studies of emotion attribution and schema activation. *Motivation and Emotion, 4,* 193–216.

Di Matteo, M. R., and Friedman, H. S. (1982). *Social psychology and medicine.* Cambridge, MA: Oegeschlager, Gunn, & Hain.

Dion, K. K., and Dion, K. L. (1975). Self-esteem and romantic love. *Journal of Personality, 43,* 39–57.

Dishman, R. K. (1982). Compliance/adherence in health related exercise. *Health Psychology, 1,* 237–267.

DiVasto, P. V., Pathak, D., and Fishburn, W. R. (1981). The interrelationship of sex guilt, sex behavior, and age in an adult sample. *Archives of Sexual Behavior, 10,* 119–122.

Dixit, N. (1985). *The effect of verbal contact and spatial positioning on job satisfaction, job performance, and interpersonal attraction: An experimental investigation.* Unpublished doctoral dissertation, State University of New York at Albany.

Doherty, W. J. (1983). Impact of divorce on locus of control orientation in adult women: A longitudinal study. *Journal of Personality and Social Psychology, 44,* 834–840.

Dollard, J., Doob, L., Miller, N., Mowrer, O. H., and Sears, R. R. (1939). *Frustration and aggression.* New Haven: Yale University Press.

Donnerstein, E. (1980). Aggressive erotica and violence against women. *Journal of Personality and Social Psychology, 39,* 269–277.

Donnerstein, E., and Donnerstein, M. (1976). Research in the control of interracial aggression. In R. G. Geen and E. C. O'Neal (eds.), *Perspectives on aggression.* New York: Academic Press.

Donnerstein, E., and Wilson, D. W. (1976). The effects of noise and perceived control upon ongoing and subsequent aggressive behavior. *Journal of Personality and Social Psychology, 34,* 774–781.

Dovidio, J. H., Evans, N., and Tyler, R. B. (1986). Racial stereotypes: The contents of their cognitive representations. *Journal of Experimental Social Psychology, 22,* 22–37.

Downey, L. (1980). Intergenerational change in sex behavior: A belated look at Kinsey's males. *Archives of Sexual Behavior, 9,* 267–317.

Drachman, D., de Carufel, A., and Insko, C. A. (1978). The extra credit effect in interpersonal attraction. *Journal of Experimental Social Psychology, 14,* 458–465.

Driscoll, R., Davis, K. E., and Lipetz, M. E. (1972). Parental interference and romantic love: The Romeo and Juliet effect. *Journal of Personality and Social Psychology, 24,* 1–10.

Duck, S. (1985). Social and personal relationships. In S. R. Miller and M. L. Knapp (eds.), *The handbook of interpersonal communication.* Beverly Hills, CA: SAGE.

Duck, S., and Gilmour, R. (eds.). (1981). *Personal relationships. 1: Studying personal relationships.* London: Academic Press.

Duffy, M., Bailey, S., Beck, B., and Barker, D. G. (1986). Preferences in nursing home design: A comparison of residents, administrators, and designers. *Environment and Behavior, 18,* 246–257.

Duke, M. P. (1986). Personality science: A proposal. *Journal of Personality and Social Psychology, 50,* 382–385.

Dutton, D. G., and Aron, A. P. (1974). Some evidence for heightened sexual attraction under conditions of high anxiety. *Journal of Personality and Social Psychology, 30,* 510–517.

Dutton, D. G., and Lake, R. A. (1973). Threat of own prejudice and reverse discrimination in interracial situations. *Journal of Personality and Social Psychology, 28,* 94–100.

Duval, S., and Wicklund, R. A. (1972). *A theory of objective self-awareness.* New York: Academic Press.

Eagly, A. H., and Carli, L. (1981). Sex of researchers and sex-typed communications as determinants of sex differences in influence-ability: A meta-analysis of social influence studies. *Psychological Bulletin, 90,* 1–20.

Eagly, A. H., and Chaikin, S. (1984). Cognitive theories of persuasion. In L. Berkowitz (ed.), *Advances in experimental social psychology,* vol. 17 (pp. 267–359). New York: Academic Press.

Eagly, A. H., and Steffen, V. J. (1984). Gender stereotypes stem from the distribution of women and men into social roles. *Journal of Personality and Social Psychology, 46,* 735–754.

———. (1986). Gender and aggressive behavior: A meta-analytic review of the social psychologial literature. *Psychological Bulletin,* in press.

Eagly, A. H., and Wood, W. (1982). Inferred sex differences in status as a determinant of gender stereotypes about social influence. *Journal of Personality and Social Psychology, 43,* 915–928.

Earn, B. M. (1982). Intrinsic motivation as a function of extrinsic financial rewards and subjects' locus of control. *Journal of Personality, 50,* 360–373.

Ebbesen, E. B., and Bowers, R. J. (1974). Proportion of risky to conservative arguments in a group discussion and choice shift. *Journal of Personality and Social Psychology, 29,* 316–327.

Ebbesen, E. B., Kjos, G. L., and Konecni, V. J. (1976). Spatial ecology: Its effects on the choice of friends and enemies. *Journal of Experimental Social Psychology, 12,* 505–518.

Edney, J. J. (1972). Property, possession, and permanence: A field study in human territoriality. *Journal of Applied Social Psychology, 2,* 275–282.

Eidelson, R. J. (1980). Interpersonal satisfaction and level of involvement: A curvilinear relationship. *Journal of Personality and Social Psychology, 39,* 460–470.

Eisen, S. V. (1979). Actor-observer differences in information inferences and causal attribution. *Journal of Personality and Social Psychology, 37,* 261–272.

Eisenberger, R., and Shank, D. M. (1985). Personal work ethic and effort training affect cheating. *Journal of Personality and Social Psychology*, 49, 520–528.

Eisenman, R. (1982). Sexual behavior as related to sex fantasies and experimental manipulation of authoritarianism and creativity. *Journal of Personality and Social Psychology*, 43, 853–860.

Eiser, J. R. (1983). Smoking, addiction, and decision-making. *Journal of Applied Social Psychology*, 32, 11–28.

Eiser, J. R., and van der Pligt, J. (1984). Attitudinal and social factors in adolescent smoking: In search of peer group influence. *Journal of Applied Social Psychology*, 14, 348–363.

————. (1986). Smoking cessation and smokers' perceptions of their addiction. *Journal of Social and Clinical Psychology*, 4, 60–70.

Ekman, P., and Friesen, W. V. (1975). *Unmasking the face.* Englewood Cliffs, NJ: Prentice-Hall.

Elder, G. H., Jr., and MacInnis, D. J. (1983). Achievement imagery in women's lives from adolescence to adulthood. *Journal of Personality and Social Psychology*, 45, 394–404.

Elliott, G. C., and Meeker, B. F. (1984). Modifiers of the equity effect: Group outcome and causes for individual performance. *Journal of Personality and Social Psychology*, 46, 586–597.

————. (1986). Achieving fairness in the face of competing concerns: The difference effects of individual and group characteristics. *Journal of Personality and Social Psychology*, 50, 754–760.

Ellis, H. (1899). *Studies in the psychology of sex.* New York: Random House. 1936.

Ellis, S., Rogoff, B., and Cramer, C. C. (1981). Age segregation in children's social interactions. *Developmental Psychology*, 17, 399–407.

Ellsworth, P. C., and Carlsmith, J. M. (1973). Eye contact and gaze aversion in an aggressive encounter. *Journal of Personality and Social Psychology*, 28, 280–292.

Ellsworth, P. C., and Langer, E. J. (1976). Staring and approach: An interpretation of the stare as a nonspecific activator. *Journal of Personality and Social Psychology*, 33, 117–122.

Elms, A. C., and Milgram, S. (1966). Personality characteristics associated with obedience and defiance toward authoritative command. *Journal of Experimental Research in Personality*, 1, 282–289.

English, E. H., and Baker, T. B. (1983). Relaxation training and cardiovascular response to experimental stressors. *Health Psychology*, 2, 239–259.

Enzle, M. E., Hansen, R. D., and Lowe, C. A. (1975). Causal attribution in the mixed-motive game: Effects of facilitory and inhibitory environmental factors. *Journal of Personality and Social Psychology*, 31, 50–54.

Epstein, L. H. (1984). The direct effects of compliance on health outcome. *Health Psychology*, 3, 385–393.

Epstein, S. (1979). The stability of behavior: I. On predicting most of the people much of the time. *Journal of Personality and Social Psychology*, 37, 1097–1126.

Erber, R. and Fiske, S. T. (1984). Outcome dependency and attention to inconsistent information. *Journal of Personality and Social Psychology*, 47, 709–726.

Erkut, S., Jaquette, D. S., and Staub, E. (1981). Moral judgment-situation interaction as a basis for predicting prosocial behavior. *Journal of Personality*, 49, 1–14.

Eron, L. D. (1982). Parent-child interaction, television violence, and aggression of children. *American Psychologist*, 37, 197–211.

Erwin, P. G., and Calev, A. (1984). Beauty: More than skin deep? *Journal of Social and Personal Relationships*, 1, 359–361.

Evans, G. W. (1979). Behavioral and physiological consequences of crowding in humans. *Journal of Applied Social Psychology*, 9, 27–46.

————. (1981). Environmental stress: Introduction. *Journal of Social Issues*, 37, 1–3.

Evans, G. W., Jacobs, S. V., and Frager, N. B. (1982). Behavioral responses to air pollution. In A. Baum and J. E. Singer (eds.), *Advances in environmental psychology*, vol. 4. Hillsdale, NJ: Erlbaum.

Evans, M. C., and Wilson, M. (1949). Friendship choices of university women students. *Educational and Psychological Measurement*, 9, 307–312.

Evans, R. I., Raines, B. E., and Hanselka, L. (1984). Developing data-based communications in social psychological research: Adolescent smoking prevention. *Journal of Applied Social Psychology*, 14, 289–295.

Eye of the storm. (1970). ABC TV (film).

Eysenck, H. J. (1986). Can personality study ever be scientific? *Journal of Social Behavior and Personality*, 1, 3–19.

Fagin, P. F. (1985). What can be done about pornography. In D. A. Scott (ed.), *Pornography—Its effects on the family, community and culture.* Washington, DC: Child and Family Protection Institute.

Fajardo, D. M. (1985). Author race, essay quality, and reverse discrimination. *Journal of Applied Social Psychology*, 15, 255–268.

Fazio, R. H. (1981). On the self-perception explanation of the over-justification effect. *Journal of Experimental Social Psychology*, 17, 417–426.

————. (1986). How do attitudes guide behavior? In R. M. Sorrentino and E. T. Higgins (ed.), *The handbook of motivation and cognition.* New York: Guilford Press.

Fazio, R. H., Chen, J., McDonel, E. C., and Sherman, S. J. (1982). Attitude accessibility, attitude-behavior consistency, and the strength of the object-evaluation association. *Journal of Experimental Social Psychology*, 18, 339–357.

Fazio, R. H., Cooper, M., Dayson, K., and Johnson, M. (1981). Control and the coronary-prone behavior pattern: Responses to multiple situational demands. *Personality and Social Psychology Bulletin*, 7, 97–102.

Fazio, R. H., Lenn, T. M., and Effrein, E. A. (1984). Spontaneous attitude formation. *Social Cognition*, 2, 217–234.

Fazio, R. H., Powell, M. C., and Herr, P. M. (1983). Toward

a process model of the attitude-behavior relation: Accessing one's attitude upon mere observation of the attitude object. *Journal of Personality and Social Psychology, 44,* 723–735.

Fazio, R. H., Sanbonmatsu, D. M., Powell, M. C., and Kardes, F. R. (1986). On the automatic activation of attitudes. *Journal of Personality and Social Psychology, 50,* 229–238.

Feather, N. T. (1985). Attitudes, values, and attributions: Explanations of unemployment. *Journal of Personality and Social Psychology, 48,* 876–889.

Feather, N. T., and Tiggermann, M. (1984). A balanced measure of attributional style. *Australian Journal of Psychology, 36,* 267–283.

Feinberg, R. A., Miller, F. G., and Ross, G. A. (1981). Perceived and actual locus of control similarity among friends. *Personality and Social Psychology Bulletin, 7,* 85–89.

Feldman-Summers, S., and Norris, J. (1984). Differences between rape victims who report and those who do not report to a public agency. *Journal of Applied Social Psychology, 14,* 562–573.

Felman, Y. M., Young, A. W., Siegal, F. P., and Scham, M. (1983). Sex and herpes. *Medical Aspects of Human Sexuality, 17*(1), 24L, 24N, 24Q–24R, 24W, 24Z, 24BB, 24DD, 24HH.

Fenigstein, A. (1984). Self-consciousness and overperception of self as target. *Journal of Personality and Social Psychology, 47,* 860–870.

Fenigstein, A., Scheier, M. F., and Buss, A. H. (1975). Public and private self-consciousness: Assessment and theory. *Journal of Consulting and Clinical Psychology, 43,* 522–527.

Ferguson, T. J., and Rule, B. G. (1983). An attributional perspective on anger and aggression. In R. G. Green and E. I. Donnerstein (eds.), *Aggression: Theoretical and empirical reviews* vol. 1, (pp. 41–74). New York: Academic Press.

Feshbach, S. (1984a). The catharsis hypothesis, aggressive drive, and the reduction of aggression. *Aggressive Behavior, 10,* 91–101.

———. (1984b). The "personality" of personality theory and research. *Personality and Social Psychology Bulletin, 10,* 446–456.

Feshbach, S., and Singer, R. D. (1971). *Television and aggression.* San Francisco: Jossey-Bass.

Festinger, L. (1957). *A theory of cognitive dissonance.* Evanston, Ill.: Row, Peterson.

Festinger, L., and Carlsmith, J. M. (1959). Cognitive consequences of forced compliance. *Journal of Abnormal and Social Psychology, 58,* 203–211.

Festinger, L., Schachter, S., and Back, K. (1950). *Social pressures in informal groups: A study of a housing community.* New York: Harper.

Fiedler, F. E. (1978). Contingency model and the leadership process. In L. Berkowitz (ed.), *Advances in experimental social psychology,* vol. 11. New York: Academic Press.

Fiedler, F. E., and Garcia, J. E. (1987). *Leadership: Cognitive resources and performance.* New York: Wiley.

Fincham, F. D., and Roberts, C. (1985). Intervening causation and the mitigation of responsibility for harm doing. II. The role of limited mental capacities. *Journal of Experimental Social Psychology, 21,* 178–194.

Findley, M. J., and Cooper, H. M. (1983). Locus of control and academic achievement: A literature review. *Journal of Personality and Social Psychology, 44,* 419–427.

Firestone, I. J., Lichtman, C. M., and Colamosca, J. V. (1975). Leader effectiveness and leadership conferral as determinants of helping in a medical emergency. *Journal of Personality and Social Psychology, 31,* 343–348.

Fischer, C. S. (1982). *To dwell among friends: Personal networks in town and city.* Chicago: University of Chicago Press.

Fishbein, M. (1982). Social psychological analysis of smoking behavior. J. R. Eiser (ed.), *Social psychology and behavioral medicine* (pp. 179–197). NY: Wiley.

Fisher, J. D., and Baum, A. (1980). Situational and arousal-based messages and the reduction of crowding stress. *Journal of Applied Social Psychology, 10,* 191–201.

Fisher, J. D., Bell, P. A., and Baum, A. (1984). *Environmental psychology* (2nd ed.). New York: Holt, Rinehart, & Winston.

Fisher, J. D., and Byrne, D. (1975). Too close for comfort: Sex differences in response to invasions of personal space. *Journal of Personality and Social Psychology, 32,* 15–21.

Fisher, J. D., DePaulo, B. M., and Nadler, A. (1981). Extending altruism beyond the altruistic act: The mixed effects of aid on the help recipient. In J. P. Rushton and R. M. Sorrentino (eds.), *Altruism and helping behavior.* Hillsdale, NJ: Erlbaum.

Fisher, J. D., Harrison, C. L., and Nadler, A. (1978). Exploring the generalizability of donor-recipient similarity effects. *Personality and Social Psychology Bulletin, 4,* 627–630.

Fisher, J. D., Nadler, A., and Whitcher-Alagna, S. (1982). Recipient reactions to aid. *Psychological Bulletin, 91,* 27–54.

Fisher, J. D., Rytting, M., and Heslin, R. (1976). Hands touching hands: Affective and evaluative effects of an interpersonal touch. *Sociometry, 39,* 416–421.

Fisher, W. A. (1980a). *Erotophobia-erotophilia and performance in a human sexuality course.* Unpublished manuscript, University of Western Ontario, London, Ontario.

Fisher, S. (1980b). Personality correlates of sexual behavior in black women. *Archives of Sexual Behavior, 9,* 27–35.

———. (1984). Predicting contraceptive behavior among university men: The roles of emotions and behavioral intentions. *Journal of Applied Social Psychology, 14,* 104–123.

Fisher, W. A., Byrne, D., Edmunds, M., Miller, C. T., Kelley, K., and White, L. A. (1979). Psychological and situation-specific correlates of contraceptive behavior among university women. *Journal of Sex Research, 15,* 38 – 55.

Fisher, W. A., Byrne, D., and White, L. A. (1983). Emotional barriers to contraception. In D. Byrne and W. A. Fisher (eds.), *Adolescents, sex, and contraception* (pp. 207 – 239). Hillsdale, NJ: Erlbaum.

Fisher, W. A., Byrne, D., White, L. A., and Kelley, K. (1986, in press). Erotophobia-erotophilia as a dimension of personality. *Journal of Sex Research.*

Fisher, W. A., and Gray, J. (1983, November). *Erotophobia-erotophilia and couples' sexual behavior during pregnancy and after childbirth.* Paper presented at the meeting of the Society for the Scientific Study of Sex, Chicago.

Fiske, S. T., and Taylor, S. E. (1984). *Social cognition.* Reading, MA: Addison-Wesley.

Fleischer, R. A., and Chertkoff, J. M. (1986). Effects of dominance and sex on leader selection in dyadic work groups. *Journal of Personality and Social Psychology, 50,* 94 – 99.

Fleming, R., Baum, A., and Singer, J. E. (1984). Toward an interpretive approach to the study of stress. *Journal of Personality and Social Psychology, 46,* 939 – 949.

Foa, U. G. (1976). Resource theory of social exchanges. In J. S. Thibaut, J. Spence, and R. Carson (eds.), *Contemporary topics in social psychology.* Morristown, NJ: General Learning Press.

Folkes, V. S. (1982). Forming relationships and the matching hypothesis. *Personality and Social Psychology Bulletin, 8,* 631 – 636.

Folkman, S. (1984). Personal control and stress and coping processes: A theoretical analysis. *Journal of Personality and Social Psychology, 46,* 839 – 852.

Forbes, R. J., and Jackson, P. R. (1980). Non-verbal behaviour and the outcome of selection interviews. *Journal of Occupational Psychology, 53,* 65 – 72.

Ford, C. S., and Beach, F. A. (1951). *Patterns of sexual behavior.* New York: Harper.

Ford, M. R., and Lowery, C. R. (1986). Gender differences in moral reasoning: A comparison of the use of justice and care orientations. *Journal of Personality and Social Psychology, 50,* 777 – 783.

Forest, D., Clark, M. S., Mills, J., and Isen, A. M. (1980). Helping as a function of feeling state and nature of the helping behavior. *Motivation and Emotion.*

Forsyth, D. R. (1983). *An introduction to group dynamics.* Monterey, Calif.: Brooks/Cole.

Foss, R. D. (1983). Community norms and blood donation. *Journal of Applied Social Psychology, 13,* 281 – 290.

Fox, J., and Guyer, M. (1978). Public choice and cooperation in N-person prisoner's dilemma. *Journal of Conflict Resolution, 22,* 468 – 481.

Franck, K. (1980). Friends and strangers: The social experience of living in urban and nonurban settings. *Journal of Social Issues, 36,* 52 – 71.

Frank, S. (1983, October 16). 'We' conquering 'me' era, as sexual revolution fades. *Albany Times-Union,* C-1, C-3.

Freedman, J. L. (1984). Effect of television violence on aggressiveness. *Psychological Bulletin, 96,* 227 – 246.

Freedman, J. L., and Fraser, S. C. (1966). Compliance without pressure: The foot-in-the-door technique. *Journal of Personality and Social Psychology, 4,* 195 – 202.

Freedman, J. L., Heshka, S., and Levy, A. (1975). Population density and pathology: Is there a relationship? *Journal of Experimental Social Psychology, 11,* 539 – 552.

Freedman, J. L., Klevansky, S., and Ehrlich, P. I. (1971). The effect of crowding on human task performance. *Journal of Applied Social Psychology, 1,* 7 – 26.

Freud, S. (1905). *Three contributions to the theory of sex.* New York: Dutton, 1962.

——— . (1930). *Civilization and its discontents.* London: Hogarth.

——— . (1933). *New introductory lectures on psych-analysis.* New York: Norton.

Frick, R. W. (1985). Communicating emotion: The role of prosodic features. *Psychological Bulletin, 97,* 412 – 429.

Friedland, N. (1982). A note on tax evasion as a function of the quality of information about the magnitude and credibility of threatened fines: Some preliminary research. *Journal of Applied Social Psychology, 12,* 54 – 59.

Friedman, M., and Rosenman, R. H. (1959). Association of a specific overt behavior pattern with increases in blood cholesterol, blood clotting time, incidence of arcus senilis and clinical coronary heart disease. *Journal of the American Medical Association, 169,* 1286 – 1296.

Fromm, E. (1956). *The art of loving.* New York: Harper.

Fultz, J., Batson, C. D., Fortenbach, V. A., McCarthy, P. M., and Varney, L. L. (1986). Social evaluation and the empathy-altruism hypothesis. *Journal of Personality and Social Psychology, 50,* 761 – 769.

Funder, D. C., and Ozer, D. J. (1983). Behavior as a function of the situation. *Journal of Personality and Social Psychology, 44,* 107 – 112.

Gabrielcik, A., and Fazio, R. H. (1983). Priming and frequency estimation: A strick test of the availability heuristic. *Personality and Social Psychology Bulletin, 10,* 85 – 89.

Gaertner, S. L., and Dovidio, J. F. (1977). The subtlety of white racism, arousal, and helping behavior. *Journal of Personality and Social Psychology, 35,* 691 – 707.

Galle, O. R., Gove, W. R., and McPherson, J. M., (1972). Population density and pathology: What are the relationships for man? *Science, 176,* 23 – 30.

Gallup, G. (1978, October 18). Gallup youth survey. *Indianapolis Star.*

Galton, F. (1870). *Hereditary genius: An inquiry into its laws and consequences.* (Republished: New York, Horizon, 1952).

Gangestad, S., and Snyder, M. (1985). On the nature of

self-monitoring: An examination of latent causal structure. In P. Shaver (ed.), *Review of personality and social psychology*, vol. 6 (pp. 65–85). Beverly Hills, CA: SAGE.

Garcia, L. T. (1986). *Exposure to pornography and attitudes about women and rape: A correlational study.* Manuscript submitted for publication.

Garcia, L. T., Brennan, K., DeCarlo, M., McGlennon, R., and Tait, S. (1984). Sex differences in sexual arousal to different erotic stories. *Journal of Sex Research, 20,* 391–402.

Garwood, S. G., Cox, L., Kaplan, V., Wasserman, N., and Sulzer, J. L. (1980). Beauty is only "name" deep: The effect of first-name in ratings of physical attraction. *Journal of Applied Social Psychology, 10,* 431–435.

Gastorf, J. W. (1980). Time urgency of the Type A behavior pattern. *Journal of Consulting and Clinical Psychology, 48,* 299.

Gastorf, J. W., and Teevan, R. C. (1980). Type A coronary-prone behavior pattern and fear of failure. *Motivation and Emotion, 4,* 71–76.

Gatchel, R. J., and Proctor, J. D. (1976). Physiological correlates of learned helplessness in man. *Journal of Applied Psychology, 85,* 27–34.

Geen, R. G. (1968). Effects of frustration, attack, and prior training in aggressiveness upon aggressive behavior. *Journal of Personality and Social Psychology, 9,* 316–321.

———. (1978). Some effects of observing violence upon the behavior of the observer. In B. A. Maher (ed.), *Progress in experimental personality research*, vol. 8. New York: Academic Press.

———. (1981). Behavioral and physiological reactions to observed violence: Effects of prior exposure to aggressive stimuli. *Journal of Personality and Social Psychology, 40,* 868–875.

Geen, R. G., and Donnerstein, E. (eds.) (1983). *Aggression: Theoretical and empirical reviews.* New York: Academic Press.

Geen, R. G., and Gange, J. J. (1977). Drive theory of social facilitation: Twelve years of theory and research. *Psychological Bulletin, 84,* 1267–1288.

Geer, J. H., and Fuhr, R. (1976). Cognitive factors in sexual arousal: The role of distraction. *Journal of Consulting and Clinical Psychology, 44,* 238–243.

Geier, J. G. (1969). A trait approach to the study of leadership in small groups. *Journal of Communication, 17,* 316–323.

Geiselman, R. E., Haight, N. A., and Kimata, L. G. (1984). Context effects on the perceived physical attractiveness of faces. *Journal of Experimental Social Psychology, 20,* 409–424.

Geller, D. M. (1980). Responses to urban stimuli: A balanced approach. *Journal of Social Issues, 36,* 86–100.

Geller, E. S., Erickson, J. B., and Buttram, B. A. (1983). Attempts to promote residential water conservation with educational, behavioral, and engineering strategies. *Population and Environment, 6,* 96–112.

Georgoudi, M., and Rosnow, R. L. (1985). Notes toward a contextualist understanding of social psychology. *Personality and Social Psychology Bulletin, 11,* 5–22.

Gerard, H. B. (1983). School desegregation: The social science role. *American Psychologist, 38,* 869–877.

Gerard, H. B., Wilhelmy, R. A., and Conolley, E. S. (1968). Conformity and group size. *Journal of Personality and Social Psychology, 8,* 79–82.

Gergen, K. J., Ellsworth, P., Maslach, C., and Seipel, M. (1975). Obligation, donor resources, and reactions to aid in three cultures. *Journal of Personality and Social Psychology, 31,* 390–400.

Gergen, K. J., Hepburn, A., and Fisher, D. C. (1986). Hermeneutics of personality description. *Journal of Personality and Social Psychology, 50,* 1261–1270.

Gerrard, G. (1986). Are men and women really different? In K. Kelley (ed.), *Females, males, and sexuality.* Albany: SUNY Press.

Gerrard, M. (1977). Sex guilt in abortion parents. *Journal of Consulting and Clinical Psychology, 45,* 708.

———. (1980). Sex guilt and attitudes toward sex in sexually active and inactive female college students. *Journal of Personality Assessment, 44,* 258–261.

———. (1982). Sex, sex guilt, and contraceptive use. *Journal of Personality and Social Psychology, 42,* 153–8.

Gerrard, M., and Gibbons, F. X. (1982). Sexual experience, sex guilt, and sexual moral reasoning. *Journal of Personality, 50,* 345–359.

Gerrard, M., McCann, L., and Geis, B. (1982). The antecedents and prevention of unwanted pregnancy. In A. Rickel, M. Gerrard, and I. Iscoe (eds.), *Social and psychological problems of women: Prevention and crisis intervention.* New York: McGraw-Hill.

Gibbons, F. X. (1978). Sexual standards and reactions to pornography: Enhancing behavioral consistency through self-focused attention. *Journal of Personality and Social Psychology, 36,* 976–987.

Gilbert, D., and Jones, (1986). *Journal of Personality and Social Psychology, 50,*

Gillen, B. (1981). Physical attractiveness: A determinant of two types of goodness. *Personality and Social Psychology Bulletin, 7,* 277–281.

Gilligan, C. (1982). *In a different voice.* Cambridge, MA: Harvard University Press.

Gillis, J. S., and Avis, W. E. (1980). The male-taller norm in mate selection. *Personality and Social Psychology Bulletin, 6,* 396–401.

Gioia, D. A., and Sims, H. P., Jr. (1985). Self-serving bias and actor-observer differences in organizations: An empirical analysis. *Journal of Applied Social Psychology, 15,* 547–563.

Glass, D. C. (1977). *Behavior patterns, stress, and coronary disease.* Hillsdale, NJ: Erlbaum.

———. (1983). Behavioral, cardiovascular and neuroendocrine responses to psychological stressors. *International Review of Applied Psychology, 32,* 137–151.

Glass, D. C., Krakoff, L. R., Finkelman, J., Snow, B., Contrada, R., Kehoe, K., Mannucci, E. G., Isecke, W., Collins, C., Hilton, W. F., and Elting, E. (1980). Effect of task overload upon cardiovascular and plasma catecholamine responses in Type A and B individuals. *Basic and Applied Social Psychology, 1,* 199–218.

Glass, D. C., and Singer, J. E. (1972). *Urban stress.* New York: Academic Press.

Glenn, N., and Hill, L. (1977). Rural-urban differences in attitudes and behavior in the United States. *The Annals of the American Academy of Political and Social Science, 429,* 36–50.

Glenn, N. D., and Weaver, C. N. (1979). Attitudes toward premarital, extramarital, and homosexual relations in the U. S. in the 1970s. *Journal of Sex Research, 15,* 108–118.

Godfrey, D. K., Jones, E. E., and Lord, C. G. (1986). Self-promotion is not ingratiating. *Journal of Personality and Social Psychology, 50,* 106–115.

Goethals, G. R. (1986). Fabricating and ignoring social reality: Self-serving estimates of consensus. In J. Olson, C. P. Herman, and M. P. Zanna (eds.), *Relative deprivation and social comparison: The Ontario symposium on social cognition IV.* Hillsdale, NJ: Erlbaum.

Goethals, G. R., Cooper, J., and Naficy, A. (1979). Role of foreseen, foreseeable, and unforeseeable behavioral consequences in the arousal of cognitive dissonance. *Journal of Personality and Social Psychology, 37,* 1179–1185.

Goethals, G. R., and Zanna, M. P. (1979). The role of social comparison in choice shifts. *Journal of Personality and Social Psychology, 37,* 1469–1476.

Gold, J. A., Ryckman, R. M., and Mosley, N. R. (1984). Romantic mood induction and attraction to a dissimilar other: Is love blind? *Personality and Social Psychology Bulletin, 10,* 358–368.

Goldband, S. (1980). Stimulus specificity of physiological response to stress and the Type A coronary-prone behavior pattern. *Journal of Personality and Social Psychology, 39,* 670–679.

Goldberg, R., and Tull, R. M. (1984). *The psychosocial dimensions of cancer.* New York: Free Press.

Goldstein, J. H., Davis, R. W., and Herman, D. (1975). Escalation of aggression: Experimental studies. *Journal of Personality and Social Psychology, 39,* 670–679.

Goldstein, M. J., Kant, H. S., and Hartman, J. J. (1974). *Pornography and sexual deviance.* Berkeley: University of California Press.

Goleman, D. (1985, August 20). New studies examine sexual guilt. *New York Times.*

———. (1986, April 8). Studies point to power of nonverbal signals. *New York Times,* C-1, C-6.

Gondola, J. C. (1985). The enhancement of creativity through long and short term exercise programs. *Journal of Social Behavior and Personality, 1,* 77–82.

Gonzales, M. Hope, Davis, J. M., Loney, G. L., LuKens, C. K., and Junghans, C. M. (1983). Interactional approach to interpersonal attraction. *Journal of Personality and Social Psychology, 44,* 1192–1197.

Gormley, F. F., and Aiello, J. R. (1982). Social density, interpersonal relationships, and residential crowding stress. *Journal of Applied Social Psychology, 12,* 22–236.

Gormly, A. V. (1979). Behavioral effects of receiving agreement or disagreement from a peer. *Personality and Social Psychology Bulletin, 5,* 405–408.

Gormly, J. P. (1983). Predicting behavior from personality trait scores. *Personality and Social Psychology Bulletin, 9,* 267–270.

Gormly, J. B., and Gormly, A. V. (1981). Approach-avoidance: Potency in psychological research. *Bulletin of the Psychonomic Society, 17,* 221–223.

Gotay, C. C. (1981). Cooperation and competition as a function of Type A behavior. *Personality and Social Psychology Bulletin, 7,* 386–392.

Gottlieb, J., and Carver, C. S. (1980). Anticipation of future interaction and the bystander effect. *Journal of Experimental Social Psychology, 16,* 253–260.

Gouaux, C. (1971). Induced affective states and interpersonal attraction. *Journal of Personality and Social Psychology, 20,* 37–43.

Gould, R., and Sigall, H. (1977). The effects of empathy and outcome on attribution: An examination of the divergent-perspectives hypothesis. *Journal of Experimental Social Psychology, 13,* 480–491.

Granberg, D., and King, M. (1980). Cross-lagged panel analysis of the relation between attraction and perceived similarity. *Journal of Experimental Social Psychology, 16,* 573–581.

Graziano, W., Brothen, T., and Berscheid, E. (1978). Height and attraction: Do men and women see eye-to-eye? *Journal of Personality, 46,* 128–145.

Green, R. (1985, September). *Exposure to explicit sexual materials and sexual assault: A review of behavioral and social science research.* Paper presented at the U. S. Justice Department Hearings, Houston.

Green, S. E., and Mosher, D. L. (1985). A causal model of sexual arousal to erotic fantasies. *Journal of Sex Research, 21,* 1–23.

Green, S. K., Buchanan, D. R., and Heuer, S. K. (1984). Winners, losers, and choosers: A field investigation of dating initiation. *Personality and Social Psychology Bulletin, 10,* 502–511.

Greenbaum, P., and Rosenfield, H. W. (1978). Patterns of avoidance in response to interpersonal staring and proximity: Effects of bystanders on drivers at a traffic intersection. *Journal of Personality and Social Psychology, 36,* 575–587.

Greenberg, J. (1980). Attention focus and locus of performance causality as determinants of equity behavior. *Journal of Personality and Social Psychology, 38,* 579–585.

———. (1982). Approaching equity and avoiding inequity in groups and organizations. In J. Greenberg and R. L. Cohen (eds.), *Equity and justice in social behavior.* New York: Academic Press.

————. (1983). Self-image vs. impression management in adherence to distributive justice standards: The influence of self-awareness and self-consciousness. *Journal of Personality and Social Psychology, 44*, 5–19.

————. (1986). Differential intolerance for inequity from organizational individual agents. *Journal of Applied Social Psychology, 16*, 191–196.

Greenberg, J., and Musham, C. (1981). Avoiding and seeking self-focused attention. *Journal of Research in Personality, 15*, 191–200.

Greenberg, J., & Pyszczynski, T. (1985). The effect of an overheard slur on evaluations of the target: How to spread a social disease. *Journal of Experimental Social Psychology, 21*, 61–72.

Greenberg, J., Pyszczynski, T., and Solomon, S. (1982). The self-serving attributional bias: Beyond self-presentation. *Journal of Experimental Social Psychology, 18*, 56–67.

Greenberg, J., Williams, K. D., and O'Brien, M. K. (1986). Considering the harshest verdict first: Biasing effects on mock juror verdicts. *Personality and Social Psychology Bulletin, 12*, 41–50.

Greenberg, M. S., and Ruback, R. B. (1982). *Social psychology of the criminal justice system.* Monterey, CA: Brooks/Cole.

Greendlinger, V. (1985). *Dispositional and situational variables as predictors of rape proclivity in college men.* Unpublished doctoral dissertation, State University of New York at Albany.

Greendlinger, V., and Byrne, D. (1985). *Propinquity and affiliative needs as joint determinants of classroom friendships.* Manuscript submitted for publication.

————. (1986). Coercive sexual fantasies of college males as predictors of self-reported likelihood to rape and overt sexual aggression. *Journal of Sex Research.*

Greenwald, A. G. (1968). Cognitive learning, cognitive response to persuasion, and attitude change. In A. Greenwald, T. Brock, and T. Ostrom (eds.), *Psychological foundations of attitudes* (pp. 148–170). New York: Academic Press.

Gregersen, E. (1982). *Sexual practices: The story of human sexuality.* New York: Franklin Watts.

————. (1986). Human sexuality in cross-cultural perspective. In D. Byrne and K. Kelley (eds.), *Alternative approaches to the study of sexual behavior* (pp. 87–102). Hillsdale, NJ: Erlbaum.

Griffitt, W. (1970). Environmental effects on interpersonal affective behavior: Ambient effective temperature and attraction. *Journal of Personality and Social Psychology, 15*, 240–244.

Griffitt, W., and Kaiser, D. L. (1978). Affect, sex guilt, gender, and the rewarding-punishing effects of erotic stimuli. *Journal of Personality and Social Psychology, 36*, 850–858.

Griffitt, W., May, J., and Veitch, R. (1974). Sexual stimulation and interpersonal behavior: Heterosexual evaluative responses, visual behavior, and physical proximity. *Journal of Personality and Social Psychology, 30*, 367–377.

Griffitt, W., and Veitch, R. (1971). Hot and crowded: Influence of population density and temperature on interpersonal affective behavior. *Journal of Personality and Social Psychology, 17*, 92–98.

————. (1974). Preacquaintance attitude similarity and attraction revisited: Ten days in a fall-out shelter. *Sociometry, 37*, 163–173.

Groff, B. D., Baron, R. S., and Moore, D. L. (1983). Distraction, attentional conflict, and drivelike behavior. *Journal of Experimental Social Psychology, 19*, 359–380.

Gross, A. E., and Fleming, I. (1982). Twenty years of deception in social psychology. *Personality and Social Psychology Bulletin, 8*, 402–408.

Grusec, J. E., and Redler, E. (1980). Attribution, reinforcement, and altruism: A developmental analysis. *Developmental Psychology, 16*, 525–534.

Gully, K. J., and Dengerink, H. A. (1983). The dyadic interaction of persons with violent and nonviolent histories. *Aggressive Behavior, 9*, 13–20.

Gutek, B. A. (1985). *Sex and the workplace.* San Francisco: Jossey-Bass.

Gyllenhammer, P. G. (1977, July-August). How Volvo adapts work to people. *Harvard Business Review*, pp. 102–113.

Haan, N., Weiss, R., and Johnson, V. (1982). The role of logic in moral reasoning and development. *Developmental Psychology, 18*, 245–256.

Hackman, J. R., Lawler, E. E., III and Porter, L. W. (1983). *Perspective on behavior in organizations.* (2nd ed.) New York: McGraw-Hill.

Haley, W. E., and Strickland, B. R. (1986). Interpersonal betrayal and cooperation: Effects on self-evaluation in depression. *Journal of Personality and Social Psychology, 50*, 386–391.

Hall, E. T. (1966). *The hidden dimension.* New York: Doubleday.

Hamilton, D. L., Dugan, P. M., and Trolier, T. K. (1985). The formation of stereotypic beliefs: Further evidence for distinctiveness-based illusory correlations. *Journal of Personality and Social Psychology, 48*, 5–17.

Hamilton, D. L., and Gifford, R. K. (1976). Illusory correlation in interpersonal perception: A cognitive basis of stereotypic judgments. *Journal of Experimental Social Psychology, 12*, 392–407.

Hamilton, D. L., Swap, W. C., and Rubin, J. Z. (1981). Predicting the effects of anticipated third party intervention: A template-matching approach. *Journal of Personality and Social Psychology, 41*, 1141–1152.

Hamilton, G. V. (1929). *A study in marriage.* New York: Boni.

Hamilton, V. L. (1978). Obedience and responsibility: A jury simulation. *Journal of Personality and Social Psychology, 36*, 126–146.

Hampson, S. E. (1983). Trait ascription and depth of acquaintance: The preference for traits in personality descriptions and its relation to target familiarity. *Journal of Research in Personality, 17,* 398–411.

Hansen, R. D. Commonsense attribution. (1980). *Journal of Personality and Social Psychology, 39,* 996–1009.

Harackiewicz, J. M., Manderlink, G., and Sansone, C. (1984). Rewarding pinball wizardry: Effects of evaluation and cue value on intrinsic interest. *Journal of Personality and Social Psychology, 47,* 287–300.

Harding, C. M., Eiser, J. R., and Kristiansen, C. M. (1982). The representation of mortality statistics and the perceived importance of causes of death. *Journal of Applied Social Psychology, 12,* 169–181.

Harkins, S. G., Latané, B., and Williams, K. (1980). Social loafing: Allocating effort or taking it easy? *Journal of Experimental Social Psychology, 16,* 457–465.

Harkins, S. G., and Petty, R. E. (1982). The effects of task difficulty and task uniqueness on social loafing. *Journal of Personality and Social Psychology, 43,* 1214–1229.

Harries, K. D., and Stadler, S. J. (1983) Determinism revisited: Assault and heat stress in Dallas. *Environment and Behavior, 15,* 235–256.

Harrigan, J. A., and Rosenthal, R. (1983). Physicians' head and body positions as determinants of perceived rapport. *Journal of Applied Social Psychology, 13,* 496–509.

Harris, M. B., Harris, R. J., and Bochner, S. (1982). Fat, four-eyed, and female: Stereotypes of obesity, glasses, and gender. *Journal of Applied Social Psychology, 12,* 503–516.

Hartsough, D. M., and Myers, D. G. (1985). *Disaster work and mental health prevention and control of stress among workers.* Washington, DC: National Institute of Mental Health.

Hartsough, D. M., and Savitsky, J. C. (1984). Three Mile Island: Psychology and environmental policy at a crossroads. *American Psychologist, 39,* 1113–1122.

Harvey, J. H., and Weary, G. (1984). Current issues in attribution theory and research. *Annual Review of Psychology, 35,* 427–459.

Harvey, J. M. (1971). Locus of control shift in administrators. *Perceptual and Motor Skills, 33,* 980–982.

Hassett, J. (1981, November). But that would be wrong . . . *Psychology Today,* pp. 34–35, 37–38, 41, 44, 46, 49–50.

Hastie, R. (1984). Causes and effects of causal attribution. *Journal of Personality and Social Psychology, 46,* 44–55.

Hastie, R., and Kumar, P. A. (1979). Person memory: Personality traits as organizing principles in memory for behaviors. *Journal of Personality and Social Psychology, 37,* 25–38.

Hastrup, J. L., Hotchkiss, A. P., and Johnson, C. A. (1985). Accuracy of knowledge of family history of cardiovascular disorders. *Health Psychology, 4,* 291–306.

Hatch, O. G. (1982). Psychology, society, and politics. *American Psychologist, 37,* 1031–1037.

Hatfield, E. (1983a). Passionate love scale. Personal communication.

———. (1983b). What do women and men want from love and sex? In E. R. Allgeier & N. B. McCormick (eds.), *Changing boundaries: Gender roles and sexual behavior.* Palo Alto, CA: Mayfield.

Hatfield, E., and Sprecher, S. (1986). *Mirror, mirror . . . The importance of looks in everyday life.* Albany, NY: State University of New York Press.

Hatfield, E., and Walster, G. W. (1981). *A new look at love.* Reading, MA: Addison-Wesley.

Hathaway, S. R., and McKinley, J. C. (1940). A multiphasic personality schedule (Minnesota): I. Construction of the schedule. *Journal of Psychology, 10,* 249–254.

Haynes, R. B., Taylor, D. W., and Sackett, D. L. (eds.) (1979). *Compliance in health care.* Baltimore: Johns Hopkins University Press.

Haynes, S., Feinleib, M., and Kannel, W. (1980). The relationship of psychosocial factors to coronary heart disease in the Framingham Study: Eight-year incidence of coronary heart disease. *American Journal of Epidemiology, 111,* 37–58.

Hays, R. B. (1984). The development and maintenance of friendship. *Journal of Social and Personal Relationships, 1,* 75–98.

Heard, A. (1985). Porn in the USA. *New Republic, 193*(16), 12, 14.

Heath, L. (1984). Impact of newspaper crime reports on fear of crime: Multimethodological investigation. *Journal of Personality and Social Psychology, 47,* 263–276.

Hechinger, F. M. (1980, December 30). Studies examine the issue of ethics. *New York Times,* pp. C1, C3.

Heerwagen, J. H., Beach, L. R., and Mitchell, T. R. (1985). Dealing with poor performance: Supervisor attributions and the cost of responding. *Journal of Applied Social Psychology, 15,* 638–655.

Hefner, H. M. (1986). Sexual McCarthyism. *Playboy, 33*(1), 58–59.

Heiby, E., and Becker, J. D. (1980). Effect of filmed modeling on the self-reported frequency of masturbation. *Archives of Sexual Behavior, 9,* 115–121.

Heider, F. (1985). *The psychology of interpersonal relations.* New York: Wiley.

Heimberg, R. G., Acerra, M. C., and Holstein, A. (1985). Partner similarity mediates interpersonal anxiety. *Cognitive Therapy & Research, 9,* 443–453.

Heisler, G. (1974). Ways to deter law violators: Effects of levels of threat and vicarious punishment on cheating. *Journal of Consulting and Clinical Psychology, 42,* 577–582.

Helmreich, R. L., Spence, J. T., and Gibson, R. H. (1982). Sex-role attitudes: 1972–1980. *Personality and Social Psychology Bulletin, 8,* 656–663.

Hemstone, M., and Jaspars, J. (1982). Explanations for racial discrimination: The effects of group decision on intergroup attributions. *European Journal of Social Psychology, 12,* 1–16.

Henderson, J. and Taylor, J. (1985, November 17). Study finds bias in death sentences: Killers of whites risk execution. *Times Union*, p. A–19.

Hendrick, C., and Hendrick, S. (1986). A theory and method of love. *Journal of Personality and Social Psychology, 50*, 392–402.

Henley, N. M. (1973). The politics of touch. In P. Brown (ed.), *Radical psychology*. New York: Harper & Row.

Heshka, S., and Nelson, Y. (1972). Interpersonal speaking distance as a function of age, sex, and relationship. *Sociometry, 35*, 491–498.

Hicks, R. A., Allen, J. G., Armogida, R. E., Gilliland, M. A., and Pellegrini, R. J. (1980). Reduction in sleep duration and Type A behavior. *Bulletin of the Psychonomic Society, 16*, 109–110.

Higgins, E. T., Rholes, W. S., and Jones, C. R. (1977). Category accessibility and impression formation. *Journal of Experimental Social Psychology, 13*, 141–154.

Hill, C. T., Rubin, Z., and Peplau, L. A. (1976). Breakups before marriage: The end of 103 affairs. *Journal of Social Issues, 32*, 147–168.

Hill, C. T., and Stull, D. E. (1981). Sex differences in effects of social and value similarity in same-sex friendship. *Journal of Personality and Social Psychology, 41*, 488–502.

Hiltrop, J. M., and Rubin, J. Z. (1982). Effects of intervention mode and conflict of interest on dispute resolution. *Journal of Personality and Social Psychology, 42*, 665–672.

Hilts, P. J. (1981, July 31). Poll shows school censorship rising. *Albany Times Union*, 1, 4.

Hinsz, V. B., and Davis, J. H. (1984). Persuasive arguments theory, group polarization, and choice shifts. *Personality and Social Psychology Bulletin, 10*, 260–268.

Hirschman, R. S., Leventhal, H., and Glynn, K. (1984). The development of smoking behavior: Conceptualization and supportive cross-sectional survey data. *Journal of Applied Social Psychology, 14*, 184–206.

Hirt, E., and Kimble, C. E. (1981). The home-field advantage in sports: Differences and correlates. Paper presented at the Midwestern Psychological Association, Detroit.

Hochschild, A. R. (1983). *The managed heart*. Berkeley, CA: University of California Press.

Hoffman, L. W. (1979). Maternal employment: 1979. *American Psychologist, 34*, 859–865.

Hoffman, M. L. (1981). Is altruism part of human nature? *Journal of Personality and Social Psychology, 40*, 121–137.

Hokanson, J. E., Burgess, M., and Cohen, M. E. (1963). Effects of displaced aggression on systolic blood pressure. *Journal of Abnormal and Social Psychology, 67*, 214–218.

Holahan, C. J. (1986). Environmental psychology. In M. R. Rosenzweig and L. W. Porter (eds.), *Annual review of psychology*, vol. 37 (pp. 381–407). Palo Alto, CA: Annual Reviews Inc.

Hollander, E. P. (1978). *Leadership dynamics: A practical guide to effective relationships.* New York: Free Press.

Holmes, D. S., McGilley, B. M., and Houston, B. K. (1984). Task-related arousal of Type A and Type B persons: Level of challenge and response specificity. *Journal of Personality and Social Psychology, 46*, 1322–1327.

Holmes, D. S., Solomon, S., Cappo, B. M., and Greenberg, J. L. (1983). Effects of transcendental meditation versus resting on physiological and subjective arousal. *Journal of Applied Social Psychology, 44*, 1245–1252.

Holtzworth-Munroe, A., and Jacobson, N. S. (1985). Causal attributions of married couples: When do they search for causes? What do they conclude when they do? *Journal of Personality and Social Psychology, 48*, 1398–1412.

Hoon, P., Wincze, J., and Hoon, E. (1977). A test of reciprocal inhibition: Are anxiety and sexual arousal in women mutually inhibitory? *Journal of Abnormal Psychology, 86*, 65–74.

Hoppe, C. M. (1979). Interpersonal aggression as a function of subject's sex, subject's sex role identification, opponent's sex, and degree of provocation. *Journal of Personality, 47*, 317–329.

Horvath, T. (1979). Correlates of physical beauty in men and women. *Social Behavior and Personality, 7*, 145–151.

Hosch, H. M., and Platz, S. J. (1984). Self-monitoring and eyewitness accuracy. *Personality and Social Psychology Bulletin, 10*, 289–292.

House, R. J., and Baetz, M. L. (1979). Leadership: Some generalizations and new research directions. In B. M. Staw (ed.), *Research in organizational behavior.* Greenwich, Conn.: JAI Press.

Houston, B. K. (1983). Psychophysiological responsivity and the Type A behavior pattern. *Journal of Research in Personality, 17*, 22–39.

Hovland, C. I., Lumsdaine, A., and Sheffield, F. (1949). Experiments on mass communication. *Studies in social psychology in World War II, 226.* Princeton, NJ: Princeton University Press.

Hovland, C. I., and Weiss, W. (1952). The influence of source credibility on communication effectiveness. *Public Opinion Quarterly, 15*, 635–650.

Howard, G. S. (1985). The role of values in the science of psychology. *American Psychologist, 40*, 255–265.

Hoyer, W. D., and Jacoby, J. (1983). Three-dimensional information acquisition: An application to contraceptive decision-making. In R. P. Bagozzi and A. Tybout (eds.), *Advances in consumer research, 10*, 432–435.

Hudson, W. W., Murphy, G. J., and Nurius, P. S. (1983). A short-form scale to measure liberal vs. conservative orientations toward human sexual expression. *Journal of Sex Research, 19*, 258–272.

Huesmann, L. R. (1982). Television violence and aggressive behavior. In D. Pearl, L. Bouthilet, and J. Lazar (eds.), *Television and behavior*, vol. 2. *Technical reviews* (pp. 220–256). Washington, DC: National Institute of Mental Health.

Hughes, M. T. (1981, July 26). To cheat or not to cheat? *Albany Times-Union*, pp. B-1, B-3.

Hughes, S. K. D. (1974). Criticism and interaction. Unpublished doctoral dissertation, Boston University.

Hull, J. G. (1981). A self-awareness model of the causes and effects of alcohol consumption. *Journal of Abnormal Psychology, 90*, 586–600.

Hull, J. G., and Levy, A. S. (1979). The organizational functions of the self: An alternative to the Duval and Wicklund model of self-awareness. *Journal of Personality and Social Psychology, 37*, 756–768.

Hull, J. G., and Young, R. D. (1983). Self-consciousness, self-esteem, and success-failure as determinants of alcohol consumption in male social drinkers. *Journal of Personality and Social Psychology, 44*, 1097–1109.

Hull, J. G., Young, R. D., and Jouriles, E. (in press). Applications of the self-awareness model of alcohol consumption: Predicting patterns of use and abuse. *Journal of Personality and Social Psychology*.

Humphries, C., Carver, C. S., and Neumann, P. G. (1983). Cognitive characteristics of the Type A coronary-prone behavior pattern. *Journal of Personality and Social Psychology, 44*, 177–187.

Hunt, M. (1974). *Sexual behavior in the 1970s*. Chicago: Playboy.

Hunter, J. E., and Schmidt, F. L. (1983). Quantifying the effects of psychological interventions on employee job performance and work-force productivity. *American Psychologist, 38*, 473–478.

Huston, T. L., Ruggiero, M., Conner, R., and Geiss, G. (1981). Bystander intervention into crime: A study based on naturally-occurring episodes. *Social Psychology Quarterly, 44*, 14–23.

Hyland, M. E. (1985). Do person variables exist in different ways? *American Psychologist, 40*, 1003–1010.

Ickes, W. (1984). Compositions in black and white: Determinants of interaction in interracial dyads. *Journal of Personality and Social Psychology, 47*, 330–341.

Ickes, W., Reidhead, S., and Patterson, M. (1986). Machiavellianism and self-monitoring: As different as "me" and "you." *Social Cognition, 4*, 58–74.

Ickes, W., and Turner, M. (1983). On the social advantages of having an older, opposite-sex sibling: Birth order influences in mixed-sex dyads. *Journal of Personality and Social Psychology, 45*, 210–222.

Imada, A. S., and Hakel, M. D. (1977). Influence of nonverbal communication and rater proximity on impressions and decisions in simulated employment interviews. *Journal of Applied Psychology, 62*, 295–300.

Imig, D. (1985). Cited in C. R. Creekmore, Cities won't drive you crazy. *Psychology today, 17*, 46–53.

Insko, C. A. (1985). Balance theory, the Jordan paradigm, and the Wiest tetrahedron. In L. Berkowitz (ed.), *Advances in experimental social psychology*. New York: Academic Press.

Insko, C. A., Sedlak, A. J., and Lipsitz, A. (1982). A two-valued logic or two-valued balance resolution of the challenge of agreement and attraction effects in p-o-x

triads, and a theoretical perspective on conformity and hedonism. *European Journal of Social Psychology, 12*, 143–167.

Insko, C. A., Smith, R. H., Alicke, M. D., Wade, J., and Taylor, S. (1985). Conformity and group size: The concern with being right and the concern with being liked. *Personality and Social Psychology Bulletin, 11*, 41–50.

Isen, A. M. (1984). Toward understanding the role of affect in cognition. In R. S. Wyer, Jr., and T. K. Srull (eds.), *Handbook of social cognition*, vol. 3. Hillsdale, NJ: Erlbaum.

Isen, A. M., Clark, M., and Schwartz, M. F. (1976). Duration of the effect of good mood on helping: "Footprints on the sands of time." *Journal of Personality and Social Psychology, 34*, 385–393.

Isen, A. M., Horn, N., and Rosenhan, D. L. (1973). Effects of success and failure on children's generosity. *Journal of Personality and Social Psychology, 27*, 239–247.

Isen, A. M., Johnson, M. M. S., Mertz, E., and Robinson, G. F. (1985). The influence of positive affect on the unusualness of word associations. *Journal of Personality and Social Psychology, 48*, 1413–1426.

Istvan, J., Griffitt, W., and Weidner, G. (1983). Sexual arousal and the polarization of perceived sexual attractiveness. *Basic and Applied Social Psychology, 4*, 307–318.

Izard, C. (1977). *Human emotions*. New York: Plenum.

Izraeli, D. N., and Izraeli, D. (1985). Sex effects in evaluating leaders: A replication study. *Journal of Applied Psychology, 70*, 540–546.

Izraeli, D. N., Izraeli, D., and Eden, D. (1985). Giving credit where credit is due: A case of no sex bias in attribution. *Journal of Applied Social Psychology, 15*, 516–530.

Jaccard, J., Brinberg, D., and Ackerman, L. J. (in press). Assessing attribute importance: A comparison of six methods. *Journal of Consumer Research*.

Jackson, C. N., and King, D. C. (1983). The effects of representatives' power within their own organizations on the outcome of a negotiation. *Academy of Management Journal, 26*, 178–185.

Jackson, L. A. (1983). The influence of sex, physical attractiveness, sex role, and occupational sex-linkage on perceptions of occupational suitably. *Journal of Applied Social Psychology, 13*, 31–44.

Jacoby, J. (1976). Consumer psychology: An octennium. In M. R. Rosenzweig and L. W. Porter (eds.), *Annual review of psychology*, vol. 27, (pp. 331–358). Palo Alto, CA: Annual Reviews.

———. (1984). Perspectives on information overload. *Journal of Consumer Research, 10*, 432–435.

Jacoby, J., Chestnut, R. W., and Silberman, W. (1977). Consumer use and comprehension of nutrition information. *Journal of Consumer Research, 4*, 119–128.

Jacoby, J. F., Kolla, D. T., and Blackwell, R. D. (1973). *Consumer behavior*. NY: Holt, Rinehart, & Winston.

Jacoby, J., and Mazursky, D. (1984). Linking brand and retailer images: Do the potential risks outweigh the potential benefits? *Journal of Retailing, 60,* 105–122.

Jaffe, Y., Malamuth, N., Feingold, J., and Feshbach, S. (1974). Sexual arousal and behavioral aggression. *Journal of Personality and Social Psychology, 30,* 759–764.

James, W. (1899). *Talks to teachers on psychology.* New York: Henry Holt.

———. (1950). *The principles of psychology.* New York: Dover.

Janda, L. H., O'Grady, K. E., Nichelous, J., Harsher, D., Denny, C., and Denner, K. (1981). Effects of sex guilt on interpersonal pleasuring. *Journal of Personality and Social Psychology, 40,* 201–209.

Janis, I. L. (1954). Personality correlates of susceptibility to persuasion. *Journal of Personality, 22,* 504–518.

———. (1982). *Groupthink: Psychological studies of policy decisions and fiascoes,* 2nd ed. Boston: Houghton Mifflin.

Jay, S. M., Ozolins, M., Elliott, C. H., and Caldwell, S. (1983). Assessment of children's distress during painful medical procedures. *Health Psychology, 2,* 133–147.

Jeavons, C. M., and Taylor, S. P. (1985). The control of alcohol-related aggression: Redirecting the inebriate's attention to socially appropriate conduct. *Aggressive Behavior, 11,* 93–101.

Jellison, J. M., and Oliver, D. F. (1983). Attitude similarity and attraction: An impression management approach. *Personality and Social Psychology Bulletin, 9,* 111–115.

Jenkins, B. M. (1983). *Some reflections on recent trends in terrorism.* Rand Corporation.

Jenkins, C. D., Zyzanski, S. J., and Rosenman, R. H. (1979). *Jenkins Activity Survey.* New York: Psychological Corporation.

Jenkins, C. D., Zyzanski, S. J., Ryan, T. J., Flessas, A., and Tannenbaum, S. I. (1977). Social insecurity and coronary-prone Type A responses as identifiers of severe atherosclerosis. *Journal of Consulting and Clinical Psychology, 45,* 1060–1067.

Jennings, J. W., Geis, F. L., and Brown, V. (1980). Influence of television commercials on women's self-confidence and independent judgment. *Journal of Personality and Social Psychology, 38,* 203–210.

Jessor, R., Costa, F., Jessor, L., and Donovan, J. E. (1983). Time of first intercourse: A prospective study. *Journal of Personality and Social Psychology, 44,* 608–626.

Johansson, G., Collins, A., and Collins, V. P. (1983). Male and female psychoneuroendocrine response to examination stress: A case report. *Motivation and Emotion, 7,* 1–9.

Johnson, B. L., and Kilmann, P. R. (1975). The relationship between recalled parental attitudes and internal-external control. *Journal of Clinical Psychology, 31,* 40–42.

Johnson, J. T., Jemmott, J. B., III, and Pettigrew, T. F. (1984). Causal attribution and dispositional inference: Evidence of inconsistent judgments. *Journal of Experimental Social Psychology, 20,* 567–585.

Johnson, T. E., and Rule, B. G. (1986). Mitigating circum-

stance information, censure, and aggression. *Journal of Personality and Social Psychology, 50,* 537–542.

Jones, A. P. (1984). Organizational reward systems: Implications for climate. *Motivation and Emotion, 8,* 259–274.

Jones, E. E. (1964). *Ingratiation: A social psychological analysis.* New York: Appleton-Century-Crofts.

Jones, E. E., and Davis, K. E. (1965). From acts to dispositions: The attribution process in person perception. In L. Berkowitz (ed.), *Advances in experimental social psychology,* vol. 2. New York: Academic Press.

Jones, E. E., and McGillis, D. (1976). Corresponding inferences and the attribution cube: A comparative reappraisal. In J. H. Harvey, W. J. Ickes, and R. F. Kidd (eds.), *New directions in attribution research,* vol. 1. Hillsdale, NJ: Erlbaum.

Jones, E. E., and Nisbett, R. E. (1971). *The actor and the observer: Divergent perceptions of the causes of behavior.* Morristown, NJ: General Learning Press.

Jones, J. W. (1981). Dishonesty, burnout, and unauthorized work break extensions. *Personality and Social Psychology Bulletin, 7,* 406–409.

Jones, W. H. (1982). Loneliness and social behavior. In L. A. Peplau and D. Perlman (eds.), *Loneliness: A sourcebook of current theory, research, and therapy.* New York: Wiley.

Jones, W. H., Freeman, J. A., and Goswick, R. A. (1981). The persistence of loneliness: Self and other determinants. *Journal of Personality, 49,* 27–48.

Jones, W. H., Hannson, R., and Phillips, A. L. (1978). Physical attractiveness and judgments of psychotherapy. *Journal of Social Psychology, 105,* 79–84.

Jones, W. H., Hansson, R., and Smith, T. G. (1980). *Loneliness and love: Implications for psychological and interpersonal functioning.* Unpublished manuscript, University of Tulsa.

Jones, W. H., Hobbs, S. A., and Hockenbury, D. (1982). Loneliness and social skill deficits. *Journal of Personality and Social Psychology, 42,* 682–689.

Jorgensen, R. S., and Houston, B. K. (1981). The Type A behavior pattern, sex differences, and cardiovascular response to and recovery from stress. *Motivation and Emotion, 5,* 201–214.

Kabanoff, B. (1985). Potential influence structures as sources of interpersonal conflict in groups and organizations. *Organizational Behavior and Human Decision Processes, 36,* 113–141.

Kagehiro, D. K., and Werner, C. M. (1981). Divergent perceptions of jail inmates and correctional officers: The "blame the other expect to be blamed" effect. *Journal of Applied Social Psychology, 11,* 507–528.

Kahneman, D., and Tversky, A. (1982a). On the psychology of prediction. In D. Kahneman, P. Slovic, and A. Tversky (eds.), *Judgment Under Uncertainty* (pp. 48–68). New York: Cambridge University Press.

———. (1982b). Psychology pf preferences. *Scientific American,* pp. 161–173.

Kandel, D. B. (1978). Similarity in real-life adolescent

friendship pairs. *Journal of Personality and Social Psychology, 36,* 306–312.

Kandel, D. B., Single, E., and Kessler, R. C. (1976). The epidemiology of drug use among New York State high school students: Distribution, trends, and change in rates of use. *American Journal of Public Health, 66,* 43–53.

Kanekar, S., Pinto, N. J. P., and Mazumdar, D. (1985). Causal and moral responsibility of victims of rape and robbery. *Journal of Applied Social Psychology, 15,* 622–637.

Kanin, E. J., and Parcell, S. R. (1977). Sexual aggression: A second look at the offended female. *Archives of Sexual Behavior, 6,* 67–76.

Kantola, S. J., Slyme, G. J., and Nesdale, A. R. (1983). *Journal of Applied Social Psychology, 13,* 164–182.

Kaplan, M. F., and Miller, L. E. (1978). Reducing the effects of juror bias. *Journal of Personality and Social Psychology, 36,* 1443–1455.

———. (1979). Effects of juror's identification with the victim depends on likelihood of victimization. *Law and Human Behavior.*

Kaplan, R. M., Atkins, C. J., and Reinsch, S. (1984). Specific efficacy expectations mediate exercise compliance in patients with COPD. *Health Psychology, 3,* 223–242.

Kaplan, R. M., and Bush, J. W. (1982). Health-related quality of life measurement for evaluation research and policy analysis. *Health Psychology, 1,* 61–80.

Karlin, R. A., Rosen, L., and Epstein, Y. (1979). Three into two doesn't go: A followup of the effects of overcrowded dormitory rooms. *Personality and Social Psychology Bulletin, 5,* 391–395.

Karniol, R. (1982). Behavioral and cognitive correlates of various immanent justice responses in children: Deterrent versus punitive moral systems. *Journal of Personality and Social Psychology, 43,* 881–820.

Kasl, S. V. (1980). Cardiovascular risk reduction in a community setting: Some comments. *Journal of Consulting and Clinical Psychology, 48,* 143–149.

Kassin, S. M., and Juhnke, R. (1983). Juror experience and decision making. *Journal of Personality and Social Psychology, 44,* 1182–1191.

Kassin, S. M., and Wrightsman, L. S. (1983). The construction and validation of a juror bias scale. *Journal of Research in Personality, 17,* 423–442.

Katkovsky, W., Crandall, V. C., and Good, S. (1967). Parental antecedents of children's beliefs in internal-external control of reinforcement in intellectual achievement situations. *Child Development, 28,* 765–776.

Katzell, R. A., and Guzzo, R. A. (1983). Psychological approaches to productivity improvement. *American Psychologist, 38,* 468–472.

Kaufman, M. T. (1980, November 16). Love upsetting Bombay's view of path to altar. *New York Times,* 12.

Kelley, H. H. (1972). Attribution in social interaction. In E. E. Jones et al. (eds.), *Attribution: Perceiving the causes of behavior.* Morristown, NJ: General Learning Press.

Kelley, H. H., and Michela, J. L. (1980). Attribution theory and research. *Review of Psychology, 31,* 457–501.

Kelley, K. (1985a). The effects of sexual and/or aggressive film exposure on helping, hostility, and attitudes about the sexes. *Journal of Research in Personality, 19,* 472–483.

———. (1985b, September). *Testimony presented to the U. S. Attorney General's Commission on Pornography.* Paper presented at the U. S. Justice Department Hearings, Houston.

———. (1985c). Sexual attitudes as determinants of the motivational properties of exposure to erotica. *Personality and Individual Differences, 6,* 391–393.

———. (1985d). Sex, sex guilt, and authoritarianism: Differences in responses to explicit heterosexual and masturbatory slides. *Journal of Sex Research, 21,* 68–85.

———. (1985e). Sexual fantasy and attitudes as functions of sex of subject and content of erotica. *Imagination, Cognition and Personality, 4,* 339–347.

———. (1986). *Health correlates of self-destructiveness.* Manuscript submitted for publication, State University of New York at Albany.

———. (1986). *Females, males, and sexuality.* Albany, NY: State University of New York Press.

Kelley, K., and Byrne, D. (1983). Assessment of sexual responding: Arousal, affect, and behavior. In J. Cacioppo and R. Petty (eds.), *Social psychophysiology.* New York: Guilford Press.

Kelley, K., Byrne, D., Przybyla, D. P. J., Eberly, C. C., Eberly, B. W., Greendlinger, V., Wan, C. K., and Grosky, J. (1985). Chronic self-destructiveness: Conceptualization, measurement, and initial validation of the construct. *Motivation and Emotion, 9,* 135–151.

Kelley, K., Cheung, F., Rodriguez-Carrillo, P., Singh, R., Wan, C. K., and Becker, M. C. (1986). Chronic self-destructiveness and locus of control in cross-cultural perspective. *Journal of Social Psychology.*

Kelley, K., Miller, C. T., Byrne, D., and Bell, P. A. (1983). Facilitating sexual arousal via anger, aggression, or dominance. *Motivation and Emotion, 7,* 191–202.

Kelley, K., and Musialowski, D. (1986a, April). *Female sexual victimization and effects of warnings about violent pornography.* Paper presented at the meeting of the Eastern Psychological Association, New York City.

———. (1986b). *Personality correlates of chronic self-destructiveness.* Manuscript submitted for publication, State University of New York at Albany.

Kelman, H. C. (1967). Human use of human subjects: The problem of deception in social psychological experiments. *Psychological Bulletin, 67,* 1–11.

Kenney, D. A., and Zaccaro, S. J. (1983). An estimate of variance due to traits in leadership. *Journal of Applied Psychology, 68,* 678–685.

Kenrick, D. T. (1986). How strong is the case against contemporary social and personality psychology? A response to Carlson. *Journal of Personality and Social Psychology, 50,* 839–844.

Kenrick, D. T., Cialdini, R. B., and Linder, D. E. (1979). Misattribution under fear-producing circumstances:

Four failures to replicate. *Personality and Social Psychology Bulletin, 5,* 329–334.

Kenrick, D. T., and Gutierres, S. E. (1980). Contrast effects and judgments of physical attractiveness: When beauty becomes a social problem. *Journal of Personality and Social Psychology, 38,* 131–140.

Kenrick, D. T., and Johnson, G. A. (1979). Interpersonal attraction in aversive environments: A problem for the classical conditioning paradigm? *Journal of Personality and Social Psychology, 37,* 572–579.

Kenrick, D. T., and MacFarlane, S. W. (1986). Ambient temperature and horn honking: A field study of the heat/aggression relationship. *Environment and Behavior, 18,* 179–191.

Kenrick, D. T., and Stringfield, D. O. (1980). Personality traits and the eye of the beholder: Crossing some traditional philosophical boundaries in the search for consistency in all the people. *Psychological Review, 87,* 88–104.

Kent, G. G., Davis, J. D., and Shapiro, D. A. (1981). Effect of mutual acquaintance on the construction of conversation. *Journal of Experimental Social Psychology, 17,* 197–209.

Keown, C., Slovic, P., and Lichenstein, S. (1984). Attitudes of physicians, pharmacists, and lay persons toward seriousness and need for disclosure of prescription side effects. *Health Psychology, 3,* 1–11.

Kerber, K. W. (1984). The perception of nonemergency helping situations: Costs, rewards, and the altruistic personality. *Journal of Personality, 52,* 177–187.

Kernis, M. H., and Wheeler, L. (1981). Beautiful friends and ugly strangers: Radiation and contrast effects in perceptions of same-sex pairs. *Personality and Social Psychology Bulletin, 7,* 617–620.

Kerr, N. L. (1978a). Beautiful and blameless: Effects of victim awareness and responsibility on mock juror verdicts. *Personality and Social Psychology Bulletin, 4,* 479–482.

———. (1978b). Severity of prescribed penalty and mock jurors' verdicts. *Journal of Personality and Social Psychology, 36,* 1431–1442.

———. (1981). Social transition schemes: Charting the group's road to agreement. *Journal of Personality and Social Psychology, 41,* 684–702.

———. (1983). Social transition schemes: Model, method, and applications. In J. H. Davis and H. Brandstatter (eds.), *Group decision making processes.* New York: Academic Press.

Kerr, N. L., and MacCoun, R. J. (1985). The effects of jury size and polling method on the process and product of jury deliberation. *Journal of Personality and Social Psychology, 48,* 349–363.

Kiecolt-Glaser, J. K., Glaser, R., Williger, D., Stout, J., Messick, G., Sheppard, S., Ricker, D., Romisher, S. C., Briner, W., Bonnell, G., and Donnerberg, R. (1985). Psychosocial enhancement of immuno-competence in a geriatric population. *Health Psychology, 4,* 25–42.

Kiesler, C. A. (1985). Psychology and public policy. In E. M. Altmaier and M. E. Meyer (eds.), *Applied specialties in psychology* (pp. 375–390). New York: Random House.

Kiesler, C. A., Collins, B. E., and Miller, N. (1969). *Attitude change: A critical analysis of theoretical approaches.* New York: Wiley.

Kiesler, C. A., and Kiesler, S. B. (1969). *Conformity.* Reading, MA: Addison-Wesley.

Kiesling, S. (1983, February). Miles from A's to B's. *American Health, 25.*

Kilham, W., and Mann, L. (1974). Level of destructive obedience as a function of transmitter and executant roles in the Milgram obedience paradigm. *Journal of Personality and Social Psychology, 29,* 696–702.

King, L. (1986, June 2). Sex habits explored in new survey. *Albany Times Union,* A-5.

Kinsey, A. C., Pomeroy, W., and Martin, C. (1948). *Sexual behavior in the human male.* Philadelphia: W. B. Saunders.

Kinsey, A. C., Pomeroy, W., Martin, C., and Gebhard, P. (1953). *Sexual behavior in the human female.* Philadelphia: W. B. Saunders.

Kipnis, D. (1984). *The powerholders.* Chicago: University of Chicago Press.

Kirmeyer, S. L. (1984). Observing the work of police dispatchers: Work overload in service organizations. In S. Oskamp (ed.), *Applied social psychology annual 5: Applications in organizational settings* (pp. 45–66). Beverly Hills, CA: Sager.

Kirscht, J. P. (1983). Preventive health behavior: A review of research and issues. *Health Psychology, 2,* 277–301.

Kleinke, C. L., Meeker, F. B., and LaFong, C. (1974). Effects of gaze, touch, and use of name on evaluation of "engaged" couples. *Journal of Research in Personality, 7,* 368–373.

Kleinke, C. L., and Staneski, R. A. (1980). First impressions of female bust size. *Journal of Social Psychology, 110,* 123–134.

Klentz, B., and Beaman, A. L. (1981). The effects of type of information and method of dissemination on the reporting of a shoplifter. *Journal of Applied Psychology, 11,* 64–82.

Klirs, E. G., and Revelle, W. (1986). Predicting variability from perceived situational similarity. *Journal of Research in Personality, 20,* 34–50.

Knapp, M. L. (1978). *Nonverbal communication in human interaction.* New York: Holt, Rinehart, & Winston.

Knight, G. P. (1980). Behavioral similarity, confederate strategy, and sex composition of dyad as determinants of interpersonal judgments and behavior in the prisoner's dilemma game. *Journal of Research in Personality, 14,* 91–103.

Knight, G. P., and Dubro, A. F. (1984). Cooperative, competitive, and individualistic social values: An individualized regression and clustering approach. *Journal of Personality and Social Psychology, 46,* 98–105.

Knowlton, W. A., Jr., and Mitchell, T. R. (1980). Effects of casual attributions on a supervisor's evaluation of subordinate performance. *Journal of Applied Psychology,* 65, 459–466.

Knox, R. E., and Safford, R. K. (1976). Group caution at the race track. *Journal of Experimental Social Psychology,* 12, 317–324.

Koch, J. L., Tung, R., Gmelch, W., and Swent, B. (1982). Job stress among school administrators: Factorial dimensions and differential effects. *Journal of Applied Psychology,* 67, 493–499.

Kogan, N., and Wallach, M. A. (1964). *Risk taking: A study in cognition and personality.* New York: Holt, Rinehart, & Winston.

Kohlberg, L. (1981). *The philosophy of moral development.* New York: Harper & Row.

Komorita, S. S., and Lapworth, C. W. (1982). Cooperative choice among individuals versus groups in an N-person dilemma situation. *Journal of Personality and Social Psychology,* 42, 487–496.

Konecni, V. J. (1975). Annoyance, type and duration of post-annoynance activity, and aggression: The "carthartic" effect. *Journal of Experimental Psychology: General,* 104, 76–102.

Konecni, V. J., Libuser, L., Morton, H., and Ebbesen, E. G. (1975). Effects of a violation of personal space on escape and helping responses. *Journal of Experimental Social Psychology,* 11, 288–299.

Koop, C. E. (1983). Perspectives on future health care. *Health Psychology,* 2, 303–312.

Korte, C. (1980). Urban-nonurban differences in social behavior and social psychological models of urban impact. *Journal of Social Issues,* 36, 29–51.

————. (1981). Constraints on helping in an urban environment. In J. P. Rushton and R. M. Sorrentino (eds.), *Altruism and helping behavior.* Hillsdale, NJ: Erlbaum.

Krafft-Ebing, R. von. (1886). *Psychopathia sexualis.* Philadelphia: F. A. Davis, 1894.

Krantz, D. S., and Glass, D. C. (1984). Personality, behavior patterns, and physical illness: Conceptual and methodological issues. In W. D. Gentry (ed.), *Handbook of behavioral medicine* (pp. 38–86). New York: Guilford.

Krantz, D. S., Grunberg, N. E., and Baum, A. (1985). Health psychology. In M. R. Rosenzweig and L. W. Porter (eds.), *Annual review of psychology,* vol. 36, pp. 349–383. Palo Alto, CA: Annual Reviews, Inc.

Kremer, J. F., and Stephens, L. (1983). Attributions and arousal as mediators of mitigation's effects on retaliation. *Journal of Personality and Social Psychology,* 45, 335–343.

Kruglanski, A. W., Friedland, N., and Farkesh, E. (1984). Lay persons' sensitivity to statistical information: The case of high perceived applicability. *Journal of Personality and Social Psychology,* 46, 503–518.

Krulewitz, J. E., and Nash, J. E. (1980). Effects of sex role attitudes and similarity on men's rejection of male homosexuals. *Journal of Personality and Social Psychology,* 38, 67–74.

Krupat, E., and Guild, W. (1980). Defining the city: The use of objective and subjective measures of community description. *Journal of Social Issues,* 36, 9–28.

Kuhlman, D. M., and Marshello, A. F. J. (1975). Individual differences in game motivation as moderators of pre-programmed strategy effects in prisoner's dilemma. *Journal of Personality and Social Psychology,* 32, 922–931.

Kuiper, N. A., MacDonald, M. R., and Derry, P. (1983). Parameters of self-reference in depression. In J. Suls and A. G. Greenwald (eds.), *Social psychological perspectives on the self,* vol. 2 (pp. 191–217). Hillsdale, NJ: Erlbaum.

Kulik, J. A., and Brown, R. (1979). Frustration, attribution of blame, and aggression. *Journal of Experimental Social Psychology,* 15, 183–194.

Kupferberg, S. (1980). The party line: Tupperware and capitalism. *The New Republic,* 183(24), 10–13.

Kurtines, W. M. (1986). Moral behavior as rule governed behavior: Person and situation effects on moral decision making. *Journal of Personality and Social Psychology,* 50, 789–791.

Kutchinsky, B. (1985). Pornography and its effects in Denmark and the United States. *Comparative Social Research,* 8.

La Chance, L. C., Chestnut, R. W., and Lubitz, A. (1977). The "decorative" female model: Sexual stimuli and the recognization of advertisements. *Journal of Advertising,* 6, 11–14.

Lamberth, J., Krieger, E., and Shay, S. S. (1982). Juror decision making: A case of attitude change mediated by authoritarianism. *Journal of Research in Personality,* 16, 419–434.

Lamm, H., and Myers, D. G. (1978). Group-induced polarization of attitudes and behavior. In L. Berkowitz (ed.), *Advances in experimental social psychology.* New York: Academic Press.

La Morto-Corse, A. M., and Carver, C. S. (1980). Recipient reactions to aid: Effects of locus of initiation, attributions, and individual differences. *Bulletin of the Psychonomic Society,* 16, 265–268.

Landers, A. (1977, March 28). "Like spouse?" Poll startles. *Field Enterprises.*

Laner, M. R. (1983). Courtship abuse and aggression: Contextual aspects. *Sociological Spectrum,* 3, 69–83.

Langer, E. J. (1983). *The psychology of control.* Beverly Hills, CA: Sage.

Langer, E. J., Bashner, R. S., and Chanowitz, B. (1985). Decreasing prejudice by increasing discrimination. *Journal of Personality and Social Psychology,* 49, 113–120.

Langer, E. J., and Imber, L. (1980). The role of mindfulness in the perception of deviance. *Journal of Personality and Social Psychology,* 39, 360–367.

LaRocco, J. M. (1985). Effects of job conditions on worker perceptions: Ambient stimuli vs. group influence. *Journal of Applied Social Psychology,* 15, 735–757.

Larson, J. R., Jr. (1985). Supervisor's performance feedback to subordinates: The inpact of subordinate performance valence and outcome dependence. *Organizational Behavior and Human Decision Processes, 37,* 391–408.

Latané, B., and Dabbs, J. M., Jr. (1975). Sex, group size, and helping in three cities. *Sociometry, 38,* 180–194.

Latané, B., and Darley, J. M. (1970). *The unresponsive bystander: Why doesn't he help?* New York: Appleton-Century-Crofts.

Latané, B., and Rodin, J. (1969). A lady in distress: Inhibiting effects of friends and strangers on bystander intervention. *Journal of Experimental Social Psychology, 5,* 189–202.

Latané, B., Williams, K., and Harkins, S. (1979). Many hands make light the work: The causes and consequences of social loafing. *Journal of Personality and Social Psychology, 37,* 822–832.

Latané, B., and Wolf, S. (1981). The social impact of majorities and minorities. *Psychological Review, 88,* 438–453.

Lau, R. R. (1982b). Origins of health locus of control beliefs. *Journal of Personality and Social Psychology, 42,* 322–334.

Lau, R. R., and Hartman, K. A. (1983). Common sense representations of common illnesses. *Health Psychology, 2,* 167–185.

Lau, S. (1982a). The effect of smiling on person perception. *Journal of Social Psychology, 117,* 63–67.

Laudenslager, M. L., and Reite, M. L. (1984). Losses and separations: Immunological consequences and health implications. *Review of personality and social psychology: Emotions, relationship and health,* vol. 5, (pp. 285–312). Beverly Hills, CA: Sage Publications.

Laughlin, P. R. (1980). Social combination processes of cooperative problem-solving groups on verbal intellective tasks. In M. Fishbein (ed.), *Progress in social psychology.* Hillsdale, NJ: Erlbaum.

Laughlin, P. R., and Earley, P. R. (1982). Social combination models, persuasive arguments theory, social comparison theory, and choice shift. *Journal of Personality and Social Psychology, 42,* 273–280.

Lavrakas, P. J. (1975). Female preferences for male physiques. *Journal of Research in Personality, 9,* 324–334.

Lawler, E. E., III (1982). Strategies for improving the quality of work life. *American Psychologist, 37,* 486–493.

———. (1985, January/February). Quality circles after the fad. *Harvard Business Review,* pp. 65–71.

Lawler, E. J., and MacMurray, B. K. (1980). Bargaining toughness: A qualification of level-of-aspiration and reciprocity hypotheses. *Journal of Applied Social Psychology, 34,* 885–894.

Lazarus, R. S. (1984). On the primacy of cognition. *American Psychologist, 39,* 124–129.

Lazarus, R. S., and Folkman, S. (1984). *Stress, appraisal and coping.* New York: Springer.

Lebo, C. P., and Oliphant, K. P. (1968). Music as a source of acoustical trauma. *Laryngoscope, 78,* 1211–1218.

Lee, L. (1984). Sequences in separation: A framework for investigating endings of the personal (romantic) relationship. *Journal of Social and Personal Relationships, 1,* 49–73.

Lee, R. V. (1980). The case for chastity. *Medical Aspects of Human Sexuality, 14*(12), 57–58.

Lefcourt, H. M. (1982). *Locus of control: Current trends in theory and research,* 2nd ed. Hillsdale, NJ: Erlbaum.

Leippe, M. R. (1985). The influence of eyewitness non-identifications on mock-jurors' judgments of a court case. *Journal of Applied Social Psychology, 15,* 656–672.

Lemery, C. R. (1983). *Children's sexual knowledge as a function of parent's affective orientation to sexuality and parent-child communication about sex: A causal analysis.* Unpublished master's thesis, University of Western Ontario, London, Ontario.

Lenfant, C., and Schweizer, M. (1985). Contributions of health-related biobehavioral research to the prevention of cardiovascular diseases. *American Psychologist, 40,* 217–220.

Lentz, S. L., and Zeiss, A. M. (1984). Fantasy and sexual arousal in college women: An empirical investigation. *Imagination, Cognition and Personality, 3,* 185–202.

Leo, J. (1983). Waterbeds and willow worlds. *Time, 122*(5), p. 71.

———. (1985). Getting a headlock on wedlock. *Time, 126*(19), p. 96.

Leonard, K. E., and Taylor, S. P. (1983). Exposure to pornography, permissive and nonpermissive cues, and male aggression toward females. *Motivation and Emotion, 7,* 291–299.

Lepper, M., and Greene, D. (eds.) (1978). *The hidden costs of reward.* Hillsdale, NJ: Erlbaum.

Lesnik-Oberstein, M., and Cohen, L. (1984). Cognitive style, sensation-seeking, and assortative mating. *Journal of Personality and Social Psychology, 46,* 112–117.

Leung, K., and Bond, M. H. (1984). The impact of cultural collectivism in reward allocation. *Journal of Personality and Social Psychology, 47,* 793–804.

Leventhal, G. S. (1976). The distribution of rewards and resources in groups and organizations. In L. Berkowitz (ed.), *Advances in experimental social psychology,* vol. 9. New York: Academic Press.

Leventhal, H., and Nerenz, D. (1983). Implications of stress research for the treatment of stress disorders. In D. Meichenbaum and M. Jarenko (eds.), *Stress reduction and prevention* (pp. 5–38). NY: Plenum Press.

Leventhal, H., Singer, R., and Jones, S. (1965). The effects of fear and specificity of recommendation upon attitudes and behavior. *Journal of Personality and Social Psychology, 2,* 20–29.

Levine, M. P., and Moore, B. S. (1979, September). *Trans-situational effects of lack of control and coronary-prone behavior.* Paper presented at the meeting of the American Psychological Association, New York.

Levinger, G. (1980). Toward the analysis of close relationships. *Journal of Experimental Social Psychology, 16,* 510–544.

Levitt, M. J. (1980). Contingent feedback, familiarization, and infant affect: How a stranger becomes a friend. *Developmental Psychology, 16,* 425–432.

Levy, S. (1979). Authoritarianism and information processing. *Bulletin of the Psychonomic Society, 13,* 240–242.

Levy, S. M., Herberman, R. B., Maluish, A. M., Schlien, B., and Lippman, M. (1985). Prognostic risk assessment in primary breast cancer by behavioral and immunological parameters. *Health Psychology, 4,* 99–113.

Lewin, K., Lippitt, R., and White, R. K. (1939). Patterns of aggressive behavior in experimentally created "social climates." *Journal of Social Psychology, 10,* 271–299.

Leyens, J. P., Camino, L., Parke, R. D., and Berkowitz, L. (1975). Effects of movie violence on aggression in a field setting as a function of group dominance and cohesion. *Journal of Personality and Social Psychology, 32,* 346–360.

Liebert, R. M., and Baron, R. A. (1972). Some immediate effects of televised violence on children's behavior. *Developmental Psychology, 6,* 469–475.

Liebert, R. M., Sprafkin, J. N., and Davidson, E. S. (1982). *The early window: Effects of television on children and youth* (2nd ed.). New York: Pergamon.

Liem, R., and Raymono, P. (1982). Health and social costs of unemployment. *American Psychologist, 37,* 1116–1123.

Linder, D. E., Cooper, J., and Jones, E. E. (1967). Decision freedom as a determinant of the role of incentive magnitude in attitude change. *Journal of Personality and Social Psychology, 6,* 245–254.

Linn, R. T., and Hodge, G. K. (1982). Locus of control in childhood hyperactivity. *Journal of Consulting and Clinical Psychology, 50,* 592–593.

Linville, P. W. (1982). The complexity-extremity effect and age-based stereotyping. *Journal of Personality and Social Psychology, 42,* 183–211.

Lipson, A. L., Przybyla, D. P. J., and Byrne, D. (1983). Physical attractiveness, self-awareness, and mirror-gazing behavior. *Bulletin of the Psychonomic Society, 21,* 115–116.

Littlel, L. (1981, August 17). Sad country tunes may turn your brown eyes red. *Albany Times-Union,* p. 1.

Lockard, J. S., Kirkevold, B. C., and Kalk, D. F. (1980). Cost-benefit indexes of deception in nonviolent crime. *Bulletin of the Psychonomic Society, 16,* 303–306.

Locke, E. A., Shaw, K. N., Saari, L. M., and Latham, G. P. (1981). Goal setting and task performance: 1969–1980. *Psychological Bulletin, 90,* 125–152.

Locksley, A., Ortiz, V., and Hepburn, C. (1980). Social categorization and discriminatory behavior: Extinguishing the minimal intergroup discrimination effect. *Journal of Personality and Social Psychology, 39,* 773–783.

Loftus, E. F. (1980). *Eyewitness testimony.* Cambridge, MA: Harvard University Press.

Logan, J., and Molotch, H. (in press). *Urban fortunes.* Berkeley, CA: University of California Press.

Lord, C. G., Ross, L. and Lepper, M. R. (1979). Biased assimilation and attitude polarization: The effects of prior theories on subsequently considered evidence. *Journal of Personality and Social Psychology, 37,* 2098–2109.

Lorenz, K. (1966). *On aggression.* New York: Harcourt, Brace, & World.

———. (1974). *Civilized man's eight deadly sins.* New York: Harcourt, Brace, Jovanovich.

Loye, D., Gorney, R., and Steele, G. (1977). An experimental field study. *Journal of Communication, 27,* 206–216.

Lueger, R. J. (1980). Person and situation factors influencing transgression in behavior-problem adolescents. *Journal of Abnormal Psychology, 89,* 453–458.

Lumpkin, J. R. (1986). The relationship between locus of control and age: New evidence. *Journal of Social Behavior and Personality, 1,* 245–252.

Lurigio, A. J., and Carroll, J. S. (1985). Probation officers' schemata of offenders: Content, development, and impact on treatment decisions. *Journal of Personality and Social Psychology, 48,* 112–126.

Lynch, M. D., Norem-Hebeisen, and Gergen, K. J. (1981). *Self-concept: Advances in theory and research.* Cambridge, MA: Ballinger.

Lynn, M., and Shurgot, B. A. (1984). Responses to lonely hearts advertisements: Effects of reported physical attractiveness, physique, and coloration. *Personality and Social Psychology Bulletin, 10,* 349–357.

Maas, A., and Brigham, J. C. (1982). Eyewitness identifications: The role of attention and encoding specificity. *Personality and Social Psychology Bulletin, 8,* 54–59.

Maas, A., and Clark, R. D., III (1984). Hidden impact of minorities: Fifteen years of minority influence research. *Psychological Bulletin, 95,* 428–450.

Mackie, D. M. (1986). Social identification effects in group polarization. *Journal of Personality and Social Psychology, 40,* 720–728.

MacKinnon, D. W. (1933). *The violation of prohibitions in the solving of problems.* Unpublished doctoral dissertation, Harvard University, Cambridge.

Maddux, J. E., and Stoltenberg, C. D. (1983). Clinical social psychology and social clinical psychology: A proposal for peaceful coexistence. *Journal of Social and Clinical Psychology, 1,* 289–299.

Madigan, R. M. (1985). Comparable worth judgments: A measurement properties analysis. *Journal of Applied Psychology, 70,* 137–147.

Magoun, H. W. (1981). John B. Watson and the study of human sexual behavior. *Journal of Sex Research, 17,* 368–378.

Major, B., Carrington, P. I., and Carnevale, P. J. D. (1984). Physical attractiveness and self-esteem: Attributions for praise from an other-sex evaluator. *Personality and Social Psychology Bulletin, 10,* 43–50.

Major, B., and Deaux, K. (1982). Individual differences in justice behavior. In J. Greenberg and R. Cohen (eds.), *Equity and justice in social behavior.* New York: Academic Press.

Major, B., and Konar, E. (1984). An investigation of sex differences in pay expectations and their possible causes. *Academy of Management Journal, 27,* 777–792.

Major, B., Vanderslice, V., and McFarlin, D. B. (1985). Effects of pay expected on pay received: The confirmatory nature of initial expectations. *Journal of Applied Social Psychology, 14,* 399–412.

Malamuth, N. M. (1981). Rape proclivity among males. *Journal of Social Issues, 37,* 138–157.

———. (1984). Violence against women: Cultural and individual cases. In N. M. Malamuth and E. Donnerstein (eds.), *Pornography and sexual aggression.* New York: Academic Press.

———. (1985, September). *The mass media as an indirect cause of sexual aggression.* Paper presented at the U. S. Justice Department Hearings, Houston.

———. (1986). Predictors of naturalistic sexual aggression. *Journal of Personality and Social Psychology., 50,* 953–962.

Malamuth, N. M., Check, J. V. P., and Briere, J. (1986). Sexual arousal in response to aggression: Ideological, aggressive, and sexual correlates. *Journal of Personality and Social Psychology, 50,* 330–340.

Malamuth, N. M., and Donnerstein, E., (eds.) (1984). *Pornography and sexual aggression.* New York: Academic Press.

Malinowski, B. (1929). *The sexual life of savages in North-Western Melanesia.* New York: Halcyon House.

Mallick, S. K., and McCandless, B. R. (1966). A study of catharsis of aggression.

Malloy, T. E., and Kenny, D. A. (1986). The social relations model: An integrative method for personality research. *Journal of Personality, 54,* 199–225.

Manning, M. M., and Wright, T. L. (1983). Self-efficacy expectancies, outcome expectancies, and the persistence of pain control in childbirth. *Journal of Personality and Social Psychology, 45,* 421–431.

Marks, E. L., Penner, L. A., and Stone, A. V. W. (1982). Helping as a function of empathic responses and sociopathy. *Journal of Research in Personality, 16,* 1–20.

Marks, G., and Miller, N. (1982). Target attractiveness as a mediator of assumed attitude similarity. *Personality and Social Psychology Bulletin, 8,* 728–735.

Marks, G., Miller, N., and Maruyama, G. (1981). Effect of targets' physical attractiveness on assumptions of similarity. *Journal of Personality and Social Psychology, 41,* 198–206.

Marks, M. L. (1986). The question of quality circles. *Psychology Today, 20,* (3), pp. 36–38, 42, 44, 46.

Markus, H. (1978). The effect of mere presence on social facilitation: An unobtrusive test. *Journal of Experimental Social Psychology, 14,* 389–397.

Markus, H., and Smith, J. (1982). The influence of self-schemata on the perception of others. In N. Cantor and J. Kihlstrom (eds.), *Personality, cognition, and social interaction.* Hillsdale, NJ: Erlbaum.

Markus, H., and Zajonc, R. B. (1985). The cognitive perspective in social psychology. In G. Lindzey and E. Aronson (eds.), *Handbook of social psychology.* New York: Random House.

Marshall, W. L. (1985, September). *The use of pornography by sex offenders.* Paper presented at the U. S. Justice Department Hearings, Houston.

Marshall, W. L., and Barbaree, H. E. (1984). A behavioral perspective of rape. *International Journal of Law and Psychiatry, 7,* 51–77.

Martens, R. (1969). Palmar sweating and the presence of an audience. *Journal of Experimental Social Psychology, 5,* 371–374.

Martin, D. J., Abramson, L. Y., and Alloy, L. B. (1984). The illusion of control for self and others in depressed and nondepressed college students. *Journal of Personality and Social Psychology, 46,* 125–136.

Martindale, D. A. (1971). Territorial dominance behavior in dyadic verbal interactions. *Proceedings of the Annual Convention of the American Psychological Association, 6,* 305–306.

Maruyama, G., and Miller, N. (1981). Physical attractiveness and personality. In B. Maher (ed.), *Advances in Experimental Research on Personality,* vol. 10. New York: Academic Press.

Maslach, C., and Jackson, S. E. (1984). Burnout in organizational settings. In S. Oskamp, *Applied social psychology annual 5: Applications in organizational settings* (pp. 133–153). Beverly Hills, CA: Sage.

Massey, A., and Vandenburgh, J. G. (1980). Puberty delay by a urinary cue from female house mice in feral populations. *Science, 209,* 821–822.

Masters, W. H., and Johnson, V. E. (1960). The human female: Anatomy of sexual response. *Minnesota Medicine, 43,* 31–36.

———. (1962). The sexual response cycle of the human female: III. The clitoris: Anatomic and clinical considerations. *Western Journal of Surgery, 70,* 248–257.

———. (1963). The sexual response of the human male: I. Gross anatomic considerations. *Western Journal of Surgery, 71,* 85–95.

———. (1966). *Human sexual response.* Boston: Little, Brown.

Mathes, E. W., Adams, H. E., and Davies, R. M. (1985). Jealousy: Loss of relationship rewards, loss of self-esteem, depression, anxiety, and anger. *Journal of Personality and Social Psychology, 48,* 1552–1561.

Mathews, K. E., and Canon, L. K. (1975). Environmental noise level as a determinant of helping behavior. *Journal of Personality and Social Psychology, 32,* 571–577.

Matlin, M. W., and Zajonc, R. B. (1968). Social facilitation of word associations. *Journal of Personality and Social Psychology, 10,* 455–460.

Matthews, K. A. (1977). Caregiver-child interactions and the Type A coronary-prone behavior pattern. *Child Development, 48,* 1752–1756.

———. (1982). Psychological perspectives on the Type A behavior pattern. *Psychological Bulletin, 91,* 293–323.

Matthews, K. A., and Brunson, B. I. (1979). Allocation of attention and the Type A coronary-prone behavior pattern. *Journal of Personality and Social Psychology, 37,* 2081–2090.

Matthews, K. A., Glass, D. C., and Richins, M. (1977). The mother-son observation study. In D. C. Glass, *Behavior patterns, stress, and coronary disease.* Hillsdale, NJ: Erlbaum.

Matthews, K. A., Helmreich, R. L., Beane, W. E., and Lucker, G. W. (1980). Pattern A, achievement striving, and scientific merit: Does pattern A help or hinder? *Journal of Personality and Social Psychology, 39,* 962–967.

Matthews, K. A., and Siegel, J. M. (1983). Type A behaviors by children, social comparison, and standards for self-evaluation. *Developmental Psychology, 19,* 135–140.

Matthews, K. A., Siegel, J. M., Kuller, L. H., Thompson, M., and Varat, M. (1983). Determinants of decisions to seek medical treatment by patients with acute myocardial infarction symptoms. *Journal of Personality and Social Psychology, 44,* 1144–1156.

May, J. L., and Hamilton, P. A. (1980). Effects of musically evoked affect on women's interpersonal attraction and perceptual judgments of physical attractiveness of men. *Motivation and Emotion, 4,* 217–228.

Mayer, F. S., Duval, S., Holtz, R., and Bowman, C. (1985). Self-focus, helping request salience, felt responsibility, and helping behavior. *Personality and Social Psychology Bulletin, 11,* 133–144.

McAdams, D. P., and Losoff, M. (1984). Friendship motivation in fourth and sixth graders: A thematic analysis. *Journal of Social and Personal Relationships, 1,* 11–27.

McAllister, H. A., and Bregman, N. J. (1983). Self-disclosure and liking: An integration theory approach. *Journal of Personality, 51,* 202–212.

McArthur, L. A. (1972). The how and what of why: Some determinants and consequences of causal attribution. *Journal of Personality and Social Psychology, 22,* 171–193.

McArthur, L. Z., and Eisen, S. V. (1976). Achievements of male and female storybook characters as determinants of achievement behavior by boys and girls. *Journal of Personality and Social Psychology, 33,* 467–473.

McCain, G., Cox, V. C., Paulus, P. B., Luke, A., and Abadzi, H. (1985). Some effects of reduction of extraclassroom crowding in a school environment. *Journal of Applied Social Psychology, 15,* 503–515.

McCallum, D. M., Harring, K., Gilmore, R., Drenan, S., Chase, J. P., Insko, C. A., and Thibaut, J. (1985). Competition and cooperation between groups and between individuals. *Journal of Experimental Social Psychology, 21,* 301–320.

McCaul, K. D., Glasgow, R. E., Schafer, L. C., and O'Neill, H. K. (1983). Commitment and the prevention of adolescent cigarette smoking. *Health Psychology, 2,* 253–365.

McCauley, C., Coleman, G., and DeFusco, P. (1977). Commuters' eye contact with strangers in city and suburban train stations: Evidence of short-term adaptation to interpersonal overload in the city. *Environmental Psychology and Nonverbal Behavior, 2,* 215–225.

McCauley, C., and Taylor, J. (1976). Is there overload of acquaintances in the city? *Environmental Psychology and Nonverbal Behavior, 1,* 41–55.

McClelland, D. C., Alexander, C., and Marks, E. (1982). The need for power, stress, immune function, and illness among male prisoners. *Journal of Applied Psychology, 91,* 61–70.

McClelland, D. C., and Boyatzis, R. E. (1982). Leadership motive pattern and long-term success in management. *Journal of Applied Psychology, 67,* 737–743.

McClelland, D. C., Clark, R. A., Roby, T. B., and Atkinson, J. W. (1949). The effect of the need for achievement on thematic apperception. *Journal of Experimental Psychology, 37,* 242–255.

McCrae, R. R., and Costa, P. T., Jr. (1984). Personality is transcontextual: A reply to Veroff. *Personality and Social Psychology Bulletin, 10,* 175–179.

McDonald, P. J., and Eilenfield, V. C. (1980). Physical attractiveness and the approach/avoidance of self-awareness. *Personality and Social Psychology Bulletin, 6,* 391–395.

McDougall, W. (1908). *Introduction to social psychology.* London: Methuen.

McGaughey, K. J., and Stiles, W. B. (1983). Courtroom interrogation of rape victims: Verbal response mode use by attorneys and witnesses during direct examination vs. cross-examination. *Journal of Applied Social Psychology, 13,* 78–87.

McGovern, L. P. (1976). Dispositional social anxiety and helping behavior under three conditions of threat. *Journal of Personality, 44,* 84–97.

McGovern, L. P., Ditzian, J. L., and Taylor, S. P. (1975). The effect of one positive reinforcement on helping with cost. *Bulletin of the Psychonomic Society, 5,* 421–423.

McGovern, T. V., Jones, B., and Morris, S. E. (1979). Comparison of professional vs. student ratings of job interviewee behavior. *Journal of Consulting Psychology, 26,* 176–179.

McGrath, J. E. (1984). *Groups: Interaction and performance.* Englewood Cliffs, NJ: Prentice-Hall.

McGuire, W. J. (1969). The nature of attitudes and attitude change. In G. Lindzey and E. Aronson (eds.), *Handbook of social psychology,* vol. 3. Reading, MA: Addison-Wesley.

McGuire, W. J., and Papageorgis, D. (1961). The relative efficacy of various types of prior belief-defense in producing immunity against persuasion. *Journal of Abnormal and Social Psychology, 62,* 327–337.

McKillip, J., and Riedel, S. L. (1983). External validity of matching on physical attractiveness for same and opposite sex couples. *Journal of Applied Social Psychology, 13,* 328–337.

McMullin, E. (1983). Values in science. In P. D. Asquith and T. Nickles (eds.), *Proceedings of the 1982 Philosophy of Science Association,* vol. 2, (pp. 3–23). East Lansing, MI: Philosophy of Science Association.

McQuay, D. (1985, December 1). It's hard to identify winners of the sexual revolution. *Albany Times Union*, pp. D-1, D-10.

Mead, M. (1969). *Sex and temperament in three primitive societies.* New York: Dell.

Meecham, W. C., and Smith, H. G. (1977, June). *British journal of audiology.* Quoted in N. Napp, Noise drives you crazy-jets and mental hospitals. *Psychology Today*, p. 33.

Meer, J. (1986). The strife of bath. *Psychology Today*, 20(5), p. 6.

Mehrabian, A. (1968). Relationship of attitude to seated posture, orientation, and distance. *Journal of Personality and Social Psychology, 10*, 26–30.

Mehrabian, A., and Russell, J. A. (1974). *An approach to environmental psychology.* Cambridge, MA: MIT Press.

Meindl, J. R., and Lerner, M. J. (1983). The heroic motive: Some experimental demonstrations. *Journal of Experimental Social Psychology, 19*, 1–20.

———. (1985). Exacerbation of extreme responses to an out-group. *Journal of Personality and Social Psychology, 47*, 71–84.

Mendelsohn, R., and Orcutt, G. (1979). An empirical analysis of air pollution dose-response curves. *Journal of Environmental Economics and Management, 6*, 85–106.

Mending broken families. (1986, March 17). *New Republic*, pp. 7–8.

Merari, A., ed. (1985). *On terrorism and combating terrorism.* University Publications of America.

Messé, L. A., and Sivacek, J. M. (1979). Predictions of others' responses in a mixed-motive game: Self-justification or fales consensus? *Journal of Personality and Social Psychology, 37*, 602–607.

Messé, L. A., and Watts, B. L. (1983). Complex nature of the sense of fairness: Internal standards and social comparison as bases for reward evaluations. *Journal of Personality and Social Psychology, 45*, 84–93.

Messick, D. M., and Sentis, K. P. (1979). Fairness and preference. *Journal of Experimental Social Psychology, 15*, 418–434.

Meyer, D., Leventhal, H., and Gutman, M. (1985). Common-sense models of illness: The example of hypertension. *Health Psychology, 4*, 115–135.

Meyer, J. P., and Mulherin, A. (1980). From attribution to helping: An analysis of the mediating effects of affect and expectancy. *Journal of Personality and Social Psychology, 39*, 201–210.

Meyer, J. P., and Pepper, S. (1977). Need compatibility and marital adjustment in young married couples. *Journal of Personality and Social Psychology, 35*, 331–342.

Michelini, R. L., and Snodgrass, S. R. (1980). Defendant characteristics and juridic decisions. *Journal of Research in Personality, 14*, 340–350.

Middlekauf, R. (1982). *The glorious cause.* NY: Oxford University Press.

Middlemist, R. D., Knowles, E. S., and Matter, C. F. (1976). Personal space invasions in the lavatory: Suggestive evidence for arousal. *Journal of Personality and Social Psychology, 33*, 541–546.

Milardo, R. M., Johnson, M. P., and Huston, T. L. (1983). Developing close relationships: Changing patterns of interaction between pair members and social networks. *Journal of Personality and Social Psychology, 44*, 964–976.

Milgram, S. (1963). Behavioral study of obedience. *Journal of Abnormal and Social Psychology, 67*, 371–378.

———. (1964). Group pressure and action against a person. *Journal of Abnormal and Social Psychology, 69*, 137–143.

———. (1965a). Liberating effects of group pressure. *Journal of Personality and Social Psychology, 1*, 127–134.

———. (1965b). Some conditions of obedience and disobedience to authority. *Human Relations, 18*, 57–76.

———. (1970). The experience of living in cities. *Science, 167*, 1461–1468.

———. (1974). *Obedience to authority.* New York: Harper.

———. (1977). *The individual in a social world.* Reading, MA: Addison-Wesley.

Miller, D. T., and Ross, M. (1975). Self-serving biases in the attribution of causality: Fact or fiction? *Psychological Bulletin, 82*, 313–225. *Research in organizational behavior*, vol. 3. Greenwich, Conn.: JAI Press.

Miller, N., and Brewer, M. (1984). *Groups in contact: The Psychology of desegregation.* New York: Academic Press.

Miller, N., Maruyama, G., Beaber, R. J., and Valone, K. (1976). Speed of speech and persuasion. *Journal of Personality and Social Psychology, 34*, 615–624.

Miller, S. M., Lack, E. R., and Asroff, S. (1985). Preference for control and the coronary-prone behavior pattern: "I'd rather do it myself." *Journal of Personality and Social Psychology, 49*, 492–499.

Millham, J. (1974). Two components of need for approval score and their relationship to cheating following success and failure. *Journal of Research in Personality, 8*, 378–392.

Mischel, W. (1968). *Personality and assessment.* New York: Wiley.

———. (1977). On the future of personality measurement. *American Psychologist, 32*, 246–254.

———. (1985, August 25). *Personality: Lost or found? Identifying when individual differences make a difference.* Paper presented at the meeting of the American Psychological Association, Los Angeles.

Mitchell, H. E. (1979). *Informational and affective determinants of juror decision making.* Unpublished doctoral dissertation, Purdue University.

Mitchell, H. E., and Byrne, D. (1982). Minimizing the influence of irrelevant factors in the courtroom: The defendant's character, judge's instructions, and authoritarianism. In K. M. White and J. C. Speisman (eds.), *Research approaches to personality* (pp. 174–183). Monterey, CA: Brooks/Cole.

Mitchell, T. R., Green, S. G., and Wood, R. S. (1981). An

attributional model of leadership and the poor performing subordinate: Development and validation. In B. M. Staw and L. L. Cummings (eds.),

Mitchell, T. R., and Kalb, L. S. (1982). Effects of job experience on supervisor attributions for a subordinate's poor performance. *Journal of Applied Psychology, 67,* 181–188.

Money, J. (1985, September). *Pornography as related to criminal sex offending and the history of medical degeneracy theory.* Paper presented at the U. S. Justice Department Hearings, Houston.

Monson, T. C., and Hesley, J. W. (1982). Causal attributions for behaviors consistent or inconsistent with an actor's personality traits: Differences between those offered by actors and observers. *Journal of Personality and Social Psychology, 18,* 416–432.

Monson, T. C., Hesley, J. W., and Chernick, L. (1982). Specifying when personality traits can and cannot predict behavior: An alternative to abandoning the attempt to predict single-act criteria. *Journal of Personality and Social Psychology, 43,* 385–399.

Moreland, R. L., and Zajonc, R. B. (1979). Exposure effects may not depend on stimulus recognition. *Journal of Personality and Social Psychology, 37,* 1085–1089.

———. (1982). Exposure effects in person perception: Familiarity, similarity, and attraction. *Journal of Experimental Social Psychology, 18,* 395–415.

Morell, M. A., and Katkin, E. S. (1982). Jenkins Activity Survey scores among women of different occupations. *Journal of Consulting and Clinical Psychology, 50,* 588–589.

Morgan, C. D., and Murray, H. A. (1938). Thematic Apperception Test. In H. A. Murray, *Explorations in personality.* New York: Science Editions.

Morgan, C. J. (1978). Bystander intervention: Experimental test of a formal model. *Journal of Personality and Social Psychology, 36,* 43–55.

Moriarty, T. (1975). Crime, commitment, and the responsive bystander: Two field experiments. *Journal of Personality and Social Psychology, 31,* 370–376.

Morris, D., Collett, P., Marsh, P., and O'Shaughnessy, M. (1979). *Gestures: Their origins and distribution.* London: Cape.

Morris, W. N., and Miller, R. S. (1975). The effects of consensus-breaking and consensus-preempting partners on reduction of conformity. *Journal of Personality and Social Psychology, 11,* 215–223.

Morris, W. N., Miller, R. S., and Spangenberg, S. (1977). The effects of dissenter position and task difficulty on conformity and response to conflict. *Journal of Personality, 45,* 251–266.

Morris, W. N., Worchel, S., Bois, J. L., Pearson, J. A., Rountree, C. A., Samaha, G. M., Wachtler, J., and Wright, S. L. (1976). Collective coping with stress: Group reactions to fear, anxiety, and ambiguity. *Journal of Personality and Social Psychology, 33,* 674–679.

Morrison, D., Siegal, M., and Francis, R. (1984). Control, autonomy, and the development of moral behavior: A

social-cognitive perspective. *Imagination, Cognition, and Personality, 3,* 337–351.

Moscovici, S. (1980). Toward a theory of conversion behavior. In L. Berkowitz (ed.), *Advances in experimental social psychology,* vol. 13, (pp. 209–239). New York: Academic Press.

———. (1985). Social influence and conformity. In G. Lindzey and E. Aronson (eds.), *Handbook of social psychology,* vol. II. New York: Random House.

Moscovici, S., and Faucheux, C. (1972). Social influence, conforming bias, and the study of active minorities. In L. Berkowitz (ed.), *Advances in experimental social psychology,* vol. 6, (pp. 149–202) New York: Academic Press.

Mosher, D. L. (1968). Measurement of guilt in females by self-report inventories. *Journal of Consulting and Clinical Psychology, 32,* 690–695.

Mosher, D. L., and Anderson, R. D. (1986). Macho personality, sexual aggression, and reactions to guided imagery of realistic rape. *Journal of Research in Personality, 20,* 77–94.

Mosher, D. L., and O'Grady, K. E. (1979). Sex guilt, trait anxiety, and females' subjective sexual arousal to erotica. *Motivation and Emotion, 3,* 235–249.

Moskowitz, D. S. (1982). Coherence and cross-situational generality in personality: A new analysis of old problems. *Journal of Personality and Social Psychology, 43,* 754–768.

Moss, M. K., and Page, R. A. (1972). Reinforcement and helping behavior. *Journal of Applied Social Psychology, 2,* 360–371.

Muecher, H., and Ungeheuer, H. (1961). Meteorological influence on reaction time, flicker-fusion frequency, job accidents, and medical treatment. *Perceptual and Motor Skills, 12,* 163–168.

Mueser, K. T., Grau, B. W., Sussman, S., and Rosen, A. J. (1984). You're only as pretty as you feel: Facial expression as a determinant of physical attractiveness. *Journal of Personality and Social Psychology, 46,* 469–478.

Mugny, G. (1975). Negotiations, image of the other and the process of minority influence. *European Journal of Social Psychology, 5,* 209–229.

Mullen, B., Atkins, J. L., Champion, D. S., Edwards, C., Hardy, D., Story, J. E., and Vanderklok, M. (1985). The false consensus effect: A meta-analysis of 115 hypothesis tests. *Journal of Experimental Social Psychology, 21,* 262–283.

Mullen, B., Futrell, D., Stairs, D., Tice, D., Baumeister, R., Dawson, K., Riordan, C., Radloff, C., Kennedy, J., and Rosenfeld, P. (in press). Newscasters' facial expressions and voting behavior of viewers: Can a smile elect a president? *Journal of Personality and Social Psychology.*

Munsterberg, H. (1907). *On the witness stand: Essays in psychology and crime.* New York: McClure.

Murnen, S. K., and Allgeier, E. R. (1986). *Estimations of parental sexual frequency and parent-child communication.* Manuscript submitted for publication.

Murphy-Berman, V., Berman, J. J., Singh, P., Pachauri, A., and Kumar, P. (1984). Factors affecting allocation to needy and meritorious recipients: A cross-cultural comparison. *Journal of Personality and Social Psychology, 46,* 1267–1272.

Murray, D. M., Johnson, C. A., Luepker, R. V., and Mittelmark, M. B. (1984). The prevention of cigarette smoking in children: A comparison of four strategies. *Journal of Applied Social Psychology, 14,* 274–288.

Murray, D. M., and Wells, G. L. (1982). Does knowledge that a crime was staged affect eyewitness performance? *Journal of Applied Social Psychology, 12,* 42–53.

Murray, H. A. (1962). *Explorations in personality.* New York: Science Editions. (Originally published, 1938.)

Murstein, B. I. (1972). Physical attractiveness and marital choice. *Journal of Personality and Social Psychology, 22,* 8–12.

———. (1980). Love at first sight: A myth. *Medical Aspects of Human Sexuality, 14*(9), 34, 39–41.

Musante, L., Gilbert, M. A., and Thibaut, J. (1983). The effects of control on perceived fairness of procedures and outcomes. *Journal of Experimental Social Psychology, 19,* 223–238.

Musialowski, D. (1986). *Quality of worklife disease prevention, and productivity.* Unpublished manuscript, State University of New York at Albany.

Myers, D. G., Burggink, J. B., Kersting, R. C., and Schlosser, B. S. (1980). Does learning others' opinions change one's opinions? *Personality and Social Psychology Bulletin, 6,* 253–260.

Nadler, A., and Fisher, J. D. (1983). Recipient reactions to aid: Research and theory validation. In L. Berkowitz (ed.), *Advances in experimental social psychology.* New York: Academic Press.

Nadler, A., Fisher, J. D., and Itzhak, S. B. (1983). With a little help from my friend: Effect of a single or multiple act of aid as a function of donor and task characteristics. *Journal of Personality and Social Psychology, 44,* 310–321.

Nadler, A., Mayseless, O., Peri, N., and Chemerinski, A. (1986). The role of threat to self-esteem and perceived control in recipient reaction to help: Theory development and empirical validation. *Journal of Personality, 53,* 23–35.

Nahemow, L., and Lawton, M. P. (1975). Similarity and propinquity in friendship formation. *Journal of Personality and Social Psychology, 32,* 205–213.

Narayanan, V. K., and Nath, R. (1982). A field test of some attitudinal and behavioral consequences of flexitime. *Journal of Applied Psychology, 67,* 214–218.

Nasby, W., and Yando, R. (1982). Selective encoding and retrieval of affectively valent information. *Journal of Personality and Social Psychology, 43,* 1244–1255.

Nathan, P. E. (1983). Failures in prevention: Why we can't prevent the devastating effect of alcoholism and drug abuse. *American Psychologist, 38,* 459–467.

Neale, M. A., and Bazerman, M. H. (1985). The effects of framing and negotiator overconfidence on bargaining behaviors and outcomes. *Academy of Management Journal, 28,* 34–49.

Near, J. P., Smith, C. A., Rice, A. R. W., and Hunt, R. G. (1983). Job satisfaction and nonwork satisfaction as components of life satisfaction. *Journal of Applied Psychology, 13,* 126–144.

Neimeyer, G. J., and Neimeyer, R. A. (1981). Functional similarity and interpersonal attraction. *Journal of Research in Personality, 15,* 427–435.

Nelkin, D., and Brown, M. S. (1984). *Workers at risk: Voices from the workplace.* Chicago: University of Chicago Press.

Nemeth, C. J. (in press). Differential contributions of majority and minority influence. *Psychological Review, 93.*

Nesbit, P., and Steven, G. (1974). Personal space and stimulus intensity at a southern California amusement park. *Sociometry, 37,* 105–115.

Netanyahu, B. (ed.). (1986). *Terrorism: How the West can win.* New York: Farrar, Straus, and Giroux.

Newcomb, T. M. (1961). *The acquaintance process.* New York: Holt, Rinehart and Winston.

———. (1981). Heiderian balance as a group phenomenon. *Journal of Personality and Social Psychology, 40,* 862–867.

Nicola, J. A. S., and Hawkes, G. R. (1986). Marital satisfaction of dual-career couples: Does sharing increase happiness? *Journal of Social Behavior and Personality, 1,* 47–60.

Nida, S. A., and Koon, J. (1983). They get better looking at closing time around here, too. *Psychological Reports, 52,* 657–658.

Nieva, V. F., and Gutek, B. A. (1981). *Women and work: A psychological perspective.* New Yorker: Praeger Publishers.

Nisbett, R. E., Caputo, C., Legant, P., and Marecek, J. (1973). Behavior as seen by the actor and as seen by the observer. *Journal of Personality and Social Psychology, 27,* 154–164.

Nisbett, R. E., and Kunda, Z. (1985). Perception of social distributions. *Journal of Personality and Social Psychology, 48,* 297–311.

Nisbett, R. E., and Ross, L. (1980). *Human inference: Strategies and shortcomings of social judgment.* Englewood Cliffs, NJ: Prentice-Hall.

Nisbett, R. E., and Wilson, T. D. (1977). Telling more than we can know: Verbal reports on mental processes. *Psychological Review, 84,* 231–259.

Norman, J., and Harris, M. (1982, January 13). Students talk about their education. *Albany Times-Union,* p. 11.

Normoyle, J., and Lavrakas, P. J. (1984). Fear of crime in elderly women. Perceptions of control, predictability, and territoriality. *Personality and Social Psychology Bulletin, 10,* 191–202.

Nowicki, S., Jr. (1982). Competition-cooperation as a mediator of locus of control and achievement. *Journal of Research in Personality, 16,* 157–164.

Nyquist, L. V., and Spence, J. T. (1986). Effects of dispositional dominance and sex role expectations on leadership behaviors. *Journal of Personality and Social Psychology, 50,* 87–93.

O'Grady, K. E. (1982a). "Affect, sex guilt, gender, and the reward-punishing effects of erotic stimuli": A reanalysis and reinterpretation. *Journal of Personality and Social Psychology, 43,* 618–622.

———. (1982b). Sex, physical attractiveness, and perceived risk for mental illness. *Journal of Personality and Social Psychology, 43,* 1064–1071.

Ohbuchi, K., and Izutsu, T. (1984). Retaliation by male victims: Effects of physical attractiveness and intensity of attack of female attacker. *Personality and Social Psychology Bulletin, 10,* 216–224.

Ohbuchi, K., and Kambara, T. (1985). Attacker's intent and awareness of outcome, impression management, and retaliation. *Journal of Experimental Social Psychology, 21,* 321–330.

Ohbuchi, K., and Ogura, S. (1984). The experience of anger (1): The survey for adults and university students with Averill's questionnaire (Japanese). *Japanese Journal of Criminal Psychology, 22,* 15–35.

Olbrisch, M. E., Weiss, S. M., Stone, G. C., and Schwartz, G. E. (1985). Report of the National Working Conference on Education and Training in Health Psychology. *American Psychologist, 40,* 1038–1041.

Oldham, G. R., and Brass, D. J. (1979). Employee reactions to an open-plan office: A naturally-occurring quasi-experiment. *Administrative Science Quarterly, 24,* 267–284.

O'Malley, M. N. (1983). Interpersonal and intrapersonal justice: The effect of subject and confederate outcomes on evaluations of fairness. *Journal of Experimental Social Psychology, 13,* 121–128.

O'Malley, M. N., and Andrews, L. (1983). The effect of mood and incentives on helping: Are there some things money can't buy? *Motivation and Emotion, 7,* 179–189.

O'Malley, M. N., and Becker, L. A. (1984). Removing the egocentric bias: The relevance of distress cues to evaluation of fairness. *Personality and Social Psychology Bulletin, 10,* 235–242.

Orinova, G. (1981, November). A woman's-eye view of Russia. *Cosmopolitan,* pp. 194, 196.

Ortega, D. F., and Pipal, J. E. (1984). Challenge seeking and the Type A coronary-prone behavior pattern. *Journal of Personality and Social Psychology, 46,* 1328–1334.

Oskamp, S. (ed.) (1984). *Applied social psychology annual, 5.* Beverly Hills, CA: Sage.

O'Sullivan, C. S., and Durso, F. T. (1984). Effects of schema-incongruent information on memory for stereotypical attributes. *Journal of Personality and Social Psychology, 47,* 55–70.

Otten, M. W. (1977). Inventory and expressive measures of locus of control and academic performance: A five-year outcome study. *Journal of Personality Assessment, 41,* 644–649.

Pagan, G., and Aiello, J. R. (1982). Development of personal space among Puerto Ricans. *Journal of Nonverbal Behavior, 7,* 59–68.

Page, R. A. (1977). Noise and helping behavior. *Environment and Behavior, 9,* 559–572.

Page, R. R. (1978). Environmental influences on prosocial behavior: The effect of temperature. Paper presented at the Midwestern Psychological Association meeting, Chicago.

Pallak, M. S., Cook, D. A., and Sullivan, J. J. (1980). Commitment and energy conservation. *Applied Social Psychology Annual, 1,* 235–253.

Palmer, J., and Byrne, D. (1970). Attraction toward dominant and submissive strangers: Similarity versus complementarity. *Journal of Experimental Research in Personality, 4,* 108–115.

Paloutzian, R. F., and Ellison, C. W. (1979, May). Emotional, behavioral, and physical correlates of loneliness. Paper presented at the UCLA Research Conference on Loneliness, Los Angeles.

Pantin, H. M., and Carver, C. S. (1982). Induced competence and the bystander effect. *Journal of Applied Social Psychology, 12,* 100–111.

Park, B., and Rothbart, M. (1982). Perception of out-group homogeneity and levels of social categorization: Memory for the subordinate attributes of in-group and out-group members. *Journal of Personality and Social Psychology, 42,* 1051–1068.

Parke, R. D., Berkowitz, L., Leyens, J. P., West, S. G., and Sebastian, R. J. (1977). Some effects of violent and nonviolent movies on the behavior of juvenile delinquents. In L. Berkowitz (ed.), *Advances in experimental social psychology,* vol. 10. New York: Academic Press.

Parsons, J. E., Adler, T., and Meece, J. L. (1984). Sex differences in achievement: A test of alternate theories. *Journal of Personality and Social Psychology, 46,* 26–43.

Parsons, J. E., and Goff, S. B. (1980). Achievement motivation: A dual modality. In L. J. Fyans (ed.), *Recent trends in achievement motivation: Theory and research* (pp. 349–373). Englewood Cliffs, NJ: Prentice-Hall.

Patterson, A. (1978). Territorial behavior and fear of crime in the elderly. *Environmental Psychology and Nonverbal Behavior, 2,* 131–144.

Patterson, M. L. (1973). Compensation in nonverbal immediacy behaviors: A review. *Sociometry, 36,* 237–252.

———. (1976). An arousal model of interpersonal intimacy. *Psychological Review, 83,* 235–245.

Paulus, P. B. (1980). Crowding. In P. B. Paulus (ed.), *Psychology of group influence.* Hillsdale, NJ: Erlbaum.

Paulus, P. B., Aunis, A. B., Seta, J. J., Schkade, J. K., and Matthews, R. W. (1976). Crowding does affect task performance. *Journal of Personality and Social Psychology, 34,* 248–253.

Paulus, P. B., and McCain, G. (1983). Crowding in jails. *Basic and Applied Social Psychology, 4,* 89–107.

Peele, S. (1984, December). The question of personality. *Psychology Today,* pp. 54, 55–56.

Pendleton, M. G., and Batson, C. D. (1979). Self-presentation and the door-in-the-face technique for inducing compliance. *Personality and Social Psychology Bulletin, 5,* 77–81.

Penk, W. (1969). Age changes and correlates of internal-external locus of control scales. *Psychological Reports, 25,* 856.

Penley, L. E. (1982). An investigation of the information processing framework of organizational communication. *Human Communication Research, 8,* 348–365.

Pennebaker, J. W., Dyer, M. A., Caulkins, R. S., Litowitz, D. L., Ackerman, P. L., Anderson, D. B., and McGraw, K. M. (1979). Don't the girls get prettier at closing time: A country and western application to psychology. *Personality and Social Psychology Bulletin, 5,* 122–125.

Penrod, S., and Hastie, R. (1980). A computer simulation of jury decision making. *Psychological Review, 87,* 133–159.

Peplau, L. A., and Perlman, D. (1982). Perspectives on loneliness. In L. A. Peplau and D. Perlman (eds.), *Loneliness: A sourcebook of current theory, research, and therapy.* New York: Wiley.

Perlman, D., Gerson, A. C., and Spinner, B. (1978). Loneliness among senior citizens: An empirical report. *Essence, 2*(4), 239–248.

Perlman, D., Josephson, W., Hwang, W. T., Begum, H., and Thomas, T. L. (1978). Cross-cultural analysis of students' sexual standards. *Archives of Sexual Behavior, 7,* 545–558.

Peters, L. H., Hartke, D. D., and Pohlmann, J. T. (1985). Fiedler's contingency theory of leadership: An application of the meta-analysis procedures of Schmidt and Hunter. *Psychological Bulletin, 97,* 274–285.

Peters, L. H., O'Connor, E. J., Weekley, J., Pooyan, A., Frank, B., and Erenkrantz, B. (1984). Sex bias and managerial evaluations: A replication and extension. *Journal of Applied Psychology, 69,* 349–352.

Peters, T. J., and Waterman, R. H., Jr. (1982). *In search of excellence: Lessons from America's best-run companies.* New York: Warner Books.

Peterson, C., and Raps, C. S. (1984). Helplessness and hospitalization: More remarks. *Journal of Personality and Social Psychology, 46,* 82–83.

Peterson, E. A., Augenstein, J. S., Tanis, D. C., and Augenstein, A. G. (1981). Noise raises blood pressure without impairing auditory sensitivity. *Science, 211,* 1450–1452.

Petty, R. E., and Cacioppo, J. T. (1981). *Attitudes and persuasion: Classic and contemporary approaches.* Dubuque, Iowa: Wm. C. Brown.

———. (1985). The elaboration likelihood model of persuasion. In L. Berkowitz (ed.), *Advances in experimental social psychology,* vol. 19. New York: Academic Press.

Petty, R. E., Ostrom, T. M., and Brock, T. C. (1981). *Cognitive responses in persuasion.* Hillsdale, NJ: Erlbaum.

Petty, R. E., Wells, G. L., and Brock, T. C. (1976). Distraction can enhance or reduce yielding to propaganda:

Thought disruption versus effort justification. *Journal of Personality and Social Psychology, 34,* 874–884.

Pfeffer, J. (1985). Organizations and organization theory. In G. Lindzey and E. Aronson (eds.), *Handbook of social psychology,* 3rd. ed., vol. 2, (pp. 379–440). New York: Random House.

Phares, E. J. (1978). Locus of control. In H. London and J. E. Exner, Jr. (eds.), *Dimensions of Personality.* New York: Wiley.

Phelps, E. J. (1981). *The maid of the North.* New York: Holt, Rinehart and Winston.

Phillis, D. E., and Gromko, M. H. (1985). Sex differences in sexual activity: Reality or illusion? *Journal of Sex Research, 21,* 437–448.

Phillips, D. P. (1983). The impact of mass media violence on U. S. homicides. *American Sociological Review, 48,* 560–568.

Piliavin, J. A., Callero, P. L., and Evans, D. E. (1982). Addiction to altruism? Opponent-process theory and habitual blood donation. *Journal of Personality and Social Psychology, 43,* 1200–1213.

Piliavin, J. A., Dovidio, J. F., Gaertner, S. L., and Clark, R. D., III. (1981). *Emergency intervention.* New York: Academic Press.

Pines, A., and Aronson, E. (1983). Antecedents, correlates, and consequences of sexual jealousy. *Journal of Personality, 51,* 108–136.

Pinto, R. P., and Hollandsworth, J. G., Jr. (1984). A measure of possessiveness in intimate relationships. *Journal of Social and Clinical Psychology, 2,* 273–279.

Pittner, M. S., Houston, B. K., and Spiridigliozzi, G. (1983). Control over stress, Type A behavior pattern, and response to stress. *Journal of Personality and Social Psychology, 44,* 627–637.

Pliner, P., Hart, H., Kohl, J., and Saari, D. (1974). Compliance without pressure: Some further data on the foot-in-the-door technique. *Journal of Experimental Social Psychology, 10,* 17–22.

Pocs, O., and Godow, A. G. (1977). Can students view parents as sexual beings? *The Family Coordinator, 26,* 31–36.

Pollack, L. M., and Patterson, A. H. (1980). Territoriality and fear of crime in elderly and nonelderly homeowners. *Journal of Social Psychology, 111,* 119–129.

Pomazal, R. J., and Clore, G. L. (1973). Helping on the highway: The effects of dependency and sex. *Journal of Applied Social Psychology, 3,* 150–164.

Pomeroy, W. B. (1972). *Dr. Kinsey and the Institute for Sex Research.* New York: Harper & Row.

Powell, M. C., and Fazio, R. M. (1984). Attitude accessibility as a function of repeated attitudinal expression. *Personality and Social Psychology Bulletin, 10,* 139–148.

Powers, P. C., and Geen, R. S. (1972). Effects of the behavior and the perceived arousal of a model on instrumental aggression. *Journal of Personality and Social Psychology, 23,* 175–184.

Prentice-Dunn, S., and Rogers, R. W. (1982). Effects of public and private self-awareness on deindividuation and aggression. *Journal of Personality and Social Psychology, 43,* 503–513.

———. (1983). Deindividuation in aggression. In R. Geen and E. Donnerstein (eds.), *Aggression: Theoretical and empirical reviews.* New York: Academic Press.

———. (1984). Assessing subjects' reactions to deception methodology by means of the ethics monitoring card. Paper presented at the meetings of the Southeastern Psychological Association, New Orleans, LA.

Prentice-Dunn, S., and Spivey, C. B. (1986). Extreme deindividuation in the laboratory: Its magnitude and subjective components. *Personality and Social Psychology Bulletin, 12,* 206–215.

Pretty, G. H., and Seligman, C. (1984). Affect and the overjustification effect. *Journal of Personality and Social Psychology, 46,* 1241–1253.

Price, G. H., and Dabbs, J. M. (1974). Sex, setting, and personal space: Changes as children grow older. *Personality and Social Psychology Bulletin, 1,* 362–363.

Price, K. H., and Garland, H. (1981). Compliance with a leader's suggestions as a function of perceived leader/members competence and potential reciprocity. *Journal of Applied Psychology, 66,* 329–336.

Price, R. A., and Vandenberg, S. G. (1979). Matching for physical attractiveness in married couples. *Personality and Social Psychology Bulletin, 5,* 398–400.

Pritchard, R. D., Dunnette, H. D., and Jorgenson, D. O. (1972). Effects of perceptions of equity and inequity on worker performance and satisfaction. *Journal of Applied Psychology, 56,* 75–94.

Pruitt, D. G. (1981). *Negotiation behavior.* New York: Academic Press.

———. (1983). Integrative agreements: Nature and antecedents. In M. H. Bazerman and R. J. Lewicki (eds.), *Negotiation in organizations.* Beverly Hills, CA: Sage.

Pruitt, D. G., and Rubin, J. Z. (1986). *Social conflict: Escalation, stalemate, and settlement.* New York: Random House.

Pryor, J. B., Gibbons, F. X., Wicklund, R. A., Fazio, R. H., and Hood, R. (1977). Self-focused attention and self-report validity. *Journal of Personality, 45,* 514–527.

Przybyla, D. P. J. (1985). *The facilitating effects of exposure to erotica on male prosocial behavior.* Unpublished doctoral dissertation, State University of New York at Albany.

Przybyla, D. P. J., and Byrne, D. (1984). The mediating role of cognitive processes in self-reported sexual arousal. *Journal of Research in Personality, 18,* 54–63.

Przybyla, D. P. J., Byrne, D., and Allgeier, E. R. (1986). *Expressive behavior as a function of erotophobia-erotophilia.* Manuscript submitted for publication.

Przybyla, D. P. J., Byrne, D., and Kelley, K. (1983). The role of imagery in sexual behavior. In A. A. Sheikh (ed.), *Imagery: Current theory, research, and application.* New York: Wiley.

Przybyla, D. P. J., Murnen, S., and Byrne, D. (1985). *Arousal and attraction: Anxiety reduction, misattribu-tion, or response strength?* Unpublished manuscript, State University of New York at Albany.

Pursell, S. A., and Banikiotes, P. G. (1978). Androgyny and initial interpersonal attraction. *Personality and Social Psychology Bulletin, 4,* 235–243.

Putallaz, M., and Gottman, J. (1981). Social skills and group acceptance. In S. R. Asher and J. M. Gottman (eds.), *The development of children's friendships.* New York: Cambridge University Press.

Raboch, J., and Bartak, V. (1980). Changes in the sexual life of Czechoslovak women born between 1911 and 1958. *Archives of Sexual Behavior, 9,* 495–502.

Raine, A., Roger, D. B., and Venables, P. H. (1982). Locus of control and socialization. *Journal of Research in Personality, 16,* 147–156.

Rajecki, D. W., Kidd, R. F., and Ivins, B. (1976). Social facilitation in chickens: A different level of analysis. *Journal of Experimental Social Psychology, 12,* 233–246.

Rajecki, D. W., Nerenz, D. R., Freedenberg, T. G., and McCarthy, P. J. (1981). Components of aggression in chickens and conceptualizations of aggression in general. *Journal of Personality and Social Psychology, 37,* 1902–1914.

Ramirez, J., Bryant, J., and Zillmann, D. (1983). Effects of erotica on retaliatory behavior as a function of level of prior provocation. *Journal of Personality and Social Psychology, 43,* 971–978.

Rapaport, K., and Burkhart, B. (1984). Personality and attitudinal characteristics of sexually coercive college males. *Journal of Abnormal Psychology, 93,* 216–221.

Rasmussen, K. G., Jr. (1984). Nonverbal behavior, verbal behavior, resume credentials, and selection interview outcomes. *Journal of Applied Psychology, 69,* 551–556.

Raviv, A., and Palgi, Y. (1985). The perception of social-environmental characteristics in Kibbutz families with family-based and communal sleeping arrangements. *Journal of Personality and Social Psychology, 49,* 376–385.

Reardon, R., and Rosen, S. (1984). Psychological differentiation and the evaluation of juridic information: Cognitive and affective consequences. *Journal of Research in Personality, 18,* 195–211.

Reed, D., and Weinberg, M. S. (1984). Premarital coitus: Developing and established sexual scripts. *Social Psychology Quarterly, 47,* 129–138.

Regan, D. T. (1971). Effects of a favor and liking on compliance. *Journal of Experimental Social Psychology, 7,* 627–639.

Reimanis, G. (1971). *Effects of experimental IE modification techniques and home environment variables on IE.* Paper presented at the meeting of the American Psychological Association, Washington, DC.

Reis, H. T., Nezlek, J., and Wheeler, L. (1980). Physical attractiveness in social interaction. *Journal of Personality and Social Psychology, 38,* 604–617.

Reis, H. T., Wheeler, L., Kernis, M. H., Spiegel, N., and Nezlek, J. (1985). On specificity in the impact of social participation on physical and psychological health. *Journal of Personality and Social Psychology, 48,* 456 – 471.

Reis, H. T., Wheeler, L., Spiegel, N., Kernis, M. H., Nezlek, J. and Perri, M. (1982). Physical attractiveness in social interaction: II. Why does appearance affect social experience? *Journal of Personality and Social Psychology, 43,* 979 – 996.

Research and Forecasts, Inc. (1981). *The Connecticut Mutual Life report on American values in the '80s: The impact of belief.* Hartford: Connecticut Mutual Life Insurance Co.

Revenson, T. A. (1981). Coping with loneliness: The impact of causal attributions. *Personality and Social Psychology Bulletin, 7,* 565 – 571.

Rhodewalt, F. (1984). Self-involvement, self-attribution, and the Type A coronary-prone behavior pattern. *Journal of Personality and Social Psychology, 47,* 662 – 670.

Rhodewalt, F., and Davison, J., Jr. (1983). Reactance and the coronary-prone behavior pattern: The role of self-attribution in response to reduced behavioral freedom. *Journal of Personality and Social Psychology, 44,* 220 – 228.

Rhodewalt, F., Hays, R. B., Chemers, M. M., and Wysocki, J. (1984). Type A behavior, perceived stress, and illness: A person-situation analysis. *Personality and Social Psychology Bulletin, 10,* 149 – 159.

Rholes, W. S., Bailey, S., and McMillan, L. (1982). Experiences that motivate moral development: The role of cognitive dissonance. *Journal of Experimental Social Psychology, 18,* 524 – 536.

Rice, R. W., Instone, D., and Adams, J. (1984). Leader sex, leader success, and leadership process: Two field studies. *Journal of Applied Psychology, 69,* 12 – 31.

Rice, R. W., Near, J. P., and Hunt, R. G. (1980). The job satisfaction/life satisfaction relationship: A review of empirical research. *Basic and Applied Social Psychology, 1,* 37 – 64.

Riggio, R. E. (1986). Assessment of basic social skills. *Journal of Personality and Social Psychology, 51,* 649 – 660.

Riggio, R. E., and Friedman, H. S. (1986). Impression formation: The role of expressive behavior. *Journal of Personality and Social Psychology, 50,* 421 – 427.

Riggio, R. E., and Woll, S. B. (1984). The role of nonverbal cues and physical attractiveness in the selection of dating partners, *Journal of Social and Personal Relationships, 1,* 347 – 357.

Riordan, C. (1978). Equal-status interracial contact: A review and revision of a concept. *International Journal of Intercultural Relations, 2,* 161 – 185.

Riordan, C. A., Quigley-Fernandez, B., and Tedeschi, J. T. (1982). Some variables affecting changes in interpersonal attraction. *Journal of Experimental Social Psychology, 18,* 358 – 374.

Riordan, C. A., and Tedeschi, J. T. (1983). Attraction in aversive environments: Some evidence for classical conditioning and negative reinforcement. *Journal of Personality and Social Psychology, 44,* 683 – 692.

Riskind, J. H., and Wilson, D. W. (1982). Interpersonal attraction for the competitive person: Unscrambling the competition paradox. *Journal of Applied Social Psychology, 12,* 444 – 452.

Rittle, R. H. (1981). Changes in helping behavior: Self- versus situational perceptions as mediators of the foot-in-the-door effect. *Personality and Social Psychology Bulletin, 7,* 431 – 437.

Roberts, M. C., Wurtele, S. K., Boone, R., Metts, V., and Smith, V. (1981). Toward a reconceptualization of the reciprocal imitation phenomenon: Two experiments. *Journal of Research in Personality, 15,* 447 – 459.

Robinson, I., and Jedlicka, D. (1983). *Journal of Marriage and the Family, 45.*

Robinson, M. (1985). Jesse Helms, take stock: Study shows Rather bears no liberal bias. *Washington Journalism Review, 7,* 14 – 17.

Robinson, W. L. V., and Calhoun, K. S. (1983). Sexual fantasies, attitudes, and behavior as a function of race, gender, and religiosity. *Imagination, Cognition and Personality, 2,* 281 – 290.

Rodgers, J. L., Billy, J. O. B., and Udry, J. R. (1984). A model of friendship similarity in mildly deviant behaviors. *Journal of Applied Social Psychology, 14,* 413 – 425.

Rodin, J. (1985). The application of social psychology. In G. Lindzey and E. Aronson (eds.), *Handbook of Social Psychology,* 3rd ed., vol. 2, (pp. 805 – 881). New York: Random House.

Rodin, J., Solomon, S. K., and Metcalf, J. (1979). Role of control in mediating perceptions of density. *Journal of Personality and Social Psychology, 36,* 988 – 999.

Rodrigues, A., and Newcomb, T. M. (1980). The balance principle: Its current state and its integrative function in social psychology. *Interamerican Journal of Psychology, 14,* 85 – 136.

Rogers, M., Miller, N., Mayer, F. S., and Duvall, S. (1982). Personal responsibility and salience of the request for help: Determinants of the relation between negative affect and helping behavior. *Journal of Personality and Social Psychology, 43,* 956 – 970.

Rogers, R. W. (1980). Subjects' reactions to experimental deception. Unpublished manuscript, University of Alabama.

———. (1983). Preventive health psychology: An interface of social and clinical psychology. *Journal of Social and Clinical Psychology, 1,* 120 – 127.

Rogers, R. W., and Ketcher, C. M. (1979). Effects of anonymity and arousal on aggression. *Journal of Psychology, 102,* 13 – 19.

Rogers, R. W., and Prentice-Dunn, S. (1981). Deindividuation and anger-mediated interracial aggression: Unmasking regressive racism. *Journal of Personality and Social Psychology, 41,* 63 – 73.

Rogers, T. B., Kuiper, N. A., and Kirker, W. S. (1977). Self-reference and the encoding of personal information. *Journal of Personality and Social Psychology*, 35, 677–688.

Rohe, W. M. (1982). The response to density in residential settings: The mediating effects of social and personal variables. *Journal of Applied Social Psychology*, 12, 292–303.

Rohner, R. P. (1974). Proxemics and stress: An empirical study of the relationship between living space and roommate turnover. *Human Relations*, 27, 697–702.

Rook, K. S., and Dooley, D. (1985). Applying social support research: Theoretical problems and future directions. *Journal of Social Issues*, 41, 5–28.

Rook, K. S., and Peplau, L. A. (1982). Perspectives on helping the lonely. In L. A. Peplau and D. Perlman (eds.), *Loneliness: A sourcebook of current theory, research, and therapy.* New York: Wiley.

Rorschach, H. (1921). *Psychodiagnostics.* Berne: Hans Huber.

Rose, S. M. (1984). How friendships end: Patterns among young adults. *Journal of Social and Personal Relationships*, 1, 267–277.

Rosen, R. H., Herskovitz, L., and Stack, J. M. (1982). Timing of the transition to nonvirginity among unmarried adolescent women. *Population Research and Policy Review*, 1, 153–170.

Rosen, S., Tomarelli, M. M., Kidda, M. L., Jr., and Medvin, N. (1986). Effects of motive for helping, recipient's inability to reciprocate, and sex on devaluation of the recipient's competence. *Journal of Personality and Social Psychology*, 50, 729–736.

Rosenbaum, M. E. (1980). Cooperation and competition. In P. B. Paulus (ed.), *The psychology of group influence.* Hillsdale, NJ: Erlbaum.

———. (1986). The repulsion hypothesis: On the nondevelopment of relationships. *Journal of Personality and Social Psychology.*

Rosenfield, D., Folger, R., and Adelman, H. F. (1980). When rewards reflect competence: A qualification of the overjustification effect. *Journal of Personality and Social Psychology*, 39, 368–376.

Rosenfield, D., Greenberg, J., Folger, R., and Borys, R. (1982). Effect of an encounter with a black panhandler on subsequent helping for blacks: Tokenism or conforming to a negative stereotype? *Personality and Social Psychology Bulletin*, 8, 664–671.

Rosenhan, D. L., Salovey, P., and Hargis, K. (1981). The joys of helping: Focus of attention mediates the impact of positive affect on altruism. *Journal of Personality and Social Psychology*, 40, 899–905.

Rosenman, R. H., and Friedman, M. (1974). Neurogenic factors in pathogenesis of coronary heart disease. *Medical Clinics of North America*, 58, 269–279.

Ross, L. (1977). The intuitive psychologist and his shortcomings: Distortions in the attribution process. In L. Berkowitz (ed.), *Advances in experimental social psychology*, vol. 10. New York: Academic Press.

Ross, L., Greene, D., and House, P. (1977). The "false consensus effect": An egocentric bias in social perception and attribution processes. *Journal of Experimental Social Psychology*, 13, 279–301.

Ross, L., Lepper, M. R., and Hubbard, M. (1975). Perseverance in self-perception and social perception: Biased attributional process in the debriefing paradigm. *Journal of Personality and Social Psychology*, 32, 880–892.

Ross, M., Layton, B., Erickson, B., and Schopler, J. (1973). Affect, facial regard, and reactions to crowding. *Journal of Personality and Social Psychology*, 28, 69–76.

Roter, D. L. (1984). Patient question asking in physician-patient interaction. *Health Psychology*, 3, 395–409.

Rotter, J. B. (1954). *Social learning and clinical psychology.* Englewood Cliffs, NJ: Prentice-Hall.

———. (1966). Generalized expectancies for internal versus external control of reinforcement. *Psychological Monographs*, 80 (Whole No. 609).

———. (1980). Trust and gullibility. *Psychology Today*, 14(5), pp. 35–38, 40, 42, 102.

Rotter, J. B., and Hochreich, D. J. (1975). *Personality.* Glenview, IL: Scott, Foresman.

Rotton, J., and Frey, J. (1985a). Air pollution, weather, and violent crimes: Concomitant time-series analysis of archival data. *Journal of Personality and Social Psychology*, 49, 1207–1220.

———. (1985b). Psychological costs of air pollution: Atmospheric conditions, seasonal trends, and psychiatric emergencies. *Population and Environment*, 7, 3–16.

Rotton, J., Frey, J., Barry, T., Milligan, M., and Fitzpatrick, M. (1979). The air pollution experience and physical aggression. *Journal of Applied Social Psychology*, 9, 397–412.

Routh, D. K., and Ernst, A. R. (1984). Somatization disorder in relatives of children and adolescents with functional abdominal pain. *Journal of Pediatric Psychology*, 9, 427–437.

Rozin, P., Millman, L., and Nemeroff, C. (1986). Operation of the laws of sympathetic magic in disgust and other demains. *Journal of Personality and Social Psychology*, 50, 703–712.

Rubin, J. Z. (1980). Experimental research on third-party intervention in conflict: Toward some generalizations. *Psychological Bulletin*, 87, 379–391.

Rubin, J. Z., and Friedland, N. (1986). Theater of terror. *Psychology Today*, 20(3), pp. 18–19, 22, 24, 26–28.

Rubin, Z. (1974). From liking to loving: Patterns of attraction in dating relationships. In T. L. Huston (ed.), *Foundations of interpersonal attraction.* New York: Academic Press.

———. (1980). *Children's friendships.* Cambridge, MA: Harvard University Press.

———. (1982). Children without friends. In L. A. Peplau and D. Perlman (eds.), *Loneliness: A sourcebook of current theory, research, and therapy.* New York: Wiley.

———. (1985). Deceiving ourselves about deception: Comment on Smith and Richardson's "Amelioration of deception and harm in psychological research."

Journal of Personality and Social Psychology, 48, 252 – 253.

Rubin, Z., Peplau, L. A., and Hill, C. T. (1981). Loving and leaving: Sex differences in romantic attachments. *Sex Roles, 7,* 821 – 835.

Rule, B. G., Bisanz, G. L., and Kohn, M. (1985). Anatomy of a persuasion schema: Targets, goals, and strategies. *Journal of Personality and Social Psychology, 48,* 1127 – 1140.

Rusbult, C. E. (1980). Commitment and satisfaction in romantic associations: A test of the investment model. *Journal of Experimental Social Psychology, 16,* 172 – 186.

———. (1983). A longitudinal test of the investment model: The development (and deterioration) of satisfaction and commitment in heterosexual involvements. *Journal of Personality and Social Psychology, 45,* 101 – 117.

Rusbult, C. E., Johnson, D. J., and Morrow, G. D. (1986). Impact of couple patterns of problem solving on distress and nondistress in dating relationships. *Journal of Personality and Social Psychology, 50,* 744 – 753.

Rusbult, C. E., Musante, L., and Soloman, M. (1982). The effects of clarity of decision rule and favorability of verdict on satisfaction with resolution of conflicts. *Journal of Applied Social Psychology, 12,* 304 – 317.

Rusbult, C. E., and Zembrodt, I. M. (1983). Responses to dissatisfaction in romantic involvements: A multi-dimensional scaling analysis. *Journal of Experimental Social Psychology, 19,* 274 – 293.

Rusbult, C. E., Zembrodt, I. M., and Gunn, L. K. (1982). Exit, voice, loyalty, and neglect: Responses to dissatisfaction in romantic involvements. *Journal of Personality and Social Psychology, 43,* 1230 – 1242.

Russ, R. C., Gold, J. A., and Stone, W. F. (1980). Opportunity for thought as a mediator of attraction to a dissimilar stranger: A further test of an information seeking interpretation. *Journal of Experimental Social Psychology, 16,* 562 – 572.

Russell, D. (1982). The measurement of loneliness. In L. A. Peplau and D. Perlman (eds.), *Loneliness: A sourcebook of current theory, research, and therapy.* New York: Wiley.

Russell, D., Peplau, L. A., and Cutrona, C. E. (1980). The revised UCLA Loneliness Scale: Concurrent and discriminant validity evidence. *Journal of Personality and Social Psychology, 39,* 472 – 480.

Russell, D. E. H., and Trocki, K. F. (1985, September). *The impact of pornography on women.* Paper presented at the U. S. Justice Department Hearings, Houston.

Russell, J. A., Ward, L. M., and Pratt, G. (1981). Affective quality attributed to environments: A factor analytic study. *Environment and Behavior, 13,* 259 – 288.

Rüstemli, A. (1986). Male and female personal space needs and escape reactions under intrusion: A Turkish sample. *International Journal of Psychology.*

Rutkowski, G. K., Gruder, C. L., and Romer, D. (1983).

Group cohesiveness, social norms, and bystander intervention. *Journal of Personality and Social Psychology, 44,* 545 – 552.

Saegert, S. (1978). High density environments: Their personal and social consequences. In A. Baum and Y. M. Epstein (eds.), *Human response to crowding.* Hillsdale, NJ: Erlbaum.

Sanders, G. S. (1982). Social comparison as a basis for evaluating others. *Journal of Research in Personality, 16,* 21 – 31.

———. (1983). An attentional process model of social facilitation. In A. Hare, H. Blumberg, V. Kent, and M. Davies (eds.), *Small groups.* London: Wiley.

———. (1984a). Effects of context cues on eyewitness identification responses. *Journal of Applied Social Psychology, 14,* 386 – 397.

———. (1984b). Self-presentation and drive in social facilitation. *Journal of Experimental Social Psychology, 20,* 312 – 322.

Sanders, G. S., and Baron, R. S. (1977). Is social comparison irrelevant for producing choice shifts? *Journal of Experimental Social Psychology, 13,* 303 – 314.

Sanders, G. S., Baron, R. S., and Moore, D. L. (1978). Distraction and social comparison as mediators of social facilitation effects. *Journal of Experimental Social Psychology, 14,* 291 – 303.

Sanders, G. S., and Mullen, B. (1983). Accuracy in perceptions of consensus: Differential tendencies of people with majority and minority positions. *European Journal of Social Psychology, 13,* 57 – 70.

Sanders, G. S., and Simmons, W. (1983). The use of hypnosis to enhance eyewitness accuracy: Does it work? *Journal of Applied Psychology, 68,* 70 – 77.

Satow, K. L. (1975). Social approval and helping. *Journal of Experimental Social Psychology, 11,* 501 – 509.

Scandura, T. A., and Graen, G. B. (1984). Moderating effects of initial leader-member exchange status on the effects of a leadership intervention. *Journal of Applied Psychology, 69,* 428 – 436.

Schachter, S. (1951). Deviation, rejection, and communication. *Journal of Abnormal and Social Psychology, 46,* 190 – 207.

———. (1959). *The psychology of affiliation.* Standord, CA: Stanford University Press.

Schachter, S., and Singer, J. (1962). Cognitive, social, and physiological determinants of the emotional state. *Psychological Review, 69,* 379 – 399.

Schaffner, P. E. (1985). Specious learning about reward and punishment. *Journal of Personality and Social Psychology, 48,* 1377 – 1386.

Schank, R. C., and Abelson, R. P. (1977). *Scripts, plans, goals, and understanding: An inquiry into human knowledge structures.* Hillsdale, NJ: Erlbaum.

Scheier, M. F., and Carver, C. S. (1985). Optimism, coping, and health: Assessment and implications of generalized outcome expectancies. *Health Psychology, 4,* 219 – 247.

Schindler, B. A. (1985). Stress, affective disorders, and immune function. *Medical Clinics of North America, 69,* 585–597.

Schlenker, B. R. (1980). *Impression management: The self-concept, social identity, and interpersonal relations.* Belmont, CA: Brooks/Cole.

———. (1982). Self-contemplations. *Contemporary Psychology, 27,* 615–616.

Schmidt, D. E., and Keating, J. P. (1979). Human crowding and personal control: An integration of the research. *Psychological Bulletin, 86,* 680–700.

Schneider, F., and Mockus, Z. (1974). Failure to find a rural-urban difference in incidence of altruistic behavior. *Psychological Reports, 34,* 294.

Schopler, J., and Stockdale, J. (1977). An interference analysis of crowding. *Environmental Psychology and Nonverbal Behavior, 1,* 81–88.

Schriesheim, J. F. (1980). The social context of leader subordinate relations: An investigation of the effects of group cohesiveness. *Journal of Applied Psychology, 65,* 183–194.

Schullo, S. A., and Alperson, B. L. (1984). Interpersonal phenomenology as a function of sexual orientation, sex, sentiment, and trait categories in long-term dyadic relationships. *Journal of Personality and Social Psychology, 47,* 983–1002.

Schulte, L. (1986). The new dating game. *New York, 19*(9), pp. 92–94, 96, 98, 103–104, 106.

Schultz, N. R., Jr. (1984). Loneliness: Correlates, atrributions, and coping among older adults. *Personality and Social Psychology Bulletin, 10,* 67–77.

Schultz, N. R., Jr., and Moore, D. W. (1984). Loneliness: Correlates, attributions, and coping among older adults. *Personality and Social Psychology Bulletin, 10,* 67–77.

Schuster, E., and Elderton, E. M. (1906). The inheritance of psychical characters. *Biometrika, 5,* 460–469.

Schwab, D. P., and Grams, R. (1985). Sex-related errors in job evaluation: A "real-world" test. *Journal of Applied Psychology, 70,* 533–539.

Schwartz, B., and Barsky, S. (1977). The home advantage. *Social Forces, 55,* 641–661.

Schwartz, S. (1973). Effects of sex guilt and sexual arousal on the retention of birth control information. *Journal of Consulting and Clinical Psychology, 41,* 61–64.

Schwartz, S. H., and Gottlieb, A. (1980). Bystander anonymity and reactions to emergencies. *Journal of Personality and Social Psychology, 39,* 418–430.

Schwarzwald, J., Bizman, A., and Raz, M. (1983). The foot-in-the-door paradigm: Effects of second request size on donation probability and donor generosity. *Personality and Social Psychology Bulletin, 9,* 443–450.

Schwarzwald, J., Raz, M., and Zvibel, M. (1979). The applicability of the door-in-the-face technique when established behavioral customs exist. *Journal of Applied Social Psychology, 9,* 576–586.

Schweder, R. A. (1975). How relevant is an individual difference theory of personality? *Journal of Personality, 43,* 455–484.

Scitovsky, T. (1980, October). Why do we seek more and more excitement? *Stanford Observer,* p. 13.

Scott, J. (1985). *Violence and erotic material: The relationship between adult entertainment and rape.* Paper presented at the meeting of the American Association for the Advancement of Science, Los Angeles.

Scott, J. A. (1984). Comfort and seating distance in living rooms: The relationship of interactants and topic of conversation. *Environment and Behavior, 16,* 35–54.

Scott, K. P., and Feldman-Summers, S. (1979). Children's reactions to textbook stories in which females are portrayed in traditionally male roles. *Journal of Educational Psychology, 71,* 396–402.

Sebba, R., and Churchman, A. (1983). Territories and territoriality in the home. *Environment and Behavior, 15,* 191–210.

Segal, M. W. (1974). Alphabet and attraction: An unobtrusive measure of the effect of propinquity in a field setting. *Journal of Personality and Social Psychology, 30,* 654–657.

Sex news. (1985, December). *Penthouse,* 54.

Shaffer, D. R., and Graziano, W. G. (1980). Effect of victims' race and organizational affiliation on receiving help from blacks and whites. *Personality and Social Psychology Bulletin, 6,* 366–372.

———. (1983). Effects of positive and negative moods on helping tasks having pleasant or unpleasant consequences. *Motivation and Emotion, 7,* 269–278.

Shaffer, D. R., Rogel, M., and Hendrick, C. (1975). Intervention in the library: The effect of increased responsibility on bystanders' willingness to prevent a theft. *Journal of Applied Social Psychology, 5,* 303–319.

Shaffer, D. R., and Smith, J. E. (1985). Effects of preexisting moods on observers' reactions to helpful and nonhelpful models. *Motivation and Emotion, 9,* 101–122.

Shaffer, D. R., Smith, J. E., and Tomarelli, M. (1982). Self-monitoring as a determinant of self-disclosure reciprocity during the acquaintance process. *Journal of Personality and Social Psychology, 43,* 163–175.

Shanab, M. E., and Yahya, K. A. (1977). A behavioral study of obedience in children. *Journal of Personality and Social Psychology, 35,* 530–536.

Shea, J. D. C. (1981). Changes in interpersonal distances and categories of play behavior in the early weeks of preschool. *Developmental Psychology, 17,* 417–425.

Shelom, K. J., Walker, J. L., and Esser, J. K. (1985). A choice of alternative strategies in oligopoly bargaining. *Journal of Applied Social Psychology, 15,* 345–353.

Shelton, M. L., and Rogers, R. W. (1981). Fear-arousing and empathy-arousing appeals to help: The pathos of persuasion. *Journal of Applied Social Psychology, 11,* 366–378.

Shepherd, J. W., Ellis, H. D., and Davies, G. M. (1983). *Identification evidence: A psychological evaluation.* Aberdeen, Scotland: Aberdeen University Press.

Sheppard, B., and Vidmar, N. (1980). Adversary pretrial procedures and testimonial evidence: Effects of lawyer's role and Machiavellianism. *Journal of Personality and Social Psychology, 39,* 320–332.

Sherif, M. (1935). A study of some social factors in perception. *Archives of Psychology,* No. 187.

Sherif, M., Harvey, O. J., White, B. J., Hood, W. E., and Sherif, C. W. (1961). *Intergroup conflict and cooperation: The Robbers cave experiment.* Norman: Institute of Group Relations.

Sherman, S. J. (1980). On the self-erasing nature of errors of prediction. *Journal of Personality and Social Psychology, 16,* 388–403.

Sherman, S. J., Cialdini, R. B., Schwartzman, D. F., and Reynolds, K. D. (1985). Imagining can heighten or lower the perceived likelihood of contracting the disease: The mediating effect of ease of imagery. *Personality and Social Psychology Bulletin, 11,* 118–127.

Sherman, S. J., Presson, C. C., and Chassin, L. (1984). Mechanisms underlying the false consensus effect: The special role of threats to the self. *Personality and Social Psychology Bulletin, 10,* 127–138.

Sherman, S. J., Presson, C. C., Chassin, L., Corty, E., and Olshavsky, R. (1983). The false consensus effect in estimates of smoking prevalence: Underlying mechanisms. *Personality and Social Psychology Bulletin, 9,* 197–207.

Shiffman, S. (1984). Cognitive antecedents and sequelae of smoking relapse crises. *Journal of Applied Social Psychology, 14,* 296–309.

Shigetomi, C. C., Hartmann, D. P., and Gelfand, D. M. (1981). Sex differences in children's altruistic behavior and reputations for helpfulness. *Developmental Psychology, 17,* 434–437.

Shirley, C. E. (1984). Alcoholism and drug abuse in the workplace . . . there is a way out. *Office Administration and Automation, 45,* 24–27, 90.

Shotland, R. L., and Heinold, W. D. (1985). Bystander response to arterial bleeding: Helping skills, the decision-making process, and differentiating the helping response. *Journal of Personality and Social Psychology, 49,* 347–356.

Shotland, R. L., and Mark, M. M. (1985). *Social science and social policy.* London: Sage.

Shupe, L. M. (1954). Alcohol and crimes: A study of the urine alcohol concentration found in 882 persons arrested during or immediately after the commission of a felony. *Journal of Criminal Law and Criminology, 33,* 661–665.

Shure, G. H., Meeker, R. J., and Hansford, E. A. (1965). The effectiveness of pacifist strategies in bargaining games. *Journal of Conflict Resolution, 9,* 106–117.

Shute, G. E., Howard, M. M., and Steyaert, J. P. (1984). The relationships among cognitive development, locus of control, and gender. *Journal of Research in Personality, 18,* 335–341.

Siegel, J. M., and Steele, C. M. (1980). Environmental distraction and interpersonal judgments. *British Journal of Social and Clinical Psychology, 19,* 23–32.

Sigall, H., and Ostrove, N. (1975). Beautiful but danger-

ous: Effects of offender attractiveness and nature of the crime on juridic judgment. *Journal of Personality and Social Psychology, 31,* 410–414.

Sigelman, C. K., Berry, C. J., and Wiles, K. A. (1984). Violence in college students' dating relationships. *Journal of Applied Social Psychology, 5,* 530–548.

Sigusch, V., and Schmidt, G. (1973). Teenage boys and girls in West Germany. *Journal of Sex Research, 9,* 107–123.

Sims, H. P., and Manz, C. C. (1984). Observing leader verbal behavior: Toward reciprocal determinism in leadership theory. *Journal of Applied Psychology, 69,* 222–232.

Singer, J. E., Lundberg, U., and Frankenhaeuser, M. (1978). Stress on the train: A study of urban commuting. In A. Baum, J. E. Singer, and Valins, S. (eds.), *Advances in environmental psychology,* vol. 1. Hillsdale, NJ: Erlbaum.

Singer, J. L. (1984). The private personality, *Personality and Social Psychology Bulletin, 10,* 7–30.

Sistrunk, F., and McDavid, J. W. (1971). Sex variable in conforming behavior. *Journal of Personality and Social Psychology, 17,* 200–207.

Sivacek, J., and Crano, W. D. (1982). Vested interest as a moderator of attitude-behavior consistency. *Journal of Personality and Social Psychology, 43,* 210–221.

Skevington, M. (1981). Intergroup relations and nursing. *European Journal of Social Psychology, 22,* 43–59.

Skinner, B. F. (1986). What is wrong with daily life in the Western World? *American Psychologist, 41,* 568–574.

Smeaton, G., and Byrne, D. (1986, in press). The effects of "R"-rated violence and erotica, individual differences, and victim characteristics on acquaintance rape proclivity. *Journal of Research in Personality.*

Smith, A., and Stansfeld, S. (1986). Aircraft noise exposure, noise sensitivity, and everyday errors. *Environment and Behavior, 18,* 214–226.

Smith, A. J. (1957). Similarity of values and its relation to acceptance and the projection of similarity. *Journal of Psychology, 43,* 251–260.

Smith, D. E., Gier, J. A., and Willis, F. N. (1982). Interpersonal touch and compliance with a marketing request. *Basic and Applied Social Psychology, 3,* 35–38.

Smith, R. J., and Knowles, E. S. (1979). Attributional consequences of personal space invasions. *Personality and Social Psychology Bulletin, 4,* 429–433.

Smith, S. S., and Richardson, D. (1983). Amelioration of deception and harm in psychological research: The important role of debriefing. *Journal of Personality and Social Psychology, 5,* 1075–1082.

———. (1985). On deceiving ourselves about deception: Reply to Rubin. *Journal of Personality and Social Psychology, 48,* 254–255.

Smith, T. W., and Anderson, N. B. (1986). Models of personality and disease: An interactional approach to Type A behavior and cardiovascular risk. *Journal of Personality and Social Psychology, 50,* 1166–1173.

Smith, T. W., and Brehm, S. S. (1981a). Cognitive correlates of the Type A coronary-prone behavior pattern. *Motivation and Emotion, 5,* 215–223.

———. (1981b). Person perception and the Type A coronary-prone behavior pattern. *Journal of Personality and Social Psychology, 40,* 1137–1149.

Smith, T. W., Houston, B. K., and Stucky, R. J. (1984). Type A behavior, irritability, and cardiovascular response. *Motivation and Emotion, 8,* 221–230.

Snow, B. (1978). Level of aspiration in coronary-prone and noncoronary-prone adults. *Personality and Social Psychology Bulletin, 4,* 416–419.

Snyder, C. R., and Fromkin, H. L. (1980). *Uniqueness: The human pursuit of difference.* New York: Plenum.

Snyder, M., and Cunningham, M. R. (1975). To comply or not to comply: Testing the self-perception explanation of the "foot-in-the-door" phenomenon. *Journal of Personality and Social Psychology, 31,* 64–67.

Snyder, M., Gangestad, S., and Simpson, J. A. (1983). Choosing friends as activity partners: The role of self-monitoring. *Journal of Personality and Social Psychology, 45,* 1061–1072.

Snyder, M., Grether, J., and Keller, K. (1974). Staring and compliance: A field experiment on hitchhiking. *Journal of Applied Social Psychology, 4,* 165–170.

Snyder, M., and Ickes, W. (1985). Personality and social behavior. In G. Lindzey and E. Aronson (eds.), *The handbook of social psychology,* 3rd ed., vol. I (pp. 883–947). New York: Random House.

Snyder, M., and Monson, T. C. (1975). Persons, situations, and the control of social behavior. *Journal of Personality and Social Psychology, 32,* 637–644.

Snyder, M., and Simpson, J. A. (1984). Self-monitoring and dating relationships. *Journal of Personality and Social Psychology, 47,* 1281–1291.

Snyder, M., and Swann, W. B. (1976). When actions reflect attitudes: The politics of impression management. *Journal of Personality and Social Psychology, 34,* 1034–1042.

Solano, C. H., Batten, P. G., and Parish, E. A. (1982). Loneliness and patterns of self-disclosure. *Journal of Personality and Social Psychology, 43,* 524–531.

Solomon, R. C. (1981, October). the love lost in cliches. *Psychology Today,* pp. 83–85, 87–88.

Sommer, R. (1969). *Personal space.* Englewood Cliffs, NJ: Prentice Hall.

———. (1980). Environmental psychology—a blueprint for the future. *APA Monitor, 11,* 47.

Sommer, R., and Becker, F. D. (1969). Territorial defense and the good neighbor. *Journal of Personality and Social Psychology, 11,* 85–92.

Sorrels, J. P., and Kelley, J. (1984). Conformity by omission. *Personality and Social Psychology Bulletin, 10,* 302–305.

Spears, R., van der Pligt, J., and Eiser, J. R. (1985). Illusory correlation in the perception of group attitudes. *Journal of Personality and Social Psychology, 48,* 863–875.

Spiegel, D. (1985). Trance, trauma, & testimony. *Stanford Magazine, 13*(4), 41–44.

Spielberger, C. D., and Stenmark, D. E. (1985). Community psychology. In E. M. Altmaier and M. E. Meyer (eds.), *Applied specialties in psychology* (pp. 75–97). New York: Random House.

Sprecher, S., DeLamater, J., Neuman, N., Neuman, M., Kahn, P., Orbuch, D., and McKinney, K. (1984). Asking questions in bars: The girls (and boys) may not get prettier at closing time and other interesting results. *Personality and Social Psychology Bulletin, 10,* 482–488.

Srull, T. K., and Wyer, R. S. (1979). The role of category accessibility in the interpretation of information about persons: Some determinants and implications. *Journal of Personality and Social Psychology, 37,* 1660–1672.

Staats, A. W., and Burns, G. L. (1982). Emotional personality repertoire as cause of behavior: Specification of personality and interaction principles. *Journal of Personality and Social Psychology, 43,* 873–881.

Stake, J. E. (1983). Factors in reward distribution: Allocator motive, gender, and Protestant ethic endorsement. *Journal of Personality and Social Psychology, 44,* 410–418.

Stapp, J., and Fulcher, R. (1984). The employment of 1981 and 1982 doctorate recipients in psychology. *American Psychologist, 39,* 1408–1423.

Stasser, G., and Titus, W. (1985). Pooling of unshared information in group decision making: Biased information sampling during discussion. *Journal of Personality and Social Psychology, 48,* 1467–1478.

Staub, E., Tursky, B., and Schwartz, G. (1971). Self-control and predictability: Their effects on reactions to aversive stimulation. *Journal of Personality and Social Psychology, 18,* 157–162.

Stech, F., and McClintock, C. G. (1981). Effects of communication timing on duopoly bargaining outcomes. *Journal of Personality and Social Psychology, 40,* 664–674.

Steck, L., Levitan, D., McLane, D., and Kelley, H. H. (1982). Care, need, and conceptions of love. *Journal of Personality and Social Psychology, 43,* 481–491.

Steele, C. M., and Southwick, L. (1985). Alcohol and social behavior I: The psychology of drunken excess. *Journal of Personality and Social Psychology, 48,* 18–34.

Steffen, V. J., and Eagly, A. H. (1985). Implicit theories about influence style: The effects of status and sex. *Personality and Social Psychology Bulletin, 11,* 191–205.

Steinberg, R., and Shapiro, S. (1982). Sex differences in personality traits of female and male master of business administration students. *Journal of Applied Psychology, 67,* 306–310.

Steiner, I. D. (1972). *Group process and productivity.* New York: Academic Press.

———. (1976). Task-performing groups. In J. W. Thibaut, J. T. Spence, and R. C. Carson (eds.), *Contemporary topics in social psychology.* Morristown, NJ: General Learning Press.

Stephan, W., Berscheid, E., and Walster, E. (1971). Sexual arousal and heterosexual perception. *Journal of Personality and Social Psychology, 20,* 93–101.

Stephan, W. G. (1985). Intergroup relations. In G. Lindzey and E. Aronson (eds.), *Handbook of social psychology* (3rd ed.). New York: Random House.

Sterling, B., and Gaertner, S. L. (1984). The attribution of arousal and emergency helping: A bidirectional process. *Journal of Experimental Social Psychology, 20,* 586–596.

Stern, G. S., Harris, J. R., and Elverum, J. (1981). Attention to important versus trivial tasks and salience of fatigue-related symptoms for coronary-prone individuals. *Journal of Research in Personality, 15,* 467–474.

Stern, L. D., Marrs, S., Millar, M. G., and Cole, E. (1984). Processing time and the recall of inconsistent and consistent behaviors of individuals and groups. *Journal of Personality and Social Psychology, 47,* 253–262.

Stewart, J. E., II (1980). Defendant's attractiveness as a factor in the outcome of criminal trials: An observational study. *Journal of Applied Social Psychology, 10,* 348–361.

Stock, W. (1985, September). *The effect of pornography on women.* Paper presented at the U. S. Justice Department Hearings, Houston.

Stock, W. E., and Geer, J. H. (1982). A study of fantasy-based sexual arousal in women. *Archives of Sexual Behavior, 11,* 33–47.

Stokols, D. (1972). On the distinction between density and crowding: Some implications for future research. *Psychological Review, 79,* 275–277.

Stone, A. A., and Neale, J. M. (1984). Effects of severe daily events on mood. *Journal of Personality and Social Psychology, 46,* 137–144.

Stone, L. (1977). *The family, sex and marriage in England: 1500–1800.* New York: Harper.

Stoner, J. A. F. (1961). A comparison of individual and group decisions involving risk. Unpublished master's thesis, School of Industrial Management, MIT.

Storms, M., and Thomas, G. C. (1977). Reactions to physical closeness. *Journal of Personality and Social Psychology, 35,* 412–418.

Straus, M. A., Gelles, R. J., and Steinmetz, S. K. (1980). *Behind closed doors: Violence in the American family.* Garden City, NJ: Anchor Books.

Streeter, L. A., Krauss, R. M., Geller, V., Olson, C., and Apple, W. (1977). Pitch changes during attempted deception. *Journal of Personality and Social Psychology, 35,* 345–350.

Stringer, M., and Cook, N. M. (1985). The effects of limited and conflicting stereotypic information on group categorization in Northern Ireland. *Journal of Applied Social Psychology, 15,* 399–407.

Strom, J. C., and Buck, R. W. (1979). Staring and participants' sex: Physiological and subjective reactions. *Personality and Social Psychology Bulletin, 5,* 114–117.

Strube, M. J., and Garcia, J. E. (1981). A meta-analytic investigation of Fiedler's contingency model of leadership effectiveness. *Psychological Bulletin, 90,* 307–321.

Strube, M. J., and Lott, C. L. (1984). Time urgency and the Type A behavior pattern: Implications for time investment and psychological entrapment. *Journal of Research in Personality, 18,* 395–409.

Strube, M. J., Lott, C. L., Heilizer, R., and Gregg, B. (1986). Type A behavior pattern and the judgment of control. *Journal of Personality and Social Psychology, 50,* 403–412.

Strube, M. J., and Ota, S. (1982). Type A coronary-prone behavior pattern: Relationship to birth order and family size. *Personality and Social Psychology Bulletin, 8,* 317–323.

Strube, M. J., Turner, C. W., Cerro, D., Stevens, J., and Hinchey, F. (1984). Interpersonal aggression and the Type A coronary-prone behavior pattern: A theoretical distinction and practical implications. *Journal of Personality and Social Psychology, 47,* 839–847.

Strube, M. J., and Werner, C. (1984). Personal space claims as a function of interpersonal threat: The mediating role of need for control. *Journal of Nonverbal Behavior, 1984, 8,* 195–206.

Sue, D. (1979). Erotic fantasies of college students during coitus. *Journal of Sex Research, 15,* 299–305.

Suedfeld, P. (1982). Aloneness as a healing experience. In L. A. Peplau and D. Perlman (eds.), *Loneliness: A sourcebook of current theory, research, and therapy.* New York: Wiley.

Suinn, R. M. (1982). Intervention with Type A behaviors. *Journal of Consulting and Clinical Psychology, 50,* 797–803.

Sulman, F. G., Levy, D., Levy, A., Pfeifer, Y., Superstein, E., and Tal, E. (1974). Ionometry of hot, dry desert winds (sharav) and application of ionizing treatment to weather-sensitive patients. *International Journal of Biometeorology, 18,* 393.

Suls, J., and Fletcher, B. (1985). The relative efficacy of avoidant and nonavoidant coping strategies: A meta-analysis, *Health Psychology, 4,* 249–288.

Summers, G., and Feldman, N. S. (1984). Blaming the victim versus blaming the perpetrator: An attributional analysis of spouse abuse. *Journal of Social and Clinical Psychology, 2,* 339–347.

Sundstrom, E., and Altman, I. (1974). Field study of dominance and territorial behavior. *Journal of Personality and Social Psychology, 30,* 115–125.

Sundstrom, E., and Sundstrom, M. G. (1977). Personal space invasions: What happens when the invader asks permission? *Environmental Psychology and Nonverbal Behavior, 2,* 76–82.

Sundstrom, E., Town, J., Brown, D., Forman, A., and McGee, C. (1982). Physical enclosure, type of job, and privacy in the office. *Environment and Behavior, 14,* 543–560.

Sunnafrank, M. J., and Miller, G. R. (1981). The role of initial conversations in determining attraction to similar and dissimilar strangers. *Human Communication Research, 8,* 16–25.

Swap, W. C. (1977). Interpersonal attraction and repeated

exposure to rewarders and punishers. *Personality and Social Psychology Bulletin, 3,* 248–251.

Sweeney, P. D., and Gruber, K. L. (1984). Selective exposure: Voter information preferences and the Watergate affair. *Journal of Personality and Social Psychology, 46,* 1208–1221.

Sypher, B. D., and Sypher, H. E. (1983). Perceptions of communication ability: Self-monitoring in an organizational meeting. *Personality and Social Psychology Bulletin, 9,* 297–304.

Tabachnik, N., Crocker, J., and Alloy, L. B. (1983). Depression, social comparison, and the false-consensus effect. *Journal of Personality and Social Psychology, 45,* 688–699.

Tajfel, H. (1982a). *Social identity and intergroup relations.* Cambridge: Cambridge University Press.

————. (1982b). Social psychology of intergroup relations. In M. R. Rosenzweig and L. R. Porter (eds.), *Annual review of psychology,* vol. 33, (pp. 1–39). Palo Alto, CA: Annual Reviews.

Tajfel, H., and Turner, J. (1979). An intergrative theory of intergroup conflict. In W. G. Austin and S. Worchel (eds.), *The social psychology of intergroup relations.* Monterey, CA: Brooks/Cole.

Talarico, S. M. (1985). *Courts and criminal justice.* Beverly Hills, CA: Sage.

Tanford, S., and Penrod, S. (1984). Social influence model: A formal integration of research on majority and minority influence processes. *Psychological Bulletin, 95,* 189–225.

Taormina, R. J., and Messick, D. M. (1983). Deservingness for foreign aid: Effects of need, similarity, and estimated effectiveness. *Journal of Applied Social Psychology, 13,* 371–391.

Taylor, F. W. (1911). *The principles of scientific management.* NY: Harpers Brothers.

Taylor, M. S., Locke, E. A., Lee, C., and Gist, M. E. (1984). Type A behavior and faculty research productivity: What are the mechanisms? *Organizational Behavior and Human Performance, 34,* 402–418.

Taylor, R. B., and Lanni, J. C. (1981). Territorial dominance: The influence of the resident advantage in triadic decision making. *Journal of Personality and Social Psychology, 41,* 909–915.

Taylor, R. B., and Stough, R. R. (1978). Territorial cognition: Assessing Altman's typology. *Journal of Personality and Social Psychology, 36,* 418–423.

Taylor, S. E., and Crocker, J. (1981). Schematic bases of social information processing. In E. T. Higgins, C. P. Herman, and M. P. Zanna (eds.), *Social cognition: The Ontario symposium.* Hillsdale, NJ: Erlbaum.

Taylor, S. E., Lichtman, R. R., and Wood, J. V. (1984). Attributions, beliefs about control, and adjustment to breast cancer. *Journal of Personality and Social Psychology, 46,* 489–502.

Taylor, S. E., and Thompson, S. C. (1982). Stalking the elusive "vividness" effect. *Psychological Review, 89,* 155–181.

Taylor, S. P., and Leonard, K. E. (1983). Alcohol and human physical aggression. In R. Geen and E. Donnerstein (eds.), *Aggression: Theoretical and empirical reviews.* New York: Academic Press.

Terman, L. M., Buttenwieser, P., Ferguson, L. W., Johnson, W. B., and Wilson, D. P. (1938). *Psychological factors in marital happiness.* New York: McGraw-Hill.

Tesser, A., Campbell, J., and Smith, M. (1984). Friendship choice and performance: Self-evaluation maintenance in children. *Journal of Personality and Social Psychology, 46,* 561–574.

Tesser, A., and Paulhus, D. L. (1976). Toward a causal model of love. *Journal of Personality and Social Psychology, 34,* 1095–1105.

Thelen, M. H., Frautschi, N. M., Roberts, M. C., Kirkland, K. D., and Dollinger, S. J. (1981). Being imitated, conformity, and social influence: An integrative review. *Journal of Research in Personality, 15,* 403–426.

Thibaut, J. W., and Walker, L. (1975). *Procedural justice: A psychological analysis.* Hillsdale, NJ: Erlbaum.

Thomas, G. C., Batson, C. D., and Coke, J. S. (1981). Do good Samaritans discourage helpfulness? Self-perceived altruism after exposure to highly helpful others. *Journal of Personality and Social Psychology, 40,* 194–200.

Thomas, M. H. (1982). Physiological arousal, exposure to a relatively lengthy aggressive film, and aggressive behavior. *Journal of Research in Personality, 16,* 72–81.

Thompson, R. A., and Hoffman, M. L. (1980). Empathy and the development of guilt in children. *Developmental Psychology, 16,* 155–156.

Thompson, W. C., Cowan, C. L., and Rosenhan, D. L. (1980). Focus of attention mediates the impact of negative affect on altruism. *Journal of Personality and Social Psychology, 38,* 291–300.

Tice, D. M., and Baumeister, R. F. (1985). Masculinity inhibits helping in emergencies: Personality does predict the bystander effect. *Journal of Personality and Social Psychology, 49,* 420–428.

Toch, H. (1980). *Violent men,* rev. ed. Cambridge, MA: Schenkman.

————. (1985). The catalytic situation in the violence equation. *Journal of Applied Social Psychology, 15,* 105–123.

Toi, M., and Batson, C. D. (1982). More evidence that empathy is a source of altruistic motivation. *Journal of Personality and Social Psychology, 43,* 281–292.

Toris, C., and DePaulo, B. M. (1985). Effects of actual deception on interpersonal perceptions. *Journal of Personality and Social Psychology, 47,* 1063–1073.

Triplett, N. (1898). The dynamogenic factors in pacemaking and competition. *American Journal of Psychology, 9,* 507–533.

Tunnell, G. (1980). Intraindividual consistency in personality assessment: The effect of self-monitoring. *Journal of Personality, 48,* 220–232.

Turk, D. C., Litt, M. D., Salovey, P., and Walker, J. (1985).

Seeking urgent pediatric treatment: Factors contributing to frequency, delay, and appropriateness. *Health Psychology, 4,* 43–59.

Turk, D. C., Rudy, T. E., and Salovey, P. (1984). Health protection: Attitudes and behaviors of LPNs, teachers, and college students. *Health Psychology, 3,* 189–210.

Turkington, C. (1986, February). High court weighs value of research by social scientists. *APA Monitor, 17*(2), 1, 30.

Tversky, A., and Kahneman, D. (1971). The belief in the "law of small numbers." *Psychological Bulletin, 76,* 105–110.

———. (1973). Availability: A heuristic for judging frequency and probability. *Cognitive Psychology, 5,* 207–232.

———. (1982). Judgment under uncertainty: Heuristics and biases. In D. Kahneman, P. Slovic, and A. Tversky (eds.), *Judgment under uncertainty* (pp. 3–20). New York: Cambridge University, Press.

Tyler, T. R., and Cook, F. L. (1984). The mass media and judgment of risk: Distinguishing impact on personal and societal level judgments. *Journal of Personality and Social Psychology, 47,* 693–708.

Tyler, T. R., and Lavrakas, P. J. (1983). Support of gun control: The influence of personal, sociotropic, and ideological concerns. *Journal of Applied Social Psychology, 13,* 392–405.

Ulshak, F. L., Nathanson, L., and Gillan, P. B. (1981). *Small group problem solving: An aid to organizational effectiveness.* Reading, MA: Addison-Wesley.

Umberson, D., and Hughes, M. (1984, August). *The impact of physical attractiveness on achievement and psychological well-being.* Paper presented at the meeting of the American Sociological Association, San Antonio, Texas.

Unger, R. K., Hilderbrand, M., and Madar, T. (1982). Physical attractiveness and assumptions about social deviance: Some sex-by-sex comparisons. *Personality and Social Psychology Bulletin, 8,* 293–301.

Utne, M. K., Hatfield, E., Traupmann, J., and Greenberger, D. (1984). Equity, marital satisfaction, and stability. *Journal of Social and Personal Relationships, 1,* 323–332.

Vallacher, R. R., and Wegner, D. M. (1985). *A theory of action identification.* Hillsdale, NJ: Erlbaum.

———. (1986). Action identification theory: The representation and control of behavior. *Psychological Review.*

Vallone, R., Ross, L., and Lepper, M. R. (1985). The hostile media phenomenon: Biased perception and perceptions of medial bias in coverage of the Beirut massacre. *Journal of Personality and Social Psychology, 49,* 577–585.

Van der Pligt, J. (1984). Atrributional false consensus, and valence: Two field studies. *Journal of Personality and Social Psychology, 46,* 57–68.

Van der Pligt, J., and Eiser, J. R. (1983). Actors' and observers' attributions, self-serving bias, and positivity bias. *European Journal of Social Psychology, 13,* 95–104.

Van de Ven, A. H., and Delbecq, A. L. (1974). The effectiveness of nominal, Delpihi, and interacting consensus group formats: The case of the structured problem. *Decision Sciences, 10,* 358–370.

van Komen, R. W., and Redd, W. H. (1985). Personality factors associated with anticipatory nausea/vomiting in patients receiving cancer chemotherapy. *Health Psychology, 4,* 189–202.

Veitch, R., and Griffitt, W. (1976). Good news, bad news: Affective and interpersonal effects. *Journal of Applied Social Psychology, 6,* 69–75.

Ventimiglia, J. C. (1982). Sex roles and chivalry: Some conditions of gratitude to altruism. *Sex Roles, 8,* 1107–1122.

Verbrugge, L., and Taylor, R. B. (1985). Cited in C. R. Creekmore, Cities won't drive you crazy. *Psychology Today, 17,* 46–53.

Vinokur, A., and Burnstein, E. (1974). Effects of partially shared persuasive arguments on group-induced shifts: A group problem-solving approach. *Journal of Personality and Social Psychology, 29,* 305–315.

Vinokur, A., Burnstein, E., Sechrest, L., and Wortman, P. M. (1985). Group decision making by experts: Field study of panels evaluating medical technologies. *Journal of Personality and Social Psychology, 49,* 70–84.

Vroom, V. H., and Yetton, P. W. (1973). *Leadership and decision-making.* Pittsburgh, PA: University of Pittsburgh Press.

Wagner, P. J., and Curran, P. (1984). Health beliefs and physician identified "worried well". *Health Psychology, 3,* 459–474.

Wagner, R. K., and Sternberg, R. J. (1985). Practical knowledge in real-world pursuits: the role of tacit knowledge. *Journal of Personality and Social Psychology, 49,* 436–458.

Walker, J. (1983). *Sexual activities and fantasies of university students as a function of sex role orientation.* Unpublished honors thesis, University of Western Ontario, London, Ontario.

Walker, L., and Lind, E. A. (1984). Psychological studies of procedural models. In G. M. Stephanson and J. H. Davis (eds.), *Progress inapplied social psychology,* vol. 2, (pp. 293–313). New York: Wiley.

Wallach, M. A., and Wing, C. W. (1968). Is risk a value? *Journal of Personality and Social Psychology, 9,* 101–106.

Wallston, B. S., Wallston, K. A., Forsberg, P. R., and King, J. E. (1984). Measuring desire for control of health processes. *Journal of Personality and Social Psychology, 47,* 415–426.

Walster, E., and Festinger, L. (1962). The effectiveness of "overheard" persuasive communications. *Journal of Abnormal and Social Psychology, 65,* 395–402.

Walster, E., Walster, G. W., and Berscheid, E. (1978). *Equity: Theory and research.* Boston: Allyn and Bacon.

Walster (Hatfield), E., Walster, G. W., and Traupmann, J.

(1978). Equity and premarital sex. *Journal of Personality and Social Psychology, 36*, 82–92.

Warner, R. B., and Sugarman, D. B. (1986). Atrributions of personality based on physical appearance, speech, and handwriting. *Journal of Personality and Social Psychology, 50*, 792–799.

Warriner, G. K., McDougall, G. H. G., and Claxton, J. D. (1984). Any data or none at all? Living with inaccuracies in self-reports or residential energy consumption. *Environment and Behavior, 1*, 503–526.

Watson, J. B. (1929). Introduction. In G. V. Hamilton and K. Macgowan, *What is wrong with marriage?* New York: Boni.

Watts, B. L. (1982). Individual differences in circadian activity rhythms and their effects on roommate relationships. *Journal of Personality, 50*, 374–384.

Wegner, D. M., and Vallacher, R. R. (1986). Action identification. In R. M. Sorrentino and E. T. Higgins (eds.), *Handbook of cognition and motivation* (pp. 550–582). New York: Guilford Press.

Weidner, G., and Matthews, K. A. (1978). Reported physical symptoms elicited by unpredictable events and the Type A coronary-prone behavior patterns. *Journal of Personality and Social Psychology, 36*, 1213–1220.

Weigel, R. H., and Loomis, J. W. (1981). Televised models of female achievement revisited: Some progress. *Journal of Applied Social Psychology, 11*, 58–63.

Weinberg, R. S., Hughes, H. H., Gritelli, J. W., England, R., and Jackson, A. (1984). Effects of preexisting and manipulated self-efficacy on weight loss in a self-control program. *Journal of Research in Personality, 1*, 352–358.

Weiner, B. (1980). A cognitive (attribution) emotion-action model of motivated behavior: An analysis of judgments of helpgiving. *Journal of Personality and Social Psychology, 39*, 186–200.

Weiner, N., Latané, B., and Pendey, J. (1981). Social loafing in the United States and India. Paper presented at the Joint Asian Meetings of the International Association for Cross-Cultural Psychology and the International Council of Psychologists. Taipei, Taiwan.

Weinstein, N. D. (1983). Reducing unrealistic optimism about illness susceptibility. *Health Psychology, 2*, 11–20.

———. (1984). Why it won't happen to me: Perceptions of risk factors and susceptibility. *Health Psychology, 3*, 431–457.

Weis, D. L. (1983). Reactions of college women to their first coitus. *Medical Aspects of Human Sexuality, 17*(2), 60CC, 60GG–60HH, 60LL.

Weisinger, H., and Lobsenz, N. M. (1981). *Nobody's perfect: How to give criticism and get results.* New York: Warner Books.

Weiss, S. M. (1982). Health psychology: The time is now. *Health Psychology, 1*, 81–91.

Wells, G. L. (1984). The psychology of lineup identification. *Journal of Applied Social Psychology, 14*, 89–103.

Wells, G. L., and Murray, D. M. (1983). What can psychology say about the *Neil v. Biggers* criteria for judging eyewitness accuracy? *Journal of Applied Psychology, 68*, 347–362.

Wells, G. L., Wrightsman, L. S., and Miene, P. K. (1985). The timing of the defense opening statement: Don't wait until the evidence is in. *Journal of Applied Social Psychology, 15*, 758–772.

Werner, C. M., Brown, B. B., and Damron, G. (1981). Territorial marking in a game arcade. *Journal of Personality and Social Psychology, 41*, 1094–1104.

West, S. G., and Brown, T. J. (1975). Physical attractiveness, the severity of the emergency, and helping: A field experiment and interpersonal simulation. *Journal of Experimental Social Psychology, 11*, 531–538.

West, S. G., Whitney, G., and Schnedler, R. (1975). Helping a motorist in distress: The effects of sex, race, and neighborhood. *Journal of Personality and Social Psychology, 31*, 691–698.

Wexley, K. N., and Yukl, G. A. (1984). *Organizational behavior and personnel psychology.* Homewood, IL: Richard D. Irwin.

White, G. L. (1980a). Inducing jealousy: A power perspective. *Personality and Social Psychology Bulletin, 6*, 222–227.

———. (1980b). Physical attractiveness and courtship progress. *Journal of Personality and Social Psychology, 39*, 660–668.

———. (1981). Some correlates of romantic jealousy. *Journal of Personality, 49*, 129–146.

White, L. A. (1979). Erotica and aggression: The influence of sexual arousal, positive affect, and negative affect on aggression. *Journal of Personality and Social Psychology, 37*, 591–601.

White, R. K. (1977). Misperception in the Arab-Israeli conflict. *Journal of Social Issues, 33*, 190–221.

Wichman, H. (1970). Effects of isolation and communication on cooperation in a two-person game. *Journal of Personality and Social Psychology, 16*, 114–120.

Wicker, A. W. (1969). Attitudes versus actions: The relationship of verbal and overt behavioral responses to attitude objects. *Journal of Social Issues, 25*, 41–78.

Wiggins, J. S., Wiggins, N., and Conger, J. C. (1968). Correlates of heterosexual somatic preference. *Journal of Personality and Social Psychology, 10*, 82–90.

Wilder, D. A. (1977). Perception of groups, size of opposition, and social influence. *Journal of Experimental Social Psychology, 13*, 253–268.

———. (1984). Intergroup contact: The typical member and the exception to the rule. *Journal of Experimental Social Psychology, 20*, 177–194.

Wilke, H., and Lanzetta, J. T. (1982). The obligation to help: Factors affecting response to help received. *European Journal of Social Psychology, 12*, 315–319.

Williams, J. E., and Best, D. L. (1982). *Measuring sex stereotypes: A third-nation study.* Beverly Hills, CA: Sage.

Williams, J. G., and Solano, C. H. (1983). The social reality of feeling lonely: Friendship and reciprocation. *Personality and Social Psychology Bulletin, 9, 237–242.

Williams, K. (1986, February 7). The role of appraisal salience in the performance evaluation process. Paper presented at a colloquium, SUNY-Albany.

Williams, K., Harkins, S., and Latané, B. (1981). Identifiability as a deterrent to social loafing: Two cheering experiments. Journal of Personality and Social Psychology, 40, 303–311.

Williams, K. B., and Williams, K. D. (1983). Social inhibition and asking for help: The effects of number, strength, and immediacy of potential help givers. Journal of Personality and Social Psychology, 44, 67–77.

Willis, F. N., Jr., and Hamm, H. K. (1980). The use of interpersonal touch in securing compliance. Journal of Nonverbal Behavior, 5, 49–55.

Wills, G. (1977). Measuring the impact of erotica. Psychology Today, 11(3), pp. 30–31, 33–34, 74, 76.

Wilson, T. D., Dunn, D. S., Bybee, J. A., Hyman, D. B., and Rotondo, J. A. (1984). Effects of analyzing reasons on attitude-behavior consistency. Journal of Personality and Social Psychology, 47, 5–16.

Wilson, T. D., and Linville, P. W. (1982). Improving the academic performance of college freshmen: Attribution therapy revisited. Journal of Personality and Social Psychology, 42, 367–376.

Wilson, T. D., and Stone, J. I. (1985). Limitations of self-knowledge: More on telling more than we can know. Review of Personality and Social Psychology.

Winer, D. L., Bonner, T. O., Jr., Blaney, P. H., and Murray, E. J. (1981). Depression and social attraction. Motivation and Emotion, 5, 153–166.

Winick, C. (1985). A content analysis of sexually explicit magazines sold in an adult bookstore. Journal of Sex Research, 21, 206–210.

Winslow, C. N. (1937). A study of the extent of agreement between friends' opinions and their ability to estimate the opinions of each other. Journal of Social Psychology, 8, 433–442.

Wishnoff, R. (1978). Modeling effects of explicit and non-explicit sexual stimuli on the sexual anxiety and behavior of women. Archives of Sexual Behavior, 7, 455–461.

Wispé, L. (1986). The distinction between sympathy and empathy: To call forth a concept, a word is needed. Journal of Personality and Social Psychology, 50, 314–321.

Witenberg, S. H., Blanchard, E. B., McCoy, G., Suls, J., and McGoldrick, M. D. (1983). Evaluation of compliance in home and center hemodialysis patients. Health Psychology, 2, 227–237.

Wittenbraker, J., Gibbs, B. L., and Kahle, L. R. (1983). Seat belt attitudes, habits, and behaviors: An adaptive amendment to the Fishbein model. Journal of Applied Social Psychology, 1, 406–421.

Wohlwill, J. F., and Kohn, I. (1973). The environment as experience by the migrant: An adaptation level view. Representative Research in Social Psychology, 4, 135–164.

Wolchik, S. A., Beggs, V., Wincze, J. A., Sakheim, D. K., Barlow, D. H., and Mavissakalian, M. (1980). The effects of emotional arousal on subsequent sexual arousal in men. Journal of Abnormal Psychology, 89, 595–598.

Wolf, S. (1985). Manifest and latent influence of majorities and minorities. Journal of Personality and Social Psychology, 48, 899–908.

Wolf, S., and Latané, B. (1983). Majority and minority influence on restaurant preferences. Journal of Personality and Social Psychology, 45, 282–292.

Wolfe, B. M., and Baron, R. A. (1971). Laboratory aggression related to aggression in naturalistic social situations: Effects of an aggressive model on the behavior of college students and prisoner observers. Psychonomic Science, 24, 193–194.

Wolfle, L. M., and Robertshaw, D. (1982). Effects of college attendance on locus of control. Journal of Personality and Social Psychology, 43, 802–810.

Wood, W. (1982). Retrieval of attitude-relevant information from memory: Effects on susceptibility to persuasion and on intrinsic motivation. Journal of Personality and Social Psychology, 42, 798–810.

Wood, W., Polek, D., and Aiken, C. (1985). Sex differences in group task performance. Journal of Personality and Social Psychology, 48, 63–71.

Worchel, S. (1974). The effect of three types of arbitrary thwarting on the instigation to aggression. Journal of Personality, 42, 301–318.

Worchel, S., and Brown, E. H. (1984). The role of plausibility in influencing environmental attributions. Journal of Experimental Social Psychology, 20, 86–96.

Worchel, S., and Teddlie, C. (1976). The experience of crowding: A two-factor theory. Journal of Personality and Social Psychology, 34, 36–40.

Wortman, C. B., and Linsenmeier, J. A. W. (1977). Interpersonal attraction and techniques of ingratiation in organizational settings. In B. M. Staw and G. R. Salancik (eds.), New directions in organizational behavior. Chicago: St. Clair Press.

Wright, P. H. (1984). Self-referent motivation and the intrinsic quality of friendship. Journal of Social and Personal Relationships, 1, 115–130.

Yaffe, M., and Nelson, E. (1982). The influence of pornography on behavior. London: Academic Press.

Yagoda, B. (1980). How Hollywood manipulates film ratings. Saturday Review, 7(12), 39–42.

Yandrell, B., and Insko, C. A. (1977). Attributions of attitudes to speakers and listeners under assigned-behavior conditions: Does behavior engulf the field? Journal of Experimental Social Psychology, 13, 269–278.

Yarber, W. L., and Fisher, W. A. (1983). Affective orientation to sexuality and venereal disease preventive behaviors. Health Values, 7, 19–23.

Yarber, W. L., and McCabe, G. P. (1985). Importance of sex education topics: Correlates with teacher characteristics and inclusion of topics of instruction. Health Education.

Yarber, W. L., and Whitehill, L. L. (1981). The relationship between parental affective orientation toward sexuality and responses to sex-related situations of preschool-age children. *Journal of Sex Education and Therapy, 7,* 36–39.

Yarnold, P. R., and Grimm, L. G. (1982). Time urgency among coronary-prone individuals. *Journal of Abnormal Psychology, 91,* 175–177.

Yates, B. T., and Mischel, W. (1979). Young children's preferred attentional strategies for delaying gratification. *Journal of Personality and Social Psychology, 37,* 286–300.

Yates, S. M., and Aronson, E. (1983). A social psychological perspective on energy conservation in residential buildings. *American Psychologist, 38,* 435–444.

Yinon, Y., and Sharon, I. (1985). Similarity in religiousness of the solicitor, the potential helper, and the recipient as determinants of donating behavior. *Journal of Applied Social Psychology, 15,* 726–734.

Yinon, Y., Sharon, I., Gonen, Y., and Adam, R. (1982). Escape from responsibility and help in emergencies among persons alone or within groups. *European Journal of Social Psychology, 12,* 301–305.

Young, J. E. (1982). Loneliness, depression, and cognitive therapy: Theory and application. In L. A. Peplau and D. Perlman (eds.), *Loneliness: A sourcebook of current theory, research, and therapy.* New York: Wiley.

Youngs, B. (1984). Drug abuse among superintendents and principals. *American School and University, 57,* 35–40.

Yukl, G. (1974). Effects of the opponent's initial offer, concession magnitude, and concession frequency on bargaining behavior. *Journal of Personality and Social Psychology, 30,* 323–335.

Zaccaro, S. J. (1984). Social loafing: The role of task attractiveness. *Personality and Social Psychology Bulletin, 10,* 99–106.

Zajonc, R. B. (1965). Social facilitation. *Science, 149,* 269–274.

———. (1968). Attitudinal effects of mere exposure. *Journal of Personality and Social Psychology Monographs Supplement, 9,* 1–27.

———. (1984). On the primacy of affect. *American Psychologist, 39,* 117–123.

Zajonc, R. B., Heingartner, A., and Herman, E. M. (1969). Social enhancement and impairment of performance in the cockroach. *Journal of Personality and Social Psychology, 13,* 83–92.

Zajonc, R. B., and Sales, S. M. (1966). Social facilitation of dominant and subordinate responses. *Journal of Experimental Social Psychology, 2,* 160–168.

Zanna, M. P., and Olson, J. M. (1982). Individual differences in attitudinal relations. In M. P. Zanna, E. T. Higgins, and C. P. Herman (eds.), *Consistency in social behavior: The Ontario Symposium,* vol. 2. Hillsdale, NJ: Erlbaum.

Zarski, J. J. (1984). Hassles and health: A replication. *Health Psychology, 3,* 243–251.

Zeichner, A., and Phil, R. O. (1980). Effects of alcohol and instigator intent on human aggression. *Journal of Studies on Alcohol, 41,* 265–276.

Zeiss, A. M. (1982). Expectations for aging on sexuality in parents and average married couples. *Journal of Sex Research, 82,* 47–57.

Zilbergeld, B., and Evans, M. (1980, August). The inadequacy of Masters and Johnson. *Psychology Today.*

Zillmann, D. (1971). Excitation transfer in communication-mediated aggressive behavior. *Journal of Experimental Social Psychology, 7,* 419–434.

———. (1979). *Hostility and aggression.* Hillsdale, NJ: Erlbaum.

———. (1983a). Transfer of excitation in emotional behavior. In J. T. Cacioppo and R. E. Petty (eds.), *Social psychophysiology.* New York: Guilford Press.

———. (1983b). Arousal and aggression. In R. G. Geen and E. Donnerstein (eds.), *Aggression: Theoretical and empirical reviews.* New York: Academic Press.

———. (1984). *Connections between sex and aggression.* Hillsdale, NJ: Erlbaum.

Zillmann, D., Baron, R. A., and Tamborini, R. (1981). Social costs of smoking: Effects of tobacco smoke on hostile behavior. *Journal of Applied Social Psychology, 11,* 548–561.

Zillmann, D., and Bryant (1984). Effects of massive exposure to pornography. In N. M. Malamuth and E. Donnerstein (eds.), *Pornography and sexual aggression.* New York: Academic Press.

———. (1986). *Pornography's impact on sexual satisfaction.* Manuscript submitted for publication.

Zillmann, D., Katcher, A. H., and Milavsky, B. (1972). Excitation transfer from physical exercise to subsequent aggressive behavior. *Journal of Experimental Social Psychology, 8,* 247–259.

Zillmann, D., and Mundorf, N. (in press). Effects of sexual and violent images in rock-music videos on music appreciation. *Communication Research.*

Zillmann, D., Weaver, J. B., Mundorf, N., and Aust, C. F. (1986). Effects of an opposite-gender companion's affect to horror on distress, delight, and attraction. *Journal of Personality and Social Psychology, 51,* 586–594.

Zimbardo, P. G. (1970). The human choice: Individuation, reason, and order versus deindividuation — impulse, and chaos. In W. J. Arnold and D. Levine (eds.), *Nebraska Symposium on Motivation, 1969.* Lincoln: University of Nebraska Press.

———. (1977). *Shyness: What it is and what you can do about it.* Reading, MA: Addison-Wesley.

Zlutnick, S., and Altman, S. (1972). Crowding and human behavior. In J. Wohlwill and D. Carson (eds.), *Environment and the social sciences: Perspectives and applications.* Washington, DC: American Psychological Association.

Zuckerman, M., Driver, R., and Koestner, R. (1982). Discrepancy as a cue to actual and perceived deception. *Journal of Nonverbal Behavior, 7,* 95–100.

Zuckerman, M., and Feldman, L. S. (1984). Actions and

occurrences in attribution theory. *Journal of Personality and Social Psychology, 46,* 541–550.

Zuckerman, M., Miserandino, M., and Bernieri, F. (1983). Civil inattention exists — in elevators. *Personality and Social Psychology Bulletin, 9,* 578–586.

Zuckerman, M., Schmitz, M., and Yosha, A. (1977). Ef-

fects of crowding in a student environment. *Journal of Applied Social Psychology, 7,* 67–72.

Zukier, H., and Pepitone, A. (1984). Social roles and strategies in prediction: Some determinants of the use of base-rate information. *Journal of Personality and Social Psychology, 47,* 349–360.

SUBJECT INDEX

NAME INDEX